CONTROLLING THE ATOM

CONTROLLING THE ATOM

The Beginnings of
Nuclear Regulation 1946–1962

GEORGE T. MAZUZAN
and
J. SAMUEL WALKER

UNIVERSITY OF CALIFORNIA PRESS
Berkeley   Los Angeles   London

University of California Press
Berkeley and Los Angeles, California

University of California Press, Ltd.
London, England

Library of Congress Cataloging in Publication Data

Mazuzan, George T.
 Controlling the atom.

 Bibliography: p. 500
 Includes index.
 1. Atomic power—Law and legislation—United States—
History. 2. Radioactive substances—Safety regulations—
United States—History. I. Walker, J. Samuel. II. Title.
KF2138.M39   1984   343.73'0925   84-2485
ISBN 0-520-05182-3   347.303925

Printed in the United States of America

1 2 3 4 5 6 7 8 9

CONTENTS

PREFACE AND
ACKNOWLEDGMENTS

This book traces the early history of nuclear power regulation in the United States. It focuses on the Atomic Energy Commission (AEC), the federal agency that until 1975 was primarily responsible for planning and carrying out programs to protect public health and safety from the hazards of the civilian use of nuclear energy. It also describes the role of other groups that figured significantly in the development of regulatory policies, including the congressional Joint Committee on Atomic Energy, federal agencies other than the AEC, state governments, the nuclear industry, and scientific organizations. And it considers changes in public perceptions of and attitudes toward atomic energy and the dangers of radiation exposure. The context in which regulatory programs evolved is a rich and complex mixture of political, legislative, legal, technological, scientific, and administrative history.

The basic purpose of this book is to provide the Nuclear Regulatory Commission (NRC), which inherited responsibility for nuclear safety after Congress disbanded the AEC, and the general public with information on the historical antecedents and background of regulatory issues. In that regard, the volume falls into the category of "public history," a field that has had its practitioners for years but has only recently gained prominence within the historical profession. The fundamental premise of public history, and one to which we fully subscribe, is that understanding the history of any given problem is essential to approaching it knowledgeably. Policymakers run the risk of "reinventing the wheel" when they make judgments on problems they face unless they are well informed about the context in which previous decisions of a similar nature were made, what alternatives were considered and why certain ones were chosen, and what personal and impersonal forces shaped a particular policy. The same holds true for members of the general public, whether their concerns center on nuclear-plant safety, allocation of water resources, air pollution, or any other issue. History, in other words, is a useful component of sound public policy. Although it cannot offer definitive guidance on resolving problems, history does provide a unique and valuable perspective. The point is not to belabor the often misleading aphorism that "those who fail to study the past are condemned to repeat it," but rather to recognize that both continuity and change in history need to be understood to deal effectively with the present.

Although we have tried to reconstruct fully the context of regulatory development during the 1950s and early 1960s, we have not written a comprehensive account of the history of atomic energy or the activities of the Atomic Energy Commission. Regulation was but one of the AEC's three major statutory functions; the agency was also responsible for developing and testing nuclear weapons and for encouraging private industry to expand the peaceful applications of atomic energy. While we have attempted to show how the agency's military and promotional duties influenced regulatory policies, we have limited our discussion of those other programs to their impact on regulation. Our description of the controversy over fallout from nuclear-bomb testing, for example, recounts the ways in which the debate affected regulatory matters but does not attempt to provide an analysis of all aspects of the issue. The same pattern applies to our accounts of the AEC's efforts to promote the use of nuclear energy for peaceful purposes.

While preparing this volume, we have striven to meet the exacting standards of historical scholarship in conducting research, reconstructing the sequence of events, and evaluating decisions and actions within the context of their historical setting. The Nuclear Regulatory Commission placed no restrictions, either explicitly or implicitly, on our access to documents or on the structure, approach, direction, or conclusions of this volume. We exercised our independent professional judgment throughout the project, and we wish to emphasize that we, and not the Commission, bear full responsibility for the book's contents.

Our work on this book benefited immeasurably from the assistance of many people both within and outside the NRC. Since the agency's history program began in 1977, it has received strong support from the members of the Commission. Commissioners Victor Gilinsky and Richard T. Kennedy were particularly instrumental in establishing the office, and both maintained a personal interest in the project throughout their tenures on the Commission.

A legion of NRC staff members cheerfully rendered invaluable aid by searching agency files, locating printed materials, obtaining books and articles, and providing a wide variety of administrative services. Although they are too numerous to name, we thank them collectively for their help. Two individuals deserve special mention: James D. Nuse for his unfailing knowledge of congressional materials and legislative histories, and Myrna L. Steele for her expert advice on procurement and publication matters.

Several people in the agency read the manuscript in whole or in part and offered criticism from the vantage point of their own areas of expertise. We thank them for the donation of their time as well as for their commentary: Frederick D. Anderson, Peter A. Bradford, Allen Brodsky, Richard E. Cunningham, Peter J. Garcia, Victor Gilinsky, Albert P. Kenneke, G. Wayne Kerr, Morton W. Libarkin, Thomas E. Murley, R. G. Page, Jerome D. Saltzman, Leo E. Slaggie, and Royal J. Voegeli. James G. Beckerley and William C. Parler, both of whom were participants in or close observers of many of the events covered in this book, took a particularly keen interest in the project. They constantly allowed us to refer to them for information, criticisms, and advice that clearly went beyond the call of their official duties.

Mary C. Hood, who worked with us as a research assistant and skilled typist, merits our deep appreciation. She spent many long hours on the tedious tasks that support historical research.

Roger R. Trask, our predecessor and the NRC's first historian, inaugurated and gave initial direction to the program. We hope this volume measures up to the high standards he set for the work of this office.

We are grateful to the archivists and librarians in many institutions who made our research easier. We are particularly indebted to Roger M. Anders of the Department of Energy, who not only was relentlessly efficient in digging out Atomic Energy Commission records for us but also smoothed the process of declassification when it was necessary. David R. Kepley of the National Archives and Donald A. Ritchie of the U.S. Senate Historical Office facilitated our access to the records of the Joint Committee on Atomic Energy and performed key roles in opening Committee files for public examination. We are also grateful for the assistance of Edward J. McCarter, R. Michael McReynolds, John J. Rumbarger, and C. Edward Schamel of the National Archives; Robert S. Wood of the Herbert Hoover Library; James W. Leyerzapf and Rodney

Soubers of the Dwight D. Eisenhower Library; E. William Johnson of the John F. Kennedy Library; Warner W. Pflug of the Walter P. Reuther Library at Wayne State University; Mary Jo Pugh of the Bentley Historical Library at the University of Michigan; and William Jankos of the University of Southern California Library. Arthur Lazell of the Division of Radiological Health of the U.S. Public Health Service offered much-appreciated help in our research of Public Health Service records.

In addition to NRC staff members who commented on draft chapters, we benefited from the critiques of experts outside the agency who generously took time to review materials we sent them. Richard G. Hewlett, formerly chief historian of the Atomic Energy Commission and the Department of Energy, not only read sections of our manuscript but also offered valuable advice from his experiences in running a government history program for many years. Jack M. Holl, Hewlett's successor at the Department of Energy, shared his research findings on atomic-energy policy during the Eisenhower years with us. We also profited from the observations of others who read parts of the manuscript: Walter D. Claus, Leo Goodman, Kenneth C. Hall, Lee M. Hydeman, Ralph E. Lapp, Daniel J. Metlay, Arthur W. Murphy, James T. Ramey, and Lauriston S. Taylor. We especially appreciate the efforts of Spencer R. Weart of the American Institute of Physics and Allan M. Winkler of the University of Oregon, who interrupted their own research on the history of nuclear energy to provide us detailed and informed comments on the entire manuscript.

We are grateful to the people who granted interviews and shared their experiences and perspectives with us. Their names are listed in the Select Bibliographic Essay at the end of the book.

Finally, we are indebted to the University of California Press and especially to editor John R. Miles. This volume was subjected to the review, selection, and editorial procedures that other scholarly books undergo, and we are most appreciative of the support, encouragement, and assistance we have received from Dr. Miles and the press.

George T. Mazuzan
J. Samuel Walker

Washington, D.C.

I

TOWARD THE PEACEFUL ATOM

From the moment the American people first learned about the awesome power of the nuclear bombs that devastated Hiroshima and Nagasaki, Japan, the dawn of the atomic age aroused ambivalent emotions. Americans felt pride in the herculean scientific, technical, and industrial effort that had unleashed the vast energy of nuclear fission, and gratitude that the use of atomic bombs had brought a quick and decisive end to World War II. At the same time they experienced a profound sense of uneasiness about the implications of the new weapon for the future of the nation and the world. As events unfolded in the immediate postwar years, symbols associated with atomic energy presented a disquieting image of the technology to the American public. Within a year after the end of the war, neighborhood movie-theater newsreels and the nation's newspapers showed atomic explosions being tested by the government at the Bikini atoll in the Pacific Ocean. A 1946 *March of Time* episode, "Atomic Power," dramatized the development of atomic weapons, and the first of many American motion pictures about atomic war, *The Beginning or the End*, was released to movie houses across the land the same year. Two books on the destructive power of atomic weapons became best-sellers. John Hersey's *Hiroshima*, published in late 1946, grippingly described the effect of the bomb on the city's inhabitants. It had previously appeared as an article in the *New Yorker*, whose editors emphasized their "conviction that few of us have yet comprehended the all but incredible destructive power of this weapon, and that everyone might well take time to consider the terrible implications of its use." The second book, *No Place to Hide*, was a log kept by David Bradley, a young Army Medical Corps doctor assigned to monitor radioactivity during the 1946 Bikini tests. Excerpted first in the *Atlantic Monthly* in 1948,

Bradley's diary entries graphically related an experience that convinced him that there was no real defense against atomic weapons and that radioactivity could affect the land and its people for centuries. The most common symbol of the atomic era, the gigantic fireball and mushroom-shaped cloud created by the explosion, was joined by others that were less dramatic but still unsettling. Increasingly familiar yellow-and-magenta radiation signs depicted the invisible, silent, and odorless hazards of atomic energy. Government labels, such as "restricted data," and technical terms sounding vaguely ominous, such as "fissionable materials" or "gamma rays," contributed to an almost science-fiction-come-true image of an astonishing technology that, if not properly controlled, might lead to Armageddon.[1]

The fearful images of atomic energy were balanced, though not overshadowed, by soaring projections of the potential benefits that peaceful uses of the new technology might offer. Politicians, scientists, journalists, and business leaders predicted that the atom could eventually be harnessed for a breathtaking array of applications to raise standards of living throughout the world. Senator Joseph C. O'Mahoney of Wyoming declared that atomic energy "might bring us greater freedom than we had dared dream of before—greater freedom from toil, from hunger, and from disease." Nuclear physicist Alvin M. Weinberg told the Senate's Special Committee on Atomic Energy in December 1945: "Atomic power can cure as well as kill. It can fertilize and enrich a region as well as devastate it. It can widen man's horizons as well as force him back into the cave." *Newsweek* reported that "even the most conservative scientists and industrialists [are] willing to outline a civilization which would make the comic-strip prophecies of Buck Rogers look obsolete." Observing that ideas for civilian uses of atomic energy ranged "from the practical to the fantastic," it cited a few examples: atomic-powered airplanes, rockets, and automobiles, large electrical-generating stations, small "home power plants" to provide heat and electricity in individual homes, and tiny atomic generators wired to clothing to keep a person cool in summer and warm in winter.[2]

Developing atomic energy for peaceful applications, as even the most enthusiastic proponents recognized, would take many years. The immediate challenge facing American leaders in the postwar period was to direct atomic activities in a way that would win the nation's confidence in the judicious use of the technology for both military and peaceful purposes. Shortly after the war ended, Congress began deliberations on a law intended to achieve those objectives while maintaining, at least for the time being, strict government control over atomic energy.

It took almost a year from the time of the Japanese bombings for the Congress and the executive branch to reach agreement on the Atomic Energy Act of 1946, which President Harry S Truman signed on 1 August. Planning for effective management of the atom had started in the War Department in 1944 and had resulted in the introduction in the fall of 1945 of the May-Johnson bill, named after its sponsors, Senator Edwin C. Johnson of Colorado and Representative Andrew J. May of Kentucky. Hoping to push the bill through Congress quickly, its supporters ran into unexpected opposition from atomic scientists and others who wanted extended public hearings on such an important matter. In response to a rising crescendo of protest, the Senate created a special committee to investigate the issue and recommend legislation. Under the leadership of freshman senator Brien McMahon of Connecticut, a new draft was drawn up. Acrimonious debate and much compromise took place in the spring and summer of 1946 before the law was finally enacted, establishing the Atomic Energy Commission. The fight over the bill was largely a struggle over civilian or military domination of the new agency. The May-Johnson bill implied military control; the McMahon bill eventually compromised the issue by affirming civilian control while leaving "military applications" of atomic energy at a top policy level. It created a Military Liaison Committee that had its own access through the civilian armed-forces secretaries to the president.

Civilian direction of the agency did not mean liberalized control of the atom by the government. Provisions in the law gave the government exclusive authority over the development and application of atomic energy; ownership of fissionable materials and the facilities for producing and using them were to remain a government monopoly. The statute required security investigations for everybody who worked for the Atomic Energy Commission or its contractors and created a new special atomic-information category called "restricted data." In addition, the act tightly controlled patents owned by the government as well as any that might be developed through government-financed work. Furthermore, cooperation with other countries in atomic-energy activities was severely circumscribed. Ironically, the government monopoly of the atom was championed by some of the most conservative politicians in the Congress, men who throughout their political careers had fought encroachment by big government.[3]

The broad acceptance of such far-reaching control of atomic energy reflected the historical legacy of the Manhattan Project and contemporary anxiety about international politics. The Manhattan Project had been conceived in wartime with the specific purpose of developing an atomic bomb. The program's focus on weaponry did not end with the defeat of Japan and public knowledge of the bomb. The beginning of the Cold War between the United States and the Soviet Union heightened the determination to continue the American monopoly over atomic-weapons technology until an acceptable international-control scheme could be worked out. In addition, the military planned to stockpile atomic bombs as well as undertake research on and development of more sophisticated nuclear weapons.

The 1946 law defined the Atomic Energy Commission's principal functions: to produce fissionable material for weapons and to develop and manufacture weapons as military requirements dictated. In order to meet those basic demands, the agency took on other related responsibilities. For example, it had to assure and develop an adequate supply of uranium, engage in research-and-development programs, and protect the atomic secrets inherent in its operations. The 1946 act also encouraged the Commission to develop peaceful uses of atomic energy, though this function remained secondary to weapons production. Consequently, the new agency postponed major initiatives on civilian applications until the weapons program was on a sound footing.[4]

Along with the technical-control aspects of the act, the organizational arrangement to manage the agency had concerned the legislators. They finally settled on a commission with five full-time members, appointed by the president on a staggered five-year-term basis. The lawmakers believed that the far-reaching policy decisions the agency would make could be produced best through the deliberative process of a multi-headed body. To handle the day-to-day operations they created an agency executive officer, called the general manager. Congress also established four operating divisions—production, research, engineering, and military applications—with each director selected by the Commission.[5]

President Truman recruited five distinguished Americans to serve as the first commissioners. He first nominated Sumner Pike, a businessman and former member of the Securities and Exchange Commission, and quickly added Lewis Strauss. For chairman, Truman enlisted David E. Lilienthal. Then serving as head of the Tennessee Valley Authority, Lilienthal had proved himself an able administrator. Furthermore, he had coauthored the Acheson-Lilienthal plan, the first effort to formulate United States policy on international control of the atom. The TVA chief had the strong backing of Vannevar Bush and James B. Conant, two key administrators of the Manhattan Project.

Late in October 1946 Truman selected William W. Waymack and Robert F. Bacher to round out the first Commission. Pulitzer Prize winner Waymack was the editor of the Des Moines *Register and Tribune* and a director of the Federal Reserve Bank of Chicago. Bacher was the only scientist on the Commission. A highly respected physicist, he also had the strong endorsement of Bush. Bacher had worked at Los Alamos during the war years and had recently returned to his academic post at Cornell University.

Truman was proud of his choices, particularly of the fact that they were nonpartisan nominees. Indeed, four of the five were registered Republicans: Pike, Strauss, Waymack, and Bacher; Lilienthal was an independent. While the confirmation proceedings turned out to be less than *pro forma* affairs—they dragged on acrimoniously throughout the first months of 1947—the five nominees began informally in the fall of 1946 to face the imposing organizational tasks ahead of them.[6]

By establishing a commission-type organization, Congress expected a collegial, deliberative approach toward policymaking. The first five members seemed well suited to carry out that concept. Lilienthal possessed the right temperament and experience to fill the chairman's role. Throughout his tenure he attempted to develop a consensus on policy issues among his colleagues.

Among the five, Strauss turned out to be least suited to the deliberative approach. He often displayed his impatience for action that conflicted with the approach of his colleagues. A strong-willed man, Strauss had a remarkable talent for attracting or stirring controversy despite his own claim that he never had enemies before coming to Washington. Bald, bespectacled, with an owlish-looking face, Strauss had a ramrod posture and a superbly tailored figure. He was intelligent, articulate, and displayed an air of old-world courtliness and charm. Even his enemies conceded his executive brilliance and tactical mastery. One close observer noted, however, that when he was piqued, Strauss's expression varied "between childish indignation and pouting martyrdom." Mostly self-educated, Strauss through his own ambition, drive, and ability had advanced from humble origins to acquire wealth and power. Born in 1896, he started in the business world as a shoe salesman. He served as private secretary to Herbert Hoover between 1917 and 1919, securing the appointment on his own brash initiative following encouragement from his mother. Strauss earned financial success after becoming a full partner at age thirty-two in the Wall Street investment house of Kuhn, Loeb and Company. During the Second World War he served in Washington as a navy reserve officer, eventually becoming special assistant to Secretary of the Navy James V. Forrestal and achieving flag-officer rank. Truman appointed him to the Commission just after he had resumed his business career with Kuhn, Loeb. After the appointment Strauss soon found himself in the minority of many four-to-one decisions. Nevertheless, he spearheaded the establishment of a detection system that picked up radiation from the Soviet Union's first atomic explosion in 1949; and soon after, he played a large role in starting the hydrogen-bomb program. On that issue he met the combined opposition of his fellow commissioners and the scientists on the AEC's prestigious General Advisory Committee, chaired by J. Robert Oppenheimer. In 1950 he left the Commission to resume his career in the world of high finance; three years later he returned as AEC chairman.[7]

An operating philosophy emerged from the early Commission meetings. The five men believed that up to then, atomic-energy questions had benefited from a nonpartisan approach. By acting prudently and seeking to build a consensus for their decisions, they hoped to keep atomic energy out of the political arena. Lilienthal had applied the nonpartisan principle quite successfully at TVA, and his leadership reflected an attempt to continue it at the Atomic Energy Commission.[8]

The commissioners adopted an operational mode that avoided specialization. Lilienthal and Pike were experienced public administrators, and both believed that having each commissioner informed on all policy matters was preferable to diluting the collegial system with specifically assigned functional areas. They had learned the pitfalls of such practices at the Tennessee Valley Authority and the Securities and Exchange Commission and had no difficulty convincing their three colleagues that the strength of the Commission depended on all five drawing on their different concepts of the public interest to forge policy decisions. This never meant there would be total agreement on every issue; it merely assured total participation by all the commissioners.

The Commission's first job after its establishment was to take over administration of the Manhattan Project's operations. General Leslie Groves, who headed the Project throughout its existence, had hoped for a much earlier transfer of functions, but legislative wrangling over the 1946 law caused delay. The vast enterprise, administered chiefly from Oak Ridge, Tennessee, but including vital installations in Los Alamos, New Mexico, Hanford, Washington, and Chicago, Illinois, suffered during the interim period. With the postwar emphasis on phasing out and reconverting military operations, Groves accomplished a remarkable management task in keeping the wartime project from completely falling apart. But the year-and-a-half delay took a toll in loss of manpower and deferments in both project development and needed construction. When the transfer finally occurred on 30 December 1946, the Commission inherited an atomic program that retained the basic foundations laid in the war years but that had suffered an appreciable loss of momentum after the end of hostilities.[9]

At an early stage the Commission made a practical organizational decision by retaining the Manhattan Project's contractor system. The agency had no mandate to do this, but in view of the circumstances it had no workable alternatives. The Commission readily saw that it would be unrealistic for the agency to hire directly the many scientists, engineers, and technicians that contractors for the Manhattan Project had enlisted from private industry and universities. Only at the risk of great delay and major disruptions to the program could the Commission have reversed the Manhattan Project's established contractor policy. Even if reality dictated retention of the contractor system, the Commission might have entertained a long-range plan for eventual direct government hiring and operation. But none of the commissioners believed strongly that it was desirable or advantageous.

This was a significant decision. Since private companies under contract would operate the nation's atomic plants and laboratories, the Commission relied on an already trained cadre to develop the new technology. In view of the Atomic Energy Act's prohibition against private ownership of fissionable materials and the facilities for using or producing them, the decision on contractors also turned out to be the one practical way of allowing access for segments of private industry to at least some nuclear fundamentals. Another benefit accrued from the contractor policy: it allowed the AEC to operate initially with a small administrative staff that in turn delegated a large share of administrative controls to program offices and field operations. This concept fitted well into Lilienthal's public-administration philosophy of decentralization, and its application probably was the most lasting imprint he made on the Atomic Energy Commission.[10]

After much debate the drafters of the 1946 act had recognized that a five-man commission was ill suited for the daily conduct of agency operations. The law made a distinction between policy and operations. To perform the latter functions, the statute established the position of general manager and underscored its importance by making it a presidential appointment subject to Senate confirmation. To assure an integration of policy and administration, the Congress gave the commissioners advisory authority to the president on the appointment or removal of the general manager. Clearly, though, he was meant to direct the agency's day-to-day operations while the commissioners focused on overall policies and priorities.[11]

Carroll L. Wilson, the first general manager, served the agency from late 1946 to 1950. In large measure the choice of Wilson was due to his commitment to Lilienthal's decentralized approach to agency administration. Both men were convinced that the principal technical and managerial strength had to be located in the hands of the division directors and in the field managers' offices. As critical as delegation of authority was under this philosophy, a strong general manager was still necessary. Wilson personally discharged responsibility for all aspects of internal management. Gifted with an unflappable personality, he soon established a working relationship with the commissioners on the one hand and his key staff members on the other.[12]

Wilson and the commissioners immediately built a workable organization and recruited staff members. Long-range planning and staff judgment on technical and scientific matters rested in the four statutory program divisions: Research, Engineering, Military Application, and Production; and in two divisions subsequently created by the Commission: Raw Materials, and Biology and Medicine. The division directors reported to Wilson, though he authorized them to exchange information directly with their counterparts in the field offices and on the contractor staffs.

Throughout 1947 the commissioners and Wilson organized the necessary central management offices: Security and Intelligence, Organization and Personnel, Budget, Comptroller, General Counsel, and a Public and Technical Information Service. Those office heads also reported to Wilson; additionally, the comptroller and general counsel reported directly to the Commission on particular fiscal and legal matters.[13]

Formal staff papers were used to place policy problems and recommended solutions before the commissioners. To handle the paperwork the Commission established a secretariat. The secretary, who reported to the general manager, developed the agenda for Commission meetings, provided assistance to the staff in preparation of the staff papers, and kept the records and minutes of Commission meetings and actions.[14]

In 1947 the Commission organized five decentralized field offices—New York, Oak Ridge, Chicago, Hanford, and Santa Fe—built on the Manhattan Project model but with substantive differences. The Manhattan Project had been a nationwide enterprise with major operation control emanating from its Oak Ridge headquarters. The Commission decentralized that authority while keeping the geographic distribution of the offices. Responsibility for agency operations rested with the field-office managers. Under the policy framework established by the Washington-based commissioners and coordinated by the general manager, the field-office managers assumed delegated authority to negotiate contracts, to establish certain positions and make appointments, and to take general administrative actions necessary to carry out the assigned functions of their offices. Wilson insisted that the managers bring only those problems to him that raised new policy questions of a complex nature or that affected the total agency operation.[15]

Most agency activities took place in the field. Several of the field sites traced their beginnings to the Manhattan Project. Oak Ridge had been the field headquarters of the wartime project. Selected for its isolation, dependable power supply from TVA, and topography, Oak Ridge was initially used for isotope-separation facilities necessary in the process of making uranium 235 for atomic bombs. Several production factories were constructed there during the war, including an electromagnetic-separation plant, a thermal-diffusion plant, and a gaseous-diffusion plant. The first two processes were discontinued and placed on standby status in September 1945 in favor of the more efficient and economical gaseous-diffusion process, which expanded and continued operation under a contract with the Union Carbide and Carbon Chemicals Company. In this process, uranium in the form of a gas (uranium hexafluoride) is forced through thin, porous barriers. Because the lighter gas molecules, containing the uranium 235, move at a higher velocity than the heavy molecules containing uranium 238, the lighter ones pass through each barrier more frequently than do the heavy ones, producing a slight enrichment in the lighter isotope. Hundreds of these separation stages are required to effect a significant separation of uranium 235 from uranium 238. In addition, a vast array of other technical facilities were constructed at the Oak Ridge site. For example, a scaled-up model of Enrico Fermi's Chicago pile, which generated the first nuclear chain reaction in 1942, was built to provide design data for the full-blown production reactors that later would be constructed at the AEC's reservation at Hanford, Washington. In 1946 Oak Ridge also became the short-lived site for a cooperative effort to build the world's first power reactor. Called the Daniels pile, after designer and chemist Farrington Daniels, the project brought together for the first time some of American industry's promising young engineers for study and work on peaceful applications of atomic energy. Westinghouse sent John W. Simpson and Nunzio J. Palladino, Allis-Chalmers was represented by Harold Etherington, and General Electric sent Harry E. Stevens. The AEC canceled the Daniels project in 1947, however, when it transferred power-reactor development to Chicago's Argonne National Laboratory.[16]

The other major production facility was the Hanford Engineer Works near Richland, Washington. It functioned as a center for production of the plutonium used in atomic bombs. Three large water-cooled, graphite-moderated reactors were built during the war, and several more were constructed in the postwar years. The Hanford Works also housed three chemical-separation plants that recovered and purified the plutonium from irradiated fuel elements. The isolation and vastness of the area had been major reasons for selection of the site. Important, too, were geological formations that could hold the immense weight of the reactors, large volumes of water from the Columbia River for cooling the machines, and tremendous amounts of electrical power available from nearby hydroelectric stations. The Du Pont Company initially ran the facility for the government; in 1946 the General Electric Company became the prime contractor.[17]

Tucked away on a high mesa in northern New Mexico, the Los Alamos complex constituted a third major facility of the Manhattan Project. This weapons research-and-development center, renamed after the war the Los Alamos Scientific Laboratory, had been the key meeting ground for scientists working on the bomb, and it remained the major facility for development of atomic weapons. The University of California operated it for the AEC. In 1950 the agency contracted with the university to open a second weapons-research center in Livermore, California, near San Francisco. The Livermore Laboratory concentrated on developing new and improved types of nuclear weapons. Since the university had been a pioneer in atomic research, it was a logical contractor for those facilities.

Since 1936 the university had operated its own Radiation Laboratory in Berkeley, which had contributed greatly to the nuclear sciences. There researchers had identified plutonium and renowned physicist Ernest O. Lawrence had invented the cyclotron. As a tribute to Lawrence's accomplishments, both the Livermore and the Radiation Laboratories were named for him after his death in 1958.[18]

The AEC's domain included other highly specialized supporting facilities. The original Metallurgical Laboratory at the University of Chicago became the Argonne National Laboratory. In a major decision in late December 1947 the Commission designated Argonne as the chief laboratory for reactor development work. In subsequent years, scientists at the suburban Chicago facility designed several experimental reactors, most of which were constructed at the AEC's new National Reactor Testing Station at Arco, Idaho, twenty-five miles west of Idaho Falls. The Chicago operations office supervised the laboratory's work.[19]

The New York office ran the AEC's uranium-procurement operations and its Health and Safety Laboratory. It also supervised the new Brookhaven National Laboratory on Long Island, which Associated Universities, a consortium of eastern schools, ran under contract to the AEC. The laboratory originated and developed as a center for nonmilitary research.[20]

Truman's decision in 1950 to build the hydrogen bomb spawned development of other major production facilities. The gigantic Savannah River reactor complex near Aiken, South Carolina, by 1953 was producing not only tritium for thermonuclear warheads but also plutonium. Du Pont operated the facility for the AEC. Two new gaseous diffusion plants also were constructed at Paducah, Kentucky and Portsmouth, Ohio. Those plants operated under contract to private industry and came under the AEC's decentralized field-office system.[21]

A unique means of congressional oversight provided in the 1946 act monitored the overall operations of the AEC. Congress created the Joint Committee on Atomic Energy, which practically from the beginning acted as a powerful and sometimes highly critical watchdog of the Commission. The legislative history of the 1946 law does not show where the idea for the Joint Committee originated. But all the legislators familiar with plans for the new agency were cognizant of the vast powers they were giving to the executive branch and must have felt that some legislative device was essential to restrict the independence of the agency and to protect their traditional congressional prerogatives. The Joint

Committee was one of the few committees established by statute rather than by the rules of each House. Moreover, it was the only joint committee of Congress authorized to receive proposed legislation and recommend it to the Congress.[22]

The Joint Committee consisted of eighteen members, nine from the Senate and nine from the House, with not more than five senators or five representatives from the same political party. The law vested the group with full jurisdiction over "all bills, resolutions, and other matters in the Senate or the House of Representatives relating primarily to the Commission or to the development, use, and control of atomic energy." An important proviso also required the Commission to keep the Joint Committee "fully and currently informed with respect to the Commission's activities." The Joint Committee could appoint its own staff as well as utilize the services, information, facilities, and personnel of the executive branch.[23]

The Joint Committee performed four broad functions. The legislative function, in practice, did not become important until after passage of the 1954 Atomic Energy Act, which opened the technology to commercial enterprise. Thereafter, the group considered and recommended several amendments to the act in order to keep the law up to date as atomic-energy applications rapidly developed. When the Joint Committee considered amendments, it sent identical bills and reports containing recommendations to each House simultaneously. In considering presidential appointments the committee conducted hearings and formally advised the Senate of its position on confirmation. The Joint Committee's watchdog function over the AEC was particularly important during the period 1946–1954, when most AEC activities were secret, but it continued to carry out that role more publicly after passage of the 1954 law. The committee also assumed a policy-and-review function under which either the Joint Committee or individual members proposed policy changes or innovations in the atomic-energy program. Finally, the Joint Committee provided an information service. It conducted and published studies and held public hearings on many nonclassified aspects of the AEC's programs. Its collection of materials was a valuable public source in the rapidly changing technical field. Overall, the Joint Committee provided energetic leadership and close scrutiny of the AEC's policies on military applications of atomic energy and continuing oversight of the major civilian applications, particularly atomic-power generation.[24]

Although researchers in the Manhattan Project had concentrated on building a bomb, they had thought fleetingly about the possibility of developing an atomic-power reactor that would generate electricity. The 1946 act clearly indicated that the main purpose of atomic development, at least in the short term, applied to weapons development. However pressing that goal might have been, the Congress also contemplated the eventual use of atomic energy for peaceful purposes. The act's Declaration of Policy stated that the nation looked toward the day when "the development and utilization of atomic energy shall, so far as practicable, be directed toward improving the public welfare, increasing the standard of living, strengthening free competition in private enterprise, and promoting world peace." In effect, that declaration challenged the AEC to find some way to allow private enterprise to take advantage of the new technology without jeopardizing military secrets. During the period 1946–1954 two movements slowly unlocked the government's atomic monopoly. The Commission initiated one by considering future civilian uses in its reactor-development work on military applications. Industry attempted the other one through pressure for direct participation in atomic matters with the goal of establishing the feasibility of an atomic-power industry.[25]

Key AEC officials believed that private industry could best undertake power-reactor development. But until national-security considerations allowed loosening the restrictions of the 1946 act and until the agency could further explore power-reactor designs, it moved slowly on peaceful applications of atomic energy. The initial emphasis on building a weapons stockpile, the shortage of uranium, the need for secrecy, and President Truman's decision in January 1950 to proceed with work on the hydrogen bomb, relegated power-reactor development to a secondary priority. Nonetheless, the AEC undertook research on power reactors that eventually merged with industry's interest in opening up the technology.[26]

The idea of using atomic energy for electrical generation was based on the assumption that nuclear fission could replace fossil fuels as the basic energy source to convert water into steam to drive a turbine. Soon after the Second World War, atomic-power advocates promoted research aimed at replacing heat generated by fossil fuels with heat produced by a reactor. The basic physical phenomenon of nuclear fission that the physicists, engineers, and industrialists wanted to exploit is the splitting of a nucleus of an atom into two or more separate nuclei accompanied by the release of a large amount of energy. The reaction can be induced by a nucleus absorbing a neutron, or it can occur spontaneously, because of the unstable nature of some of the heavy isotopes. But among the heavy isotopes few can be readily excited to the state where the fission reaction occurs. Those few are limited to the isotopes of atomic number 90 (thorium) and above.

Nearly all the fissions in the fuel of a reactor result from neutron absorption in an isotope of atomic number 90 or higher. Only a few of these "fissionable" heavy isotopes can be used as reactor fuel: uranium 233, uranium 235, plutonium 239, and plutonium 241. Uranium 235 is a naturally occurring fissionable isotope that is used in the reactor fuel of all of today's commercial nuclear power plants in the United States. There also are artifically produced heavy isotopes suitable for fuels; these are uranium 233 (produced by irradiation of thorium 232 in a reactor) and plutonium 239 (produced by irradiation of uranium 238).

In reactor fuels, one or more fissionable isotopes are incorporated in the fuel elements. Usually the elements consist of metal sheaths that look like giant curtain rods. Each rod encases a large number of pellets of fissionable material in ceramic (oxide) form. Gathered in bundles, called subassemblies, the rods are placed in the reactor vessel in a regular geometric arrangement that permits the circulation of coolant over each rod to extract fission heat. This is the core of the reactor.

The number of neutrons produced varies with the different fissionable isotopes and with the energy of the absorbed neutron that causes the reaction. In an operating reactor the probability that a neutron will cause fission is highly (and generally inversely) dependent on the kinetic energy of the incident neutrons—that is, whether the neutron is "fast" or "slow."

The neutrons that are produced in the fission process are fast and are less likely to cause fission than slower neutrons. As a consequence, in the most common type of power reactor the kinetic energy of the fission neutrons is reduced to a value where it is more likely to cause fission. This is done by interposing between the fuel rods a medium that will slow down or "thermalize" the fission neutrons and do so without absorbing too many. The medium used, called the moderator, acts as a control factor to maintain the chain reaction. Ordinary or light water, graphite, heavy water, and organic materials have been used as moderators in commercial and experimental reactors. Fast reactors operate under somewhat different conditions and are designed to sustain a chain reaction using fast or high-energy neutrons; they require no moderator.

The amount and configuration of the moderator determines the degree of slowing down that occurs and, as a consequence, the amount of fuel necessary to maintain the chain reaction—that is, to keep the fission process going. As a practical matter, more fuel is put into the reactor than the amount that would just sustain a chain reaction. Because this additional fuel would create a "supercritical" reactor in which the chain reaction would continually increase beyond the capability of the reactor cooling system, it is necessary to include among the fuel bundles control devices known as control rods. Composed of materials that readily absorb the neutrons that are causing the fission, the control rods can be injected quickly into the core to shut off the chain reaction. When the control rods are taken out of the core, the neutron population builds up and the fission chain reaction begins again.

About 90 percent of the total energy released in an atomic reactor manifests itself as heat at or near the point of fission—that is, within the fuel in the core. The magnitude of this energy can be appreciated by considering that the fission of all the atoms in one pound of uranium 235 would yield about ten million kilowatt-hours of thermal energy or heat. In a power reactor a fluid, or reactor coolant, removes the fission heat from the core.[27] The choice of coolant determines many of the basic features of a power-reactor design. In light-water reactors the coolant also serves as the moderator. Coolant properties often directly determine the operating pressure and directly or indirectly limit the operating temperature of power reactors. The heat-transfer characteristics of a coolant also have an important bearing on the allowable power density in the reactor core. As different reactor concepts were developed, a variety of coolants were studied experimentally. Sodium, light water, certain organic fluids, and heavy water were extensively investigated in the development of power reactors.

A major concern in reactor technology is associated with the products of the fission process. Fission products include many radioactive isotopes that are important in a number of ways. Their radioactivity can damage the fuel elements and thus limit the time fuel can be allowed to remain in the reactor. In addition, fission products are the sources of most of the radioactivity in irradiated fuel. Because of this latter consideration, reactor design and operation had to provide for control and containment of fission products under both normal and abnormal conditions. Adequate protection of the safety and health of the general population from the hazards of fission products became a requirement in power-reactor design.

In 1947 top AEC officials anticipated that building atomic-power reactors for large-scale use would occur only in the distant future. Walter Zinn, director of the Argonne National Laboratory, where reactor research was a prime concern, reported that the best hope for power reactors rested with machines that would generate power and at the same time create or "breed" more fissionable material than they consumed. The shortage of existing stocks of uranium and the priority for using uranium in military applications made the so-called breeder reactor especially attractive. The possibility of breeding was based on the fact (experimentally confirmed during the Manhattan Project) that each fissioning nucleus of uranium or plutonium released more than two neutrons. One neutron was needed to sustain the chain reaction; the second would, in principle, be available for capture by the nucleus of a "fertile" atom such as uranium 238 or thorium 232 to create an atom of fissionable material to replace the original fissioning nucleus. Because more than two neutrons were emitted in the fission process, the possibility of creating more than the one replacement fissionable nucleus was envisioned. Thus a breeder would produce heat for power while at the same time produce more fissionable material than it consumed.

By 1947 the AEC had two experimental breeder reactors in early design stages. At Argonne, Zinn worked on the design for a small "fast" breeder (one without a moderator and using highly enriched fuel). This experimental breeder was constructed and commenced operation at the Idaho test facility in 1951. At General Electric's Knolls Atomic Power Laboratory near Schenectady, New York, researchers were investigating another type of breeder reactor, the "intermediate" breeder, so called because the chain reaction was sustained by neutrons with energies intermediate between slow and fast neutron energies. But they saw its construction as far in the future.[28]

By late 1948 the AEC had developed a five-reactor research plan that included the fast and intermediate breeders. The other three were a high-flux reactor, later called the materials-testing reactor, that was designed to test reactor fuels and materials for both military and civilian applications; a submarine-propulsion reactor, a thermal, water-cooled type that came under the direction of an ambitious naval officer, Captain Hyman Rickover, and was supported by Argonne and Westinghouse; and Oak Ridge's homogeneous reactor, based on a concept that eliminated the need to fabricate fuel elements and offered the possibility of continuous chemical processing of the fuel.[29]

The year 1949 witnessed both progress and setbacks for power-reactor development. Early in the year the Commission found an able director for its newly created Division of Reactor Development. Lawrence R. Hafstad, a physicist and former director of research at the Johns Hopkins University Applied Physics Laboratory, was a highly regarded scientist who brought considerable administrative skills to the post. In the spring the Commission settled on the Idaho location for a reactor test site. Those were positive signs that the government reactor program was taking shape.

But when the United States discovered in September that the Soviet Union had detonated its first atomic device the previous month, a renewed emphasis on military weapons and military reactor applications kept the development of civilian power reactors consigned to a low priority. The subsequent atomic-arms race also helped establish a preference among various reactor designs by giving an edge to Rickover's pressurized-light-water reactor for submarine propulsion.[30]

Nevertheless, some policy groundwork had been laid for power-reactor technology that could be exploited by private industry. For example, in October 1947 Chairman Lilienthal remarked to the Economics Club of Detroit that atoms for power lay far in the future. He noted how the continuing need for government secrecy precluded any private-industry initiative to use the technology. But the door was not completely closed. Lilienthal announced that the AEC was establishing an Industrial Advisory Group that would be allowed to survey classified agency activities for commercial possibilities.[31]

Headed by James W. Parker, president of the Detroit Edison Company, the committee included senior officials of the electric-power industry and industrial-research corporations. After a year's work the group's final report recommended that more technical information be declassified and published and that more contact be allowed between AEC staff, contractors, and industry representatives. The report, however, did not indicate what was perhaps the committee's most positive contribution to atomic-power development. Its work provided knowledge of Commission activities to its members, who were influential leaders of American industry.[32]

One persistent outsider influenced Lilienthal more than the members of the Parker committee. Philip Sporn, president of American Gas and Service Corporation in New York, frequently pleaded at length with the AEC chairman for more information on reactors. In turn, Lilienthal encouraged the AEC staff to take action in this area. In August 1949 the

Commission permitted a private advisory committee under Sporn's direction to examine AEC classified information related to power reactors. This set a basis for further technical cooperation between industry and the agency. But the Commission's military requirements, intensified by the Soviet atomic detonation the same month, sidetracked at least temporarily any further exploration of direct industrial participation in atomic-power development. Lilienthal resigned in February 1950 and was replaced as chairman in July by Gordon Dean.[33]

As a private citizen Lilienthal explained his frustration in attempting to open the atomic monopoly even slightly. He began a well-publicized article in Collier's in June 1950 with the statement that "no Soviet industrial monopoly is more completely owned by the state than is the industrial atom in free-enterprise America." He pointed his finger at the culprit—the Atomic Energy Act of 1946—and emphasized that the law should be repealed so that the industrial atom could be developed "in accord with the American system." His piece became the opening salvo of an effort to create a political atmosphere conducive to making changes in the 1946 act.[34]

At the same time that Lilienthal issued his challenge, a close friend, Charles A. Thomas of the Monsanto Chemical Company, proposed to the Commission that his company be allowed to design, construct, and operate atomic-power plants at its own expense to produce both power and plutonium. Thomas was no newcomer to the atomic field. He was aware of the AEC's earlier attempts to establish closer ties with industry and recognized the agency's pressing need in 1950 to increase plutonium production because of the new demands for weapons. Thomas's suggestion for a dual-purpose reactor, therefore, appealed to agency requirements as well as to the hope of the industry for direct participation in atomic-power development. He saw two benefits to industry if his proposals were accepted. The agency would allow industry access to classified technical information, and the sale of plutonium to the government would offset the expected noncompetitive cost of atomic power, making the dual-purpose reactor attractive to the power industry. After extensive examination of the Thomas proposal in the summer of 1950, the AEC staff concluded that the agency should allow Monsanto representatives to study the agency's reactor-development program to determine the feasibility of development and construction of the proposed reactor. In the fall a similar proposal for industry participation came jointly from the Detroit Edison Company and the Dow Chemical Company. The AEC thought that more proposals from other companies might be forthcoming; accordingly, the Commission in December established a general policy on industrial reactor-development.[35]

Announced in January 1951 as the Industrial Participation Program, the policy limited proposals to surveys of existing reactor data. The AEC would grant security clearances to a number of industry technical personnel, and each industrial group would submit a feasibility report on its reactor concept to the Commission. If a project produced a promising reactor design, the AEC would consider government financing for a company's development work.[36]

The announcement of the Industrial Participation Program immediately brought two more proposals, one from the Commonwealth Edison Company of Chicago, and a joint one from the San Francisco–based Bechtel Corporation and the Pacific Gas and Electric Company. Encouraged by the initial proposals, the AEC announced a second round in 1952. A wide range of industrial, research, and electric-power concerns either joined the initial groups or submitted proposals of their own during that round.[37]

Most study groups incorporated the dual-purpose machine in their concepts; however, they suggested a variety of designs. The Monsanto proposal studied a graphite-moderated, sodium-cooled 150-megawatt reactor that would also produce plutonium. The Detroit Edison–Dow Chemical team concentrated on a fast-breeder concept. Commonwealth Edison initially evaluated a helium-cooled, graphite-moderated machine fueled with natural uranium as well as a reactor moderated and cooled by pressurized heavy water and fueled with natural uranium. Later the Chicago-based company submitted additional proposals to study homogeneous and sodium-graphite reactors, and an intermediate power breeder similar to the Knolls Atomic Power Laboratory design. The Bechtel–Pacific Gas and Electric group investigated a heavy-water-moderated, light-water-cooled reactor using natural uranium, and a sodium-cooled breeder. These initial studies took time, since the companies had first to gain knowledge of reactor technology. Clearly, though, the program produced evidence that some industrial leaders were willing to move ahead if the restrictive terms of the 1946 act were eased.[38]

While industry and the AEC worked on reactor development, the Joint Committee contributed significantly to changing the political atmosphere. Until 1952 the committee had not paid much attention to commercial development because it had been fully engrossed in the agency's propulsion- and production-reactor programs for the military. In the summer of 1952, however, the Joint Committee began its own investigations that eventually resulted in opening atomic technology to private development.

By the fall of 1952 the Joint Committee staff had compiled a four-hundred page information-laden document entitled "Atomic Power and Private Enterprise." The compendium presented in rich detail the current history of commercial power-reactor development. It included papers that discussed law, technology, secrecy, and the roles of government and industry; it incorporated speeches by AEC commissioners and other agency personnel; and it showed the positive results of an informal opinion-poll of "company executives, Government officials, scientists, lawyers, and others" with regard to opening the technology to private enterprise. The poll left no doubt that technological developments had created a strong interest in domestic nuclear-power application. The overall document also showed that the 1946 act lacked the flexibility to address the administrative and financial arrangements necessary for commercial development. In summary, the report indicated the complexity of the issues the government faced if it was to devise a national nuclear-power policy. The Joint Committee intended to use the information as a basis for hearings it scheduled for the following summer.[39]

In a statement opening the public hearings in June 1953, Joint Committee members emphasized that it was "necessary to develop a public understanding of the subject [of private development of atomic power] before determining whether a legislative expression of national policy should be made." Over the course of the month-long sessions, more than fifty individuals representing forty-six companies, organizations, and government agencies presented their views. All who testified seemed to agree that atomic power was important to the future economy not only of the United States but of the world. Most maintained that in order to bring about power-reactor development, government assistance was necessary, particularly in the areas of research and development, investment, public health and safety, and defense and security. Joint Committee chairman W. Sterling Cole suggested that the AEC should develop plans for "research and development in the field of atomic power components, pilot plants, and prototypes," so that the private sector would have guidelines to follow in planning its own participation. If nothing more, the hearings showed an auspicious climate on Capitol Hill for legislative changes to promote private development of reactor technology.[40]

The policy statement that retiring AEC chairman Gordon Dean presented to the Joint Committee hearings was a compromise between the AEC staff's proposed approach to atomic power and the views of the newly elected Dwight D. Eisenhower administration. Early staff drafts had envisioned government development of atomic power with private assistance. By contrast, Eisenhower's advisers, especially those on the National Security Council, called for more private development with government assistance. Dean's statement followed a middle course, suggesting that both government and industry should participate, but leaving in question how much financial support each one would contribute. Dean suggested, and his designated successor Lewis Strauss reiterated in his closing statement, that successful development would not totally depend on either industry or government alone, but rather on a joint venture that would draw the best from the government's technological expertise and the competitive nature of the free-enterprise system. The hearings reinforced this view in making it clear that private industry was not prepared to assume the full cost of development and that government support would be necessary.[41]

The summer hearings gave support to AEC plans to go forward with funding of a major power-reactor development project the agency was considering at the time. The Commission negotiated with the Duquesne Light Company and the Westinghouse Electric Corporation to design, build, and operate a demonstration pressurized-light-water reactor with a sixty-megawatt electric capacity at Shippingport, Pennsylvania. Since the 1946 act prohibited private ownership, the Commission would retain title to the reactor while Duquesne Light owned the electrical portion— that is, the turbine and related electrical-generating facilities. Duquesne would operate the plant, pay the AEC for the steam, and distribute the power through its electrical grid. Westinghouse would design the facility.

The choice of Westinghouse as the prime design contractor and the light-water reactor concept were based on the company's successful venture with Hyman Rickover's submarine-propulsion project, whose land-based light-water prototype had achieved criticality in March 1953 and had generated power in May. Rickover's naval reactors group had worked with Westinghouse's Pittsburgh-based Bettis Atomic Power Laboratory. The success of the navy project prompted the AEC to ask Rickover to work with the company on the Shippingport reactor.

The pressurized-light-water reactor constructed at Shippingport employed ordinary water as both moderator and coolant and was pressurized to keep the coolant stream from boiling. The reactor coolant circulated in a closed primary loop that included a steam generator. In passing through the steam generator the primary-loop coolant transferred heat to water flowing through a secondary loop, thereby generating steam that was fed to a steam turbine. Several considerations led to the selection of this type of reactor for the Shippingport project. Rickover's previous work with pressurized-water reactors had brought the technology to an advanced development stage relative to that of other concepts. Experience had shown that pressurized-water reactors were stable in operation, had advantageous safety characteristics, and could achieve high power densities. Furthermore, ordinary water had good heat-transfer properties, and engineers were well acquainted with its use as a heat-exchange medium. The Shippingport project greatly enhanced the commercial prospects of the light-water reactor design over other competing reactor systems.

Even with the relatively advanced and proven design of the light-water machine, the cost of the Shippingport project was more than private industry was prepared to commit. So in 1953 the AEC funded the plant. In spite of and, in fact, because of the restrictive provisions of the 1946 law, Shippingport was important in involving industry more intimately in the development of central atomic-power stations. A more subtle significance pointed to the need for statute revision if private rather than government projects were to proceed.[42]

Throughout 1953, private-sector interest in peaceful uses of atomic power became increasingly evident. The Joint Committee's study underscored this trend, as did the founding in the spring of the Atomic Industrial Forum, an organization of businessmen, engineers, scientists, and educators interested in atomic-energy development. The Forum served as a stimulant to industrial participation; its board of directors included executives of large corporations and universities who had a direct stake in atomic development. Likewise, the Eisenhower administration, with its decidedly conservative and business-oriented disposition, strengthened the climate for a change in the law that would allow private enterprise to enter more fully into the atomic age.

The interest of government and industry leaders in atomic power arose from a number of considerations. One was projected national-energy requirements. Although conventional fuels were plentiful for the short term, experts predicted that the United States would need sizable amounts of atomic power for electrical generation in the foreseeable future. In a 1952 report that commanded wide attention, the President's Materials

Policy Commission, chaired by William S. Paley, suggested that world shortages of fossil-fuel sources might become serious as early as 1975. While acknowledging the many existing uncertainties about the costs and feasibility of harnessing atomic energy for power production, it urged that development proceed to help meet future demands. Witnesses at the Joint Committee's 1953 hearings made the same point, maintaining that atomic power would be an important component of America's long-range energy requirements.[43]

The projected energy demands of the United States were hardly enough in themselves to give a sense of urgency to the atomic-power program. America's need for electricity from nuclear fission appeared to be at least a generation away, allowing ample time for a measured pace of development. Other considerations, however, were of much more immediate significance. The most prominent centered on the implications of fostering the growth of atomic power for America's international prestige and leadership. Although the United States could meet its energy requirements for many years without using atomic energy, in other nations the need for new sources of power was more pressing.

Many authorities from inside and outside the government emphasized the vital importance of maintaining America's preeminent position in nuclear technology. They echoed the statement of Gordon Dean during the Joint Committee's hearings: "It would be a major setback to the position of this country in the world to allow its present leadership in nuclear power development to pass out of its hands." The strides Great Britain was making in the field were disturbing enough, but the possibility that the Soviet Union might surpass the United States in peaceful atomic progress was even more ominous. "We cannot be indifferent to the enormous psychological advantage that the Soviets would gain if they demonstrated to a tense and divided world the ability to put the atom to work in peacetime civilian pursuits," declared California congressman Chet Holifield, a member of the Joint Committee. "The United States will not take second place in the contest." AEC commissioner Thomas E. Murray addressed the same issue in a speech in October 1953, depicting a "nuclear power race" in which the "stakes are high." He added: "Once we become fully conscious of the possibility that power hungry countries will gravitate toward the USSR if it wins the nuclear power race, . . . it will be quite clear that this power race is no Everest-climbing, kudos-providing contest."[44]

Related to the concern for maintaining American leadership in nuclear power and enhancing its position in the world was an impulse to employ atomic technology for constructive purposes rather than exclusively for military requirements. "The elemental force of the split atom—the force which protects this nation in the form of atomic weapons—will someday be harnessed to make this world nearer our hearts' desires," remarked Joint Committee chairman Cole. "We have a positive obligation to show decent people everywhere—by deed as well as by word—that we wish to share the benefits of peaceful atomic energy with all free peoples." The most dramatic statement of the desire to turn atoms into plowshares was President Eisenhower's address, "Atomic Power for Peace," before the United Nations General Assembly on 8 December 1953. Since assuming office the previous January, the president had become increasingly concerned about the growing arms race and finding means to make its implications clear to the American people. The Soviet detonation of a thermonuclear device in August had intensified his determination to explain frankly the perils of nuclear war. For months, Eisenhower's advisors worked on a draft speech, but the president found them too negative in emphasizing the destructiveness of atomic energy. He finally decided on a more positive approach that would point out the horror of nuclear war while at the same time offering hope through expanding the beneficial uses of atomic energy.[45]

In his United Nations speech Eisenhower cited the threat of "human degradation and destruction" but coupled it with a proposal to apply scientific resources and knowledge for more exalted purposes. He called for the creation of an International Atomic Energy Agency to accept contributions of fissionable materials from the nuclear powers. The agency would allocate its supplies for "the peaceful pursuits of mankind." In this way, the president suggested, "the contributing powers would be dedicating some of their strength to serve the needs rather than the fears of mankind." Eisenhower's speech was partly propaganda; and, as he privately acknowledged, his proposal, if adopted, would favor the United States because it possessed larger stockpiles of nuclear arms than the Soviets. But it also embodied a sincere urge on the part of the president and many other authorities to transform atomic energy into a peaceful and positive asset to serve the entire world.[46]

Eisenhower's United Nations speech not only set the tone for a new foreign-policy initiative but also for a new domestic atomic policy. In a February 1954 message to Congress the president requested fundamental changes in the 1946 Atomic Energy Act, further alerting the nation that his administration would place greater emphasis on both peaceful and private development of atomic power. Eisenhower argued that general progress in nuclear science and technology had outdistanced the most optimistic predictions of 1946, making the existing legislation "inconsistent with the nuclear realities of 1954." Along with recommendations for relaxing the 1946 law to allow friendly nations to share in restricted data and research on atomic energy, he called on Congress to amend the statute to encourage private domestic development of the technology. He favored unlocking the government monopoly because he believed that private industry could "assure the greatest efficiency and progress at the least cost to the public." The president wanted the new industry to proceed under government supervision, "with careful regulation to protect the national security and the public health and safety."[47]

By 1954, then, a confluence of perceptions and developments led to a sweeping revision of the 1946 Atomic Energy Act and an end to the government's monopoly on nuclear technology. The technical know-how for building atomic-power plants was available. A long-term need for new sources of energy was widely accepted. A number of private concerns had expressed deep interest in the use of atomic energy if they could get access to information and if they received government assistance. And the widespread desire to enhance America's international prestige, maintain its world leadership, and promote the beneficial applications of atomic energy infused a heightened sense of urgency to inaugurating a full-scale atomic-power program.

As early as May 1953 the AEC staff had prepared draft legislation that would embody a new approach to atomic power through amendment of the 1946 act. Thorny questions regarding patents, use of source material, international cooperation, use of classified information, and monopolization by those companies that had gained competence by holding AEC contracts were the important issues the staff and the commissioners addressed. After customary submission to the Bureau of the Budget and review and criticism by other agencies, the AEC sent two draft pieces of amending legislation, one dealing with the international and security aspects of atomic energy, the other with private participation, to the Joint Committee in February 1954.[48]

Corbin Allardice, the Joint Committee staff director, reviewed the AEC bills and determined that a single piece of legislation would be preferable to the AEC amendments. Chairman Cole later explained to his House colleagues why the AEC drafts were objectionable. Those bills, he said, "gave the President such rather complete, unlimited, and unrestricted authority, both in the domestic and in the international field," that he refused to introduce them. He insisted that they would not have been acceptable to the Joint Committee and certainly not the entire House.

Consequently, Cole, Joint Committee vice-chairman Bourke Hickenlooper, Allardice, and committee counsel George Norris, Jr. drafted a new consolidated bill. Norris, with extensive industrial experience, was particularly helpful in writing portions of the legislation that would bring private industry into the atomic-energy field. Considered by some as the father of the 1954 act, Norris selected the Federal Communications Act of 1934 as a model for the new legislation and extracted almost verbatim the licensing provisions of that law for the atomic bill. The initial draft was then thoroughly discussed in committee. Cole later commented: "The Joint Committee . . . spent 5 weeks, I believe, going through that bill, paragraph by paragraph, line by line and item by item." By April 1954 the bill was ready.[49]

The committee scheduled both executive-session hearings and public hearings that opened on 3 May and ran until 18 June. Initially, the Joint Committee met with the commissioners in closed session to gather their views on the proposed legislation. The first meeting on 3 May, however, turned to concerns among the commissioners over their collegial role in running the agency. The exchange of views, particularly between Chairman Strauss and Commissioner Thomas E. Murray, underscored the personal bitterness that had arisen between the two men and foreshadowed future policy conflicts within the Commission.[50]

President Truman had appointed Murray to the Commission in May 1950, shortly after Strauss had left. A millionaire by inheritance, Murray was the son of an immigrant Irishman who made a fortune through construction of power-generating stations in New York that later became the nucleus of the Consolidated Edison network. Trained in mechanical engineering at Yale, the younger Murray became an industrialist in his own right after moving into his family's electrical-manufacturing business. In his early career he acquired more than two hundred electrical and welding patents and became president of the Metropolitan Engineering Company. Furthermore, he was an influential director of its parent organization, the Murray Manufacturing Company, which made welding devices and electrical switches.

A devout religious and family man, Murray exhibited strong character and moral convictions. He attended Roman Catholic mass every day and built private chapels in his Long Island home and Park Avenue apartment. He presided over a family of eleven children and took great pride in the fact that two of his sons were Jesuit priests. His frail appearance was coupled with a bashful voice and gentle manner that outwardly belied a strong will and stubborn pride. When he believed he was on the correct side of an issue, he was a tenacious fighter. In his sixties when he joined the Commission, Murray took enormous pride in what he thought the atom could do to better the condition of the world. He viewed nuclear technology as a divine gift that the United States had a moral duty to develop to prove the superiority of its capitalistic society.[51]

Henry DeWolf Smyth and Eugene M. Zuckert were also old hands, having served on the Commission since 1949 and 1952 respectively. Both would leave before the year was out. Smyth, a brilliant Princeton physicist who had worked on the Manhattan Project, replaced Bacher as the scientist on the Commission. Zuckert, a Yale-educated lawyer, had helped organize the new Department of the Air Force in 1946 and became assistant secretary the following year, experiences that gave him a keen sense for administration. The fifth commissioner was Joseph Campbell, on leave from his position as treasurer of Columbia University, who had joined the Commission in the same month as Strauss.

The issue that caused disagreement centered on language in the Joint Committee bill that designated the chairman as "principal officer" of the Commission. It brought to a head the role Strauss had followed since his appointment the previous July as both chairman and special adviser to the president on atomic energy. To Murray in particular, and to a lesser degree to Smyth and Zuckert, the "principal officer" phrase indicated that Strauss sought to undermine the equality and collegiality among the commissioners that had generally prevailed since the agency's establishment. Strauss pointed out that the 1946 act did not delineate the chairman's responsibilities in relation to those of the commissioners, and that no consensus had developed on how to clarify the situation. He argued that the chairman should have more authority than the 1946 act had granted.[52]

Murray's views reflected the personal animosity that had grown between him and Strauss. He expressed his concern that "centralization of authority in the chairman" might "invalidate the effectiveness of the commission form of organization." In a comment directed at Strauss, Murray told the Joint Committee that "exploitation of the indefinite meaning of principal officer would pave the way to a de facto one-man commission." The issue was not resolved until Murray submitted to the Joint Committee suggested clarifying language for the principal-officer section, stipulating that each commissioner have "equal authority and responsibility" and "full access to all information." The Joint Committee then revised the bill. It designated the chairman as "official spokesman" rather than "principal officer" and incorporated Murray's suggestion that each member of the Commission "have equal responsibility and authority" in all actions.[53]

The Committee's debate on the principal-officer issue revealed tension among the commissioners just at the time when the agency was about to be given expanded responsibilities. The issue underscored the legal ambiguities defining the role of the chairman and the commissioners, which, in effect, allowed the chairman's position to be based on the personality and operating style of a particular incumbent. Lilienthal and Dean had largely avoided problems because their personalities had bridged any potential major disagreements. But it appeared that Strauss was placing his imprint on the Commission through his combative style. The problem was deepened further by Strauss serving both as chairman and as special adviser to the president, which allowed him access to information denied the other commissioners.

In addition to personality conflicts among the commissioners, some substantive policy differences arose between the Joint Committee and the AEC on the proposed legislation. Two major areas involved ownership of fissionable material and the always complicated question of patents. The Joint Committee bill required government ownership of fissionable materials; the AEC argued it would be impractical for the government to retain ownership if it was going to allow private ownership of reactors. Much discussion took place on the subject both in executive session and in the public hearings. Generally, private industry supported the AEC argument. But the Joint Committee, sensing that Congress would never pass a bill that allowed private ownership of fissionable material sufficient to make weapons, insisted on continued government control.[54]

The patent question arose from the section that abolished the special patent provisions of the 1946 act without substituting any transition for licensing of patents developed under government contract. Strauss, reflecting not only the agency view but that of President Eisenhower, argued for a transition period of compulsory licensing of patents developed under government contract. This would prevent monopoly of the industry by a few companies that had secured an advantage as contractors to the AEC. This issue also received prolonged discussion in the public hearings, and was set in a larger contextual argument over industrial monopoly. The AEC's position prevailed as Congress completely revised the section on patents in its bill requiring licensing for a five-year period. After a sustained argument over this issue in a later House-Senate conference, it remained intact in the final bill.[55]

The purpose of the revisions of the 1946 act was to allow atomic technology to enter the mainstream of American industrial life. In remarks to the House in April when the original bill was introduced, Sterling Cole indicated that the major intent of the act was to "give a material and substantive start in law to a new atomic industry." The Joint Committee's hearings and the long, hot summer debate resulted in a thorough analysis of the bill's provisions, including heated exchanges on whether the government should allow private industry to produce atomic power, and if so, on what terms. Industrial spokesmen quite naturally favored amending the 1946 law in order to foster a civilian atomic-power industry, although some had reservations about the draft bill. Walker L. Cisler, president of the Detroit Edison Company, stated that industry was eager to participate in the development of atomic power. Cisler bluntly put the responsibility on the legislators: "The question Congress must consider is whether at this critical period in the development, industry using its own funds, will be given the opportunity to perform its natural function of seeking out economic methods of utilizing this natural energy resource and making the resulting benefits available to all in a normal manner, or whether industry is to be restricted in its opportunities by a continuation of the existing law. In our minds we must proceed along natural and traditional lines."[56]

Alfred Iddles, president of the Babcock and Wilcox Company, a major industrial-equipment manufacturer, argued that the inclusion of private enterprise in the development of atomic power "can only be attained if the basis of participation is made sufficiently attractive for investment of private capital." He thought that elements of the draft bill, especially the licensing provisions and government retention of ownership of special nuclear materials, would reduce interest in private investment. Francis K. McCune, general manager of the Atomic Products Division of General Electric, spoke about the problem of regulation. Although he thought it "inevitable that atomic energy will be one of the most heavily regulated of all American industries," he maintained that the regulatory structure need not be an obstacle to development. "To the degree that the rules of the game established by the act are clear, the Commission and industry will be able to work together, and will be able to avoid disputes about what may, or may not, be done. This is the most important single condition to the successful growth of a regulated industry."[57]

In closing his February 1954 message to Congress proposing new atomic-energy legislation, President Eisenhower recommended authorizing the AEC "to establish minimum safety and security regulations to govern the use and possession of fissionable material." In accordance with his emphasis on the greatest possible encouragement of private development of atomic energy, he urged flexibility in the licensing and regulatory provisions of the law.[58]

Congress followed his advice. The legislators thought it would reflect poorly on them if they wrote legislation that was too specific or too rigid. They used broad statutory language and left implementation to the experts: the engineers, scientists, attorneys, and businessmen whose task would be to apply their special skills and knowledge to make the general law work. Throughout the 1954 act's sections on licensing and regulation, the phrase "to protect the health and safety of the public" stated the objectives of those functions in the most general of terms.[59]

Although the goal of protecting public health and safety was cited frequently throughout the act, the legislative history revealed little discussion on the subject or attempts to define the dangers to health and safety. The Senate and House reports on the legislation contrasted conditions in 1946 with those in 1954. In 1946, the reports said, "there was little experience concerning the health hazards involved in operating atomic plants," while by 1954 it had become "evident that greater participation in power development need not bring with it attendant hazards to the health and safety of the American people." The 1954 legislation left specific standards in the area of public health and safety to the AEC. As a consequence, the agency faced the task of developing both a regulatory organization and a licensing mechanism that would grow side by side with the new industry. How well it could perform that function was unknown at the time, but there appeared little concern on the part of the administration, members of the Joint Committee, or the Commission about whether it could carry out its responsibilities for public health and safety.[60]

Congress finally passed the new Atomic Energy Act in August 1954, despite the objections of some legislators who complained that it would lead to private monopoly of atomic power and preclude public-power initiatives. Eisenhower signed the measure into law on 30 August.[61]

The 1954 law provided a new and optimistic symbol to stand beside the negative ones that had dominated since the Hiroshima and Nagasaki bombings of 1945. Although the law reaffirmed national policy on military applications of the atom, it added some wider dimensions. The new law embodied the positive aspects of atomic technology and reflected the changing technological, political, and industrial milieu by instructing the AEC to provide "a program to encourage widespread participation in the development and utilization of atomic energy for peaceful purposes." Although the Commission still would spend most of its time building and testing weapons, retain ownership of fissionable materials, and hold vast files of restricted data on atomic technology, it had acquired new authority to develop a technology from which many important benefits were expected. In guiding the transition of atomic energy from strict government control to commercial use by private enterprise, the AEC also assumed responsibility for protecting public health and safety from the hazards that would accompany industrial growth.

II

THE PRINCIPLES OF
RADIATION PROTECTION

The possibility that workers in atomic plants or the general public could be exposed to radiation in concentrations high enough to cause serious injury was the paramount danger of the expanding use of peaceful atomic energy and the central focus of the Atomic Energy Commission's regulatory policies. Although scientists and health experts had recognized and studied the harmful effects of radiation for many years, radiation hazards did not become a source of sustained public interest until the mid-1950s. At that time, nuclear-bomb testing by the United States, Great Britain, and the Soviet Union generated widespread concern about the health implications of radioactive fallout. The fallout question greatly increased public awareness of radiation and stirred contentious debate about the magnitude of its risks. Scientists divided in their opinions about fallout hazards, largely because empirical evidence was inadequate and inconclusive. The issues of what levels of exposure were acceptable and how to balance the dangers of radiation against its benefits inevitably involved subjective assessments and political judgments. The fallout controversy was the key factor in stirring political responses and defining public attitudes toward radiation during the late 1950s and early 1960s. It also exerted a major impact on the AEC's formulation of radiation-protection standards for its peacetime atomic programs.

Initially, the general public had viewed radiation more with fascination than with fear. One form of radiation was first identified in 1895 when German physicist Wilhelm Konrad Roentgen discovered X rays. The announcement of Roentgen's findings generated a wave of excitement that was fueled by numerous newspaper and magazine articles, public demonstrations of X-ray machines, promises that unwanted body hair could be removed, and experiments on therapeutic uses of X rays. Scientific interest in X rays soon led to the detection of other forms of radiation that were produced by radioactivity. After French physicist Henri Becquerel discovered natural radioactivity in 1896, Pierre and Marie Curie elaborated on his work and isolated the highly radioactive element radium in 1898. Information—and much misinformation—about radium was disseminated in a plethora of books, articles, editorials, and lectures. The element was credited with a rich variety of beneficial uses, such as curing cancer and blindness, determining an unborn child's sex, and changing skin pigment. In the popular hoopla over the wonders of X rays and radium, the hazards of radiation were generally overlooked, though concern that X rays might compromise feminine modesty inspired at least one firm to promote lead-lined undergarments.[1]

Scientific investigators quickly learned, however, that radiation could cause much more serious problems. Researchers who worked with X rays and radioactive materials reported loss of hair, skin irritations, and in some cases severe burns in exposed areas. Within a short time after the discovery of X rays and radioactivity some scientists and physicians had concluded that heavy doses of radiation could produce sterility, bone disease, and cancer. Those and other harmful consequences arose from the ionizing effect of radiation on human cell structure, a process that was incomprehensible at the time and incompletely understood even much later. Radiation is energy, whether in the form of X rays or in the form of alpha or beta particles or gamma rays, which are emitted as the atomic nuclei of radioactive elements undergo spontaneous disintegration. The products of radioactive decay differ from one another in mass, electrical charge, and power of penetration. When radiation passes through matter and collides with surrounding atoms, it can alter their structure, often by stripping electrons from them. This creates fragments called ions. Such changes in the composition of a cell's atoms can cause mutations or cell death and ultimately lead to serious biological injury. The severity of hazard depends on a number of variables, including the dose of radiation absorbed, the rate at which it is received, the sensitivity of different body organs, and the form of radiation to which one is exposed. Gamma rays from natural radioactive decay and X rays from man-made machines can penetrate far inside the body from external sources; alpha and beta particles are too weak to penetrate deeply from outside but are harmful if breathed or swallowed and lodged in internal organs.[2]

Reports of injuries caused by X rays created signs of public concern that galvanized professional efforts to promote precautions against X-ray hazards. As early as 1913 the German Roentgen Society developed a list of guidelines to shield X-ray operators from excessive exposure, and the British Roentgen Society took similar action two years later. In response to a significant increase in the use—and misuse—of X rays during World War I, a group of British radiologists and physicians formed a radiation-protection committee in 1921 and issued a series of more detailed recommendations for safeguarding workers from the harmful effects of X rays and radium. During the 1920s growing recognition of serious health problems stemming from overexposure to radium prompted professionals to devote even more attention to devising protective measures against radiation. Their activities culminated in 1928, when the Second International Congress of Radiology organized the International X-Ray and Radium Protection Committee, which was originally composed of five members from different countries. The following year, representatives of four professional societies and several X-ray equipment manufacturers in the United States formed an eight-member American counterpart of the international committee, the Advisory Committee on X-Ray and Radium Protection. The American committee established an informal connection with the U.S. National Bureau of Standards because of its leadership in radiation research and because the international committee had asked the Bureau to designate an official U.S. delegate to its meetings. The Bureau agreed to publish reports of the national committee, though it stipulated that it would not officially endorse the committee's recommendations.[3]

Both the international and the U.S. committees were informal groups of experts who gathered periodically to discuss findings, provide information, and offer guidance on radiation protection. Neither had any official standing or statutory authority; their influence derived from the respect their members commanded. Contacts between the committees and overlaps in their memberships contributed to a general consensus in their positions. Lauriston S. Taylor, a Cornell-trained physicist who had joined the National Bureau of Standards in 1927 to organize an X-ray standards program, served as chairman of the American committee and U.S. representative on the international body.

In their initial meetings each committee refrained from bold new statements, though they did adopt suggestions for safeguarding radiation workers that enlarged and refined earlier proposals. In 1934, however, both the American and the international committees took an unprecedented step by recommending a quantitative "tolerance dose" of radiation. During the 1920s scientists had researched and discussed the possibility of defining a numerical level below which radiation would not cause observable injury, but knowledge and experimental data were too limited to allow development of specific criteria. Only after more information became available did radiation experts feel confident enough to propose a tolerance dose. The levels they recommended were based on a unit of measurement that had recently gained wide acceptance, the roentgen (r). A roentgen indicated the quantity of X rays or gamma rays that would produce a specified degree of ionization under prescribed conditions. The U.S. committee agreed on a tolerance dose of 0.1 r per day for whole-body exposure to radiation and 5 r per day for fingers. The international committee set a whole-body limit of 0.2 r per day from X rays, though unlike the American group, it excluded radium-produced gamma rays from its recommendations.[4]

Although the international committee's tolerance dose for X rays was twice as permissive as that of the U.S. committee, the discrepancy resulted not from any fundamental disagreement but from differences in rounding off similar figures calculated from available data. Both groups based their recommendations on evidence that they acknowledged was incomplete, and neither claimed that its tolerance dose was definitive. They believed that available information made their proposals reasonable and provided an adequate margin of safety for persons in normal health working in average conditions. The radiation experts did not regard the exposure levels as inviolable rules; a person who absorbed more than the recommended limits would not necessarily suffer harm. Both committees recognized that exposure to radiation in any amount might be detrimental, but they considered levels below the tolerance dose to be generally safe and unlikely to cause permanent damage "in the average individual." Their recommendations represented a tentative effort to establish practical guidelines that would reduce injuries to radiation workers. Although the tolerance doses were based on imperfect knowledge and unproved assumptions, they were an important advance in the theory and practice of radiation protection.[5]

In addition to their efforts to control the dangers of X rays, radiation experts became increasingly concerned about the effects of "internal emitters" taken into the body. Unlike X rays, which can penetrate deeply through the skin from external sources, the alpha and beta particles that internal emitters give off are too weak to penetrate into vital human tissue from outside the body. But if they enter the body by consumption of irradiated food or liquids or by breathing contaminated air, their radioactivity poses grave hazards because of the damage it can cause in surrounding tissue. Scientists initially became aware of the effects of internal radiation from tragic experiences with radium. During the 1920s medical reports first cited the harmful and sometimes fatal consequences suffered by workers who painted radium dials on watches and who frequently licked their brushes to a point to facilitate their task. Other illnesses and fatalities resulted from usage of radium for its alleged curative powers. Physicians sometimes prescribed radium-spiked water or injected radium intravenously to treat a variety of disorders ranging from acne to heart disease, and some companies sold radium solutions as an all-purpose health tonic. Cases of cancer, other serious diseases, and deaths attributable to ingestion of radium generated wide publicity and concern during the 1920s and 1930s and helped spur scientific investigation on the effects of the element. Researchers learned that once inside the body, radium tends to settle in bone tissue, where it is virtually impossible to dislodge and impervious to medical treatment. Therefore, it was essential to prevent harmful concentrations of the element from entering the body. On the basis of extensive research and deliberation on what constituted a safe level of radium, the U.S. Advisory Committee on X-Ray and Radium Protection advised in 1941 that any worker who showed a deposit of more than 0.1 micrograms of radium should change employment immediately. It also recommended a maximum concentration of radon gas, a decay product of radium, in the air in working places.[6]

The findings and recommendations of the American radiation-protection committee provided the basis for radiological health programs during the wartime Manhattan Project. The Project's Health Division, established in the Metallurgical Laboratory at the University of Chicago in mid-1942 and headed by University of California radiologist Robert S. Stone, confronted some formidable problems. Not only was existing scientific understanding of radiation from X rays and radium tenuous and problematical, but experiments with nuclear reactions created many new radioactive substances about which even less was known. Furthermore, the effort to build an atomic bomb exposed many more people to radiation than the relatively few who had worked earlier with X rays and radium. Mindful of the severe injuries resulting from ignorance of the harmful effects of X rays and radium in previous years, the Health Division insisted on conservative standards and practices to safeguard employees of the Manhattan Project. For radiation from external sources it adopted the level recommended by the U.S. Advisory Committee on X-Ray and Radium Protection, and for internal emitters it set a goal of preventing any exposure at all. The objectives could not always be achieved; cases of overexposure inevitably occurred. The most serious were accidents in August 1945 and May 1946 that each claimed the life of a researcher who received acute doses of radiation. But overall, the Manhattan Project compiled a remarkable safety record, especially in light of the extraordinary exigencies of time and the many uncertainties about the nature of the materials being handled. Research done by the Health Division significantly enhanced scientific knowledge about the biological effects of radiation and led to the development of improved instruments for detection and measurement of it.[7]

The dawn of the atomic age made a careful reassessment of prewar radiation-protection precepts and practices essential. In the immediate postwar years, both the American and the international radiation-protection committees made organizational changes, modified their philosophy of radiological safety, and lowered their suggested exposure levels. Since its activities would inevitably extend beyond X rays and radium, in 1946 the U.S. body adopted a new name, the National Committee on Radiation Protection (NCRP). It reaffirmed Lauriston Taylor as chairman, enlarged the membership of its "main committee" to twenty-six, and created several subcommittees to study specific problems. The NCRP included among its new members representatives of government agencies concerned with radiation protection, such as the U.S. Public Health Service, military departments, and the Atomic Energy Commission. The committee was determined to preserve its independence and avoid undue influence by the government, though it maintained its ties with the National Bureau of Standards and accepted limited funds from the AEC to defray travel expenses of its members.[8]

The relationship between the NCRP and the AEC was informal and generally cooperative, but at times it was uneasy. The AEC took a keen interest in the committee's activities because the NCRP's recommendations indirectly affected its operations. When the AEC learned that the NCRP was considering lowering the tolerance dose for radiation workers, it pressed for information in advance of formal publication. Despite the reluctance of some members, the NCRP agreed to give the AEC preliminary guidance on what its new exposure levels were likely to be. The committee was less accommodating on another AEC request. In February 1947 the AEC asked to review an updated edition of an NCRP handbook on X-ray protection prior to publication to make certain that it contained no restricted data. The request caused the NCRP "considerable concern." It replied that it would submit potentially sensitive material that the AEC was legally obliged to protect, but found it unnecessary and undesirable to do so with publications on subjects outside the AEC's jurisdiction, such as the X-ray handbook. The AEC accepted that argument while reiterating its insistence that the NCRP guard against the inadvertent disclosure of classified information.[9]

Shortly after its 1946 reorganization, the NCRP reassessed its position on radiation-exposure limits. Largely though not solely because of genetic considerations, it abandoned the concept of "tolerance dose," which assumed that exposure to radiation below the specified limits was generally harmless. Experiments in genetics with fruit flies indicated that reproductive cells were highly susceptible to damage from even small amounts of radiation and that mutant genes could be inherited from a parent with no obvious radiation-induced injuries. At least for genetic effects, most scientists had rejected the supposition before World War II that exposure to radiation was biologically innocuous below a certain threshold. The NCRP took action that reflected the consensus of opinion by replacing the terminology of "tolerance dose" with "maximum permissible dose," which it thought better conveyed the idea that no quantity of radiation was certifiably safe. It defined the permissible dose as that which, "in the light of present knowledge, is not expected to cause appreciable bodily injury to a person at any time during his lifetime," and explicitly acknowledged the possibility of suffering deleterious consequences from radiation in amounts below the allowable limits. But the NCRP emphasized that the permissible dose was based on the belief that "the *probability* of the occurrence of such injuries must be so low that the risk would be readily acceptable to the average individual."[10]

The number of people working with radiation sources was still too small to threaten significant changes in the genetic composition of the entire population, and the NCRP pointed out that for the present, genetic considerations were not a "limiting factor" in setting permissible occupational levels. Nevertheless, genetic effects of radiation not only could have painful consequences for individuals but also were "likely to add to the number of undesirable genes present in the population." Because of the growth of atomic-energy programs and the substantial increase in the number of individuals who were subject to injuries from radiation, the NCRP revised its recommendations on radiation protection. It reduced the permissible dose for whole-body exposure from external sources to 50 percent of the 1934 level. It measured the new whole-body limit of 0.3 r per six-day week by exposure of the "most critical" tissue in blood-forming organs, gonads, and lenses of the eyes; higher limits applied for less sensitive areas of the body. For persons over forty-five years old the committee set values twice as high as the basic levels because older individuals were less likely to have children and pass mutant genes to succeeding generations. Although the NCRP did not formally publish its recommendations on permissible limits from external sources until 1954, it had agreed on its main conclusions by 1948.[11]

The NCRP also devoted careful attention to internal emitters. In the postwar period the major peril of internal emitters stemmed not so much from misuse of radium as from the growing numbers of and expanded work with radioactive isotopes. Nearly every element has three or more isotopes, which have identical chemical properties but differ slightly in their nuclear composition. Only a few isotopes are naturally radioactive. Most radioactive isotopes are produced artificially in particle-accelerating machines or in nuclear reactions. Uranium fission in an atomic reactor or bomb, for example, creates as by-products many radioactive isotopes that do not occur naturally. The onset of the atomic age, therefore, greatly increased the number of radioactive isotopes in existence. Although under controlled conditions they serve useful purposes in research, industry, agriculture, and medicine, they can pose grave dangers if they enter the atmosphere or water supply. After a four-year study by one of its subcommittees, the NCRP published in 1953 a handbook citing maximum permissible amounts in the human body and concentrations in air and water of a long list of radioactive isotopes. The committee based its recommendations on existing knowledge of X-ray, gamma-ray, and radium injuries, comparison with the effects of naturally radioactive isotopes, experiments with animals, and limited clinical experience with humans. To provide an adequate margin of safety, it proposed permissible levels as low as one-tenth of the numerical values derived from the available data.[12]

In the case of internal emitters, as with external sources of radiation, the NCRP did not regard its maximum permissible doses as final or definitive. Despite increased knowledge and greater experience, many uncertainties about the effects of radiation remained. In establishing exposure levels the NCRP considered both the risks inherent in and the benefits derived from radiation. It worried that if it recommended limits that were impractically low, it would unduly discourage use of radioactive materials. Therefore, it set levels that seemed attainable and at the same time offered reasonable assurance that radiation workers would not suffer harm. The NCRP believed its recommendations were conservative enough to make the chances of serious injury statistically slight.

The activities of the international committee, which was renamed the International Commission on Radiological Protection (ICRP), followed the example of the NCRP in the early postwar years. It too enlarged its membership, formed several subcommittees to examine specific problems, and abandoned the use of "tolerance dose" in favor of "maximum permissible dose." The ICRP also lowered its suggested occupational whole-body exposure from external sources to match that of the American committee (0.3 r per week) and issued recommendations for internal emitters which duplicated those of the NCRP. In its only major departure from the NCRP, the ICRP proposed a maximum permissible dose of one-tenth the occupational levels in case of exposure by large numbers of people. The basic recommendations of both committees applied only to radiation workers. But in view of the growing scientific recognition of the genetic effects of radiation and the possibility that the general population, or at least a significant part of it, might be exposed in accidental or emergency situations, the ICRP agreed in 1953 on reducing the occupational level by a factor of ten. Although the NCRP had established the same limit for minors under age eighteen, it refused to do so for the entire population. The committee wished to avoid the appearance of a double standard of protection, one for radiation workers and one for the general public. While the ICRP's recommendations on the issue were arbitrary and tentative, they represented the first formal effort to establish radiation-protection guidelines for large groups outside "controlled areas."[13]

Knowledge of the findings and recommendations of the NCRP and ICRP was confined mostly to scientific circles. The general public remained largely unaware of radiation hazards other than those associated with atomic warfare. The use of atomic bombs against Japan gave the public a dramatic introduction to the effects of radiation, and an outpouring of books, articles, and popular films provided constant reminders. But public attitudes toward radiation, whether shaped by accounts as moving as John Hersey's *Hiroshima* or by horror films featuring giant radioactive ants, reflected concerns about atomic weapons rather than about dangers from civilian uses of radioactive substances. Although abuse of X rays and radium became less common as scientific recognition of their risks increased, continuing misuse testified to prevailing public innocence about potentially harmful exposure to radiation-producing machines and materials. As late as 1953, for example, an American company advertised contraceptive jelly containing radium. Many shoe stores used X-ray devices called fluoroscopes to fit customers, which posed some hazards for patrons and even greater ones for the employees who operated the machines. Some hospitals X-rayed newborn babies for the sole purpose of showing the parents their offspring's bone structure.[14]

In the mid- and late 1950s the American public's unfamiliarity with the dangers of radiation outside the immediate vicinity of an atomic explosion gave way to growing anxiety, largely generated by reports about radioactive fallout from atomic-weapons tests. The development and testing of hydrogen bombs not only heightened fears about the effects of a nuclear war but also alerted the public to the risks of radiation exposure from any source. Recognition of the fact that one could suffer deleterious consequences from radiation without being near the site of a nuclear blast gradually became more widespread. A harbinger of future events occurred when the AEC conducted a series of atomic (but not hydrogen) bomb tests at its Nevada Proving Grounds in the spring of 1953. One shot on 19 May spread radioactive particles over areas more than a hundred miles from the test site. The AEC advised residents of St. George, Utah to stay indoors until the radioactive cloud passed over and stopped traffic on main highways in southern Utah and northern Nevada to check for contamination. Agency officials insisted that radiation levels were too low to be harmful, but doubts about those assurances arose when southern Utah sheepmen complained about extraordinarily heavy losses in their herds at the time of the tests. After conducting an investigation, the AEC announced in January 1954 that the sheep deaths could not be attributed to radiation exposure, though it failed to cite the uncertainty about its conclusions among some scientific authorities who worked on the inquiry. The AEC's report, as the *New York Times* observed, "was not much consolation to the sheepmen, but by the same token implied reassurance to the population at large." The test series, the dispersion of radioactivity to inhabited areas, and the sheep losses attracted public attention, but the reaction was generally restrained.[15]

The hazards of radioactive fallout became a subject of much more widespread publicity, comment, and concern after a U.S. hydrogen-bomb test in the Pacific in March 1954 accidentally contaminated a Japanese fishing vessel. Although the boat, named the *Lucky Dragon*, was eighty to ninety miles from the test site at the time of the blast, it was showered by radioactive ash. Members of the crew suffered skin irritations and burns, nausea, loss of hair, and other afflictions of radiation. One of the men died within six months, either directly from exposure to radiation or, more likely, indirectly—from hepatitis caused by a blood transfusion administered to treat the symptoms of "atomic sickness." News of the fate of the *Lucky Dragon* created a panic in Japan and alerted the world to a new atomic peril. Although the AEC initially described its test explosion as "routine," it soon became apparent that the United States had detonated a weapon of startling dimensions. It was not only much larger than previous bombs but also spread incontestably dangerous levels of radioactivity far beyond the immediate vicinity of the blast.[16]

The destructive power of the atomic bombs dropped on Japan in World War II and in subsequent tests derived from the force of the blast, heat, and radiation within a relatively limited area. High-yield thermonuclear bombs, such as those tested by the United States in 1954, greatly extended the radius of the area affected by the blast, and also, if detonated at or near ground level, spewed radioactive debris over thousands of square miles. The most lethal fallout was that which immediately followed the blast. The fallout that showered the *Lucky Dragon* contaminated a cigar-shaped area about 220 miles in length downwind and up to 40 miles in width with high levels of radiation. Because most of the radioisotopes created by such an explosion are short-lived, the major portion of radiation disappeared fairly rapidly. But longer-lived radioactive particles could be carried by the winds around the entire globe. Although their radioactivity gradually decreased, the low levels of radiation they emitted still could pose a health hazard when they descended to the earth over an extended period of time. The longer-lasting radioisotope that seemed most worrisome was strontium 90. On the basis of studies of the consequences of a nuclear war, the AEC had concluded in 1953: "Of the radioisotopes resulting from the detonation of nuclear weapons, strontium-90 appears to be critical in the determination of hazardous long-range effects." It has chemical properties similar to those of calcium and, if inhaled or swallowed, collects in bones and gives off radiation internally. If strontium 90 settles on edible plants or in the soil, it can contaminate food supplies. Thus, radioactive fallout not only threatened those in the vicinity of or directly downwind from an atomic blast but potentially affected people in every part of the world.[17]

The opening of a more perilous phase of the nuclear-arms race and stories about the menace of fallout generated concern throughout the world. "Talk and worry over the H-bomb's radioactive 'fall-out' is spreading," reported *Time* magazine in November 1954. To offset press accounts on the subject, which Chairman Strauss described as "very naturally . . . treated in a sensational manner," and to provide guidance to the public on how to protect itself in case of an atomic strike, the Atomic Energy Commission prepared a report on the effects of thermonuclear weapons and radioactive fallout. Strauss pressed for early publication of the statement after its completion, but objections from other administration officials, particularly Secretary of State John Foster Dulles, delayed its release until 15 February 1955. In a dispassionate and straightforward manner the AEC's report described the awesome power of hydrogen bombs and the dangers of widespread radioactive fallout they produced. It concluded, however, that "simple precautionary measures" could greatly diminish the perils of fallout if the United States was attacked with thermonuclear weapons. It also maintained that fallout from nuclear testing did not expose the American population to significant levels of radiation or pose a hazard to public health. The AEC argued that the risks of fallout from test explosions were small compared to the national-security benefits they provided. "The study and evaluation of weapons effects and civil defense protection measures must be a necessary duty of our government," the statement declared. "The degree of risk must be balanced against the great importance of the test programs to the security of the nation and of the free world."[18]

The AEC's attempts to calm public fears produced, at best, mixed results. The agency intended its February report to be reassuring, but the information it presented was unavoidably disquieting. The new bombs and the threat of fallout, wrote Michael Straight in the *New Republic*, heralded "a foreboding future." A series of U.S. tests of small atomic bombs in Nevada in early 1955 and Soviet hydrogen blasts later in the year raised levels of radioactivity over large areas and rekindled public anxieties. Despite public opinion polls that revealed a remarkable degree of ignorance about the nature of fallout, news about the effects of nuclear explosions called attention to the hazards of radiation in general. A series of articles on radiation in the *Chicago Sun-Times* in January 1955, for example, emphasized the implications of fallout but also warned about the potential dangers of peaceful applications of atomic energy. "The atomic age's golden promise is tarnished by a widely held scientific prediction," wrote reporter Carl Larsen. "It is that eventually man will have to limit his exposure to radiation sharply. . . . As the atoms-for-peace program gets into high gear, wider policing of radiation hazards is being urged."[19]

Although the biological consequences of exposure to heavy radiation doses were clear, scientists remained uncertain about the effects of low-level radiation and the degree of risk it posed. Most agreed with the AEC that bomb tests had not raised levels of radiation enough to be harmful, but some believed that the Commission was too sanguine, especially about the genetic implications of fallout. Convinced that the AEC's position was scientifically sound, Strauss in early 1955 requested the National Academy of Sciences to undertake a study of the effects of radiation in hopes that it could provide an authoritative assessment of the issue. The Rockefeller Foundation agreed to finance the project. In accepting the assignment, Dr. Detlev W. Bronk, president of the National Academy, "welcomed the opportunity to make a dispassionate and objective effort to clarify the issues which are of grave concern as well as great hope to mankind." He appointed over a hundred prominent scientists, most drawn from the academic world but some from government and industry, to six committees to examine various aspects of radiation: genetics, pathology, agriculture and food supplies, meteorology, oceanography, and radioactive-waste disposal.[20]

The National Academy issued its report on 12 June 1956. In some ways its findings were reassuring. Contrary to widely circulated speculation, it denied that nuclear-bomb tests had caused discernible changes in climate or weather conditions. In its assessment of the effects of radioactive fallout, the study concluded that the amount of radiation produced by weapons tests to that time did not present a major health hazard. Compared with the exposure the U.S. population received from X rays and from natural background radiation that comes from cosmic rays and radioactive substances in rocks and the soil, the doses from fallout were small. The report also declared: "It appears that radiation problems, if they are met intelligently and vigilantly, need not stand in the way of the large-scale development of atomic energy."[21]

In most respects, however, the National Academy's determinations were deeply disturbing, especially in their emphasis on the genetic effects of radiation. Since the "inheritance mechanism" seemed much more sensitive to radiation than other body cells, the growing use of atomic energy raised particularly acute problems in the area of genetics. Even small doses of radiation trigger at least some mutations in reproductive cells, and the damage is cumulative. Therefore, people exposed to low-level radiation over an extended period of time might well escape any visible injury to themselves but still undergo genetic changes with profound consequences for their progeny, even if the effects did not appear for several generations.

Radiation-induced genetic disorders would be tragic in individual cases, the study declared, but the implications for the population as a whole were even more alarming. If the entire population, or a significant part of it, received radiation in amounts "a great deal more than the average" from natural background, not only would large numbers of unborn children "be definitely handicapped," but harmful mutations would be added to the population's genetic pool and increase the risks for future generations. The genetic consequences of radiation would not be immediately obvious but could cause enormous damage over a long period of time. Therefore, although the report maintained that the levels of radiation produced by fallout to that time were relatively inappreciable, it cautioned that "there remains a proper concern to see to it that the fallout does not increase to more serious levels." It was also essential to make certain that the risks of overuse of X rays, peaceful applications of atomic energy, and radioactive-waste disposal be recognized and vigorously controlled. The study acknowledged that its findings on genetics were based on limited evidence and that many existing uncertainties could be resolved only through further research. But it was unequivocal in its basic recommendation: "We ought to keep all our expenditures of radiation exposure as low as possible. From the point of view of genetics, they are all bad."[22]

While stressing genetic risks, the National Academy report cited other existing and potential hazards of radiation. It pointed out that concern about fallout had obscured other sources of radiological contamination that could prove to be more serious as the application of atomic energy for peaceful purposes became more widespread. The construction and operation of large numbers of atomic-power plants inevitably involved risks, especially if they indiscriminately or routinely released radioactive gases into the air. Although the chances of a major accident in a power plant seemed "highly unlikely in a properly designed reactor," utmost caution was required to avoid such a catastrophe. Radioactive wastes that would grow in volume as atomic energy activities expanded posed perplexing problems for which no satisfactory solution had been found. In addition to calling for careful consideration of long-range issues, the report urged that the use of X rays, which were the source of highest average exposure to radiation other than natural background, "be reduced as much as is consistent with medical necessity."[23]

The National Academy's study did not find the difficulties of ensuring radiological safety insurmountable. It called for "careful, integrated planning" in atomic development and warned: "A large part of the information that is needed to make intelligent plans is not yet at hand." The report pointed out that scientists knew more about radiation than other man-made environmental hazards, such as new medicinal drugs and industrial chemicals. But it stressed that more research was required to understand the dangers of radiation more fully and deal with them more effectively. Although it was the most comprehensive and authoritative statement for the general public to that time on the effects of radiation, it made no claim to being definitive. It also cautioned that increased scientific data and technical knowledge were not enough in themselves to resolve controversies over the problems of radiation protection. The ethical, political, economic, and military questions about relative risks and benefits that the use of atomic energy inevitably raised could not be answered by scientific information alone.[24]

The Atomic Energy Commission was generally pleased with the National Academy's report. The findings on the genetic effects of radiation, remarked Charles L. Dunham, director of the AEC's Division of Biology and Medicine, included "nothing in it that we cannot without too much effort live with." Strauss observed that the AEC was well acquainted with the data in the report, but he publicly hailed it as a "constructive and independent study" that rendered a "public service of major importance." He was particularly gratified that both the National Academy and the United Kingdom Medical Research Council, which simultaneously issued a report on radiation that reached conclusions similar to those of the American scientists, supported the AEC's position on the risks of atomic-weapons testing. He thought it unlikely that the findings of either study would require major changes in the AEC's military or civilian programs.[25]

The National Academy's survey commanded wide attention and generated considerable concern. "It is impossible to read the report," commented the *Washington Post*, "without a feeling of profound apprehension." A staff member of the Joint Committee on Atomic Energy observed that the study had made the subject of radiation a "national issue," and numerous editorials and articles highlighted the National Academy's emphasis on the hazards of X rays and nonmilitary uses of atomic energy. Within a short time the report and other publications had created so many misgivings about X rays that physicians complained that their patients were resisting legitimate X-ray treatment. "This whole x-ray scare has really gone to the ridiculous," declared one radiologist.[26]

The AEC had anticipated and accepted the possibility that some accounts would overstate or misinterpret the dangers cited by the National Academy, but it was disturbed by stories that it viewed as unduly exaggerated or misleading. One such article was written by noted critic and moviemaker Pare Lorentz for *McCall's* magazine. The cover of the magazine featured in large bold print: "Radioactivity Is Poisoning Your Children." Lorentz called for an end to atomic testing by all nations, suggested that atomic-power plants were unnecessary, and argued that radioactive-waste disposal was contaminating the oceans. "It is not a question of *whether* we have polluted the earth," he wrote. "It is a question of *how much* we have polluted it." Lorentz recommended that even though the AEC had done "a creditable job" in radiation safety within its areas of jurisdiction, overall responsibility for radiation protection should be vested in the U.S. Public Health Service or some organization "concerned not with weapons but with health." Commissioner Willard F. Libby privately decried the "*McCall* scare article" as a "terrible thing." In a letter to the editor of the magazine he defended the AEC's efforts to protect public health and stressed that natural background yielded much more radiation than atomic energy. In another instance, AEC officials found amusing, and quickly denied, rumors that Strauss was so worried about radiation that he refused to eat seafood until it was checked with a Geiger counter. But such reports, whether as gloomy as the *McCall's* article or as outlandish as the story about Strauss's culinary habits, testified to increasing public awareness of and apprehension about the perils of radiation.[27]

Despite their rising concern about radiation after the 1954 Pacific bomb tests, the American people accepted the Eisenhower administration's contention that the risks of fallout were less disturbing than the dangers of falling behind the Soviets in the nuclear-arms race. In the 1956 presidential election, Democratic candidate Adlai Stevenson questioned the administration's position on fallout and advocated a nuclear-test ban but failed to win broad support or discernibly undermine public confidence in Eisenhower's policies.[28]

The following spring, however, intensified qualms about the threat of radiation produced considerable debate and criticism of the AEC's position. Bomb testing by the United States, Great Britain, and the Soviet Union generated worldwide protests, though only the Soviet explosions produced high levels of fallout. A statement of famed philosopher and humanitarian Albert Schweitzer expressing alarm over fallout and a response by the AEC's Libby denying that it posed appreciable risks attracted wide attention. The controversy was fueled by a petition initiated by Nobel Prize–winning chemist Linus Pauling and signed by nearly two thousand American scientists. The petition cited the dangers of fallout "to the health of human beings all over the world" and appealed for an international agreement to end nuclear-bomb tests. The White House received so many letters and petitions urging a test ban that Strauss told Eisenhower that the "pressure has at least earmarks of organization," a charge that the president aired at a press conference. Although the public reaction to the radiation issue demonstrated no signs of panic or hysteria, opinion polls underscored the marked increase in concern about fallout. A survey taken in April 1955 revealed that only 17 percent of the respondents knew what was meant by fallout from a hydrogen bomb, but a May 1957 poll showed that 52 percent of those questioned believed that fallout was a "real danger," compared with 28 percent who did not think so and 20 percent who did not know.[29]

In March 1957 the Joint Committee on Atomic Energy announced plans to hold hearings to gather information and educate the public on the nature, hazards, and latest scientific assessments of radioactive fallout. It created a Special Subcommittee on Radiation, chaired by Chet Holifield, to conduct the investigation. Holifield, a liberal Democrat from California, had taken a keen interest in nuclear energy after the explosion of the first atomic bomb and had served on the Joint Committee since its inception. He developed considerable expertise on atomic-energy issues despite his lack of a high school diploma or formal scientific

training. Born in 1903, Holifield left his home in Arkansas before grad-
uating from high school and drifted to California. At age nineteen he
established his own cleaning business in suburban Los Angeles and a
few years later converted it to a menswear shop. He suffered two major
setbacks in the early 1930s, however. A freak hunting accident confined
him to a bed or wheelchair for four years, and the depression hurt his
business badly. Holifield's personal woes turned his attention to politics.
He became active in local and state Democratic organizations, and successfully managed the congressional campaign of his friend Jerry Voorhis
in 1940. Two years later he won his own seat in Congress from a newly
created district. Short and stocky in build, the mustachioed congressman
was gentle in manner but sometimes displayed an acid tongue in criticizing opponents. His attacks on the AEC so annoyed Strauss that he
privately sneered at Holifield as "the part-time nuclear physicist and
haberdasher." Holifield played an instrumental role in ensuring civilian
control of atomic energy after World War II and in congressional efforts
to push development of the hydrogen bomb a few years later. His advocacy of producing and testing hydrogen weapons did not, however,
preclude his concern about the effects of radioactive fallout. He hoped
that the Joint Committee hearings on fallout would "result in valuable
contributions to the knowledge of radiation, the lack of which is now
the basis of so much controversy."[30]

When the hearings were held in late May and early June of 1957, they
highlighted some uncertainties and differences of opinion among experts
about the risks of radiation and raised questions about the position and
performance of the AEC. The issue that generated the most debate
among scientists who testified at the hearings was whether or not a
threshold, or level of exposure below which no perceptible injury occurred, existed for the somatic (nongenetic) effects of radiation. The
witnesses agreed that there was no threshold for genetic damage and
that even small doses of radiation caused some mutation in reproductive
cells. But they expressed conflicting views on whether a similar process
took place in less sensitive organs. If so, it meant that exposure to
radiation in any amounts increased the chances that a person would
develop leukemia or cancer or other radiation-induced illnesses, proportional to the dose received. If not, it implied that there was a level
at which exposure to radiation was safe, at least for somatic effects.
Presentations of data and round-table discussions failed to produce a
consensus on the question.[31]

Opinion also divided on whether or not fallout that reached the earth's stratosphere after a bomb detonation returned to ground level in a uniform pattern. Lester Machta of the United States Weather Bureau tentatively suggested that stratospheric fallout was deposited unevenly when it fell to earth over a period of years, and that the heaviest concentrations descended on the northern temperate zones, including the northern United States. The AEC's Libby questioned Machta's findings, though he qualified his objections under interrogation from Senator Clinton P. Anderson. On other important matters, such as levels of radiation given off from natural sources and the biological effects of strontium 90, the scientific experts expressed uncertainty rather than disagreement. In either case, they concurred on the need for further research on radiation.[32]

Various scientists who testified at the hearings commented on the AEC's role in the fallout controversy. Several applauded the AEC for providing valuable data on fallout and for sponsoring independent research without pressuring scientists to produce results that supported its own position. But a number of witnesses, including some who praised the AEC on those grounds, also criticized aspects of the agency's program. Bentley Glass, a geneticist from Johns Hopkins University, complained that the AEC focused its research on the physical properties of atomic energy and slighted the biological consequences. He suggested that the "unbalance" would continue unless a biologist or geneticist were appointed as an AEC commissioner. Indiana University professor Hermann J. Muller, who had received a Nobel Prize for his pioneering work on the genetic effects of radiation, agreed with Glass that the AEC underemphasized biological problems. He also bemoaned "prolonged official reluctance" to acknowledge and clearly explain publicly the risks of radiation exposure, even in small doses. Muller argued that such a policy was self-defeating because it undermined confidence in public officials once the facts became widely known. "The only defensible or effective course for our democratic society," he declared, "is to recognize the truth, to admit the damage, and to base our case for continuance of the [bomb] tests on a weighing of the alternative consequences."[33]

Ralph E. Lapp, a physicist and free-lance writer who published widely in laymen's terms on atomic-energy questions, presented a sharp rebuke of the AEC. Two years earlier Lapp had used data from a speech of Commissioner Libby and from Japanese scientists to accurately compute fallout patterns from the bomb test that had contaminated the *Lucky Dragon*. He published his findings before the AEC issued its February

1955 report on thermonuclear weapons, stirring attacks on the agency for withholding information. Lapp pursued that theme during the fallout hearings by contending that the AEC should have made facts about fallout available more promptly so that scientists and the public could assess the risks more knowledgeably. He also accused AEC officials of making "reckless or unsubstantiated statements" on the dangers of fallout. Lapp cited specifically the claim of one AEC spokesman in 1955 that the level of fallout would have to be increased "by a million" to cause harm, another by Libby the same year that exposure from fallout could be fifteen thousand times greater without creating somatic hazards, and a 1957 statement by an agency official that bomb tests did not produce "the slightest possible effect" on humans.[34]

Other witnesses offered similar criticisms by suggesting that the AEC placed an overly benign interpretation on the fallout data it published. A. H. Sturtevant, a professor of genetics at the California Institute of Technology, observed that even though the genetic and biological risks of bomb testing to an individual were statistically small, they still posed an appreciable hazard to the national or world population as a whole. In absolute numbers, many people, even if they represented a low percentage of the population, could be adversely affected by fallout. Sturtevant also countered the argument of AEC officials that the risks of fallout were statistically less significant than those that people encountered routinely, such as driving a car or swimming in the ocean. He pointed out that people accepted the risks of normal activities voluntarily, but had no control over or freedom of choice regarding the perils of radioactive fallout. Walter Selove, a University of Pennsylvania physicist, echoed the same general theme. He spoke as a representative of the Federation of American Scientists, an organization that focused on the "interrelation between science and public affairs." Selove maintained that the AEC's dual functions of developing weapons and assessing fallout hazards predisposed the agency to understate the health risks created by bomb testing. "It can readily be seen," he said, "that decisions felt to be necessary in one area might conflict with and unduly influence decisions in the other." Selove commended the AEC for its measurements of fallout and the "steady release" of its data, but he urged that an "independent group of qualified scientists" be appointed to study and evaluate fallout and other radiation problems.[35]

The chief spokesman for the AEC at the fallout hearings was Commissioner Willard Libby. As an acknowledged authority on nuclear energy and the only professional scientist then serving as a commissioner, Libby took the lead in defining and articulating the AEC's position on the technical aspects of fallout. He was well qualified to fill the role. After receiving his Ph.D. in chemistry from the University of California at Berkeley in 1933, he taught at his alma mater and at Princeton University. He joined the Manhattan Project in 1941 and for four years worked on separating the isotopes of uranium. After the war he became a professor at the University of Chicago, where he conducted research on natural radioactivity. He won wide recognition and eventually a Nobel Prize in chemistry for perfecting an "atomic calendar," a method of using radioactive carbon 14 to determine accurately the age of fossils, artifacts, and other remains of distant times. Tall, red-haired, and solemn in his bearing, Libby exuded so much energy and creativity in his research that he earned the nickname "Wild Bill." He was politically conservative; *Time* magazine oversimplified but exaggerated only slightly in describing his basic philosophy as "bigger bombs and more bombs" providing the best way to prevent war. Eisenhower appointed him to the Atomic Energy Commission in 1954 on the recommendation of Strauss. Libby's many technical speeches and publications on radioactive fallout received respect and praise from other scientists, even those who questioned his conclusions that bomb tests posed only slight and justifiable health risks. "People have got to learn to live with the facts of life," he once declared, "and part of the facts of life are fallout."[36]

In his testimony Libby addressed some of the criticisms of the AEC cited by other witnesses. He agreed that more research on and greater understanding of the biological implications of radiation were needed, and indicated that the AEC would enlarge its program in that field. "In reading the testimony before the committee," he commented, "I am impressed with the disparity in our knowledge of the biological effects as compared to our knowledge of the physical facts about fallout." Libby acknowledged that publication of the AEC's fallout data had sometimes been delayed because of security considerations, but affirmed that with the exception of "certain facts" relating to intelligence and weapons design, the agency had publicly issued all of its "significant information" on fallout. "Our policy," he declared, "is to discover the truth about fallout and to make it public." Under skeptical inquiries from Congressman Holifield and Senator Anderson he denied that the AEC interpreted the facts to suit its own position or deliberately misled the public about the dangers of fallout. Libby insisted that the hazards of fallout were "relatively small." He added that "the critical and essential question is, 'Are they tolerable?'" That question, he stressed, required political and sociological, rather than purely scientific, judgments. Libby reiterated his strong opinion that the rapid development of new weapons and delivery systems made continued bomb testing essential for national defense. In the absence of an international disarmament agreement, he argued, the risks were necessary for the survival of the free world.[37]

The fallout hearings produced no startling revelations, but they achieved Holifield's main objective of disseminating information and illuminating scientific opinions on fallout. Within two years the Joint Committee distributed about twenty thousand copies of the transcripts of the hearings. Strauss thought the hearings "ended more agreeably than might have been the case." Nevertheless, they highlighted some reservations about the AEC's position on fallout, and criticism of the agency continued. Eight members of Congress urged Eisenhower to create a National Radiation Institute of Health to conduct research on radiation risks. Some scientists suggested that because of the inherent conflict in the AEC's weapons development and health and safety functions, the U.S. Geological Survey should be given responsibility for evaluating the hazards of radiation. The *Nashville Tennessean* reproached the president and the AEC for "hesitation in laying their facts on the line," and a Nevada farmer was quoted as saying of the agency, "I wouldn't believe them on a stack of Bibles."[38]

Chet Holifield assailed the AEC in an article published in the *Saturday Review.* He accused the AEC of deliberately delaying release and "selective use" of fallout data. "I believe from our hearings," he wrote, "that the Atomic Energy Commission approach to the hazards from bomb test fall-out seems to add up to a party line—'play it down.'" Holifield contended that the AEC tended to minimize the risks of fallout because of its competing responsibilities: "The AEC is charged with the responsibility of weapon development and they are doing a good job in this field, but an adverse judgment on their part on bomb testing could conflict with their primary mission." He called for an international conference of scientists to assess the dangers of fallout and other sources of radiation. Meanwhile, protests calling for a ban on nuclear testing were gaining support and recognition. The AEC maintained its position that fallout caused only minor risks. But as public apprehension about radiation grew, so did doubts about the agency's credibility and performance in protecting public health.[39]

As public awareness of radiation hazards increased after 1954, the International Commission on Radiological Protection and the National Committee on Radiation Protection reconsidered their recommendations on permissible levels of exposure for radiation workers and the general public. The ICRP met in April 1956 and agreed to lower its suggested maximum occupational dose from external sources to 5 rems per year for whole-body exposure. The rem had recently gained preference over the roentgen (r) as the basic unit of measurement. For gamma- and X-ray radiation, 1 rem equals 1 r. The rem is a more useful unit because it indicates the biological effect of radiation doses more precisely. The ICRP adopted the adjusted level to conform with the proposals of the soon-to-be-published report of the National Academy of Sciences. The new recommendation of 5 rems per year represented a reduction by a factor of three from the previous level of 0.3 r per week or 15 per year. To provide further protection from genetic consequences by limiting exposure of younger persons most likely to have children, the ICRP specified total permissible accumulated doses at various ages (50 rems to age thirty, 100 rems to age forty, and 200 rems to age sixty). It also lowered its recommendations for whole-population exposure by corresponding proportions.[40]

The NCRP issued similar guidelines in a preliminary statement published in January 1957 and, after some revisions, released in final form in April 1958. Like the ICRP, the American committee was influenced not only by scientific considerations, especially the findings of the National Academy of Sciences, but also by the "public clamor" that had arisen over radiation exposure. The NCRP recommended an average whole-body dose from external sources of 5 rems per year. In response to the concern of some members that a firm numerical level was too inflexible, the committee offered a formula to prorate the permissible limit by age. As long as a total accumulated lifetime dose was not exceeded, a worker could receive up to 12 rems in a given year (that is, if his exposure was below the 5-rem average limit in previous years). The NCRP cautioned, however, that a dose of 12 rems in a single year was permissible only when adequate records of past exposure existed, and even then "should be regarded as an allowable but not usual condition." It still refrained from explicitly setting a level for whole-population exposure, though it specified that the maximum permissible dose for persons living or working near sources of radiation but outside "controlled areas" should not be greater than one-tenth of the levels recommended for radiation workers.[41]

The sharp reductions by both the ICRP and the NCRP in their suggested maximum permissible doses stirred speculation that the previous levels had been dangerously high. Lauriston Taylor, who was still serving as a member of the international group and chairman of the American body, denied that the earlier limits had provided inadequate protection. He pointed out that no evidence existed to show that radiation workers had suffered harm under the older standards and that in most cases they received much less exposure than even the new levels allowed. Taylor explained that the recent revisions reflected the growing use of atomic energy and the scientific consensus that occupational and general-population exposure to radiation should be kept to a minimum. The ICRP and the NCRP were still trying to balance the hazards and the benefits of radiation in their recommendations by setting levels that seemed generally safe without being impractical. As Taylor declared in 1956: "Any radiation exposure received by man must be accepted as harmful. Therefore, the objective should be to keep man's exposure as low as possible and yet, at the same time, not discontinue the use of radiation altogether."[42]

The Atomic Energy Commission adopted the recommendations of the NCRP in formulating regulations for radiation protection in the civilian atomic-energy program. The AEC had used the NCRP's occupational maximum permissible doses in its own installations and operations since its establishment in 1947.

Passage of the 1954 Atomic Energy Act required the agency to draw up new regulations that applied to its licensees and the general public. The AEC's standards did not diverge quantitatively from the proposals of the NCRP, but they did differ in their legal status. The NCRP's recommendations were strictly advisory while the AEC's regulations carried statutory authority in the areas of jurisdiction assigned the agency in the 1954 act.[43]

In July 1955 the AEC published for public comment proposed radiation-protection standards. It used the recommended doses of the NCRP for both external radiation and internal emitters and established a limit of one-tenth of the occupational level for members of the public potentially affected by the operations of AEC licensees. After considering the criticisms it received, the AEC made several revisions in its preliminary proposals, but the numerical exposure limits remained unchanged. The final version of the AEC's regulations became effective in February 1957. After the NCRP reduced its recommended doses, the AEC followed suit. In April 1959 the agency published for public comment revised regulations that incorporated the changes recommended by the NCRP the previous year. It limited occupational whole-body exposure from external sources to an average of 5 rems per year. In cases where adequate records existed, the AEC allowed a dose of up to 12 rems during a single year if the 5-rem annual average was not exceeded. Like the NCRP, the AEC believed that the occupational-exposure limits provided ample protection for most individuals, but it did not guarantee that its standards offered absolute safety for all radiation workers. Population limits outside controlled areas remained one-tenth of the occupational levels. The AEC received "a very substantial number" of comments on its draft regulations, many of which argued that the lower standards were unnecessary. The agency made no major revisions in its numerical levels, however, and issued the new standards in July 1960. They became effective 1 January 1961.[44]

The NCRP's determinations were of crucial importance for AEC programs, but the agency neither dictated to nor dominated the committee. The NCRP continued to guard its independence from undue government influence, and its changes in permissible doses sometimes aroused the misgivings of AEC officials. In June 1956, for example, Strauss indicated concern about the ICRP's sharp reduction in maximum exposure levels, which the NCRP adopted a short time later. Libby assured him, however, that the new recommendations were not "too bad for us" because "we now live within this new limit anyhow" and "they say [bomb] testing isn't dangerous in any way, at least at the present rate."[45]

Within a short time after the *Lucky Dragon* incident in 1954, radiation protection became an issue of widespread national and international concern. Although the growing debate centered on radiation produced by weapons testing, it called attention to and influenced policies toward other possible sources of radioactive contamination. Scientists had recognized and carefully considered the effects of radiation long before they became a matter of public notice, and the ICRP and NCRP had devised recommendations for protecting radiation workers from excessive exposure. In the absence of conclusive data, their proposed limits were not absolute standards but imprecise estimates that reflected a conservative application of the best available information. Both organizations compensated for the uncertainties in knowledge about radiation by formulating recommendations that they believed erred on the side of caution. They worked on the assumption that exposure to radiation should be held to a minimum but that occupational limits should not be so low as to be practically unattainable. They lowered their permissible levels in the 1950s in response to changing scientific views, expanding uses of atomic energy, and increasing public concern about radiation. By using the NCRP's recommendations in its regulations for occupational-exposure limits in its areas of jurisdiction, the AEC accepted the judgment of acknowledged experts in the field of radiation protection on what constituted generally safe and achievable doses for atomic workers.

The question of population exposure to low-level radiation was much more controversial. Scientists generally agreed that any exposure to radiation by large segments of the population was potentially harmful, particularly because of genetic mutation. But they differed on the severity of the risk. Some geneticists argued that radiation caused less permanent damage to reproductive cells than most of their colleagues supposed. Scientific opinion was even more divided on the somatic effects of radiation, ranging from views that small doses produced no cell damage to theories that the chances of radiation-induced diseases were directly proportional to the amount absorbed. Scientific authorities generally maintained that doses of radiation produced by fallout were not a significant health peril on a short-term basis, though they worried about the effects if bomb testing continued over a long period. Some, however, insisted that existing levels of fallout would cause irreparable harm both to large numbers of living individuals and to future generations. The lack of consensus among experts on those and other issues engendered frustration for laymen trying to evaluate the dangers of fallout and other sources of radiation. Senator Anderson complained of that problem during the 1957 fallout hearings. "How would we go about getting a jury that would give some sort of answer that the common people can trust?" he asked. "You get one group of scientists together, and they say one thing, and you get another group together, and they say another thing. What does a man who is not a scientist have that he can tie to?"[46]

Anderson's question was unanswerable, partly because of the need for expanded research but largely because the issues raised by the fallout debate required philosophical, moral, and political judgments that sci-

entific evidence alone could not resolve. As radiation protection proceeded from a rather arcane scientific problem of safeguarding a limited
number of workers to a public issue involving questions of national
security and the health of millions of people and their unborn progeny,
it inevitably created controversies. Scientists, politicians, journalists, and
members of the general public held divergent views about the level of
risk from radiation that was acceptable. The arguments focused on
whether the national-security benefits of nuclear-bomb testing justified
the hazards of radioactive fallout. The AEC, as the most visible proponent of official policy, was positioned in the center of the debate. The
agency acknowledged that fallout produced some harmful effects, but
maintained that the advantages of testing far outweighed the dangers
to public health.

The AEC, as even its critics conceded, sponsored important research
and published a great deal of valuable scientific data on fallout. But the
agency undermined its own credibility by consistently placing the most
benign interpretation on available information. Although most scientists
agreed that existing levels of radiation from weapons testing were relatively insignificant, the air of certainty with which the AEC offered its
assurances glossed over the undetermined and unexplored aspects of
radiation effects in general and fallout in particular. Moreover, the agency
did not, and because of existing unknowns could not, convincingly
counter arguments that fallout would present a growing threat in future
years if testing continued. Nor did it have an answer to those who
pointed out that fallout affected, in absolute terms, large numbers of
people who assumed its risks involuntarily. The AEC's tendency to
minimize the potential implications of testing reflected its commitment
to weapons development and its conviction that fallout was much less
dangerous than falling behind the Soviets in the arms race. But even
some supporters of the AEC's stance urged the agency to spell out as
clearly as possible the potential genetic and somatic effects of fallout and
allow the public to balance the risks and benefits of nuclear testing.[47] By
failing to delineate the hazards more frankly and leaving announcements
about many worrisome repercussions of fallout to its critics, the agency
intensified doubts about its position and damaged its public image.

III

THE STRUCTURE OF
ATOMIC REGULATION

The radiation-protection regulations were but one part of a series of safety rules and procedures that the Atomic Energy Commission devised in the mid-1950s. Despite the uncertainties among experts about the effects of radiation, the AEC could draw on a considerable body of scientific knowledge and experience in drafting its radiation-protection standards. It had much less scientific and technical data on which to base its other regulations as it attempted to balance the need for safety with the goal of stimulating the growth of an atomic industry.

The 1954 Atomic Energy Act established a national policy for the development and regulation of a new atomic industry and made the AEC responsible for both functions. A key section of the law encouraged "widespread participation in the development and utilization of atomic energy for peaceful purposes and to the maximum extent consistent with the common defense and security and with the health and safety of the public." Additional paragraphs told the AEC how to carry this out: through research activities that included assistance to private enterprise, by providing to industry government-owned "special nuclear materials" (plutonium, uranium 233, and uranium enriched in the isotope 233 or in the isotope 235) used as fuel in power reactors, by releasing hitherto classified "restricted data" for use in domestic development of atomic facilities, by licensing private atomic plants, and by continued inspection of such facilities and enforcement of regulations.[1] Various program divisions in the agency geared up for this new challenge—to put atomic energy to work for wider use. The engineers and scientists in the agency's far-flung laboratories and offices as well as the Washington-based commissioners viewed their mandate as an exciting adventure.

The new act recognized the dangerous nature of the technology. Throughout, the words "health and safety of the public" acknowledged potential hazards and underscored the basic goal of the AEC's regulatory function.[2]

The question facing the agency was how to perform both its developmental and its regulatory duties without doing injustice to one or both functions. Commissioner Willard Libby, in an early 1955 discussion with his colleagues on establishing the agency's regulatory framework, expressed a feeling that was widespread in the AEC: "Our great hazard is that this great benefit to mankind will be killed aborning by unnecessary regulation. There is not any doubt about the practicability of isotopes and atomic power in my mind. The question is whether we can get it there in our lifetime." One way to balance the two responsibilities would have been for Congress to create separate developmental and regulatory agencies. That idea had crossed the minds of members of the Joint Committee when they considered atomic-energy legislation in 1954. But at the time there were compelling reasons to combine the two functions in a single agency. Technical manpower was at a premium. Two separate agencies would of necessity have drawn from the same pool of human resources with the real possibility of shortchanging each other. The technology was in such an early stage that two organizations, one performing research and development, the other regulating, would have worked at cross-purposes, perhaps frustrating the overall goal of building a viable atomic industry. Consequently, the risk of a conflict of interest in making one agency perform two contradictory functions appeared a small price to pay for the anticipated benefits.[3]

Prior to passage of the 1954 act, no central regulatory office existed in the AEC. The safety of reactors was solely a government problem, since all of them were owned and operated by the agency. The AEC had shown its concern for reactor safety by establishing, in June 1947, a blue-ribbon advisory group known as the Reactor Safeguard Committee. Composed of some of the nation's best atomic experts and chaired by physicist Edward Teller, the committee evaluated technical health and safety aspects of reactor hazards and submitted recommendations to the general manager. Teller, chairman for six years, later described those early times: "The committee was about as popular—and also as necessary—as a traffic cop. Some of my friends, anxious for reactor progress, referred to the group as the Committee for Reactor Prevention, and I was kidded about being assigned to the AEC's Brake Department." The Commission appreciated the committee's frank comments but was careful to define how much advice it would seek. For example, on policy issues such as balancing overall AEC program considerations with factors bearing on health and safety, the Commission would not approach the committee. The commissioners believed that they had nondelegable authority in this area and should not give undue weight to the opinions of the Reactor Safeguard Committee.[4]

The agency broadened its safety program in the fall of 1950 by creating a second advisory group, the Industrial Committee on Reactor Location Problems, to balance the "technical and scientific aspects of reactor hazards, as developed by the Reactor Safeguard Committee, against the nontechnical aspects of reactor locations." This new committee drew its members from a wide spectrum of the scientific and industrial communities. The group reviewed, for example, the problems of locating specific government reactors, taking into account such matters as the density of surrounding population, property values, and hydrological and seismic factors. Recognizing that the responsibilities of the two committees were becoming more closely related, the Commission merged their functions in July 1953 and reorganized them into the Advisory Committee on Reactor Safeguards.[5]

In discussing the original Reactor Safeguard Committee's early work, Teller told of the concern over evaluating the hazards of reactors:

> We could not follow the usual method of trial and error. This method was an integral part of American industrial progress before the nuclear age, but in the nuclear age it presented intolerable risks. An error in the manufacture of an automobile, for instance, might kill one to ten people. An error in planning safety devices for an airplane might cost the lives of 150 people. But an error allowing the release of a reactor's load of radioactive particles in a strategic location could endanger the population of an entire city. In developing reactor safety, the trials had to be on paper because actual errors could be catastrophic.[6]

Recognizing this danger, the Reactor Safeguard Committee established what Teller called a "simple procedure." For each reactor, it asked the designers to "imagine the worst possible accident and to design safety apparatus guaranteeing that it could not happen." Teller went on: "The committee reviewed each reactor plan, trying to imagine an accident even worse than that conceived by the planner. If we could think of a plausible mishap worse than any discussed by the planner, his analysis of the potential dangers was considered inadequate. In most cases, the required discussion created a reasonable spirit of caution, and we could advise the Atomic Energy Commission that the reactor would be sufficiently safe."

This procedure, based mostly on theory because of so little experience with reactors, was not acceptable to the first engineer on the original committee, who told Teller that safeguards should be based on actual experience rather than on theory. Since the government reactors were so new, the engineer was of the opinion that safeguards could not be established. He resigned after the committee's first meeting, citing the pressure of other duties. The committee, nonetheless, had little choice but to use this procedure with all AEC contractors. For the first time in any major industrial development it attempted to foresee the possible accidents or disasters and to take steps to prevent them.[7]

By 1951 the AEC elaborated on Teller's "simple procedure" by requiring a hazards-summary report on each planned facility. It identified the necessary information about the hazards that would result from the operation of a new or significantly modified reactor. In most cases the agency required the report prior to a decision on the construction of a proposed reactor at a given site; however, the procedure also provided for a preliminary hazards-summary report for those few instances when a decision had to be made before sufficient detailed information was available to write the regular report.[8]

The report had to include a description of the reactor and the site, a detailed plan of operation, a schedule of chemical processing and disposal of reactor fission products, the methods of disposal of radioactive effluents, and a description of the safety mechanisms of the reactor. More specific information was required on potential hazards, incorporating the data used in the safety-evaluation procedure described by Teller. The designer had to list all the known potentially hazardous features and include the experimental information, calculations, and assumptions used in evaluating those hazards. The report required information on steps taken to minimize the risks and an estimate, if a failure should occur, on the extent of any release of radioactive material and the damage to be expected.[9]

Regarding the site of a reactor, the report required consideration of hydrological data including the expected drainage of liquids in case of a major accident, seismic data including estimates of potential damage that might occur in the event of earthquakes of various intensities, and atmospheric conditions including an assessment of dangers to the surrounding population and industries. In addition, contractors had to provide information on the distribution of population and list vital industrial, defense, and public-service installations within the possible hazard radius of the facility.[10]

This extensive report became a standard document by which the AEC staff and the Safeguard Committee judged the hazards of a reactor. The staff first reviewed it, then sent the report to the committee. It considered the report in two ways. If there were no new or unusual problems either in the report or in the staff comments on it, the committee passed judgment without a formal meeting. If major issues or new types of reactors were involved, the staff and representatives of the contractor were called before the committee to provide additional information.[11]

By maintaining the standards set by its predecessor groups, the Advisory Committee on Reactor Safeguards was highly influential in all areas of reactor safety. AEC general counsel William Mitchell, reporting to the Joint Committee in 1955 on the safety features of the new regulatory program, observed with considerable pride that the AEC's "extraordinary reactor safety record" owed much to the "strict criteria laid down by the Reactor Safeguards Committee." Since all safety questions were referred to that group prior to passage of the 1954 act, it was logical that the committee would continue to play a vital role in licensing procedures once the law was enacted.[12]

After 1954, practical reasons prevented the Safeguards Committee from continuing as the only group reviewing reactor hazards. Its members were part-time consultants and the workload under the expanded reactor program began to place an increasing burden on them. For example, between the spring of 1954 and April 1955, seven full committee meetings were held, compared to only twenty meetings in the six years between 1947 and 1953. In addition, several subcommittees met to consider specific reactor problems prior to each main Safeguards Committee session. Recognizing this problem, General Manager Kenneth Nichols recommended the formation of a full-time reactor hazards evaluation staff to analyze reactor safety problems.[13]

The Commission created a Reactor Hazard Evaluation Staff in April 1955, initially placed under Alfonso Tammaro, assistant general manager for research and industrial development. Tammaro told the Commission that he needed the additional responsibility "like I need a hole in the head." But he conceded that until the AEC staff, including himself, had finished "groping our way" on regulatory organization, it was best that the hazards group come under his supervision.[14]

The Commission assigned several functions to the hazard-evaluation group. It developed health and safety standards, guides, and codes for all reactors, whether AEC-owned or privately owned. From a safety standpoint it assessed new reactor proposals and significant modifications in existing reactors. In addition, it provided administrative assistance to the Safeguards Committee and assumed responsibility for preparing a comprehensive plan for conducting investigations of major reactor accidents.[15]

Tammaro told the commissioners that while this was the beginning of a permanent regulatory staff, it would remain in a transitional phase until further study could be made on the staff's proper place and functions within the AEC. Commissioner Libby asked if the transition could be made without affecting reactor development. Nichols replied that unless there was a transition, the reactor work might be stalled. In the interim period the Safeguards Committee would continue to function as it had in the past, as both an advisory and a working group. Tammaro hoped that over the long term the Safeguards Committee could eventually assume its proper role as a purely advisory committee to the general manager.[16]

Over the next five months, both the activities and the place of the hazard-evaluation group were discussed within several staff divisions, principally in the Division of Reactor Development and the newly created Division of Civilian Application. By September 1955, recently appointed general manager Kenneth Fields had reached the conclusion that the functions of the Hazards Evaluation Staff belonged with the licensing duties of the Division of Civilian Application.[17]

The formation of the Hazards Evaluation Staff and its eventual addition to Civilian Application was part of an evolving agency reorganization that began shortly after passage of the 1954 act. Although the AEC had administered limited licensing functions under the 1946 law, they were peripheral to the agency's primary responsibilities of producing weapons-grade nuclear material and building atomic bombs. Previous licensing activities had involved control of isotopes and source material available for research, domestic and export control of production facilities for fissionable material and important component parts, and control of access to AEC-held patents. The 1954 law greatly broadened the scope of the licensing program, but the objectives of the earlier licensing functions still applied: guarding national security by regulating the distribution and use of materials and equipment, protecting public health and safety, and stimulating private enterprise to use materials, information, and techniques developed in the infant atomic-energy program.

Early licensing activities were decentralized. The Division of Construction and Supply had a Licensing Controls Branch that administered all phases of the program for exports of equipment and materials, and the control of domestic transactions involving non-AEC-owned source materials (nuclear materials, other than special nuclear material, containing by weight 1/20 of 1 percent or more of uranium and/or thorium). This small unit processed reports and license applications. The Patent Branch, a part of the general counsel's office, administered and issued licenses to use AEC-owned patents. Before 1954, over three hundred patent licenses had been issued to American corporations and individuals. The Isotopes Division at the Oak Ridge Operations Office conducted the largest and oldest AEC licensing function. It handled applications for stable isotopes, radioisotopes, and irradiation services. Since the summer of 1946, under the direction of Paul C. Aebersold, this division had stood out as one of the AEC's best examples of the peaceful uses of atomic energy by providing isotopes for medical therapy.[18]

To build a functional regulatory organization and to develop the rules necessary to proceed with its expanded licensing responsibilities, General Manager Nichols in October 1954 named Harold L. Price, an agency attorney, to head a task force on regulation. Price, a University of Virginia Law School graduate, had practiced law privately for a short time before joining the Department of Agriculture in 1936. He subsequently served in the general counsel's office of the War Production Board and as general counsel in the Civilian Production Administration before joining the AEC in 1947 as the chief law officer at the Oak Ridge Operations Office. In 1951 the Commission appointed him deputy general counsel. Price was an indefatigable worker with good organizational ability. His appointment was the beginning of a lengthy career as the chief regulator in the AEC.[19]

Price's group prepared a recommendation for the commissioners that called for establishing a Division of Civilian Application. At the same time a temporary division, called the Division of Licensing, was created to carry on the AEC's interim licensing functions until the recommendations of Price's organizational study could be implemented.[20]

Price's staff study recommended an organization that not only carried out licensing functions but also promoted the civilian uses of atomic energy. The report noted that the Joint Committee had emphasized and encouraged maximum participation by private interests in its recent hearing on "Development, Growth and State of the Atomic Energy Industry." Those annual hearings were required under section 202 of the 1954 act (they quickly became known as "202" hearings) and mandated the Joint Committee to hold meetings within the first sixty days of each congressional session to receive information on the industry's progress. Joint Committee members frequently commented at the first "202" hearings in January and February on the need for the AEC to keep licensing regulations and procedures as simple as possible and to process licenses expeditiously so as to encourage private participation.[21]

The plan Price presented to the commissioners analyzed the existing hodgepodge of licensing and regulatory activities within the AEC and proposed an organization that would establish in one office the responsibility for "carrying out the licensing and related activities set forth in the Act." The new division would have several functions. Its foremost task would be to develop regulations affecting the licensing process. The division would also set pricing schedules for AEC-furnished materials and services as well as prices paid by the agency for materials produced or returned by the licensees. It would handle requests and authorize access to restricted data and control export authorizations of equipment and materials. To carry out those functions, the plan recommended that the division head be delegated power to issue licenses.[22]

In bringing this matter to the Commission, both Price and Fields emphasized that the new division would establish an agency focal point for all civilian interests apart from the AEC's own programs. The activities of the Licensing Controls Branch in the Division of Construction and Supply, the licensing activities of the Oak Ridge Isotopes Division, and functions conducted by the abolished Industrial Liaison Branch in the Division of Reactor Development would be shifted to Civilian Application. Patent licensing, however, would remain with the general counsel, as would all compliance functions that were centered in an expanded Division of Inspection. Fields was open-minded as to where the organization would fit in the overall AEC structure. But he was careful to point out that all technical questions on any private power-reactor proposal still would be referred to the appropriate program divisions. The Civilian Application Division would act as the administrative coordinator. Price foresaw only a small technical staff for the proposed division. He told the Commission that the unit would need some technical competence "to understand what the people outside are saying and to be sure they get steered to the right place in the Commission and also to understand what the other divisions of the Commission are saying on technical matters as they relate to license application."[23]

The name "Civilian Application" worried some commissioners. Libby in particular zeroed in on its implication. "It is not possible to segregate to one division such an enormous task such as civilian application," he said. "It is the business of ten divisions of the AEC and the Commission, constant and continuing, and so with the understanding that the function of this new division is to take care of the paper work and serve as the focal point, but that your responsibility is not to develop new and unseen use primarily—I am then willing to go along." Price replied that the reason for the name was to make it clear that it was an agency focal point. The program divisions would do the technical work and analysis on any given civilian project. Still dubious about the name, the Commission nonetheless approved the new organization.[24]

The organizational staff paper did not mention the recently created Hazards Evaluation Staff assigned to the general manager. The only reference to safety in the paper was a statement that the proposed new division would review requests for licenses to determine "technical and administrative factors involved, including technology, safety, security, financing, and the need for advice and assistance of program and staff divisions in processing the license of agreement." The main thrust of the report and the subsequent Commission discussion of it was to streamline the licensing organization to help the agency go forward in its promotion of civilian uses. But within a short time the Hazards Evaluation Staff joined Price's division and assumed an increasingly important role in its activities.[25]

By the end of 1955 Price had his division organized. It was small, consisting of three branches plus the hazards staff (soon changed to a branch) and the Oak Ridge Isotopes Extension. With the exception of the Oak Ridge detail, the division was located in the newly acquired Matomic building at 1717 H Street in downtown Washington. Eighty-five staff members worked in Washington with the remaining fifty-eight at Oak Ridge. From its eighth-floor offices the Licensing Branch under Lyall E. Johnson carried out the basic administrative paperwork on licenses for reactors, operators, and source and special nuclear materials. The Foreign Activities Branch, headed by Bernard B. Smyth, administered requests by Americans engaging in overseas activities. The Policy and Program Branch, under Charles Manly, carried on both regulatory and promotional functions by determining the need for regulations and assisting companies wanting to engage in atomic-energy activities.[26]

The Hazards Evaluation Branch quickly became a key element in the division. When it was transferred from the assistant general manager's office, it was manned by a reactor engineer, a reactor physicist, and two secretaries. Within a year its staff increased to fourteen professionals and five clerical assistants. At the time of transfer, chemical engineer Charles D. Luke also moved to Civilian Application as technical assistant to Price to help in the hazards-evaluation staff's work on reactor standards, guides, and codes. Luke had joined the AEC in the summer of 1954 as director of the Office of Classification after a lengthy career as chairman of the chemical engineering department at Syracuse University.[27]

To man the division, General Manager Fields recruited from both inside and outside the agency. In conjunction with Price he made several key appointments. Price had already chosen one of his two authorized deputy directors in June 1955, when he hired Frank Pittman from the AEC's Production Division. An old atomic-energy hand, Pittman had joined the agency in 1948; before that time he worked in plutonium production at Los Alamos. Trained in chemical engineering at the Massachusetts Institute of Technology, he taught there in the early 1940s before going to work in private industry. After a second deputy director for hazards evaluation was named, Pittman worked primarily in the promotional aspects of the division.[28]

With encouragement from Chairman Strauss, the AEC lured C. Rogers McCullough into full-time government service as Price's deputy director for hazards evaluation. Teller's successor as chairman of the Safeguards Committee after its reorganization in 1953, McCullough previously had served as chairman of the Industrial Committee on Reactor Locations Problems. Also trained in chemistry at MIT, he had spent many years doing research in chemistry and nuclear engineering with the Monsanto Chemical Company. He had earned an excellent reputation in the nuclear community and in government circles as an expert on reactor safety. He wrote frequently in trade and scholarly journals and often testified before the Joint Committee. Monsanto placed him on leave of absence to take the government job, which he held from late summer 1956 to mid-1957. In addition, McCullough continued as the Safeguards Committee chairman, performing a dual role that concerned some members of the committee.[29]

Price also recruited Clifford K. Beck from North Carolina State College to work in hazards evaluation. Beck's nuclear career, like that of many of his colleagues, dated back to the Manhattan Project. After the war he served as director of the Gaseous Diffusion Project at Oak Ridge. He returned to his native North Carolina in 1949, where he chaired the Physics Department at North Carolina State. There he initiated a reactor project that led to the licensing of the first university research reactor. In addition, he developed an academic program that awarded the first doctoral degrees in nuclear engineering. Initially, Beck took a leave of absence to become scientific adviser to Price. By the end of 1956 he had agreed to Price's request that he stay permanently with the agency and become chief of the Hazards Evaluation Branch.[30]

While Price was recruiting staff and dealing with organizational matters, he was also implementing the regulatory program by writing and issuing regulations. Shortly after the 1954 act had become law, Nichols had outlined for the commissioners the major problems facing the AEC in licensing reactors. The greatest obstacle, he thought, would be the complexity of licensing activities, particularly in terms of procedural problems and the immediate and long-term development of regulations. For example, no regulations were in effect in the areas either of domestic and foreign distribution of special nuclear materials or of operators' licenses. And where regulations presently existed, in such areas as domestic and foreign distribution of source materials and production of special nuclear materials, considerable revision would be required. By Nichols's estimate, at least "six months of solid work" lay ahead in the preparation of the new regulations.[31]

The AEC approached its regulatory responsibility keenly aware of the effect its rules would have on the growth of the industry. The task was to regulate a potentially dangerous technology for an industry that would have to go through a developmental period of unknown duration without assurance that the results would be favorable. Chairman Strauss later told the Joint Committee that AEC regulations "should not impose unnecessary limitations or restrictions upon private participation in the development of the atom's civilian uses, . . . should not interfere with management practices, and . . . should be enforceable in a practical and uniform manner." Devising such regulations became a critical aspect of Harold Price's job. To write clear regulations that covered the necessary legal, safety, and technical points but still allowed flexibility for the developing industry proved to be a difficult task. Even so, Price and his colleagues felt pressure from the commissioners as well as the industry to turn regulations out as rapidly as possible.[32] They issued key rules during 1955 and early 1956, and others followed in succeeding years.

The 1954 law guided agency rule-making. Since the 1946 act preserved a government monopoly except in regard to the licensing of by-product materials (any radioactive material other than source or special nuclear material, formed in the process of producing or utilizing source or special nuclear material) and source materials, there had been no need to give great consideration to the public-health and public-safety aspects of atomic power. But the 1954 law provided the authority for the transition from a government monopoly to private enterprise and required the AEC to closely regulate the new industry. The law did so in general terms, but it left no doubt about the importance of health and safety factors.

Sections of the 1954 act reflected the state of the technology by establishing two classes of licenses for atomic facilities. One section authorized the AEC to issue commercial or "class 103" licenses (after the section number in the law) whenever it had determined that a facility had been "sufficiently developed to be of practical value for industrial or commercial purposes." Since the agency and the Joint Committee interpreted "practical value" to mean that atomic facilities had to be judged economically competitive with other energy sources, issuance of class-103 licenses was postponed until the industry had passed through its research and development phase.[33]

Instead, early power reactor facilities received "class-104" licenses under the terms of section 104. Reactors used in medical therapy, university research, and power demonstration came under this category. A key phrase authorized reactor licenses that would lead to the "demonstration of the practical value . . . for industrial or commercial purposes." Class-104 licenses, then, covered all power reactors used during the developmental period until the industry could find a design that would eventually meet the "practical value" criterion of a class-103 commercial license. Furthermore, section 104 specifically instructed the AEC to impose the minimum amount of regulation on a licensee consistent with the public health and safety. In other words, a class-104 license indicated that the government wanted to encourage the new industry to undertake research and development under minimum regulation that would lead to major advances in power-reactor technology.[34]

The law recognized the technology's potential danger. It referred to safety considerations in every context in which it discussed the agency's licensing and regulatory authority. For example, section 103 restricted the issuance of a license to persons "who are equipped to observe and who agree to observe such safety standards . . . as the Commission by rule may establish," and who agreed to make available to the AEC such data as it determined necessary "to protect the health and safety of the public." Section 104 directed the AEC to impose regulations on a licensee to fulfill the agency's obligations to protect public health and safety. Section 182, in describing requirements for license applications, gave the AEC broad authority to prescribe what information should be furnished. In any event, the applicant had to provide enough specific data so that the AEC could determine that the facility would "provide adequate protection to the health and safety of the public."[35]

The licensing mechanism of the law made this clear. Using the 1934 Federal Communications Act as a precedent, the Atomic Energy Act of 1954 stipulated that license issuance would be a two-step procedure. Applicants would first be issued a construction permit, defined as a form of a license and treated in all procedural respects as a license. Once an application for a construction permit was "otherwise acceptable to the Commission," which in large measure meant adherence to the AEC's regulations on health and safety, the applicant would be granted a permit and could proceed with construction. After the applicant completed construction according to the terms of the original construction permit and to any modifications subsequently approved, the Commission would issue a license allowing the applicant to load fuel and operate the reactor.[36]

The AEC followed a standard government procedure in issuing its regulations. It sent out a draft regulation for a thirty-day public-comment period through notice and publication in the *Federal Register*. It could then make revisions in light of the comments received. The regulation was then published in final form in the *Federal Register*. This simple procedure, in reality, masked the thought and work that was necessary to ready each regulation for initial and final publication.

Price called on various people from within and without the AEC to help him establish the regulatory program. Shortly after taking his regulatory position, he and Nichols in December 1954 organized an internal *ad hoc* group, named the Licensing Review Committee, that was drawn from the program divisions and the legal staff. The committee reviewed all draft regulations prior to presentation to the commissioners. To write the regulations, Price enlisted Robert Lowenstein, an attorney in the general counsel's office, and at various times General Counsel Mitchell assigned several lawyers to the project as they were needed. James

Morrisson, Lee Hydeman, Herzel Plaine, and William Berman intermittently participated in drafting the regulations. They, in turn, called
on many technical staff people to assist them, but particularly relied on
Frank K. Pittman, C. A. Rolander, Jr., Charles G. Manly, and David
Saxe. Lowenstein recalled the workload as "being massive." He remembered the number of secretaries who resigned and the many overtime
hours expended on the task.[37]

Nichols and Price also wanted to be sure that those who would be
affected by the regulations had an opportunity to see what was being
developed. The Commission approved their proposal to hold a series
of conferences with industry groups to explain the proposed rules. Nichols
told the commissioners that such meetings would lead to sounder policy
determinations as well as reduce misunderstanding about the intent and
scope of the regulations. The staff suggested that the meetings be held
before the Commission initiated final action on the regulations.[38]

The agency set rules for the conferences that minimized the possibility
of violation of the antitrust laws, established the meetings as purely
advisory, required that information discussed at the session be made
public, and ensured that a cross section of the affected groups was
represented. Subsequently the regulators held several meetings in March
1955 with representatives of four selected groups: utilities, vendors, the
chemicals industry, and research organizations.[39]

The early regulations covered eight parts under Title 10 of the *Code of
Federal Regulations,* the standard codification of general and permanent
rules issued by the government. The first dealt with production and
utilization facilities (Part 50) and included definitions as to what constituted a "production" and a "utilization" facility. The second set up the
domestic licensing process for special nuclear materials (Part 70). Not
only did this part spell out the application requirements and the criteria
for approval of licenses, it also outlined the accounting and physical-
security requirements for the material. The third group covered operators' licenses (Part 55) while the fourth set contained standards for
protection against radiation (Part 20).[40]

Security regulations composed another group (Part 25), which established requirements for the safeguarding of classified information by
licensees. The next two sets were revisions of current regulations on
control of source materials (Part 40) and the control of by-product materials (Part 30). Finally, the agency issued regulations on the rules of
practice (Part 2) that dealt with administrative procedures to be followed

in connection with the issuance, amendment, transfer, suspension, and revocation of licenses.[41]

The regulations on radiation protection, production and utilization facilities, distribution of special nuclear material, and operators' licenses were written first because they had an immediate bearing on the development of central-station power reactors. Even as the rules were under consideration in 1955, the agency received applications from Consolidated Edison of New York and Commonwealth Edison in Chicago for construction permits for proposed atomic-power plants. The agency handled the initial docketing of these applications under interim licensing arrangements, but it placed added pressure on Price's staff to promulgate final rules.

Price started the rule-writing process in December 1954 by presenting to the Commission a report on the proposed definitions of production and utilization facilities. This was the initial point for determining what types of machines were to be licensed. The 1954 act allowed the agency considerable flexibility to decide what facilities were production or utilization units. According to the law, the determination depended on whether a device was capable of producing or utilizing special nuclear material (plutonium, uranium 233, or uranium 235) in such quantity as to be of significance to the common defense and security or to affect public health and safety. What would be subject to licensing rested on the key words "significant quantity." The staff's definition established the base quantity for both production and use facilities at a hundred grams per year—a level above which agency experts believed both national security and public health and safety might be affected. Because of this hundred-gram floor, production facilities would not include cyclotrons, synchrocyclotrons, or linear ion accelerators that were capable of producing only insignificant (less than a hundred grams per year) quantities of special nuclear material.[42]

The production-facility definition had other exceptions. It would not extend to machines that were capable of increasing the uranium-235 content of uranium to an amount less than 10 percent by weight. The staff placed this exception in the definition in order to exclude standard industrial equipment, such as centrifuges and distillation columns, that were capable of enriching normal uranium only slightly, but would otherwise fall under the definition of a production facility because they could handle uranium in such large quantities that a yearly production of a hundred grams of uranium 235 might be achieved. In addition, certain types of reactors, regardless of their potential production capability, were not included as production facilities. Instead, these reactors were labeled utilization facilities. They included machines designed for powering mobile equipment like aircraft or ships, producing steam or heat for nonweapons purposes, medical therapy, research and development, and irradiation of materials other than source materials or special nuclear materials.[43]

The definition for utilization facility also had exceptions. Not included were electronuclear machines (cyclotrons, synchrocyclotrons, and linear ion accelerators), X-ray generators, and any equipment utilizing by-product materials. Those devices historically had not been licensed by the AEC even under the 1946 act although they were used widely in private research and clinical medicine. The staff believed that since the nation possessed no monopoly over "know-how" regarding the manufacture and operation of those types of machines, and since their production potential was negligible, they posed no threat to national security. The staff reasoned that since the machines were run in the province of research and medical circles by people trained in their operation, there was no overriding reason to assert federal control for health and safety reasons. In the case of by-product devices, the AEC already exercised authority over use of by-product materials, which the staff believed was broad enough to encompass health and safety factors.[44]

A lengthy section of Price's report discussed definitions of "component parts" that the Commission might consider licensing. Examples included drive rod mechanisms, specialized pumps, and motors. Subsequently, however, the Licensing Review Committee recommended omitting such items from regulation. Price explained to the Commission that the rationale for omission was that those items could do no harm to health and safety or to national security until they became part of a reactor, at which time the AEC would gain licensing control. Price noted that components could be exported, but he assured the Commission that the Commerce Department, which ran the export-control program, would have the items on its export list. In addition, information on many hardware components was classified. This gave additional control through the classification regulations.[45]

Both the Commission and several industry groups reviewed the production and utilization facility regulation prior to publication for initial public comment in April 1955. Yet some unresolved issues remained. Originally the regulation called for licensing of plants where nuclear fuels were fabricated into various shapes for insertion into reactors. After lengthy consideration the Commission decided that those plants should be excluded in the final rule because the special-nuclear-materials regulation provided for fuel-element fabrication with all needed safeguards. The question of creditors' rights also posed some uncertainties. The original section of the facility regulation granted approval for foreclosure by a creditor in the event of a bankruptcy proceeding. The creditor, however, would not be able to assume the license without making reapplication to the AEC. This raised questions among both the commissioners and the industry groups that could not be answered readily. The section was deleted in the final draft. Price noted at that time that the agency would have to schedule further rule-making on the issue after his group consulted experts in the mortgage-banking field.[46]

Certain sections of the facility regulations were relatively easy to write because there was some guidance from the 1954 act. The act spelled out the requirements for class-103 and class-104 licenses, and they were copied into the regulations. Itemized information required in an application was framed within the statutory criteria of safety to the public. For example, the necessary information required on financial qualifications reflected the belief of Joint Committee members that an applicant who was not financially qualified might take shortcuts in construction that could affect the facility's safety.[47]

The AEC developed other sections, however, with little guidance except the tenet of minimum regulation. Price told the Commission that the section on technical data the applicant had to provide for the Hazards Summary Report was based on borrowed and modified information that the "Reactor Safeguard Committee gets when it looks over reactors at the present." But the rules provided only general guidance on the standards against which the regulators would judge the submitted data. A key section broadly stated that a license would be granted if the application provided "reasonable assurance" that the applicant would "comply with the regulations," if the applicant was "technically and financially qualified" to construct and operate the facility, and if issuance of the license would not be "inimical to the common defense and health and safety of the public." In effect this meant that the burden of judging the quality of an application fell on technical appraisals by the agency. Both government and industry officials knew that final publication of the regulations did not preclude further revision and amendment as standards were developed for a maturing atomic industry. The early regulation was broadly fitted to the needs of a rapidly changing nuclear technology and a multifaceted research-and-development program.[48]

To provide as much freedom as possible for the developers to experiment as they progressed in their construction, Price's task force included in the regulations an "extended time for providing technical information" that allowed the AEC to issue a conditional or provisional construction permit even though all the technical information required for the application had not been submitted. The staff qualified this type of permit by requiring that it be given sufficient information to provide "reasonable assurance that a facility . . . can be constructed . . . without undue risk to the health and safety of the public and that the omitted information will be supplied."[49]

Both the applicant and the AEC benefited from this provision. The fact that the applicant would be issued a permit, albeit conditional, would give the company some assurance that a construction permit would be converted to an operating license. For the agency, issuing a conditional construction permit provided the flexibility to investigate proposed reactor designs that had not yet proved themselves. AEC officials assumed that outstanding safety questions would be satisfied by the time the reactor was ready to operate.

In such a potentially dangerous technology, this appeared to be a less than cautious safety philosophy. The AEC, however, believed that its safety provisions were adequate. General Manager Kenneth E. Fields told the Joint Committee in early 1956 that the agency's regulatory procedures guaranteed a careful evaluation of every proposed atomic reactor. They ensured that all hazards had been recognized, that "all reasonable steps" were being taken to "minimize the probability of the occurrence of an accident," and that if an accident did occur its consequences would be minimal. The regulatory program relied greatly on the technical competence of the designers and operators as well as the agency hazards staff, and included constant checks on the reactor operator for compliance with the agency's rules and regulations. The AEC recognized that the conditional construction permit was not the ideal licensing procedure. But because the power reactors under consideration were still being developed and useful standards and codes could only be written as the facilities became more standardized, the AEC had to be flexible. Fields observed: "This is the type of construction permit that we will probably have to issue for all the power demonstration reactors, and even for many of the research, testing, and medical reactors, for the next few years."[50]

The framers of the 1954 act expected private industry to begin to invest in atomic research and development and power-plant construction and thereby reduce the role government had played to that time. But the AEC would exercise major responsibilities for speeding progress in the peaceful uses of atomic energy. The agency maintained authority to fund and construct large-scale atomic reactors for production and for research-and-development purposes. The law prohibited the AEC from using reactors to sell or distribute electricity, which was clearly to be a function of private industry. In the fall of 1954 the Commission determined that a flexible industry-government partnership was needed to develop power-reactor technology as rapidly as possible and to spread the results of research and development among vendors and utilities.[51]

Four months after the law went into effect, the AEC announced its plan to encourage industry to take advantage of the statute's provisions through a Power Demonstration Reactor Program. The AEC began the program largely because industry had indicated little immediate interest in reactor development under the terms of the 1954 act. Despite the enthusiasm expressed by some utility spokesmen, the overall response of the industry to the opportunity for atomic development was restrained. In addition to the hazards of the technology, the financial uncertainties of nuclear power contributed to a sense of caution and fostered an attitude of wait-and-see among utility executives. The capital and operating costs of nuclear power were sure to be much higher than those of fossil-fuel plants, at least in the early stages of development, and the prospects of realizing short-term profits from atomic stations were dim. As an American Management Association symposium concluded in 1957: "The atomic industry has not been—and is not likely to be for a decade—attractive so far as quick profits are concerned." When Lewis Strauss made his oft-quoted statement in 1954 that nuclear power could provide electricity "too cheap to meter," he was referring to long-range hopes rather than to immediate realities. He knew as well as industry analysts that the heavy investments required were a major impediment to the growth of nuclear power.[52]

As inducements for industry, the agency through its demonstration program waived for seven years the established fuel-use charges for the loan of source and special nuclear materials that the government owned under the law. In addition, it offered to perform, without charge, "certain mutually agreed upon research and development work" in its national laboratories. Finally, the AEC offered subsidies, under a fixed-sum contract, for other research-and-development work on proposed reactor designs. This last provision had two aims. First, it fixed a dollar ceiling on AEC participation, thus placing the economic risks of a project squarely on the industry. Second, the AEC could share the research-and-development information it acquired with all interested parties, which would avoid the charge that the agency was giving an advantage to any one firm.[53]

No single reactor design had established priority as the mainstay of the power-reactor industry when the AEC announced the demonstration program in January 1955. Although the pressurized-light-water reactor being constructed at Shippingport seemed to have a lead over other alternatives, it was by no means obvious that the light-water models would dominate the field. The demonstration program was intended to show which one or several were most practical and reliable. Consequently, the program encouraged research on many reactor designs between 1955, when it began, and 1963, when it ended. Under the initial guidelines, industry had to submit proposals by 1 April 1955. Because the AEC indicated that it might make subsequent requests for proposals, those submitted before the initial deadline fell under what became known as the "first round" of the demonstration program.

Four industry proposals came in under round one. A selection board composed of five members from the Division of Reactor Development and assisted by a technical advisory group of engineers and physicists reviewed and evaluated them. It used five general criteria to make its determinations: (1) probable contribution of the proposed project toward achieving competitive nuclear power, (2) cost to the AEC, (3) financial risk (construction delays, cost overruns from unforeseen technical problems) to be taken by the proposer, (4) competence and responsibility of the proposer, and (5) assurances given against abandonment of the project.[54]

One of the four proposals, from the Nuclear Power Group, headed by the Commonwealth Edison Company of Chicago, was withdrawn from the program even after a favorable evaluation by the selection panel. The Nuclear Power Group decided, in August 1955, to waive its request for research-and-development aid from the AEC and to proceed privately. The project eventually culminated in the construction of a power reactor in Dresden, Illinois. It was the first large-scale dual-cycle boiling-light-water reactor and effectively demonstrated that concept's feasibility for electrical generation. The General Electric Company, a pioneer in boiling-water reactors, designed the project.

Long a leader in the electrical business, General Electric had been an innovator in developing one of the few large industrial scientific research laboratories at Schenectady, New York before World War II. The company entered the nuclear field in 1946 when it replaced the Du Pont Company in running the Manhattan Project's production reactors at Hanford, Washington. In exchange, the government agreed to provide an atomic-development laboratory near the company's Schenectady headquarters. Established in the fall of 1946, the Knolls Atomic Power Laboratory worked on the navy's submarine-propulsion program, which gave General Electric scientists and engineers experience that could be applied later in power-reactor development. In 1953 the company initiated its commercial nuclear operations when it decided to focus on boiling-water reactor technology at its new Vallecitos Atomic Laboratory near Pleasanton, California. Initially drawing heavily on AEC research on boiling-water reactors carried out at Argonne National Laboratory, General Electric determined that the direct cycle characteristic of the boiling-water reactor was a key feature it wished to exploit because it could cut the capital cost of a reactor without jeopardizing safety. Unlike the pressurized-water reactor being constructed by Westinghouse at Shippingport, the boiling-water reactor allows the coolant to boil in the core. The steam is then fed directly to the turbine generator through a steam drum, thus eliminating the need for the costly steam generator that pressurized-water reactors use. The company developed this technology with its experimental Vallecitos reactor. Fourteen months after start of construction, the AEC in August 1957 granted the experimental plant the first operating license issued to a privately owned reactor. In the meantime General Electric had contracted with its old customer, the Commonwealth Edison Company, to supply the Dresden facility. General Electric became the leading and eventually the only vendor for boiling-water reactors.[55]

Of the other three first-round projects, the proposal of the Yankee Atomic Electric Company to build a 175-megawatt electric pressurized-water reactor at Rowe, Massachusetts proceeded most smoothly. Shippingport, then under construction, also was a pressurized-water reactor, but Yankee Atomic's concept, like Shippingport a Westinghouse reactor, was different because it operated at lower pressures. Delay over a disagreement about the nature of the AEC research and development to be conducted under the proposal hampered the signing of a contract until June 1956. Construction went almost on schedule and Yankee Atomic began operation in 1960.

The Consumers Public Power District of Nebraska proposed under round one to build a small sodium graphite reactor at Hallam that was designed by Atomics International. With respect to technical feasibility the selection board rated the design as about on a par with that of the pressurized-water reactor. There were, however, several unknowns, the most important of which was the lack of significant operating experience with a sodium-cooled reactor to that time. Finalization of a contract was delayed until September 1957, primarily because Consumers was unable to assume the financial risk for the plant. The two parties resolved the problem by agreeing that the AEC would own the reactor, terms made possible under round two of the demonstration program. Construction began in 1959 and the reactor went critical in 1962.

The Power Reactor Development Company, a consortium led by the Detroit Edison Company, signed a contract with the AEC for a fast-breeder reactor in mid-1956. The last of the round-one proposals, the Power Reactor Development Company's plant became involved in a legal and political dispute that resulted in long delays.[56]

In addition to the round-one proposals, the AEC granted in May 1956 a construction permit to Consolidated Edison Company of New York to build a pressurized-water reactor on the Hudson River at Indian Point, New York, approximately twenty-four miles north of the center of New York City. Top management in the company disliked government intrusion and believed that private enterprise should underwrite the development of commercial atomic power. On that basis Consolidated Edison proceeded with the Indian Point plant without participating in the Power Demonstration Reactor Program. The facility began operation in 1962.[57]

The first round of the demonstration program represented the AEC's attempt to speed up reactor development by private industry with a minimum of government subsidy. While generally viewed by the industry as a promising start toward private atomic development, the program drew some complaints. None of the proposed reactors in round one were small in scale. The AEC aimed at large-scale prototype reactors. Critics, particularly the Rural Electrification Administration and small publicly and privately owned utilities, complained that the terms of round one effectively precluded them because they lacked the capital necessary to participate. In addition, they were more interested in smaller-scale plants suitable for their generating needs. The agency attempted to satisfy the program's critics by announcing round two in September 1955, which enlarged the AEC's role. Under this round the agency offered to finance and retain ownership of the reactor portion of the facility, much as the earlier Shippingport contract had provided. By retaining ownership the agency accomplished two objectives. First, it avoided conflict with that section of the 1954 law which prohibited direct subsidy of reactor construction. Even more important, it allowed smaller con- sumer-owned utilities to join the program without making an enormous capital outlay as was required in the first round. Under the second round, reactor size was limited to power output ranging from five to forty megawatts electric. Proposals had to be submitted by 1 February 1956.[58]

Six municipally or cooperatively owned facilities filed proposals. A seventh came from the University of Florida. The selection board found four of the proposals acceptable for further negotiation, but after more than a year, agreements had not been reached because of the continuing reluctance of the utilities to assume the financial risks. This lack of prog- ress created a good deal of consternation, particularly among Joint Com- mittee members who wanted a more vigorous reactor program, even if it meant a major government reactor-construction program. A change in the rules resulted, allowing the AEC to contract directly with the equipment manufacturer for the design and development of a reactor and with the utility for the site and conventional generating facilities. Even with this additional provision only two of the original proposals under round two were negotiated and consummated: an Allis-Chalmers Manufacturing Company closed-cycle boiling-water reactor sponsored by the Rural Cooperative Power Association in Elk River, Minnesota and an Atomics International organic-cooled and -moderated reactor owned by the City of Piqua, Ohio.[59]

In response to increased Joint Committee pressure to expand the re- actor program the AEC announced a third round in January 1957. The agency aimed this phase at encouraging private utilities to finance con- struction of advanced reactor designs under terms similar to those of round one. It received several proposals, a number of which led to new projects. The designs included a seventeen-megawatt electric heavy- water pressure-tube reactor at Parr, South Carolina with a design quite different from those of the typical heavy-water reactors being developed in Canada; a boiling-water reactor at Big Rock Point in Michigan that tested different fuel elements; the Pathfinder plant in South Dakota that implemented an advanced nuclear-fueled superheater; and a high-tem- perature gas-cooled reactor at Peach Bottom, Pennsylvania. The AEC undertook negotiations, entered into contracts, and issued construction permits for those plants in the late 1950s and early 1960s. Finally, in August 1962, the AEC announced a modified third round of the demonstration program calling for proposals for "large . . . base load, electrical generating facilities" that would demonstrate reactors "as reliable sources of electrical power." In other words, only proven reactor-concepts were eligible. By the end of the program in 1963, the light-water reactor family had emerged as the future workhouse of the atomic industry.[60]

While it licensed the first demonstration reactors under the utilization regulations, the agency also spent considerable time in 1955 on two other sets of rules that applied to power reactors. Regulations on special nuclear materials and on operators' licenses were necessary to implement the 1954 Atomic Energy Act. Under the law, the government retained title to all special nuclear material because of its strategic importance in making atomic bombs. So Congress imposed upon the Commission the responsibility to protect special nuclear material against loss, diversion, and unauthorized use. Since national-security considerations gave special nuclear materials a high strategic value, the foremost concern of Price's task force was to develop rules to safeguard them. The Atomic Energy Act specifically told the Commission that special nuclear materials must be distributed so that no user would be "permitted to construct an atomic bomb," and under standards that would "protect health and minimize danger to life and property."[61] Although in certain forms special nuclear material needed to be controlled because of health and safety considerations, the strategic aspects were critical in the development of regulations.

The agency required a license to possess special nuclear material. A power-reactor owner applied for a materials license concurrently with a submission for a utilization-facility license. The AEC insisted on this procedure to assure a facility of adequate supplies of fuel for the duration of its forty-year license period. Agency officials thought it would be unrealistic to expect private groups to make substantial investments for reactor construction without guarantees that special nuclear material would be available at the time of operation. Fuel fabricators and processors, unlike reactor owners, would not receive an assured supply of material, although they, too, would normally make application to possess special nuclear materials at the same time they applied for their facility license. The issuance of a materials license to a fuel fabricator or a processor was analogous to a hunting license because both had to solicit business from reactor owners. Consequently, their supply of material came out of the allocations granted to reactor owners. To accommodate this, the regulation provided for transfer of special nuclear materials from one licensee to another.[62]

The key problem in developing the regulation concerned the extent to which the agency should impose detailed rules for accountability and safeguarding the material. The first draft from Price's task force warily incorporated detailed procedures. The authors attempted a compromise that would satisfy the 1954 act's forceful provisions but would not be too burdensome on the licensees. The draft instructed licensees to establish double-entry accounting records and internal control procedures, directed licensees to take measurements of special nuclear material shipped or received, and required physical inventories as well as the submission to the AEC of material balance reports. Elaborate safeguard details were also written in the sections on protection of the material. Reviewing this draft in early February 1955, the commissioners thought the stringent provisions were too detailed and exacting. Commissioners Libby and Murray suggested rethinking the regulation to modify the more formidable requirements. Price's drafters went back to work.[63]

The new draft completely eliminated the sections on accountability procedures and provisions for safeguards. The rule merely stated that the AEC could incorporate additional requirements in this area. Because of its bearing on national security, this was a major policy decision that the Commission studied and discussed at length. Price carried the argument for the elimination of the procedures. He commented that the AEC should stay out of the licensee's business. "We don't care," Price argued, "whether he keeps the records on the back of an envelope or where, just so he has them and we can come and look at them." The premise for allowing a licensee to keep his own accounts was based on the inherent monetary value of the material. Price said what the government was telling the licensee was that "he is the one on the hook for the dollar value, and will protect it out of self interest."[64]

The same premise applied to safeguarding the material. "It is more valuable than gold," Price noted at a later meeting with the commissioners. "Banks know how to protect gold. We think these companies know how to protect this material." From a different perspective, Strauss challenged Price's argument. The value of the material did not bother Strauss, but possible diversion to a potential enemy did. "To the extent that weapons grade material or spiked material is involved, covert operations could accumulate enough to make a weapon," Strauss suggested. When Nichols answered that the criminal penalties were a serious impediment to clandestine activities, Strauss retorted that an enemy was not much concerned with a violation of American law. But Price assured Strauss that the regulators were relying on more than criminal penalties. "We believe," he said, "that the financial investment that the licensee has in the material will give him the incentive, and that he will just out of his own self interest give it the kind of guarding and protecting that will satisfy what we regard as the kind of protection that the strategic value would require." Price further assured Strauss that the agency's inspection program would add another obstacle to any possible covert operation. Nichols capped the discussion by mentioning the other side of the regulatory problem that struck a sympathetic note with Strauss. "The minute you start writing rules," Nichols said, "you get into a most difficult problem here of interfering with private business." The regulation carried as written.[65]

The third set in the initial group of regulations discussed by the Commission—operators' licenses—was approved with some reluctance. When discussing the draft 1954 act in executive session with the Joint Committee in May 1954, the agency took a position that licensing operators of atomic facilities would be unduly burdensome for the AEC. Strauss argued that it was more appropriate to license the plant and make the facility's management responsible for its own operators. Congressman Carl Hinshaw of California and Senator John Bricker of Ohio immediately took Strauss to task. Hinshaw reminded the AEC chairman that the Joint Committee had considered this section carefully and "came to the conclusion that the public interest . . . made it highly desirable for the Commission not only to license these people, but to examine into their knowledge of the situation before they operated the facilities, because it is rather a dangerous thing to do in some instances." Bricker added his support: "Pulling the wrong lever might not only be of interest to the company, but of interest to the public generally, or the whole community. It [operators] ought to be licensed by the authority that knows more about this subject." Meekly, Strauss replied, "Very well, sir," and a section on operators' licenses was included in the 1954 act. Price's task force finished the first draft of the operators'-license regulation in February 1955, and the Commission approved it for discussion with the industry groups in March.[66]

The Commission did not hold its first substantive discussion of the regulation, however, until 6 April. Price reported that all the advisory industry groups agreed with the original AEC position that the agency should not regulate this area. Strauss suggested to his colleagues that the Commission write to the Joint Committee, reiterate the agency position, back it up with the testimony from the industry groups, and ask for an amendment eliminating the section. He said he was concerned over the amount of work that Price's group would have to put into the regulations. But Price cautioned Strauss against that approach. He thought it would be difficult to make a stronger case now than the Commission had made at the time of the hearings. Price assured Strauss that the regulation was relatively simple. In addition, he observed that only four people in the country would be affected by it immediately, those being the operators of the first private research reactor at North Carolina State College. This was all the more reason, argued Price, for not going to the Joint Committee for an amendment. The agency should wait until it had acquired experience with more operators.[67]

The task force wrote the regulation as simply as possible. The rule required an applicant to take an operating test and pass a medical examination. It also took care of people who were already trained in government contract and navy reactor programs by waiving the requirements for operators who could prove their qualifications to the AEC. Price believed that the regulation imposed minimum demands that still met the main objective of protecting the health and safety of the public. He said the task force was inclined to follow the example of the Civil Aeronautics Administration in licensing pilots. "They examine the man's competence, his health," Price said. "They leave it to the management to determine if he is reliable and trustworthy. In view of the tremendous investment that the companies will have in these plants, . . . we thought that this was a proper case where we could say that the selection of reliable people is the responsibility of management, and that it would be getting into the management function to some extent to be trying to determine that kind of qualification." The Commission agreed.[68]

Even while these regulations were being developed and the Division of Civilian Application was being organized, processing of applications for construction permits began. As the licensing process evolved, it proceeded along both formal and informal lines involving personnel not only in the Civilian Application Division but in several other program units as well. Because all reactor designs were developmental, whether they were carried out privately or under the government-sponsored power-demonstration program, the applicants benefited from an early and informal discussion of their proposals with the AEC staff. Those meetings determined, first, whether the projects were feasible, and second, whether they included the necessary technical data, financial information, and safety provisions required under the regulations in the formal application.[69]

At the preliminary meetings, which were numerous and long, the staff emphasized that the initiative for the safety of the reactors rested with the applicant. Consequently, the applicant's engineers and scientists had to review every phase of the proposed reactor design and operating procedure to assure that the probability of a serious operating mishap had been brought to an acceptably low level. In addition, the applicant had to provide information on a second line of defense to prevent serious consequences should an accident occur. The preliminary informal discussions highlighted such matters as the relationship between the site and the reactor containment; the fact that the applicant had to select a site on the basis of complete knowledge of all radiological factors and had to consider the hydrology, meteorology, and seismology of a site; and the requirement that an applicant look at the population density of the surrounding areas and plan for the probable population distribution in future years. In addition, it was necessary to determine whether the surrounding areas were used for industrial, commercial, agricultural, or residential purposes, and whether the surface or ground waters that might be subject to contamination by the proposed reactor were used for human or animal consumption. The discussions more than merely underscored the applicant's responsibility for the safety of a proposed project. Outstanding technical problems were isolated so that the applicant could resolve them before submitting a formal request for a license. The agency staff provided not only guidance but also information from current state-of-the-art research conducted by AEC laboratories. All this facilitated not only the licensing process but the development of the reactor industry.[70]

The AEC's rules of practice established the formal procedures for processing the application. After being docketed by the Civilian Application Division, the application received an administrative review for completeness. This process checked the items required by the 1954 act and the implementing regulations. Key information included data on the financial and technical qualifications of the applicant, the earliest and latest dates for completion of the project, a request for allocation of special nuclear material, the nature of restricted data within the application, and the inclusion of the hazards-summary report. Any missing data had to be supplied by the applicant before the process moved forward.[71]

Several AEC divisions then worked on the application. Throughout, the Division of Inspection kept abreast of the proposed design, technical aspects, and construction progress. The Division of Finance conducted a review of the applicant's financial qualifications. The Division of Reactor Development reviewed the application to determine the technical competence of the applicant and the reasonableness of the special-nuclear-material request. The Nuclear Materials Management Division calculated the facility's special-nuclear-materials requirements. The Division of Production, under whose supervision AEC reprocessing plants operated, gave advice on whether existing or proposed AEC reprocessing facilities could handle the fuel returns from the applicant's facility.[72]

The Hazards Evaluation Branch in Civilian Application performed the critical task of reviewing the hazards-summary report. In addition, the Safeguards Committee conducted an independent review. Those two reviews constituted the heart of the application process. Much of the information in the hazards-summary report already had been discussed with the applicant in the preliminary informal meetings. The document now included the applicant's best technical opinion as to what could possibly take place in the reactor that might result in the release of radioactive materials from its core and conclusions on the effectiveness of the facility's containment and isolation in minimizing the consequences of such occurrences. The staff review of the report judged the safety of the reactor by use of much of the same procedure as Teller's original committee. In this process the regulators often sought the advice of the Safeguards Committee and held additional meetings with the applicant to discuss further any questions raised by the report. The staff's goal was to arrive at a point where it believed there was reasonable assurance that the reactor could be operated safely or at least that any unresolved safety problems could be mitigated over the intervening construction period. After construction was completed, the applicant was required to submit a final updated hazards-summary report before the construction permit was converted to an operating license.[73]

Evaluation of applications was a formidable task. Everyone in the nuclear field recognized that an accident could destroy the fledgling industry or at least set it back many years. Excessive caution, though, if it did not recognize established principles of reliable reactor design and operation or if it overloaded the machines with unnecessary and expensive safeguards, might also have a negative impact on development of the industry. The problem was to find the appropriate balance despite many unanswered questions about atomic energy. Both the AEC regulators and the applicants lacked definitive safety standards and criteria against which to judge a reactor application. A technology marked by many reactor designs, all in the developmental stage, made it even more difficult to apply uniform standards. Even with the experience gained by the mid-1950s, many gaps in technical knowledge remained to be resolved before the regulators could devise standards with greater certainty. Concerned about this, Rogers McCullough wrote in 1957 that a "discussion of unknowns in reactor safety could be lengthy indeed." He itemized some of them: knowledge of the properties of steel and other metals under stress in a reactor was not complete; means of quantifying the effect of various forms of radiation on reactor materials needed more study; the question of the reaction of water with aluminum, zirconium, uranium, and thorium needed more theoretical and experimental work; and in the event of a major reactor accident, the measures required to decontaminate a large area or minimize radiation exposure were uncertain. Consequently, the hazards staff and the Safeguards Committee had to give a great amount of individual attention to the design details of each reactor.[74]

Unknowns in the technology presented special problems for the agency. When questioned by the Joint Committee, AEC officials admitted readily that they had not "reached the stage where there are rules of thumb which can be applied to the hazards evaluation of reactors." The agency's policy had to be a cautious, deliberate approach on issuing detailed criteria since nearly every reactor application "presented new problems or required the reconsideration of problems in new contexts." In spite of the lack of codes or formulas, the AEC believed it could move forward in the safe licensing of reactors. General Manager Fields reported to the Joint Committee in 1957: "We can identify a good many elements or factors which must be evaluated in consideration of the safety aspects of reactors. We can, also, in the case of some of these factors provide general guides against which we attempt to evaluate the pertinent information available for the particular reactor. Not all of such factors would require consideration in connection with every reactor, and the general guides stated for these factors might need to be revised or modified in connection with particular reactors."[75]

The Division of Reactor Development's ongoing research-and-development programs at the various national laboratories gave considerable attention to safety issues that provided knowledge for the regulators. This research was carried out on a specific safety-program basis and, in some instances, on an individual reactor-project basis. For example, some experiments designed to obtain safety information were done with the Boiling Reactor Experiments (BORAX I-V) and the experimental breeder reactor. The BORAX experiments, conducted at the Idaho test station by Argonne Laboratory, were designed to study the feasibility and operating characteristics of boiling-light-water reactors. In particular, the early tests dealt with inherent control conditions of such reactors. The first of five experimental reactors built between 1953 and 1962, BORAX-I, started up in 1953, was the first boiling-light-water reactor. After a long series of experiments that demonstrated the technical feasibility and inherent stability of the concept, BORAX-I was subjected to an extreme power-excursion experiment that resulted in partial meltdown of the core. More important for safety considerations, however, the experiment dramatically confirmed the self-quenching characteristic of a steam void that reduced the reactivity of the system. Argonne's experimental breeder reactor, also constructed at the Idaho test station, was put through a series of experiments that provided valuable safety information; they included operating through a zone of temperature instability combined with rapid power increases. In addition, other test reactors were in a design or construction phase. Individual programs also were run that tested metal-water reaction, metal ignition, reactor fuses, containment, and reactor instrumentation and control.[76]

While the agency spent an increasing amount of money on safety-research projects, the regulators had no control over the program other than to request information on safety-related questions that were raised by the licensing process. There was much cooperation between the hazards-evaluation staff in the Division of Civilian Application and the Reactor Development Division staff. In addition, the regulatory staff received research results from applicants for reactor facilities, licensees, and their manufacturers. But in those days, when the Commission placed top priority on the successful development of a nuclear industry, it sought to maintain flexibility, cut red tape, and increase administrative efficiency. So it appeared only natural that safety research should be an important part of the agency's larger research and development program.[77]

Following its evaluation and review of an atomic-facility application, Price's division submitted a staff paper to the general manager that analyzed all pertinent facts on the proposed facility and presented its recommendations on issuing the construction permit and the allocation of special nuclear material. After review by the general counsel, the recommendation along with the independent Safeguards Committee appraisal was sent to the Commission for its decision. If it was approved, Price issued a construction permit.[78]

The construction permit might have conditions placed on it. Fields had told the Joint Committee that conditions probably would be common in the case of the early reactors since most were in the development stage and the applicants often could not provide initially all the technical data needed for the AEC to make a conclusive judgment on the safety of the machines. But as long as the regulatory staff agreed that the applicant could furnish the answers before submission of the final hazards-summary report, a conditional permit could be issued under terms in the regulations allowing "extended time for providing technical information." This permitted the construction of developmental reactors without violating any known safety considerations. Theoretically, it also provided an incentive to the licensee to resolve safety issues, because a conditional construction permit indicated that the holder had to remove the conditions before an operating license would be issued. At the same time the conditional permit guaranteed fuel for the reactor and allowed construction to proceed side by side with continuing technical refinement.[79]

Semisecrecy surrounded the agency's evaluation of an application. In 1956 the AEC established a Public Document Room at its downtown Washington building, where enumerated items about an application were deposited for public inspection. They included "records of license and access permit applications and issuances, comments from interested persons on proposed regulations, and records of licensing hearings." But the regulatory-staff safety analysis on its review of an application, and Safeguards Committee safety reports, were considered internal documents. In addition, all meetings between the applicant and agency staff as well as Commission meetings where decisions were made on an application were closed. Minutes of those meetings were not made available. Only the Commission's decision was disclosed. Even the Joint Committee was not routinely informed of the staff's and the Safeguards Committee's recommendations on proposed facilities.[80]

The Commission's rules of practice, subject under the Atomic Energy Act of 1954 to the Administrative Procedures Act of 1946, allowed public participation. The rules specified that an applicant or an intervenor could request a hearing, or the Commission, on its own initiative, could order a hearing prior to taking action on an application. Since it was unlikely that the Commission or an applicant would request a hearing, the only real possibility for such action would be based on a request from an intervenor. Yet since little information was available before a construction permit was issued upon which a potential intervenor might base a petition for a hearing, an intervention could in practice occur only after the agency issued a permit. AEC rules specified that the Commission would order a hearing if a valid petition was received within thirty days after the issuance of a license.[81]

Issuing an operating license was the second principal step in the licensing process. Several years usually intervened between the construction-permit issuance and the conversion to an operating license. During that time the licensee regularly sent supplementary information to the Division of Civilian Application to bring the application up to date and to fulfill any conditions that had been placed on the construction permit. When the applicant was ready to convert his license, he submitted a final hazards-summary report. As in the earlier construction-permit review, the regulatory staff and the Safeguards Committee formally reviewed the report. Recommendations again were forwarded through the general manager to the Commission, which, if it decided favorably, authorized Price to issue the operating license. At this time the licensee also received authorization to possess the source material, special nuclear material, or by-product material used or produced during the facility's operation.[82]

President Eisenhower had explicitly stated a goal of minimum regulation for the new atomic-energy industry, and his philosophy had been incorporated in the 1954 Atomic Energy Act. When General Manager Kenneth Nichols discussed the early regulatory program with the commissioners in February 1955, he told them that the concept was "to get into the licensee's business as little as possible." Describing the Joint Committee discussion of the regulatory program at the recently held "202" hearings, Nichols concluded that the majority of its members also felt that way.[83] The subsequent development of regulations and a regulatory organization by the AEC implemented the national policy set in the White House and in Congress. Minimum regulation that protected national security and public health and safety appeared as the only logical way to proceed if the new industry was to be allowed the necessary flexibility to develop fully. Because the technology was in a developmental stage and was years away from maturity as a competitive industry, Price and his regulators established the safety program in a general way in order to adjust to fast-moving developments and existing imponderables. They knew the system had imperfections. But sharp criticism and major challenges to their regulatory procedures came sooner than they had expected.

IV

INSURING
AGAINST CATASTROPHE:
PRICE-ANDERSON

Everyone involved in the atomic-power program in the mid-1950s accepted the fact that atomic technology posed significant potential danger. The 1954 act acknowledged the hazards by its many references to the need for protection of public health and safety. Both government officials and private promoters recognized that to develop a successful atomic-power industry careful attention to reactor design, construction, and operation was essential. Effective regulation was equally necessary to reduce the chances of a reactor accident and to mitigate any serious consequences if such an accident occurred. The government's impressive safety record since the war years with its own reactors contributed a sense of optimism that future reactor operations, both government-owned and privately owned, would remain free of major accidents. Atomic proponents, nonetheless, acknowledged that the ideal of zero risk could never be achieved. To guard against what they considered a remote but real possibility that a catastrophe might occur, government authorities and industry leaders strongly supported some type of liability insurance to cover the emerging private atomic industry. Lack of such insurance protection, they believed, could stall or even stop the private development of atomic power.

The story of enactment of the insurance-indemnity program (the Price-Anderson Act) between 1954 and 1957 is a key element in understanding the AEC's dual promoter/regulator role as the agency moved on an uncharted course to fulfill its mandate under the 1954 law. The Commission had to license a technology that was considered safe but still involved the risk of a catastrophic accident. In order to promote the new industry by providing insurance coverage for a major nuclear accident, the AEC entered the private-insurance field in a novel way never before employed by government, industry, or insurance underwriters. Consequently, the two years leading to the passage of the Price-Anderson law gave important firsthand experience to the atomic and insurance industries, the AEC, and the Joint Committee in dealing with the complex ramifications of atomic development.

Francis K. McCune, general manager of the Atomic Products Division of the General Electric Company, first brought the insurance problem to the Joint Committee's attention during the 1954 hearings on revisions to the atomic law. Under the 1946 act the question of liability had not been considered because all facilities were owned by the government and, therefore, were self-insured. But with the advent of private ownership and development the liability problem seemed likely to arise. McCune told the Joint Committee that private enterprise's inability to secure adequate insurance coverage would be a serious obstacle to growth of an atomic industry. He believed private enterprise should carry its own insurance to the extent that the insurance industry could offer protection. But he suggested that the government should make some provision for insurance above whatever limits were privately available "to protect both industry and innocent people against the kind of catastrophe that we hope will never come." McCune thought such coverage would probably be necessary if the goal of widespread atomic industrial progress was to be achieved.[1]

McCune recognized that in urging government insurance assistance he was at odds with his own request and the call of private industry in general for increased freedom from government control in atomic affairs. But the problem of liability, he noted, "is bigger than any that business has ever had to face." In the event of a major atomic accident, it was "entirely possible for damage to exceed the corporate assets of any given contractor or insurance company."[2]

The 1954 law, however, included no provision permitting the AEC to insure any licensee's operation. On the contrary, although it gave the AEC authority to include "hold harmless" provisions in its contracts for the management and operation of Commission-owned plants, the new statute contained a section that specifically required licensees who used special nuclear material (which they leased from the AEC) to make the

United States and the Commission unaccountable for any damages resulting from the use or possession of the material. In other words, the government assumed no liability for damages that arose because of faulty nuclear material that caused an accident. The law's legislative history shows no further discussion on the liability question. For at least two reasons Congress did not address McCune's concerns in the statute. First, the background research and data on the insurance problem were not available to the Joint Committee at the time. The committee and its staff knew that to wait for an investigation on the liability question would delay passage of the law. Second, no immediate need for an indemnity provision existed. All concerned with private atomic development realized it would take years before liability coverage would be required, which would occur only when the first privately owned reactor began operation. McCune merely had identified a future problem; in 1954 it was not urgent.[3]

Within a short time, however, both the AEC and the Joint Committee began looking more closely at the insurance question. Joint Committee staff counsel George Norris suggested in December 1954 that a panel composed of atomic industry and insurance leaders be formed to "sort out the major questions on which decisions are needed." Although such a group did not materialize until 1956, the AEC on its own began security-clearance procedures in late 1954 for several insurance executives so that they could study AEC data and make recommendations to the agency.[4]

When AEC officials informed the Joint Committee at the annual "202" hearings in 1955 that industry probably could not acquire enough private insurance to meet its needs and might require supplemental government coverage, the news irked Chet Holifield. Several AEC witnesses insisted that the lack of adequate insurance was potentially detrimental to private atomic development and that the matter demanded further detailed study. Holifield appeared mystified. "It is interesting to me," he commented, "that all these industrial groups which beat tom-toms and put articles in national magazines and built up a great propaganda drive that now is the time for private industry to come in and do a job, are suddenly becoming a little coy. They don't want to plunge in. They are putting their big toe in the water, and say it is a little cold; will the Government give us a little incentive?"[5]

Notwithstanding Holifield's comment, a parade of industry witnesses emphasized the potential impact of the insurance problem. Paul W. McQuillen, an attorney with the New York law firm of Sullivan and

Cromwell and chairman of the Legal Committee of Atomic Power Development Associates, hoped that the industry's worry would be shared by Congress. He cautioned that private industry was unlikely ever to be able to underwrite the whole risk of atomic accidents, though he added that it should be able to carry a substantial amount of the load.[6]

General Electric's director of research, C. G. Suits, testified for the National Association of Manufacturers that while the probability of a serious atomic accident could be reduced through careful design and proper location of reactors, it would never reach zero. "It is this extremely improbable but not entirely negligible accident," he said, "for which insurance has thus far been sought unsuccessfully." Suits emphasized that industry willingly and realistically recognized the unusual hazards of atomic power, and added that "from the nature of those risks . . . protection must be accomplished by insurance." Later in the hearings, General Electric's McCune echoed Suits's concern about the inability to obtain adequate insurance for atomic risks. He considered it a great problem for the industry and recommended that the Joint Committee study the situation and invite insurance representatives to give their views.[7]

Hudson R. Searing, president of Consolidated Edison Company of New York, presented a slightly different perspective to the Joint Committee. In announcing that his company planned to construct and operate a reactor without any federal financial assistance from the AEC's Power Demonstration Reactor Program, Searing also noted that Con Ed was a large company and accordingly could assume substantial risks. Thus the lack of an insurance program was not a deterrent to its initial plans. He pointed out that he could say this now because the risk from the reactor would not arise for three or four years and he felt confident that by that time the "insurance industry will know a great deal more about the hazards involved and will work out some solutions to the problem." He emphasized that his company did not underestimate the liability problem. Although the issue would not slow Con Ed's project, he said, "in the case of smaller companies it may operate as a serious deterrent to their going ahead." To encourage those companies to participate promptly in the reactor program, Searing urged some form of government insurance protection.[8]

Foster Wheeler Corporation president Earle W. Mills suggested what might be done in more specific terms. Since an atomic catastrophe might easily exceed the resources of any private insurance underwriter, or even groups of underwriters, he told the Joint Committee that for some time to come, the government should provide a legal umbrella to relieve the underwriters until experience with reactors could bring reductions of the risks to "reasonable commercial dimensions." Mills believed industry had to determine how much insurance was needed and then seek as much coverage as possible from private companies. If the private capacity still proved insufficient, the government could supplement the difference. But Mills cautioned: "Government should not subsidize this insurance protection any more than is necessary."[9]

Throughout 1955 the National Industrial Conference Board, the Association of Insurance Counsels, the Federal Bar Association, the United States Chamber of Commerce, and the American Bar Association held sessions at their annual meetings in attempts to develop better understanding of atomic insurance questions. Lawyers, insurance and utility executives, scientists, and engineers participated in the discussions, which had the effect of giving increasing weight to the immediacy of the problems associated with insuring private reactors. In addition, at the Geneva International Conference on the Peaceful Uses of Atomic Energy, experts presented a number of papers that called attention to the complexities of the topic.[10]

Not surprisingly, the AEC took the lead in attempting to determine the magnitude of the problem and to devise possible solutions. By March 1955 the agency had cleared ten executives of the fire and casualty insurance industry to study its records, visit its facilities, and talk with key government officials. In June this Insurance Study Group wrote a preliminary report on its findings that the AEC widely publicized. The study emphasized that the fundamental difficulty of insuring atomic reactors was that the "catastrophe potential, although remote, [was] more serious than anything [then] known in industry." As a result the authors could draw only tentative conclusions pending additional study.[11]

The report outlined some specific concerns. It affirmed that physical damage to reactors and related machinery could probably be handled in the same way that boilers and machinery were covered in other industries. But radioactive contamination of equipment and containment buildings resulting from reactor failure presented new problems requiring further investigation to determine the scope of coverage needed. The report also raised questions about insuring against loss of use of a facility if an accident happened. Other industries frequently purchased this type of business-interruption insurance. But the study group believed that if such coverage were to be made available during the early development of industrial atomic power, it would be very limited in amount. Another issue requiring futher study involved reactors located near large existing industrial plants. The possible damage to other facilities might exceed the capacity of the insurance industry.[12]

The insurance executives considered the most serious problem to be third-party liability—the possibility of widespread damage to property or harm to persons beyond the boundaries of the plant property. Claims might be made directly by the person suffering injury or loss, or they might arise as subrogation actions on the part of insurers who were called upon to pay the third parties. The study group cited as examples claims for property losses or decontamination paid by property insurers, and workmen's-compensation losses arising from injuries to employees in neighboring plants. They reported that claims of those types, in the event of a catastrophic accident, might amount to an extremely high aggregate total.[13]

Some of the insurance executives' conclusions were less disquieting. They contended that the insurance problem was complicated by the experimental nature of the power-reactor development program but noted that as knowledge of the hazards accumulated, the insurance market could be expected to increase its capacity. The study group suggested a continuing liaison effort between the insurance industry and the AEC that would build confidence in the technology among the insurers. But the insurance spokesmen warned that in order to promote insurability of atomic-energy enterprises in the future, "it is believed absolutely necessary that the present Reactor Safeguards Committee or a similar committee continue to function and that stringent safety standards be maintained as a condition precedent to licensing." Finally, the group disclaimed any intention to recommend "whether or not legislation should be proposed under which the Government might assume liabilities in excess of those normally covered by [private] insurance."[14]

After studying the report, Civilian Application Division director Harold Price, controller Don S. Burrows, and general counsel William Mitchell reported jointly to the Commission that they believed the insurance industry would be able to write substantial amounts of insurance on atomic risks. But the three AEC officials could not provide clear evidence at that time that those amounts would be adequate; consequently, they expressed uncertainty about the need for the agency to request legislation authorizing government insurance. The Insurance Study Group would continue to meet; but to get other viewpoints, Price planned to send letters to organizations that had submitted proposals under the power-demonstration program as well as to vendor corporations requesting comments on the preliminary conclusions of the insurance executives. Mitchell told the Commission he hoped the responses would clarify whether government assistance might be required.[15]

The agency effort produced mixed reactions. General Electric's McCune and Ray L. Schacht of the Consumers Public Power District wanted prompt legislative action. What the industry needed, McCune wrote, was insurance against extraordinary risks, and "at the present time the only way to provide such insurance is by legislation." Schacht thought the study group's report indicated that the insurance industry would have to develop an increased capacity in order to meet the current requirements of the Power Demonstration Reactor Program. Convinced that the insurance industry would not be able to respond adequately, Schacht urged a legislative program that would provide government assistance. Commonwealth Edison suggested that the national interest required a quick resolution of the problem. The Chicago-based utility recommended "some form of Congressional assurance under which the Government would assume the risk beyond a specified large limit in the event of a major catastrophe." But responses from Detroit Edison, Westinghouse, Yankee Atomic, and Consolidated Edison indicated uncertainty and a willingness to wait for results of further study by the insurance industry.[16]

As a contingency, Clark Vogel of the AEC's general counsel's office drafted an insurance bill which he, Mitchell, and Price discussed with the Insurance Study Group on 24 October 1955. The insurers reported at the meeting that the industry probably could write twenty-five million dollars of liability coverage for each atomic plant and that it had been working on a plan through which members of the insurance industry could make specific commitments to a pool of insurers. Moving a little closer to committal, they thought that under those circumstances it seemed reasonable that the AEC proceed with drafting legislation, at least until insurers could state more precisely what coverage they could offer. The study group hoped to be more specific by the time they met in December.[17]

Both the organization of the insurance industry and the amount of coverage it could provide presented major obstacles to solving the atomic insurance problem. The numerous companies in the public-liability field were divided between stock insurance companies and mutual insurance companies. Furthermore, both stock and mutual companies were split between the underwriters of personal damage and underwriters of property damage, although in a few instances companies bridged the two fields. The insurers realized that not one or two or even several of the largest companies jointly could underwrite the amount of insurance the atomic industry indicated it would require.[18] Insurance leaders, therefore, worked on solving the problem by organizing the industry into syndicates or pools. The study group sent invitations to all American insurance companies to participate. A sizable number elected to join, and by May 1956 three syndicates had been organized.

One syndicate, the Nuclear Energy Property Insurance Association, consisted of stock property-insurance companies that were willing to retain for each company's account a minimum of twenty-five thousand dollars to cover atomic activities. The association acted as an agency to offer property coverage for reactors, fuel-fabrication plants, and fuel-reprocessing facilities. Stock liability insurers formed a second pool, the Nuclear Energy Liability Insurance Association, through which its members could offer insurance protection (other than workmen's compensation, which would be handled through regular insurance policies) against liability due to radiation hazards connected with reactors, fuel-reprocessing facilities, and the transportation of wastes. Like the property syndicate, minimum individual-company membership required a reserve of twenty-five thousand dollars for atomic insurance. Both stock syndicates indicated to the AEC that they would be able to offer jointly about fifty million dollars of coverage per atomic installation.[19]

Mutual companies made up the third syndicate. The Mutual Atomic Energy Insurance Pool differed from the other two. Its members covered both third-party liability and physical damage, separately or combined, in a net amount retained directly by each participating insurance company. This pool hoped to provide from eleven to fifteen million dollars of insurance for each atomic facility. Thus the level of private-property and liability insurance available for each installation totaled approximately sixty to sixty-five million dollars. This represented an unprecedented undertaking by the insurance companies; the largest amount made available to other American industries had never exceeded fifteen million.[20]

While the AEC set in motion the activities of the insurance companies, the Joint Committee, in January 1956, received the report of a blue-ribbon panel (named the McKinney Panel after its chairman, New Mexico news-paper publisher Robert McKinney) that it had asked to appraise the growth of the peaceful uses of atomic energy. Along with other requests the Joint Committee had asked the panel to recommend any legislative or policy actions needed to speed the development of private atomic energy. Part of the wide-ranging final report dealt with the insurance question. It encouraged the reviews that the AEC and the insurance industry were carrying out but concluded that at least two to three years remained "in which to conduct research and accumulate knowledge and experience before any substantial private activity can be delayed or stopped because of the inability to obtain adequate insurance." Con-sequently, the panel viewed a "federal atomic insurance program as a threat to private atomic enterprise, not a benefit," and thought it should be considered as a last resort. The McKinney panel was not satisfied that the time had arrived to consider the need for federal involvement.[21]

In early 1956 the AEC staff reached the same conclusion. After meeting with the insurance-industry advisory group in January, Mitchell, Bur-rows, and Price reported to the Commission that the atomic industry should "further consider the adequacy of private insurance coverage which will be available." Any Commission decision on whether to rec-ommend legislation providing insurance coverage in excess of that pri-vately available should be based on whether failure to offer government coverage would impede the atomic-energy program. The staff members emphasized their opinion that the Commission's judgment would be based not on "new technical information or on new evaluations of ex-isting information" but on whether the atomic industry would proceed without government coverage.[22]

Nonetheless, in anticipation that government assistance might be needed, the staff raised several unresolved questions. No determination had been made as to what type of assistance was most desirable. Three forms had been suggested: direct government excess-coverage insur-ance, in which the government would provide extra insurance beyond that available through private insurance; general indemnity, in which the government would give general protection to the atomic industry against uninsured liability to the public; and limitation of liability com-bined with public protection through a special disaster-insurance plan. In addition, the question of rates remained open, particularly if excess-coverage insurance were to be selected. To date, no definitive rate studies had been made by the insurance industry, although indications were that each reactor project would be evaluated separately. Finally, a major question existed on whether to set an upper limit on the amount of government assistance provided. Only continued investigation by the AEC and the insurance industry could answer some of these questions.[23]

The Joint Committee's "202" hearings in February and March 1956 provided another forum to discuss the latest insurance developments. AEC witnesses outlined the progress to date but hesitated again to recommend a federal program. Sterling Cole expressed his dismay that the McKinney panel had not investigated the matter thoroughly and suggested that if the AEC or the Joint Committee failed to find a solution, the industry would be discouraged from moving into the atomic-power field. Congressman Melvin Price went further. Fearing a deadlock if something was not done, he told his colleagues that he had directed the Joint Committee staff to investigate the question of third-party liability. He asked Joint Committee chairman Anderson to "set aside a special meeting or hearing on this particular matter."[24]

As a former insurance executive, Senator Anderson was the best-equipped member of the Joint Committee to deal with the insurance problem. Born in North Dakota, the son of a Swedish immigrant farmer, in 1895, Anderson had by 1917 completed three years of college. Rejected that year for Army officer's training because of a tubercular infection, he left home for a nine-month rest at a New Mexico sanatorium and decided to remain in the Southwest. Taking a job as a reporter for the *Albuquerque Herald*, then switching to the *Albuquerque Journal*, he became the latter's managing editor in 1922. But a recurrence of tuberculosis forced him to seek a job out of doors, so he turned to selling insurance and in 1925 started his own agency. While operating his business, he also became active in New Mexico Democratic politics, handling several state and federal jobs during the depression. In 1940 he became a full-time politician when he was elected to the first of three terms in the U.S. House of Representatives. In Washington he developed a poker-table companionship with Senator Harry Truman, who, as president, named Anderson his secretary of agriculture in 1945. Returning to electoral politics in 1948, Anderson ran successfully for the Senate. Because of the importance of atomic energy in New Mexico, he eagerly sought appointment to the Joint Committee, which he secured in 1951. He quickly emerged as an influential member of the committee and became its chairman for the first time in 1954 (the chairmanship rotated between the Senate and the House each session of Congress). The tall, curly-haired Anderson was a dedicated and hardworking legislator who won the respect of his colleagues for the knowledge he acquired of the nation's atomic-energy programs. He was not, however, a genial, outgoing type, and when aroused he could be petulant and vindictive. He was plagued by illness throughout his life; in addition to tuberculosis he suffered from diabetes, shingles, and a heart ailment (Eisenhower speculated rather illogically in 1958 that Anderson's bitter animosity toward Lewis Strauss might be attributed to the Senator's diabetic condition). In considering liability protection for the atomic industry, Anderson's experience in the insurance field gave him solid credentials to play a leading role in discussions of the complex issue.[25]

If Senator Anderson needed further encouragement to address the insurance problem promptly, he received it over the next few days from several industry witnesses. Commonwealth Edison's chairman, Willis Gale, told the Joint Committee that if reactors were to be built, coverage of catastrophe risk had to be provided. Like most industry leaders, he believed the hazard to be extremely remote. Since the development of competitive atomic power was "in the interest of all the people," Gale asked, "why not have the risk shared by all the people through the Federal Government?" Detroit Edison's Walker Cisler backed Gale: "The absolute necessity of insurance against a catastrophe involving extensive public liability, in adequate amount, cannot be overstressed." In a discussion of the McKinney Panel report, Philip Sporn, president of American Gas and Electric Corporation, talked about the dilemma the insurance question placed on the industry. Experience with reactors would provide more data about the possibilities of catastrophic occurrences. But Sporn said the atomic industry could not complete and operate reactors, thus accumulating the needed data, "without some form of assurance that the potentially very great claims resulting from a major catastrophe could be satisfied." The logical solution rested with the federal government, Sporn emphasized.[26]

Anderson wanted both a broader and more in-depth perspective on the problem. Accepting Melvin Price's earlier advice, he announced toward the close of the "202" hearings that the Joint Committee would sponsor a unique advisory seminar in mid-March 1956. Representatives of the insurance and atomic industries were invited, along with the AEC and interested members of the legal community. Even as the staff worked out the details, Price and Cole responded to the atomic industry's plea and introduced separate legislation amending the 1954 law to authorize liability protection for reactor owners.[27]

The two bills were the first legislative attempts to deal with liability.

Price introduced his bill on 1 March. It provided for a ten-year period within which the AEC, upon individual requests from utilities, would enter into an agreement to indemnify an owner, operator, manufacturer, designer, and builder of a production and utilization facility against uninsured liability to the public for bodily injury, death, or property damage arising from atomic hazards. Before such agreements could be effected, however, the AEC had to be assured that nongovernmental insurance against such liability under normal contingencies had been obtained. Cole's bill, introduced on 7 March and considered by some attorneys to be of doubtful constitutionality, proposed to limit liability in the event of a catastrophic accident. It set a ceiling of "twice the original capital cost" of an individual facility. This sum would apply to all contractors and subcontractors of the licensee in the design, construction, or operation of an atomic-power facility. If an accident occurred in which damages exceeded such an aggregate amount, the licensee could apply to an appropriate U.S. District Court for an order limiting the liability as well as one apportioning a claimant's payments "upon appropriate proof of damage." The bills needed refinement, but in effect they precluded any immediate AEC decision to initiate a legislative proposal. In addition, the bills signaled to industry that some form of liability relief might be forthcoming.[28]

A week before the Joint Committee seminar, the Atomic Industrial Forum released a much-awaited preliminary report, "Financial Protection against Atomic Hazards," prepared by the Legislative Drafting Research Fund of Columbia University. In November 1955 the industry group had concluded that although the insurance community might be able to marshal a sizable amount of coverage, "there would yet remain a large potential liability for which it might be prudent and desirable to make provision." Seeking an independent legal study on the question, the Forum engaged the Legislative Drafting Fund, which over the years had provided technical drafting assistance for several pieces of important national legislation. New York attorney Arthur W. Murphy, the executive director of the study, wrote the report. Columbia Law School professors John M. Kernochan, the Fund director, and John G. Palfrey supervised the work. When the Forum contracted for the study, it required that a preliminary draft be submitted by 1 March 1956. Although coincidental, the release of the report in early March came at a time when industry, AEC, and Joint Committee views were merging in support of legislative action to include some federal role in the solution of the problem. Consequently, the preliminary report turned out to be more significant than the final report that was published in 1957.[29]

The Forum scheduled a meeting for 8 March at its New York City headquarters to discuss the report. Representatives of the atomic and insurance industries attended. Copies of the report were also sent to the AEC, to the Joint Committee, and to the scheduled participants at the upcoming Joint Committee seminar.[30]

The report succinctly presented an overview of the problem and suggested general solutions. Murphy pointed out that because basic research had not yet been completed, the material presented was necessarily tentative. In spite of this reservation, the author believed it was advantageous to set out at an early stage some of the relevant considerations and possible approaches to the problem.[31]

More than half of the report identified the problem and its effect on the atomic industry, the public, and the government. Most of the conclusions were familiar: the chance of a catastrophic accident was considered small; although current efforts by the insurance industry would offer liability coverage many times greater than that available to other industries, the magnitude of a catastrophic accident still could not be fully covered; the reluctance of the atomic industry to proceed without additional coverage was "a serious immediate threat to the vital national interest" of atomic-power development; and the public would have to bear a major share of the losses. The key conclusion, however, assumed an active role for the AEC in providing liability coverage "in view of its special relation to atomic energy."[32]

Since the 1954 act gave the government a polymorphous role, Murphy wrote, by making the AEC a "sponsor, participant, regulator, guardian and mediator," the agency's conduct sometimes appeared ambivalent. Nevertheless, unless the agency's responsibility to public health and safety was to be narrowly defined, the AEC's functions should include "provision for compensating the public for damage suffered as a result of the atomic energy program." To date, that had not been accomplished; in fact, under the current special-nuclear-materials licensing program, the "hold harmless" clause shifted all responsibility to the private atomic industry. On the basis of this argument the report concluded that the AEC should participate in resolving the problem.[33]

The remainder of the report considered the government role. Any program adopted had to include requirements for the private atomic industry to protect itself against liability to third parties and for the public to be protected. Murphy reviewed other government insurance programs, including crop insurance, bank-deposit insurance, and a proposal for flood insurance, but found they offered few precedents for atomic-energy questions. The report briefly touched on three considerations that had to be addressed: the extent of government intervention, or at what point in any indemnity program the government would begin activities and limit its liability; the fees to be charged industry for government participation; and the feasibility of compelling the industry to take on whatever liability protection the government program offered. Because of its preliminary nature the report proposed few answers to those questions; it promised further analysis in its final form. Despite the difficulty of assessing the report's impact precisely, it seems clear that the force of its argument for government participation in the liability area was influential. Furthermore, it helped change the focus of the liability question from one of protecting industry against catastrophic liability to one in which the need to protect the public was of equal importance. The report's release came at an opportune time because it helped produce a consensus at the Joint Committee's March 1956 seminar on the need for legislation that included a major government role.[34]

The two-day seminar was the first meeting together for most of those involved in the insurance question. After months of investigation, reports, and small-group meetings, all participants were quite knowledgeable about the problems involved. The Joint Committee believed that the informal seminar atmosphere, closed to outside participants, would be the best way to exchange ideas and evaluate possible solutions that had been proposed. Accordingly, the Joint Committee established a flexible agenda. In the opening session, Price, Mitchell, and Rogers McCullough outlined government experience to date and summarized the technical features of reactor safety and potential hazards. The participants used the remainder of the two days to discuss four questions: what the operators wanted, what the manufacturers wanted, what the insurance community would give, and what needed to be done.[35]

The informal atmosphere of the seminar encouraged a frank exchange of views. Utility and vendor representatives, though gratified by the insurance industry's willingness to provide an unprecedented amount of liability coverage, emphasized that even those amounts were inadequate for catastrophic accidents. They thought that since the realistic limits of possible damage were incalculable, nothing short of complete indemnification would be adequate if private development was to proceed expeditiously. In a significant change of policy from his earlier position, Consolidated Edison's Searing said his company would go ahead and construct its reactor but would not put fuel rods in it unless the insurance problem was solved. Other utility spokesmen indicated that they would not even begin construction. The insurance representatives, still working on organizing their syndicates, generally opposed government participation in their business. They expressed hope that any legislation would take the form of indemnification rather than insurance. Although AEC representatives expressed no opinion on the advantages and disadvantages of a government role, the consensus of the seminar supported some legislative action to guarantee government protection above that of private companies.[36]

In his statement to the seminar, William Mitchell emphasized that Congress must decide whether such protection was necessary. That decision, he observed, would be made when the Joint Committee considered the Price and Cole bills that recently had been introduced. Although the general counsel remarked that the AEC was not prepared at that time to make any recommendations, in fact the commissioners had already discussed the matter and had agreed that they would encourage a government program if the private sector could not offer adequate protection. Staff work on an AEC proposal began shortly after the seminar.[37]

While Mitchell, Price, and Burrows developed the AEC's plan, the Joint Committee staff readied its own guidelines for legislation that incorporated certain features of the Price and Cole bills. Senator Anderson made the proposal public in a letter that also announced hearings on the subject beginning 15 May 1956. The Joint Committee's main recommendation was that the government offer indemnity of as much as five hundred million dollars above any third-party liability insurance provided by private carriers. Damages over the government ceiling would be handled by special legislation. The proposal also limited the liability of the licensees and equipment manufacturers to the total amount of private insurance plus the government indemnity. The government would charge a minimum annual fee per reactor for its indemnity coverage with proceeds going to AEC's safety research-and-development program. Refinement of specific language for a bill continued for a month before Anderson formally introduced his measure in the Senate on 25 May.[38]

Joint Committee staff director James T. Ramey had collaborated with

Anderson to arrive at the five-hundred-million-dollar figure. With politics in mind and no hard evidence on what might be a realistic number, Ramey had suggested five hundred million as simply representing the halfway point between zero and a billion dollars. Anderson readily accepted the number. In a later discussion the senator presented his rationale for the figure. He thought that ceilings on insurance policies were worthwhile and important and therefore an upper-limit figure in the proposed bill seemed desirable. Anderson noted additionally that if no upper limit was placed on the amount of government indemnity, some budget-conscious legislators would skeptically view what unlimited indemnity represented. So he attempted to please both his political colleagues and the atomic industry. Anderson said he wanted to "find something" that would take care of the pressing need for liability coverage while at the same time would "be able to be carried into law and not disturb anybody who is worried about the budget situation." Questioning whether any bill could pass Congress that incorporated "a blank check that says we will take care of every reactor accident no matter what the claims may total," Anderson remarked that if the industry was not pleased with the five-hundred-million-dollar figure, "it might end up being satisfied with nothing at all."[39]

The AEC staff had drafted a much simpler proposal that it readied for Commission consideration by the end of April. The AEC bill featured an unlimited indemnity approach that acknowledged that claims might exceed those usually handled by insurance. It also recognized the difficulty of assessing the amount of coverage needed because the chance of a catastrophe seemed so remote that the probability of risk could not be calculated in a meaningful way for insurance purposes. The bill granted the Commission authority, over a ten-year period, to indemnify, above the limits provided by private insurance, each owner, operator, manufacturer, designer, and builder of a facility against third-party liability for the life of the facility. In addition, it required the Commission to use the services of private insurance companies to the "maximum practical extent."[40]

Unlike the earlier Cole bill as well as the proposal suggested by Anderson, the AEC staff thought that its measure averted a possible constitutional challenge over limiting the amount of liability. Even more important, unlimited-liability coverage assured full compensation to the public. The staff also thought administration of its program would be simpler than the other plans and, through indemnification rather than direct insurance, avoided government competition with the insurance industry.[41]

The staff selected the unlimited-liability feature after reviewing other feasible approaches including direct insurance to the atomic industry, reinsurance of the insurance industry, and the limited-liability concept. Direct insurance and reinsurance were eliminated because of administrative overhead as well as undesirable competition with the insurance industry. The staff pointed out that the major problem, not only with some form of insurance that had a top dollar figure but also with a limited-indemnity program, was in determining "such limits on a realistic basis." In discussing the alternatives the staff made a strong and repeated argument that setting realistic limits was not only an arbitrary, impractical exercise but might well result in inadequate coverage for compensation to the public.[42]

The staff also gave careful attention to the definition of the limits to which a licensee would be liable under private insurance and above which the government indemnification would take effect. Since the atomic industry repeatedly argued that private insurance coverage would be inadequate, the simplest procedure would be for the government's indemnification to be limited to claims above the available private coverage. The staff also considered a number of other alternatives for defining limits below the available top amount of private insurance. Those included formulas related to cost of a facility; value of fissionable material on hand; power levels; fission-product activity; combinations of power levels and geographic areas subject to radioactive damage coupled with estimates of potential damages; and judgments based on such factors as the need for the facility, its size, cost, use, design, and location, owner's financial status, and cost of insurance.[43]

The staff concluded that any of those alternatives would establish relatively arbitrary limits that seemed unreasonable in specific cases. It argued that on the one hand the simpler examples failed to give weight to significant factors but that on the other hand the more complex approaches resulted in basing analyses on a great number of arbitrary assumptions. In addition, all the examples involved unreasonably complex and time-consuming studies. In the final analysis, the staff thought that allowing the atomic and insurance industries more time to work out the problem would be a better solution at that time than attempting to provide a government solution through specifically defined legislation. Such an approach would resolve any concern about companies

planning large facilities because they would undoubtedly insure or assume the risk up to the limits of available private insurance. Smaller
reactors, the staff observed, were of less concern because they might
not require protection against liability above the levels of insurance they
could buy from private insurers. Consequently, the proposed bill simply
provided for indemnification above the limits of available private
insurance.[44]

Although the Commission agreed with the staff's recommendations,
the standard review of proposed legislation by the Bureau of the Budget
brought two modifications to the bill that the Commission reluctantly
accepted. The staff proposal assessed each licensee a nominal hundred-
dollar fee to cover administrative costs incurred by the AEC. The bill
envisioned no charge for the indemnification itself because such fees
appeared inapplicable to the unlimited-indemnity concept. The staff had
argued that determining such a fee must take into account the amount
of coverage provided. Since the size of the risk and the probability of
accidents were extremely difficult if not impossible to estimate, it appeared impractical to base any charge on those factors. The Bureau of
the Budget countered that if industry paid no indemnity fee, a precedent
might be established for providing this service free of charge. In other
words, since indemnification protected a licensee above a defined level
provided by private insurance, it had monetary value. Unless those
benefiting were assessed for the program, they would be receiving a
subsidy. The Commission deferred to the Budget Bureau argument and
added a section making an annual charge at "reasonable" rates set after
considering the insurance industry's premiums for the basic coverage.[45]

The Bureau of the Budget also strongly urged a reinsurance program
in which the insurance industry would write the additional insurance
with the government reinsuring the underwriters. The idea resulted
from the administration's experience with a pending flood-relief bill that
included the reinsurance concept. More or less as a sop to the Budget
Bureau the Commission added a reinsurance provision to its bill, but
included it as an alternative to the indemnity plan it clearly favored.
The reinsurance item also established an "atomic hazard indemnity fund"
where proceeds from payments collected would be deposited. Such a
mechanism was common to both private and government insurance
programs.[46]

Congressman Cole introduced the Commission bill, and the commissioners testified at the Joint Committee hearings on the insurance ques-

tion the week of 15 May 1956. The purpose of the hearings was to publicize the facts about and possible solutions to the indemnity problem. Testimony revealed little that was new to the participants since the earlier private work on the problem had already created a consensus that some federal involvement was necessary. Early in the hearings Cole pointed out that the basic issues were familiar to everyone and that the Joint Committee had been on notice for two years that atomic-power development would be stalled until the insurance question was resolved. The main questions facing the Joint Committee concerned the level and the method of federal participation. The AEC presented its answers to those questions on the first day. Harold Price and Mitchell were key figures among the agency contingent that trooped into the House Caucus Room at the Capitol. Chairman Strauss and General Manager Kenneth Fields added weight to the agency position, while Commissioner Libby and Rogers McCullough spoke as experts on reactor safety and the consequences of accidents.[47]

After Strauss opened the hearings with a plea for the legislation to promote more quickly the use of atomic power, Harold Price told the Joint Committee that the Commission based its bill on several assumptions. First, he said, "we do not expect to have a catastrophic accident in this field but we cannot guarantee against it." Next he acknowledged the lack of solid data on the probabilities of a major accident, although he reiterated, "we are sure that the risk is extremely remote." And finally, since no one had had experience with such an accident, it was impossible "to know the magnitude of the losses." The AEC bill incorporated those assumptions through its principle of unlimited-liability coverage by the government above amounts provided by the insurance carriers.[48]

Although Price affirmed that the AEC would be satisfied with either direct indemnity or government reinsurance, he made his preference clear by acknowledging that the insurance industry objected to a government reinsurance program. Under either method the government would take on the total liability for the amount in excess of the basic insurance. Price asserted, however, and testimony by members of the insurance industry unanimously backed him, that the insurance industry thought that by providing the unprecedented sixty million dollars of basic insurance, it had taken care of its part of the insurance problem. The insurance industry regarded the special catastrophe problem as something beyond its obligations. Consequently, the insurers argued that government indemnity was the best approach. Quite aware of their position from his extensive contacts with insurance executives, Price made an effective argument for indemnity without badly tarnishing the Bureau of the Budget's reinsurance recommendation.[49]

Mitchell testified on the legal provisions of liability. Under questioning on indemnity versus reinsurance, he left the matter open for the Joint Committee to decide. He thought the agency could accomplish its objective of resolving the problem either by indemnity and reinsurance or by indemnity only. The choice seemed clear to the Joint Committee. Indemnity raised no opposition; objections from the insurance industry tipped the balance against reinsurance.[50]

One of the major points in the AEC bill—unlimited indemnity—at first attracted little attention. Price initially introduced the concept by remarking that "since the size of the risk involved cannot be accurately estimated, we recommend that the legislation not place any ceiling on the amount of the indemnity." Although the AEC had considered the five-hundred-million-dollar limit proposed by Senator Anderson, Price told the Joint Committee that it had concluded that that amount or "any other particular figure" had "no sound basis." The Commission opposed a limit on indemnity until more experience and data were available. The agency's position did not imply that it anticipated accidents causing damage in excess of the coverage that the insurance industry would offer. Price's statement maintained that the licensing procedure established by the agency was designed to give "reasonable assurance" that such large accidents would not occur. A nagging doubt nevertheless remained. "It is because we cannot guarantee against the remote possibility of a catastrophe," Price stated, "that we are recommending legislation in this field."[51]

McCullough, Libby, and Fields discussed the state of reactor technology, current knowledge of contamination effects in the event of an accident, and AEC procedures to prevent such an occurrence. Ironically, the information presented allowed Senator Anderson to undercut the agency's position on unlimited liability. McCullough acknowledged that reactor technology was "still very young" and there were "no standards by which we can judge reactors at this stage of the game." Rather, he said, engineering judgment had been and would continue to be used for some time to determine that the "hazard is acceptably low." He emphasized that for the first time in any major industrial development an attempt was being made to foresee possible accidents or disasters and to take positive steps to prevent them. After briefly describing the known dynamics of runaway reactors, the Advisory Committee on Reactor Safeguards chairman maintained that the excellent safety record to that time could be sustained through existing methods: "careful reactor design by competent people, careful, conscientious, and skillful operation, and adequate maintenance—and, I would like to add, a good deal of luck."[52]

Willard Libby discussed with the Joint Committee what could happen in the "worst possible case" reactor accident that would totally release its fission products. But he differentiated between maximum possible damage and the more likely probable damage in the event of a reactor failure. He also testified that estimates of consequences were necessarily theoretical because, fortunately, "practical experience with reactor failure has been minimal." The danger arose from the fission products accumulated during the operating period, and not just from the additional fission products generated instantaneously in a runaway accident.[53]

Using the latest theoretical appraisal made by Frank Pittman, the deputy director of Civilian Application who had assistance from the staff of the Division of Biology and Medicine, Libby described the lethal conditions if all fission products were released. A reactor of a hundred thousand thermal kilowatts would affect only the immediate vicinity of the reactor, whereas a reactor in the range of millions of thermal kilowatts extended the harmful dose to distances of ten to fifty miles. A full release from a hundred-thousand-thermal-kilowatt reactor might kill between twenty and fifty people in a region with a population density of two hundred to five hundred people per square mile. Even with fairly prompt evacuation, Libby said, between three hundred and five hundred people might be exposed to "possibly damaging levels of radiation." Libby reminded his audience that these calculations were strongly dependent upon the time and height of the release and the meteorological conditions.[54]

Libby also estimated contamination resulting from release of 1 percent of one hundred days' accumulated fission products at full power in a ten-thousand-thermal-kilowatt reactor: "In an area of 1 to 5 square miles, crops would probably be unfit for use, within this same area perhaps one-half square mile would have to be temporarily evacuated, perhaps 50 to 100 acres would be unusable for about 2 years without thorough decontamination; and in addition, of course, there might be a few acres near the site which would be more heavily contaminated." He reiterated that the damage would be influenced greatly by terrain and wind pat-

terns. Rainfall would also change the possible effects. The area immediately surrounding the plant would be more heavily contaminated, but
conversely, rainfall would decrease the damage farther out. Bodies of
water would be contaminated both by direct fallout and by secondary
leaching from the land into streams. Libby thought direct fallout could
make close-in bodies of water unusable for some time; leaching would
be less of a problem because it would take longer. Monitoring of water
downstream from the accident nonetheless would be required.[55]

Libby translated into dollar figures the property damage for a worst
possible case: "explosive rupture of the core of the reactor and complete
release of all the accumulated fission products after 100 days of operation
at full power." For a ten-thousand-thermal-kilowatt reactor, the property
damage would range from five to twenty-four million dollars; for a
hundred-thousand-thermal-kilowatt reactor, the estimate increased from
fifty to two hundred million dollars.[56]

Senator Anderson quizzed Libby on this estimate. On the basis of the
figures the commissioner had cited, Anderson wanted to know if there
was any point in talking about damage over a billion dollars, or even
five hundred million. When Libby replied that his totals were "pretty
conservative," Anderson inquired why the AEC could not place a top
limit on the coverage the government would extend to industry. Citing
the five-hundred-million-dollar amount that the Joint Committee had
suggested in addition to the sixty million the insurance industry would
provide, Anderson asked whether that would not be relatively complete
coverage. Libby realized that his estimations had undercut the Commission's argument for unlimited indemnity. Making the best of this
uncomfortable situation, he replied, "Though I speak with an air of
certainty, I am not sure these figures are absolutely the upper limits to
maximum possible loss. I think the assumptions given in calculating
these figures are reasonable assumptions. But you might have conditions, Senator, which make them worse."[57]

The Commission later changed its figures. On 13 June Kenneth Fields
sent a letter to the Joint Committee clarifying Libby's testimony. Fields
noted that Libby used figures based on thermal kilowatts since in general
discussion of reactor hazards, engineers and scientists used thermal
output because many machines such as experimental and research reactors produced no electrical power. Now using an arbitrary conversion
ratio of one electrical kilowatt to four thermal kilowatts, Fields provided
new figures to the committee. In an accident with a release of 1 percent

of the fission products from a hundred-thousand-electrical-kilowatt facility, the property damage range might be in the order of two million
dollars to eight million. In the remote possibility of release of one hundred
percent of the fission products from such a facility, the AEC estimated
the range of damage from 130 million dollars to six hundred million.
For a two-hundred-thousand-electrical-kilowatt facility with one hundred
percent release of fission products, the new property damage estimate
increased from a low of 180 million dollars to a high of nine hundred
million. Of the three central-power-station reactors being planned or
under construction at the time, Shippingport would have an electrical-
power output of ninety thousand kilowatts, Commonwealth Edison's
Dresden facility two hundred thousand electrical kilowatts, and Consolidated Edison's Indian Point plant 265 thousand kilowatts. While Fields'
letter clarified the situation somewhat, it apparently had no effect on
the disposition of the Joint Committee to keep the bill's five-hundred-
million-dollar government limit.[58]

At the completion of the testimony of McCullough, Libby, and Fields,
Senator Anderson noted that their remarks revealed how carefully the
"Commission is going into this and how many precautions it has taken
to safeguard health." So he wondered aloud why the indemnity program
was necessary. But in the next breath he commented that if the hazard
was not very great, the government might easily undertake the program
without jeopardizing its financial credit. Senator Henry Jackson interrupted Anderson's meandering thoughts to remind the chairman that
an accident might occur. "The important thing," Jackson said, "is not
how many accidents occur, but the total damages that have to be met
by someone." He told Anderson that he could not assume that because
the chance of an accident was small, the total amount of damages would
be correspondingly low. It seemed to Anderson, though, that if Libby's
estimates were correct, there would not be much monetary risk to the
government even if it underwrote the program beyond sixty million
dollars. Harold Price agreed with both senators. "We think," he said,
"the risk is that kind of remoteness and that is the basis of our presentation. The difficulty is, as Senator Jackson says, with all our safety
requirements and our record, we can't guarantee against that one that
might happen."[59]

On the basis of this testimony, combined with the remarks by insurance and atomic industry representatives throughout the remainder of
the week, Anderson introduced the formal Joint Committee bill (S. 3929)

on 25 May. The measure followed the lines of the proposal he had made earlier. It authorized the Commission to determine the amount of financial protection a licensee must have to protect the public against atomic accidents. Beyond this amount the government would indemnify reactor owners for sums up to five hundred million dollars. If a runaway reactor caused damages beyond those combined amounts, additional federal contributions might be granted after congressional consideration. If funds available still were insufficient, apportionment proceedings could be held to divide the total indemnity among those suffering property or bodily damage. In addition, the bill provided liability protection for designers, builders, and suppliers of parts for reactors. A few days later, Melvin Price introduced a companion bill in the House of Representatives, thus informally identifying the Joint Committee's liability legislation as the Price-Anderson bill.[60]

The Price-Anderson package obviously differed from the Commission bill; it was a compromise between the AEC and the original Joint Committee position. Price-Anderson limited liability; however, it allowed for damages beyond the limit. The bill made no provisions for an alternate reinsurance program. Before reporting the measure out of committee for consideration by the full Congress, the Joint Committee scheduled another day for hearings in mid-June. In the meantime, Mitchell analyzed the Joint Committee bill for the commissioners when they met on 4 June.[61]

The Commission by that time had concluded that some form of indemnity legislation was needed at the current congressional session in order to assure industry that financial protection would be available. Commissioner Vance emphasized the point at the meeting. He suggested that if the Price-Anderson bill was satisfactory to industry, the Commission should support it, particularly if it appeared more likely to pass than the AEC bill. The other commissioners agreed. They decided that they would not offer detailed comment on the Price-Anderson bill because such an approach might impede its enactment by precipitating further study and discussion. The Commission directed Mitchell to revise the AEC statement to incorporate any drafting or clarifying revisions of the Joint Committee bill, but not to question the desirability of any of the bill's main features.[62]

By the time it held its final session on the insurance bill, the Joint Committee had agreed on what form of legislation would be reported to the Congress. Melvin Price chaired the session, which was attended only by Congressmen Paul J. Kilday of Texas and James E. Van Zandt of Pennsylvania. Vance and Mitchell traveled to Capitol Hill to present the Commission's observations on the proposal.[63]

Vance briefly reviewed the earlier hearings and acknowledged that experts unanimously agreed that the amount of liability insurance available from the industry would not provide adequate protection to the public. He emphasized that prompt legislation either in the form of the Price-Anderson bill or the Commission bill would eliminate this deterrent to the development of private atomic power. Although Vance paid AEC allegiance to the Bureau of the Budget in suggesting that the Commission favored incorporating into the Price-Anderson bill an alternative reinsurance program along with a reserve fund to support it, he followed the earlier Commission position by not strongly advocating it. When Price pressed Vance on which bill the agency favored, the commissioner evaded a direct reply: "I frankly believe that the passing of some bill at this session of Congress is more desirable than the selection of a particular bill." When Price asked what would happen if a bill were not passed, Vance answered flatly that the power-reactor program would be delayed.[64]

The hearings ended one phase of the indemnity problem and demonstrated a textbook example of political compromise. The Joint Committee issued its two identical reports later in June that called for a five-hundred-million-dollar limit on the government's part of the indemnity package.[65] The committee denied the AEC's appeal for unlimited indemnity, but the agency was willing to compromise in order to increase the chances for passage of an indemnity program. It was satisfied that alternate government reinsurance was not included in the bill, though its ostensible support for such a provision placated the Bureau of the Budget. In doing so the AEC recognized the insurance industry's objections to government reinsurance, and the agency's lukewarm advocacy of reinsurance indicated its acceptance of the industry's position.

One key member of the Joint Committee voiced dissent to the Price-Anderson bill. In a separate opinion filed with the two reports, Chet Holifield conveyed his feeling that the bill would provide a financial climate in which private industry could take undue risks with public health and safety. As evidence he cited the refusal of the "hardheaded insurance companies" to place full-coverage policies on atomic reactors and Commissioner Libby's testimony regarding the consequences of worst possible accidents. "An aye vote," Holifield told his congressional colleagues, "means you are willing to take the gamble, not just with dollar liability but with hundreds of thousands of human lives in every urban center where these atomic reactors will be placed and where they may blow up, melt down, or leak deadly gas, liquids, or finely divided particles into nearby cities." Considering it premature to take such "blind risks with human lives" before more knowledge and operating experience had been acquired, Holifield advocated constructing reactors at isolated government sites "under Government supervision and where direct Government responsibility is exercised."[66]

Holifield had championed that course of action through sponsorship of a controversial bill that had been winding its way through the Congress since spring. The measure reflected the anxiety that Democrats felt about the present state of the administration-backed reactor program, which primarily relied on the private sector to develop atomic power. Concerned that private reactor development was not moving rapidly forward and that it was placing too much emphasis on one or two reactor designs, the Gore-Holifield bill directed the AEC to build and operate a number of different prototype reactors as a supplemental part of the Power Demonstration Reactor Program. The bill stirred contentious debate in the Joint Committee. It was strongly supported by Democratic members, who contended that the United States was falling behind Great Britain and the Soviet Union in the quest for practical and economical atomic power. Cosponsor Albert Gore, a senator from Tennessee, insisted that the nation was engaged in "a race in which anything other than victory is a disastrous defeat," and Holifield declared that "if we are going to obtain the lead in the development of electrical kilowatts on an economic basis in the world, it must be through a crash effort of the Government." The administration and the AEC sharply disagreed, arguing that private industry, under the power-demonstration program, provided the best vehicle to develop atomic power. Strauss told the Joint Committee that "we have a civilian power program that is presently accomplishing far more than we had reason to expect in 1954."

Although the Joint Committee reported Gore-Holifield favorably, it won support from few Republicans and encountered difficulties in the Congress, particularly in the House. Like the indemnity legislation, the objective of Gore-Holifield was to accelerate atomic-power development; but unlike Price-Anderson, it provoked significant political differences. The Democrats on the Joint Committee regarded the indemnity and the government-reactor bills as parts of a coordinated program. So the fate of Price-Anderson in the Eighty-fourth Congress depended on Congress' decision on the Gore-Holifield legislation.[67]

With campaigning for the 1956 elections already under way, Congress wanted to finish its business before the end of July. Coming to the floor so late in the session, Gore-Holifield soon emerged as the keystone to passage not only of Price-Anderson but of several other bills important to the AEC. Measures on appropriations, authorization for an atomic-powered merchant ship, amendments to the Public Utility Holding Company Act, and salary increases for key AEC personnel could be affected. Strauss, following the legislative action closely, sensed correctly that linkage of those bills amounted to a Democratic tactic "of applying pressure on us" to support Gore-Holifield.[68]

Already completed Senate action gave credence to Strauss's analysis. Anticipating a close floor fight in the House, the Senate Democratic leadership, prompted by Senator Anderson, had called Gore-Holifield for a vote because it felt the bill stood a better chance of passage in the upper chamber. In turn, success in the Senate could influence the House vote. After a brief debate, the Senate, on 12 July, voted for the bill by forty-nine to forty.[69]

The pressure to which Strauss referred had started before the rancorous House debate began, pitting the Democratic majority against the Republican supporters of the administration. The Democrats' political strategy in the House called for bringing the bill to a vote under any circumstances because they thought little could be lost whatever the outcome. Whether the bill passed or failed, the Republicans could be attacked for attempting to block progress in achieving the development of atomic power. In either case, the Democrats thought they would gain an issue for use in the elections.[70]

Virginia congressman Howard Smith, chairman of the Rules Committee, called the bill for consideration on 24 July. He cautioned his colleagues to listen carefully to the ensuing debate because "there is violent disagreement between the Atomic Energy Commission which is opposed to the construction of these [government-sponsored] reactors, and the Congressional Joint Committee on Atomic Energy which promotes this bill and is in favor of it." Ramifications of the bill became clearer, however, when Republican whip Charles A. Halleck's opening statement claiming dissatisfaction with the measure was answered by the Democratic floor leader of the House, John W. McCormack. The powerful Massachusetts congressman warned that failure of Gore-

Holifield could cause delay on the indemnity bill, "which, of course, is of vital concern to private interests—what we call the big fellows—in this particular bill."[71]

Even after Sterling Cole offered several amendments aimed at making the bill innocuous and thus palatable to the Republicans, Halleck announced that the administration would not accept it. He feared that because the session was drawing to a close, an amended bill rapidly developed in conference might be reported out that would be acceptable to a majority of the House. On a subsequent motion to recommit the bill, the Republicans, supported by coal-state Democrats opposed to atomic-power development, prevailed on a 203–191 roll-call vote.[72]

Later that evening, Strauss received a call from Republican congressman John Phillips, who jubilantly reported the day's action on Gore-Holifield. Strauss thought over the situation. "It occurred to me," he wrote in a memo to his files the next day, "that the Democrats, smarting under this defeat, might undertake as a reprisal to defeat or fail to call up for consideration S. 4112 and H.R. 12050, the insurance bill." In the morning, Strauss went to the White House, where President Eisenhower was already meeting with Republican legislative leaders, Senator William Knowland, Congressman Joseph Martin, and Halleck. When Strauss entered the room, Eisenhower turned to atomic energy matters and expressed his strong antagonism to the Gore-Holifield measure. "I read this _____ bill called the Gore bill," he declared, "and let me tell you right now I would have vetoed it if it had passed." He then asked Strauss to discuss the importance of the indemnity legislation. Knowland and Halleck said that they would give it immediate priority.[73]

On his own, Strauss pursued action on the bill. He called Joint Committee vice-chairman Carl Durham and encouraged him to ensure that the measure did not die in that session. He also persuaded Eisenhower to write letters to both the Senate and House urging quick action. But the Democrats refused to move. When Halleck asked majority floor leader McCormack on 25 July when the bill would be considered, he received only a vague answer. Two days later, Halleck chastised the Democratic leadership for their tactics: "It comes with poor grace from those who lost in the other fight to erect this roadblock in the way of progress of the programs that promise so much for the future." But his warning that "if you will not do it in this Congress, then some of us will see to it that it is the first order of business in the next one" admitted that further efforts to pass indemnity legislation in the 1956 session would be futile. The Price-Anderson bill was not called up in the Eighty-fourth Congress.[74]

Lack of success in passing the Price-Anderson bill in that Congress did not mean that the effort had been futile. The preliminary work had been completed, the views of all parties had been heard, and organization of insurance pools had been started. Most important, however, the industry, the AEC, and the Joint Committee had forged agreement on the concept of limited government assistance. Time still remained before lack of an indemnity program might cause reactor owners to retreat from their plans. Barring unforeseen problems, Joint Committee members and AEC officials hoped that the next Congress would be able to view the Price-Anderson legislation in a more favorable political climate. The off-year elections would be over, and by 1957 the passions aroused by the Gore-Holifield measure might have subsided. But even as the votes were being tallied on the Gore-Holifield bill, a power-reactor licensing controversy was developing in the summer of 1956 that would leave its imprint not only on the indemnity bill but on the whole AEC process of reactor licensing and regulation.

V

THE POWER REACTOR
DEVELOPMENT COMPANY
CONTROVERSY

Just as the Price-Anderson and Gore-Holifield bills were undergoing congressional consideration in the summer of 1956, the Atomic Energy Commission voted favorably on a construction-permit application from the Power Reactor Development Company (PRDC) for a research-and-development fast-breeder reactor. The PRDC case touched off a major controversy between the AEC and the Joint Committee. It underscored the difficulties the agency faced in promoting privately owned power reactors while at the same time assuring that the licensing process afforded adequate protection to the public from the hazards inherent in nuclear power. The PRDC episode was a case study of existing AEC procedures in licensing atomic reactors. Even more important, it started a series of events that greatly influenced the future structure of the regulatory and licensing system.[1]

In December 1951 Walker L. Cisler, an early advocate of atomic power, had become president of the Detroit Edison Company, one of the Midwest's largest utilities. Cisler already had recognized the possibilities for the use of atomic energy in the generation of electricity and had promoted the direct participation of industry in what was still a government monopoly. Trained in engineering at Cornell, Cisler was a leader in the electric-utility industry. Handsome, articulate, pragmatic, and confident, he moved with ease among top government officials as well as in the industrial, social, and civic circles of Detroit. Probably more than anyone else at Detroit Edison, Cisler was responsible for the utility's early leadership in the atomic-power field. He was a key industry witness at the 1953 Joint Committee hearings on power development and the 1954 hearings on revising the Atomic Energy Act. At the later hearing Cisler emphasized how aggressively his company, in association with several others, had prepared to build a full-sized atomic-power plant.[2]

Detroit Edison became one of the first utilities to propose and negotiate a contract with the AEC under the terms of the Power Demonstration Reactor Program. Cisler organized a new nonprofit technical consortium, Atomic Power Development Associates (APDA), composed of forty-two utility, manufacturing, and engineering interests, to design and conduct research and development on a fast-breeder reactor. The group named Cisler its president and enlisted physicist and Nobel laureate Hans Bethe as a consultant and nuclear engineer Alfred Amorosi as its technical director. While preliminary discussions on the project were held throughout 1955 with the staff of the AEC Division of Reactor Development, Cisler formed still another combine, the Power Reactor Development Company, which would construct, own, and operate the reactor. Cisler also headed that company.[3]

In August 1955 the AEC accepted Detroit Edison's proposal to construct a hundred-megawatt electric fast-breeder plant as part of the power-demonstration program. The technical advisory group of the AEC's selection board noted that much research and development would still have to be carried out under the agency's experimental breeder-reactor program and that successful development of the project would in large measure depend on progress it made. Nonetheless, the Commission determined that the proposal gave sufficient "promise of significantly advancing power reactor technology" to allow negotiations leading to a contract between the utility and the government to proceed.[4]

The nine-hundred-acre tract where the reactor would be built was located in farming country at Lagoona Beach on the western shore of Lake Erie, about seven miles north of Monroe, Michigan, a city of twenty thousand. While Monroe County was basically rural, the adjacent area was urban. Detroit lay twenty-nine miles north, Toledo, Ohio thirty miles south. Also close to the site were Dearborn and Ypsilanti, Michigan to the northwest, and Windsor, Ontario across the lake.

The proposed PRDC fast-neutron breeder reactor required the greatest technological sophistication among the designs submitted under the first round of the power-demonstration program. Atomic reactors can be classified in various ways, one of which is based on the average speed or energy of the neutrons that cause fission. The nuclear chain reaction depends upon the fact that neutrons, released by the fission of atomic nuclei, strike the nuclei of other fissionable atoms and in turn cause them to fission. Neutrons released when a uranium-235 nucleus fissions have speeds of about ten thousand miles per second. In the more common "thermal" reactors, such as the Shippingport facility, a moderator such as water is used to slow down the neutrons, so that most fissions are caused by neutrons moving at speeds of about one mile per second. In a fast-neutron reactor, like the proposed PRDC design, there is no moderator; as a result most fissions are caused by neutrons traveling at speeds of several thousand miles per second.

The breeder concept incorporated an optimum chain-reaction arrangement structure to maximize the neutron economy so that there would be excess neutrons for breeding. Within such an arrangement some of the neutrons released in the fission process, instead of striking other fissionable atoms and causing them to split, may be absorbed by a "fertile" atom—uranium 238 or thorium 232—and convert it to a fissionable atom. In the PRDC reactor the nonfissionable (and fertile) uranium 238 was to be converted into plutonium, which, like uranium 235, is a fissionable material. Because of its particular design the PRDC reactor would "breed" (that is, generate fissionable plutonium from uranium 238) at a rate equal to or greater than its consumption of uranium 235.[5]

The PRDC design consisted of a core of uranium enriched in the isotope uranium 235, surrounded by a blanket of uranium depleted in uranium 235 and contained in a stainless-steel reactor vessel. To extract the heat generated in the fission process, liquid sodium would circulate through the core and the blanket in the "primary coolant loop" and into three heat exchangers which would transfer the heat to a secondary liquid-sodium loop. The secondary loop in turn would provide the heat source for three U-shaped tube steam generators whose steam would be used to make electricity in a conventional turbine-generator unit. The portion of the plant containing radioactive material (that is, the core and primary loop) would be enclosed in a gastight steel containment building, while the steam generators, turbine generator, and associated equipment would be located in a conventional building next to the containment.[6]

The liquid-sodium coolant constituted a serious hazard. If exposed to water or air, the sodium could explode or burn. Sodium, however, possesses excellent heat-transfer properties which, combined with its high boiling point, would permit operation at high temperature with a low-pressure system. APDA designers believed that safety precautions could be built into the system that would offset the dangers from use of sodium. Precautions would include a secondary coolant loop of sodium in order to separate the radioactive sodium coolant in the primary loop from the water in the turbine-generator loop. The APDA design group concluded that a heat exchanger (or steam generator) to transfer heat from radioactive sodium to water or steam would create an unacceptable risk—the risk of a reaction of radioactive sodium and water. If a secondary loop were to be used, such a chemical reaction would be nonradioactive.[7]

The PRDC maintained regular contact with the AEC Reactor Development Division from late 1954 through 1955. While PRDC officials did not apply for a construction permit until January 1956, they followed a generally established informal procedure of keeping in touch with the AEC staff to resolve design and safety problems before submission of the formal application.

One critical group Cisler's organization had to satisfy was the AEC's Advisory Committee on Reactor Safeguards, the outside reactor experts who judged health and safety factors. At that point in the development of the AEC's civilian reactor program, the committee played a major role in evaluating reactor safety because the AEC had only recently established its own hazards-evaluation staff. Before applying for a construction permit, PRDC officials met with the Safeguards Committee. In turn, the committee established a three-man fast-reactor subcommittee to review the PRDC's plans. It was headed by Harvey Brooks, professor of engineering and applied physics at Harvard University; his two colleagues were chemical engineer Manson Benedict of the Massachusetts Institute of Technology and Donald A. Rogers of the Allied Chemical and Dye Corporation.

In their first meeting with Brooks's subcommittee on 3 March 1955, PRDC representatives went over the preliminary design of the proposed fast breeder as well as safety aspects of several alternative features. The two groups held a second meeting in Detroit on 20 April. The subcommittee reached several preliminary conclusions, including approval for construction at Lagoona Beach, the PRDC's preferred site, without requiring that a prototype be built and operated at a remote site. The subcommittee, however, strongly urged further testing and experimentation by both the company and the AEC.[8]

When the full Safeguards Committee met informally to review the PRDC's preliminary plans on 30 June 1955, the proposed site raised many questions. After hearing the presentation of Cisler's group, the committee held lengthy discussions. It considered the site desirable in a number of respects: hydrology, meteorology, and seismology were suitable for the type and size of the reactor. The committee warned, however, that assumptions about the reactor's safety based on the PRDC's calculations had "not been established experimentally, and must be so before the operation of such a reactor could possibly be recommended for a site so close to a populated area." Echoing the reservations of Brooks's subcommittee, the full Safeguards Committee suggested an experimental analytical program that "ought to answer unequivocally" certain safety questions. Members were worried, for example, about the large size of the PRDC reactor. In addition to uncertainties about siting near population centers, other questions remained unanswered. What would happen if excess fuel was loaded into the reactor? What would happen to the reactor's stability as plutonium was formed? Until such queries could be satisfactorily resolved, the committee experts insisted that much more work had to be done before they would even consider formal approval of reactor construction.[9]

Solution of some of the known safety problems of breeder reactors depended on continuing research in the AEC's experimental-breeder program. The Experimental Breeder Reactor–I (EBR–I), developed and operated by Argonne National Laboratory at the AEC's Idaho test facility, was the first reactor to produce electricity and to demonstrate the technical feasibility of breeding. It had been in operation since late 1951. As a small-scale experimental power reactor, EBR–I supplied only 1.7 megawatts of electricity, but it had been employed for experiments in fast-neutron physics and radiation damage that provided useful information both to the agency and to the PRDC. In 1954 the AEC approved plans to build a much larger unit, the Experimental Breeder Reactor–II (EBR–II), that would produce 15 megawatts of electricity. With regard to power, control, fuel handling, and other features, it would more closely resemble a large central-station reactor. Much of the equipment for a full-scale power plant would also be used—pumps, heat exchangers, valves, and flow meters. Construction, however, was not planned to begin until 1956, with operation in 1959, much too late to serve as a prototype for the PRDC reactor.[10]

Experiments with EBR–I revealed two particular properties of fast-breeder reactors critically important to their safety. Any reactor should have a "negative temperature coefficient," where reactivity decreases as the temperature of the core rises. This makes the system somewhat self-regulating. The opposite, a "positive temperature coefficient," is undesirable since reactivity will increase as the temperature rises. Reactivity is a direct measure of how much a reactor is above or below criticality. When a reactor is generating heat at a constant rate (that is, the rate of fissioning is constant), the reactivity is exactly zero. If the reactivity is slightly above zero, the fissioning rate will steadily increase, with the rate of increase depending on how much above zero the reactivity is. When the reactivity is increased above a certain level, the reactor becomes "prompt critical" and the fissioning rate increases so rapidly that effective operator control becomes impossible. A reactor is always operated well below the prompt-critical condition. Experiments on EBR–I and calculations based on those experiments revealed a positive temperature coefficient under certain conditions. The other reactor property important to safety, called the "Doppler coefficient," depends on the change in absorption characteristics of the nuclear-fuel atoms due to thermal motion. Again, a negative effect is desirable because it provides a degree of self-regulation; a positive effect would make operator control of the power level extremely difficult. Calculations based on experiments with EBR–I in 1954 and 1955 showed some positive Doppler characteristics. The Argonne scientists decided to run further experiments.

On 29 November 1955 one such experiment on the EBR–I resulted in a partial fuel meltdown of the core. A meltdown is the most critical problem any reactor can have. When the fuel melts, its behavior can become unpredictable. Even though the fissioning stops, the heat generated by the fission products may cause the core to melt through the bottom of the reactor vessel—the idea of melted fuel heading through the earth that was later dubbed the "China syndrome." Or the molten fuel might react with the coolant or with the air (if the reactor vessel is penetrated), causing a chemical explosion that might breach the containment and release radioactive materials into the outside environment. The scientists knew in advance that the nature of the EBR–I experiment made a meltdown possible, so they took extra precautions—starting the reactor at low power, then slowly increasing the power level while drastically reducing coolant flow rates. They had developed plans to "scram" the reactor quickly if the temperature reached a dangerous level. To scram a reactor means to stop the nuclear chain reaction. After a reactor is shut down, the fission process stops and the only heat generated is that of the fission products. But there was a misunderstanding in signals between the reactor operator and the chief scientist. The operator, on order, started to drop the control rods by means of a motor-driven mechanism rather than by an alternate method that would have reduced the reactivity much faster. When the scientist noticed this, he hit the faster scram control to stop the reactor. The whole incident took place within two seconds, and yet the core partially melted. Later analysis of the data led to the conclusion that this "excursion" was due to the increase in reactivity caused by a thermal distortion or bowing of the fuel rods in the core.[11]

Data from this experiment and the earlier ones were incorporated in the refined design of the PRDC reactor. By January 1956 the PRDC was confident enough about its progress to file a formal application with the AEC Division of Civilian Application for a construction permit. The hundreds of pages of documents placed in the AEC licensing docket on the facility reflected not only the work of the PRDC staff but also the informal liaison work done by the AEC staff and the Safeguards Committee.[12] Even so, more briefings, consultations, and analyses by the PRDC and the AEC were required before a permit could be expected.

A series of meetings in February and March 1956 between PRDC representatives and members of the fast-breeder subcommittee of the Safeguards Committee turned up many unresolved safety questions. The subcommittee analyzed new physics calculations on the temperature, power, and bowing problems. The AEC staff scrutinized the PRDC report on the Lagoona Beach site. On 20 March the subcommittee met in Detroit with PRDC officials to review the status of the design. After a discussion of the project by PRDC general manager Robert Hartwell, Argonne's fast-reactor expert David Okrent described the several EBR–I experiments, including the excursion on 29 November, and related how those calculations applied to the PRDC reactor. He noted that more experiments were planned.[13]

Discussion turned to hypothetical accidents. Technical Director Amorosi told the subcommittee that the PRDC wanted to analyze more realistic accident scenarios than had yet been scrutinized in order to test the design of the PRDC reactor containment. Consultant Bethe reviewed recent British calculations on a hypothetical fast-reactor meltdown due to loss of the sodium coolant. He considered the British assumptions on energy release unrealistic but thought such an accident might be containable. Another technical assistant on the PRDC team, Wayne Jens, a physicist, described to the subcommittee three hypothetical accidents that he had been studying. In the first, the sodium coolant boiled out of the core and the core was compressed by the surrounding blanket. He calculated the total energy output in such an accident to be equivalent to the explosion of five tons of TNT. The second accident postulated a hydrogenous substance penetrating the core and causing a high rate of reactivity increase. His last accident hypothesized part of the fuel melting and falling to the bottom of the reactor, melting a hole in the chamber, and forming a critical mass. The remainder of this scenario envisioned the rest of the core falling on this mass. For the last two accidents, Jens had not yet calculated the energy released. Members of the subcommittee agreed that no firm conclusions could be reached and that without further study of those types of accidents no informed judgments of the proposed reactor could be made.[14]

Professor Henry J. Gomberg, a nuclear engineer at the University of Michigan's Engineering Research Institute and a PRDC consultant, briefly reported to the subcommittee on the progress of his work for the company. He was studying the probability of radiation exposure and its severity for the nearby population in the event of an accidental release of fission products from the Lagoona Beach reactor. While noting that his work took into account the surrounding population distribution and meteorological variables, his conclusions remained tentative at the time of the meeting. Finally, Walter McCarthy, the head of nuclear engineering for the PRDC, told the subcommittee about the latest estimated temperature coefficients for the reactor. Both PRDC officials and fast-reactor subcommittee members recognized the outstanding problems in this area and agreed that while solutions appeared feasible, much more experimental work was needed.[15]

Cisler and his design group believed they could adequately resolve the technical uncertainties before the facility was constructed and the company applied for an operating license. The anticipated date for operation was 1959 or 1960. On that basis they pushed for issuance of the construction permit. The full Advisory Committee on Reactor Safeguards scheduled a meeting to review the PRDC application before sending its recommendation to AEC general manager Kenneth Fields.[16]

The meeting took place at the Chicago office of the Argonne National Laboratory on 3 June 1956. Rogers McCullough, Safeguards Committee chairman, conducted the session as Cisler, McCarthy, Bethe, and Amorosi presented the PRDC data. Committee members then reviewed the information in executive session. At the conclusion, McCullough faced the task of writing a formal recommendation to Fields that reflected the composite view of the committee. Dated 6 June 1956, this letter started a series of events with ramifications that took years to resolve.[17]

Near the beginning, McCullough hinted at the problems the committee faced in reviewing the application. "The proposed PRDC reactor," he wrote, "represents a greater step beyond the existing state of the art than any other reactor of comparable power level which has been proposed by an industrial group." Even though the committee saw no available "facts or calculations" that indicated the proposed reactor was not safe for the Lagoona Beach site, the committee believed "there is insufficient information available at this time to give assurance that the PRDC reactor can be operated at this site without public hazard." The committee thought it doubtful that enough experimental information could be obtained before the PRDC's scheduled application for an operating license to ensure "safe operation of this reactor" unless the AEC expanded its fast-reactor research. Even if the AEC intensified its efforts, the committee still found it "impossible to say" that sufficient data could be developed within the proposed time schedule to permit safe operation.[18]

Determining the causes of the undesirable positive temperature coefficient that EBR–I had shown required more experimentation. The committee believed that "a clear demonstration must be given that a coefficient of this magnitude cannot exist in the PRDC design." To provide greater understanding of the temperature coefficient problem, it called for study of a new EBR–I core designed to ensure against the bowing characteristics shown in the 29 November partial meltdown. To demonstrate the proposed reactor's safety, the committee recommended that extensive studies of oscillator experiments on the PRDC design with a simulator would need to be conducted. Specifically, the committee wanted data showing "a negative prompt temperature coefficient of sufficient magnitude to prevent a fuel meltdown."[19]

The Safeguards Committee also suggested a program to determine fully whether the various negative coefficients were sufficient to prevent meltdown under any conceivable circumstances. It included simulator studies to provide information on a wide range of temperature coefficients and oscillator studies on the proposed EBR–I reactor. After the PRDC reactor was completed, a gradual "start-up" should be carried out so that additional data could be obtained before the reactor operated at full power.[20]

On the question of containment, the committee thought that insufficient evidence had been presented to assure that a "credible supercriticality accident" resulting from a core meltdown "would not breach the container." To remove the uncertainties, it suggested a theoretical and experimental program, including mechanical mock-up studies to determine distortion of the core due to sudden melting and design studies of the reactor structure with supporting mock-up experiments to "assure that free fall of core parts cannot reassemble a critical mass suddenly."[21]

Finally, the committee insisted that the AEC place greater emphasis on the EBR–II program. McCullough wrote in the letter: "The EBR–II . . . is the only program now constituted which could provide engineering information and operating experience on a high-power-density fast reactor in advance of the scheduled date for operation of the PRDC reactor." In other words, EBR–II, still in the advanced design stage, would be the only prototype close to the plans for the PRDC reactor. The committee further emphasized that if the suggested theoretical and experimental program on the containment capabilities was not possible or did not give adequate assurance of containment integrity following credible accidents, then the EBR–II should be converted to a genuine prototype of the PRDC reactor. Operating experience on fast reactors, the committee noted, "is not wholly reassuring." Although the EBR–I incident was not directly relevant to the PRDC reactor, the committee pointed out that "the origin of this unstable coefficient [on the EBR–I] has not been clearly established and therefore its possible occurrence in the PRDC design cannot be definitely excluded on the basis of present experimental information."[22]

The letter ended by commending the willingness of the PRDC "to risk its capital and prestige in advancing the development of this reactor concept." Nevertheless, the committee warned, the PRDC should not take further steps so bold "as to risk the health and safety of the public."[23]

The committee's unfavorable comments shocked PRDC officials, and the AEC was even more stunned since the report expressed grave reservations about the adequacy of its own fast-breeder research program. Fields wanted more information on the bases of the Safeguards Committee's position, as did Harold Price, director of the Division of Civilian Application, and Kenneth Davis, director of the Division of Reactor

Development. Price arranged a meeting with the fast-reactor subcommittee on 21 June 1956. Subcommittee chairman Brooks explained the situation to the AEC staff in the context of the viewpoints expressed at the 3 June Safeguards Committee meeting. Brooks said that the letter represented a compromise on which the whole committee agreed and that the recommendations reflected the more cautious majority. He himself belonged to a smaller, more optimistic minority, while his subcommittee colleague, Manson Benedict, represented the conservative majority. The committee had adopted its conclusions unanimously; the only divergence among the members related to the determination that it was "impossible to say" specifically how likely the suggested experimental program was to provide the desired assurance on the PRDC reactor. Brooks observed that his own confidence level on that conclusion was "about 95%," but some members' confidence was "as low as 50%."[24]

Not satisfied that he had explained the committee's position fully to the AEC, Brooks wrote a detailed letter to Price a few days later amplifying his comments at the 21 June meeting. He asserted that if the AEC conducted a vigorous experimental and analytical program, the question of temperature coefficients could be resolved to the point where low-power oscillator experiments could be run on the completed PRDC reactor at the Michigan site. But he saw little prospect that the question of a meltdown accident could be resolved experimentally or theoretically "in a manner which will be convincing to all the people [committee members] concerned." They would not agree that the hazard from a meltdown was acceptably low without first obtaining operating experience on a reactor much closer in design to the PRDC reactor than was the EBR–I. Brooks, too, wanted results from EBR–II before the committee finally decided whether an operating license for the PRDC reactor was advisable. Furthermore, he indicated that some Safeguards Committee members favored a prototype at a remote site regardless "of the outcome of the proposed experiments." Brooks stated that he did not know whether the AEC should issue a construction permit, but that he believed the Safeguards Committee's duty was to take the most conservative position in assessing possible public hazard and leave it to the Commission, "fully aware of what the risks are, to decide what probability of an accident they are willing to accept, taking into consideration the national importance of the program under review."[25]

After Brooks read the minutes of his 21 June meeting with the AEC officials, he wrote another letter, this time to Joshua D. Holland, the

Safeguards Committee's executive secretary. He wanted to place on the record "one viewpoint which was perhaps not adequately presented at the meeting." In Brooks's opinion, the lack of a prototype reactor was the one serious safety argument against issuing a license to the PRDC:

> In any technology as new and untested as that of fast sodium-cooled reactors there are likely to be serious surprises which were not anticipated by the designers. Experience indicates that such surprises always occur in connection with any new development, even when the technology is much more thoroughly tested than in the case of the fast reactor. Many of these surprises can be matters of apparently trivial detail which may nevertheless seriously influence the safety or operability of the reactor. The purpose of a prototype is primarily to minimize the possibility of such surprises rather than to find the answer to specific technical questions which are anticipated now, and which presumably can be answered on a piecemeal basis by experiment and theory.

Brooks noted that it was "probably wrong to single out the PRDC reactor in this regard," because his strictures undoubtedly applied to all industrial programs. Yet, while he was confident that the suggested experimental program would satisfy the temperature coefficient and meltdown questions, he would not "express an equal degree of confidence with respect to the overall [research-and-development] program." A prototype would help dispel doubts and give the Safeguards Committee reassurance on the "elimination of possible surprises" that generally troubled them.[26]

The disagreement among members of the Safeguards Committee reflected the state of atomic technology at the time. The experts knew the dangers involved and believed the promotion of civilian atomic power depended on protecting public health and safety. Despite hope for a successful fast breeder, the committee felt obliged to emphasize the serious questions about the PRDC reactor. Its recommendation implied that both the AEC and PRDC lacked sufficient knowledge to guarantee control over the unique features and problems of the fast reactor. In the Safeguards Committee's collective thinking, the AEC experimental program had not progressed to the point where a large-scale facility could be operated with acceptable risk. McCullough's letter, underscoring the need for a greatly accelerated experimental program, stressed the committee's concern. Even then, the most cautious members wanted nothing less than a full-scale prototype at a remote site. The less conservative members carefully restrained their optimism about the eventual safety of the reactor. The committee took its work seriously and undoubtedly recognized the difficulties its recommendations would create for fast-breeder development.

While discussions of the PRDC project were taking place at the staff level, the Atomic Energy Commission had been involved throughout 1956 with members of the Joint Committee in the debate, centered on the Gore-Holifield bill, over the best way to accelerate atomic-power development. Strauss and other administration officials believed that private industry, under the Power Demonstration Reactor Program, provided the best means to accomplish the objective. But Joint Committee Democrats favored an additional government program to build prototype power reactors. As the 1956 national elections approached, the bill underscored the long-standing political issue of private versus public power.

At the time, the Commission, in addition to Strauss, Murray, and Libby, included Harold S. Vance and John Von Neumann. Vance, whom President Eisenhower appointed in 1955, was a businessman-engineer who had served as chairman of the Studebaker-Packard Corporation's executive committee. John Von Neumann, a mathematician renowned for his work in computer design and construction, had also been appointed in 1955. He had recently received the AEC's first Enrico Fermi Award, established for outstanding achievement related to the development and use of atomic energy. A long illness, however, which began in the summer of 1955 and ended with his death in January 1957, prevented Von Neumann from participating in much of the Commission's business during 1956. Among the five, Murray and Strauss clashed frequently, mostly on issues involving small atomic weapons development, and Murray had been the only commissioner to support the Gore-Holifield bill. In many ways Murray played the role of outspoken dissenter on the Commission just as Strauss had done under Lilienthal.[27]

Although the Joint Committee oversaw all AEC activities, the traditional power that the House Appropriations Committee exercised often injected it into discussion of AEC programs. A 1956 agency supplemental request for fifty-five million dollars for research and development and thirty-five million for construction related to civilian atomic-power development provided the Subcommittee on Public Works of the Appropriations Committee an opportunity in late June 1956 to review all aspects of the AEC's civilian power-reactor program—just when political controversy was beginning to peak over Gore-Holifield. Appropriations

Committee chairman Clarence Cannon of Missouri, one of the most powerful Democrats in Congress and a strong supporter of public power, used week-long subcommittee hearings to vent open hostility toward the AEC's private-industry approach and in particular toward Strauss's leadership. Cannon's acerbic criticism frequently exasperated many of his colleagues as well as the testifying commissioners. Under sharp questioning, Strauss and Murray revealed information that set off the public controversy over the pending PRDC construction permit.[28]

On the fourth day of the hearings, 28 June, Cannon badgered Strauss about the fact that the AEC was not building power reactors and private companies such as the PRDC appeared to be making little progress. He was concerned that the nation was falling behind other countries in power technology. "It is a matter of great disappointment," Cannon said, "that you have not come here with a program to maintain a lead, if you had a lead. But from all the evidence submitted, that appears to be doubtful." He cited the PRDC project as an example of long negotiations under the Power Demonstration Reactor Program that had proceeded with no "intention of building this reactor at any time in the determinable future."

Strauss, agitated, replied, "I do not see that at all, Mr. Chairman. They [PRDC] have already spent eight million dollars of their own money to date on this project. I told you they were breaking ground on August 8. I have been invited to attend the ceremony; I intend to do so." The fact that the PRDC was ready to break ground, said Strauss, showed that they were "businessmen whose word is good." In the context of the discussion, Strauss emphasized the point that private industry was moving forward at a reasonably fast pace. But in his anxiety to impress the subcommittee he had inadvertently revealed publicly that he planned to attend groundbreaking ceremonies for a reactor whose construction permit was still under consideration by his agency.[29]

Over a month before the Advisory Committee on Reactor Safeguards had met on the breeder-reactor application, the PRDC had selected 8 August 1956, as the groundbreaking date for the plant. Cisler informed various officials, including Strauss, not only of the date but about the intention of the company trustees to name the project in memory of celebrated atomic pioneer Enrico Fermi. Cisler assumed a construction permit would be issued by that time. In mid-June he sent invitations to the ceremonies. The invitation list included such notables as Eisenhower, Strauss, and Senator Anderson.[30]

A previous commitment kept Commissioner Murray from attending the 28 June hearings, but he testified the following day. Cannon asked Murray's opinion on the ability of the PRDC to design and construct a fast-breeder reactor. In the presence of his three fellow commissioners Murray declared that the fast-breeder concept was an important part of the development program but needed more funds to prove its worth. To underscore his point, Murray read into the subcommittee record the conclusions of the Safeguards Committee on the safety of the PRDC reactor. Noting that the subcommittee had cut the AEC's request for fifty-five million dollars to fifteen million, he revealed those conclusions in order to support the agency's request for more money for research and development. "Now, I submit," Murray said, "that we need more money, and our staff agreed in April that we did need more money, to carry on research and development in order to solve the problems of the Detroit Edison Company and other problems related thereto, in order to get on with a vigorous civilian power reactor program. I ask this committee to reestablish the research and development figures so as to include the original figures that were submitted in the supplemental budget."[31]

Murray was also concerned with the safety implications of the Safeguards Committee letter. On the same day that he publicly disclosed parts of it before the appropriations subcommittee, he went to Senator Anderson to tell him about the letter. According to Anderson's memoirs, Murray revealed the information to him because he felt the AEC "intended to ignore the signs of danger and grant the construction permit anyway."[32] Animosity between Murray and Strauss probably also played a part in Murray's decision to speak to Anderson. In any event, the news innervated Anderson's long-standing personal feud with Strauss, which had flourished because of policy differences between the two strong-willed, proud, and determined men. The information about the Safeguards Committee's views set the stage for a major confrontation between the AEC and the Joint Committee.

The disclosures by Strauss and Murray angered not only Anderson but the other members of the Joint Committee, who jealously guarded their statutory mandate to be kept "fully and currently informed" on atomic matters. In this case the Joint Committee had received no report on the Safeguards Committee's conclusions. It was also annoyed that Murray had given the information, not to the Joint Committee, but to a House subcommittee.

At the direction of Anderson, James T. Ramey, staff executive director for the Joint Committee, immediately telephoned the AEC to ask for a copy of the Safeguards Committee letter. Fields, Price, and William Mitchell, AEC general counsel, discussed the request but had taken no action on it when Anderson sent a formal letter on 9 July demanding the report. Price opposed giving Anderson the information because he believed that such reports were internal matters and should not be made available when a decision on a construction permit was pending.[33]

At a Commission executive session on 11 July, Fields presented a draft reply to Anderson's request. Murray was not present at the meeting. Both the staff and the commissioners were concerned over the precedent that would be created by the release of what they considered an internal document, even though part of it had already been made public by Murray's testimony before the Cannon subcommittee. Fields opened the discussion by arguing that the request was "every bit as serious an inroad on privacy as any request we have had . . . in the sense that this is a matter that is under consideration." It would, he said, "seriously affect our abilities to carry out our regulatory functions if this is any kind of precedent." Fields conceded that perhaps there was reason to provide the report in this case, but added that it would raise questions of confidentiality about the agency among "companies and others who are requesting licenses under our regulatory program."[34]

Discussion turned to Murray's disclosure to the appropriations subcommittee. General Counsel Mitchell and Commissioner Libby noted that since he had read only the conclusions into the record, most of the report remained confidential. Strauss contended that the importance was not in how much was disclosed. He emphasized "the fact that we had such a letter, that it was an unfavorable recommendation, [and] was compromised at that time without Commission action having been taken." Commissioner Vance attempted to provide a broader view of the problem. He suggested that the Commission deal with two separate points. First was a general question about the agency position on matters of this kind. The second was the specific problem that in this case the report had been partially disclosed. He asked whether it was better not to reveal any more than already divulged, "or is it better to make the whole thing in effect available to the committee?"[35]

Fields and Price, both concerned about the broader implications of revealing the document, were even more worried that the report, standing alone, would be misinterpreted. Price told the commissioners that he had acquired an interpretation of the letter quite different from his original impression after discussing it in detail with his staff and members of the Safeguards Committee. "That is why," Price said, "documents like this ought to be privileged." Vance suggested that the reply to the Joint Committee clarify the role of the advisory committees because he believed it failed to understand their functions. Fields, reflecting on Murray's testimony before Cannon's committee, thought Murray left the impression that the Safeguards Committee actually made the decision. Libby also feared that Murray's statement would create problems "where we have to make a decision contrary to the advice of our advisory committee." Price interjected that the Commission might not have to make a decision against the Safeguards Committee's advice. "We have argued back and forth with them [the Safeguards Committee] and sometimes we have revised the conditions. We work them out until they are satisfied and we are satisfied."[36] In other words, Price argued that the report would give a misleading impression if read out of the context of the internal give-and-take of the licensing process.

Using Fields's draft, the group worked on the reply. The letter opened with an explanation of how the Safeguards Committee's recommendation fitted in the review process for a construction permit—a recommendation that had not yet been acted upon by the Commission. Under the circumstances, the Commission considered it inappropriate to disclose the contents of "advice and recommendations which are currently under review," and it believed that "the Joint Committee *in the ordinary course* [emphasis supplied] will support such a position." The letter noted that "under any other procedure the independence of the staff of the Commission or advisory committees to the Commission would be seriously impaired in the future, the value of their contribution would be greatly diminished, and the regulatory functions of the Commission would be correspondingly impeded."[37]

The draft acknowledged that the requested report had been in part introduced into the record of the Cannon committee by Commissioner Murray. That action, the letter stated, was "unilateral . . . on the part of Commissioner Murray, taken without prior consultation with the Commission."[38]

The original draft of the final paragraph agreed that under the circumstances the letter would be delivered, but only with the understanding that it would not be regarded as a precedent. Discussion followed on whether to incorporate further reservations on releasing the letter. Vance suggested that in sending the report the Commission request that the Joint Committee not make it a matter of record. Both Libby and Strauss agreed. Subsequently the last sentence of the reply asked that the Safeguards Committee letter "be treated as administratively confidential" by the Joint Committee. The AEC sent its reply on 13 July.[39]

The Joint Committee refused to accept the report under the "administratively confidential" qualification. On 13 July, Ramey wrote to Fields, returning the Safeguards Committee letter and stating that Senator Anderson "could not receive the report under these conditions." Four days later, Anderson followed with a letter to Strauss in which he repeated his request for the report without conditions. The senator insisted that there was "an overriding public interest in permitting the Joint Committee, the Congress itself, the people in areas surrounding reactor locations, and local and state governments and affected organizations, to know the facts concerning hazards in locating these reactors."[40]

On 16 July Anderson informed Michigan governor G. Mennen Williams of the substance of the Safeguards Committee report. Williams, who had appointed an executive committee of state officials to study how Michigan could best encourage atomic development, met with his committee on the same day to discuss the information Anderson had given him. Albert E. Heustis, the state health commissioner, had already heard of the report through press sources who knew about Murray's testimony before the Cannon subcommittee, and he had talked to Harold Price that morning. Price told him that the report was only one part of the PRDC case then under active review by the AEC. An angry Williams, insisting that he should be fully informed of the Safeguards Committee report, disclosed to his advisors that he had requested a copy of it from the AEC.[41]

The following day, Fields answered Governor Williams's request. The general manager took the same position as the agency had done in its reply to the Joint Committee. Fields explained the role of the Safeguards Committee and how its recommendations would be considered in evaluating the PRDC application. He told Williams that the AEC would send copies of the available public documents of the PRDC application and its amendments and would be willing to meet with Williams in the near future to discuss the safety aspects of the application. But he refused to release the Safeguards Committee report.[42]

The four commissioners met on 18 July to discuss the new developments. Strauss read the letters from Ramey and Anderson. Fields and Mitchell said they would draft a reply but would still hold to the AEC position. Strauss, showing his continuing anger at Murray and his frustration with the growing controversy, blurted out, "I can only say I certainly regret the introduction of that letter into the testimony." The matter continued to irritate Strauss so much that at a Commission meeting on 1 August, he read a statement into the record outlining the circumstances under which Murray revealed the Safeguards Committee report. "The letter was an intra-agency letter from an advisory committee and the Commission had not had an opportunity to consider it," Strauss stated. "It was read without prior notice or knowledge or consent of the members of the Commission, and in my opinion a disregard of the best interests of our aims. The purpose of this statement on my part is to say that I feel we should disavow it as a precedent, and that we continue in the future as in the past to hold the policy of the Commission to preserve the inviolability of reports and recommendations from advisory bodies as privileged communications within the Commission and within the Executive Branch of the government." Murray, sitting silently throughout the reading, retorted that he might submit a rejoinder. He never did.[43]

The Commission's new reply to the Joint Committee emphasized that its wish that the report be kept "administratively confidential" was a request and not a condition. "We renew our request," the letter stated, "which your committee is not bound to honor but which we are bound to make." It closed with an offer to appear before the Joint Committee in executive session to discuss the broad question of privilege. The Joint Committee did not respond and the privilege matter rested. Both parties had made their point; related events soon transcended the issue.[44]

Meanwhile, Price's Division of Civilian Application worked on its recommendation to the Commission on the PRDC reactor construction permit. The staff knew it must reconcile the Safeguards Committee's position with its own more optimistic views if a favorable recommendation was to be presented. On 11 July 1956 the PRDC, obviously in response to the Safeguards Committee's report, had filed an amendment to its application that acknowledged the company's responsibility to the public for the safety of the reactor design and operation. It also had submitted a summary of the experimental program it would conduct as well as a report on the containment of possible accidents.[45]

The staff paper to the Commission specifically commented on the points raised by the Safeguards Committee. In each case the staff was satisfied that the PRDC had taken or would take adequate measures to address the committee's concerns before an operating license was issued. For example, in response to the committee's comment that there was insufficient information currently available to give assurance that the reactor could be operated at the proposed site without endangering the public, the staff observed that both it and the PRDC agreed. It argued, however, that there was sufficient basis for believing the safety problems could be solved. The staff analysis concurred that the AEC fast-reactor program should be accelerated and that solutions to the problems cited by the Safeguards Committee could take longer than the PRDC's planned schedule. But the staff believed the difficulties could be resolved in time.[46]

On the question of accidents that might breach the containment, the staff agreed with the Safeguards Committee that more theoretical and experimental research was needed to evaluate all possible contingencies. The staff argued, however, that such studies were unlikely to "remove all possibilities of meltdown," and it doubted that design features "can remove all probability of a secondary critical accumulation if meltdown does occur." Yet on the basis of studies completed, the staff concluded that the containment could hold the "maximum credible accident in this reactor."[47]

The staff report commented on Harvey Brooks's 17 July letter to Price in which he outlined the different points of view among Safeguards Committee members on the "gaps" in fast-reactor knowledge that could become apparent as design and operation proceeded. The staff acknowledged that there would be gaps. But it believed they would have "negligible probability of making the reactor unsafe with containment." The main question that remained, the staff stated, was whether solutions to newly discovered safety problems could be resolved "within the time schedules now contemplated by the PRDC."[48]

The staff described the proposed PRDC program to resolve the hazard problems as outlined in its amended application. Included were a study of the EBR–I core, simulator and oscillator experiments for clarification of the behavior of fast reactors, further tests on the Doppler effect, and theoretical studies on the magnitude of meltdown accidents together with methods of coping with them if they occurred. In short, the PRDC now planned to perform many of the tests recommended by the Safeguards Committee.[49]

Though admitting that the PRDC reactor was a scale-up from the EBR–I "of unprecedented magnitude," the AEC staff felt optimistic that the combination of the PRDC program and an expanded AEC effort utilizing the EBR–II would satisfy the safety questions. Therefore, it recommended issuance of a construction permit.[50]

On the afternoon of Thursday, 1 August, the AEC met to discuss and decide on the construction permit. Price presented the staff's case, as was his custom, and key members stood by to answer technical questions. After a brief background statement on the PRDC reactor, Price turned to the safety considerations. He observed that among those working on the case there were no differences "as to what the known safety problems are." There were, however, "differences of opinion with respect to this project that relate to the degree of optimism or pessimism among various people as to the likelihood that these problems can be satisfactorily resolved." Price proposed issuing a construction permit with the provision that the problems had to be resolved before a final operating license would be issued.[51]

Strauss asked for discussion of the paper. Commissioner Murray, turning to McCullough, who was present to answer questions on the Safeguards Committee's position, asked if there had been any change in its views since the 6 June report. McCullough replied that there had not. Murray then declared: "On that basis, I am opposed to the issuance of this construction permit at this time." Reporting a week later to his committee colleagues, McCullough felt obliged to amplify on his statement to Murray:

> You will also be interested to know that Commissioner Murray asked me if I had any change of view with regard to the letter of June 6th. I replied I had not. This was not a clear-cut exchange, since obviously I could not change a unanimous opinion of the Committee without consulting it. Personally, on the points covered by the letter of June 6th I had no changes to offer. In view of the . . . clear intent [of the AEC] to tie the fast reactor program and the PRDC project together, I feel that the Commission has not gone against the advice of the Committee and that the situation is satisfactory. The thing that is important is to keep clearly in mind that experimental data must be accumulated on the important hazards problems. I hope the Committee concurs in my belief that this is temporarily a happy solution to the PRDC problem.[52]

At the 1 August meeting, Commissioner Vance strongly urged that in the proposed permit and in the press release, the adjective "conditional" be used. According to the AEC's regulations, the permit was by definition conditional, but he wanted the fact to be emphasized because of the questions already publicly raised over the safety of the reactor.

"It seems to me that we cannot go too far in stating very clearly that we are not going to allow this reactor to operate unless and until we are satisfied that it can be done with safety to the public." Price affirmed that he had gone over the provisional nature of the permit with the company and that it fully understood. Vance recognized this but insisted on stressing the conditional aspect. "We are doing something," he said, "that we ordinarily would not do, in that we would not ordinarily issue a construction permit unless we were satisfied that the reasonable safety requirements had been met." But in this case, Vance argued, there was good reason to grant the permit. "It may be some time before reasonable assurance can be obtained. If we were to delay the construction permit until then, it might delay a very important program. If we didn't think that the chances were very good that all these problems would be resolved, we would not issue the permit. We do think they are good." Strauss and Libby agreed.[53]

Vance's reference to the publicity over the reactor's safety stemmed in part from hostile criticism about the AEC's licensing procedure made on the House floor during debate on the Gore-Holifield bill. Representative John D. Dingell of Michigan, for example, had inserted three news items into the record from the *Detroit News*, the *Toledo Blade*, and the *Wall Street Journal* which questioned the extent of the safety problems at the PRDC plant. Dingell told his House colleagues that he did not "wish to leave the question of safety . . . to an agency which is neither candid nor apparently concerned with the health of this or future generations." He urged that any federal funds for the plant be withheld "until all safety problems have been resolved for the protection of the public."[54]

When Strauss polled the commissioners, three assented to the conditional permit and Murray voted no. Murray requested that the press release include an indication that the vote was not unanimous. His three colleagues disagreed. Vance turned to Murray: "Tom, it seems if we start the practice on every piece of publicity going out of here we have to say that there is a split vote on the proposition, it is something that we should not do." With Murray remaining silent, the other three commissioners then discussed and agreed upon a number of revisions to the press release. Alert to the sensitivity of the Joint Committee, they ordered Price to inform it before notifying the state of Michigan, the PRDC, and the public. The agency officially issued the permit on 4 August.[55]

The Joint Committee reacted immediately after the permit was issued.

Chairman Anderson declared that the permit set a "dangerous pattern in the early stages" of AEC quasi-judicial activity. He charged the agency with conducting "star chamber" proceedings because it never made the Safeguards Committee report public. Further, he regretted that the state of Michigan had been precluded from participation in the decision. Anderson pledged that the Joint Committee would "ascertain the full facts involved in this precipitate action." He would ask Congress to consider reorganizing the AEC into two separate units, one for promotion and the other for regulatory and licensing functions. In addition, he wanted safety questions made public before a construction permit was issued.[56]

In a separate statement Chet Holifield minced no words in attacking Strauss and the AEC. He coupled the announcement by Strauss that he would attend the 8 August groundbreaking ceremonies with the timely issuance of the construction permit. Strauss, Holifield said, "has decided to make good on his testimony." Charging the chairman with proceeding in a "reckless and arrogant manner," the California congressman called upon the president to direct the AEC to rescind the construction permit until the Safeguards Committee could make an "unequivocal report assuring the safety of the plant." He, too, intended to sponsor legislation separating the functions of the agency. The people of the United States, Holifield said, "have a right to objective judicial review of safety matters divorced from any promotional objectives which may dominate AEC thinking." He closed by congratulating Murray for opposing the decision. In its customary way the White House forwarded Holifield's telegram to Strauss for a draft reply. In a return memo accompanying his suggested draft, Strauss noted that mere acknowledgment of Holifield's telegram would have been sufficient since "he was simply sending it for the record." Combative as usual, Strauss added: "He [Holifield] ignores the fact that the permit in question is a 'conditional' permit and was plainly so stated. However, he has ignored the facts in many other instances."[57]

In one context the PRDC reactor controversy was an aberration. Using the same procedure, the Commission had issued two construction permits before considering the PRDC application. No uproar accompanied those decisions. But the PRDC reactor was different. The other two were light-water reactors, with which the AEC and atomic experts had more experience and more confidence that they could be operated safely. The fast breeder, admittedly an advanced design, was bound to raise questions that had not yet been resolved. Nonetheless, under the Power

Demonstration Reactor Program the AEC encouraged different designs such as the fast breeder. Since development of atomic energy through private and competitive enterprise was a primary goal of the 1954 Atomic Energy Act, the AEC and Congress viewed alternative reactor designs as necessary to the accomplishment of this purpose.

The Atomic Energy Act required that reactors be safe. Furthermore, the people working on the safety of the new reactor designs recognized the dangerous aspects of the technology and realized that if atomic reactors were to assume a place in the nation's arsenal of energy sources, they had to be safe. The Advisory Committee on Reactor Safeguards, the PRDC designers and engineers, Price's hazards staff, and the AEC Division of Reactor Development (charged with providing research data to companies like the PRDC under the Power Demonstration Reactor Program) all viewed safety research as inseparable from development research. The major problem in evaluating reactor designs in this early stage lay in the lack of theoretical and experimental studies on safety features and, in the case of the PRDC reactor, lack of operating experience with a prototype. Since Price's division had no independent research capability of its own, it had to rely on the other groups for the bulk of its information. Price's recommendation to the Commission for the PRDC construction permit reflected, therefore, his staff's attempt to reconcile the views of the other three groups.

The informal discussions that were a part of the AEC's licensing process also promoted conciliation. The many private meetings among representatives of the PRDC, the Safeguards Committee and its subcommittee, and AEC divisions allowed Price's staff to develop what it considered the best expert judgment in its final recommendation to the Commission. In the course of developing the technology, the give-and-take procedures in discussion, analysis, and planning—isolated from public participation—appeared to the AEC to be the appropriate way to arrive at a decision.

The AEC's procedures failed to give early public notification that could have provided a basis for input from the public, which in turn might have influenced the decision to construct the reactor at Lagoona Beach. Moreover, the general public either supported atomic-power development or was apathetic toward it. There were no public-interest groups actively opposing the development of the technology. The outside groups that took a direct interest in atomic policies—the Joint Committee on Atomic Energy, the House and Senate Appropriations Committees, and, in the PRDC case, the state of Michigan—also were eager to promote the use of atomic energy for peaceful purposes. Among them the Joint Committee was the only body in a position to perform the traditional oversight role vis-à-vis the AEC. As elected representatives of the public point of view, members of the Joint Committee strongly voiced their concern over the PRDC proceedings to the agency and to the public. By the end of the summer of 1957 the Joint Committee further reacted to the PRDC case by enacting legislation that required the AEC to develop formal procedures with the objective of creating a more open licensing process.

VI

THE PRDC IN COURT

The controversy over the PRDC reactor did not end with the AEC's decision to grant the company a provisional permit. Unexpectedly, the agency received three identical intervention petitions on 31 August 1956 requesting suspension of the permit while a hearing was held on the reactor's safety, the PRDC's financial qualifications, and the legality of the AEC's conduct in issuing the permit. All came from American Federation of Labor–Congress of Industrial Organizations (AFL-CIO) unions: the International Union of Electrical, Radio and Machine Workers, the United Paperworkers of America, and the United Automobile, Aircraft, and Agricultural Implement Workers of America, each of which had substantial memberships in the Detroit-Toledo area.[1]

Reasons other than the issues cited in the petitions, especially politics and the chronic issue of public versus private power, helped persuade the union leadership to intervene. Political considerations arose because 1956 was an election year. The matter of public or private financing was important to labor because of the AFL-CIO's support for both federally funded atomic-power projects and more aid to smaller public and co-operative utilities.

Organized labor, a traditional supporter of the Democratic Party, never was happy with President Eisenhower's favoritism toward large private-business interests. The field of atomic energy was no exception. Labor had opposed many of the changes in the atomic law in 1954, citing fear of industry monopolization by private utilities. Once the law became effective and the AEC embarked on its Power Demonstration Reactor Program, labor leaders maintained that the program gave advantages to the larger private interests at the expense of smaller, publicly owned utilities. Labor's spokesmen testified often before the Joint Committee in support of an expanded role for publicly owned power. In this area the AFL-CIO worked closely with the American Public Power Association, a lobbying group representing public-power interests. The first round of the AEC's Power Demonstration Reactor Program decidedly favored the larger and better-financed private utilities, but the second round, announced in September 1955, broadened the program to attract the participation of small, publicly owned utilities. Their lack of technical and especially financial resources, however, limited their contribution despite the AEC's efforts to include them.[2]

In the middle of the growing controversy over the best way to develop an atomic industry, the AEC issued the PRDC provisional construction permit. Even Democrats with short memories remembered that nine days earlier the Republicans in the House, with strong administration backing, had narrowly defeated the Gore-Holifield bill, the Democratic attempt, with labor support, to bolster the civilian power program by directing the AEC to construct and operate six different prototype power reactors. In this heated political context, and with the fall election on most politicians' minds, the PRDC decision took on a new dimension. Anderson and Holifield as well as several labor leaders recognized that the AEC decision on the PRDC reactor offered both the Democrats and the AFL-CIO a political opportunity that could be exploited to embarrass the Republicans. But the best tactical course to pursue was less obvious.

At a press conference hastily called after the AEC announced its decision on 4 August, Holifield urged that legal procedures be taken to stop construction. He told the press that he was wiring Michigan governor Williams to take action "necessary to protect life and property in his state." The California congressman added: "If I were the Governor of Michigan, I would take legal steps to prevent construction of any reactor which has not been declared free of hazard." In a private meeting later that day in Holifield's office, Anderson, Holifield, and Joint Committee staff director Ramey met with labor official Leo Goodman to discuss different courses of action. Goodman was the secretary for the Staff Subcommittee on Atomic Energy of the AFL-CIO and an adviser to Walter P. Reuther of the United Automobile Workers. Someone suggested the possibility of Joint Committee legal action, but that choice was ruled out as unrealistic and probably illegal. Holifield asked Goodman if a local union could establish a picket line at the upcoming PRDC groundbreaking ceremony. Goodman dismissed that idea because it would violate provisions of the Taft-Hartley Act. Then, as Holifield had publicly suggested earlier, the group considered encouraging Governor Williams to take legal action. Anderson had already talked to Williams; and later, labor leaders urged the Michigan chief executive to intervene. Their efforts proved futile. Williams later told syndicated columnist Raymond Moley that he "got snagged" into the controversy after Anderson's call questioning the safety of the reactor. Later in August, Williams accepted the conclusion of his own Atomic Energy Study Committee that the conditions in the construction permit provided "adequate safeguards for the public, operators and the risk investment of PRDC in the plant itself." Discussion at the 4 August meeting in Holifield's office also keyed on the possibility of legal intervention by the labor unions. Ramey advised Goodman that if the unions decided to take action, the Joint Committee staff could provide them with informal technical support. Goodman took this information back to his colleagues. In the meantime, Anderson contacted Reuther and suggested that the United Automobile Workers intervene since the union represented so many workers in the area of the PRDC reactor.[3]

Late in August, union staff leaders Donald Montgomery and Goodman, along with General Counsel Benjamin Sigal of the Machine Workers Union, met with Harold P. Green, a former AEC attorney knowledgeable about atomic law, and James Grahl, a nuclear physicist working for the American Public Power Association. They discussed petitioning the AEC for a hearing within the allowable thirty-day period after issuance of the permit. Grahl listed the technical issues that should be raised in such a petition. Montgomery, in a subsequent memo to Reuther, urged the UAW chief to act. Montgomery argued that the time was "ripe to expose" the AEC construction permit for the PRDC reactor because it demonstrated "that Strauss is prepared to disregard or relax safety requirements simply to prove his ideological point that private enterprise can and will build reactors." Montgomery cited the Safeguards Committee report as proving that "the Monroe project is years away from demonstrating that this kind of reactor can be safe" while also supporting "the very point we have been making—that only the government can cope with the technological problems involved at this stage." He recommended that locals of "southeast Michigan and northwest Ohio in the Toledo area of Ohio should initiate steps to challenge the granting of this construction permit" and predicted that other national groups would join such a move. Consequently, the unions acted.[4]

Reuther publicly explained the intervention as a move to protect the interests of the whole nation. "We have been motivated," he told an interviewer in September, "by our desire to have brought before the American people, the full facts as they relate to the Monroe reactor. We would be performing a broad public service by merely trying to get a public hearing, where the experts could lay before all the American people all of the facts, and remove the doubts and fears." He hoped the proceeding would show that the PRDC could go ahead with the project. But, he cautioned, "if the facts show otherwise, then certainly the public safety must be protected." Questioned about the political nature of the issue, particularly the question of public versus private power, Reuther pointedly downgraded that controversy. "Nothing could be more tragic," he said, "than to get a dispute over safety standards involved in an ideological discussion between public power versus private power." Rather he summarized it as a simple matter: "Is the reactor . . . a safe reactor? Will it not jeopardize the health and safety of the people in this great area?" Reuther added: "If those questions are met, then the reactor being built by private enterprise has our blessing, has our support, and we wish them well—and we wish them the earliest possible date of operation."[5]

The petitions to intervene activated for the first time certain provisions of the AEC's existing regulations on procedural matters. The "Rules of Practice for Domestic Licensing Proceedings" had been written in 1955 by the general counsel's staff and Price's Division of Civilian Application. Based on requirements of the Atomic Energy Act of 1954 and the general administrative law encompassed in the Administrative Procedure Act of 1946, the rules set out quasi-judicial procedures in connection with the issuance of licenses as well as administrative functions related to agency licensing activities. In preparing the rules, AEC lawyers considered the future needs of the agency by drawing on the practices of other government agencies as well as the recommendations of several bar associations. After waiting the prescribed thirty-day public-review period and making some minor revisions, the AEC had promulgated the final rules on 5 March 1956.[6]

The rules provided three methods of allowing public participation when the AEC reviewed a request for a construction permit. The Commission could give public notice of its intention to issue a permit and afford parties fifteen days to ask for a hearing. It could, on its own initiative, schedule a hearing prior to granting a permit, or it could, "without formally expressing an advanced intention, or without hearing," award a permit and allow parties thirty days in which to request a hearing. The AEC followed the last procedure in promulgating its first three power-reactor construction permits, including the one to the PRDC.[7]

The staff's analysis of the proposed rules of practice had observed that giving prior public notification of intent to issue a permit would be useful in reactor licensing. "There may often be special conditions proposed if a license is to be issued," the paper stated, "which may not match the application. There may be interveners in opposition to, or support of, the application for a license. The notice of proposed action issued in advance would give the applicant an opportunity to decide whether he can and should accept any special conditions proposed, and will apprise persons who may have reason to intervene of the likely proposal they must face in deciding that their interests do or do not need protection by their participation in a hearing."[8]

The staff disregarded its earlier advice in presenting the PRDC case to the commissioners in early August. Despite the available alternatives and the obvious concern of the Joint Committee over the Safeguards Committee's misgivings about the PRDC reactor, the staff failed to present the three options to the commissioners when they discussed the PRDC permit. Had the staff made a case for the alternatives, and had the commissioners selected one of them, Senator Anderson's "star chamber proceeding" charge might have been avoided. Instead, the method followed, although legally correct, appeared as a *fait accompli* to those outside the agency.

When the unions decided to act in the PRDC case, they requested a public hearing on three issues: the legality of the Commission's conduct in issuing the permit, the safety of the reactor, and the financial qualifications of the PRDC. In addition, they asked for suspension of the permit pending the hearing. The company, afforded an opportunity to answer the petition, stated that while it could find no justifiable cause for the unions' objections, it would wait for the AEC to determine the petitioners' right to intervene. The PRDC affirmed that it was willing to present evidence on the merits of the permit. The company did, however, ask the AEC to deny the unions' request to suspend the permit. Since this was the first time in agency history that an intervention petition had been filed, the Commission held several meetings to discuss the hearing request and the legalities on how to proceed.[9]

With the PRDC intervention, the Commission instituted a new internal procedure in handling its regulatory matters. Until that time, regulatory items were included as necessary on the general agenda of Commission meetings. Now the Commission began conducting separate meetings at which it considered only regulatory issues. For the first few meetings the PRDC case was the sole topic, but as time went on, all regulatory problems brought before the commissioners were presented at the designated sessions. It represented a short step in the agency's attempt to separate regulatory from developmental business.[10]

General Counsel William Mitchell presented the staff's proposed "Notice of Hearing and Order" on the intervention at the first Commission regulatory meeting on 26 September. He recommended that the Commission allow the petitioners a hearing, adding that by doing so it would not necessarily be accepting the validity of the petitioners' grounds for intervention. Strauss inquired about the legal implications of Commission participation in a review of its own decision. Mitchell replied that the purpose of the hearing was to develop additional facts or considerations that the Commission might have overlooked in making its earlier judgment, and then either to reaffirm, modify, or reverse the earlier action. He pointed out that the Commission's own conduct and procedures in issuing the construction permit on 4 August would not be examined in the hearing.[11]

The Commission carefully considered the important question of the status of the construction permit. Mitchell said the Commission could either continue it in effect or suspend it. The staff had recommended that the Commission allow the unions and the PRDC to present arguments on the point. But Strauss and Libby indicated that they opposed suspension, and Strauss told his colleagues that Commissioner Vance, who was not present at the meeting, agreed with his position. Mitchell denied the request for suspension and declared the Commission would reserve final judgment until after the hearing. Harold Price observed that suspension during the hearings should not be a significant question since their ultimate purpose was to determine the permit's status.[12]

Commissioner Murray dissented on the construction-permit suspension. At a meeting on 28 September, he had learned from Rogers McCullough that the position of the Safeguards Committee on the PRDC application had not changed because it had received no new information. Consequently, on 8 October, Murray cast a negative vote on that part of the order, commenting that "under these circumstances I am of the opinion that this permit should be suspended pending conclusion of the hearing in this matter."[13]

Between the first Commission meeting on the petitions and the 8 October session at which it approved the final formal order, the Commission made several modifications and additions. The order granted the unions' request for a hearing and listed five specific issues: (1) whether sufficient information was available to provide assurance that the reactor could be constructed and operated at the Lagoona Beach site "without undue risk to the health and safety of the public," (2) whether reasonable assurance existed that the technical information omitted from the application could be supplied, (3) whether the PRDC was financially qualified to build and operate the facility, (4) whether any exemptions to AEC regulations should be granted to the PRDC, and (5) if the issues in the proceeding were resolved in favor of continuing the construction permit, what additional conditions, if any, should be attached to it.

On 8 October the commissioners also discussed the 6 June Safeguards Committee report that the AEC still held in confidence. The unions' petitions alleged that the report had been "suppressed by the AEC." In ensuing consultations with the staff, the commissioners learned that in mid-June Harold Price had given a copy of the report to PRDC officials. At the 8 October meeting, Price explained that in June he had believed the commissioners knew that the PRDC had a copy of the report because its contents had been outlined in an information paper. Consequently, it did not seem inappropriate to him to give the PRDC a copy of the document. But Price's action was inconsistent with the privileged-document argument the commissioners had used so strongly in July when they asked the Joint Committee to keep the report "administratively confidential." They now decided they had no choice but to release it publicly.

In a letter to the Joint Committee transmitting the hearing order, the Commission, without detailing its reasons for shifting its stance, acknowledged its error: "Reviewing the circumstances in connection with your request for this document and the Commission's handling of this document, our request that it be treated as 'Administratively Confidential' was a mistake."[14]

Although the release of the document closed one controversial part of the agency's regulatory proceedings in the PRDC case, it left a disagreeable impression on the Joint Committee. In a statement to the press, Senator Anderson announced the agency's decision and made the most out of the AEC's uncomfortable position. "I'm glad the Atomic Energy Commission has admitted its mistake," he said. "I can only add that it is always a mistake to deal with unclassified matters on a secret or confidential basis." By that time the Joint Committee had begun its previously announced inquiry into AEC licensing procedures. Ensuring that reports of the Safeguards Committee were made public was high on the list of topics under study.[15]

With the order issued, the AEC had to develop its procedures and define the role the agency would take in the upcoming hearing. The general counsel's office assumed primary responsibility for working out the details, but the Division of Civilian Application also played an important part since it had processed the PRDC's request for a license. AEC lawyers used the 1946 Administrative Procedure Act as their legal guide and also drew on the experience of other federal regulatory agencies. After receiving the petitions, Mitchell immediately enlisted on a borrowed basis the assistant hearing examiner of the Federal Communications Commission, Jay A. Kyle. The 8 October order that set the case for hearing specified that Kyle would hear the case and then send a certified hearing record to the Commission. The general procedure to be followed then required the Commission to make an initial decision based on the hearing record. Further time would be allowed for the parties to file exceptions to the Commission's initial decision. After reviewing the exceptions, the Commission would issue a final decision. If any party wanted redress, the case could be subjected to judicial review by the federal courts.[16]

Since the commissioners planned to use the outside hearing examiner only to hear the case and retain the authority to make the decision themselves, the AEC staff's role at the hearing had to be determined. Both Mitchell and Price agreed that an *ad hoc* "separated" AEC staff should be established to represent the agency at the hearing. Its purpose would be to separate staff members participating in the hearing from all other staff members who were free to advise the commissioners in deciding the case. The Administrative Procedure Act provided for this type of arrangement, and it had been used regularly at several federal regulatory agencies. In explaining the separated-staff concept to the commissioners at the 8 October meeting, Mitchell emphasized that the special staff's main task would be to develop as complete a record as possible at the hearing. Strauss, stung by the controversy already surrounding the case, inquired whether such separation would eliminate allegations of AEC partiality. Mitchell thought not, but at least its use might blunt some criticism. Although the commissioners approved using the separated-staff concept, Strauss cautioned everyone that the procedure was limited to the PRDC case and should not be viewed as a precedent for future hearings in any other cases.[17]

Two questions concerning the activities of the separated staff caused sharp disagreement between Price and Mitchell. The questions arose over the objectives of the staff at the hearing and over the supervisory authority the deputy general manager, Richard W. Cook, who headed the separated staff, could exercise over the counsel assigned to the staff. On the one hand, Price argued that since the Commission had already made a decision in the case, the separated staff should develop a record at the hearing that supported the Commission's prior action. He also thought that the separated staff should ensure that all relevant facts not brought out by the other parties were fully aired at the hearing. Price also believed that Cook should control all activities of the staff. On the other hand, Mitchell viewed the primary objective of the separated staff as making certain that all relevant evidence was introduced. Disagreeing with Price, he insisted that the staff should take no position regarding the Commission's previous decision. And he maintained that the attorneys assigned to the separated staff should exercise independent professional judgment not subject to the authority of Cook, who was not a lawyer.[18]

The Commission discussed the matter on 18 October. Murray disliked Price's recommendation, which would support the Commission's prior action without providing any affirmative obligation to assist the intervenors in proving their case. He thought this would conflict with the need to assure the public that the agency was seeking an unbiased resolution to the case. Mitchell reminded Murray that under either procedure the separated staff would compile as full a record as possible. The Commission reached no decision that day. Subsequent consultation among the staff resulted in a December compromise announced by the general manager. On the question of objectives, the separated staff would "ensure that all relevant facts not brought out by the other parties are fully developed at the hearing," while Price's recommendation on the issue of supervision was accepted. Subsequent assignments to the separated staff included people from several AEC divisions. Cook supervised the staff, assisted by Frank Pittman, Price's deputy director, and Edward Diamond, the deputy general counsel. James L. Morrisson, trial attorney in the general counsel's office, handled the actual proceedings at the hearing.[19]

Although the hearing had originally been scheduled for November, additional motions to the Commission by both the intervenors and the PRDC delayed it until 8 January 1957. The unions, in reply to the 8 October order, asked for Commission reconsideration on the issue of suspension of the construction permit; the PRDC asked that the specific item on the financial qualifications of the company be eliminated from the list of issues. In addition, the unions asked the Commission for access, without prior security clearance, to certain restricted data that they considered relevant to the case. The Commission denied the first two motions, and the touchy question of access to restricted data was not settled until after the hearing began in January.[20]

The unions charged that the Commission had acted illegally in issuing the construction permit. The Commission thought it had eliminated that issue through its 8 October order, but the unions continued to press their point. The Commission announced in December, therefore, that such an allegation would not be treated as an issue in the hearings. If the unions still wanted to pursue the matter after completion of the hearing, the Commission would be willing then to accept briefs on the legal issues. The AEC based its position on the premise that the hearings were a continuing part of the licensing process and that their sole purpose was to determine "what order should be issued in the public interest at the conclusion of the hearing and not to determine what the [legal] situation was on August 4, 1956."[21]

Two other AEC actions caused great consternation among the union attorneys and led them to charge that the agency deliberately placed the unions at a disadvantage. In mid-December, Harold Price wrote to all AEC employees and consultants regarding their participation in the case, which the unions viewed as an attempt by the AEC to keep expert witnesses from testifying fully at the hearing. Second, the unions' previous request for access to restricted data that they believed was essential in presenting their case had not been answered by the agency. Those circumstances made the AEC appear unwilling to make its performance on the issuance of the PRDC reactor construction permit clear, especially when they received attention in the press.

Price's 14 December letter directed AEC employees not to appear voluntarily at any formal AEC hearing except as a witness for the agency. If subpoenaed, employees could appear as witnesses for the unions, but even then they would remain subject to the direction of the Commission. AEC consultants, Price advised, could appear voluntarily, but were warned that such appearances might violate the conflict-of-interest laws and make them liable to criminal prosecution. Two days earlier the Commission had countered the union claim that the AEC was a party to the case by rejecting the unions' statements on the illegality of the 4 August construction permit. Now, however, Price's letter implied that this was indeed a case against the AEC. When the unions learned about the letter, they reacted immediately. Benjamin Sigal, the principal attorney for the union legal team, complained to Strauss about Price's "unwarranted" interpretation of the conflict-of-interest laws. To come under those laws, said Sigal, a proceeding must involve "a claim against the United States or a demand for money or property, neither being the case here." This prompted AEC general manager Fields to explain on 25 January that Price's statement was meant to apply to cases where consultants testified in connection with matters on which they performed services under their agreements with the Commission. Fields's explanation, however, came too late to help the unions. Since the AEC effectively controlled the nation's atomic-energy affairs, few experts were willing to risk their careers by voluntarily testifying in the face of the Price directive. Over the course of the hearings no atomic experts testified voluntarily for the unions. Public assertions that the AEC had "muzzled" its staff and consultants embarrassed the agency.[22]

The unions' motions for access to restricted data, the special category of classified defense information concerning atomic weapons and special nuclear materials, without prior security clearance became a sensitive issue not only to the AEC but to the general public. In the mid-1950s most people generally regarded atomic energy as unique and mysterious because of its technical novelty and because the atomic-weapons program enshrouded AEC operations. Through their petitions the unions sought to make AEC secrecy a major issue. Ultimately, the way the agency handled the matter defused the issue. Nonetheless, it added to the adversarial circumstances under which the PRDC hearing took place.

In their initial 21 November 1956 motion on the issue the unions demanded access to restricted data that they considered relevant to the case. Specifically, the union attorneys identified seventy-three documents they wanted, along with any other classified information "to which PRDC or APDA has had access in connection with the facility." Three of the four union attorneys on the case did not have security clearances and refused to apply for them. Instead they insisted that the restricted data they wished to examine bore no relation to national security. They pointed out that the data had been made available to private companies and persons under the AEC access program that authorized nongovernment applicants to obtain restricted data that were useful in the civilian application of atomic energy. They argued that this situation, in effect, gave the data they wanted the status of "published" records and stripped the government security classification of any meaning. Consequently, the unions requested that the information be officially declassified. In addition, the unions contended that to require intervenor attorneys to submit to AEC security requirements for access to information that was essential to preparation of the case was a denial of free speech and due process under the First and Fifth Amendments of the Constitution. The unions asked for a hearing on those questions.[23]

The legal staff took considerable time to reply to the intervenors because it had to check each requested document. Meanwhile, the hearing began on 8 January. While this concerned the commissioners because any delay in finalizing the access issue might adversely affect the unions' ability to present its case, they ultimately denied the unions' request for access and for a hearing on the motion.[24]

In reaching this decision, the commissioners accepted the general counsel's advice that the classification of the material was justified because of its relationship to atomic weapons, military propulsion reactors, and material production-reactor programs. The commissioners declared, however, that the intervenors' motion had accelerated the declassification process for their requested documents. But they also insisted that declassification would have taken place anyway, although admittedly at a slower pace. "It is unfortunate but nonetheless true," the Commission stated in its formal memorandum on the issue, "that information which is of need and use in the development of civilian uses of atomic energy bears a relationship in varying degrees to the military uses."[25]

The commissioners rejected the unions' argument that restricted data already made available to a large number of access-permit holders compromised the classification of the data. AEC lawyers cited the Atomic Energy Act, which limited dissemination of classified information to properly cleared persons. The agency's regulations implemented the statute in its rules of practice by specifying that if data became involved in an adjudicatory hearing, it could be made available only to access-permit holders (the PRDC had acquired access permits). The AEC also curtly dismissed the union charge of violation of constitutional rights by commenting that the agency was not "the forum for debating or deciding such an issue. The security requirements are imposed by and under the Atomic Energy Act." Actually, the AEC memorandum pointed out, its rules of practice minimized the problem of restricted data for any uncleared counsel. Under agency procedures, "declassification review is facilitated, the parties are under obligation to avoid introducing Restricted Data, prior notice of intention to offer Restricted Data in evidence is required, provision is made for substituting unclassified statements for Restricted Data, and there are strict limitations on the admissibility of the classified evidence." The commissioners closed their statement with the suggestion that the unions' attorneys "promptly proceed with applications for access."[26]

Although the Commission denied the unions' motion, a review of the seventy-three requested documents resulted in full or partial declassification of fifty-eight of them. Twelve of the remaining fifteen documents involved British information and remained classified for either security reasons or because of understandings with the British government. An additional document was a classification guide, and the other two were withheld because they were intra-agency communications prepared by agency consultants for use within the AEC. Consequently, the release of the documents muted the union criticism of the agency, and secrecy as an issue in the PRDC case generated little further notice.[27]

The PRDC case had created the public impression that the AEC had ignored and then tried to conceal the Safeguards Committee's adverse recommendation. The implications of the AEC's dual role of regulating as well as promoting the PRDC project as part of its Power Demonstration Reactor Program initially attracted considerable public notice. Although the Commission could argue that it had acted as a responsible regulator in scheduling a hearing, rejecting the PRDC's attempt to restrict the issues, declassifying as many documents as possible, and instructing a separated staff to act as public counsel, the hearing itself became the crucial test of the agency's regulatory commitment. For the first time, the safety of an atomic facility would be scrutinized in a public proceeding.

The hearing opened the morning of 8 January 1957 in a small examiner's room in the Post Office Department building on Pennsylvania Avenue. Hearing Examiner Jay Kyle delayed the start for nearly an hour so that more folding chairs could be brought in to accommodate the unexpected swarm of newsmen and attorneys. The hearing dragged on intermittently until 7 August 1957, much longer than anticipated when it had been scheduled in December 1956. Legal maneuvering and objections accounted for much of the delay. The hearing record, totally unclassified when finally completed, contained 457 pages of written narrative testimony and 3,919 pages of stenographic transcript. The PRDC called seven witnesses, the union four, and the AEC staff six. Most of the seventeen witnesses had been involved in the application and review of the construction permit for the AEC: General Manager Kenneth Fields; W. Kenneth Davis, head of Reactor Development; Harold Price of Civilian Applications; Rogers McCullough, Price's deputy and chairman of the Safeguards Committee; committee members Harvey Brooks, Donald Rogers, Manson Benedict, Abel Wolman, and Mark Mills; and Norman Hilberry, deputy director of Argonne National Laboratory. In addition, Walter McCarthy, Alfred Amorosi, and Hans Bethe from PRDC and its technical consulting group, Atomic Power Development Associates, presented testimony.[28]

The hearing initially attracted considerable attention in the press. But once the technical and legal complexities of the proceeding began to lengthen, it was quickly relegated to the back pages of a few newspapers. By August, the hearing had few outside observers. The limited press interest was regrettable since the hearing was the first in the history of atomic-power technology and regulation in which the public had access to thoughtful statements by some of the nation's outstanding experts discussing safety problems of fast reactors. But the case soon lost much of its news value because the openness of the hearing showed that nothing was being concealed. In addition, the adversarial relationship between the AEC and the unions that was spawned by the case was mitigated considerably by the general knowledge that the three intervening unions favored atomic development. Over the course of the hearings and the subsequent court appeals, union officials, especially Walter Reuther, publicly affirmed their continuing support of atomic power.[29]

The PRDC presented its evidence first. Initially represented in the case by the Detroit law firm of Miller, Canfield, Paddock and Stone, in December 1956 Walker Cisler also retained the prestigious Washington firm of Covington and Burling. W. Graham Claytor, Jr., a senior partner at Covington and Burling, became the chief counsel in the proceeding for the PRDC. The company's lawyers contended that their data would "fully support an affirmative finding by the Commission" on the two main safety issues: whether there was sufficient information that the reactor could be operated safely and whether there was "reasonable assurance that any technical information which has been omitted from the application will hereafter be supplied." The PRDC's witnesses repeated generally familiar or previously submitted information. Some new data, however, had come to light since issuance of the provisional construction permit on 4 August.[30]

Professor Hans Bethe's testimony revealed significant new findings to support his theory that oscillatory power experiments could be used to explore the behavior of a fast reactor under abnormal conditions. He explained how an experiment could prove the theory: "If the reactor has an instability at some high power, let us say 300 megawatts of heat, one can predict this instability very well from experiments at much lower power, let us say at 50 to 100 megawatts. This is precisely the purpose of these experiments, namely to get advance warning of instabilities long before these instabilities actually occur. . . . It is my opinion that safety tests with the help of a reactor oscillator can be carried out without danger to public safety and that the tests will give all the information required to insure safe operation of the reactor subsequently." In cross-examination by Sigal, Bethe concluded that the most important safety question involved the temperature coefficient. The cause of the positive temperature coefficient in the EBR–I accident had to be determined to ensure that the same kind of instability would not occur in the PRDC reactor.[31]

Manson Benedict, one of the Safeguards Committee members who opposed the construction permit in 1956, wrote his narrative testimony after reading the transcript of Bethe's testimony. He commented that he subscribed "to Dr. Bethe's view that the oscillator tests at low power can give, without hazard, an indication of the limits within which a reactor can be operated under stable conditions." He continued, however, that the present state of knowledge regarding the causes of instabilities in EBR–I did not permit him to conclude that the design of the PRDC reactor would not have similar defects. More research had to be done before an experiment at low power could be tried on the PRDC reactor. Such a test should be deferred, Benedict believed, "until the causes of instability of EBR–I have been identified, until the validity of oscillator tests on fast reactors has been established."[32]

In developing the unions' case, Benjamin Sigal, the talented general counsel of the machinists' union, cross-examined several members of the Safeguards Committee—Rogers McCullough, Donald Rogers, Harvey Brooks, and Mark Mills—who had submitted the 6 June 1956 report.

Sigal asked each witness whether he still agreed with the findings in that report. He then inquired whether they still believed that the Safeguards Committee's recommended experimental programs could be accomplished by the proposed completion date for the reactor. All four members affirmed their support for the content of the 6 June report. Each one also pointed out that more information was currently available and that experimental work was progressing, but all stood by the earlier recommendations in the report. In this way Sigal developed his main contention on the safety issue: that the Safeguards Committee report to the Commission continued to be valid, although additional steps had been started to improve the safety of the machine. Sigal's point was that such up-to-date testimony could not be taken lightly by the Commission when they reviewed the record.[33]

In addition to the safety question, the other major issue brought before the hearing concerned the financial qualifications of the PRDC to construct and operate the proposed facility. The Commission had raised the matter in 1956 when it issued the construction permit. The PRDC had secured a fifteen-million-dollar loan commitment from several banks, but the consortium had not obtained formal monetary commitments from all its member companies. The AEC staff had considered this as inadequate financial information. Consequently, the Commission thought that it could not find that the PRDC was financially qualified at that time to build and operate the facility as well as to pay the AEC charges for use of its special nuclear material. By implication, the lack of financial resources could also affect the safety of the PRDC reactor. The 4 August construction permit required the PRDC to submit to the agency within one year the financial information necessary to enable the Commission to judge further the company's qualifications.[34]

Ernest R. Acker, president of the Central Hudson Gas and Electric Corporation and chairman of the PRDC's Financial Committee, testified at the hearing on the financial status of the company. His appearance, the lengthiest of any witness at the hearing, covered five full days in March 1957. Acker disclosed that the total estimated cost for research, development, construction, and preoperational testing of the reactor amounted to $43,216,000. He presented evidence that the PRDC had obtained commitment for $23,540,000 from twenty-one member companies, the loan agreement with several banks for fifteen million dollars, and an agreement with Atomic Power Development Associates, the consulting firm established to give technical assistance to the PRDC, to cover seven million dollars in research, development, and equipment contributions. In addition, the PRDC had requested the Internal Revenue Service to exempt it from federal income-tax liability during construction as a nonprofit scientific enterprise. Although a final ruling had not been made at the time of Acker's testimony, Internal Revenue subsequently ruled favorably on the PRDC request.[35]

Sigal's cross-examination of Acker attempted to show how the PRDC's financial status was, at best, tentative, largely because of the loose organizational structure of the PRDC and the APDA. Sigal devoted considerable attention to analyzing the APDA. For example:

> Sigal: How does this operate, then Mr. Acker? Does the APDA send out a call for a certain amount of money to each member and ask them to contribute that amount?
> Acker: No, not a specific amount. It sends out a statement of its budget for the coming year sometime early in the year and asks the members to make commitments in amounts that represent their respective interest and each company makes its own contribution on the basis of such interest.
> Sigal: How can you possibly be assured of having enough money to meet your budget if the contribution in each case is entirely voluntary and presumably no contributor knows what the other contributors are going to give? How do you get what you need for your budget?
> Acker: We get it because of the interest of the member companies in forwarding the project.
> Sigal: And you just rely on that?
> Acker: We rely absolutely on that, Mr. Sigal.[36]

A short while later, Sigal asked Acker similar questions on the PRDC organization:

> Sigal: Mr. Acker, there are now 21 members of PRDC, is that correct?
> Acker: That is correct.
> Sigal: Is there any obligation on the part of these members to continue their membership for any particular length of time?
> Acker: No.
> Sigal: Aside from any written commitment which these members may have given to PRDC is there any additional commitment for contributions by these members to PRDC?
> Acker: No.[37]

In this manner Sigal attempted to show that the company, unlike other utilities embarking on an atomic-power program, did not have adequate long-range financial resources. In his post-hearing brief, Sigal reemphasized that the PRDC relied on APDA for research, development, and equipment contributions totaling several million dollars but that APDA members had made no specific commitments for contributions for 1957 or thereafter. Furthermore, APDA members could withdraw at any time. Likewise, Sigal argued, the members of PRDC had no obligation to continue their membership and had made no contributions beyond those originally pledged.[38]

Midway through the hearing, the AEC publicly announced the signing of a contract with the PRDC under the Power Demonstration Reactor Program. The agreement provided the company with up to $4,450,000 over a three-year period in the form of research-and-development work in AEC facilities, consultant services, and training assistance for reactor-plant operators and maintenance personnel. In addition, the AEC waived its normal charge for use of nuclear fuel for up to five years. The terms were standard for such contracts, and the agreement had been in the negotiation stage well before the PRDC controversy arose. But the AEC blundered in the timing of the announcement. It further complicated the proceedings of the hearings and in a broader sense again pointed up the difficulty of promotion and regulation by the same agency. Benjamin Sigal, after observing this dual role for several years, labeled it "an invitation to schizophrenia."[39]

The AEC publicly attempted to dissociate the contract from the regulatory process. In issuing a press release on the contract, the agency noted that the agreement "recognizes that the company must obtain necessary licenses and regulatory approvals before it may operate the reactor plant" and added that the contract was not a representation by the Commission that any of the necessary licenses or approvals would be granted. The agency hoped its word would be taken on faith.[40]

Moneys for the AEC services still had to be authorized in the AEC budget. The agency requested $1.5 million in fiscal year 1958 and the remainder of the nearly $4.5 million in 1959 and 1960. The Commission saw no problem in this because it was a small part of the total agency outlay under the Power Demonstration Reactor Program. Labor, however, viewed the authorization as another means to question the agency's method of conducting business. Walter Reuther and Benjamin Sigal used the fiscal year 1958 authorization hearings held by the Joint Committee's Subcommittee on Legislation in the late spring and early summer of 1957 to argue against what they considered a blatant conflict of interest—the negotiation of the contract while the PRDC case was in the hearing process.[41]

On 27 June 1957 Reuther and Sigal went before the Joint Committee subcommittee "to seek redress and to seek relief." Reuther charged that the AEC, in completing the contract with the PRDC, acted in an irresponsible way and disregarded the public interest. He cited his union's intervention in the case and drew extensively on the hearing testimony of the Safeguards Committee members who had made the 6 June 1956 report. Then came the contract that Reuther said prejudged the outcome of the hearings. He told the Joint Committee: "We do not believe that we are going to get redress of our problem [through adjudication], or any assurance that the health and the safety of the people in the area in which this reactor is being built—we have no assurance that the AEC can be relied upon to protect the public interest." He asked the legislators "not to authorize one cent of Federal funds to permit the construction of this reactor" until a prototype had been built and tested at a remote location.[42]

Following Reuther's testimony, Sigal called the issuance of the contract while conducting the hearing "indefensible." He believed such situations placed a "great, if not intolerable, strain on the integrity of the administrative processes." The Commission, Sigal charged, "has effectively precluded itself from rendering an independent judgment on the issues raised in the current proceeding before it." He asserted that the contract was so contrary to public policy that it should be null and void. "There is a conflict of interest here," Sigal emphasized.[43]

The Reuther and Sigal testimony impressed some Joint Committee members. Senator Albert Gore, for example, told subcommittee chairman Holifield that the matter "raises a serious question as to the propriety of approval of this authorization." Joint Committee chairman Carl T. Durham of North Carolina later told reporters that the committee did not want to authorize the contract until the safety question had been resolved. The Joint Committee's subsequent majority report on the authorization bill disapproved the requested funds for the PRDC contract. The report cited the hearing testimony of the Safeguards Committee members that Reuther and Sigal had emphasized in their presentation to the legislation subcommittee. In place of approving moneys for the PRDC contract the Joint Committee authorized $1.5 million for research and development "in the art of the fast breeder reactor generally, anticipating that this special sum will be expended by AEC in its own laboratories . . . to gain experience."[44]

Joint Committee member Sterling Cole subsequently asked Strauss to comment on the amended authorization. As expected, the AEC chairman vehemently protested the exclusion of the PRDC contract funds. His reply to Cole pointed out that PRDC had already spent "very substantial sums in reliance on the Commission's understanding to provide this assistance." The contract, Strauss stated, "was entered into in good faith. . . . We believe that under the circumstances PRDC in justice is entitled to assurance that the appropriations . . . are authorized." He then turned to the intervention proceeding. "Apparently," Strauss wrote, "the reason urged for not authorizing the necessary funds is the possibility that the PRDC reactor may be determined later to be unsafe." That was a wrong assumption, he asserted. "The contract does not constitute a determination of any of the issues presented in the proceeding and is without prejudice to their determination in that proceeding."[45]

Strauss's letter to Cole became a partial basis for a disqualification motion by Sigal at the close of the hearings on 7 August. The union attorney remarked that it was with some regret that he had to ask Kyle to act on his motion that Strauss disqualify himself from further participation in the case. But Sigal argued that the AEC chairman had prejudged the issues and would not be able to give them impartial consideration. He cited the Strauss letter to Cole as well as an earlier statement by Strauss at the August 1956 groundbreaking ceremony for the PRDC reactor. At that time the AEC chairman had claimed that the opposition to the construction permit was part of "the attack on the free enterprise development of nuclear power in this country." Kyle informed Sigal that he could not rule on such a motion and suggested that Sigal present it directly to the Commission. Subsequently, in October, Sigal petitioned the Commission for Strauss's disqualification. The Commission considered the motion later that year.[46]

By the time Kyle sent the certified case record to the Commission on 29 November 1957, its make-up had changed considerably from the time the construction permit had originally been issued. President Eisenhower's decision not to reappoint "dissenter" Thomas Murray when his term expired at the end of June 1957 was perhaps the most significant change. It eliminated the acrimonious friction that had prevailed between Murray and Strauss. In the fall, Eisenhower appointed two new commissioners—John Forrest Floberg and John S. Graham—filling the Murray vacancy and the opening created when John Von Neumann died in February.[47]

Floberg, a Harvard Law School graduate, was a practicing attorney in Washington at the time of his appointment. He had served as a lieutenant commander in the navy during World War II. President Truman appointed the politically independent Floberg to the position of assistant secretary of the navy in 1949, a post he held until the end of the Democratic administration. Floberg succeeded Murray. Graham, born in 1905, had graduated from the University of North Carolina and from the law school of the University of Virginia. After serving in World War II he held positions as executive assistant to two different Treasury Department under secretaries. In 1948 Truman appointed Graham, a Democrat, as under secretary of the treasury, where he served until the end of the administration. At the time of his AEC appointment to replace Von Neumann, he was working in Washington as a financial and business consultant.

At a regulatory meeting on 27 November 1957 the new Commission met to discuss future procedures in the PRDC case. Strauss first turned to the union motion to disqualify him from participating further in the proceeding. The chairman solicited the view of his colleagues. Libby, a strong and consistent Strauss supporter, said the chairman was not biased to the point where he could not reach a fair judgment in the case. He urged his fellow commissioners to take this position. Strauss, showing his sensitivity on the point, expressed concern that if he participated even in procedural matters he might give the intervenors evidence that the Commission could not be impartial in reaching a decision on the case. Edward Diamond, the acting general counsel, supported Strauss's reasoning. The chairman decided that until a final decision was made on the disqualification motion, he would withdraw from all discussions on the PRDC.[48]

The Commission next decided to hear oral arguments before issuing its initial decision. It hoped to do this in January 1958, but other agency business prevented some commissioners from taking the time needed to study the lengthy record. So not until 29 May 1958 was oral testimony heard. In the meantime, Strauss's tenure as chairman was drawing to an end; his term expired on 30 June. Although the general counsel advised Strauss that there was nothing in law requiring him to disqualify himself, and his colleagues had no intention to move against him, the chairman decided not to participate in the proceedings because the termination of his appointment was so near. In an additional development, Commissioner Libby suffered a protracted illness that prevented him from attending the oral testimony. Consequently he, too, removed himself from acting on the initial decision. Thus by the time the AEC finally issued its initial decision in December 1958, only one commissioner—Harold Vance—had participated totally in the case from the time the controversial 1956 construction permit had set off the intervention.[49]

The long delay irritated the unions. Benjamin Sigal, on the eve of the second anniversary of the intervention, wrote to John A. McCone, Strauss's successor as AEC chairman, complaining about the Commission's slowness in reaching a decision. He noted that construction of the reactor was "going on apace because the Commission declined to suspend its conditional construction permit pending disposition of the intervenors' objections." Sigal recognized the many issues the Commission had to consider, but still it seemed to him that enough time had elapsed to allow the Commission to have completed a thorough consideration of the case.[50]

Aided by Courts Oulahan, an AEC attorney hired by General Counsel Loren Olson to assist in writing the Commission opinion, Commissioners Vance, Floberg, and Graham issued the long-awaited decision on 10 December 1958 (McCone did not participate because he assumed the chairmanship after the date of the oral argument). Floberg and Vance submitted a joint opinion. Graham concurred in a separate opinion. The accompanying order continued the provisional construction permit but amended the original one by adding some requirements. The PRDC, at three-month intervals, now had to report significant changes or developments relating to the status of technical investigations on safety aspects of the project. The company also had to report to the AEC on its financial condition at six-month intervals.[51]

The Floberg-Vance commentary stressed the importance of the Safeguards Committee advice given in its 6 June 1956 report:

> The spectrum of expert testimony on the safety of the proposed PRDC design was surprisingly narrow. The report of the Reactor Safeguards Committee referred to in Interveners' brief can be literally accepted by the Commission, as it was by many of the witnesses, as meaning that the state of human knowledge at the time the report was prepared would not support an absolute guarantee that there would be no safety problem in the operation of the reactor; but it also permits the conclusion that going forward with the construction phase of this project would, by the very nature of the information developed in the course of evolving design, help to remove doubt concerning safety and would tend to provide an increasingly firm foundation for the reasonable assurance

required by the statute that the project could be *operated* without undue risk to public health and safety. Of one thing there can be certainty: until the questions raised by the Reactor Safeguards Committee have been answered to the satisfaction of the Commission, there will be no license to operate the PRDC reactor.[52]

Floberg and Vance emphasized that Commission jurisdiction on safety would not end when an operating license was issued. The agency would take appropriate action if "newly discovered scientific knowledge could conceivably indicate an unanticipated hazard even after some years of operation." In his concurring opinion Graham added that "continuance of this construction permit is not to convey to the applicant that it has gained any assurance of favorable action if, and when, an application is made for a permit to operate the reactor facility."[53]

The Commission gave the contesting parties twenty days to file exceptions to its decision of 10 December. Owing to the press of other commitments as well as the year-end holidays, the Commission later extended the time limit. The unions filed their exceptions and supporting brief on 14 January 1959. A short time later, the AEC separated staff and the PRDC filed replies to the intervenors' exceptions.[54]

The unions' brief argued the illegality of the AEC's original 1956 decision. Sigal took exception to the way the Commission interpreted the 1954 act as well as its own regulations in issuing the construction permit. Citing the AEC regulation that allowed extended time to an applicant to provide technical information, Sigal acknowledged that while the agency could issue a construction permit without all the necessary information, the regulation stipulated that it still must be "satisfied that it has information sufficient to provide reasonable assurance that a facility . . . can be constructed and operated at the proposed location without undue risk to the health and safety of the public and that the omitted information will be supplied." Sigal argued that the AEC took "extraordinary latitude" with this regulation in its "crucial" findings leading to issuance of this permit.[55] He specifically disputed two Commission findings.

He challenged one finding by submitting "that it has not yet been positively established that a fast breeder reactor of the general type and power level proposed by the Applicant can be *operated* without a credible possibility of releasing significant quantities of fission products to the environment." Sigal complained that more than two years and four months after the AEC originally issued the construction permit, it still

could not find sufficient information, as the regulation required, to provide assurance that the reactor could be operated safely. Citing the
Commission's opinion that an anticipated growth of knowledge about
the reactor as well as its belief in the improbability of an accident would
guarantee the future safe operation of the reactor, Sigal asserted that
neither the statute nor the regulations were satisfied by "such easy-
going assurances." He noted that the regulation required "reasonable
assurance of safe operation *at the time the construction permit is issued.*"
Sigal wrote that it was "faint consolation to the millions of people who
live within commuting distance of Lagoona Beach, and who may be
injured in a nuclear accident, that the PRDC reactor can eventually be
operated safely."[56]

The other "crucial" Commission finding on safety cited by Sigal declared that "reasonable assurance in the record" indicated that the PRDC
reactor "can be constructed and will be able to be operated at the location
proposed without undue risk to the health and safety of the public."
Sigal pointed out that the regulation required that a facility "can be
constructed and operated" without undue risk to the public. By using
different words, Sigal argued, the AEC "has clearly failed to make the
finding required by its own regulation before a construction permit can
be issued" and had consequently violated the law in affirming the permit. On the basis of those objections he asked that the permit be
suspended.[57]

In reply, the AEC brief dismissed the unions' concern as unnecessary
quibbling over wording. The separated staff argued that it would not
object to "the slight alteration of the finding necessary to conform to the
precise wording of the regulation."[58]

After reviewing the appeal briefs the Commission prepared a final
decision. Drafted by Oulahan, the ruling was ready by the first of May
for Commission consideration. Once again, only Commissioners Vance,
Floberg, and Graham acted on the matter, with Floberg as chairman.
Meeting informally on several occasions during the month of May, the
commissioners worked with Oulahan and prepared the document for
formal approval at a regulatory meeting on 26 May. By that time, Graham
declared, the case had received the Commission's "most careful and
mature consideration."[59]

The commissioners broadened their scope of review in the final decision because of the exceptions and brief filed by the unions. An equally
compelling fact was that the case was the first intervention.[60]

The commissioners noted in their introduction that the proceeding required them for the first time to "construe and apply several provisions of the Atomic Energy Act of 1954 and our own regulations which relate to the issuance of construction permits and licenses for power reactors." They outlined the intervenors' attack on the AEC's interpretation of relevant statutory provisions and rules, the unions' charge that the AEC had "uncontrolled discretion" in granting construction and operating licenses, and their assertion that the agency's decision to grant the construction permit swept aside any limitations imposed by the statute and the regulations. The commissioners also observed that the unions claimed, with respect to safety and financial qualifications, that the same findings were necessary for issuing both a construction permit and an operating license. In the detailed explanation that followed, the commissioners rejected the unions' arguments.[61]

In the opinion of the commissioners, the critical point was whether the "distinction between a construction permit and an [operating] license is only in the name." The commission argued that the distinction was substantive. Citing the law and its own rules, as well as those of other administrative agencies, the commissioners asserted that the "very fact the construction permit is referred to as the natural precursor of the [operating] license emphasizes the distinction between them." They acknowledged the ostensible plausibility of the unions' contention, however, that "construction of the reactor inevitably means operation," a contention the intervenors supported with the argument that the "heavy investment in the reactor always will generate irresistible pressure for its operation so as to protect the investment itself."[62]

The Commission countered that point by insisting that it did not interpret the law that way. It contended that the PRDC reactor was an excellent example of how the agency applied the regulations. The Commission emphasized that "PRDC has been on notice since before the first shovel of dirt was moved that its construction permit is *provisional* upon further demonstration of many technical and financial facts, including the complete safety of the reactor." Citing PRDC testimony at the hearing that waived any commitment for an operating license, the commissioners declared that the "possibility that the Commission would be in any way bound cannot be visualized." They denied the unions' implication. "In view of the wording of the provisional construction permit, it is perfectly clear that PRDC is assuming a substantial financial risk with its eyes wide open, and that generation of any pressure from such ingredients would be quite absurd." The commissioners concluded that their interpretation of the regulations was, contrary to what the intervenors argued, "neither novel nor illegal."[63]

But to clarify some of the findings contested by the unions, the commissioners supplied the additional phrase "for the purposes of this conditional construction permit" in several places in their written opinion. They reemphasized that their findings applied only to the construction permit and not to a future operating license. The question of the reactor's safety, the main issue itemized by the Commission on 8 October 1956 when it originally ordered the hearing in the case, was particularly crucial. The three commissioners found "reasonable assurance in the record, for the purposes of this provisional construction permit, that a utilization facility of the general type proposed in the PRDC application and amendments thereto can be constructed and operated at the location without undue risk to the health and safety of the public." With those revisions the Commission issued its final order and ended its first formal agency adjudicatory proceeding. It was still subject to review, however, by the federal courts.[64]

The issue reverted to the unions for further action, and it surprised no one that the intervenors petitioned for review of the AEC decision in federal court. Spokesmen for the unions had stated earlier that they would go as far as legally possible to try to obtain a determination favorable to them. On 25 July 1959 the unions filed a petition for review in the United States Court of Appeals for the District of Columbia. Because of court delays, however, oral arguments were not presented until 23 March 1960.[65]

The unions' brief before the appeals court seized upon the modified language in the AEC's final decision, describing it as illegal and inadequate. Their statement contended that the AEC regulation required "reasonable assurance, *not limited to the purposes of a provisional construction permit*," that the PRDC reactor could be both constructed and operated without undue risk to the public. The argument in the brief cited the legislative history of the 1954 act:

> It was the intention of Congress, in establishing a two step licensing procedure, that an applicant who received a permit to construct a nuclear reactor should have substantial assurance that if the reactor is built in accordance with the conditions of the permit a license to operate will be granted, and therefore the essential finding with respect to safety should be made at the time the construction permit is issued. This

protects the paramount interest of the public in safety, and at the same time encourages private industry to invest the very large sums of money required for such construction.

The unions insisted that the AEC had not met the provisions of the law. Indeed, it had failed to fulfill its own main requirement that a positive safety finding not be limited to the "purposes of this provisional construction permit." The unions concluded that the 1954 act required the AEC to make the same safety determination at both the construction permit and operating license stages. On the one hand, the brief of the unions declared, if the AEC interpretation of its own regulation (section 50.35) allowed the agency to employ different standards for a provisional construction permit, then the regulation violated the law. On the other hand, if the AEC interpretation of its regulation was in accordance with the law, then the Commission did not make the finding required by its own regulations on the PRDC project.[66]

The Commission brief countered this argument by drawing a clear dichotomy between the standards applicable to construction permits and those applicable to operating licenses. Further, agency lawyers maintained, the regulation being questioned was a valid interpretation of the Atomic Energy Act. The regulation, the AEC brief stated, "carried out the Congressional distinction between the issuance of construction permits and operating licenses. It prescribes safety standards for provisional construction permits on the basis of the developmental nature of nuclear power technology, of which Congress was aware." Finally, the Commission brief maintained that it followed its own regulations and that the controversial phrase "for the purposes of this construction permit" did not invalidate its action. The AEC insisted that the phrase "was obviously intended to do no more than reemphasize the policy behind the two-step licensing procedure and the use of provisional permits."[67]

On 10 June 1960 a three-member panel of the court of appeals, in a two-to-one opinion, upheld the unions by declaring the PRDC construction permit illegal. Circuit Judges Henry W. Edgerton and David L. Bazelon formed the majority; Judge Warren E. Burger wrote a dissenting opinion.[68]

Judge Edgerton's majority opinion, in deciding for the unions, found that the AEC had an obligation to use the same standards in judging a construction-permit application as it did for a subsequent operating license. On the basis largely of a detailed review of the 1954 act Edgerton concluded: "It seems certain that if the Act did not require, as a condition to the issuance of a construction permit, a finding that the proposed facility can be operated without undue risk to the health and safety of the public, the Act would not require the issuance of a license when the permitted construction is carried out."[69]

Edgerton turned to the AEC findings and concluded that they were both inadequate and ambiguous. He centered on the key finding: "The Commission finds reasonable assurance . . . for the purposes of this provisional construction permit, that a utilization facility . . . can be constructed and operated . . . without undue risk to the health and safety of the public." The judge pointed out the difference in wording between the AEC's initial and final decisions, particularly the insertion of the phrase "for the purposes of this provisional construction permit." The AEC's interpretation, Edgerton wrote, skirted the issue of whether the facility could be operated without undue risk. Rather, he emphasized, it was merely a finding that "there was sufficient likelihood that a facility can be operated . . . without undue risk so that, in the Commission's opinion, it is appropriate to issue a 'provisional' construction permit." But Edgerton found that was not sufficient to meet the act's requirements.[70]

The opinion cited other internal inconsistencies in the Commission's findings. Taken together, they implied to the court that while it seemed reasonable that scientific research would eventually establish that the PRDC reactor could be operated safely, the evidence currently available did not establish the fact. The court disliked the existing uncertainty. "In view of the nature, size, and location of the project," the majority opinion stated, "we think the findings should be free from ambiguity."[71]

Finally, in a particularly controversial section of its opinion, the two-judge majority took it upon themselves to review the proposed site of the PRDC reactor. Although reactor experts had testified at the Commission hearing that chances were exceedingly small that a major accident would occur, Edgerton suggested that the testimony demonstrated the "'possibility of a major disaster, even though it was a low probability.'" He continued: "We think it clear from Congressional concern for safety that Congress intended no reactor should, without compelling reasons, be located where it will expose so large a population to the possibility of a nuclear disaster." The record, Edgerton wrote, did not show that the "Commission found compelling reasons or saw that such reasons were necessary."[72]

In his dissent, Judge Burger wrote that in a technological area such as the development of atomic energy in which so much scientific uncertainty prevailed, the AEC must be allowed to proceed on a step-by-step basis. He suggested that his colleagues, in their majority opinion, were "undertaking to assume responsibilities which Congress vested in the Commission." They were, in effect, telling the agency it had made an unwise decision. The Court majority assumed, Burger charged, that once the Commission had "permitted PRDC to invest its millions in the plant they are 'bound' or 'likely' to relax their notion of what is safe or dangerous in order to bail out the investors." He refused to believe that the AEC would act "to make a finding of safety which is not supported by substantial scientific evidence."[73]

The court of appeals handed down its decision on Friday, 10 June 1960, and directed that construction at the site stop within fifteen days. The ruling stunned officials at both the PRDC and the AEC. Contacted by the press Friday night, Chairman McCone said he had not had enough time to consider all the implications but that the commissioners would gather at a special meeting on Monday morning to discuss them. The court's decision, McCone said, raised issues "of great importance to the Commission and to industry in connection with . . . public health and safety." A UAW spokesman, pleased that the decision justified its position, said the court showed "that no one, the AEC especially, should brush aside the opinions of atomic scientists who serve on the Advisory Committee on Reactor Safeguards."[74]

At the special Monday morning meeting on 13 June the commissioners discussed courses of action in light of the decision. If the agency did nothing, not only would the PRDC be affected, but so would previous construction permits issued to other companies. In addition, the whole licensing scheme that the agency had developed would be undermined. The choice was clear. The commissioners directed General Counsel Loren Olson to consult with Department of Justice officials to begin an appeal process. On Tuesday, McCone personally called Attorney General William P. Rogers to discuss the matter. Rogers told McCone that he recognized the importance of the case and would assign his best legal talent to it. A short time later, the AEC and the PRDC petitioned the appeals court for a rehearing *en banc*—that is, by the total membership of the court—but it denied the petition on 25 July. So that construction at the plant site could continue, the PRDC then successfully applied for a stay of the court-of-appeals order while the AEC and the Justice Department filed a petition for certiorari with the United States Supreme Court asking it to review the court-of-appeals record. The PRDC also petitioned the high court. On 19 November 1960 the Supreme Court issued a writ granting the review and placed the case on its docket.[75]

The Supreme Court heard the oral arguments on 26 and 27 April 1961. By then, the John F. Kennedy administration had taken office and made new appointments to the Justice Department. Robert F. Kennedy had become attorney general and Archibald Cox had been appointed solicitor general. Cox, who presented the case before the Supreme Court, was a highly respected legal scholar as well as a practicing attorney. While both Justice and AEC lawyers worked on the case, Lionel Kastenbaum, who worked at both Justice and the general counsel's office of the AEC, prepared much of both the petition for certiorari and the government's brief in the Supreme Court. Benjamin Sigal remained as the unions' principal attorney, lengthening his involvement in the case to nearly six years since the labor organizations initially intervened. Covington and Burling attorney Graham Claytor continued to represent the PRDC.

In issuing the writ the high court agreed to consider two main questions and a subsidiary one. One was whether the AEC had the legal authority to license a power reactor near a large city without showing compelling reasons for the location, and the other was whether the 1954 act permitted the AEC to license the construction and operation of atomic-power plants in two steps. The subsidiary question related to the latter main one: whether the Commission really addressed the safety issues as required by its own regulations or whether its findings were as ambiguous as the court of appeals had found.[76]

Two aspects of the Supreme Court proceeding were noteworthy. First, the justices avoided the question of whether the PRDC reactor could be proved to be sufficiently safe. Appellate courts traditionally do not resolve such issues because it is not considered a judicial function. Although a main issue on which the Commission originally granted a hearing to the unions was the sufficiency of information available to provide assurance that the reactor could be constructed and operated at the site without undue risk to the health and safety of the public, the high court would not resolve the matter. But the second issue that the unions pressed—that the AEC violated its own regulations in initially issuing the construction permit—the Supreme Court would review. No matter which way the Court ruled, that legal issue would be decided.

The government's brief before the Supreme Court made a straight-forward argument that the 1954 act authorized the Commission's regulations. Agency action under those regulations should be sustained as long as its choice among existing alternatives was "one which a rational person could have made." Furthermore, the brief stated, Congress, by taking no action, acquiesced in the Commission's practice (after initially criticizing its issuance of the original construction permit), thereby confirming that the agency regulations were in agreement with the 1954 act. Turning to the question of the location of the PRDC reactor, the government lawyers contended that neither the law nor the regulations required the Commission to demonstrate "compelling reasons" before approving a site. The government maintained that the appeals court erred in questioning the proposed location because it usurped the Commission's function of investigating and evaluating reactor sites. In addition, the brief asserted that the appeals court's statement contradicted the undisputed technical testimony given during the hearings. This was especially serious, the brief went on to note, "where judges not trained in complicated scientific and technical matters undertake to substitute their conclusions for the findings of the expert body established by Congress."[77]

Sigal's brief for the unions restated what he had submitted so often before—that the AEC violated the 1954 act and its own regulations in granting the PRDC construction permit. The appeals court had an obligation, which it had fulfilled, to reconcile the AEC's administrative interpretation with the broad statutory policies laid down by Congress. Even when administrative action was discretionary, the regulations were binding on the agency. The AEC in this case illegally mishandled its authority.[78]

The Joint Committee on Atomic Energy, especially Senator Anderson, had followed the case from its beginning with great interest. Shortly after Cox presented the government's case before the Supreme Court, Anderson called to his attention the section in the government's brief regarding Congress' alleged acquiescence in the AEC's handling of the case. The argument irritated Anderson. He told Cox that Joint Committee criticism had been muted only because ethical considerations restrained it while the case was under litigation. This did not mean that the Joint Committee thought the AEC had handled the case correctly. "The basis of the original Congressional criticism of the initial handling of the PRDC case," wrote Anderson, "applies with much the same force and conviction to each succeeding phase of PRDC's history." Furthermore, he said, this criticism affected "the issues now before the court."

He hoped the statements regarding the Joint Committee's position in the government's brief would not prejudice a "fair consideration of the case."[79]

Cox replied to Anderson that the Joint Committee's position must be considered in the context of the question before the Court on whether the Atomic Energy Act permitted the AEC to license private reactors in two stages. The key feature of this procedure, which the government brief defended, left the PRDC and the AEC "free to work out unresolved safety problems during the progress of construction, *provided that the Commission has enough assurance before construction starts that solutions will be forthcoming.*" The Commission, Cox wrote, had frequently acted in this manner "with what appears to be the full concurrence of the Joint Committee." The appeals court, however, held the procedure to be contrary to the statute. If the Supreme Court upheld that ruling, it meant that construction permits already granted for several reactors were issued illegally. More specifically, Cox hinted strongly to Anderson that Congress had acquiesced in the two-step procedure: "Unless my memory is playing tricks, Jim Raney [sic] told me some time ago that if the circuit court's decision was affirmed on this point (not others), the statute would have to be amended so as to authorize the two-step procedure."[80]

Cox, not wishing to antagonize Anderson, played down their differences. "Your earnest desire, which I share," he wrote, "is that an unsafe atomic reactor should not be built near a large metropolitan area like Detroit. The critical question whether the PRDC reactor can be proved sufficiently safe will come up in the hearings which will be held before the Atomic Energy Commission upon the PRDC application for a license to operate. This all-important question is not before the Supreme Court and, so far as I can see, the present case could not be properly expanded to include it."[81]

On 12 June 1961 the Supreme Court announced a seven-to-two vote in favor of the government's position. Justice William J. Brennan, Jr. wrote the majority opinion, while Justice William O. Douglas, with the concurrence of Justice Hugo L. Black, issued a dissenting view.

The main question before the Court, Brennan wrote, was whether the AEC in issuing a construction permit must make the "same definitive finding of safety of operation" as it would have to make before it issued an operating license. To answer that, the Court reviewed the 1954 act and the AEC regulations. First, it determined that Congress "contemplated a step-by-step procedure." Second, the Court found that before licensing the operation of a reactor, the Commission "will have to make a positive finding that operation of the facility will 'provide adequate protection to the health and safety of the public.'" But the statute did not make clear, and so it became "the center of controversy in this case," whether the Commission "must also have made such a finding when it issued PRDC's construction permit."[82]

AEC regulation section 50.35 continued to be the crucial issue in the case. Brennan's opinion noted the regulation elaborated upon and described in fuller detail the step-by-step procedure contemplated by the statute. Furthermore, the Court found, the regulation "was a valid exercise of the rule-making power conferred upon the AEC by statute." And it required that "some finding as to the safety of operation be made before a provisional construction permit is granted." The real question nonetheless, Brennan stated, "is whether that first finding must be backed up with as much conviction as to the safety of the final design of the specific reactor in operation as the second, final finding must be." Brennan and the majority thought the "weight of the argument" supported the government and the PRDC that regulation 50.35 permitted the AEC "to defer a definitive safety finding until operation is actually licensed." The Court offered commonsense reasoning for this: "For nuclear reactors are fast-developing and fast-changing. What is up to date now may not, probably will not, be as acceptable tomorrow. Problems which seem insuperable now may be solved tomorrow, perhaps in the very process of construction itself. We see no reason why we should not accord to the Commission's interpretation of its own regulation and governing statute that respect which is customarily given to a practical administrative construction of a disputed provision."[83]

Lack of action by the Congress to challenge this procedure reinforced the Court's support of the AEC's procedures. Citing the responsibility of the Joint Committee, under section 202 of the law, to oversee the development, growth, and state of the atomic-energy industry, Brennan's opinion emphasized that "no change in this procedure has ever been suggested by the Committee, although it has on occasion been critical of other aspects of the PRDC proceedings not before us." He wrote on: "We think it fair to read this history as a de facto acquiescence in and ratification of the Commission's licensing procedure by Congress."[84]

In the Court's opinion the AEC had complied with the statute and regulations fully. As a capstone to this section of the opinion the majority cited the key finding in the Commission's final decision where it determined with reasonable assurance that the PRDC reactor could be constructed and operated without undue risk. The Court observed that the finding was in the "very words of Reg. 50.35" except for insertion of the phrase "for the purposes of this construction permit." The additional phrase, to which the unions had attached great importance, was "merely declaratory of the nature of the proceeding . . . and in no way denigrated the finding as to safety of the operation."[85]

Brennan reviewed particular parts of the legislative history of the 1954 law, "since the Court of Appeals relied heavily on this," and concluded that the lower court's interpretation was based on parts of that history taken out of context. Turning specifically to the AEC's authority to license reactors near a large city without "compelling reasons," he quickly dismissed the issue. Noting that the issue had been raised by the court of appeals, he observed that it was unclear "whether respondents [the unions] have abandoned that contention in this Court and it is likewise uncertain whether they ever presented it to the Commission, a step which would ordinarily be a prerequisite to its consideration by the Court of Appeals." In any event, he concluded, "the position is without merit."[86]

Justice Douglas based his short dissenting opinion on his interpretation of the legislative history. He maintained that the Commission had a legal obligation to make a finding on the safety of the facility at the time the construction permit was issued. Instead, the AEC had presupposed—"contrary to the premises of the Act—that safety findings can be made *after construction is finished.*" Douglas found that socially irresponsible. "When that point is reached," he wrote, "when millions have been invested, the momentum is on the side of the applicant, not on the side of the public." Douglas wrote that the Commission's interpretation, although approved by the Court majority, was, "with all deference, a light-hearted approach to the most awesome, the most deadly, the most dangerous process that man has ever conceived."[87]

The Supreme Court decision mirrored the analysis Cox had given earlier to Anderson. The solicitor had maintained that the Commission's findings were exactly those required by the statute and the AEC regulations. He also had found no basis in the 1954 act for the appeals court's interpretation on the issue of locating reactors near a large metropolitan area. Even more significant was Cox's view on the correctness of the Commission's findings, on which the Supreme Court could not and would not rule. "The Atomic Energy Act," wrote Cox, "directs the Commission to resolve disputed questions of safety. It gives the courts no power to second-guess the Commission." That meant the Commission could make mistakes "which no one else can correct; and if the mistake is bad enough, tragedy may follow." Congress nonetheless was right in assuming that the AEC would be less likely to misjudge the safety of a reactor than would a court. In any event, the safety question was not finally resolved, and the AEC would again face it when the PRDC filed its application for an operating license. In addition, the passage of time meant that a different Commission might bring a fresh perspective to the controversy over the project.[88]

The Commission discussed the Supreme Court decision the afternoon of 12 June 1961. Pleased that the Court had upheld the agency after such a protracted procedure, Commissioner Graham recommended to the attending staff that they not exaggerate the effects of the decision. Publicly the agency expressed no opinion. Chairman Glenn T. Seaborg, who had assumed office on 1 March 1961, asked if this would end legal appeals in the PRDC case. Lionel Kastenbaum, the AEC attorney who had prepared the government's brief and now reviewed the decision for the Commission, replied that although the question of AEC's right to grant an operating license to the PRDC might precipitate litigation, it probably would not.[89]

The high-court decision brought the PRDC case back into the news headlines. The *New York Times* highlighted it as "an important test case for the atomic energy program."[90] Indeed it was, since the Supreme Court's decision verified the legality of the 1954 act's two-step licensing procedure as well as the AEC's implementing regulations. The decision carried great implications not only for those few facilities already in the construction- and operating-license stage but for the entire future of the licensing program. Had the AEC not been sustained by the Supreme Court, it would have meant, at the very least, significant delays in the civilian atomic-power program while the Congress and the agency developed new procedures to license private reactors. The agency staff prudently refrained from proclaiming an unqualified victory, however, for a broader review of the whole PRDC case revealed some continuing problems inherent in the licensing process that had not been resolved by the Court.

The Supreme Court decision, for example, did not resolve the safety questions raised by the Advisory Committee on Reactor Safeguards. The high court did not judge those issues. By confirming the legality of the two-step procedure, it left the ultimate safety decision to the time when the Commission considered the operating license. Moreover, by implication the Supreme Court affirmed that it lacked the technical expertise to evaluate regulatory matters. The law gave that responsibility to the AEC, and if the Court had attempted to answer safety questions, it would have been second-guessing the Commission. The justices avoided that role because they did not view it as a judicial function.

In a broader context the PRDC case underscored the problems inherent in balancing regulatory matters with promotional ones in an administrative agency. No court could resolve the philosophical and organizational problems that had to be addressed in the wider question of how to meet the goals set for civilian atomic power without jeopardizing the congressional mandate of protecting public health and safety. Throughout the time the case was under litigation the Joint Committee on Atomic Energy and the AEC grappled with those issues by independently considering ways to separate the two roles without actually splitting the agency. The details of the compromises reached underscored the difficulties of the problems and the unlikelihood of ever settling them by court decree.

The PRDC reactor case, as part of the developmental Power Demonstration Reactor Program, brought into play many elements that showed the difficulty in implementing the dual role established by the Atomic Energy Act. Although the agency ultimately "won" the case, the manner in which it handled the early proceedings undermined confidence in its judgment on safety issues. The bungling of the Safeguards Committee report in the administrative process, the seeming suppression of witnesses, the ill-timed issuance of the PRDC contract while the case was under agency adjudication, and the long delays between completion of the hearings and Commission decisions while construction on the facility continued unabated suggested that the agency was overzealous in pursuing its promotional functions. The AEC's conduct in the case contributed heavily to the beginning of a credibility problem over its regulatory role. Although the agency took some positive steps, such as separating its hearing staff and declassifying certain restricted data as quickly as possible, the Commission had difficulty offsetting the negative view it had projected to those interested or involved in the PRDC affair. Of greater immediate significance, as a result of the Commission's early handling of the PRDC case the Joint Committee on Atomic Energy forced some unwanted changes in the agency's regulatory program.

VII

LICENSING REFORM AND PRICE-ANDERSON

The prolonged legal contest was but one of several important ramifications of the PRDC controversy. It directly influenced other aspects of the AEC's regulatory program, including the final form of the Price-Anderson legislation, the internal regulatory organization of the agency, the availability of safety reports, and the opportunity for greater public participation in the licensing process. Following his public blast against the Commission in the immediate aftermath of its issuance of the PRDC construction permit, Chairman Anderson ordered staff director James Ramey to investigate the AEC's reactor-licensing procedures and regulatory organization. Shortly thereafter, the Joint Committee staff undertook a study of three fundamental questions: first, whether to require a public hearing on each application for a construction permit and operating license; second, whether all reports on reactor safety should be made public; and third, whether regulatory responsibilities should be separated from the developmental and operational functions of the AEC.[1]

Ramey was a key figure in directing this work. An honors graduate of Amherst College and Columbia University School of Law, he had been in government service since 1941 when he joined the Tennessee Valley Authority as a staff attorney. There Ramey gained the regard of David Lilienthal, and in January 1947 he moved to the newly established AEC, where Lilienthal had assumed the chairmanship. In October he became the chief counsel at the Chicago field office. Through eight years of experience in the legal management of agency research and development contracts Ramey acquired broad knowledge of the atomic-energy program. This attracted the attention of the Joint Committee, which in April 1956 appointed him staff executive director. He quickly assumed a key role in the formulation of Joint Committee policies and positions. By the time of the PRDC controversy in the summer of 1956, Ramey's influence was apparent. Although he assigned staff attorney David Toll to undertake the study on the organization and administration of the AEC regulatory program, Ramey carefully supervised the project.

After Anderson received assurance from AEC general manager Kenneth Fields that the agency would cooperate fully in the investigation, Toll scheduled several meetings with the Division of Civilian Application staff. Discussions centered on background explanations and general statements by the staff on the processing of facility applications, reactor-hazards evaluations, and the functions of the division. Although he found the sessions helpful, Toll wanted more specific information. At a meeting on 7 September 1956 with Lyall Johnson, the head of the Civilian Application Licensing Branch, Toll requested copies of the Safeguards Committee reports and the staff reports on the construction-permit applications for the light-water reactors being built by the Consolidated Edison Company and the Commonwealth Edison Company. Toll felt he needed those documents to consider adequately Anderson's suggestion that such reports be made public. Furthermore, he thought that the reports would be useful to him in making an informed judgment on the question of separating regulatory from promotional functions, since they would enable him to "understand in some detail the present actions taken by the various divisions, staffs and advisory committees . . . in connection with facility license applications." Johnson referred Toll's request to Frank Pittman, the deputy director of Civilian Applications.[2]

Although Toll pressed the agency for the documents, Pittman demurred. On 11 September, Pittman told him that the matter was under study because of the "difficult policy questions involved." Pittman would not elaborate, but his reference undoubtedly was to the question already under discussion over the leaked Safeguards Committee report on the PRDC reactor that the Commission had asked the Joint Committee to hold "administratively confidential." The AEC still had not settled that issue. By early October, Toll could only report to Ramey that the agency still had reached no decision. Toll suggested taking additional steps, first through a letter from Senator Anderson to Strauss formally requesting the material. Other possible alternatives might be scheduling a hearing with the Commission on the question, or "the use of subpoenas, etc."[3]

On 5 October, Fields called Ramey and told him the agency would not release the requested documents. At a meeting the following week involving Ramey, Harold Price, and Pittman, Price gave his views on the questions of open hearings and issuing public-safety reports. He opposed both proposals because of the added administrative burden and unnecessary time spent on formalities and *pro forma* proceedings. Furthermore, Price thought publishing safety reports would decrease the candor of the statements contained in them. Everyone at the meeting agreed that the proposed requirements would probably increase public education about atomic energy and confidence in the AEC licensing process. But Price believed the same purpose would be better served by publishing composite reports on each construction permit that would include treatment of the safety problems and reactor hazards of the particular facility. While the discussion did not broach the issue of the requested documents, it indicated Price's preference for a continued informal licensing procedure that he could manage internally.[4]

Price told Ramey that the AEC was still working on a formal statement describing the functions of the Safeguards Committee and the licensing staff that he hoped would be useful to the Joint Committee in its study. But he thought that it would probably not be ready for several months. Nonetheless, on 9 and 17 October, Fields, in an attempt to be as co-operative as possible, sent to the Joint Committee several composite reports with details of the licensing process as well as considerations leading to the issuance of construction permits for the PRDC, Consolidated Edison, and Commonwealth Edison reactors. While none of those reports included verbatim copies of the Safeguards Committee proceedings or internal staff reports requested by Toll, they were detailed analyses of the licensing operations.[5]

Ramey nevertheless agreed with Toll that a review of the specifically requested documents was vital to the staff study. Ramey therefore drafted a formal letter from Anderson to Strauss. In it the Joint Committee chairman noted that although the investigation had thus far been conducted in a "spirit of mutual cooperation," he regretted that "the AEC reached this decision not to cooperate fully." He could not see how the Joint Committee staff could make an adequate investigation without full access to the pertinent documents "being held 'administratively confidential' by the AEC." Citing section 202 of the 1954 act that required the AEC to keep the Joint Committee "fully and currently informed," the senator insisted that either the documents be made available or "a complete written statement of the grounds for refusal be furnished to the Committee promptly." Sent on 16 October, Anderson's letter opened again the question of executive privilege the Commission thought it had recently resolved in the PRDC reactor dispute (the Commission released the Safeguards Committee report on the PRDC on 9 October).[6]

Meanwhile, Price and Mitchell had developed a new regulation on the agency's public records used in regulatory proceedings, which they had rushed to completion because of the AFL-CIO intervention in the PRDC case. The intervention necessitated some formal guidance for the staff in determining what documents in regulatory proceedings should be made public and placed in the AEC's public-document room. Although the agency's rules of practice and the regulation on access permits generally addressed this question, more specific guidelines were needed.[7]

The new rule generally defined public records as they applied to regulatory proceedings and listed specific inclusions. But the regulation also listed ten exceptions, one of which would withhold from the public "intra-agency and inter-agency communications, including memoranda, reports, correspondence, and staff papers prepared by members of the Commission, AEC personnel, or by any other Government agency for use within the AEC or within the executive branch of the Government." When the Commission met on 17 October to discuss the proposed rule, that exception elicited considerable comment.[8]

Commissioner Murray restated his consistent position that Safeguards Committee reports should be made public. He argued that such action would help ensure public confidence in the civilian power program. Libby countered that it might prove impossible to retain highly qualified people on the Safeguards Committee if it "were likely that their individual positions would be made public." After some discussion, Libby and Murray supported Price's suggestion that summary statements of Safeguards Committee reports be made public without identifying individual members. Murray also retreated from his original position by agreeing with Libby that even summaries need not be released in every instance, but should be determined on a case-by-case basis. Commissioner Vance thought the AEC needed more experience in handling the reports before developing a firm policy. Perhaps on occasion, he said, obviously thinking of the recent PRDC case, the Safeguards Committee might not recommend approval of a reactor that the Commission later found satisfactory. In such an instance the Commission might consider issuing a statement explaining the reasons for approval.[9]

Discussion turned to the role of the Safeguards Committee. Kenneth Fields thought that if the committee remained exclusively an advisory body, its reports should not be published. But, he said, if the committee's opinion was to be, in effect, the determining factor in approving power-reactor licenses, he believed the group should be made a statutory body. The suggestion of incorporating the Safeguards Committee into the statutory organization of the agency drew no response from the commissioners. Rather, Vance commented that because of the publicity over the PRDC report the public was aware of the committee's existence and "in the future will wish to be informed of this Committee's views on any proposed power reactor." The commissioners decided to defer voting on the regulation at that time, but on 31 October they approved its publication as originally proposed.[10]

Since the AEC had not yet replied to Anderson's 16 October letter, the Joint Committee viewed its earlier request for information in the context of the proposed regulation. When Ramey telephoned General Counsel Mitchell on 9 November, he learned that the new rule would not apply to Joint Committee requests for information. Mitchell reconsidered his opinion, however, and a few days later wrote to Ramey that his telephone statement "was not entirely accurate." The new regulation would apply to Joint Committee requests for specific internal documents, Mitchell wrote, unless those requests were individually granted by the Commission or the general manager.[11]

Ramey received further AEC views on the matter at a meeting on access to information he held a few days later with several senior members of the agency staff. Robert Hollingsworth, the assistant general manager for administration, told Ramey that the agency believed it could refuse access to "internal working papers." Richard Cook, the deputy general manager, reiterated several times at the meeting that review by the Joint Committee "was tantamount to review by the public." But he indicated that the Commission could, on its initiative, provide reports or summaries of information rather than specific documents requested. Ramey reported this information to the Joint Committee and concluded that the AEC's current policy "would tend to restrict the powers of the Joint Committee."[12]

Those developments deeply concerned Anderson, who placed much emphasis on being kept "fully and currently informed" about AEC activities. He had Ramey draft a letter to Strauss, which was never sent, that demanded an insertion in the public-records rule stating its non-applicability to requests "by the Joint Committee or other Congressional Committees for information or documents." Anderson wanted Ramey to circulate the draft letter to ranking committee members Cole, Durham, and Hickenlooper for their approval. Before sending the letter, however, Ramey learned from the AEC staff that the agency was preparing a reply to Anderson's 16 October request for the documents and that it planned to make more documents available to the Joint Committee than it had indicated previously. Anderson then backed off and directed Ramey to await the Commission reply before deciding whether to send his letter.[13]

The Commission's answer to the Joint Committee's 16 October request had been drafted by the general manager in mid-November for review by the commissioners. The first draft flatly refused to honor the Joint Committee request. Strauss opened the discussion on the draft letter at a Commission meeting on 14 November, observing that a question of precedent was involved if the documents were given to the Joint Committee because it would be difficult to "turn down other requests for miscellaneous internal Commission documents." Libby agreed with Strauss but thought the letter should express a continued desire to co-operate with the Joint Committee. Murray, consistent with his earlier position, said the Commission should not summarily deny the request for the Safeguards Committee reports, particularly in view of the Joint Committee's strong political position and the public-relations aspect of the situation. Murray added that the draft letter implied that the agency accorded the Joint Committee the same treatment as the general public. He argued that the AEC set no precedent by releasing the documents to the oversight committee, and maintained that if the agency did not release them, the Joint Committee would undoubtedly continue its efforts to gain access to them.[14]

Unconvinced by Murray's argument, Strauss countered that the AEC had already given the substantive information in the reports in other material sent to the Joint Committee. He also contended that the Safeguards Committee documents were privileged communications of the executive branch of the government. Seeking a solution, Murray thought that if the letter explained the Commission's position, an agreeable middle ground might be reached. He further inquired of Fields if members of the Safeguards Committee objected to release of their reports to the Joint Committee. No immediate answer was available, so Strauss directed the general manager to solicit the views of the Safeguards Committee. The commissioners also agreed that Fields and Vance should work on a revised draft.[15]

The growing dissension between the agency and the Joint Committee over executive privilege became more pronounced a few days later when Ramey and Toll met with several agency staff members. The topic was section 202. Ramey opened the meeting by declaring that he would not discuss the legal basis for keeping the Joint Committee fully and currently informed because the question was "cut and dried." Turning specifically to the requested documents, Ramey said the agency interpretation for withholding internal reports ran counter to the committee's understanding of section 202. Ramey emphasized that the Safeguards Committee reports were important to the Joint Committee study of AEC licensing procedures since the Safeguards Committee "is more powerful than any statutory committee and the study of its operations is a prerequisite to a thorough understanding of the administrative process." He made it clear that the Joint Committee viewed agency compliance with its request "as a duty rather than a courtesy."[16]

Ramey's strong position influenced Fields's and Vance's rewriting of the draft reply to the Joint Committee. Their draft now made an exception for the release of the requested documents. Discussing the new version with the commissioners on 28 November, Fields, with Mitchell's support, said he presently believed the Joint Committee needed the documents in its study. Besides, he said, "providing these reports . . . would forestall any charges that AEC is withholding information on the safety of power reactors." Vance added his weight to the argument, observing that although the question of executive privilege was important, "the factor of public safety involved in power reactors compels the Commission to treat [Safeguards Committee] reports in a different manner than other internal documents." He had been convinced that the agency needed to create greater public confidence in its handling of safety aspects of the power program because a "large segment of U.S. public opinion believes the AEC is unnecessarily secretive about many of its activities." Vance thought that the average layman considered the Safeguards Committee opinion more important than the scientific facts upon which its opinion was based. If the Commission withheld such reports, Vance said, it would indicate that the public "must rely solely on the AEC for a judgment on the safety of power reactors."[17]

Libby and Strauss were only partially convinced. Libby had no problem with furnishing the Joint Committee with the pertinent scientific information on which the Safeguards Committee based its findings but thought it unwise to provide the verbatim reports because of the executive-privilege precedent. Strauss worried that other AEC activities, such as weapons testing, also involved public health and safety. Conse-quently, he believed the Commission should not establish a precedent that might require the agency in the future to grant congressional com-mittees access to sensitive information.[18]

Harold Price, continuing his opposition to any release, interjected that the reports would not be very useful as public-information documents because they were "written by technical men for the use of technical men." Fields added that Safeguards Committee chairman McCullough also opposed giving the reports to the Joint Committee. But before reach-ing a final decision on releasing the documents, the commissioners wanted Fields to discuss the matter further with McCullough.[19]

McCullough conferred by telephone with the far-flung part-time Safe-guards Committee members, who collectively agreed that the requested reports should be given to the Joint Committee. A majority felt, however, that release of their proceedings should not become a customary practice. The survey of the Safeguards Committee bolstered the Vance-Fields position and persuaded the Commission to release the reports.[20]

In his reply to Anderson, Strauss set out Commission policy. Although the AEC declined to honor the Joint Committee's broad request for all future reports, it agreed to make an exception for the specific Reactor Safeguards Committee reports. Strauss explained that the Commission granted the exception because it wanted to cooperate with the Joint Committee, and in this case the reports might help the committee in its study of the licensing process. Strauss emphasized, however, that re-leasing the material was not a precedent for other documents the Joint Committee might ask to see. The original request, Strauss stated, raised "the issue of whether the Commission should depart from the long established constitutional position of the executive branch in disclosing day-to-day judgments and advice to scrutiny by the Congress." The chairman emphasized that in dispatching the reports to the Joint Com-mittee, the agency had no intention of creating a precedent "regarding the availability of other advice and recommendations of this Advisory Committee or any other advisory committee or any other internal work-ing papers prepared by employees or consultants of the Commission."[21]

So the Joint Committee won the skirmish. By itself the incident ap-peared insignificant, but viewed in the larger context of unfolding events it became an important part of the Joint Committee's effort to force the AEC to open its licensing process through publication of formal reports.

Another aspect of Senator Anderson's investigation of the licensing process raised the possibility that the Joint Committee would require the agency to hold public hearings on all reactor construction permits and operating licenses. When Anderson first broached the subject in August 1956, General Counsel Mitchell immediately prepared a staff report for the commissioners that analyzed the senator's query and suggested how to prevent such a requirement. Most agency officials thought mandatory hearings would cause extensive delays without greatly improving the licensing process.[22]

In his report, Mitchell reviewed the alternative construction-permit procedures presently available under the AEC's rules of practice. Until then, the agency had followed the procedure employed in the PRDC application: issuing a permit subject to a request for hearing within thirty days. While not yet used, the rules of practice also gave the Commission authority to order a hearing before granting a permit or issuing a notice of proposed permit and allowing fifteen days thereafter for filing requests for a hearing. Mitchell argued, that the rules were already flexible and that an amendment to the 1954 law requiring hearings on every application would be unduly restrictive. Mitchell believed that although holding hearings before a permit was issued might be desirable in some circumstances, the Commission should make that determination rather than having it mandated by law. Furthermore, he insisted, such a requirement, if enacted, would be difficult to repeal even if the AEC or the Joint Committee later found it to be no longer useful.[23]

Mitchell analyzed for the Commission the current criticism of the existing procedure. Because the industry was new, reactor technology was highly specialized with many classification controls on data and little public understanding of the degree of hazard associated with various types of reactors. Critics thought the AEC's procedures inadequate either to advise the public of the hazards or to give it "full confidence in the thoroughness of AEC's hazards review." The public understood the safety problems of other industries more clearly than it did those of the atomic-power industry. The Commission had not yet been able to publish detailed standards for reactor construction or operation that would provide better public understanding of atomic power. Furthermore, because of the top-secret nature of the weapons program the general public seemed to feel that the agency was unduly secretive about the whole technology. Consequently, AEC critics insisted that the more hearings the agency held, the more it would assure safety through the regulatory procedures and thus gain public confidence.[24]

Particularly disconcerting to Mitchell was a recommendation made at a recent legal workshop on atomic-energy problems held at the University of Michigan. Attended largely by lawyers associated with various segments of the atomic-energy industry, the workshop participants suggested that the agency hold formal public hearings on all applications for power reactors. While the recommendation carried the reservation that the procedure should "apply only during the present developmental period" of the industry, Mitchell was concerned that such a move, if enacted by Congress, would be hard to reverse at a later time.[25]

Mitchell noted that the agency could, under the present rules and at its own discretion, conduct a public hearing in every case. If the agency followed this procedure, it would be in a flexible position in the future to dispense with such hearings as a routine practice. Mitchell saw two possible reactions to that procedure. On the one hand, it might eliminate the controversy about Anderson's proposal and might result in no further congressional action on the matter. On the other hand, the procedure might only serve to encourage the Joint Committee to recommend a statutory requirement for hearings and place the AEC in an awkward position to oppose such legislation.[26]

Consequently, Mitchell recommended adoption of the alternate procedure that would require a notice of proposed action and give an applicant or an intervenor an opportunity to obtain a formal public hearing. In addition, the director of the Division of Civilian Application would submit to the general manager a detailed memorandum describing the type of reactor and its various characteristics. The document would identify each of the factors considered by the staff regarding safety, site, and financial qualifications, and the reasons why the application appeared satisfactory. The memorandum would be both published and placed in the agency public-document room along with a notice stating that the Commission proposed to issue the permit or license.[27]

Mitchell argued that this procedure would educate the public with pertinent information on each application without "a cumbersome hearing procedure." The agency could, therefore, give the public substantially the information that would go into the record if a formal hearing requirement in all cases were adopted. The general counsel admitted, though, that the suggested procedure would not completely satisfy some critics who believed that it was more important, at this developing stage of the licensing process, to have a hearing in each case. With little discussion the Commission approved Mitchell's recommendation on 12 December.[28]

Also on the agenda at the 12 December meeting were two construction-permit applications, one from Westinghouse Electric for a small test reactor, the other from AMF Atomics for an industrial research reactor. Both applications included detailed memoranda from the Division of Civilian Application that followed the format Mitchell's policy paper had suggested. Libby commented on the high quality and content of the information presented by the Civilian Application staff. Using the newly adopted procedure, the Commission authorized publishing a notice on the proposed issuance of a construction permit for each reactor along with the staff analysis. The Safeguards Committee did not review either of the applications, although Price assured the commissioners that the committee would be consulted when the construction permits were converted into operating licenses.[29]

Strauss discussed the change in the AEC's licensing procedure in a January 1957 letter to Anderson. He affirmed that the Commission recognized the need to inform the public of the "salient facts and major factors considered" in a construction permit, particularly since the AEC could not provide detailed criteria for the construction and operation of reactors at this developmental stage of the technology. But Strauss insisted that it would be counterproductive to hold hearings in all cases. Moreover, he wrote to Anderson, "it would be undesirable to take legislative action which would restrict flexibility in the establishing of administrative procedures." He stressed that the Commission, through modification of its practices, believed it was "meeting your objective . . . and no amendment to the act is necessary."[30]

The third topic Anderson wanted investigated was whether the regulatory functions of the AEC should be separated from the promotional and operational ones. Toll's meetings with the agency staff indicated that the Joint Committee study would sift ideas for a complete separation as well as for alternate organizational arrangements within the agency. To make certain the AEC had its position ready if the Joint Committee held hearings on the matter, Mitchell and Price undertook their own study of the existing regulatory organization.[31]

After reviewing the operations of the Division of Civilian Application from its inception in the fall of 1955, Mitchell and Price concluded that the agency arrangement had worked well even though it included both regulatory and developmental functions. They decided, however, that centering responsibility for both regulatory and developmental activities in a single division made the AEC "subject to criticisms, whether justified or not." So organizational changes seemed desirable, both to build public confidence and to ensure that the regulatory staff did not have its objectivity subjected to "question by actual or potential responsibilities in areas where the primary objective is encouraging the growth of the industry."[32]

Anderson had suggested the possibility of dividing regulatory and developmental duties into separate agencies; Mitchell and Price argued that such a solution presented serious difficulties. It could result in a weakening of the regulatory system, which in turn might retard the growth of the atomic-energy industry. Among the problems they associated with such a proposal, recruitment of qualified people with specialized and technical backgrounds appeared the most formidable. They maintained that the agency could only attract qualified regulators by making them a part of a "recognized competent technical team" and providing them an opportunity to participate in the "scientific cross-fertilization which is so essential to the continued growth and development of an individual's technical acumen." Since such an intellectual process would be limited in a separate agency, Price and Mitchell feared that the AEC's efforts to recruit capable regulators would be severely hampered by a complete separation of responsibilities.[33]

Even if the staffing problem could be resolved, Mitchell and Price argued that separation would present other significant disadvantages. They noted that the reservoir of technical talent and know-how that the AEC had accumulated over the years played an important part in furnishing information and advice to the regulatory staff. By supplementing the regulatory technical staff with a vast background of specialized competence, the AEC's physicists, chemists, metallurgists, and engineers who worked in other divisions made the regulatory program better than what it would be in a separate agency. If the regulators lost the ready availability of day-to-day knowledge of the operational and developmental aspects of the AEC's program, as well as firsthand contact with the agency laboratories, the difficulty of their tasks would greatly increase.[34]

Citing national policy defined in the 1954 law that the atomic-energy industry "should come into being and grow as rapidly as is consistent with the national interest," Mitchell and Price noted that health and safety considerations had to be weighed against the benefits of the new energy source if that policy were to be effective. They contended that a proper balance could only be determined by a single group with "responsibility to Congress, the President, and the people for seeing that all aspects of the new industry are considered in its orderly growth." At least in its formative stage, industry development depended greatly on a "smoothly working government-industry partnership." Such cooperation would be impeded by two separate agencies.[35]

After finding complete separation undesirable, Mitchell and Price suggested two alternatives that might be carried out within the existing organizational framework of the agency. Both plans abolished the Division of Civilian Application and replaced it with a Division of Industry Regulation and a new Office of Industrial Development, which would assume the developmental functions presently handled by Price's division. This would restrict the Division of Industry Regulation to purely regulatory activities. The two plans differed only in where the Division of Industry Regulation was placed in the AEC hierarchy. Under the first scheme it would report to the general manager just as Price did as head of Civilian Application. The second arrangement made the division report directly to the Commission.[36]

Both plans separated developmental and regulatory functions within the AEC. From a public-relations point of view, Mitchell and Price asserted that abolition of the Division of Civilian Application, "with its connotations of promotion and encouragement of the growth of the industry," would make it clear that any potential conflict between regulation and development at the division level had been eliminated. Their analysis of the two options suggested that if the new division reported directly to the Commission, it would be more independent of other AEC functions. Price and Mitchell worried, however, that under this arrangement the commissioners would have to become heavily involved in the coordination of program relationships and administrative matters. This, they argued, could lead to inefficiency by establishing parallel services and duplication of administrative tasks. Therefore, both Mitchell and Price favored the reorganization plan where the head of the regulatory division reported to the general manager.[37]

On 20 December 1956 the commission took up the reorganization paper along with a draft agency reply to Senator Anderson's queries. All agreed with the Mitchell-Price analysis that any reorganization of the AEC into separate regulatory and developmental agencies was not at that time in the best interest of building an atomic industry. On the issue of the proposed internal reorganization, Commissioner Vance remarked that he did not wish the Joint Committee to interpret such a move as an attempt to forestall a legislative division of the agency. After briefly discussing Vance's reservation the commissioners decided that they would merely inform the Joint Committee that they were actively considering regulatory reorganization. When the commissioners met again on 3 January, they agreed that in view of the pending Joint Committee study of AEC regulatory functions, internal reorganization should be deferred.[38]

Strauss, nevertheless, emphasized in a letter to Anderson the Commission's strong opposition to amending the 1954 law to establish a separate regulatory agency. He underscored the need for "singleness of administration" in order both to develop and to regulate the new industry. Regulation, he wrote, contributed to the industry's growth just as the agency's developmental and operational activities contributed to sound regulation. Particularly at this stage of development, Strauss concluded, "we believe the need for their proper balancing and effective execution argues convincingly for the continued combining of the principal atomic energy activities of the Government in one agency."[39]

By the early part of 1957, then, the agency had informed the Joint Committee of its position on the three questions posed by Anderson. The Commission objected to separation of its regulatory functions from its developmental and operational duties, though it was considering some internal reorganization; it opposed public release of Safeguards Committee and internal staff safety reports, though it was beginning to issue composite reports; and it disapproved of mandatory public hearings on each application for a construction permit and an operating license, though it had modified the procedures to make it easier for interested parties to demand a hearing in individual cases. The AEC hoped its modifications in each area would prevent the Joint Committee from taking legislative action that might curtail agency flexibility in the licensing process.

By 13 March, David Toll, assisted by consultants John Palfrey of Columbia University Law School and J. Forrester Davison of the George Washington University School of Law, had his extensive study of the AEC's licensing procedures ready for the Joint Committee. It formed the basis for a bill introduced by Anderson on 21 March 1957.[40]

Anderson was no longer the chairman of the Joint Committee because the position alternated between the Senate and House with each new Congress. When the Eighty-fifth Congress convened in January 1957, the chair for the next two years passed to North Carolina congressman Carl Durham, the former vice-chairman. In turn, Senator Anderson reverted to the position of vice-chairman; he would again assume the chair in the Eighty-sixth Congress, beginning in 1959.

Durham pointed out in the preface to Toll's published report that the study did not contain specific legislative recommendations. Rather, he wrote, it analyzed the licensing procedures and organizational arrangement of the agency to enable the legislators to determine whether the AEC's recent changes in licensing procedures were satisfactory. Durham failed to mention that the ongoing study itself was a major catalyst in bringing about the AEC actions. If the Joint Committee had not undertaken the study, the AEC would probably still have been operating under its earlier procedures. Given its impact on both the Joint Committee and the agency, the study was a milestone document in the early history of atomic licensing and regulation.[41]

In the introduction, Toll explained several policy considerations that he took into account while pursuing the study's three areas of inquiry. More public-safety reports, more public hearings, and a sharper separation of the AEC's licensing function, he argued, would enhance objectivity in the evaluation of reactor hazards, instill greater public confidence in the AEC, and increase the emphasis on safety aspects of atomic power. Toll also cited several conflicting considerations, including the advantages of top-level coordination in the entire atomic-energy program, the need for flexibility and administrative efficiency in the field, the desirability of avoiding unnecessary duplication of functions, and added burdens on scarce technical and administrative personnel.[42]

Although Chairman Durham had correctly stated that the study technically called for no specific legislative changes, Toll made subtle recommendations by his emphasis on key questions. In his discussion on public hearings, for example, he stressed both positive and negative arguments. At the end of the discussion, however, he suggested that "one might consider" defining statutorily the types of reactor facilities that would be subject to required hearings, and he closed with a reference to the University of Michigan Law School workshop, which had urged formal hearings on all applications during the industry's developmental period.[43]

Toll likewise leaned in favor of publication of safety reports, although he gave equal space to both sides of the argument. He fully discussed the evolution of reactor-hazards reports by both the AEC staff and the Safeguards Committee. But through his choice of words, Toll clearly advocated publication. Moreover, since the Safeguards Committee was so important in appraising reactor facilities, Toll suggested "it might well be made a special statutory committee by amendment to the Act defining its composition and functions and defining the occasions on which an application should be reviewed by the Committee and a public report issued."[44]

In the final section on separation of the AEC's licensing functions, Toll discussed other federal regulatory agencies and their methods of licensing. But he emphasized that separation of functions in the atomic-energy field had to be qualified by the unique nature of the developing technology. After analyzing several possibilities for reorganization, ranging from complete separation to division within the agency, Toll agreed with the AEC that the arguments against a separate agency "are perhaps more persuasive than they will be at a later stage when commercial production of atomic power is achieved." He suggested, however, that the idea of separation be further evaluated.[45]

Senator Anderson, the mover behind the study, incorporated Toll's suggestions in the bill he introduced in the Senate on 21 March. It provided for the establishment of the Reactor Safeguards Committee as a statutory body of fifteen members and required it to review each application for a power reactor or test facility. The committee's reports would be made public. In addition, Anderson's bill directed the AEC to hold a hearing on every reactor application. Introducing his bill on the Senate floor, the senator stated that it represented his own views "as to what is needed at this time insofar as new licensing procedures are concerned." But his proposed legislation clearly reflected the conclusions of Toll's study. And just as Toll's work suggested further evaluation of the AEC's regulatory organization, so Anderson remarked that he, too, was studying organizational questions and might introduce another bill on the subject. Anderson, obviously trying to cushion his past indictments of the AEC, emphasized that his bill was not intended "as a criticism of the Commission staff, nor of course, of the members of the Advisory Committee on Reactor Safeguards." He praised both groups for their efforts in helping industrial applicants and hoped that his bill would not unduly increase their workload. But he believed the "public importance of these more formal procedures warrants their adoption."[46]

Instead of holding separate hearings on Anderson's suggested amendments to the 1954 act, the Joint Committee decided to discuss them at the upcoming hearings on the resubmitted Price-Anderson indemnity bills scheduled to begin on 25 March. By coincidence, Anderson's proposals to revise the licensing process dovetailed with the topics planned for the indemnity hearings: probabilities of reactor accidents, research on reactor hazards, and the public availability of reactor safety reports.[47]

Both the AEC and the Joint Committee had worked toward passage of new indemnity legislation from the time it became apparent that the Price-Anderson bill would not be called to the floor in July 1956. The failure of Congress to act on the measure in the Eighty-fourth Congress had a compensating factor. It allowed more time to research questions that could not be readily answered the year before. For example, Commissioner Libby's testimony in May 1956 on the probabilities and financial consequences of a reactor catastrophe had pointed up the need for further research. In June, Libby had asked the staff to study decontamination problems resulting from a reactor accident affecting areas outside the reactor site. In July 1956 Anderson, in gathering information on the insurance bill, requested a comprehensive report from the AEC on estimated damage caused by reactor runaways. The Joint Committee wanted a detailed analysis of all aspects of the problem along with explanations for the basis of the premises and the assumptions used. Another subject not fully developed in 1956 was the question of policy premiums to be charged by the insurance syndicates for their basic coverage of reactor facilities. At the time of the 1956 impasse on the Price-Anderson bill, insurance actuaries were working on a set of costs, but they needed more time to make their estimates. The 1956 controversy over the safety of the PRDC reactor infused still another element into the Price-Anderson deliberations. It underscored the importance of the question Chet Holifield had raised in his dissenting report on the 1956 Price-Anderson bill: whether the indemnity program might not encourage less restrictive location of reactors. Consequently, the period between the adjournment of the Eighty-fourth Congress and reconsideration of Price-Anderson in the new session gave time to attempt resolution of those issues.[48]

In response to Senator Anderson's request for a comprehensive reactor-accident study, Harold Price and his deputy Frank Pittman had by mid-August 1956 outlined a plan to the general manager. They decided that the study should consider hazards from a hypothetical reactor accident that could result in either injury or death to humans and in either destruction or damage to property. Three basic hazards would be studied on the basis of a selected typical but hypothetical reactor design. Initially, damage to the reactor would be estimated that would reflect the magnitude of expected energy release from the maximum excess reactivity believed possible in the reactor under study. The consequent amount of damage to the reactor would determine the percentage of fission-product inventory escaping from the reactor. In turn, this would determine the radiation and contamination damage to people and property outside the reactor. Next, radiation exposure in the immediate area of the reactor would be examined on the basis of the portion of fission-products inventory released, the physical, chemical, and physiological nature of the radioactive elements escaping, and the characteristics of scattering agents such as meteorological conditions. Finally, the study would estimate contamination from the dispersing radioactive cloud in areas remote from the reactor. The plan sought damage estimates relative to the amount of radioactive materials in substances, buildings, plants, animals, streams, and land that would cause economic loss or decontamination costs.[49]

Price and Pittman admitted that existing information on many crucial aspects of the proposed study was so limited that it would "permit us to do little more than make intelligent guesses." They cited, for example, the fragmentary information on the violence of explosion due to malfunctioning of a reactor, on the fraction of fission-product inventory and the identity of isotopes that might be released, and on the atmospheric dispersal of radioactive materials. But they also reported the existence of some fairly definitive data that had not been integrated in studies to date. They hoped this type of information would allow researchers to draw some reliable conclusions in areas such as the extent of contamination from the more hazardous isotopes that might be released and the means and cost of decontamination. Both men thought the systematic study they outlined not only would be useful in setting limits to the estimation of damages but also would focus on areas where present data and research programs were inadequate.[50]

At the suggestion of the general manager, Price and Kenneth Davis, head of the Reactor Development Division, worked out an agreement with the Brookhaven National Laboratory to undertake the proposed study and to assist the agency in writing a report. Operated by a consortium of private universities under contract to the AEC, Brookhaven was a center for pure research in the peaceful development of atomic technology. Kenneth W. Downes, a Brookhaven atomic engineer and physicist, was selected to direct the project with assistance from several colleagues at the laboratory and with close cooperation from several AEC divisions. The initial projection called for a preliminary report by the end of 1956. In addition, the AEC requested Brookhaven to consider the feasibility of undertaking a longer-term program of collection, organization, and interpretation of all information on the topic as it became available. The agency hoped that updates of the initial study could be periodically issued.[51]

As the reactor-hazards study progressed in the fall of 1956, the Commission prepared its plan to promote passage of indemnity legislation when Congress reconvened in 1957. Strauss reported to his colleagues shortly after Congress failed to pass Price-Anderson in 1956 that he had received verbal assurances from industrial representatives that the bill's delay would not impede their reactor programs. Later in the year General Counsel Mitchell, reporting to the commissioners on the proposed legislative program for 1957, stated that there had been no significant changes as far as the need for a government indemnity program was concerned. Industry representatives, in spite of the assurances given to Strauss in midsummer, still held the position that they were unable to assume financial risk above the amounts of private insurance available and that some form of government indemnity was necessary. Mitchell reported that the most noteworthy development appeared to be the progress of the insurance industry. Syndicates had been organized, rating plans and inspection procedures were being developed, and claims committees were being established. Insurance executives told him that they hoped to issue policies and establish premiums by early 1957. Mitchell recommended, therefore, that the Commission support legislation similar to the aborted Price-Anderson bill because both the insurance and atomic industries had endorsed the program and the AEC had determined that it would be workable. In mid-January 1957 Mitchell sent the Commission a new version of the agency's indemnity bill that incorporated several minor revisions based on continuing liaison work with insurance executives. The commissioners approved the draft and noted that it would serve as a basis for the agency position when the Joint Committee prepared to introduce new indemnity legislation.[52]

Seeking legislative support for the indemnity bill, Strauss met at the White House with Eisenhower and four Republican congressional leaders, Senators Styles Bridges and William Knowland and Congressmen Joseph Martin and Charles Halleck. He outlined the history of earlier efforts to pass the bill and blamed Anderson for preventing the measure from coming to the floor in 1956. He maintained that private companies were continuing to invest in atomic facilities "in the confident belief that the bill would pass at this session." No one present at the strategy meeting contradicted Strauss's plea for the indemnity legislation.[53]

Hoping for early consideration and smooth passage for the proposal, the Joint Committee also began preparations for additional hearings on bills Price and Anderson reintroduced in January. Both measures were identical to the Price-Anderson bill reported in 1956 with the exception of some minor changes in wording. Durham scheduled March hearings on the indemnity bills and also included on the agenda Anderson's proposed amendments dealing with the Safeguards Committee, public hearings, and the publication of safety reports.[54]

In February the insurance syndicates sent to the Commission and the Joint Committee their provisional rate schedules on yearly liability premiums for five specific reactors that had been established by their National Bureau underwriters. They based the long-awaited figures on individual evaluation of each facility reviewed. The industry emphasized that the rates were provisional and would be reevaluated in 1958. The insurers also planned to recalculate the premiums in ten years. If no sizable losses were incurred and if technological advancement showed promise of further reducing the risks, the syndicates promised to return a large part of the premiums the policyholders had paid. Actually, this was an arrangement made between the syndicates and the Internal Revenue Service, which allowed the syndicates to collect excess premiums and pay no taxes on them so long as they were returned after ten years. Of course, the syndicates would have to pay taxes on the investment income generated by the premiums.[55]

The rates the insurance representatives set were based on dollars of liability insurance. The syndicates used the first million dollars as the base rate that the underwriters established on type, use, size, location, and containment of the facility. Rates for additional coverage over the first million dollars were set on a sliding scale ranging from 50 percent of the base rate for each of the next four million dollars to 2.5 percent of the base rate for each million dollars over forty million. Furthermore, the underwriters fixed a minimum rate for any million-dollar increment of insurance. For power reactors the rate was one thousand dollars; for research and test reactors, five hundred dollars.[56]

Two of the five initial rate quotations were on large-scale power reactors—Yankee Atomic at Rowe, Massachusetts and Commonwealth Edison at Dresden, Illinois. The yearly premium for the Yankee plant would be $130,000; for Commonwealth Edison, $250,000. The other three were research reactors: The Armour Research Foundation reactor at Chicago, $59,000; the Battelle Institute reactor at Columbus, Ohio, $55,000; and a General Electric facility at Vallecitos, California, $64,000.[57]

Harold Price and AEC comptroller Don Burrows analyzed those rates when they studied the resubmitted Price-Anderson bills and prepared comments for the scheduled Commission testimony. Their main concern was that no dollar gaps appear between the private coverage and the government indemnity. On the one hand, they noted that the cost for power-reactor insurance was unquestionably higher than normal liability insurance carried by utilities. On the other hand, they recognized that atomic-energy risks were new to the insurance industry, which lacked significant statistical data on which to calculate rates by recognized actuarial methods. Consequently, the insurance companies had to establish higher rates than those charged for well-known and time-tested industrial risks. Both men were encouraged, however, by the insurers' plan to recalculate the premiums retrospectively in ten years and possibly return a portion to the industry. Price's and Burrow's analysis indicated their strong faith that positive control over the safety aspects of atomic technology would prevent financial losses that would hinder the industry's growth.[58]

Also in preparation for the upcoming hearings, the Commission on 15 March 1957 received the Brookhaven study on catastrophic accidents in large atomic-power plants. Circulating it to the commissioners, Fields urged approval of a final version of the report by 20 March so that it could be forwarded to the Joint Committee in time for the indemnity hearings. Titled "Theoretical Possibilities and Consequences of Major Accidents in Large Nuclear Power Plants," the report soon became known by its agency document symbol: WASH–740.[59]

The study began with some general comments on reactors and radioactivity. Reactors could not explode like an atomic bomb, the authors affirmed, but "explosive nuclear energy releases in power reactors, or chemical or physical energy releases . . . in magnitude to destroy the reactor" could occur. This posed a threat to the life of personnel within the facility and could result in the complete loss of the installation. Although the explosion itself would present little hazard to the general public, the possibility of radiation exposure and contamination if fission products escaped from the reactor could cause extensive loss of life and property damage. The study focused on that aspect of a hypothetical accident. To appraise the magnitude of the hazard, the authors attempted to find the "best possible answers" to four questions. What is the probability that fission products might be released? What are the conditions affecting the distribution of fission products over public areas? What levels of exposure or contamination cause injury to people and damage to property? If such an accident occurred, how many deaths and injuries and how much damaged property would result?[60]

In seeking answers, the researchers cautioned that their appraisal necessarily relied in many instances on expert judgment because numerous crucial factors could not be established quantitatively "either by theoretical and experimental data or adequate experience." Because of those limitations, the authors declared, the "entire study hardly constitutes more than an identification of the factors that are important, the best appraisal of these factors currently possible, and a rough approximation of the magnitudes of the composite results." More definitive information might either reduce or increase the cited estimate of deaths and damages. The authors refused to set an upper limit on potential damages simply because they had no way to calculate them from existing data. Thus WASH–740 independently supported the AEC's earlier position on indemnity that had recommended unlimited liability coverage rather than the five-hundred-million-dollar limit set by the Price-Anderson bill.[61]

In seeking an answer to the question of the probability of a catastrophic reactor accident, the report concluded that such an occurrence was "exceedingly low." The authors, however, qualified that conclusion. They stated flatly that no one then knew or probably would ever know exactly how low the probability was. But in attempting to establish some basis for estimation, the study suggested three approaches. First was operating experience. If enough reactors ran for a sufficient length of time, a better indication of accident probability might be obtained. The cumulative operating history of atomic reactors since 1942, while constituting a "remarkable safety record," did not give a dependable statistical basis for computing the likelihood of accidents in the future. Historical experience indicated both positive and negative factors about the probability of major reactor accidents. On the positive side, because of limited knowledge of accident potentials, those responsible for reactor design and construction had attempted to provide wide margins of safety. Furthermore, the newness and glamor of the field of atomic energy had attracted and challenged the "most expert and competent people." In addition, the report noted that the substantial government safety-research program as well as future reactor experience should lead to even safer design. On the negative side, since several reactor types were currently being developed, unknown safety problems could arise. And in the future, the study warned, accident-free experience might lead to complacency. Additionally, as reactors became older, operators might encounter hazards not foreseen at the time of design and construction.[62]

A possible second method to assess accident probabilities was to assign approximate numerical values to separate factors which would either prevent or cause an accident, and then attempt to calculate the composite result. The study listed as examples several positive and negative considerations. Most thermal neutron reactors were inherently stable because of the phenomenon of prompt negative temperature or power coefficients. Every reactor would have a primary pressure vessel that enclosed the reactor core and an outer gastight containment designed to prevent escape of fission products into the environment. Even if fission products were released, a complex variety of environmental, meteorological, and other conditions with differing occurrence probabilities would govern the dispersal pattern of the fission products, and the likelihood of highly unfavorable combinations of all those appeared low. But a confluence of negative factors could override the positive ones. Certain types of power reactors, for example, were designed to operate under high pressures that were subject to failure. Another largely unknown factor was the long-term cumulative effect of radiation on the physical and chemical properties of reactor-systems materials, which might raise the likelihood of serious reactor failure at some time. In addition, various metals used in reactors, such as uranium and zirconium, under certain conditions not yet fully understood, could react explosively with the water present in many reactor designs. During an abnormal operation, such metal-water contact might cause chemical reactions strong enough to rupture the containment systems. Thus the list of factors indicated that it was impossible to assign dependable quantitative values to their functioning probabilities in order to determine a reliable indication of the magnitude of the safety margin.[63]

Using the best judgment of the most knowledgeable experts was the third approach in determining probabilities. But the reluctance of scientists to make quantitative estimates on such probabilities hampered this method. Some reactor experts contacted for the study held a philosophic view that such computations were impossible. Others who were approached were apprehensive because assignment of numerical estimates might convey an erroneous impression of confidence about the knowledge that constituted the basis of their judgment. A few experts, however, were willing to state numerical order-of-magnitude estimates. Those appraisals represented their degree of "feeling" for the probability, but the study underscored the point that the numbers had "no demonstrable basis in fact." Those willing to express their opinions gave three estimates. The first was for an accident that caused major damage to the reactor core but with no fission-product release outside the reactor vessel. The experts' estimates ranged from one chance in a hundred to one in ten thousand per year for each reactor. The second estimate was for a more serious accident that released significant amounts of fission products outside the reactor vessel but not outside the containment structure. The experts assigned this accident an order-of-magnitude ranging from one chance in a thousand to one in ten thousand per year. Finally, the experts made estimates on an accident that would release major amounts of fission products outside the containment. Those ranged from one chance in a hundred thousand to one in a billion per year for each reactor.[64]

Taking these estimates, the WASH–740 authors made an admittedly highly speculative projection. Using the most pessimistic estimate for the worst accident (fission-product release outside the containment), and assuming that one hundred reactors were in operation, and further assuming that each accident would kill three thousand people, they extrapolated a figure of one chance in fifty million per year that a person would be killed by a reactor accident. For comparison the authors cited the probability of a person in the United States being killed by an automobile accident as about one in five thousand per year.[65]

With this remote but quantitatively uncertain possibility that a major accident might occur, the remainder of the study dealt with the question of the extent of personal or property damage to the public. The study made no attempt to appraise the hazard or damage to the facility itself or to its personnel. But to determine public losses, the study group took a hypothetical reactor of one hundred to two hundred megawatts of electrical power, surrounded by a pressure-resistant containment building with a two-thousand-foot reactor-site boundary, and located it near a large body of water and about thirty miles from a major city. In the possible types of accidents considered, all were postulated to occur after 180 days of reactor operation when essentially full fission-product inventories had been built up in the system. The study gave special attention to the volatile fission products—that is, xenon, krypton, bromine, and iodine—and to strontium. Iodine and strontium were biologically the most hazardous.[66]

In order to indicate the range of the hazard to the public, the researchers considered three reactor-accident cases. In the first one, all the fission products were released from the reactor core, but none escaped from the containment building. The second case assumed all of the noble gases (xenon, krypton, and bromide) and iodines plus 1 percent of the strontium were released to the atmosphere. The third case, the major one or worst possible accident considered, assumed that 50 percent of all fission products were discharged to the atmosphere.[67]

The study concluded that in the first case, under the best conditions, no personal injury would be likely, and public loss would be due entirely to evacuation costs and payments for denial of use of land outside the plant boundary. In the second and third categories of accidents, with release of assumed amounts of fission products from the containment, the authors considered four separate different situations of meteorological conditions (daytime dry, daytime rain, nighttime dry, and nighttime rain) and two different particle-size distributions. In the second case, the study estimated that lethal exposure ranged from two persons to nine hundred persons, likely injuries from ten persons to thirteen thousand persons, and property damage from zero to $205,000. In the third or worst-case accident, with 50-percent release of all fission products, the lethal exposure ranged from zero to thirty-four hundred people, injuries from none to forty-three thousand, and property damage from $500,000 to a high of about $7 billion. In the worst case, the authors noted considerable uncertainty about "many of the factors, techniques and data," so the numbers reported could only be "rough approximations." Where high degrees of uncertainty existed, the researchers chose values thought to be on the pessimistic or high-hazard side. They added, however, that certain weather conditions, when combined with other imaginable extremely adverse conditions, could cause damages even greater than the envisioned worst case.[68]

The commissioners discussed the WASH–740 report at a meeting on 20 March when they took up their prepared draft testimony on the Price-Anderson bills. Harold Price commented that the report provided an assessment "insofar as practicable" of the potential hazards. Libby, the most knowledgeable commissioner on reactor hazards, remarked that the study was the best that could be prepared at the time. He suggested, and Strauss agreed, that the report and the AEC's public statement on it should emphasize that the accident cases studied were analyzed from a hypothetical point of view and that the AEC was developing plans for gaining more data on such accidents.[69]

Strauss discussed the report at length with the Joint Committee when he led off the testimony at the indemnity hearings on 25 March. He noted the lack of operating experience and, fortunately, accident experience with reactors. He added that "establishing hypothetical circumstances under which harm and damage could occur, and arriving at estimations of the theoretical extent of the consequences, proved a complex task." He emphasized, however, that the study indicated belief among experts that the probability of major reactor accidents was exceedingly low. He supported that assessment by stressing that the self-interest of the government and the industry in developing a strong atomic program dictated avoiding even a minor accident that would be unacceptable both in financial costs and in harm to public health. The study, Strauss told the Joint Committee, underscored the Commission's belief that the regulatory program "must continue with vigor to the end that the conceivable catastrophe shall never happen." But it also showed, he said, the importance of passing indemnity legislation soon.[70]

Blunt comments the next day from one key industry spokesman added significant pressure on the Joint Committee to secure passage of the Price-Anderson bill. General Electric's Francis McCune told the Joint Committee that if indemnity legislation did not pass in that session of Congress, work by his company on Commonwealth Edison's Dresden station would stop. When Pennsylvania congressman James Van Zandt questioned McCune, he learned that all of General Electric's contracts in the civilian field incorporated provisions that would halt work if liability protection could not be obtained. Furthermore, McCune observed, he did not see how other companies in the atomic field could arrive at conclusions any different from General Electric's. Probing further, Van Zandt asked whether General Electric would totally withdraw from the field if indemnity legislation was not passed. McCune answered him in terms of the potential market for civilian products of atomic energy. Without liability protection, he argued, there would be no market, and consequently, no one would remain in the field. McCune urged congressional action as the only solution. Van Zandt concluded: "In other words, this committee has the ball and we have to carry it." All agreed.[71]

The remaining two days of testimony completed the public record on the Price-Anderson bill. Most of the witnesses discussed the cost of premiums developed by the insurance pools, which had not been available a year earlier. Nearly all the witnesses endorsed the Price-Anderson bill, with the exception of several AFL-CIO representatives who were currently contesting the AEC in the PRDC case.[72]

Since Anderson had insisted that the indemnity hearings also cover his Safeguards Committee bill, he made an effort to obtain comments from several witnesses. Because the AEC had already opposed Anderson's position in earlier communications to the Joint Committee, the senator did not question AEC witnesses on his Safeguards Committee bill. He solicited instead the views of those supporting his bill. Under Anderson's prodding, Charles Haugh of the Nuclear Energy Liability Pool and Hubert Yount of the Mutual Atomic Energy Insurance Pool gave their backing. General Electric's McCune submitted a letter favoring the measure, and Arthur Berard, president of the National Electrical Manufacturers Association, endorsed the bill because it would ensure "wide dissemination of information on reactor hazards." The strongest, most vocal support, however, came from Benjamin Sigal, the AFL-CIO attorney in the PRDC case. He launched into a bitter criticism of AEC's conduct in the PRDC proceeding, implied that the Commission and industry considered safety a secondary issue, and argued that insurance was only necessary to cover their carelessness. He said the indemnity bill should not be passed without including the provisions of the Safeguards Committee bill.[73]

Buttressed by this show of support at the hearings as well as by several additional letters, Anderson later persuaded his colleagues to incorporate his Safeguards Committee amendments into the Price-Anderson bill.[74] Since the only apparent opposition came from the AEC, and the agency strongly favored the indemnity provisions, Anderson successfully combined the two measures to secure what he wanted and to forestall any attempt to sidetrack his proposals.

The Joint Committee voted favorably on 9 May 1957 to report the revised Price-Anderson bill to Congress. Chet Holifield registered the only dissent. He believed that the bill provided a substantial subsidy to the atomic-power industry, and he claimed that its proponents were trying to obscure its purposes by citing the protection it would provide to the public. Holifield's dissent made ample reference to the Brookhaven WASH–740 study, and he argued that under its worst possible case the government would assume potential liability that could reach several billion dollars. In addition, he charged, the bill would create more executive bureaucratic authority while it weakened congressional control by committing the AEC to handle undetermined liabilities in advance of appropriations.[75]

After the committee favorably reported the revised bill, Anderson requested AEC comments on the sections incorporating his three amendments making the Safeguards Committee a statutory body, requiring its reports to be made public, and mandating a public hearing in each reactor case. In response, Fields prepared an analysis for the commissioners that pointed out the difficulties the agency might encounter with the amendments. Making the Safeguards Committee a statutory group, he cautioned, would reduce the AEC's authority with respect to the status and organization of the committee. Echoing earlier agency views on the requirement that Safeguards Committee reports be published, Fields complained that the increased workload caused by such a provision would be burdensome for the committee. He also predicted that as the volume of reactor applications grew, committee members would spend substantial time on licensing tasks that might detract from the attention they could devote to other committee work, such as developing standards. Furthermore, public reports might reduce the candid opinions members traditionally expressed in the reports. And Fields thought Anderson's requirement for mandatory public hearings greatly increased the possibility of delay in issuing licenses. He discerned no advantage in this procedure over the one already adopted by the Commission the previous December, which provided public notices of the intent to issue licenses and granting them without a hearing unless one was requested. After pointing out those already familiar concerns, Fields still recommended that the Commission support the present Price-Anderson bill. Concluding that the measure was "in the public interest and in the interest of the rapid development of nuclear power," the general manager's recommendation also sought to avoid a confrontation with the Joint Committee.[76]

The Commission followed Fields's recommendation. Strauss said he was personally committed to support the bill. Vance thought it necessary to have some form of indemnity legislation passed even though the Commission might object to some parts of the bill. Libby and Murray agreed. They directed Fields to inform the Joint Committee of their support.[77] Indemnity legislation that would speed development of atomic power was important enough to the Commission that it was willing to accept, however reluctantly, Anderson's amendments to the bill.

With no significant opposition in the Senate to the Price-Anderson bill, attention focused on the House, where Melvin Price and Chet Holifield presented two hours of pro and con argument on the proposal. The debate was noteworthy for several reasons. It was the first time the indemnity issue, the most important piece of atomic-energy legislation brought to the floor since the 1954 act, was debated in either house of Congress. Nonetheless, had Holifield not spoken against it, the bill would probably have sparked little or no discussion from other House members. Despite both Price's and Holifield's efforts to underscore the bill's importance and point out some of its potential ramifications, the House had a difficult time maintaining a quorum to conduct business on the bill. The show of massive indifference reflected the deference House members afforded the Joint Committee, which had firmly established itself as the source of congressional expertise on atomic-energy matters. A favorable report from the Joint Committee, in this case despite strong dissent from a key committee member, was usually enough to gain approval for a measure with little or no discussion. Although Holifield attempted to generate opposition on the floor, the bill passed easily on a voice vote.[78]

In his floor remarks, Holifield emphasized the lack of expert knowledge about the probability of reactor accidents. He told his colleagues that the money involved in the insurance and indemnity package was of little importance. "I am thinking," the Californian said, "about a danger to human lives." He strongly supported building power reactors, but he wanted them placed at isolated sites. He once again criticized the AEC's handling of the Safeguards Committee report in the PRDC case and wondered if such a situation could happen again. Holifield admitted he had little chance of stopping the Price-Anderson bill, but he proposed an amendment that he thought would improve it. He wanted to add a requirement that adverse reports issued by the Safeguards Committee would forbid the Commission to issue a license. That, Holifield said, "would give the Reactor Committee some teeth." Holifield's comments might as well have been a soliloquy. His amendment failed overwhelmingly, indicating further the powerful influence of the Joint Committee.[79]

Strauss triumphantly informed Eisenhower of the passage of Price-Anderson, and the president signed the bill into law on 2 September.

The atomic industry, like the AEC, felt gratified. General Electric's McCune wrote to Durham that the law was a "truly significant milestone and sets the stage for continued, rapid industrial progress."[80]

The Price-Anderson Act was the product of two years of study, debate, and compromise. Everyone involved faced squarely and seriously the need to overcome the institutional interests and politics that had created some major roadblocks. From the beginning, the proposal's basic purpose was to reduce a significant impediment to the development of the atomic industry. Even Anderson's regulatory amendments were partly an effort to promote the industry, since building public confidence in the licensing process was considered by both the AEC and the Joint Committee to be essential for a strong atomic industry. The 1954 Atomic Energy Act had set the national policy for development of an atomic industry. The two-year experience leading to enactment of the Price-Anderson Act underscored the trying task of arriving at procedures that would encourage the industry while maintaining rigorous safety requirements.

Tempered with many reservations, the best expert judgment that could be obtained at that time concluded that the probability of a major catastrophic atomic accident was quite low. Although WASH–740 confirmed what most knowledgeable people already thought to be true, the Joint Committee insisted that the AEC develop a more public, open licensing procedure. It sought in that way to improve public awareness of the reactor-safety program and show that safety considerations were as important as reactor development in considering license applications. The Commission agreed on the need to reassure the public of its commitment to health and safety but hesitated to move very rapidly toward opening the process to wider public participation. Agency officials feared that to do so would cause undue delay in licensing, which would impede building a viable atomic power industry and thwart the objectives of the 1954 Atomic Energy Act. In addition, on the basis of its own experience of reviewing licenses on proposed reactors combined with an excellent safety record with its own installations, the AEC believed it was adequately protecting public health and safety.

But the Joint Committee, and most visibly Senator Anderson, took its oversight role seriously, and persistently probed the policies and activities of the AEC. Furthermore, being composed of popularly elected members of the government, the Joint Committee was undoubtedly more sensitive to public feeling than the appointed members of the

Commission. The PRDC episode was the catalyst for Joint Committee action to allow a larger public role in licensing procedures. The case underlined its concern that the AEC was insufficiently attentive to health and safety questions. The Joint Committee initially thought the 1956 indemnity legislation, designed both to develop the industry and to protect the public through its liability provisions, was adequate. However, after studying the AEC's licensing process in the aftermath of the PRDC construction permit, Anderson determined that some changes were necessary to open the agency's decisions to greater public participation. He believed his amendments would result in even faster development for the fledgling industry. In championing that course of action, Anderson received significant backing from both the insurance and the atomic industries. The AEC, faced with this combined opposition, reluctantly accepted the new regulatory amendments in order to gain the indemnity legislation.

VIII

STANDARDS DEVELOPMENT: THE REACTOR-SITE CRITERIA

In the early years of commercial atomic-power reactor development, the Atomic Energy Commission faced the important and demanding task of determining technology-based standards for regulating the private industry. If successfully established and applied, such norms would help the agency meet its twin policy objectives of promoting the industry while protecting the health and safety of the public. But in the evolving state of atomic technology in the 1950s and early 1960s, the agency found it difficult to reach agreement on technological decisions that would satisfy both goals. One of the important technical issues the AEC regulators weighed was guidance for the industry on the siting of atomic-power reactors. Although by 1962 siting criteria had resulted only in an interim measure, the AEC regarded as important the effort to provide some basic regulatory direction and to satisfy some of the agency's critics. As an example of how standards were developed, the reactor-site criteria also showed the compromises and judgments required by the changing state of the technology.

The AEC staff realized it was blazing a trail in attempting to establish technical standards for regulating the industry. Several factors made the task difficult, foremost among which was the lack of reactor operating experience. Most reactors prior to the start-up of Shippingport in December 1957 had been located at isolated sites and operated by the government. Although operating data had accumulated from those reactors, the experience to date had by no means given enough information to enable the staff to make across-the-board technical judgments. A good example had been the technical problems encountered in the licensing of the PRDC reactor. The experts in that case believed that more breeder-reactor operating experience would yield important data that would resolve some of the major unknowns in the fast-reactor technology. Similarly, in other instances case-by-case evaluations seemed to be the only course to follow. In effect, the variety of reactor types in the early years of the Power Demonstration Reactor Program prevented rapid development of uniform measurement devices. Since nearly every design presented different problems, each proposed reactor system and its site had to be evaluated individually by the agency. Even in the case of light-water reactors, with which scientists and engineers had the most experience, no comprehensive standards could be agreed upon, mainly because of the rapid changes in the technology.

Development of rules for the regulation of the atomic industry required the AEC to use several types of measurement, including standards, codes, criteria, and guides. Standards were definitive requirements that specified procedures for obtaining and confirming particular results. For example, Part 20 of Title 10 of the Code of Federal Regulations had established basic standards on radiation protection. Codes constituted special types of standards that detailed design requirements for reactor components or systems. The professional engineering and scientific societies usually drew up codes that the AEC then followed. Criteria were general performance objectives against which to judge an applicant's facility design, while guides were suggested ways to meet general criteria. Often the terms "standards" and "criteria" were used interchangeably, but technically, standards were more definitive.

AEC officials repeatedly explained to the Joint Committee the difficulty of establishing standards. Those statements were realistic appraisals of the developing state of the technology, not admissions of failure. Harold Price testified in 1956 that to attempt to write comprehensive standards at that time would be fruitless. He believed that only after certain reactor types were developed and proven could the government "spell out for each . . . what the basic hazards protection has to be." AEC general manager Kenneth Fields, talking about the hazards-summary report, the key item in every reactor application, emphasized the difficulty for reactor designers to submit a complete report at the initial application stage. The same reasons that prevented the agency from preparing standards and criteria made it difficult for designers to submit definitive hazard reports. Adequate hazards evaluation, Fields noted, could be made only on the basis of detailed and exact design specifications and operating procedures. "The power reactors that are being considered today are still being developed," he said. "Experimental programs and theoretical studies, the results of which may cause extensive design changes, are still being carried out, and will continue to be carried out for extended periods of time." Both the agency and the industry nonetheless recognized that an adequate regulatory program required careful consideration of standards, codes, criteria, and guides under which proposed sites, designs, and operating procedures could be evaluated. A major AEC regulatory objective, Fields told the Joint Committee, was to formulate "standards or codes for atomic energy equipment somewhat analogous to the codes that have been so useful in establishing safety limits for pressure vessels of various types."[1]

The reference to pressure-vessel codes in itself underscored historically the difficulty in arriving quickly at specific standards for atomic plants. Nonnuclear boilers and pressure vessels had been used for more than 150 years, but only in the twentieth century had they become safe, reliable, and standardized. Numerous boiler and pressure-vessel accidents in the nineteenth century had prompted a great number of cities and states to regulate their design, manufacture, and operation. The result was a proliferation of laws that created widespread confusion. To provide a sound technical basis for regulation, the American Society of Mechanical Engineers (ASME) created a committee in 1911 to formulate standard specifications for boiler and pressure-vessel design and construction. On the basis of the committee's work the ASME adopted its first boiler and pressure-vessel code in 1915. Over the years most states and municipalities adopted the code and incorporated it into their ordinances.[2]

The advent of atomic-power reactor technology emphasized the importance of the pressure vessel in the operation and safety of any atomic facility. The reactor vessel housed the core and contained the primary coolant. In addition it provided, internally, coolant flow direction to and through the core. Externally, the pressure vessel furnished anchor points for primary system piping, provided supports for control-rod mechanisms, and supplied facilities for fueling and refueling the core. Thus the pressure vessel, while only one component among many in a complex integrated reactor system, had to provide a high degree of dependability throughout the life of the facility. While it was similar in many respects to the design of other industrial pressure vessels subjected to the ASME code, it required special consideration because of the unique nature of atomic reactors.[3]

Recognizing this, the ASME in 1955 established a special committee to consider the problems of reactor pressure vessels. By 1963 the ASME had accepted the committee's work by incorporating a new section into its code dealing solely with the design and construction of atomic pressure vessels. The new section, like the overall code itself, drew on the standards of other professional organizations that also developed codes and specifications for pressure vessels. Thus in the area of pressure-vessel technology, the architect engineers who designed the early atomic facilities and the AEC regulators in the Hazards Evaluation Branch had a sizable body of time-tested guidance. The evolution of the pressure-vessel code demonstrated the considerable period of time needed to arrive at an acceptable minimum standard. While the ASME code exemplified what AEC officials hoped to develop for other components of a power reactor, it also indicated that atomic technology in many specific areas had not advanced to a point where codes comparable to those for pressure vessels could be formulated. Until those standards could be developed, the AEC had to rely on the best available engineering judgment to evaluate the safety of atomic facilities.[4]

The siting of private atomic-power plants became one of the major issues for standards development. From the beginning of the civilian power program, facility location was a critical issue to the utilities because it was so closely tied in with the economics of nuclear energy. The capital cost of any central power station had to consider transmission costs. If utilities were going to invest in an atomic plant, they wanted to locate the station as close as possible to the population centers they served. Therefore, the industry strongly emphasized what came to be called metropolitan siting, and development of formal site criteria became a vital part of standards development in the late 1950s and early 1960s. The siting issue demonstrated the difficult task the AEC faced in arriving at an acceptable safety standard, because, unlike the ASME when it formulated the pressure-vessel code, the agency had no widely accepted body of engineering knowledge to draw on. The rule the AEC finally adopted in 1962 was the product of experience with government-owned reactors, case-by-case evaluation of the several reactor applications in the power-demonstration program, the demands for guidance from industry and the Joint Committee, and collective knowledge about various elements of atomic technology.

The first Reactor Safeguard Committee had been created in 1947 to examine each government reactor and to advise the Commission on their hazards. Since atomic scientists recognized that the danger of a reactor derived chiefly from the large amounts of radioactive material that could be released in a catastrophic accident, the major site require-ment for reactors at that time was isolation from population centers. To determine an acceptable site on a more precise basis, the Safeguard Committee developed by 1948 an extremely conservative "rule of thumb" formula for a controlled exclusion area around a reactor. It was based on a postulated worst possible uncontained reactor accident (the early government reactors had no containment buildings) in which 50 percent of the fission products were released to the environment in a cloud that spread out from the reactor. The formula allowed for meteorological conditions and evacuation time and further assumed that at the mini-mum exclusion distance an individual would receive an extremely severe dose of 300 roentgens whole-body exposure. Taking all those assump-tions into consideration, the committee developed a formula for the radius in miles of the controlled exclusion area: multiplication of the square root of the power level in kilowatts by 0.01. According to this model, a ten-megawatt thermal reactor would need a one-mile exclusion distance, a thousand-megawatt electrical reactor a seventeen-mile exclu-sion radius.[5]

The Safeguard Committee was also concerned with the area imme-diately outside the controlled zone, which it labeled the hazard area. The committee noted that this area was a "region of real but considerably smaller hazard—hazard so small as to be considered tolerable for any individual resident because of the combined effect of safety afforded by the isolation distance and the low probability of a major reactor accident with good design and careful operation." It suggested that the hazard area could be inhabited but that it not contain any large or industrially important centers of population. Furthermore, the committee reported that it could not set the limits of the hazard area by any formula because "not only are the type and power of reactor significant but also the local meteorological, topographical, hydrological and seismological condi-tions lead to different evaluations of hazards in different directions."[6]

The Safeguard Committee never assumed that safety for populated areas depended solely on isolation of the reactors. The locations of the large government reactors at Hanford, Savannah River, and the Idaho National Reactor Testing Station were selected, in large part, because of their isolation. But other AEC facilities constructed in the early 1950s, such as the Argonne Research Reactor, near Chicago, and the Submarine Intermediate Reactor at West Milton, New York, twenty-five to thirty miles from the tri-city area of Schenectady, Troy, and Albany, signaled the need for reliance on engineered safety features that would compensate for their proximity to population centers. The General Electric designers of the West Milton reactor set a major safety precedent by enclosing it in a large steel containment structure. Shortly afterward, the Argonne reactor was enclosed in a gastight concrete building. Containment was also a major feature in the Westinghouse design of the central power station reactor at Shippingport, which also was located in a region of relatively dense population. Except for a few experimental reactors constructed at remote sites and some gas-cooled reactors, all power-reactor facilities designed in the United States after that time included provisions for containment structures. So the safety philosophy that the Reactor Safeguards Committee's exclusion distance represented gradually was superseded by the concept of engineered safety features that permitted reactors to be cited closer to populated areas. Nonetheless, the AEC devised no specific standard incorporating the relationship between distance and containment, and it continued to judge the site for each power-reactor application on a case-by-case basis.[7]

At the "202" hearings in February 1956, Kenneth Fields outlined for the Joint Committee the hazards of power-reactor operation, the agency's attempts to develop more precise standards, and the method it would employ to analyze the safety factors of each civilian-reactor proposal. Regarding sites, Fields pointed out that the growth of the private atomic-power industry would increase pressure to locate reactors near population centers. Hence, the agency assumed, the "isolation principle . . . will probably be replaced or supplemented by a principle of safe containment." Fields pledged that the agency would give careful consideration to site location in relation to the reactor design and would also take into account hydrology, meteorology, seismology, and population density as important siting considerations. Furthermore, the agency would require the designer to look at the possible future appropriateness of the site by attempting to foresee population distribution and to speculate as to whether surrounding areas would be used for commercial, industrial, agricultural, or residential purposes. The AEC would evaluate all those site characteristics in conjunction with the reactor design.[8]

On the same day that Fields testified, Joint Committee member Bourke Hickenlooper (who did not attend the hearing) coincidentally wrote to the Advisory Committee on Reactor Safeguards about the siting question. He wanted to know specifically whether the planned operations at the Shippingport reactor would create any danger to citizens in the surrounding area. He requested the same information about any commercial reactor that might be located near population centers. And he asked whether it might not be wiser to use the isolation concept in lieu of siting near areas of population.[9]

Hickenlooper received a lengthy answer a month later, though not from the Safeguards Committee. Commissioner Willard Libby replied, utilizing the occasion to elaborate the procedures the agency used to evaluate both reactor design and site. Libby placed reactor safety in the larger context of general industrial safety. There was no such thing, he wrote to Hickenlooper, as an "absolutely safe nuclear reactor—just as there [was] no such thing as an absolutely safe chemical plant or oil refinery." Consequently, there always was a "remote *possibility*" of danger to citizens around any reactor, and it was more desirable from the standpoint of safety to locate them in areas of low population density. Safety considerations, however, had to be balanced against the growth needs of the industry. To accommodate both safety and development, Libby reviewed the licensing procedures, which he assured Hickenlooper would "reduce to a reasonable minimum the probability" of an accident causing serious radiation exposure to the public.[10]

The agency's reactor-evaluation procedures, Libby declared, determined that a plant's designers had taken "all reasonable precautions" to assure a low probability for any conceivable mishap. The agency also considered a "second line of defense" by assessing the proposed site in conjunction with the reactor containment. If the review showed that containment would not allow the release of any "significant amount" of radioactive materials into the surrounding region, the agency would be satisfied despite the proximity of the reactor to a densely populated area. The converse, Libby wrote, would also be true. He fully expected that power reactors like Shippingport would rely more on the "philosophy" of containment than of isolation. But in every case there would be a "reasonable distance" between the reactor and major centers of population. The word "reasonable" was a key element in the agency's evaluation, meaning that the regulators would use engineering judgment until experience could produce quantitative standards.[11]

By 1955 the AEC had approved several sites for power reactors under the civilian program. Commonwealth Edison's Dresden, Illinois site, Consolidated Edison's Buchanan, New York location for its Indian Point facility, and the PRDC reactor at Lagoona Beach, Michigan were all located next to large population centers. All three reactors, which received construction permits within weeks after Libby's letter to Hickenlooper, were designed with containment structures. The Indian Point reactor featured a unique double containment because it was only twenty-four miles from New York City.

After passage of the Price-Anderson Act in 1957, which required the Reactor Safeguards Committee to review each reactor application, the committee often directed its attention to site considerations. In the fall of 1957, for example, it reviewed an application for a small, sixty-megawatt thermal test reactor planned by the National Aeronautics and Space Administration at a site three miles from Sandusky, Ohio. The Safeguards Committee reluctantly endorsed the site but indicated its concern by suggesting that a less populated one would have been preferable.[12]

In the summer of 1958, location became the main topic in the Safeguards Committee's evaluation of the Rural Cooperative Power Association's boiling-water reactor, planned for Elk River, Minnesota as a part of the Power Demonstration Reactor Program. In discussing the site with the Safeguards Committee, the AEC's regulatory staff raised questions about its proximity to the small town of Elk River and recommended that only a completely airtight containment would make the location acceptable. The staff based its evaluation on the applicant's projected radiation doses in a postulated maximum credible accident, which it thought were higher than acceptable for an "accident situation based on a reasonably well assured [containment] leakage rate." The company's assumption was that following a complete core meltdown, all the radioactive iodine would be released to the containment. Based on the specified containment-leakage rates in the design, the accident scenario envisioned an extremely high dose of 4800 rems to the thyroid of a person located at the exclusion-zone boundary who remained in the path of the fission-products' airborne trajectory for eight hours. Both the staff and Safeguards Committee members agreed that the quoted dose, if accepted, "may imply approval of a standard which is much too high." After wrestling with various possible design modifications and research-and-development programs that might make the actual accident consequences lower than the company estimated, however, the committee and the staff recommended approval of the site. The committee restated its policy of not considering it "desirable to locate a nuclear reactor of this power level so close to a growing community." But with specific qualifications about final containment design and further land acquisitions, it found the Elk River site acceptable. It stipulated "that the containment vessel will provide an adequate factor of safety and will meet the specified leakage rate and that the state-owned land will be acquired" (enabling the reactor to have a larger exclusion area). The committee admitted that its action represented some relaxation of previous practice in regard to exclusion distance.[13]

The commissioners raised questions about case-by-case site evaluation when they discussed the Elk River reactor at a meeting in early October 1958. They asked Safeguards Committee chairman McCullough to have his group compare the siting standards applied in three already approved reactors (the Sodium Graphite Reactor Experiment (SRE) at Santa Susana, California, the Vallecitos boiling-water reactor at Pleasanton, California, and the Shippingport reactor) with those applied to the Elk River site. Commissioner John Graham specifically wanted to know the effect future population density had on reactor siting and the determination of exclusion distance. McCullough's announcement of the Commission request at the next meeting of the committee sparked a general discussion and review of site-selection criteria.[14]

The meeting turned into a brainstorming session. One committee member pointed out that in determining sites in relation to reactor design the committee had always assumed that a maximum credible accident would occur in every case. But one member noted that the probability of such an accident had not been discussed or analyzed. In its attempt to sort out probable reactor accidents, the committee discussed whether it would be wise to accept serious irradiation of some limited number of people. In the Elk River credible-accident scenario, for example, at one level of probability, twenty-five people would receive a maximum exposure of 4800 rems to the thyroid. Was this acceptable? The committee also mulled over related issues. It was uncertain about the number of people who might be exposed in an accident, the biological implications of exposure, and the effect of such unknowns as future population densities around reactor locations. One member suggested using the philosophy of the National Committee on Radiation Protection of setting arbitrary limits and adjusting them as experience with reactor facilities increased. The Safeguards Committee reached no conclusions in its round-table discussion on how to respond to the Commission's request. It did, however, establish a subcommittee on site-selection standards and charged it with drafting a reply to the Commission comparing the site evaluations of the power reactors recently approved.[15]

The new subcommittee met for the first and only time in New York City on 26 November 1958. Hazards-evaluation branch chief Clifford Beck, who was greatly concerned with the siting problem, also attended. After reviewing several current reactor-site evaluations, the subcommittee concluded that they demonstrated general consistency. Committee member Willard P. Connor, however, noted that evenhanded evaluations would be difficult to achieve in the future. He suggested that the real guide for a reactor site should be that "almost everybody in the vicinity should have a reasonable chance of escaping serious injury in the event of a reactor accident." Aside from estimating possible accidents and attempting to find sites and suitable engineering features that would mitigate them, Connor believed the only way his objective could be attained was to provide designers and regulators with "radiation dosage criteria which represent acceptable emergency doses below the threshold of serious injury."[16]

Connor's comment led to discussion of the exclusion radius. Some committee members thought that the maximum distance might be determined by the sum of the direct and the scattered radiation resulting from the release of fission products to the containment building. In certain accident scenarios, which included leakage of fission products from the containment building, the group believed it might be necessary to increase the exclusion distance. Beck declared that he would be concerned by any exposure of a single individual to more than 25 rems whole-body dose or 200 rems to the thyroid over an eight-hour period. Subcommittee chairman Kenneth Osborn commented that perhaps they should consider whether such a wide margin of safety would produce "overprotection in this industry." Although Osborn asked fellow committee member Leslie Silverman to draft a paper on basic site-selection criteria, the full Safeguards Committee later decided against taking such an initiative. Instead it recommended that the AEC regulatory staff present its ideas to the committee for review and advice. But to provide an answer to the Commission's earlier request for a comparative evaluation of certain reactor sites, committeeman Franklin Gifford drafted a letter for the full committee to AEC chairman John A. McCone.[17]

The Safeguards Committee letter acknowledged the complexity of site evaluation. While admitting that a large number of variables had to be considered from site to site, the committee believed it brought a consistent philosophy to site assessment. The letter focused on Commissioner Graham's concern about exclusion distances and population density at the Elk River plant. It noted that all site evaluations considered reactor-design features such as containment vessels, missile shields, and biological shields as well as hydrology, meteorology, and geology in determining an adequate exclusion distance. The committee believed the Elk River site provided adequate public protection because of the reactor's engineered design features.[18]

The letter also commented on the generally low population level near Elk River. The experts took into account the potential growth of the community. Although such growth was problematical, they believed that potential dangers to an expanded population would be mitigated by the engineered features in the reactor design.[19] Despite the Safeguards Committee's assurances, it was evident to the commissioners that although case-by-case evaluations had some thread of consistency in them, more effort was needed to establish formal guidelines that would apply to all reactor applications.

Harold Price and Clifford Beck also wanted such guidance. Spurred on by the Safeguards Committee recommendation, Beck's staff developed a set of site-evaluation factors to discuss with the advisory group. Beck and Price hoped eventually to produce a draft rule that could be released for public comment. In January 1959 they began the first formal attempt to evaluate sites by means of a published set of factors.

Beck presented to the Safeguards Committee in early 1959 his list of elements that had to be considered in siting. They included exclusion distance, population density, meteorological and seismological considerations, and the hydrology and geology of the site. Exclusion distance and population density outside the exclusion area, Beck explained, were affected by the characteristics of a selected reactor, specifically by the engineered safety devices in the design and the reliance that could be placed on them. Beck told the committee that setting exclusion distances on a reasonable basis should not be too difficult as long as proper emphasis was placed on the reactor-design characteristics. As a counterproposal, committee member Harry W. Newsom, a Duke University physics professor, described a quantitative approach that he had been studying. But his colleague Willard Conner interrupted to claim that such a numerical calculation would not be feasible within his lifetime. For the present time, Conner was satisfied with the qualitative concept that Beck had proposed. The committee agreed to study Beck's list and discuss it again at its next meeting.[20]

By February the environmental subcommittee of the Safeguards Committee, which assumed the functions of the subcommittee on site criteria, had developed its own quantitative approach as a possible guide to overall reactor-safety evaluation. The full committee and members of the AEC staff discussed the new endeavor at length. The concept considered the amount of radioactive material that might be released to the environment in an accident as a function of reactor power, type, containment, and the fission products released. It also took into account the number of people potentially exposed as a function of population density and distribution combined with the meteorology of the area. Those items produced the total radiation dose in rems to the population exposed. The dose indicated one acceptable measure for the site of a particular reactor facility as it related to population density and distribution. But a limiting criterion on the number of rems allowed for a reactor site still had to be established in order for a site to be acceptable.[21]

Beck disagreed with the subcommittee's concept because it did not adequately cover all the variables that were associated with site selection. He believed it would take a long time to develop a sound mathematical formula and insisted that the regulatory program needed something more immediate. In effect, he tabled the subcommittee's quantitative attempt. In its place Beck proposed again the list of factors his staff had developed. Beck noted in particular that his staff proposal specified that small reactors (less than a hundred megawatts thermal) would require an exclusion distance of one-quarter mile. Larger reactors (presumably more than a hundred megawatts thermal) would require one-half to three-quarters of a mile. The Safeguards Committee balked at fixing such radii. Beck promised that he would review the exclusion-distance provision but at the same time notified the committee that his list of factors would be submitted to the Commission for approval for rule-making.[22]

Meeting a short time later with the commissioners, Beck and Price presented the argument that although the staff's list of factors was tentative, comment at this time from industry seemed important. Commissioner Graham agreed, but his colleague John Floberg thought the list much too vague to be effective as a regulation because it would be difficult to enforce. In spite of Floberg's reservation the Commission approved publication of the regulatory staff's recommendations and awaited public comment.[23]

The proposed list elicited so much interest from the industry that the AEC extended the usual thirty-day comment period. Most responses were negative and many objected to the references to exclusion distances—one-quarter mile minimum and one-half mile to three-quarters of a mile for larger reactors—and to the population density distances— "several miles distant from the nearest town or city and for larger reactors a distance of 10 to 20 miles from large cities." Jack K. Busby, president of Pennsylvania Power and Light Company, typified the industry commentary by arguing that it was undesirable to make such specific designations. He suggested that those factors be given consideration only in relation to the proposed type and design safeguards of a particular reactor. R. O. Welch of the Florida West Coast Nuclear Group echoed Busby by declaring that the distances the AEC proposed would "tend to become fixed in the public mind despite words of flexibility used in connection with them." Westinghouse's Robert Wells contended that public safety could not be ensured by any simple condition such as an exclusion area.[24]

At a meeting of the Atomic Industrial Forum in June, called so that industry and the AEC might exchange ideas about the published siting factors, industry representatives sharply criticized the agency's proposed rules. After Harold Price and Rogers McCullough explained the rationale for the AEC proposals, they quickly learned that Forum members thought it was too early to issue such regulations. Philip Sporn, chairman of the session, stated that any standard, no matter how "broad and super safe," would be difficult to change in future years. Guidance was fine, Sporn declared, but not in the form of a strict regulation. Other representatives followed Sporn's line of reasoning. On the one hand, for example, Titus LeClair, the research-and-development manager at Commonwealth Edison, used the case of his company's reactor to point out the vagueness of wording in the AEC proposal. "Is Dresden a large power reactor?" he asked. "It is today, but it is pretty small when compared to a plant of 500 megawatt capacity. We don't know what is large or small." He thought such words in a regulation would only lead to future problems. On the other hand, Consolidated Edison's James Fairman said that rules with set numbers could be too restrictive and might hold back progress. "We want reactors which are safe," he stated, "and we don't want to be tied down to figures which may quickly become outdated."[25]

The Forum ended its stormy session after passing several resolutions supporting further research and symposia on the problem and encouraging both the AEC and the Reactor Safeguards Committee to prepare more guidance. But the industry group specifically resolved that it was too early for the Commission to issue any firm and definitive rule governing reactor-site selection. The AEC concluded from the reaction that although industry wanted general criteria that would define the conditions of site acceptability, it preferred flexible guidelines rather than firmly set regulations. Consequently the AEC withdrew its rule-making proposal.[26]

In the fall of 1959 the Reactor Safeguards Committee spurred another attempt to devise site criteria when it requested the AEC to review broader questions of reactor hazards. The committee asked for a formal study to determine whether available technical knowledge was sufficient to set safety criteria, whether more research was needed, and whether primary reliance should be placed upon engineering judgment and experience. The proposed study suggested several topics to be reviewed: site and environment, core design, reactor kinetics, fuel elements, metallurgy and material radiation effects, instrumentation and control, chemical reactions, system interactions, and reactor organization and operating procedures. Acting quickly on the request in December 1959, the AEC general manager appointed Clifford Beck chairman of a special working group to carry out the study. It included members from several AEC divisions, the Safeguards Committee, and representatives of the atomic industry.[27]

While Beck's *ad hoc* group worked on its report, two new developments affected the siting issue. Separately from his work with the *ad hoc* committee, Beck went through several new drafts of siting criteria that he discussed throughout 1960 with the Safeguards Committee. Equally important, the Joint Committee on Atomic Energy expanded its interest in site criteria and placed pressure on the agency to establish some formal site guidance.

Joint Committee involvement in the siting issue intensified when the AEC regulatory staff informally denied a proposed location offered by Jamestown, New York for a small pressurized-water reactor that was to be built and operated by the AEC. The agency had encouraged small municipalities and public utilities to submit plans for such reactors under its Power Demonstration Reactor Program, but the Jamestown negotiation never reached the formal proposal stage. The rejection of the upstate New York site led Jamestown city officers to complain that the agency was asking them to meet site requirements that had not been in effect when they first discussed the reactor plan with AEC officials in the summer of 1959. When the case came to its attention, the Joint Committee perceived the need for more formal site criteria.[28]

Chairman McCone, testifying before the congressional oversight group in April, acknowledged that siting had become a crucial problem. He thought that the technology had reached a point where more definitive guidance should be given so that prospective power-plant contractors could proceed with some assurance. McCone told the Joint Committee that the new AEC requirements on siting should be completed soon. Later in the same hearings, Rogers McCullough, just finishing his term as chairman of the Reactor Safeguards Committee, explained that site selection involved so many complex factors that his committee had been reluctant to recommend written criteria out of fear that the siting elements would "be misinterpreted and would acquire a sanctity beyond their value." But according to McCone's earlier commitment, McCullough affirmed that the committee now believed the "time has come to put these criteria in writing."[29]

The Joint Committee indicated that it would hold the AEC to its word. James Van Zandt, a committee member from Pennsylvania, told AEC officials at the April hearing that the presence at the hearing of Congressman Charles Goodell, who represented the district that included Jamestown, was "indicative of the great interest he has in this subject." Later that year, Chet Holifield received a letter from Oliver Townsend, the director of the New York State Office of Atomic Development, suggesting hearings in 1961 on a national policy for reactor siting. Citing the scrubbed Jamestown project, Townsend made the request because he worried that without such a policy, a considerable amount of effort was wasted by launching new atomic projects only to have them "disapproved because of previously unknown safeguards considerations."[30]

Meanwhile, both the regulatory staff and the Safeguards Committee held several meetings throughout the summer and fall of 1960 to work out new site criteria. To do so first required agreement on certain assumptions and then development of criteria to mitigate any circumstances that might arise in the event of an accident. Using their collective experience with evaluating earlier reactors, both the committee and the staff agreed that determining the maximum credible accident was the logical starting point. They also decided to use light-water reactors in their deliberations because most experience had been with those machines and most currently proposed commercial reactors were of that type. After fixing the maximum credible accident, the regulators assumed they could establish and appraise appropriate engineered design safeguards in conjunction with the site evaluation.[31]

The idea of a maximum credible accident was not new, although the term had not acquired popularity until 1959 or 1960. The original Reactor Safeguard Committee had instituted a "worst case" accident scenario in the late 1940s when it evaluated the safety of the early government-owned reactors. The 1957 WASH–740 report had postulated the concept of a conceivable accident in arriving at its pessimistic conclusions, and the aborted 1959 attempt at site-criteria rule-making had used the more restrictive term "credible accident." The idea of a general accident scenario posed a difficult dilemma. On the one hand, if worst conceivable accidents were considered, only sites removed from populated areas by hundreds of miles were likely to be suitable. On the other hand, if enough engineered safeguard features were included in a reactor design to protect against worst conceivable accidents (assuming the safeguards worked and no potential accidents had been overlooked), any site would be acceptable. Both of those positions seemed unrealistic, so the regulators found a middle ground: the maximum credible accident.[32]

The search for the maximum credible accident frustrated the regulators because they could never be entirely assured that all potential accidents had been considered. In general terms, they finally decided that an accident was in the maximum credible category if it was caused by the one single equipment failure or operational error that would result in the most hazardous release of fission products. Furthermore, no other postulated credible accident could exceed the consequences of this one. In light-water reactors the regulators postulated the maximum credible accident as the complete rupture of a major or large pipe resulting in complete loss of coolant, with consequent expansion of the coolant as flashing steam, meltdown of the fuel, and partial release of the fission-product inventory to the containment atmosphere. This accident scenario assumed that the reactor's two inner safety barriers would be breached: the fuel cladding and the primary-coolant piping system. It also assumed that the outer containment, the last barrier to a major release of the fission products to the outside environment, would remain secure. While both the Safeguards Committee and the regulatory staff considered this maximum credible accident highly unlikely, it became an important element for judging both reactor design and site.[33]

Clifford Beck, who continued to spearhead the hazards-staff effort in developing the siting criteria, also led the latest technical discussions with the Safeguards Committee. Independently, both the Safeguards Committee's environmental subcommittee and Beck's staff had drawn up their own criteria. Despite some differences the two documents were remarkably similar and provided the basic grounds for discussion. The staff and the committee agreed, for example, on certain assumptions: that power reactors were expected to be located in inhabited areas, that considerable confidence existed among experts about the relatively small probability of a maximum credible accident, that the containment structure could not be breached by such an accident, and that the radioactive leakage rate from the containment to the environment would be 0.1 percent per day. Some disagreement occurred on one issue, the estimation of the upper functional limit on release of the fission-product inventory to the containment building. Through negotiation, Beck eventually reached agreement with the committee to assume that nearly 16 percent of the total fission-product inventory would be released to the containment structure in a maximum credible accident. This amounted to 100 percent of the noble gases, 50 percent of the halogens, and 1 percent of the solids. The other 84 percent remained trapped within the fuel matrix of the reactor's primary system.[34]

Those assumptions formed the starting point for determining the radiation hazard to people inhabiting the area surrounding a reactor. For those living in close proximity, the disabled reactor could become a source of direct gamma radiation, attenuated by such factors as the structural shielding, distance, decay time, and topographical shielding. For people at more distant points, the principal determinant was transport by air of the radioactive materials leaking from the containment structure. Airborne transit made several other considerations important, such as the nature of the leaking radioactive materials, release height, particle deposition with distance, the direction, speed, and variability of wind, and air temperature gradients. Many of these elements, of course, were functions of the particular area where the reactor was located. From this complex of interwoven technical factors, Beck and his staff formulated their site-selection criteria.[35]

The draft criteria, presented to the environmental subcommittee in late August 1960 and to the full Safeguards Committee a month later, established three distances for a reactor of any given power level. Beck labeled them "benchmarks"—specifically, an exclusion distance, an evacuation distance, and a population-center distance. The exclusion area, under the complete control of the reactor owner, had an outer-limit distance at which, following the onset of a maximum credible accident, the total radiation dose received by an individual in two hours would not exceed a 25-rem whole-body exposure or 300 rems to the thyroid from radioactive iodine. The 25-rem whole-body dose was taken from the accidental or emergency once-in-a-lifetime dose for radiation workers recommended by the National Committee on Radiation Protection. While the NCRP made no specific recommendation on emergency exposure to radioactive iodine and there was disagreement among the experts, many believed that 300 rems to the thyroid was a safe upper-limit figure. The second benchmark was the evacuation area that immediately surrounded the exclusion area. The evacuation area had an outer-limit distance at which an individual would receive the same dose limit as one received at the exclusion distance, but for the entire duration of the accident instead of during the two-hour period specified in the first benchmark.[36]

Since a small theoretical possibility existed that a more serious accident than the maximum credible accident might occur, Beck's group thought it prudent to provide the third benchmark in the criteria. The population-center distance, the length from the reactor to the nearest boundary of a population area containing more than twenty-five thousand residents, was defined either in terms of the projected effects in the event of a contained maximum credible accident or in terms of the distance that would prevent any lethal exposure in the event of a conceivable accident in which the containment was breached. In the most serious accident of the latter kind, the scenario assumed a complete puff release from the containment of 100 percent of the noble gases, 25 percent of the halogens, and 1 percent of the solids. Beck's staff fixed the population center distance at 133⅓ percent of the evacuation distance.[37]

Appended to the criteria, as a sample, were methods used to calculate the benchmark distances. By simplifying assumptions, specifying that certain secondary factors were ignored, and arbitrarily fixing the values of certain key elements, the computations were a practical and necessary exercise in light of the highly complex phenomena that varied over a wide range of values. Beck and his staff recognized the substantial degree of artificiality and arbitrariness in their determinations. They admitted that the results obtained were only approximations compared with what might be obtained if the effects of all the variables and influencing factors could be recognized. But that, they conceded, was an impossibility in the present state of the technology and particularly with the lack of operating experience. The regulatory staff nonetheless believed that because of its protective assumptions and approximations in the criteria, the net effect gave a greater margin of safety than would be the case if more precise calculations could be made. They justified the criteria not so much on their technical exactness as on the value of simply defining a basis upon which the agency could approach judgments on reactor-site suitability at that time.[38]

Beck also provided other familiar elements in the criteria that were to be used in conjunction with the benchmark distances. Earthquake history (no reactor could be located within one-half mile of a known earthquake fault), special meteorological conditions at any specific site, and geological and hydrological characteristics all might have a bearing on the consequences of an escape of radioactive material and might offset the safety provided in the distance factors. Beck also observed that where particularly unfavorable features existed, the site might still be found acceptable if the facility design included adequate engineered safeguards. Consequently, he argued, the criteria never would provide fully objective procedures for site selection. Rather, the criteria, and specifically the benchmark distances, merely defined a starting point in the site-evaluation process. But he thought the new criteria were a substantial improvement over the more subjective case-by-case method utilized to that time.[39]

The proposed criteria met opposition from the Safeguards Committee. Without taking exception to the figures set by Beck's study, the committee contended that his format would be too binding on applicants and designers if issued as regulations. The advisory group preferred a more general statement. Independently, it sent its reservations to the Commission in September 1960. Coincidentally, the Commission received at the same time the report of the general manager's *ad hoc* committee on overall reactor-safety criteria that had been chaired by Beck. On the subject of site criteria the Safeguards Committee and the *ad hoc* group were at odds with each other.[40]

The report of the general manager's *ad hoc* committee included several recommendations, among which it cautioned against any current attempt to standardize reactor design or various reactor components. The report instead urged a continuing effort by the agency to write safety guides and to tabulate safety-performance objectives that could be issued to the industry as general guides rather than as hard-and-fast regulations. The *ad hoc* group also recommended that the AEC provide guidance for the industry on the preparation of hazards-summary reports and on general licensing procedures. But in contrast with those general recommendations was a suggestion on reactor-site criteria that reflected Beck's strong feeling on the subject. The committee called for "established rules, which may of necessity involve some degree of arbitrariness, by which sites that would be considered acceptable for locations of reactors can be selected."[41]

In its report to the Commission the Safeguards Committee detailed its objections to issuing the AEC site criteria in regulation form. The committee worried that Beck's proposed criteria might become so firm that it would hamper adaptation or modification to keep pace with changes as the industry developed. From a technical viewpoint, the committee stated, the simplification represented by the criteria, if fixed by regulation, might validate some expressions that were at best approximations. Safeguards Committee chairman Leslie Silverman wrote in the report that the accuracy of the numbers selected could not be proven by experimental or empirical data. Consequently, the committee feared that the numerical estimates might give the public an unwarranted impression of certainty that could not be supported under detailed examination. Furthermore, it thought that siting regulations with set numbers would deter future efforts to develop better safety limits and at the same time would reduce an applicant's interest in remaining alert for any unforeseen disadvantages of a site.[42]

The committee emphasized that its reservations about the draft criteria did not imply an absence of bases for judging sites. It simply made the point that site selection remained largely a matter of judgment. Consequently, the committee recommended its alternative to the publication of the site criteria as a proposed regulation. Beck and his staff, the committee suggested, should present their criteria as papers in technical journals. Such articles would have the "status of the opinion of an informed technical individual, but would not . . . have the rigidity of a Commission policy statement."[43]

Despite the committee's reservations, Price and Beck presented the staff criteria to the commissioners in December 1960 for their approval to release them for public comment. After briefing the Commission on the document's essential points, Beck outlined the criticism he anticipated. He thought some would object to excessive arbitrariness in the calculation of the benchmark distances. But he believed that the imprecision of the benchmarks would be compensated by permitting adjustments that recognized differences in individual cases. He admitted that the lack of objectivity in that procedure would probably also cause criticism. But he hoped that time and substantial experience with reactors would result in more objective guidance. While acceding to the Safeguards Committee's charge that it was premature to put numbers on highly complex variables, Beck took a broader view that this method was preferable to the undefined procedures currently being used. He argued that the Safeguards Committee's concern that arbitrary figures might suppress incentive for further research into more realistic values was strictly a matter of opinion. Beck speculated that an opposite result would occur. He told the Commission that "greater efforts will be expended to 'beat the system,' to show that the real numbers for an applicant's particular reactor are quite different from and more favorable than those specified."[44]

Beck envisioned several benefits accruing from adoption of the criteria. Establishment of the benchmarks would represent a step forward from past practice, in which there were no published guidelines and the whole process was subjective. Providing a series of steps and relationships between various parameters would, he thought, demonstrate the relationship of the important factors in site selection. In addition, the calculations used in the criteria would show how large the existing margins of safety were in reactor location. And identification of the factors involved in a siting problem would guide further research that would help increase reactor safety.[45]

Although the commissioners agreed on the need for the criteria, they were concerned about the Safeguards Committee's objections. Chairman McCone, anxious to produce some rules, especially in view of his earlier commitment to the Joint Committee on Atomic Energy, wanted to move quickly on the issue. Somewhat irked at the Safeguards Committee's reservations, McCone declared that it was imperative for the agency to establish the criteria as soon as possible in order to gain the confidence of both the public and the industry. Referring to the request by the state of New York to the Joint Committee to hold hearings on siting, McCone stated he hoped to avoid such a congressional inquiry. He suggested a meeting between the Commission and the Safeguards Committee early in 1961 to work out the differences.[46]

McCone, Olson, and Graham sought a basis for compromise when they met with the Safeguards Committee at its regular monthly meeting in early January. New committee chairman Theos J. Thompson and veteran committeeman Abel Wolman led the discussion on the committee's concerns. Wolman pointed out that committee members, because of the uncertainty about the basic numbers for allowable radiation exposure, were reluctant to agree to firm regulations. He sought a different way to notify industry and the public about the qualitative and quantitative methods used to determine reactor locations. Thompson interjected that most industrial groups shared the committee's reluctance to establish firm site rules at that time. Commissioner Olson countered that the agency had an obligation to inform the public and so it was asking the Safeguards Committee's advice and concurrence. He requested that the reactor experts reconcile their differences with Beck's draft criteria in order to produce something suitable for publication.[47]

Price, Beck, and committee members Thompson and meteorologist Franklin Gifford met to discuss their differing opinions. They agreed on an important compromise that changed the concept embodied in the criteria from a rule to a guide. This satisfied the committee's apprehension that the document would assume a rigid legalistic form; as a guide it would be more flexible and thus easier to change in the future as research and experience dictated. Price and Beck accepted the change readily. They believed it was a small concession to make for the committee's concurrence.[48]

Despite the compromise, the consensus of the full Safeguards Committee still found the latest version of the AEC's site requirements unacceptable. But the group was willing to discuss the issue further with the AEC staff. Time was now important, Price told the committee. He pointed out that Joint Committee "202" hearings were scheduled for late February and that he wanted to present concrete proposals to the legislators to avoid a renewal of past criticism. Hopeful that a satisfactory set of guides could be published soon, Price promised that Beck's staff would continue to refine the siting criteria during the public-review period. He hoped the Safeguards Committee would not publicly oppose the effort, even if it did not formally approve publication of the proposed guides. The committee refused to give Price that assurance. After lengthy consideration in executive session, it informed Price that it would hold a special meeting prior to the Joint Committee hearings to consider any new compromise paper.[49]

Price, Beck, Thompson, and Gifford worked on further revisions for presentation to the special Safeguards Committee meeting. In the negotiations Thompson and Gifford insisted that the committee's list of objectives for reactor siting, which had been formally submitted to the Commission in December, be in the criteria introduction. Price and Beck easily agreed. The committee's goals, in fact, blended nicely with the staff's intent for the criteria by spelling out the basic objectives it believed achievable: that serious injury to individuals off-site should be avoided if an unlikely, but still credible, accident should occur; even if a more serious accident (not normally considered credible) should occur, the number of people killed should not be catastrophic; and the average radiation dose that large numbers of people might receive should be low.[50]

The negotiators also agreed on other deletions and changes in terminology. The "evacuation area," for example, was changed to a less ominous sounding term, "low population zone." The term "benchmark distance" was eliminated, although a table of distances and the example calculating those distances remained appended to the document. Further refinement deleted the references to "maximum credible accident" but left in the references to the assumed fission-product release. This served the same purpose.[51]

Thompson discussed the revisions with the full Safeguards Committee at its special meeting. He reported that Price had been conciliatory toward the suggested changes because he wanted committee approval before recommending publication to the Commission. Lengthy discussion among the members underscored again their conviction that the document should be presented as a guide and not as a firm rule. One cynical member pointed out that the use of the word "criteria" in the title and "guide" in the body of the document was contradictory. As in earlier discussions, the major worry among several members concerned the numbers used in the sample calculation. They thought such figures would take on an importance not intended in a guide and feared that acceptance of the numbers might limit future improvements in safer reactor designs. For this reason, if the committee accepted the sample calculation, it wanted the appendix clearly marked as an example and "not as gospel." In the end, the group accepted the criteria for publication but reserved the right to consider it further. Basically unchanged by the committee's review, with the exception of the change from a rule to a guide, the revised criteria received quick Commission approval for publication.[52]

Publication of the site guidelines satisfied the complaints of the Joint Committee on Atomic Energy. Oliver Townsend, the New York State official who had been pressuring the Joint Committee for public hearings on site criteria, continued his effort. But publication of the criteria allowed the AEC to argue successfully that the rule-making procedure would serve the same purpose as a public hearing.[53]

The new criteria generated substantial interest. Over the 120-day public-comment period, the AEC received thirty-four formal comments from individuals and organizations. Most critiques came from major utilities that were interested in building power reactors and from reactor vendors. Some professional organizations commented, such as the American Standards Association and the Society of Naval Architects and Marine Engineers. Several local, state, and federal agencies, ranging from the Bay Area (California) Pollution Control District to the State of New York Department of Health to the Maritime Administration of the Commerce Department, supplied detailed commentary. Three foreign groups also submitted their concerns: the French Power Bureau, the Japan Atomic Industrial Forum, and the Japan Atomic Power Company.[54]

The largest group of comments gave strong support to the agency's effort to issue guidance in some form. The regulators especially appreciated the positive response toward issuing exposure values with respect to potential low-probability accidents. Although the values were never intended to suggest acceptable exposures, most commentators disapproved their use as upper-limit guides. Only one comment, from J. A. Swartout at the Oak Ridge National Laboratory, questioned in detail the assumption that a 300-rem thyroid exposure was a safe conservative value. Swartout argued that the criterion implied that 300-rem thyroid exposure was "somehow equivalent to the 25 rems whole body exposure." He mentioned that three groups concerned with formulating radiation-protection standards—the International Commission on Radiological Protection, the National Committee on Radiation Protection, and the recently established Federal Radiation Council—had recommended that occupational iodine exposure for the thyroid be set at a six-to-one ratio to total-body dose. In light of this, the Oak Ridge scientist believed that only a 150-rem iodine exposure was justified. Swartout suspected that the higher thyroid-exposure value in the site criteria was based on an assumption that exposed persons could be treated in such a way as to reduce their exposure by a factor of two. If this was true, Swartout wrote to the agency, it did not appear practical or realistic. He contended that it could only be justified for a particular reactor if the facility had emergency plans that would round up all persons evacuated from the low population zone and have them treated.[55]

The Reactor Safeguards Committee had been concerned with Beck's exposure figures when it had considered the draft criteria, and at the time had asked for further clarification. In March 1961 Charles Dunham, AEC director of Biology and Medicine, discussed the subject with the committee. He mentioned that the 25-rem figure for emergency exposure was generally accepted by the radiation-standards groups but that there was no similarly acceptable figure for iodine dose to the thyroid. Thus the 300-rem number was completely arbitrary. No record of any further discussion of that figure was made and the criteria continued to use the 25-rem whole-body dose and the 300-rem thyroid exposure.[56]

The main objection to the published criteria centered on the inclusion as an appendix of the sample calculation of distances. Because exact numerical values were cited in the computation, many commentators voiced concern that the computation gave an undue rigidity to the criteria, which otherwise, they thought, allowed considerable flexibility. Furthermore, most comments noted that the example tended to emphasize the concept of reactor isolation with only minimum emphasis given for eventual substitution of engineered safeguards for the distance factor. The example's seemingly rigid concept toward isolation particularly alarmed the utilities and the reactor vendors who wanted siting closer to population centers. Suggestions for changes included deletion of the example, inclusion of additional examples, or the publication of such examples in some other form.[57]

In a closely related objection, most commentators complained that the overall criteria gave too much conceptual emphasis to the distance factors and plant isolation and not enough to the engineered safety features designed into the facilities. Atomics International submitted a typical comment: "We . . . cannot agree with the . . . instinct in the Commission's concept of a population center distance that conservatism in the building of reactors and geographical isolation of reactors are analogous. We submit that the key to conservatism . . . is reactor design, not reactor location." Philip Sporn of the American Electric Power Service Corporation, argued that conservatism in estimating safety requirements should be applied to the "safeguards which need to be incorporated in the reactor facility and to the analysis of the probability and consequences of an accident, and not in some unrelated manner to the determination of site distances." In a similar vein, Bechtel Corporation's W. Kenneth Davis wrote that "design precautions can substitute for greater isolation and these should be given full consideration."[58]

Objections to other parts of the criteria pointed out shortcomings that needed to be reviewed. Since the United States was the leader in reactor technology, its guidance was generally accepted by friendly foreign nations. The isolation distances, in this case, greatly concerned the Japanese atomic-power industry, which was confronted with limited land available for reactor sites. The opinions of Japanese officials raised an issue, not considered before, of whether the criteria should apply to foreign nations. The agency also received extensive criticism that the guides did not provide for multiple reactors at one site and that it was not clear how they might apply to mobile reactors. If the guides were applied in their existing form, several commentators pointed out, atomic-powered ships, such as the NS *Savannah*, which was about to begin sea trials, would be denied entry and operation in ports. Moreover, many comments raised an old concern that had been discussed before the criteria were issued—how future population growth might affect sites after their initial approval.[59]

As the agency received these responses, the Atomic Industrial Forum decided to take action beyond merely commenting on the proposed criteria. The Forum's standing twenty-four-member Reactor Safety Committee, after reviewing the criteria, met with Clifford Beck on 17 March. Bechtel's Davis chaired the group. In a three-hour discussion the members agreed that the published criteria were a valuable contribution toward articulation of siting policy. They were, however, almost unanimous in their opposition to two features of the criteria. They believed the document offered too many open invitations for prospective intervenors and that the emphasis on distance and isolation over engineered safeguards would establish a principle that would be difficult to change. They agreed to study the situation further and submit suggestions for revisions.[60]

Subsequently the Forum Reactor Safety Committee established a subcommittee and directed it to redraft completely the AEC criteria. Roy Shoults of General Electric chaired the group, which also included Davis, Roger Coe of Yankee Atomic Electric, James Fairman of Consolidated Edison, John Gray of Nuclear Utilities Services, Woodrow Johnson of Westinghouse, and Harold Vann of the architectural engineering firm of Jackson and Moreland. Focusing on the concerns expressed by the main committee to Beck at the March meeting, the subcommittee overhauled the criteria to give greater recognition to the importance of the engineered design of a proposed reactor in relation to population, distance, and physical characteristics of the site. In addition, they tried to keep the criteria flexible enough to accommodate future experience in reactor construction and operation.[61]

The subcommittee's redraft emphasized four changes. It limited the criteria's application to power reactors, thus excluding test reactors that had been included in the AEC draft. The group thought that since test reactors were designed for experimental operations, they should not be subject to the same rules as power stations. Also eliminated in the redraft was the sample calculation for determining distances. Such examples should be published in the scientific literature, rather than in official AEC statements, the group recommended. In that way the calculations would be generally available to the technical community but would not give undue rigidity to the criteria. In addition, the Forum members deleted the population-center distance concept on the premise that the additional distance factor determined by multiplying the low population radius by the arbitrary value of one and one-third lacked a technological basis. In lieu of that concept the group suggested that the AEC or the Federal Radiation Council develop a man-rem radiation-exposure limit expressed as a function of population, distance, and density. Finally, the redraft changed the order of several sections of the criteria in order to focus more attention on the importance of the interrelationship between reactor design, site characteristics, population density, and distance. Forum members reiterated those points in a subsequent meeting with AEC officials and Safeguards Committee members. Written comments submitted by Consolidated Edison, Allis-Chalmers, Bechtel, and Westinghouse likewise underscored the importance the industry placed on engineered safety features. Those organizations made clear their concurrence with the views of the Forum subcommittee.[62]

While the regulatory staff worked on revising the draft criteria in the fall of 1961, Clifford Beck, by now a widely recognized expert on siting policy, told meetings of the American Nuclear Society and the United States and Japanese Atomic Industrial Forums that the AEC wanted to make its criteria flexible as well as sensitive to engineered safeguards and future operating experience. He reminded his audiences that the past practice in site selection, amounting to a compromise between dependence on safeguards and some degree of isolation, was the basis upon which the AEC had prepared earlier criteria. Beck thought those principles would continue to govern formulation of any final site regulation. He affirmed, however, that each reactor and site still had to be considered on its own merits, allowing for deviation from the criteria when it was clearly justified.[63]

The regulatory staff spent numerous hours in late 1961 revising the criteria. The regulators considered all of the suggested revisions but gave particular emphasis to the Atomic Industrial Forum's redraft. A comparison of the Forum document with the revised criteria presented to the Commission in early 1962 showed whole sections extracted verbatim from the Forum's proposal. The overall effect strengthened reliance on engineered safeguards relative to isolation—a key objective of the industry group.[64]

A major change that went halfway in meeting one of the industry's objections deleted the sample calculation on determining distances. But the regulators recognized the advantage such an example could provide applicants and separately published a technical paper that included the computations and provided supplementary explanatory information. The published technical information document, commonly referred to by its agency designation TID 14844, remained as the key reference work to the basic criteria. In addition, the regulatory staff rewrote the "purpose" section of the criteria to state clearly that the criteria were guides that were subject to later revision. In the prefatory statement of considerations they added a new sentence specifying that applicants were "free—and indeed encouraged—to demonstrate to the Commission the applicability and significance of considerations other than those set forth in the guides."[65]

When the staff reviewed the critical comments on the criteria's seemingly greater emphasis on distance factors than on engineered safeguards, it concluded that the commentators were misreading the document. The new staff draft nonetheless addressed the issue by incorporating the Forum's suggested rearrangement of "factors to be considered" so that "characteristics of reactor design and proposed operation" headed the list. The revised listing included such items as the extent to which generally accepted engineering standards were applied to the reactor design, the presence of unique or unusual features that had a significant bearing on the probability or consequences of an accident, the special safety features that were engineered into the facility, and the barriers that had to be breached before a release of radioactive material to the environment could occur.[66]

The population-center distance had raised particularly strong objections from commentators because of its obviously arbitrary derivation. But only the Atomic Industrial Forum had suggested a partial alternative. It proposed deleting the concept and undertaking studies to define population centers more precisely in terms of a man-rem concept. After considering the issue, the regulators decided that it was better to leave the present population-center distance factor in the criteria because it, along with the other factors used, roughly followed the assumptions employed in existing siting practices. As a partial concession to those who had challenged the population-center distance formula, the revision stated that the AEC would study further the man-rem concept.[67]

The staff added a new section on multiple reactors at one site. It decided that if two or more machines at the same site were independent to the extent that an accident at one would not result in a simultaneous accident or disruption of operation of adjacent reactors, the distance factors in the criteria could be determined on the basis of treating the reactors individually. If interconnections existed that might affect the safety of either reactor, then the distances would be determined on the basis that all interconnected reactors emitted their postulated fission-product release simultaneously.[68]

Other objections were more easily handled. Mobile reactors were excluded. The regulators hedged on the application of the criteria to foreign countries by stating that they were based on characteristic conditions in the United States. Therefore the document might not represent the significant elements in other countries whose "national needs, resources, policies, and other factors may be greatly different." On the question of population growth the criteria remained silent. The regulatory staff simply noted that objections had been raised over the lack of specific guidance but added that the issue could not be definitively resolved. The staff thought the criteria tended to require distances that would forestall the problem for at least the near future. In the meantime it hoped accumulated experience with engineered safeguards would "make it possible to rely with more surety on such factors rather than isolation."[69]

After gaining approval of the Reactor Safeguards Committee, which thought the new document well represented the general guidelines it had wanted earlier, Price presented it to the Commission. The staff paper accompanying the document noted that the criteria did not represent a different approach to reactor siting from that used to date. Rather it represented an attempt to articulate those practices. Both Price and Beck recognized that the new regulation would not eliminate the continuing need for a large degree of subjective judgment by both the agency and industry in site selection. But they thought final publication was a significant step toward making evaluations more objective while at the same time implying an important obligation to continue the effort to define reactor siting standards more explicitly. The Commission approved the criteria on 23 March 1962. They were published on 1 June and took effect thirty days later.[70]

In establishing the site criteria the AEC codified its accumulated knowledge on evaluating sites for power reactors. Early experience with government-owned, noncontained reactors had necessitated emphasis on site isolation. That concept required rethinking with the advent of reactors for commercial power production that needed to be near electric load centers. Consequently, the regulators placed greater importance on the engineered safety features of the facilities, but without discarding isolation as a significant factor. The lengthy technical negotiations between the regulatory staff and the Reactor Safeguards Committee and subsequently with the industrial community shaped the compromises that produced that final regulation.

A major component in site evaluation involved the postulation of a maximum credible accident that might cause radioactive release to areas beyond the site. From this difficult determination the regulators next had to move to still another formidable problem—specifying potential exposure doses to persons off-site. The amount of fission products released to the environment could vary from reactor to reactor, so the margin of safety in any calculation was inexact. But by estimating the radioactive inventory released to the containment building in any particular reactor, the regulators at least had a starting point for calculating the potential radiological hazard in the surrounding area.

Beck and his staff used cautious assumptions incorporating wide safety margins about the postulated accident, exposure levels, and the meteorological characteristics of the site. Proceeding from those assumptions, they established the benchmark distances for any given reactor from various population densities. Discounting the editing changes in terminology and the reservations about the applicability of the findings to mobile reactors and foreign countries, the criteria developed by early 1960 essentially remained the basis for the final 1962 product.

The 1962 siting criteria reflected and were consistent with prior site decisions on commercial power reactors. This was shown through the application of the criteria's calculations to several reactor projects that had been proposed or were authorized for construction. The Commonwealth Edison Dresden reactor, for example, with a power level of 630 megawatts thermal, had a calculated exclusion distance of 0.5 miles, which corresponded exactly with the actual exclusion distance at the facility. Its calculated population-center distance was 9.9 miles while the actual distance to the population center was 14 miles. The 585-megawatt-thermal Indian Point reactor had a calculated 0.48-mile exclusion distance by application of the criteria, while the actual distance was only 0.3 miles. The trade-off in this case, however, was an engineered safe-guard—the use of a unique double containment building that the reg-ulators believed compensated for the reduced exclusion area. The actual distance to the population center was 17 miles, well outside the perimeter of the calculated 9.9-mile distance. The smaller 58-megawatt-thermal Elk River reactor, which had caused the Commission to question siting prac-tices in 1958, also exceeded the minimum criteria. The staff calculated its exclusion distance at 0.22 miles while the actual distance was 0.23. The population-center distance, calculated at 2.0 miles, was easily within the actual 20 miles of the nearest densely populated area.[71]

Application of the actual distances for existing reactors against the withdrawn 1959 criteria pointed out again the consistency between siting practices and criteria development. The 1959 version suggested a min-imum exclusion distance for all reactors of 0.25 miles and from 0.5 to 0.75 miles for "large reactors" (Beck had informally used 100 megawatts thermal to differentiate between large and small reactors). The large Dresden and Indian Point reactors both met the minimum suggested distance while the small Elk River facility was somewhat short with a distance of 0.23 miles. Indian Point failed the one-half mile minimum since its exclusion area covered only 0.3 miles, but again, the reactor's engineered double containment safeguard was a compensating consid-eration. In the category of population density in surrounding areas, the 1959 criteria suggested that all reactors be "several miles distant from the nearest town or city and for large reactors a distance of 10 to 20 miles from large cities." Dresden with 14 miles, Indian Point with 17 miles, and Elk River with 20 miles would have met that criterion.[72]

In a broader context, the site-criteria issue was an example of the AEC seeking to fulfill its legally mandated roles under the Atomic Energy Act of both protecting public health and safety and actively developing a new industry. The AEC regulators confidently assumed that their criteria incorporated an ample margin of safety while at the same time allowed for the industry view that commercial power reactors should be located close to population centers where the greatest demand for electricity existed. In accepting the industry position, the regulators had to place added emphasis on engineered safety features and continue to make site evaluations on a case-by-case basis.

Lewis L. Strauss (Credit: National Archives)

Thomas E. Murray (Credit: National Archives)

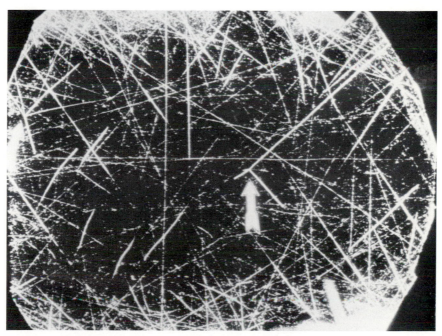

First photograph of splitting of atom, Stanford University, July 1947. (Credit: National Archives)

Reactor core being lowered into position at Shippingport (Pa.) nuclear power plant, October 1957. (Credit: National Archives)

Ceremony on occasion of first electricity generated by General Electric's prototype plant at West Milton, New York, July 1955. (Credit: National Archives)

Standing behind a brick wall, a technician at Brookhaven National Laboratory removes plug from lead shield containing radioactive tantalum. Man at his left holds Geiger counter to monitor radiation levels. (Credit: National Archives)

Willard F. Libby (Credit: National Archives)

Chet Holifield (Courtesy of Chet Holifield)

Damaged core caused by power surge in AEC's Experimental Breeder Reactor, November 1955. (Credit: National Archives)

Power Reactor Development Company's fast breeder reactor, Lagoona Beach, Michigan, July 1958. (Credit: National Archives)

Pressure vessel being moved into PRDC plant, July 1958. (Courtesy of Combustion Engineering, Inc.)

John A. McCone (Credit: National Archives)

President Kennedy at Los Alamos Scientific Laboratory, December 1962. To his right is AEC Chairman Glenn T. Seaborg and to his left is Los Alamos Director Norris Bradbury. To Bradbury's left is Senator Clinton P. Anderson. (Credit: Library of Congress)

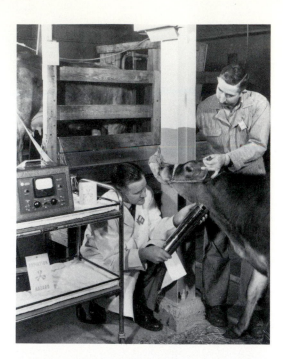

Scientists at Oak Ridge National Laboratory checking the thyroid of a heifer to detect uptake of radioactive iodine following injection. (Credit: National Archives)

Underground uranium mine. The hose on the right provided ventilation. (Credit: National Archives)

Piles of uranium ore at AEC's ore-buying station in Monticello, Utah. (Credit: National Archives)

Worker at Oak Ridge National Laboratory uses "frisker" to check for radiation on his body and clothing. (Credit: National Archives)

Steel drums containing solid radioactive wastes being loaded aboard U.S. Navy ship for disposal at sea. (Credit: National Archives)

Low-level radioactive wastes being dumped into trenches for land burial at AEC's National Reactor Testing Center, Arco, Idaho. Man on truck wears protective clothing and respirator while man to his left monitors radiation. (Credit: National Archives)

As difficult as it was to write a technical regulation that satisfied the agency's many constituencies, the AEC accepted the realities imposed by a developing industry and the rapidly changing nature of the technology. The staff analysis of the final document concluded that it was "intended as an interim measure until the state of the art allows more definitive standards to be developed." So rather than being a set of hard-and-fast standards, the criteria served as an interim guide that articulated site-selection practices used to that time. The staff admitted that application of the site criteria would not eliminate the need for a large degree of subjective judgment by both the agency and the industry. They considered it, however, a significant step forward in making site evaluations more objective.[73]

IX

THE POLITICS OF RADIATION
PROTECTION

Neither the dissension over the Power Reactor Development Company reactor nor the preparation of indemnity legislation and site criteria, despite their important implications for atomic-power development, attracted a great deal of public attention. Although all proceeded as awareness of radiation hazards was increasing, they did not generate the depth of public concern or breadth of debate that the fallout issue aroused. Questions about the risks posed by fallout from weapons testing continued to produce not only scientific disputes but also political controversy. In 1959, when fallout levels reached new peaks, growing misgivings about the AEC's performance in safeguarding public health prompted President Eisenhower to reorganize the federal government's radiation-protection programs and reduce the agency's role in evaluating fallout risks. But the changes did not end the political debate, which reemerged when fallout measurements rose again in 1961 and 1962. Only after President John F. Kennedy negotiated a ban on atmospheric weapons-testing with the Soviet Union and Great Britain did radiation protection cease being a major public and political issue and return, at least temporarily, to being a question of interest primarily to scientists.

In August 1958 Eisenhower, who was concerned about the health risks of weapons testing, anxious to slow the arms race, and hopeful of progress toward disarmament, declared a moratorium on U.S. nuclear explosions. The British agreed to the suspension, but the Soviets refused to announce whether or not they would go along. As the 31 October deadline for the moratorium approached, all three nuclear powers conducted extensive tests; the total number of experimental detonations in

1958 exceeded that of any previous year. The Soviets observed the suspension after their final shots in early November, but the profusion of tests that preceded the halt produced unprecedented levels of radioactive fallout. In early 1959 reports of disturbingly high measurements of strontium 90 in the soil, milk, and wheat in some parts of the United States generated widespread uneasiness. In New York City, readings indicated that the concentrations of strontium 90 in the soil had risen sevenfold since 1954; in Pittsburgh and Seattle they showed a fivefold increase from the previous year. Measurements of strontium 90 in milk revealed levels that were considerably higher than usual in locations as far-flung as St. Louis, Atlanta, and Mandan, North Dakota. Some samples of wheat in Minnesota exceeded the recommended maximum permissible concentration of strontium 90.[1]

Willard Libby told the Joint Committee in February 1959 that the AEC was "very concerned" about the strontium-90 content in wheat. He underscored the point in a speech denouncing the Soviet bomb explosions of the previous fall for greatly increasing the amount of radioactive debris in the atmosphere. He urged that all future testing be done underground and advised that "care and caution" must be observed to restrict radioactive contamination. Libby and other AEC spokesmen pointed out that the strontium-90 measurements, including the average levels for Minnesota wheat, were not high enough to be dangerous and pledged to continue careful monitoring to make certain they did not reach hazardous proportions.[2]

The AEC's assurances did not end public concern or deter sharp criticism. Letters from citizens worried about the fallout reports poured into the White House, Capitol Hill, and the AEC; a Miami mother of three wondered, "How could the AEC keep saying that there is no danger?" Maurice B. Visscher, head of the physiology department of the University of Minnesota and chairman of the state's atomic-energy development committee, agreed with the AEC that the strontium-90 levels in wheat were not dangerous but complained that the agency had not adequately studied the effects of fallout on the food cycle. Senator Hubert Humphrey accused the AEC of "playing down the dangers of radioactive fallout," though he found it "very interesting to note that in recent months the Atomic Energy Commission has finally come to recognize that there is a serious problem." *Saturday Review* editor Norman Cousins, a frequent critic of the AEC and a leading proponent of a nuclear-test ban, maintained that Libby's statement of concern about the strontium-

90 readings meant that the debate over whether or not nuclear testing posed significant health risks was over. "Those who opposed him," he added, "can take no satisfaction in the fact that they were right."[3]

In the midst of what *U.S. News and World Report* called a "flurry of excitement over radiation and fall-out," a new controversy intensified public apprehension and fueled attacks on the AEC. On 21 March Senator Anderson released recently declassified correspondence on the "residence time" that fallout remained in the stratosphere before descending to earth. A classified letter written by General Herbert B. Loper, assistant to the secretary of defense for atomic energy, informed the Joint Committee that new findings of the Department of Defense indicated that fallout from the stratosphere returned to earth within about two years, rather than the seven years that the AEC had previously estimated. Loper also reported that the "concentration of the strontium 90 on the surface of the earth is greater in the United States than in any other area of the world." In response to Loper's letter, Libby replied that although the AEC's estimate of seven years was probably erroneous, he had calculated from the Defense Department's data that the residence time was four years instead of two. He also questioned Loper's assertion that the United States received a disproportionate share of fallout. Both officials agreed that their conclusions were tentative and required further investigation.[4]

Anderson was furious that the Loper and Libby letters had been classified because a shorter residence time would reduce the opportunity for fission products in the stratosphere to decay to lower levels of activity before falling to earth. At his request the Defense Department, after deleting certain portions, declassified Loper's letter. But even after the removal of restricted data, Loper asked that Anderson keep the letter confidential because its conclusions were not definitive. The AEC declassified Libby's letter after excising sensitive defense data and noting the agency's reservations about Loper's estimates. In making the correspondence public, Anderson rebuked both the Defense Department and the AEC for suppressing information and declared: "As chairman of the Joint Committee, I intend to see that the essential facts [on fallout] are made available to the American people for their independent judgment." At a Joint Committee hearing on AEC appropriations he grilled Libby on why the commissioner had not mentioned Loper's calculations in his recent speech on the high levels of fallout caused by Soviet bomb tests. Libby explained that at the time the Defense Department data were still classified and reiterated that he did not agree with Loper's conclusions. He insisted that the difference in estimated residence time was only slightly meaningful in assessing fallout hazards and denied that the AEC had withheld information to mislead the public. But Anderson's release of the letters embarrassed the AEC and undermined its credibility. "Those who have been worrying about the dangers of radioactive fall-out, and charging the Administration with suppressing and distorting the unpleasant facts on this question," editorialized *Commonweal*, "seem to have been more right than their critics."[5]

AEC chairman John A. McCone acted promptly to counter the criticism directed at the agency. McCone had become chairman in July 1958 after the departure of Lewis Strauss. Eisenhower had wanted to reappoint Strauss; the president had once remarked privately that he would like to make him "permanent" chairman. But Strauss had declined, citing the hostility of certain newspapers and columnists toward him personally and his running feud with Senator Anderson as reasons to choose a different chairman. The president, after consultation with Strauss, then offered the position to McCone. McCone had compiled an impressive record in industry and government service. Born in 1902, he studied engineering at the University of California at Berkeley but left before receiving a degree. Although he began work as a riveter in an iron foundry, he quickly moved up to executive positions in the steel industry. In 1937 he cofounded the Bechtel-McCone Corporation, a heavy construction firm that built oil refineries, industrial plants, and, during World War II, ships and aircraft. After the war McCone left the company and established a prosperous business in interoceanic shipping. In 1947–48 he was a member of the President's Air Policy Commission, which made recommendations on long-range air-power planning. He then served briefly as an aide to Secretary of Defense James Forrestal and returned to Washington during the Korean War as under secretary of the air force. McCone was short in stature, levelheaded in temperament, meticulous in manner, and affable in bearing. One friend described him as a "quiet-spoken dynamo." He was a devout Roman Catholic, a lifelong Republican, and a friend and occasional golfing partner of Eisenhower. Although his views on atomic-energy issues did not differ from those of Strauss, he was anxious to avoid the bitter disputes with the Joint Committee that had afflicted the tenure of his predecessor.[6]

In a statement to the Joint Committee after the publication of the Loper-Libby correspondence, McCone declared "most emphatically and unequivocally" that he would not tolerate "the suppression of distortion of any information bearing on the safety and health of the American public." He expressed confidence that the AEC had not suppressed fallout data in the past, but pledged to take the "most vigorous and comprehensive corrective measures possible" if the Joint Committee revealed evidence showing that information had been withheld. McCone, like Libby, explained that the AEC had not published the data it received from Loper because it questioned his conclusions and because the Defense Department considered the experiments to be "highly classified." A short time later, McCone instructed AEC general manager A. R. Leudecke to investigate further "to make absolutely sure that we are not withholding or suppressing information." Although the chairman had checked his statement to the Joint Committee with the agency divisions involved in fallout matters, he still wanted to know "if there is any classified information in this area . . . precisely what it is and the basis for such classification."[7]

Eisenhower supported McCone's efforts to defend the AEC by issuing a statement declaring: "To my knowledge, there has been no suppression of information on fallout." He emphasized that the Loper-Libby letters had been classified because of the "preliminary nature of the information" that needed to be "more thoroughly evaluated" before being made public. The president's statement also commended the National Academy of Sciences for its decision, announced the previous day, to reappraise and update its 1956 report on the biological effects of radiation. Administration officials had urged the National Academy to undertake the task, and Eisenhower was pleased "that the excellent comprehensive study made under the auspices of the Academy nearly three years ago will now be brought up to date by competent scientists."[8]

McCone's and Eisenhower's attempts to repair the sullied reputation of the AEC were quickly undercut by a new report, coming from within the administration, that questioned the agency's role in protecting public health. On 26 March 1959, the day after the president's statement, the surgeon general of the United States, Dr. LeRoy E. Burney, issued the results of a review of radiation problems conducted by his agency, the U.S. Public Health Service, a division of the Department of Health, Education, and Welfare. The report, submitted by the National Advisory Committee on Radiation, which Burney had established a year earlier, urged that "ultimate authority" for radiation protection be vested in the Public Health Service. Burney had formed the advisory committee to study and recommend a comprehensive national program in radiological health. No single agency in the federal government was responsible for overseeing all aspects of radiation safety. The AEC had broad authority over the hazards arising from atomic fission, but the 1954 Atomic Energy Act gave it no regulatory jurisdiction over such potentially dangerous sources of radiation as X rays, accelerator-produced isotopes, and naturally occurring radium. Responsibility for regulating those substances rested with state governments. The U.S. Public Health Service conducted research on radiation problems, provided technical services to states, and assisted in monitoring levels of radioactivity in milk, water, and the air. The National Committee on Radiation Protection exerted great influence in the formulation of radiation-protection standards, but it was an independent body with no statutory authority. Burney, therefore, sought means to focus effective control over radiation hazards from all sources.[9]

The advisory committee's twelve members included physicians, public-health officials, geneticists, a scientist from the AEC's Brookhaven National Laboratory, and Lauriston Taylor of the National Bureau of Standards and the NCRP. The chairman was Russell H. Morgan, professor of radiology at Johns Hopkins University Medical School and radiologist-in-chief at Johns Hopkins Hospital. By October 1958 Morgan had prepared preliminary proposals recommending that the Public Health Service assume "responsibility for comprehensive control of radiation safety in the United States." His report suggested that the Service sponsor research to devise sound and uniform radiation-protection standards, give the NCRP official status by making it a part of the agency, initiate and expand education and training programs in the field of radiation control, and develop and enforce regulations "governing radiation safety problems of regional or national nature." The draft stressed that one important reason that Congress should grant the Public Health Service increased authority was that the AEC's dual functions of promoting and regulating atomic energy for peaceful purposes cast doubts on its ability to safeguard adequately public health and safety. Morgan argued that giving the AEC both roles was "unwise" because of "the possibility that the agency in its zeal to carry out its promotional activity may lose sight of its responsibilities in operational safety." He went on to say: "It is noteworthy that the dual responsibility of the Atomic Energy Commission has proven embarrassing and it may be expected to prove increasingly so in the future."[10]

The advisory committee met in March 1959 to discuss and make changes in the preliminary report before its release. Lauriston Taylor opposed the idea of making the NCRP a part of the Public Health Service; the committee accordingly deleted that proposal and affirmed that "there is much merit in the independent position which the NCRP enjoys." Several committee members thought the strong criticism of the AEC in the draft was unwarranted. Chairman Morgan accepted their position and declared: "I don't think we should give anybody the impression that we are taking pot shots at the AEC." He emphasized that he wanted to point out the inherent difficulties of carrying out both promotional and regulatory duties and he was not "trying to get at the AEC." Others agreed that dual responsibility was flawed in principle. Taylor, for example, remarked: "I don't think there is any question that [the] AEC fails to recognize that they are in an untenable situation of promoting and regulating simultaneously." The committee, therefore, toned down the draft's reproach of the AEC while retaining the statement that assigning the agency dual functions was "unwise." The committee made other revisions in the preliminary report but left unchanged the major recommendation that primary authority for radiation safety should be vested in the Public Health Service. It called for substantial budget increases to fund the Service's expanded radiation programs, urging an immediate rise of more than a million dollars over the proposed level of $1.4 million for the coming fiscal year and total expenditures of approximately $50 million during the following five years.[11]

Even before the surgeon general released the advisory committee's findings, stories about them appeared in the press. Columnist Drew Pearson accused the Eisenhower administration of "sitting on a dynamite-laden report on control of the deadly poison accumulating in our soil and food from radioactive fallout." Actually, publication of the report was delayed by a few remaining differences within the committee over the phrasing of some sections and the need to get the approval of all members for last-minute changes. Burney issued the committee's final report on 26 March, the same day he received it. The continuing concern over fallout levels and recent attacks on the AEC assured that the recommendations would command wide attention, although they dealt exclusively with peaceful uses of atomic energy rather than with fallout. The proposal to assign the Public Health Service "ultimate authority" for radiation safety won endorsements from a broad cross-section of the political spectrum. Liberal newspapers such as the *Washington Post*, journals such as *The Nation,* and political leaders such as Senators John F. Kennedy and Hubert Humphrey approved of the idea; so did more conservative voices such as the *Rocky Mountain News,* columnist William S. White, and Senator Lister Hill. In early April 1959 Hill and Congressman Kenneth A. Roberts introduced legislation designed to implement the advisory committee's recommendations by granting the Public Health Service "primary responsibility for the protection of public health and safety from radiation hazards."[12]

The AEC withheld public comment on the surgeon general's report. Neither it nor the Public Health Service viewed the advisory committee's recommendations as an effort to strip the Commission of its radiation-safety programs or control over its own installations and licensees. Still, the establishment and the proceedings of the advisory committee, which was filled largely with members whose experience centered on public health and whose professional interests paralleled those of the Public Health Service, reflected bureaucratic as well as policy considerations. The Public Health Service regarded the proposals to grant it authority for leadership and coordination of federal radiation-safety programs not only as a means to fill a void in existing arrangements but also as an opportunity to expand its own responsibilities and budget. Although the Service was not seeking to take over AEC functions (and the advisory committee's report expressly disavowed any such idea), some press accounts exaggerated the potential impact of the committee's findings by portraying a power struggle between the two agencies. Eisenhower acted to restrain the public controversy. On 3 April he announced that he had instructed Bureau of the Budget director Maurice H. Stans, with the collaboration of McCone and HEW secretary Arthur S. Flemming, to prepare a study and submit recommendations on how best to organize the efforts of federal agencies in the field of radiation protection.[13]

Eisenhower's announcement failed to quiet the debate over radiation problems because new recommendations of the National Committee on Radiation Protection soon produced another controversy. The issue stemmed from a decision of the International Commission on Radiological Protection, made public in early 1959, to advise a maximum permissible level for whole-population exposure from internal emitters of one-hundredth of the occupational limit for gonad-seeking radioisotopes and one-thirtieth of the occupational limit for radioisotopes that do not affect the reproductive cells. Most internal emitters, including strontium 90, cause somatic rather than genetic damage. The action of the ICRP put the NCRP in an awkward position. On the one hand, levels of strontium 90 in some milk samples in the United States exceeded the ICRP's new population limits, and if the NCRP adopted those levels, public anxiety surely would be amplified. On the other hand, an NCRP refusal to go along with the ICRP's recommendations would also cause concern and disapproval. To make matters more difficult for the NCRP, its subcommittee on internal emitters had nearly completed a revision of its 1953 report with no mention of a whole-population exposure limit.[14]

Predictably, when the NCRP released its findings on internal emitters in late April 1959, it stirred widespread criticism. The committee was chastised not only for failing to accept the ICRP's whole-population levels but also for raising the concentration of strontium 90 that it found an acceptable dose for radiation workers. The national and international bodies agreed on the maximum permissible occupational limit for strontium 90, and both had doubled it to make it consistent with computations used for other bone-seeking radioisotopes. But the ICRP had more than compensated for the change by recommending that the occupational levels be cut to one-thirtieth when calculating the allowable dose for whole populations. The NCRP had formed a special committee in 1958 to consider the problem of population exposure, but news of that development hardly mollified the critics. *Washington Post* science reporter Edward Gamarekian wrote that the NCRP refused to accept the ICRP's recommendations "because of the adverse effect those limits would have on the further development of nuclear weapons." Others suggested that the AEC had influenced the NCRP's position. But the AEC had not done so; indeed, its officials also questioned the NCRP's proposals. When McCone requested an explanation of the differences between the NCRP and the ICRP, an AEC staff member told him that "these revisions are believed to have been made without any consideration of the relative importance which strontium 90 has assumed in the public mind" and suggested that "the new value has perhaps less validity than the old."[15]

During the late winter and early spring of 1959, public concern over radiation rose to new levels. Although the AEC acknowledged that the potential dangers of fallout might be greater than it had previously described, it continued to insist that average levels were not high enough to create significant health hazards. The agency's statements elicited sharp attacks from the press, members of Congress, and individual citizens. Its performance in protecting public health was questioned not only from outside but also from within the administration, and a restructuring of federal programs for radiation safety was still being considered. Public apprehension about the effects of radiation was accompanied and probably exacerbated by widespread confusion. The conflicting views of eminent scientists and often divergent pronouncements of an array of agencies and organizations, including the Atomic Energy Commission, the Department of Defense, the Department of Health, Education, and Welfare, the Public Health Service, the National Advisory Committee on Radiation, the National Committee on Radiation Protection, the International Commission on Radiological Protection, the National Academy of Sciences, and the Joint Committee on Atomic Energy were enough to bewilder any individual trying to understand and assess the hazards of radiation.[16]

In an effort to update the data presented in 1957 and collect the latest scientific evaluations of fallout, especially since public concern had "risen sharply," the Joint Committee held four days of hearings in early May 1959. As chairman of the Special Subcommittee on Radiation, Chet Holifield once again presided over the sessions. In 1957 Holifield had accused the AEC of "playing down" the hazards of testing, but since that time he had adopted a position indistinguishable from the agency's on existing levels of fallout. He had concluded that fallout did not pose a significant health threat at the time and that the Soviets had promoted exaggerated fears of radiation from bomb testing. "Some of the extreme liberals have fallen for the propaganda initiated by the Soviets on this point," Holifield wrote privately. "I am not being stampeded by extreme statements of the alarmists who believe malformed babies will be born as a result of the tests." Nevertheless, in contrast with the AEC, he admitted that he was "deeply concerned" about the potential health effects of continued testing. Oral testimonies at the hearings reflected Holifield's personal views by acknowledging the risks of renewed testing but refraining from attacks on the AEC.[17]

The hearings provided additional information and commentary on the controversies of the previous few months. Charles Dunham, director of the AEC's Division of Biology and Medicine, reported that McCone's order that the AEC's classified records on fallout be reviewed had led to a complete or partial opening of "all the . . . documents that can be declassified." Dunham's statement included the most prominent example of the recently declassified material, a table showing the amount of energy yielded by fission in American, British, and Soviet bomb blasts between 1945 and 1958. *Time* magazine called that revelation the "biggest news of the hearings." Department of Defense spokesmen outlined their methods for measuring the residence time of stratospheric fallout and reiterated their position that it descended to earth in two years or less. The AEC's Libby continued to dispute the Defense Department's calculations. He agreed, however, that fallout from the Soviet tests in the Arctic remained in the stratosphere for an unusually short period because of peculiarities in the polar atmosphere and that it had contributed significantly to the high readings of strontium 90 in the United States.[18]

Because the question of federal-agency responsibilities for radiation safety was still being studied, the Joint Committee generally avoided discussion of the surgeon general's report. At one point, however, Holifield, who previously had expressed support for giving the Public Health Service primary authority in the field, voiced concern that the Service would face greater difficulties than the AEC in securing funding for radiation programs. "I know how hard it is to get appropriations for civilian agencies," he remarked, "and comparatively speaking I found it is much easier, if it is for defense." Speaking on the differences in the recommendations of the NCRP and ICRP, Lauriston Taylor vigorously denied that the NCRP considered the possible effects of its permissible doses on U.S. weapons testing. He pointed out that the American members of the ICRP had fully supported the whole-population levels for internal emitters that it had recently proposed. He emphasized that the only discrepancy between the positions of the two organizations was that the ICRP had recommended permissible limits for population groups while the NCRP had not yet done so.[19]

The hearings revealed no startling scientific findings since 1957; most of the issues that had divided or caused uncertainty among experts at that time remained unresolved. The only notable exception was that a consensus of opinion now agreed that fallout was concentrated most heavily in the Northern Hemisphere rather than distributed uniformly around the globe. The scientists who testified at the hearings or submitted written statements generally, though not unanimously, concurred that the existing levels of fallout did not represent a major health hazard, but they also believed that a resumption of bomb testing could raise concentrations high enough to be worrisome.[20]

During the late spring and summer of 1959 the Bureau of the Budget worked on the study of the roles of federal agencies in radiation protection that Eisenhower had ordered. On 28 May it presented its preliminary analysis of the problem and proposed remedies to McCone and

HEW secretary Flemming. The Bureau argued that the charges of a conflict of interest between the AEC's weapons-testing and promotional functions and its public-health and regulatory responsibilities made some changes in existing arrangements necessary to restore public confidence. But it expressed reservations about giving primary authority in radiation control to the Public Health Service because "the whole future of the use of radiation would depend on the decisions of officials whose major mission and experience is public health." The Bureau sought ways to ensure that policymakers carefully balanced the risks and the benefits of radiation. It suggested that the health effects of weapons testing would receive due consideration if the secretary of health, education, and welfare submitted a report on the subject that the president could weigh along with other relevant factors in deciding whether to authorize tests. The Bureau further advised that doubts about the AEC's objectivity in assessing fallout hazards would be alleviated and the public reassured about the low level of risk if HEW assumed responsibility for analyzing fallout data and presenting its health implications to the public.[21]

The Budget Bureau also considered the problems of establishing radiation-protection standards. It noted that the AEC and other government agencies followed the recommendations of the National Committee on Radiation Protection. Therefore the NCRP, even though it was an independent organization and "not a politically responsible body," was "inevitably making political decisions" because its standards affected a broad range of atomic-energy operations, including military programs. The Bureau proposed that the NCRP be given official status by making it a part of the AEC, HEW, or a new agency responsible for setting radiation exposure limits.[22]

Budget Director Stans, McCone, Flemming, and members of their staffs met several times to discuss the Bureau's proposals. They quickly agreed on the basic recommendations, though they made some revisions in the draft before submitting a final report to the president. Instead of restricting HEW's monitoring effort to fallout, they expanded its role to assuming "primary responsibility within the executive branch for the collation, analysis, and interpretation" of data on all sources of radiation, including natural background, radioisotopes, and X rays as well as fallout. The "toughest problem," according to McCone, was deciding on the best way to promulgate radiation-protection standards. After considering the alternatives the three officials decided that the determination of basic exposure levels should be centered in the White House. They urged the establishment of a Federal Radiation Council to advise the president in providing "general standards and guidance to executive agencies for their use in developing operating rules and regulations for radiological health protection." It would consist of the secretaries of commerce, defense, and health, education, and welfare, and the chairman of the AEC, with the president's special assistant for science and technology serving as an advisor. The Radiation Council would continue to rely on the expertise of the NCRP in making its recommendations to the president.[23]

Eisenhower accepted the Budget Bureau's recommendations. On 14 August 1959 he issued an executive order creating the Federal Radiation Council (FRC) and a few days later designated HEW secretary Flemming its chairman. In September the Joint Committee made the Council a statutory body and added the secretary of labor to its membership in a section of a law on federal and state authority in atomic regulation. The establishment of the FRC placed new responsibilities for radiation protection in the hands of the president, but his role was limited to furnishing "general standards and guidance." The Budget Bureau, after considerable discussion, decided against seeking legislation that would give the president "legally binding" authority. Federal agencies remained responsible for setting operational radiation standards within their areas of jurisdiction, and the NCRP retained its independent advisory status. Eisenhower strengthened and broadened the functions of HEW to provide a more unified and comprehensive federal program in all aspects of radiation protection and to "reassure the public as to the objectivity of Government announcements." But the basic duties and authority of the AEC were unchanged. McCone told his staff that the president's actions would have "no effect on any activities presently being undertaken by AEC."[24]

By the autumn of 1959, public anxieties about fallout had eased because of a sharp decline in strontium-90 levels, and issues that had generated controversy earlier in the year had been largely resolved. Eisenhower's creation of the Federal Radiation Council and expansion of the responsibilities of HEW ended the debate stirred by the National Advisory Committee on Radiation's report to the surgeon general. It also scuttled the Hill-Roberts bill, which had proposed vesting primary authority for radiation safety in the Public Health Service. In addition, the ICRP and NCRP curbed speculation about the differences in their positions by agreeing on whole-population exposure for both external and internal radiation. The ICRP revised its earlier proposal by recommending a limit of one-tenth of the occupational level for individuals and one-thirtieth of the occupational level as an average for the entire population. The NCRP concurred in the recommendations, at least until its ongoing study on general population exposure was complete.[25]

The decline in fallout levels, the resolution of controversies over radiation-protection standards and responsibilities, and the moratorium on bomb testing removed the fallout issue as a major source of public debate and concern between the summer of 1959 and the fall of 1961. The Public Health Service, in its new role of making official public announcements on fallout, issued periodic assurances that lingering radioactivity from bomb testing did not pose a significant public-health hazard. Other scientific analyses supported that conclusion, and one report suggested that the threat of strontium 90 from fallout was considerably less severe than experts had previously believed. In its updated survey of the biological effects of radiation, published in May 1960, the National Academy of Sciences also advanced a generally optimistic assessment of the risks of fallout accumulated to that time. It noted that scientific research since 1956 had "not brought to light any facts that call for a drastic revision of earlier recommendations." It indicated that recent studies gave some reason to believe that the genetic effects of radiation might be less ominous than they appeared in 1956, though as in its earlier report, it emphasized the "need for conservative management of all radiation sources." The National Academy reiterated its call for research "on a wide front" because "many questions about radiation hazards . . . are unanswerable with present data."[26]

Meanwhile, the recently established Federal Radiation Council was conferring on radiation problems. At their first meeting on 9 September 1959, FRC members agreed to focus their initial efforts on radiation-protection standards, and much of the Council's attention in its first months of existence was devoted to developing recommendations on exposure limits. The cabinet secretaries and agency heads who made up the Council relied on a "working group" of middle-echelon officials who met regularly to discuss and draft proposals for the Council's consideration. The working group consulted the NCRP and more than fifty scientific experts, and after lengthy discussions over the wording and emphasis of preliminary drafts, the Council presented its findings to the president in May 1960. Its proposals contained no drastic departures from the recommendations of the NCRP and ICRP; the numerical limits for whole-body occupational and population exposure from external radiation were identical with those of the two committees. The FRC did suggest, however, that it was more logical to compare whole-population levels with natural background than to base them on occupational limits, a concept that the NCRP was actively considering. The most important new proposal of the FRC was a change in terminology. Arguing that the use of "maximum permissible dose" was confusing, it adopted the term "radiation protection guide" to emphasize that the specified exposure levels did not represent inviolable limits above which a person was certain to sustain somatic injury. But it stipulated that federal agencies should make "every effort . . . to encourage the maintenance of radiation doses as far below this guide as practicable." The FRC report did not include specific guidelines for internal emitters, though it promised to undertake a "detailed study" of the problem. Eisenhower promptly approved the FRC's recommendations.[27]

In September 1961, after months of study and consultation with leading scientists, the FRC submitted its report on internal emitters to President Kennedy. Rather than provide detailed guidance on all radioisotopes, the Council focused on those that posed the greatest environmental hazard to large population groups—radium 226, strontium 89, strontium 90, and iodine 131. Radium 226 is a naturally occurring radioisotope; the other three are products of nuclear fission. On the basis of recent research the Council proposed that the exposure guides for radium 226 and strontium 90 be less restrictive than existing NCRP recommendations by a factor of three. The change in strontium-90 levels seemed reasonable because studies indicated that bone cells discriminated against it better than experts had previously believed. Therefore, a lower concentration of the isotope lodged in the skeleton than they had assumed. Balanced against those encouraging evaluations were more disturbing assessments of the dangers of strontium 89 and iodine 131. The chemical properties of strontium 89 are identical with those of strontium 90, but it disintegrates much faster. Although still viewed as much less of a hazard than strontium 90, strontium 89 represented enough of a problem for the FRC to advise restricting its intake to one-third of previous levels. Iodine 131 was even more worrisome. New data suggested that iodine 131 posed a more significant threat than scientists had recognized. If ingested or inhaled in sufficient quantity, it can cause thyroid cancer, and children are particularly susceptible. The FRC sharply reduced its guidelines for population exposure to iodine 131 to one-third of earlier NCRP levels in air and one-seventh in water. President Kennedy approved the Council's proposals on 20 September 1961. In September 1963 the AEC modified its radiation-protection regulations for licensees to conform with the FRC's recommendations; the changes became effective in November 1964.[28]

The Joint Committee on Atomic Energy observed the activities of the Federal Radiation Council with a watchful and often critical eye. Committee members worried that their oversight authority over atomic energy would be curtailed by the FRC. Their concern was exacerbated when the Council informed them that its documents and deliberations were protected by executive privilege and were not available for congressional scrutiny. The Joint Committee voiced doubts that the FRC was fulfilling its purpose of providing centralized authority and guidance to federal agencies on radiation problems. In hearings conducted in the spring of 1960, members questioned whether a staff of one full-time executive secretary was adequate to provide permanence and continuity to the FRC's work. The FRC's lack of legally binding authority caused speculation that federal agencies might ignore the Council's guidelines in issuing regulations. Overall, the Joint Committee was not satisfied that the FRC's organizational resources or administrative jurisdiction was sufficient to coordinate the activities and clarify the responsibilities of various agencies involved in radiation protection. Holifield even wondered "if there was any real reason for [having] the Federal Radiation Council."[29]

In both its 1960 report to Eisenhower on external radiation and its 1961 report to Kennedy on internal emitters, the Federal Radiation Council stated that its recommendations applied only to the government's "normal peacetime operations." It remained unclear, despite Joint Committee probing, how the FRC's guidelines should be used in assessing the hazards of radioactive fallout. As long as the moratorium on nuclear testing continued, the issue remained a relatively minor concern. But when the Soviet Union resumed atmospheric testing in September 1961, the FRC's recommendations on population exposure and the government's overall response to the renewed threat of fallout contamination assumed greatly increased importance.[30]

A few days after the Soviets began testing, Kennedy announced that the United States had "no other choice" than to conduct its own experimental detonations, but he stipulated that American shots would take place underground. By early November the Soviets had set off more than thirty blasts, climaxed by an explosion of the unprecedented size of more than fifty megatons. Kennedy then authorized preparations for a resumption of U.S. atmospheric tests, but he deferred a final decision until the Soviet shots could be evaluated and he was convinced that they made American atmospheric blasts necessary to maintain a lead in weapons technology. The president declared that he would consider U.S. atmospheric explosions with "the greatest caution and hesitancy." He was deeply concerned about the effects of radioactive fallout. During a briefing with AEC officials in February 1961, Kennedy had asked Charles Dunham why fallout was receiving much less public and press attention than it had two years before. Dunham attributed it to the fact that the peak levels from previous testing had passed. He pointed out that even the highest readings had been below the NCRP's permissible doses, but added a personal assessment that neither he nor any other AEC spokesman had ever made publicly. He told the president that if weapons testing had continued at the 1958 rate, "civilized man would have been in trouble." Dunham's statement contributed to Kennedy's reluctance to increase fallout levels by conducting atmospheric tests.[31]

The Soviet tests revived apprehension about the effects of fallout that had subsided after the summer of 1959. The immediate source of concern was iodine 131. Although scientists had recognized as early as 1954 that radioiodine from atomic fission presented potential hazards, they had given much greater attention to strontium 90. In 1957 the Public Health Service had established five monitoring stations that detected iodine 131 in milk samples.

On the basis of those measurements, California Institute of Technology biologist E. B. Lewis theorized in 1959 that small children had absorbed doses of iodine 131 that were as much as two times the amount received from natural background. Iodine 131 settles in the thyroid gland and poses the greatest danger to infants and young children because their thyroids are smaller and more sensitive to radioactive iodine than those of adults. Children are also more susceptible because the most probable source of iodine 131 is fresh milk, a major ingredient in their diets. Iodine 131 has a relatively short half-life (the time in which half of its radioactivity disappears) of eight days; the half-life of strontium 90, by comparison, is twenty-eight years. But iodine 131 tends to concentrate in cow's milk and, if ingested by cows feeding on contaminated forage, can be passed on while still dangerously radioactive to humans drinking fresh milk.[32]

By the time the Soviets resumed atmospheric testing, the Public Health Service had set up sixty milk-surveillance stations to monitor iodine 131 and other radioisotopes. It also benefited from more sensitive instruments than were available previously to measure levels of iodine 131. Between September and November of 1961 the Public Health Service recorded sharp increases in iodine-131 concentrations in milk in some parts of the country. None of the estimated doses to infant thyroids exceeded the annual guidelines of the Federal Radiation Council, which, despite the FRC's reluctance to apply them to fallout, were still used as benchmarks. But Des Moines and Minneapolis received iodine 131 that amounted to 88 percent of the FRC's annual guidelines, and Detroit, Kansas City, Omaha, and Palmer, Alaska more than 50 percent. In several other locations, single-day peaks were considerably higher than the FRC daily-exposure guidelines. The Public Health Service issued periodic assurances that the iodine-131 levels did not pose a major health hazard, and the public generally remained calm. An opinion poll taken in early December revealed that only 21 percent of those questioned agreed that "there is enough fall-out in the air right now to be a danger to people"; 61 percent disagreed.[33]

The subdued reaction to fallout that the December opinion sampling indicated did not mean that the public was indifferent. The timing of the poll partially obscured the concern created by the Soviet tests; the survey was conducted after iodine-131 levels had returned to normal and before strontium-90 concentrations began to rise. Although the public exhibited no symptoms of panic over fallout, many signals testified to an appreciable level of apprehension. *U.S. News and World Report* editor David Lawrence debunked what he called the "fallout scare" by attributing it to "many months of propaganda spread by the Communists . . . in which many Americans unwittingly participated." Other press commentary, by contrast, maintained that fallout hazards were genuinely worrisome. *Christian Century* asked, "What right have we or the Russians to pollute the atmosphere for the next 8,000 years?" It wondered whether the administration was issuing "reassuring statements concerning fallout to prepare the American people to approve atmospheric tests by our own government." A Public Health Service official found it "regrettable that publicity regarding testing of Soviet nuclear weapons has given rise to undue concern about levels of radioactivity in milk." Speaking to the National Conference on Milk and Nutrition in January 1962, President Kennedy declared that milk offered "no hazards" from radiation and announced that he had directed that it be served at every White House meal.[34]

By the early months of 1962 the United States was moving closer to a resumption of atmospheric testing. Although Kennedy continued to postpone a final decision and a January poll showed a sharp division in public opinion on the issue, many considerations weighed in favor of conducting a series of aboveground tests. American experts concluded that the Soviets had achieved significant gains with their atmospheric shots that jeopardized the U.S. lead in weapons design and capabilities. High-level Pentagon officials and many congressmen, influential members of the Joint Committee on Atomic Energy in particular, pressed for U.S. atmospheric tests. Senator Anderson, for example, declared that "atmospheric tests . . . permit greater and more rapid gains in weapons development" and, despite the fallout they produced, were necessary "to preserve the security of our country and that of the free world."[35]

Kennedy received similar advice from AEC chairman Glenn T. Seaborg. Seaborg had taken office in March 1961, replacing McCone, who resigned the chairmanship after Kennedy won the 1960 election. He brought impressive credentials to the position. Seaborg was born in 1912 in the small mining town of Ishpeming, Michigan, the son of a machinist. His family moved to California when he was ten, and he attended the University of California at Los Angeles, where he majored in chemistry and made Phi Beta Kappa. He earned a Ph.D. in chemistry from the University of California at Berkeley.

As an instructor at Berkeley, Seaborg won recognition in scientific circles for his collaboration with two other young chemists in identifying and extracting the element plutonium. During World War II he headed a Manhattan Project team charged with the difficult task of isolating enough pure plutonium to build an atomic bomb, an effort that was crucial to the development of the plutonium weapon that was dropped on Nagasaki in 1945. Seaborg harbored reservations about using the bomb, however, and along with six other scientists signed the June 1945 Franck Report to Secretary of War Henry L. Stimson. It urged that the destructive power of the bomb be demonstrated to observers at an isolated site so that Japan might be persuaded to surrender and the need to use the weapon might be averted.

After the war Seaborg returned to Berkeley, where he shared in the discovery of eight more new elements. He and nuclear physicist Edwin McMillan received a Nobel Prize in 1951 for their pioneering achievements with plutonium. After serving for several years as director of nuclear chemical research at Berkeley's Lawrence Radiation Laboratory, Seaborg became chancellor of the university in 1958. By the time he joined the AEC, therefore, he had a varied background of research, teaching, and administrative experience. A tall, rangy man, Seaborg was calm, deliberate, and thoughtful. He earned the reputation of a conciliator with a rare ability to mediate controversial issues without losing his composure or making enemies. Although a registered Democrat, he was not active in partisan politics, and he kept his views on many sensitive questions largely to himself. In his confirmation hearings Seaborg told the Joint Committee that he favored accelerating the atomic-power program but that he was unsure of how it should be done. He expressed no definite opinions on nuclear testing before becoming AEC chairman but simply declared: "I'll get all the facts, and then I'll take my position." The Soviet resumption of atmospheric testing convinced Seaborg that the United States must also conduct aboveground shots. Though not an intimate advisor of the president, he helped persuade Kennedy that in the absence of a nuclear-test ban, atmospheric blasts were necessary because underground tests provided only limited information.[36]

On 2 March 1962 Kennedy announced in a nationwide television address that the United States would resume atmospheric testing in late April unless the Soviet Union agreed to a test-ban treaty before that time. He emphasized that fallout from the blasts would be kept to a minimum. The American people overwhelmingly approved Kennedy's decision; a poll taken on 28 March indicated that 66 percent of those questioned supported U.S. atmospheric tests and only 25 percent opposed them. The ongoing negotiations with the Soviets on a test ban achieved no breakthroughs, and on 25 April the United States detonated in the Pacific the first of a series of aboveground shots.[37]

While Kennedy was still deliberating over authorizing atmospheric testing, the Federal Radiation Council submitted to him a draft of a report on the health effects of fallout that it had been preparing for several months. The Council published the final version of the study in early June 1962. It concluded that "nuclear testing through 1961 has increased by small amounts the normal risks of adverse health effects." While cautioning that estimates of fallout hazards were necessarily imprecise, the FRC argued that levels of radiation from nuclear testing were only a small percentage of natural background and were well below the recommended guidelines for peacetime atomic operations. The FRC's appraisal of fallout risks echoed the optimistic assessments offered by the AEC at the time of earlier weapons tests. The FRC departed from previous official statements on fallout, however, by providing for the first time rough estimates of how many people would be harmed. It calculated that forty deaths of 1.7 million annually in the United States could be attributed to leukemia or cancer caused by fallout and that 110 cases of serious birth defects resulting from bomb testing would show up over a period of thirty years.[38]

Despite the broad public support for atmospheric testing and the Federal Radiation Council's reassuring conclusions about fallout risks, the new series of U.S. blasts generated controversy and criticism of the administration. A *New Republic* writer sarcastically commented that the FRC's report "somewhat" eased his worry created "by the propaganda of a few lunatic-fringed groups, who claimed that fallout from atmospheric nuclear tests would cause cancer in the present generation and abnormal infants in the next." The source of greatest concern from the U.S. shots was the rising level of iodine 131 in milk in some areas of the country. The Public Health Service reported that measurements were particularly high in several midwestern states, though it stated that the concentrations were not a health problem. The Service's assurances did not go unchallenged. Republican congressman John V. Lindsay of New York found it "astounding" that public-health officials seemed so vague about the possible dangers of iodine 131. He urged the president "to provide the American people with a complete statement of the facts," and if the facts were "not available . . . to step up research in this critical area until all statistics are rendered meaningful." Several other members of Congress, on the other hand, complained that the Public Health Service was unnecessarily alarming the public about the radioactive content of milk and causing harm to the dairy industry.[39]

In the midst of the growing debate over radioactivity in milk, the Public Health Service's National Advisory Committee on Radiation issued an analysis of the question that, like its 1959 report on radiation protection, attracted widespread interest. The Service had requested the advisory committee to examine the problems of fallout contamination after the Soviet resumption of atmospheric testing in September 1961. It was particularly concerned with the advantages and disadvantages of taking countermeasures to reduce public exposure to fallout if readings reached a disturbing level. The advisory committee studied the issue for several months and submitted its findings to Surgeon General Luther L. Terry in May 1962. While Terry and White House science advisor Jerome Wiesner were reviewing the report, a spokesman for the American Federation of Labor–Congress of Industrial Organizations charged that the administration was suppressing it, an accusation that received wide media coverage. The Public Health Service hastened to issue the report and aroused the ire of the Joint Committee on Atomic Energy by failing to give it a copy in advance of publication.[40]

The advisory committee's study, contrary to some speculation before its release, did not suggest that radiation levels from fallout were more worrisome than previous official statements had indicated. Instead it recommended that the Public Health Service begin actions "to meet the radiocontamination problems of the future" that seemed likely to arise because of the growing use of atomic energy. The committee thought it vitally important that the Public Health Service extend its radiation-surveillance efforts through better coordination with state and local health laboratories and expanded scientific and technical research. To meet the demands of a comprehensive program, it called for a sixfold increase in the Service's radiation-control budget over a period of seven years. The bulk of the report discussed implementing countermeasures against iodine 131 and strontium 90 if it appeared likely that the population would "receive undue radiation exposure." Because of its short half-life, several effective means of protection from iodine 131 were available or seemed promising. Young children, lactating mothers, and pregnant women could use powdered instead of fresh milk, cows could be fed uncontaminated forage until the radioactivity in their pastureland dissipated, fresh milk could be frozen or stored for a short time, milk containing iodine 131 could be purified by an ion-exchange process, or people exposed to iodine 131 could increase their intake of stable iodine to counteract the radioactive isotope.[41]

The report explained that countermeasures against strontium 90, with its twenty-eight-year half-life, were much more difficult to devise. A number of techniques might help guard against its effects, such as preventing contaminated grass or crops from entering the food cycle, removing several inches of topsoil before planting new crops in areas showing high levels of radiation, employing ion exchange, or augmenting the amount of stable calcium consumed by humans or dairy herds likely to absorb strontium 90. For better understanding of how to deal with high concentrations of both radioisotopes, but especially with the complexities of strontium 90, the advisory committee called for an intensive research program. "Unless this effort is undertaken now," it declared, "the nation may well be faced in a few years with contamination problems which cannot easily be solved." It also emphasized that public-health officials should carefully consider all the implications of countermeasures and apply them only when the need clearly outweighed the risks. The committee cautioned that injudicious use of countermeasures could cause serious public-health hazards if, for example, people became frightened enough to stop drinking milk or drastically alter their dietary habits.[42]

The use of countermeasures against iodine 131 in milk occurred much sooner than the advisory committee had anticipated. In July 1962 the detonation of three small atomic bombs above ground at the AEC's testing site in Nevada caused iodine-131 levels to rise dramatically in nearby areas. Several daily measurements in Salt Lake City and other locations in Utah and Nevada exceeded manyfold the Federal Radiation Council's guidelines for radioiodine in milk. In response, Utah health officials arranged an agreement with a reluctant dairy industry to use milk from areas where the readings were highest for cheese and butter, which allowed time for the radioactivity to decay, and to feed cows on stored forage rather than contaminated pastureland. The countermeasures continued for a few days until iodine-131 levels dropped shortly after the end of the Nevada tests in early August. Although grocers and dairymen reported that milk sales remained normal, an AEC official who traveled to Salt Lake City found the situation "uneasy." After he explained that FRC guidelines allowed "a big safety factor" and that the recorded levels of iodine 131 would be dangerous only if they lingered for an extended period of time, the *Salt Lake Tribune* observed that "the scare over the content of radioactive iodine . . . in Utah milk subsided."[43]

In Minnesota the state health department and the dairy industry agreed to take countermeasures when iodine-131 readings increased following another Soviet resumption of atmospheric testing in August 1962. Milk producers offered farmers a price incentive for removing herds from pasture and feeding them stored forage. Health officials and industry representatives emphasized that although iodine-131 levels did not present a major hazard, they wanted to test the effectiveness of countermeasures under actual conditions in case of future emergencies. The program produced mixed results. Milk producers were discouraged that the overwhelming majority of farmers who participated lived in areas where pastureland was poor while those with good pastureland ignored the incentives for placing their herds on stored feed. Still, state health authorities were pleased with the cooperation of milk producers, and the dairy industry was gratified that the public showed no signs of panic. Milk consumption changed little during the two weeks the counter-measures were in effect.[44]

The actions of Utah and Minnesota to counteract the threat of iodine 131 raised anew the question of whether or not Federal Radiation Council guidelines applied to fallout. The AEC insisted that the guides should be used only for peaceful operations because weapons testing required risk assessments that were "different in magnitude, different in complexity of judgment and different in absolute necessity to secure [its] benefits." The AEC was concerned that strict adherence to FRC radiation guides might jeopardize its testing program by causing undue public anxiety. Despite the arguments of Public Health Service officials that the existing standards should be employed to evaluate the hazards of fallout and activate appropriate countermeasures if necessary, the FRC largely adopted the AEC's position. HEW secretary Anthony J. Celebrezze, the FRC chairman, told the Joint Committee in a letter of 17 August that although the guides had "some relevance for the assessment of fallout conditions," they were "not specifically designed for fallout situations" and were "not intended to be a dividing line between safety and danger." A few days later, he described the countermeasures "taken in some areas to reduce the intake of iodine 131" as "premature action" that "the Council would not have recommended under its interpretation of the guides." The FRC reiterated its position in a public statement on 17 September, declaring that "radiation exposures anywhere near the guides involve risks so slight that countermeasures may have a net adverse rather than a favorable effect on the public well-being." The Council promised to study the matter further and prepare a report on protective measures against fallout.[45]

The FRC's stance stirred considerable criticism. The Joint Committee, pointing to a discrepancy between the Council's position and a Public Health Service statement praising state and milk-industry countermeasures in Utah, complained that the "seemingly conflicting views . . . create much public misunderstanding." Some state health officials protested that the FRC's refusal to apply its guides to fallout meant they had to make judgments on taking countermeasures without any clear recommendations on what levels of radiation justified action. Robert

Barr of the Minnesota State Health Commission, however, declared that his state would decide independently on carrying out protective measures. "I don't intend to sit in Minnesota and watch the radioactive iodine rise," he said, "while the radiation council sits and deliberates for 30 days." Free-lance journalist Ralph Caplan assailed the administration in an article in *The Nation* for failing to develop a "coherent national protective policy" and for refusing to spell out the dangers of fallout to the American people.[46]

The harshest attack on the administration's fallout program came from Congressman Lindsay. In a speech on the floor of the House on 4 September 1962 he charged that the administration had failed to inform the public clearly about the hazards of fallout and that official statements were vague, confusing, and misleading. He called the Federal Radiation Council guidelines "the most ingenious administrative doubletalk of our time." Lindsay announced that after three months of research he had been unable to find out what the administration's fallout policy was, either because the president and his advisers did not know or because they were "deliberately being evasive." Pointing out that recent bomb tests had produced more fallout than the administration had anticipated, he urged the development of a fallout program that would ensure proper protection to the public in the event of future emergencies. Lindsay placed ultimate responsibility for the lack of a satisfactory policy on President Kennedy. "The President must put his policymaking house in order," he declared. "The people will not accept further reassurances that nothing is wrong."[47]

The condemnations of the Kennedy administration's fallout programs and pronouncements were strikingly similar to those once directed at the Eisenhower administration. As in 1957 and 1959, when rising radiation levels had generated widespread concern, in 1961–62 critics charged the government with confusion, ineptness, suppression of information, and failure to inform the public fully and frankly about the hazards of fallout. One major difference, however, was that the AEC, the target of many of the earlier attacks, remained largely in the background while the president and his close advisors, the Public Health Service, and especially the Federal Radiation Council were subjected to sharp reproach. The 1961–62 fallout controversy also highlighted the political overtones of the issue. Although the debate was never simply a matter of partisanship, as a question of major national concern it inevitably was politically tinged. Two of the leading critics of the AEC's fallout program under Eisenhower, Democrats Anderson and, particularly in 1957, Holifield, staunchly supported Kennedy's resumption of atmospheric testing and dismissed the dangers of fallout as relatively inconsequential. Lindsay and some other Republicans, by contrast, severely rebuked the Kennedy administration's performance on fallout.[48]

As the fallout debate continued in the public arena, an internal controversy over iodine 131 was brewing in the AEC. In August 1962 Harold A. Knapp, Jr., a staff member of the Fallout Studies Branch of the AEC's Division of Biology and Medicine, completed a study of radioactive iodine received by children in three locations in the United States from nuclear-weapons testing. Knapp's report was the latest of several he had done at the request of his superiors on radiation exposure from fallout. The AEC had published his earlier papers and anticipated issuing his analysis of iodine as part of its Technical Information Document series. Knapp theorized in his study that since 1953, children in areas surrounding the Nevada testing grounds had absorbed doses of iodine 131 that were much higher than previously realized and that were "genuinely disturbing." Since data on radioiodine exposures before 1961 were limited or altogether lacking, he based his findings on external radiation measurements and other available information. Knapp, who held a Ph.D. in mathematics, extrapolated what data he had and devised an intricate mathematical formula to estimate the doses of iodine 131 that children seemed likely to have received. After several other AEC staff members raised questions about the validity of Knapp's methodology and conclusions, he undertook further research and prepared a revised draft. It, too, stirred "rather sharp differences of opinion" within the AEC. Therefore, Charles Dunham, the director of the Division of Biology and Medicine, sought the advice of an *ad hoc* committee of five experts, two from AEC laboratories, one from private industry, one from the Public Health Service, and one from Cornell University. After spirited discussion among the committee members, Knapp, and other AEC scientists, Knapp wrote another draft of his paper.[49]

By the time that Knapp submitted the third version of his report in June 1963, he had left the AEC, "in accordance with a previous commitment," and taken a position with the Department of Defense. But his departure did not end the controversy over his paper, which he still wanted the AEC to publish, or the personal animosity that had developed between Knapp and the most outspoken critic of his work, Gordon M. Dunning, deputy director of the AEC's Division of Operational Safety.

Although Dunning found Knapp's third draft an improvement over the previous ones, he strongly opposed AEC publication of it on both technical and political grounds. Expressing deep reservations about the study's methodology, Dunning wrote: "Whether or not the conclusions of the paper are true may be debatable—this paper does not provide the scientific basis for a decision one way or another." Dunning argued that if the AEC published the report, it would raise questions among the press and the public about the health implications of its testing program. "We cannot hope to successfully refute the unfounded accusations of unsafe operations in Nevada from sources outside the Commission," he declared, "and at the same time sponsor an inconclusive technical report containing speculations of off-site radiation hazards." Since the existence of Knapp's paper was "probably . . . well known," Dunning recommended that to avoid the appearance of suppressing its findings, the AEC simply invite Knapp "in a matter-of-fact and bland manner" to seek publication of his report in a scientific journal.[50]

Knapp responded by calling Dunning's comments "dishonest and incompetent." More detached AEC officials remained uncertain of how to resolve the dilemma that Knapp's report created. Charles Dunham again solicited the opinions of the ad hoc committee that had reviewed the earlier draft. The reactions of committee members to Knapp's final version ranged "from favorable to completely negative." The analysis that the chairman, Wright Langham of the Los Alamos Scientific Laboratory, submitted to Dunham detailed serious reservations about the reliability of Knapp's data and about his assumptions, extrapolations, and conclusions. Nevertheless, by a vote of four to one (the Public Health Service representative dissented), the committee recommended that the AEC publish and distribute Knapp's report because it would "stimulate the scientific community's interest in the I-131 problem, which may be potentially quite important to civil defense and peaceful uses of atomic energy." Dunham then proposed that the AEC issue Knapp's paper and, to indicate the qualified nature of the endorsement of its merits by knowledgeable scientists, that it be accompanied by the ad hoc committee's comments. Although he recognized that release of Knapp's report might generate criticism of the AEC, he argued that withholding it might elicit an even more adverse reaction by making it appear that the agency was concealing "information for which the public has a genuine need." After securing Commission approval, Dunham transmitted Knapp's study along with the ad hoc committee's critique to the Joint Committee on 16

August 1963. A short time later the AEC published both reports in its Technical Information Document series.[51]

The hazards of iodine 131 were a central focus of Joint Committee hearings on radiation during the summer of 1963. Committee members voiced dismay that the Federal Radiation Council still had not explained how its guidelines for peacetime operations applied to fallout. The FRC had been actively pondering the problem since the previous summer and had drafted several papers on the subject. To compromise divergent views among its members, it contemplated raising its guideline levels for iodine 131 by a factor of ten for exposure from fallout. If that level was reached, countermeasures would be seriously considered. The FRC's working group reasoned that the risk of injury from iodine 131 would still be slight while the increased guideline levels would be less likely to interfere with weapons testing. But the proposal failed to achieve a consensus within the Council. The AEC opposed it as too inflexible, questioning "the assumption, that in an unpredictable course of events a meaningful action point can be established in absence of knowledge of the specific circumstances." Representative Melvin Price, chairman of the Joint Committee's radiation subcommittee, complained that unless the FRC settled the issue promptly, "responsible Government officials will have abdicated their solemn responsibility for dealing with this problem." FRC chairman Celebrezze promised to issue "some firm guidelines" within a year.[52]

The Joint Committee heard testimony from witnesses whose scientific investigations and conclusions were similar to those of Harold Knapp. Charles W. Mays, a University of Utah nuclear physicist, estimated that Utah infants had received annual doses of iodine 131 that exceeded Federal Radiation Council guidelines on several occasions between 1951 and 1962. He announced that since the population of Utah had "been exposed repeatedly in excess of present radiation protection guides," the state would take appropriate countermeasures in the future and "the AEC should not be surprised to receive bills for the cost of these measures." Eric Reiss, a professor of medicine at Washington University and spokesman for the Greater St. Louis Citizens' Committee for Nuclear Information, criticized the AEC even more sharply. He contended that the agency had seriously underestimated fallout hazards from its weapons tests and concluded that "in the period 1951–62, a number of local populations . . . scattered throughout the continental United States have been exposed to fallout so intense as to represent a medically unacceptable hazard to children who may drink fresh locally produced milk." Mays and Reiss acknowledged that, like Knapp, they based their findings on extrapolations from limited data. The AEC denied that large numbers of children had been exposed to significant levels of iodine 131 during the 1950s, but along with the Public Health Service it supported expanded study of cancer rates in areas most affected by fallout from continental bomb-testing.[53]

The statements of Mays and Reiss and the release of the Knapp report attracted considerable press coverage. When asked about the iodine 131 problem at a press conference on 20 August 1963, President Kennedy responded that the Utah studies were a subject of "some controversy" and added that "we do not believe that the health of the children involved has been adversely affected." But he admitted that radioiodine hazards were "a matter of concern" that made it "very desirable to get a test ban." A month earlier the United States, Great Britain, and the Soviet Union had agreed to a treaty prohibiting atmospheric testing, raising hopes that the threat of fallout would be largely eliminated. Senate approval of the treaty effectively removed the fallout issue as a matter of public controversy and concern, though it continued to generate interest and debate among scientists trying to resolve the many remaining uncertainties about the effects of radiation.[54]

The test-ban treaty marked the end of an era in the history of radiation protection. During the decade between the contamination of the *Lucky Dragon* and the three-nation agreement to end atmospheric testing, the fallout debate decisively influenced public perceptions, scientific inquiry, and government policy regarding radiation hazards. After half a century in which public attitudes toward the dangers of radiation were marked chiefly by indifference and lack of awareness, general recognition of the problem rapidly increased as a result of the fallout controversy. In a December 1961 poll asking what was "meant by 'fall-out' from an H-bomb," 57 percent of the respondents, compared with only 17 percent in 1955, answered correctly. Greater public knowledge about fallout was accompanied by heightened concern. Although the American people demonstrated no signs of panic over periodic reports of rising fallout levels, they showed unmistakable indications of appreciable anxiety. Despite government reassurances, widespread accounts of possible contamination of milk and food supplies were inevitably unsettling. Lauriston Taylor addressed the issue of public reactions when he remarked in 1961: "I spent the first 30 years of my professional life trying to scare people into doing a little something about protecting themselves from radiation. I think I'll spend the rest of my life trying to scare some common sense into them so that they will look at radiation . . . without being frightened of it."[55]

The extent to which the public linked fallout and the radiation hazards of medical and peaceful applications of atomic energy is problematic. Several well-publicized reports, such as those of the National Academy of Sciences and the National Advisory Committee on Radiation, emphasized that existing fallout levels were less cause for concern than ensuring proper control over the growing uses of atomic energy for civilian purposes. It is difficult to judge how deeply those analyses penetrated the public consciousness, but it is clear that public knowledge of radiation hazards stemmed principally from the fallout controversy. Just as the American people received their introduction to atomic energy from the explosion of the Hiroshima bomb, they became aware of the harmful long-range effects of strontium 90, iodine 131, and other products of atomic fission from the testing of nuclear weapons. Remarking on the relationship between peaceful applications of atomic energy and weapons development, one observer wrote in 1959: "In the public's mind, the two are clearly associated, and the discussion of the hazards from one . . . is applied without much considered review of the hazards [from] the other."[56]

As public concern about radiation rose in the late 1950s, confidence in the AEC's assessments of the risks of fallout diminished. The major reason that Eisenhower curtailed the agency's functions in interpreting fallout data in 1959 was that its statements had created so much controversy and suspicion. The establishment of the Federal Radiation Council and the assignment of responsibility for evaluating and publicly reporting fallout risks to the Public Health Service lowered the AEC's profile in radiation-protection matters. But they effected no substantive changes in the approach or the policies of the federal government toward radiation problems. In formulating its radiation-protection guides the FRC relied heavily on the recommendations of the NCRP, just as the AEC had done in issuing its regulations on radiation standards during the late 1950s. On the much more controversial question of assessing fallout hazards, the conclusions and announcements of the FRC and the Public Health Service echoed those made earlier by the AEC—namely, that existing levels of radiation from fallout did not present a major health threat. The only significant exception to that pattern was that the

FRC provided in 1962 estimates of how many Americans would die and how many serious birth defects would occur as a result of bomb testing. Although the numbers of people so affected were comparatively small, the FRC calculations pointed out the need for careful balancing of the risks and benefits of radiation. *Newsweek* raised the question by asking: "How much do 40 adults or 110 children weigh on the scales of policy?"[57] The Federal Radiation Council was not particularly successful in resolving those kinds of issues. It was most effective in dealing with matters that generated little debate, such as promulgating radiation-protection guides for peacetime operations. On more divisive questions, such as how its guides applied to fallout, differences of opinion and of agency priorities among its members produced bureaucratic paralysis.

The reassurances of the FRC and the Public Health Service on the dangers of fallout, like those of the AEC earlier, reflected the views of a wide segment of the scientific community and were persuasive enough to avert a frantic public reaction. But they did not prevent criticism that the government was not being candid with the American people about fallout hazards. By 1963 some scientists were adding a new source of worry to existing concerns by suggesting that during the 1950s the AEC had seriously underestimated the radiation doses that people living near the Nevada testing grounds had received from weapons tests. At the time of the nuclear-test-ban treaty, therefore, many scientific and political questions about radiation protection remained unsettled. The fallout controversy between 1954 and 1963 focused on nuclear weapons rather than peaceful atomic programs. Nevertheless, it exerted a significant impact on the regulatory activities of the AEC by stimulating scientific research that increased understanding of the nature of radiation, helping to define public perceptions of atomic energy, affecting congressional attitudes toward the AEC, altering bureaucratic arrangements within the executive branch, and influencing the formulation of radiation-protection standards.

X

THE STATES AND
ATOMIC REGULATION

When the 1954 Atomic Energy Act made nuclear technology available to private enterprise and made government regulation of the atomic industry necessary, it opened the question of what role the states should play in protecting the public from radiation hazards. Apart from a few passing references, the law did not consider the interests of the states in promoting or regulating the use of atomic energy. Traditionally the states rather than the federal government exercised primary responsibility for public health and safety functions. Officials in many states, concerned that they would be excluded from regulatory authority over atomic energy, sought to affirm and expand state jurisdiction in the field. Despite the reluctance of the Atomic Energy Commission to surrender any of its regulatory responsibilities, the arguments of the states eventually persuaded Congress to amend the 1954 act to acknowledge a state role in atomic safety. The amendment, however, did not substantially diminish the AEC's preeminence in nuclear regulation or fully resolve the disputes between the AEC and the states over their relative responsibilities in radiation protection.

Since the 1954 act did not apply to radioactive materials or radiation sources that do not result from atomic fission, such as X rays, naturally occurring radium, and accelerator-produced isotopes, responsibility for protection against radiation from those sources rested with the states. But Congress assigned the role of safeguarding against the dangers of atomic fission, inherent in dealing with nuclear reactors, most radioisotopes, and most radioactive waste, solely to the AEC. The framers of the 1954 law acted on their conviction that the states lacked the experience and technical knowledge to deal effectively and intelligently with atomic energy. They did not intend to exclude the states entirely from participation in atomic-energy issues, but they made no effort to define what functions the states might carry out.[1]

Within a short time several states took it upon themselves to examine the implications of atomic energy and decide how to deal with its potential benefits and dangers. Energy-poor New England led the way. As early as 1952 some New England business and industrial groups had concluded that nuclear power would be economically advantageous to the region. They had contacted Secretary of Commerce Sinclair Weeks and presidential assistant Sherman Adams in 1953 to propose that when the first commercial reactor was built, it be located in New England. In February 1954 the New England Governors' Conference appointed a committee of twelve citizens, including industrial leaders, utility executives, lawyers, and scientists, to study the interests and responsibilities of their states in atomic development, "particularly in the field of power generation." The committee submitted a comprehensive report in July 1955. It recommended that the New England states move aggressively to promote the use of atomic energy for a wide range of industrial, medical, and research purposes. It also urged the construction of a nuclear reactor to generate electrical power "at the earliest opportunity." An atomic-power plant, the committee reasoned, would represent an important first step toward guaranteeing New England adequate electricity in the future and would help attract industry to the area. The report recognized the economic and technical uncertainties about nuclear power and, without being specific, suggested that the states should enact safeguards against radiological dangers. But it cautioned against overly restrictive regulations that would impede industrial and technological progress. The committee incorporated its findings into a model act that provided a framework for state promotional and regulatory activities. By 1956 five New England states had adopted legislation based on the committee's recommendations. Meanwhile, the Yankee Atomic Electric Company, supported by several New England utilities, made plans for the nuclear power plant that it hoped to complete by late 1957.[2]

Other states also were exploring atomic-energy questions. In May 1954 the Texas Legislative Council commissioned a study that, in contrast with the New England report, surveyed the possible impact of atomic development in a state where other energy sources were abundant. The report, completed in May 1955, concluded that "nuclear power does not seem to pose any immediate threat to the oil and gas industry in the state." But it suggested that atomic energy, especially its industrial and medical applications, was potentially important to Texas. Governor Allen Shivers accepted the report's recommendation that an advisory committee on atomic energy be appointed to examine nuclear issues in greater detail. The committee undertook both promotional and regulatory activities. It strove to create a favorable climate for the growth of atomic industries but at the same time to encourage the adoption of state radiation-protection standards and other regulations. It opposed "federal usurpation of regulatory activity" and urged that states take a greater role in controlling atomic energy. Committee chairman Frank Norton, a Dallas attorney, wrote that "the state should accept its responsibilities to deal with health and safety aspects in the atomic field. . . . Texas is very conscious of the rights of the state and would like to do everything possible to further this philosophy."[3]

The interest of Texas in atomic energy was echoed and amplified in other southern states. Florida governor LeRoy Collins was particularly outspoken in urging the South to move promptly to capitalize on its potential benefits. In a series of addresses Collins argued that "the lack of cheap heat" had inhibited the industrial growth of the South in the past. But nuclear energy could overcome that problem and make the South economically competitive with other sections. "Nuclear energy for the South can mean economic emancipation," he declared. "It can mean for our people standards of living unmatched anywhere." He called for planning and development on a regional basis, contending that a joint venture would be more effective than efforts by individual states. Collins also suggested that the southern states frame "safe and sane nuclear codes" that would adequately protect the public without discouraging industrial growth.[4]

The Southern Governors' Conference, meeting at Point Clear, Alabama in October 1955, endorsed Collins's position. It requested the Southern Regional Education Board, an advisory body, to study possible approaches for dealing with atomic energy. The Board sponsored a series of planning sessions and workshops and presented its findings to the 1956 meeting of the southern governors. It affirmed that "the role of the state in atomic energy is a vital one" and proposed that southern states, through existing agencies, take action to encourage and regulate the use of nuclear power. It advised the states to impose uniform safety codes and "to accept the new responsibilities which nuclear plants and atomic energy activities bring." The Board also urged the creation of a regional advisory council to coordinate the atomic-energy planning of all the southern states and to disseminate information on atomic activities. The Southern Governors' Conference unanimously approved, "in principle," the Board's recommendations.[5]

Other states were also undertaking preliminary steps in atomic matters. Florida, Illinois, and Michigan set up atomic-energy study committees. New York governor Averell Harriman created a Council on the Use of Nuclear Material to coordinate the work of various state agencies, propose safety procedures, and encourage atomic development. A total of twenty-eight states made progress toward establishing radiation-protection standards, though only two—New York and California—enacted comprehensive regulations. The nation's governors adopted a resolution at their annual meeting in August 1955 asserting the role of the states in atomic regulation. Introduced by Michigan governor G. Mennen Williams, the measure called for cooperation with the federal government to frame uniform regulations that would "promote the widest possible peacetime use of atomic materials." But the governors insisted that "in the exercise of the constitutionally reserved powers of the states, it is the duty of the states to safeguard the health, welfare and safety of our own citizens."[6]

By late 1956 many states, especially those in the South and those with heavily industrial economies, had shown keen interest in the implications of atomic energy. They were eager to study the possible uses of the new technology and hopeful that it would provide many useful services. It offered an abundant and potentially inexpensive source of power for electrical generation. Nuclear power was immediately appealing in areas where fuel was scarce and costly, but it also promised to fill the nation's long-range energy needs as fossil fuels were depleted. Commenting that "nuclear fission appears at the present time to be the one new energy source that can meet world demand for energy over the next century," the New England Committee on Atomic Energy predicted that "by the end of the twentieth century the bulk of the energy supplied by electric utility systems will be from nuclear sources." The states anticipated other important benefits from nuclear energy. Radioisotopes were already being employed for a wide variety of purposes, such as measuring the thickness and studying the wear qualities of industrial products, tracing complex chemical reactions, controlling weeds and insects, and diagnosing and treating cancer and brain and blood diseases. State officials believed that expanding the applications of atomic energy in industry, agriculture, and medicine would foster economic growth and advances in public health. Furthermore, many state leaders, like their counterparts in the federal government, viewed peaceful atomic development as essential for America's international prestige and world economic leadership. They feared that the nation was falling behind Great Britain and the Soviet Union in the field of nuclear power. Rhode Island governor Dennis J. Roberts declared that "only through a stepped-up program of peacetime nuclear development . . . can America maintain its industrial and scientific leadership and greatness"; New York's Harriman asserted that "it would be shocking if the Soviets were to outstrip us."[7]

Despite their widespread interest in atomic development, the states generally confined their activities to study groups and advisory panels. In deference to the embryonic state of the technology and their own lack of experience and expertise in the field of atomic energy, they refrained from enacting safety regulations that might soon become obsolete. As the Texas Committee on Atomic Energy declared: "The Atomic Age's unknown future and constant demands for changes and new concepts makes the passage of a rigid atomic state law impractical." The states also recognized that uniformity in their regulations was necessary to avoid hindering firms that would operate across state lines. "In the exercise of their constitutional police powers," advised the Michigan Atomic Energy Study Committee, "it appears neither wise nor reasonable for the individual states to adopt non-uniform codes which could result in confusion and have the effect of retarding the peace time use of atomic energy." Since many states were anxious to encourage atomic progress, they wished to avoid imposing restrictions that might prove to be premature or cumbersome for the atomic industry.[8]

The enthusiasm of the states for promoting atomic energy coincided with that of the AEC; there was no federal-state discord in efforts to establish a favorable atmosphere for expanding the peaceful uses of atomic technology. There was, however, an emerging difference of opinion over control of atomic energy. Although they were uncertain of what their precise role should be, the states firmly believed that they should eventually play an important part in atomic regulation. They objected to the 1954 Atomic Energy Act's denial of their traditional constitutional prerogatives in health and safety matters. Many lawyers, scholars, and state officials agreed with the chairman of the Michigan Atomic Energy

Study Committee that "to permit the Atomic Energy Commission, representing the Federal Government, to come into the several states and usurp our authority and attempt to provide for the health, welfare and safety of our citizens is indeed a bad precedent."[9]

The Atomic Energy Commission intended to retain the exclusive regulatory authority granted it in the 1954 act to avert the future possibility that the states would enact a multiplicity of health and safety measures. Concerned that state activities could create "a tremendous amount of conflict and confusion," Harold Price proposed that the Commission invite representatives of all the states to a meeting to discuss federal-state relations in atomic energy. The conference, held 13–14 July 1955 and attended by representatives of thirty-eight states, revealed the basic differences of opinion between the AEC and the states. Price and other spokesmen outlined the agency's position. They expressed their intention to keep the states fully informed of Commission activities and procedures and welcomed suggestions, comments, and criticisms from the states on health and safety matters. But they did not offer to turn over any of the AEC's functions to the states. Several state representatives suggested that the agency should relinquish at least part of its regulatory authority to states with adequate staffs and sufficient technical competence. They believed that in those cases, states should play more than an advisory role in controlling the radiation hazards of atomic fission.[10]

On Price's recommendation the Commission created a panel of state authorities for further consultation on health and safety issues. The Advisory Committee of State Officials, consisting of representatives from health, labor, and legal agencies of twelve states, first met in February 1956. The state spokesmen expressed concern about the AEC's reluctance to acknowledge an active state role in atomic regulation. "Throughout the entire meeting, there constantly arose discussions of the rights of states," reported one state delegate. "The state officials present were given the impression that the Commission believes the Congress has preempted the field and believing such, was hesitant about doing anything in the line of recognition of state responsibilities." Although the AEC and state officials agreed on the need for mutual cooperation, they still held different views about what their respective roles should be.[11]

The question of federal and state jurisdiction assumed greater significance and immediacy in the summer of 1956 as a result of the controversy over licensing the Power Reactor Development Company's fast-breeder plant in Lagoona Beach, Michigan. The AEC did not make the report of the Advisory Committee on Reactor Safeguards, which cited reservations about the safety of the proposed facility, available to state officials. But when Michigan governor Williams learned of its general contents from Senator Anderson, he was angry and alarmed. Williams was a proponent of nuclear power and a supporter of the PRDC project, but he was deeply disturbed that the AEC had neither consulted with state authorities nor given them a copy of the Safeguards Committee's findings. He had been the only governor to attend the AEC's 1955 conference on state relations, and he was dissatisfied with the agency's attitude toward the states. At a meeting with a group of advisors on 16 July 1956, Williams complained that "the AEC did not appear to have given the States much support or cooperation in the past." The same day, he sent a telegram to Chairman Strauss. "It is distressing that no information regarding [the Safeguards Committee's] report has been given to the Governor of Michigan who has a constitutional responsibility for the public health and safety," he declared. "We in Michigan, who are vitally interested in such matters, have not been granted the courtesy of being sent that report."[12]

AEC general manager Fields replied that "it would be inappropriate to disclose the contents of internal documents." He pledged that the report, along with other technical advice, would receive the Commission's consideration and that the AEC would "obtain every reasonable assurenace [sic] that the health and safety of the public will be protected." The AEC's response hardly mollified Williams, who remained disgruntled and frustrated in his efforts to see the Safeguards Committee report. He received sympathy from an influential supporter, Senator Anderson. After the Commission issued the PRDC a construction permit in August 1956, Anderson wired Williams, expressing regret that "while areas between federal and state interest in safety and other matters have not been clearly delineated, the governor of the state of Michigan has apparently been precluded from being heard or participating in any decision to build this reactor." Just a few days before, Anderson had taken action toward clarifying the issue of state authority by introducing an amendment to the 1954 Atomic Energy Act.[13]

For several months Anderson and other members of the Joint Committee had considered ways to delineate more clearly the role of the states in atomic regulation. The committee had changed its position since assigning the AEC exclusive jurisdiction in the 1954 act; its leadership and staff now agreed that states with trained personnel and sufficient technical expertise should be allowed to assume some independent functions. They shifted their stance not only because of the constitutional arguments of the states but also because an enlarged definition of state authority seemed essential for atomic development. The atomic-power program was a "mirage," declared an aide to Anderson, "until the role of the states is clearly set forth and they have been given full partnership status." In January 1956 Vice-Chairman Durham introduced an amendment to the 1954 act. It required the AEC to transfer any of its health and safety functions to a state whose governor certified its competence to take over the specified duties. Committee Counsel George Norris, Jr., who drafted the Durham bill, admitted that it would allow states "to jump in precipitously before they are really ready to assume full responsibilities." But he hoped it would stimulate thinking so that "as soon as possible, and as far as possible, the health and safety regulations [would] be turned back to the States." In July 1956, in the midst of the controversy over the PRDC reactor, Anderson submitted his amendment to the 1954 act. Although less permissive than the Durham bill, it sought the same goal. The proposal authorized the AEC "to turn over such areas to the States for regulation as it finds the States are competent to assume such powers," subject to congressional review. Anderson believed that as states became better equipped to handle atomic regulation, they should be granted greater authority.[14]

Prodded by the Durham and Anderson bills, in early 1957 the Atomic Energy Commission drafted its own proposals for federal and state jurisdiction in atomic regulation. The AEC objected to the Durham bill because, in the words of General Counsel William Mitchell, it "would take the matter out of our hands." The Anderson measure, though preferable, "would put the pressure on us immediately to go into such agreements." Therefore, both congressional amendments might allow the states to assume broader authority than the AEC thought they were prepared to exercise. Commissioner Libby worried that states would plunge "into the regulatory business before they know an isotope from a cow." Harold Price argued that since the states were considering bills, some of them "pretty half baked," the Commission should press for federal legislation so "we will be in position to have a fence around . . . the states." In addition to curbing the scope of state action, the AEC found it desirable to clarify its relations with the states for other reasons. Cooperation with them would promote the adoption of uniform radiation-protection standards and "minimize the risk of inconsistencies between Federal and state regulation." Furthermore, the states could provide useful services and help alleviate potentially serious manpower shortages by assisting the AEC in inspections of the growing number of licensees and collecting environmental information on proposed sites for nuclear facilities. Finally, disputes with the states could seriously impair the growth of nuclear power because of their unquestioned control over industrial zoning and use of water supplies.[15]

On the basis of those considerations the AEC drafted an amendment to the 1954 act that allowed more active state participation in nuclear regulation than the agency had previously conceded. Although more restrictive of state functions than the Durham or Anderson bills, the AEC's proposal acknowledged that the states should exercise more than just an advisory role in protecting against atomic-radiation dangers. Its amendment specifically authorized the Commission to cooperate with the states, individually or in groups, to safeguard public health and safety. It also provided for collaboration between the AEC and states in inspecting nuclear facilities and "other services . . . as the Commission deems necessary." To improve the ability of states to deal with nuclear issues, the AEC could offer training to state employees without charge. The key section of the draft affirmed the role of states in "adopting, inspecting against, and enforcing standards for protecting the health and safety of the public from radiation hazards." But it added three important conditions. It exempted federal installations and contractors from compliance with state regulations. It also required that states adopt standards "consistent with" those of the AEC. Finally, it prohibited them from undertaking any licensing functions.[16]

The amendment proposed to establish a system of concurrent jurisdiction in which the AEC and the states would work together to ensure atomic safety. But the dual functions would not apply to licensing. The AEC wanted to avoid imposing undue burdens on the atomic industry by subjecting them to any additional licensing procedures. The draft did not authorize the Commission to relinquish any of its functions to the exclusive authority of the states, as the Durham and Anderson bills did. Strauss told Durham that "it is premature to turn over to the states sole regulatory responsibility for any of the areas in the field covered by the 1954 Act." But he added that the AEC would continue to study the question to determine whether it should turn over "some limited portions of its current regulatory jurisdiction" when the states became more technically competent. The AEC amendment was an effort to satisfy the

Joint Committee without endorsing the bolder initiatives of Durham and Anderson. It was also intended to establish an "orderly scheme" for cooperating with the states. The agency believed that it was ensuring adequate protection against atomic-radiation hazards and that state participation in safety regulation was unnecessary. But it realized that states would continue to insist on undertaking some functions and viewed its collaborative arrangement as a way to exert a restraining influence on them.[17]

The AEC sought state support for its draft amendment at a Conference on the States and Atomic Energy Development, sponsored by the Council of State Governments and held in Chicago in May 1957. Representatives of thirty-four states expressed general approval of the AEC's approach and agreement that the states were not prepared to take over major responsibility for atomic regulation. But the delegates also voiced some reservations about the AEC's proposal. They urged that the draft be considered as interim legislation because at a later time the states might want to increase their regulatory authority and assume some licensing functions. They particularly objected to the provision that state radiation standards had to be "consistent with" those of the AEC, which meant they would be identical. They thought the states should be permitted to impose stricter regulations if they chose, and unanimously recommended that the phrase "not in conflict" be substituted for the word "consistent." The AEC accepted that revision to avoid "an unnecessary states' rights dispute over the proposed legislation." It viewed cooperation with the states as the best way to deter them from passing overly rigorous laws.[18]

In addition to discussing federal legislation to delineate the role of the states in nuclear regulation, the delegates at the Chicago conference also considered state action to develop and control atomic energy. The Council of State Governments submitted a model law designed to encourage uniformity and coordination among the states in dealing with atomic matters. On the basis of the suggested legislation drafted by the New England Committee on Atomic Energy in 1955, the Council recommended that each governor appoint a "Coordinator of Atomic Development Activities" to work with the various state agencies concerned with atomic energy, including departments of health, labor, highways, public utilities, insurance, conservation, and mines. The coordinator would oversee the actions of the state agencies and keep them informed about each other's plans and programs. He would also serve as the primary contact for cooperating with the AEC and other states. The model act provided for existing agencies to carry out state responsibilities while the coordinator reviewed their activities and advised the governor on atomic-energy policies.[19]

Adoption of the model legislation, its framers believed, would provide state officials with current information on atomic energy and minimize bureaucratic confusion. It would allow for the orderly supervision of atomic activities without imposing "rigid, detailed regulations which might hamper the development of atomic energy in the State." The delegates at the Chicago meeting endorsed the model act's provisions for an atomic-energy coordinator, uniformity in various states' safety regulations, and using existing state agencies to administer atomic programs. The proposed state legislation received the approval of Senator Anderson, who called it a "very good first step," and the AEC, which regarded it as "consistent with the cooperative approach which the Commission has endeavored to undertake."[20]

While the AEC and the states were attempting to find a mutually agreeable framework for state participation in nuclear regulation, public concern about radiation hazards was increasing. The *Lucky Dragon* incident, the 1956 report of the National Academy of Sciences on radiation effects, and the growing fallout controversy called attention to the problems of radiation protection and helped spur individual states to take measures to deal with atomic energy. A meeting of state health officials in November 1957 urged prompt state action to safeguard against radiation, and many states developed new programs or expanded existing ones. By late 1958 thirteen states had approved legislation patterned on the lines suggested by the Council of State Governments, and each had installed an atomic-energy coordinator. A total of thirty states had established study committees or advisory panels to investigate and report on atomic-energy issues. Seventeen states had prohibited or sharply limited use of fluoroscope machines to fit customers in shoe stores. Seven states had adopted detailed radiation-protection regulations and twenty-two others had enacted less comprehensive standards.[21]

The states of the South were particularly active in investigating atomic-energy questions. Following the recommendations of the Southern Regional Education Board, the Southern Governors' Conference established the Regional Advisory Council on Nuclear Energy in 1957. The council undertook a wide variety of activities and sought to create, in cooperation with the states, "a healthy, vigorous, and wholesome climate for atomic progress." By setting up information programs to foster public understanding of the potential benefits of atomic energy, encouraging universities to train nuclear physicists and engineers to ease the manpower shortage in the field, and assisting electric utilities to overcome barriers that might "impede development of nuclear power plants in the South," it planned to promote aggressively the use of atomic energy. It also strongly urged that the southern states join together in a regional compact on nuclear energy. The compact would provide technical advice to the states on both developmental and regulatory issues. The council further advised the southern states to establish uniform radiation-protection regulations "as rapidly as possible." It insisted that the states should assume some of the AEC's regulatory functions to avoid the need for a "large new federal bureaucracy" and to affirm the traditional state role in protecting public health. "The states, and the South as a region," a council report declared, "should continue to be alert for a common front against *complete* Federal authority in the field of atomic energy."[22]

Like the AEC, states that established radiation-protection standards generally followed the recommendations of the National Committee on Radiation Protection. In 1955 the NCRP published a handbook that provided basic information about controlling radiation hazards and included a detailed "suggested state radiation-protection act." The committee issued the guidelines to encourage uniformity in state regulations and to deter "panicky efforts" to legislate radiation safeguards that might result from "an exaggerated notion of the seriousness of the problem" among the general public. Unlike the Council of State Governments' model act, which emphasized promotional activities, the NCRP's handbook discussed only regulation. It recommended that the states use the permissible doses for external and internal sources of radiation that the NCRP had previously published. The states that adopted radiation standards relied heavily on the NCRP's advice, but inevitably some differences and ambiguities occurred. The regulations the states developed usually dealt with areas where state authority clearly prevailed. They refrained from taking bolder steps because, in the words of two informed observers, "of confusion generated by the federal government's failure to clarify what segment of the atomic energy field it intends to occupy." Only one state, Minnesota, directly challenged federal preeminence in atomic regulation. In December 1958 its State Board of Health enacted a requirement that the owner of a nuclear reactor or facility receive the board's approval before construction or operation could proceed.[23]

The atomic industry regarded increasing state action in atomic regulation with concern. Industry spokesmen recognized that state cooperation and backing were essential for atomic progress. "It is at the local level that public understanding will be obtained or denied," declared Charles Robbins, executive manager of the Atomic Industrial Forum, in 1958. "The community will have a right to expect that local and state governments . . . are prepared to deal with [nuclear energy] properly and constructively." But the atomic industry worried that the states might impose a perplexing maze of conflicting or restrictive measures. Its representatives appealed for careful and responsible state regulations and emphasized the need for uniformity among the states. The United States Chamber of Commerce insisted, for example, that "uniformity in the regulations of the various states covering conditions of health and safety is imperative . . . if the civilian atomic energy industry is to continue to grow."[24]

W. A. McAdams, a radiation-protection consultant for General Electric, urged the states to adopt rules that, in addition to being uniform, were clear but not too specific, and sound but not overly restrictive. As an alarming example of what states might do, he cited a bill introduced in the Arizona legislature in 1958. It would have forbidden construction of nuclear reactors or missile plants within sixty miles of a city of more than ten thousand. "Such a regulation could set a precedent which would seriously jeopardize the future of the whole atomic energy industry," McAdams stated. Although killed in committee, the bill was a disquieting omen of what might happen if the question of control over atomic energy was not resolved. To end the existing uncertainty, the atomic industry had good reason to favor a clarifying amendment to the 1954 act. The AEC's proposed amendment, however, as revised after the Chicago conference, posed potential problems. A system of dual regulation, even if the AEC retained sole authority over licensing, could be unwieldy and burdensome, and the provision that states could establish stricter regulations than those of the AEC was also troublesome.[25]

Along with the states, the Atomic Energy Commission, the Joint Committee on Atomic Energy, and the atomic industry, the White House took an active interest in federal-state relations in atomic-energy matters, though its role was an indirect one. President Eisenhower supported the general principle of states' rights and wanted to arrest the gravitation of power to the national government. In June 1957 he spoke to the National Conference of Governors in Williamsburg, Virginia and gave what he privately described as a "very banal and colorless talk." It expressed, he said, "an obvious truth—that governors ought to concern themselves more with retaining states' responsibilities if they are to retain states' rights." In his address the president proposed that a task force to study a broad range of questions relating to the functions of the federal and state governments be formed. The governors accepted Eisenhower's recommendation, and within a short time the Joint Federal-State Action Committee, consisting of members appointed by the president and chairman of the governors' conference, began its work. Reflecting the views of the president, the Action Committee sought "ways and means to strengthen the Federal system by strengthening State governments as essential components of this system." Among the issues it investigated was the delegation of authority in atomic-energy programs, and it concluded that "a greater share of the responsibility for the promotion and regulation of the peacetime uses of atomic energy, particularly in the fields of health and safety, should be vested in the State governments." The Action Committee's specific recommendations on federal legislation did not differ in any significant way from the AEC's proposed amendment as revised after the 1957 Chicago conference. Although it did not contribute any original ideas for delineating federal and state roles in atomic energy, the Action Committee's call for greater state authority and Eisenhower's endorsement of it gave additional impetus to the movement to clarify the issue.[26]

By the time that the Joint Committee on Atomic Energy scheduled hearings on federal-state relations in atomic energy in early 1959, public concern over radiation had greatly intensified. The fallout controversy that arose at that time over the unprecedentedly high measurements of strontium 90 created misgivings about the AEC's performance in protecting the public from radiation hazards and indirectly helped strengthen the claims of the states for a greater role in radiation safety. The report of the Public Health Service's National Advisory Committee on Radiation, released on 26 March, not only suggested that assigning the AEC dual responsibilities for promoting and regulating atomic energy was unwise but also urged that the states be given increasing authority in the field. The advisory committee expressed confidence that the states would develop the ability to deal with radiation effectively and argued that "where regulatory controls are needed for the safety of a community, these controls may be best exercised where the authority responsible for control is not far removed from the group or groups being protected." Maurice B. Visscher, chairman of the atomic-energy study committee of

Minnesota, the only state to challenge the AEC's authority by issuing its own licensing requirements, also questioned the agency's role in radiation safety. "The fact is that the AEC has not done its practical job in the biological and medical area very well," he wrote in February 1959. "The trouble may be that the AEC is run by Commissioners who are primarily in the weapons business and don't really know enough about the biological and medical sides of things to have informed opinions as to policy in those areas."[27]

Meanwhile, the AEC was drafting new legislation on federal-state relations for consideration at the Joint Committee's hearings. The agency decided that it should make significant revisions of its 1957 proposal because of several defects that had become apparent in discussions with legal experts and industry representatives. The concurrent jurisdiction envisioned in the original bill posed several potential problems. It would require both the AEC and the states to hire staffs to perform identical functions, and qualified personnel were "very scarce." Furthermore, state legislatures might refuse to allocate funds for regulatory functions the AEC was already performing. With a dual system of authority, it seemed more likely that each component might assume the other was carrying out the necessary work and regulation might be more lax than if responsibilities were divided. Concurrent jurisdiction would create unnecessary difficulties for the atomic industry and users of radioisotopes because they would have "to deal with and satisfy the requirements of both Federal and State regulatory agencies." Another flaw in the earlier amendment was its failure to distinguish between matters primarily of state concern and those of interstate, national, and international interest that necessitated exclusive federal control. Finally, the 1957 proposal did not differentiate between states that had established satisfactory regulatory programs and those that had not. To correct those weaknesses, the AEC drafted a substantially revised amendment to the 1954 Atomic Energy Act.[28]

The bill that the AEC submitted to the Joint Committee authorized the states to assume exclusive authority in certain specified areas. After a governor and the AEC concurred that the state had established an adequate program of radiation protection that was generally compatible with AEC regulations, they could enter into a formal agreement by which the state would take over the designated licensing and regulatory functions. The proposed amendment permitted, with some exceptions, independent state control of source materials, radioisotopes, radioactive waste, and special nuclear materials in quantities small enough to avoid the possibility of an accidental chain reaction.

The AEC's proposal kept the most hazardous aspects of atomic energy under federal control. It gave the Commission exclusive jurisdiction over licensing and regulating the construction and operation of "production and utilization" facilities. It also stipulated that the AEC would regulate activities involving foreign countries, including exporting and importing and disposal in the ocean of nuclear materials. Another provision in the bill granted the AEC broad discretionary authority to license the disposal of by-product, source, or special nuclear material when it determined that their "hazards or potential hazards" required federal preemption. The proposed amendment retained some of the provisions of the AEC's 1957 bill. It authorized cooperation between the AEC and the states to perform inspections of nuclear facilities and other functions. It allowed the AEC to train state employees without charge so that the states could improve their competence in the atomic-energy field and assume the authority the amendment sanctioned.[29]

The AEC sought to satisfy all interested parties by incorporating elements of their positions into its proposal. It acknowledged the traditional state role in public health and safety by agreeing to turn over to qualified states a measure of independent authority. Although it allowed the states only limited responsibilities, it provided the means for them to gain greater experience and additional technical expertise through the AEC's training program. Furthermore, the agency affirmed that as scientific knowledge about atomic energy increased and the states became more capable of dealing with the technology, they could be permitted wider jurisdiction. The AEC's amendment also embraced important aspects of the bills introduced by Congressman Durham and Senator Anderson. Both had called for the AEC to recognize some exclusive state control over atomic energy. Durham had proposed that a state assume greater responsibility after the governor declared its ability to do so; Anderson suggested that the AEC judge the competence of the state. The AEC bill struck a compromise by authorizing federal withdrawal from some of its functions when both a governor and the Commission attested to the adequacy of the state's regulatory program. The 1959 draft also attempted to alleviate the concerns of the atomic industry. It eliminated the system of concurrent jurisdiction envisioned in the 1957 proposal. Unlike the earlier measure, as revised, it did not specifically authorize the states to establish radiation-protection standards stricter than those of the AEC.

Rather it skirted the issue by stipulating that federal and state regulations should, "to the extent feasible, be coordinated and compatible."[30]

Above all, the 1959 bill reflected the AEC's own position. After four years of debate over federal-state relations in atomic energy, the Commission had modified its thinking to the point that it now consented to grant states some independent functions in safeguarding public safety. But the amendment ensured that the AEC would partially relinquish its responsibilities only on its own terms. It would turn over authority in the specified areas on a state-by-state basis and only after it determined that each state with which it entered into an agreement had established a satisfactory regulatory program. The AEC would retain exclusive jurisdiction in states that did not sign an agreement. It still wanted to contain state activities within narrow bounds because of both regulatory and promotional considerations. It believed that few states were sufficiently prepared to assume a larger role in protecting health and safety, and it feared they might impose restrictive or ill-considered regulations that would discourage development. Even after it entered into an agreement with a state under the proposed amendment, the AEC would exercise sole jurisdiction over its most important activities, particularly all aspects of the construction and operation of nuclear power reactors. While permitting some state supervision of nuclear wastes, the AEC could control their disposal if it decided the hazards were great enough to require federal licensing. The functions that the AEC agreed to assign to qualified states, especially the regulation of isotope users, were essential for adequate radiation protection. But they dealt with the less dangerous aspects of radiological safety. They were also duties that the agency found increasingly burdensome. Delegating them to states would ease the manpower shortages the AEC faced as its regulatory workload increased.[31]

The AEC proposal received a cool response from its Advisory Committee of State Officials, which met in Washington on 5 March 1959. The state representatives complained that the area of sole AEC jurisdiction remained undefined; it was unclear, for example, whether the states could monitor gaseous and liquid effluents from a nuclear reactor. They also objected to the sections of the bill that granted exclusive authority to the AEC. On the other hand, they "did not indicate an eagerness to accept total responsibility" for the functions the amendment allowed the states to take over. The California delegate expressed dissatisfaction that the AEC would control disposal of waste materials in the ocean. Above all, the state officials disputed the bill's assumption that the federal government had legally preempted the state role in public health and safety and could return to the states whatever authority the AEC deemed appropriate. One committee member noted that "it was the opinion of the representatives of the state health departments attending this meeting that the Governor's signature would indicate the legality of the original authority of the Federal government." Therefore, he added, "this makes our acceptance of this legislation basically impossible." The AEC gave little consideration to the comments of the state officials. It believed it had framed a reasonable compromise on the question of federal-state relations. The objections of the advisory committee were not only contradictory but merely reiterated the states' position without offering any constructive alternatives.[32]

The Joint Committee held its hearings on federal and state jurisdiction in atomic regulation from 19 May through 22 May 1959. The AEC's bill received the endorsement of the Joint Federal-State Action Committee, the Council of State Governments, the National Association of Attorneys General, the South's Regional Advisory Council on Nuclear Energy, several individual states, and atomic-industry spokesmen. The hearings also highlighted some ambiguities in the legislation. It remained unclear, even after some discussion, whether or not the states could impose radiation-protection standards stricter than those of the federal government. The hearings also failed to define more precisely the jurisdiction of the AEC and the states in disposing of various kinds of nuclear wastes.[33]

The question of the role of the states in regulating nuclear reactors generated much comment but was not fully resolved. Maurice Visscher defended Minnesota's requirement that reactors meet the approval of the State Board of Health before being constructed or operated. He received little support from members of the Joint Committee or other witnesses. Senator Anderson, for example, thought that Minnesota's reactor-licensing policy "is just as wrong as it can be." But he sympathized with the need for states to investigate the safety aspects of reactors. Citing the controversy over the Power Reactor Development Company plant, he observed: "I am not so sure you can rely too completely on any one group. It might be well to have an extra group around once in a while to say we would like to look at this, too." Oliver Townsend, director of the New York Office of Atomic Development, suggested that the concern of health officials in his state about reactor safety would be eased if the state were given authority to veto the proposed site of a nuclear facility. His recommendation seemed sensible to some Joint Committee members, but other expert witnesses contended that states lacked the technical competence to make final judgments on reactor locations. The AEC held to its position that it should retain control over all aspects of regulating reactors, although, as the amendment prescribed, it pledged to consult with the states and give them the opportunity to offer advice on licensing atomic installations that remained subject to federal jurisdiction.[34]

The Joint Committee did not take action on the AEC's bill until after the Bureau of the Budget completed its study of the roles of federal agencies in radiation protection, which the president had ordered earlier in the year. After the Bureau submitted its report and Eisenhower established the Federal Radiation Council by executive order in August 1959, the committee began final consideration of the AEC's proposed amendment. It left the bill largely intact, though it added a section giving the FRC statutory authority. To emphasize the interim nature of the amendment, it inserted a statement that as states became more capable of assuming responsibilities in atomic regulation, "additional legislation may be desirable." The committee also sought to promote uniformity and discourage states from imposing standards that conflicted with the AEC's by strengthening the section of the bill that dealt with radiation-protection regulations. The original proposal had called for cooperation between the AEC and the states to establish standards that would, "to the extent feasible, be coordinated and compatible." The Joint Committee removed the words "to the extent feasible," though what constituted "compatible" standards was not defined.[35]

Senator Anderson realized that the proposed amendment did not settle all the questions about the states' role in regulating atomic energy. But "even though we may not have the final answer," he wrote, "a start has to be made in deciding what things the state is to do looking toward health and safety and what things the state must leave temporarily to the Federal Government." He urged the Senate to pass the bill promptly. Until Congress acted on the amendment, he argued, "there will be confusion and possible conflict between Federal and State regulations and uncertainty on the part of industry and possible jeopardy to the public health and safety." Both the Senate and the House approved the measure on 11 September 1959, and the president signed it into law twelve days later.[36]

The amendment established the broad outlines for delineating federal and state jurisdiction in atomic regulation. The next problem for the AEC was to devise specific criteria by which to evaluate the qualifications of states wishing to assume the authority the statute permitted them. After consulting with representatives of the Joint Federal-State Action Committee, the Council of State Governments, the National Association of Attorneys General, the Regional Advisory Council in Nuclear Energy, the AFL-CIO, the Atomic Industrial Forum, the U.S. Departments of Labor and Health, Education, and Welfare, and health departments and atomic-energy committees of several states, the agency staff in February 1960 presented to the Commission draft guidelines for signing agreements to turn over regulatory functions to the states.[37]

The proposed criteria suggested that, like the AEC's programs, "a state regulatory program should be designed to protect the health and safety of the people against radiation hazards and to encourage the constructive uses of radiation." The guidelines stressed the need for uniformity and compatibility with AEC regulations. They stipulated, for example, that permissible levels of radiation exposure imposed by states entering into agreements with the AEC (which came to be known as "agreement states") should be "no more and no less than those standards fixed by . . . the AEC." The draft criteria advised that agreement states establish a central regulatory authority and that they guard against overlapping jurisdiction at the state and local levels. The staff proposal also recommended desirable state requirements on such matters as waste disposal, records of occupational exposure to radiation, inspection of licensed facilities, enforcement procedures, and qualifications for state regulatory and inspection personnel. Although the criteria made no specific mention of control of radiation sources already under state authority, the staff argued that a state's past performance in providing protection against those hazards should be considered when assessing an application to take over additional functions under the agreements program. The draft criteria were intended to serve as a basis for discussion to establish the framework for state assumption of increased regulatory functions. "We feel the prime objective of the Commission," the staff declared, "should be to encourage the states to accept the broad regulatory responsibility as provided under the amendment."[38]

The Commission approved circulation of the draft criteria for public comment. In April 1960 Eisenhower wrote each of the fifty governors inviting their opinions on the guidelines. AEC officials met with representatives of many states and organizations to discuss and solicit reactions to the criteria. The AEC's Advisory Committee of State Officials also offered comments and proposed changes. In January 1961 the staff submitted to the Commission revised criteria incorporating suggestions received on the draft. Most of the changes were clarifications of wording, phraseology, and emphasis rather than modifications of matters of major substance. In response to several comments, for example, the AEC altered the statement on the duties of a state regulatory agency "to eliminate any intimation that [it] should have a promotional as well as a regulatory function." Although state spokesmen agreed with the desirability of uniformity in radiation-protection standards, some insisted that the draft criteria were too inflexible and that states should be permitted to impose stricter limits to adapt to local conditions or special circumstances that might arise. Therefore, the AEC deleted the phrase in the draft that called for state standards that were "no more and no less" than its own. The Commission approved the revised criteria, which even in their final form were not firm prerequisites for states wishing to enter into an agreement with the AEC. Rather they were guidelines for both the states and the AEC to use in developing the agreements by which a state could take over increased regulatory authority.[39]

Despite the state efforts that had played a major role in the enactment of the 1959 amendment and the interest of many states in the AEC's criteria, most states made little or no progress toward entering the agreements program. By early 1961, only Kentucky and New York had initiated the necessary steps to assume the responsibilities the amendment allowed. A number of considerations contributed to the inaction of the states. Some states recognized that they needed more skilled manpower and technical expertise before taking over the prescribed functions. In many states the governor lacked the legal authority to sign an agreement with the AEC and had to secure powers to act from the state legislature. Although a few state legislatures had granted the necessary authority, many others had not. In general, the states seemed more concerned with establishing the principle that they should share in atomic safety, which the 1959 amendment had affirmed, than with actually carrying out the regulatory responsibilities they were permitted to undertake.[40]

A few states declined to negotiate with the AEC for quite different reasons. Representatives of Virginia, Pennsylvania, Massachusetts, and Michigan maintained that the federal government lacked the constitutional power to preempt any of the states' health and safety functions and that entering into agreements with the AEC was therefore neither necessary nor desirable. Although Minnesota abandoned its requirement for state licensing of nuclear reactors, those four states suggested that they had the authority to regulate atomic-power plants. Michigan, mindful of its experience in the PRDC case, was particularly adamant. Commenting on the AEC's draft criteria, Michigan state health commissioner Albert E. Heustis observed that if his state signed an agreement, "we would be taking a backward step in our radiation control program." He insisted that without the monitoring of the PRDC reactor conducted by state health officials, "we would have no reliable background data with which to assure the future health and safety of the people of the state of Michigan in the Monroe area." Heustis added: "We therefore could not possibly agree to give the Atomic Energy Commission complete authority and jurisdiction . . . for the construction and operation of any production or utilization facility within the state."[41]

The states' restrained response to the agreements program generated concern and criticism from the Joint Committee, the AEC, and industry spokesmen. In Joint Committee hearings held in May 1960, Chet Holifield complained: "We were told . . . how anxious the States were to get in and do this job. . . . I am somewhat surprised in view of the case that was made to us that there has not been a little more action on the part of the States." AEC commissioner Loren K. Olson expressed disappointment to a meeting of southern attorneys general in May 1961 that the states had not moved more rapidly to take advantage of the agreements program. "We still believe it will be a successful program," he declared, "but perhaps our original optimism must now be couched in words of restraint." Charles H. Weaver, president of the Atomic Industrial Forum, worried that if agreements between the AEC and individual states were not achieved promptly, states might establish their own independent regulatory requirements. Although the atomic industry recognized the need for government safety standards, he told AEC chairman Seaborg, it was "disturbed about the possibility of being regulated by two different jurisdictions for the same purpose."[42]

Despite the general lack of progress of the states toward assuming increased regulatory authority, a few were negotiating with the AEC to enter the agreements program. Kentucky submitted an informal proposal to the AEC in July 1960. After several meetings between state officials and AEC staff members to discuss the draft, Kentucky formally presented its program for AEC consideration in July 1961. Before acting on the proposal, the Commission published it for public comment and the staff carefully reviewed it again.[43]

The staff found most of the provisions of Kentucky's proposal satisfactory, but it raised questions about two items. One concerned the extent of the authority over radioactive-waste disposal that the AEC should transfer to the state. Kentucky planned to assume responsibility for all low-level waste except that dumped into the ocean, which under the 1959 amendment remained an exclusive federal function. The AEC suggested, however, that it might retain authority over land burial of waste materials because it was uncertain that states were qualified to provide long-term supervision of disposal sites. It also indicated that federal control might be advisable because waste disposal could be most efficiently carried out on a regional basis. One AEC official noted disapprovingly that "if states assume jurisdiction in this matter each state would want a burial site within its borders." The other reservation the AEC expressed about the Kentucky program stemmed from doubts about whether the agency should relinquish jurisdiction over distribution of manufactured products containing radioactive materials. Kentucky proposed to assume licensing responsibilities for such devices, but the AEC staff worried that surrendering complete authority to the states might sacrifice uniformity in safety design and labeling for goods that were produced in one state but used in many others. The AEC asked for public comments before taking a final position on the issues of land burial of low-level waste and regulation of manufactured products.[44]

The AEC's announcement of its reservations about Kentucky's proposal generated protests from state spokesmen. John B. Breckinridge, attorney general of Kentucky, argued that many states could effectively regulate land burial of low-level waste and distribution of products containing radioactive materials. He suggested that AEC control of those functions would retard progress in the state-agreements program. The 1961 Southern Governors' Conference resolved that if the AEC retained authority in the areas under question, it would "seriously impair the development of competency and expertise within the states" and "negate the desire of the states to execute agreements." The AEC's Advisory Committee of State Officials took a similar position. In the face of strong state objections, the AEC decided not to claim exclusive jurisdiction over land burial of waste. On the issue of manufactured devices it compromised by allowing agreement states to regulate industrial products such as thickness gauges while retaining control over consumer goods such as luminous watches and lock illuminators.[45]

Once those questions were settled, the AEC and Kentucky proceeded quickly to sign an agreement. On 8 February 1962 Kentucky formally entered the agreements program and became the first state to take over regulatory duties under the provisions of the 1959 amendment. Kentucky's interest in assuming those responsibilities arose from its concern that unless the states acted, control over atomic energy would remain exclusively in the hands of the federal government. Furthermore, state officials believed that by executing authority formerly assigned to the AEC they could "create a more favorable climate for the development and use of [nuclear] materials due to the state regulatory agency's closeness to the user," provide better overall protection against radiation from sources under state jurisdiction, and more easily attract atomic industries. In May 1964 the former executive director of the Kentucky Atomic Energy and Space Authority reported that the results of the state's participation in the agreements program "border[ed] on the spectacular." He was gratified that in a little over two years the number of state licensees using atomic energy had grown from 85 to 165, that medical, industrial, and research concerns were "unanimous in their acclaim for the better and faster service in granting and amending their licenses," and that the state had licensed a commercial low-level waste disposal site that to date had buried over a hundred thousand cubic feet of waste. He maintained that "the increase in protection of the health and safety to the public and workers from all sources of ionizing radiation [had] also been dramatic."[46]

A few other states followed the example of Kentucky. California signed an agreement similar to Kentucky's and on 12 March 1962 became the second state to join the program. By May 1963 four additional states— Mississippi, New York, Texas, and Arkansas—had done likewise. The fact that four of the six states that entered into agreements with the AEC were located in the South reflected the region's particularly keen interest in atomic energy. In July 1962 the South realized one of the major goals of the Regional Advisory Council on Nuclear Energy by the creation of a regional compact, which then included eleven states and was the only organization of its kind in the nation. The Southern Interstate Nuclear Board, which administered the affairs of the compact, emphasized promotional and educational activities. But it also urged its members to adopt responsible, uniform safety regulations and to enter into agreements with the AEC to avoid a federal monopoly in guarding against the hazards of atomic fission.[47]

The 1959 amendment to the Atomic Energy Act and its subsequent implementation through the agreements program were the product of several years of uncertainty and controversy about the role of the states in regulating atomic energy. Within a short time after passage of the 1954 act, the states asserted their constitutional authority to safeguard public health and safety and challenged the right of Congress to deny those functions to the states in the field of atomic energy. Balanced against the state claims were the practical realities that in most cases they lacked the technical resources to carry out effective control of radiation hazards. For that reason, along with its fear that the states would impose diverse or conflicting safety requirements, the AEC consigned them to a strictly advisory capacity and insisted that it retain regulatory authority in its own hands. The states were concerned that their exclusion from statutory responsibilities in nuclear regulation might set a precedent that would carry over into other areas. They were determined to affirm state jurisdiction in health and safety matters by exercising at least some powers over atomic energy. In a time when federal-state relations were a subject of unprecedented study and leaders at both levels were seeking to prevent a disproportionate centralization of power, the states' constitutional arguments were the key to spurring their own action and to winning support from influential backers.[48] Only after the states' position gained sympathy in the Joint Committee on Atomic Energy and the White House did the AEC shift its stance and make a serious effort to include the states in its atomic-safety program.

Indirectly, the fallout issue further buttressed state claims. The questions it raised about the AEC's role in protecting public health helped, for example, to assure a positive administration response to the 1959 report of the Public Health Service's National Advisory Committee on Radiation, which urged that the states be given important new responsibilities in radiation protection. Doubts about the AEC's handling of radiation safety on fallout and other matters reinforced the determination of state officials to press for wider jurisdiction in the field. The controversy over the PRDC reactor in Michigan helped prompt state leaders, as well as the Joint Committee on Atomic Energy, to assert the need for increased state authority. The diminished confidence in the AEC on health and safety issues strengthened the resolve of the states and increased the credibility of their position. Reservations about the AEC's performance and priorities created interest in and support for alternatives in the area of radiological health. As a result, the AEC lost some of its authority to other federal agencies and to the states.

Yet even after passage of the 1959 amendment the AEC retained its preeminence in nuclear regulation. Even states that entered into agreements with the AEC under the provisions of the amendment were granted only limited functions. The agency avoided surrendering much of its authority for a number of reasons. The states recognized that in most cases they lacked the expertise, technical facilities, and money available to the AEC, and that they were ill prepared to assume major regulatory functions until they acquired better resources. For that purpose the amendment provided for technical training of state employees. The Joint Committee emphasized that when the states gained greater competence in dealing with radiation hazards, their jurisdiction could be extended. But once the amendment addressed the states' primary concern by affirming their constitutional right to share in atomic safety, most states moved slowly toward accepting the responsibilities they were permitted to carry out. A few, by contrast, declined to act on the grounds that the federal government had no power to circumscribe their health and safety functions and that the amendment was an unwarranted and unnecessary imposition on their traditional authority.

Finally, most states did not insist that the AEC turn over more regulatory responsibilities than the 1959 amendment conferred because, like the Commission, their primary interest was encouraging peaceful uses of atomic energy. Despite the differences between the AEC and the states over regulatory jurisdiction, they agreed that the peaceful atom promised valuable benefits and sought to provide a favorable climate for the growth of the nuclear industry. Francis J. Weber, chief of the Public Health Service's Division of Radiological Health, exaggerated when he commented that states frequently considered radiological-health matters as an "afterthought."[49] But his remark underscored the fact that the states feared that excessive regulation would interfere with atomic progress. Most were willing, therefore, to accept a secondary role and allow the AEC to carry out major regulatory responsibilities. Both the states and the AEC were alert to and concerned about the hazards of atomic energy, but they assumed that solutions to its dangers would be found as development proceeded. In what was generally regarded as a glamorous new field of technology that promised dramatic advances in energy, medicine, industry, and agriculture, promotional activities ranked higher in priority than the more mundane tasks of regulation.

The 1959 amendment and the agreements program that grew out of it represented a compromise solution to the questions about federal and state roles in atomic regulation that arose soon after passage of the 1954

Atomic Energy Act. Although the AEC, the Joint Committee, the atomic industry, and many state spokesmen found the agreements program a satisfactory way of dealing with a difficult problem, some states insisted that they should exercise greater power in regulating atomic hazards. Neither the 1959 legislation nor the agreements program fully resolved the controversy over federal and state jurisdiction in atomic regulation. Rather they embodied an effort to mitigate the existing confusion in a way that was generally acceptable to all interested parties and to reduce the possibility that federal-state differences over regulatory authority would impede atomic development.

XI

WORKERS AND
RADIATION HAZARDS

As peaceful applications of atomic energy expanded in the 1950s, so did the number of people working with potentially dangerous sources of radiation. The safety of radiation workers was a major concern of scientists, health officials, and labor representatives interested in and involved with atomic-energy programs. The public controversies over the risks that radioactive fallout from bomb testing posed for the national or world population often obscured the fact that exposure limits for large population groups were derivatives—and admittedly arbitrary ones—of radiation standards set for workers in atomic industries. The primary purpose of the recommendations of the National Committee on Radiation Protection and the radiation-protection regulations of the AEC was to prevent employees exposed to radiation from receiving excessive doses. The development of radiation standards was but one of a number of important issues that arose during the 1950s and early 1960s over providing sufficient safeguards for atomic workers. Questions and differing opinions also emerged over the adequacy of workers'-compensation laws for radiation injuries, the effectiveness of the AEC's safety requirements, and the enforcement of measures to protect uranium miners from well-recognized radiation hazards.

The radiation risks of uranium mining attracted increasing attention during the 1950s as the domestic mining industry rapidly grew. In the early post–World War II period, all of America's uranium came from abroad, and the Atomic Energy Commission was deeply concerned about ensuring an adequate supply for its weapons program. The Manhattan Project had procured small quantities of uranium concentrates from vanadium mills in the United States, but after the war the AEC's only sources of uranium were foreign mines. Most was derived from the large Shinkolobwe mine in the Belgian Congo; much smaller amounts were imported from Canada. Confronted with the gradual depletion of those mines and operational difficulties in them, the AEC sought new sources of supply at home and abroad. The outlook for domestic production, however, did not appear promising. No proven uranium reserves existed in the United States, and experts doubted that sufficient or even significant quantities of domestic ore could be found. Nonetheless, to stimulate exploration for domestic uranium, the AEC announced in April 1948 that for ten years it would pay a guaranteed minimum price of $3.50 per pound for high-grade uranium-bearing ores. It also offered a ten-thousand-dollar bonus for new discoveries of rich ore deposits in the United States. Initially, the AEC's program produced limited results; uranium supplies remained uncertain and heavily dependent on foreign mines. But some new domestic sources of ore were located, and in March 1951 the AEC extended its price incentives through 31 March 1962.[1]

A major breakthrough occurred when Charles Steen, a geologist and independent prospector, struck a rich vein of high-grade ore near Moab, Utah in 1952. Steen, who with his family had suffered through bad luck and abject poverty in his seemingly quixotic search for uranium deposits, soon converted his find into a fortune. News of Steen's discovery set off a uranium rush as prospectors and promoters undertook a feverish quest for new deposits. They succeeded far beyond expectations, locating sources of ore that belied the pessimistic presumptions of just a few years earlier. In 1948 the AEC had estimated domestic uranium ore reserves at only one million tons, but by 1957 it had raised that figure seventyfold. Most of the deposits occurred on the Colorado Plateau, which included parts of Colorado, Utah, Arizona, and New Mexico, but some were also found in other western states. The largest single ore deposit, estimated at thirty million tons, was discovered deep underground at Ambrosia Lake, New Mexico. More commonly, however, the underground mines were small operations that were sometimes of marginal profitability. In addition, some deposits were close enough to the surface to be tapped by open-pit mining.[2]

The boom in domestic mining spurred a correspondingly rapid growth in uranium milling. In the mills the ore was crushed and ground, and uranium concentrate was chemically extracted in a partially refined form called yellow cake. Although the United States had only a small milling capacity before the AEC offered its price incentives for uranium exploration, by 1957 fourteen mills were operating and eight more were under construction. Thus, in less than a decade the AEC's program prompted a startling expansion in domestic mining and milling that ended, at least temporarily, the agency's apprehensions about a shortage of raw materials. Indeed, in 1957 the AEC announced, to the consternation of the industry, that it planned to limit its uranium purchases because "we have arrived at the point where it no longer is in the interest of the Government to expand production."[3]

Accompanying the explosive rise of the domestic uranium industry were growing concerns about occupational hazards to miners. Although open-pit mines and milling operations presented some dangers to workers, safety problems were most worrisome in underground mines. Workers digging below the surface for uranium ore faced the same perils as their counterparts in other types of mines, such as exposure to toxic gases, susceptibility to silicosis, explosions, fires, and falls. But uranium mines posed additional risks because of the presence of radioactivity. Among the elements that radioactive decay of uranium yields is radium 226, which in turn produces radon 222, a radioactive gas that is undetectable to the human senses and can be a health hazard if inhaled. The decay of radon gas gives off four "daughter" products—polonium 218 (RaA), lead 214 (RaB), bismuth 214 (RaC), and polonium 214 (RaC^1)— that are an even greater health threat. The radon daughters readily cling to particles in the air and can easily be taken into the respiratory tract by breathing of mine air. Once inside the body, RaA and RaC^1 are especially dangerous because they emit alpha particles that can cause lung cancer in miners exposed to high concentrations of radon over an extended period of time.[4]

Even before the uranium boom erupted in the United States in the early 1950s, health experts had recognized that radon and its daughters posed risks for uranium miners working underground. But they were uncertain about the extent of the danger or what concentrations of radon in the atmosphere of a mine presented a significant health hazard. The only information available came from studies of the conditions in the Schneeberg (Germany) and Joachimsthal (Czechoslovakia) mines in the Erz Mountains on the German-Czech border. Opened in the fifteenth and sixteenth centuries, those mines had supplied a variety of ores, including copper, iron, silver, cobalt, arsenic, bismuth, and nickel, and since the late nineteenth century had served as sources of radium and uranium. Men who had worked in the Schneeberg and Joachimsthal mines for a period of ten years or longer had an exceedingly high mortality rate from lung cancer. Estimating that pulmonary malignancies caused 50 percent or more of the miners' deaths, experts offered numerous explanations for the unusual incidence of cancer. They theorized that conditions in the mines, such as poor ventilation, dampness, and the presence of toxic agents like nickel, cobalt, and arsenic compounds made the miners particularly susceptible to respiratory disorders; so too did the fact that workers lived far from the mines and walked for miles in the cold mountain air in clothing soaked with perspiration. By the 1920s, researchers had also identified radon gas as a major contributing factor to the lung-cancer rate among the miners. But they did not regard radon as the sole culprit. Therefore, the knowledge gained from the Schneeberg and Joachimsthal mines, though useful, did not provide definitive guidance to health officials concerned with protecting the safety of uranium miners in the United States. The extent to which the European experience could be applied to American mines remained unclear. Furthermore, scientists did not realize until the early 1950s that the daughter products were a greater health hazard than radon itself.[5]

The primary responsibility for regulating and enforcing safety standards in uranium mines rested with state governments. A number of federal agencies also took an interest in mine conditions, at least the aspects of the problem that fell within their statutory mandates. The Atomic Energy Commission's authority was restricted to a small number of mines located on federal property that the AEC had discovered itself. It leased those mines to private operators with the stipulation that they comply with established safety standards. In other mines the AEC had no clear regulatory jurisdiction. The 1946 Atomic Energy Act gave the AEC authority over source material (defined as "uranium, thorium or any other material which is deemed by the Commission, with the approval of the President, to be peculiarly essential to the production of fissionable materials") only "after removal from its place of deposit in nature." During debate on the measure, several senators raised questions about the ownership of source material, which could be sold only to the AEC. The framers of the legislation explained that in order to encourage private prospecting, title to source material would remain in private hands until removed from the ground. According to Senator Bourke Hickenlooper, "the object was to give the United States preemptive right in the material itself, [while] reserving the greatest possible freedom for private exploration amd mining development." Congress did not, however, consider the question of mine safety, perhaps because no uranium mines were then operating in the United States.[6]

Other federal agencies concerned with mine conditions also lacked clear statutory authority to regulate privately owned mines and performed only limited functions. The Department of Interior's Bureau of Mines was responsible for inspecting mines on Indian reservations and federal lands and was available for advice and technical assistance to federal and state agencies, the mining industry, and labor organizations. The Department of Labor administered and enforced the Walsh-Healy Public Contracts Act, which stipulated that federal contractors could not permit "working conditions which are unsanitary or hazardous or dangerous to the health and safety of employees." Although the AEC was the sole purchaser of uranium ore, the applicability of the Walsh-Healy Act to privately owned mines was questionable because they did not operate under federal contracts. The Public Health Service offered assistance and expertise in studying, assessing, and correcting health hazards in uranium mines but had no regulatory powers.[7]

The first state to take action on uranium-mine safety was Colorado. In August 1949 the state Department of Health appointed an advisory board to consider the potential hazards of uranium mining and milling. The panel quickly concluded that "little or nothing was known of the health hazards of the uranium-producing industry." Therefore, the state and several uranium companies requested the U.S. Public Health Service to study and analyze the health effects of working in uranium mines or mills. The Public Health Service began its investigation in the summer of 1950 and within two years reached some tentative conclusions based on observations of conditions in fifty mines on the Colorado Plateau and physical examinations of over eleven hundred workers. Since most of the miners had been digging uranium for less than three years, the survey, as expected, revealed no firm evidence of pathological injury from exposure to radiation. But the health officials found the concentrations of radioactive elements in the mines disturbing. The National Committee on Radiation Protection had proposed a maximum permissible concentration of ten micromicrocuries of radon per liter of air for continuous long-term exposure, and the Public Health Service calculated a higher allowable limit of a hundred micromicrocuries per liter of air. A curie is a unit of measure that indicates how radioactive a substance is by comparison with a standard rate of atomic disintegration. A micromicrocurie is one millionth of one millionth of a curie. The mine study revealed a median level of thirty-one hundred micromicrocuries of radon per liter of air in forty-eight mines and a median level of four thousand micromicrocuries per liter of radon daughters in eighteen mines. The Public Health Service recommended a number of measures to reduce the high levels of radiation, the most important of which was ventilation of the mines with uncontaminated air to dilute the concentrations of radon and its daughters. The Service planned to expand its investigation to obtain more comprehensive data, but the preliminary findings were troubling.[8]

The Public Health Service submitted a draft of its report to the AEC, which cooperated with the study by helping to evaluate the data and providing financial support. Jesse C. Johnson, director of the AEC's Division of Raw Materials, summarized the findings and recommendations for the commissioners and praised the Service's "sane and objective treatment of the problem." Nevertheless, Johnson, whose primary responsibility was to secure adequate supplies of uranium, worried that newspaper and magazine stories about mining hazards might "adversely affect uranium production in this country and abroad." He felt confident that radiation levels in the mines could be brought down to an acceptable level, but he feared that press accounts would distort or exaggerate the situation. The problem appeared much less threatening in the United States than abroad, where "communist propagandists may utilize any sensational statements or news reports to hamper or restrict uranium production in foreign fields, particularly at Shinkolobwe." Despite the potential difficulties the mine-safety investigation could generate for his procurement program, Johnson believed that the AEC should "lend full support" to the ongoing project. For that purpose he acquired portable ventilation equipment to test its effectiveness in reducing radon levels in the mine atmosphere, and the AEC continued to furnish funds to the Colorado Department of Health. The Public Health Service extended its survey to 157 mines in the summer of 1952 and found conditions as disquieting as those encountered previously. Concentrations of radon greater than a hundred micromicrocuries per liter of air showed up in 77 percent of the mines, and the median level of radon daughters was twelve hundred micromicrocuries. The one encouraging result of the 1952 investigation was that experiments in four mines indicated that forced ventilation could sharply diminish the concentrations of radioactive elements in the air.[9]

The results of the mine study created concern among state health officials, and in February 1955 over a hundred delegates from seven states, mining companies, the AEC, the Public Health Service, and the U.S. Bureau of Mines met in Salt Lake City at a conference called by the Industrial Commission of Utah to discuss the problem. Those attending the meeting hoped to exchange ideas and information about the legal, technical, and financial aspects of controlling uranium-mine hazards, and to reach agreement "on a realistic standard maximum allowable concentration of radon and its degradation products." At that time Colorado was the only state that had regulations on allowable concentrations of radon and its daughters, and the state commissioner of mines acknowledged that the existing standards were subject to change and difficult to enforce. The regulations stipulated that concentrations of radon and its decay products "should not exceed 100 micromicrocuries per liter of air," but they did not firmly require that mine operators achieve that level. State representatives at the conference sought guidance in devising standards by arriving at a figure that seemed technically attainable while at the same time affording adequate protection to mine workers. It was of particular importance to them because primary responsibility for uranium-mine safety remained in the hands of the states; Congress had not expanded the AEC's authority in the 1954 Atomic Energy Act.[10]

Spokesmen for mine operators at the conference expressed concern for protecting their employees from excessive radiation exposure, but they also outlined the difficulties they faced in reducing radon levels. One company representative declared: "We could not possibly get down to 100 micromicrocuries. It just is impossible." He reported that in many cases ventilation could not provide enough uncontaminated air quickly enough to all areas of a mine to assure that radon concentrations would not exceed a one-hundred-micromicrocurie limit. Other industry officials agreed that ventilation, though useful, was not always effective in diluting radon in the mine atmosphere to the desired level. They also cited other problems in controlling radon concentrations, such as the difficulty of sealing off areas of a mine where work was completed because of radon's high powers of penetration, and the fact that radon levels in one place could vary greatly from season to season, month to month, or even day to day. Mine operators were obviously concerned about the expense of ventilation and other protective measures. One company spokesman estimated that fifty percent of the existing mines, especially the small, marginal operations, might cease production if faced with costly regulatory requirements.[11]

By the end of the two-day meeting, the conferees settled on target figures for permissible "working levels" in the mines of a hundred micromicrocuries of radon per liter of air and three hundred micromicrocuries of radon daughter products. In response to a company representative's comment that the goals could not be achieved, the chairman of the Industrial Commission of Utah declared: "We're going to set up the standard that we're going to shoot at even though we can't attain it." A Colorado Public Health Department official recommended that operators reduce their employees' exposure by moving them from place to place inside and outside the mines because the proposed limit was based on an eight-hours-a-day five-days-a-week work schedule. Throughout the meeting, state regulators, health experts, and industry spokesmen demonstrated concern but little sense of urgency about conditions in the uranium mines. They were confident that the risks to miners were not cause for alarm. A University of Utah physician told the assembly that "it is much more hazardous to drive up South Temple Street or particularly to ski up at Alta than it is to work in a radiation mine," and one company representative said he was pleased and "rather amazed" that speakers at the conference "all have indicated there is no immediate danger in this radiation." A short time after the meeting ended, two prominent Colorado health officials delivered an equally sanguine assessment of uranium-mining hazards to a conference of industrial hygienists. They maintained that uranium miners on the Colorado Plateau would avoid the high incidence of lung cancer so prevalent among workers at Schneeberg and Joachimsthal because "we have a more complete understanding of the problem and of the steps that are necessary to reduce the exposure of men to these hazards."[12]

By late 1958, however, the Public Health Service's continuing study of the pathological effects of uranium mining had shown more ominous portents. In a letter to the AEC's Charles Dunham, director of the Division of Biology and Medicine, Surgeon General LeRoy Burney disclosed that forty-four of the thirty-two hundred men whom the Service was examining and maintaining records on had worked in mines containing uranium before 1941 and had at least one year of underground experience. Of that group, sixteen had died, four from lung cancer. Burney acknowledged that the sampling was too limited to draw firm conclusions. But he observed that if mortalities from lung cancer among uranium miners continued at the rate of the preliminary data, it would indicate "that our American experience is not inconsistent with the experience of the miners at Schneeberg and Joachimsthal." The surgeon general expressed further concern about surveys showing that about fifteen hundred men in three hundred mines were working in "uncontrolled or poorly controlled environments." The problem was particularly acute in older, smaller mines, where readings of radon daughters ran as high as fifty times greater than the recommended working level of three hundred micromicrocuries per liter of air. The Public Health Service had found "little, if any improvement" in conditions during the previous two years. Burney believed that the new findings made "consideration of what additional measures should be taken" advisable. While the Public Health Service planned to expand its efforts to educate mine operators and workers about radiation hazards, the surgeon general suggested that the AEC might be in a position to take stronger action because it was the sole buyer of uranium ore. He argued that an AEC requirement that mines abide by state health standards would be an effective way to bring about prompt improvement in mine conditions.[13]

Dunham circulated Burney's letter for the information of the commissioners and sought legal advice on the matter from AEC general counsel Loren K. Olson. Olson replied that the agency's statutory authority for regulating privately owned uranium mines was "very doubtful." He found no evidence in the legislative histories of the 1946 and 1954 Atomic Energy Acts suggesting that Congress intended the AEC to enforce uranium-mine safety, and noted that, by comparison, federal jurisdiction over coal-mining practices derived from an explicit and detailed congressional mandate. Therefore, he concluded that the federal government could undertake responsibility for regulating uranium-mine conditions only after receiving specific authorization from Congress, and even then he was "highly dubious" that the AEC should be the administering agency. Advising Burney of the AEC's position on 1 March 1959, General Manager A. R. Luedecke proposed that the Public Health Service invite representatives of federal agencies concerned with mine safety to discuss whether the problem seemed serious enough to require action, whether increased federal authority over the mines was desirable, and what means the federal government could use to encourage the states to take appropriate measures.[14]

Burney quickly acted on the AEC's suggestion. On 20 May 1959 twenty-six representatives from the Public Health Service, the AEC, the Department of Labor, and the Department of the Interior agreed that the health hazards in uranium mines appeared grave enough to justify federal action. They urged the establishment of a smaller group composed of one member from each of their agencies to develop specific recommendations. Accordingly, an interagency committee, chaired by M. Allen Pond, a staff assistant for HEW secretary Arthur Flemming, was formed. By November the committee completed its report. After reviewing the existing authority of federal agencies for regulating mine conditions, it concluded that the jurisdiction of the national government was both limited and ill-defined. The Department of Labor, under the Walsh-Healy Public Contracts Act, possessed the only conceivable federal enforcement power. The solicitor of the Labor Department had recently argued in an internal memorandum that Walsh-Healy applied to privately owned mines because "as a practical matter the mine owner at every stage of the relationship has produced ore for the Government." But even if that opinion were accepted, the interagency committee doubted that enforcement of Walsh-Healy would fully settle the problem. The Labor Department lacked the technical staff needed to carry out the provisions of the measure in the uranium mines; and furthermore, requiring compliance with Walsh-Healy would not solve the technical difficulties of controlling radon levels.[15]

The committee decided that the first step in improving mine safety should be "to impress upon the States the seriousness of this problem and the need to assume their rightful responsibilities" rather than seek increased federal authority "at this time." It recommended that a conference of governors from the uranium-mining states be called to inform them about the existence of significant hazards and encourage them to correct conditions in the mines. The committee did not clarify why it believed the states would be better equipped than the Labor Department to deal with the technical problems in the mines, though it emphasized that mine safety was traditionally a state function. Transferring responsibility to the federal government would undoubtedly have stirred controversy and caused delay, especially since the states had made their position on jurisdictional issues clear in the development of the 1959 amendment permitting a state role in atomic regulation. The committee's major proposal for a conference of governors won the endorsement of Secretary Flemming, but the heads of the other agencies represented on the committee persuaded him to postpone such a meeting until the recently established Federal Radiation Council could set a radiation exposure limit for the uranium mines.[16]

Meanwhile, the radiation perils in the mines were beginning to attract some congressional and public notice. In March 1959 the Joint Committee on Atomic Energy held six days of hearings on occupational radiation hazards. Although the sessions focused on other matters, they included discussion of the health risks of uranium mining. Duncan A. Holaday, chief of the Public Health Service's Salt Lake City occupational-health field station, summarized the Service's findings on radon concentrations and potential effects. He suggested that existing problems seemed controllable and added that if action was not taken, "uranium miners will continue to have dangerous exposures to radioactive materials." The AEC's Harold Price aired the agency's view that its authority over privately owned mines was "highly questionable." James A. Brownlow, president of the AFL-CIO's Metal Trades Department, urged that the AEC "promptly and adequately move" to reduce radon levels in the mines. If it lacked the statutory power to do so, he recommended an amendment to the Atomic Energy Act to authorize federal enforcement of safe working conditions for miners. The Joint Committee, despite Congressman Melvin Price's statement that the information it received on mining hazards "caused great concern" among the members, considered no measures to clarify or expand federal jurisdiction. The following year, in hearings on radiation-protection criteria, members and staff of the Joint Committee again raised questions about mine safety, but their interest did not produce any action to alleviate the problem. At best, the hearings helped call attention to the nature and magnitude of the risks of radiation exposure to uranium miners. In the midst of the 1959 sessions, for example, the *Denver Post* noted Holaday's testimony and reported that the Colorado Department of Health was seeking emergency funding to inspect conditions in the state's four hundred mines because "many Colorado uranium miners are inhaling radioactive gases that can cause lung cancer."[17]

Although the AEC lacked regulatory jurisdiction over privately owned uranium mines, it took action to correct unhealthy conditions where its authority over raw materials clearly prevailed—uranium-ore processing mills and the few mines that it leased to private operators. Occupational radiation hazards in the mills were less acute than in uranium mines because workers were not exposed as miners were to high concentrations of radon in small enclosed areas. Still, crushing the ore to remove the uranium produced airborne dust containing radioactive materials that posed a health threat. Furthermore, milling operations created potential environmental problems. Liquid waste products stored in holding ponds could contaminate the ground through seepage. In some cases, mill operators dumped waste directly into adjacent streams or rivers. In addition, solid ore residues called tailings, stored in large piles at the mill site, could be carried by winds in the form of radioactive dust to surrounding areas. The tailings had to be controlled by wetting down, covering, or growing grass on the piles.[18]

Uranium mills operated under AEC licenses and were required to meet the agency's radiation-protection regulations that first became effective in 1957. In February of that year the AEC initiated a preliminary survey of twelve of the twenty-five mills then in service to determine whether they conformed with the standards. It found that exposure of workers to radioactivity in the air and levels of radiation released to the environment from liquid effluents in milling operations exceeded the allowable limits, though not in amounts that posed "an immediate hazard to the health and safety of the employees [or] to the public." The risks would become significant only if the radiation levels remained above permissible limits for an extended period of time. The AEC then expanded its study to all mills and held meetings with their owners to offer guidance on controlling radiation levels. A second round of inspections that began in January 1959 revealed that in many cases the mills had "not exerted sufficient effort to comply with the regulations." One particularly troubling problem resulted from the practices of the Vanadium Corporation of America's mill in Durango, Colorado, which discharged radioactive materials into the Animas River without determining whether such action raised concentrations of radioactivity in the water above permissible limits. The Animas River provided water for a large number of people in Colorado and New Mexico, and the Public Health Service had found the radioactive content of the water to be as high as 160 percent above allowable concentrations.[19]

In light of its findings, the AEC directed owners of eleven mills to submit detailed outlines on the measures they would take to correct deficiencies in their operations. The agency did not believe the situation serious enough to suspend any licenses immediately, but it threatened to do so if a mill failed to act promptly to meet the regulations. Among the companies receiving those orders was the Vanadium Corporation of America. In addition, the AEC participated in a meeting with the firm sponsored by the Public Health Service, which had a statutory role in the matter under the federal Water Pollution Control Act of 1956. The AEC pledged to "take whatever steps are necessary" to ensure that the mill would comply with radiation-protection standards, and company officials promised to reduce the pollution to acceptable proportions within four months. Other mill owners also responded quickly to the AEC's pressure. By May 1960 the agency was satisfied that the mills it had cited were making adequate progress in improving health and safety conditions. It maintained surveillance over all operating mills to ensure compliance with the regulations.[20]

In addition to enforcing its radiation standards in the mills, the AEC took action to reduce radon concentrations in the uranium mines where its authority prevailed. In July 1959 the Bureau of Mines, at the AEC's request, began inspections of seventeen mines on government property that the Commission leased to private companies. Most of the mines were small operations, and their aggregate production represented only about 1.3 percent of total domestic output. The Bureau of Mines sampling showed three mines with average radon-daughter concentrations of less than three hundred micromicrocuries per liter of air, one with an average of between one and three times the working level, seven with an average of three to ten times, and six with an average of greater than ten times the working level. After receiving the results of the survey, AEC officials met with company representatives and insisted that they install adequate ventilation and take other appropriate measures to decrease the radioactivity in the leased mines. By June 1960 conditions demonstrated significant improvement. Three of the mines had closed because of exhaustion of their ore reserves. Of the other fourteen, eight had average radon-daughter concentrations of less than three hundred micromicrocuries per liter of air, five had an average of one to two times the working level, and one had an average of three times the working level. In four of the mines, operators suspended work in sections where readings were particularly high until additional ventilation equipment was placed in service. The AEC reported that "the recent inspections . . . indicate that most mine operators can, without prohibitive cost, reduce radon concentration to or below the working level."[21]

The uranium-producing states were much less successful in controlling radon levels in the approximately seven hundred privately owned mines within their jurisdictions. Utah and New Mexico joined Colorado in passing laws to protect uranium miners from radiation hazards, but the measures, particularly in Colorado and Utah, were not vigorously enforced. In Colorado the state Public Health Department conducted inspections of the state's four hundred mines with emergency funding provided for one year by the legislature in July 1959. The *Denver Post* reported in May 1960 that twelve mines had been ordered to shut down temporarily because of concentrations of radon daughters that averaged fifty times the working level. Paul W. Jacoe, chief of the department's occupational-health division, told the *Post* that over half of the state's mines exceeded the limit of three hundred micromicrocuries per liter of air and affirmed that "in most cases, radiation levels above the permissible can be controlled through proper mine ventilation." He expressed hope that the legislature would authorize funds for a permanent inspection system. The health department, however, received little cooperation from the state Bureau of Mines, which was responsible for enforcing safety requirements. The bureau refused to confirm the report on mine closings or to disclose how many mines it had directed to curtail operations. G. A. Franz, the deputy commissioner of mines, denounced Jacoe's statements. He acknowledged that up to 98 percent of Colorado's mines would have to suspend work if forced to abide by the three-hundred-micromicrocurie concentration of radon daughters, but publicly declared: "Our business is to keep the mines open." One U.S. Public Health Service official, Senior Surgeon Louis S. Gerber, submitted a discouraging report after discussing mine conditions with Colorado and Utah health authorities. He found the situation in Colorado troubling, but in Utah it seemed even worse. "At least in Colorado," Gerber wrote, "some key people appear to have more concern with the problems than is true in Utah," where "there are no funds, nor personnel, nor any backing from the Industrial Commission."[22]

In November 1960 M. Allen Pond, who had chaired the federal interagency committee on uranium-mine hazards the previous year, urged his boss, HEW secretary Flemming, to renew his call for a meeting with governors of states with uranium mines. The committee's recommendation for a conference had been shelved until the Federal Radiation Council could consider the problem, but the FRC, preoccupied with other matters, had made little progress toward developing radiation-protection guidelines for uranium mines. Advising against further delay, Pond contended that an early meeting with the governors was essential because "the evidence is abundantly clear that the radiation levels in a large number of mines are far in excess of any reasonable standard that might be suggested" by the FRC. On the positive side, the AEC's actions in its leased mines had "successfully demonstrated that it is possible to provide effective control measures." Flemming accepted Pond's argument, and the AEC, the Department of Labor, and the Department of the Interior agreed that a conference with the governors of the uranium-mining states should be held promptly.[23]

A two-day meeting opened in Denver on 15 December 1960. Secretary Flemming, Governors Steve McNichols of Colorado, George D. Clyde of Utah, John Burroughs of New Mexico, J. J. Hickey of Wyoming, a spokesman for Governor Ralph Herseth of South Dakota, federal officials from the Public Health Service, the Bureau of Mines, the Department of Labor, and the AEC, several state health authorities, representatives from the Council of State Governments and organized labor, and a few news reporters attended. Harold J. Magnuson, chief of the Public Health Service's Division of Occupational Health, presented the latest findings on mine conditions and worker mortality. Though still preliminary, they were even gloomier than earlier indications. Of a total of 3,317 miners examined since 1950, 108 had died. Lung cancer had caused 5.5 percent of the deaths in that group. More alarming was the fact that among a group of 907 miners who had worked underground for more than three years, five of forty-four mortalities were attributed to respiratory malignancies. That figure was almost five times as high as the mortality rate from lung cancer among the general male population in Arizona, New Mexico, Utah, and Colorado. Furthermore, sputum tests that detected minute changes in cell structure showed a sharp rise in the percentage of miners with suspected cancer cells in their lungs. The Public Health Service's most recent survey of radon-daughter concentrations in 371 mines was also discouraging. One-third of the 1,802 samplings taken in those mines were less than the working level, but the percentages of measurements between three and nine times and over ten times the working level had increased between 1958 and 1959.[24]

Although the governors initially seemed dubious about the severity of radiation hazards in uranium mines, the information they received convinced them that the problem was serious. Colorado's McNichols, a former official of the Uranium Ore Producers Association, raised a series of pointed questions. He suggested that the AEC should regulate mine conditions but received no support from the other governors. He also argued that enforcing a level of three hundred micromicrocuries of radon daughters per liter of air would close a large number of mines and that requiring installation of ventilating equipment would impose substantial financial burdens on mine owners. Nathan Woodruff, director of the AEC's Office of Health and Safety, countered McNichols by pointing out that the AEC's experience with its leased mines showed that radon concentrations could be lowered significantly without high costs to operators. McNichols did not press his points in private sessions. But in comments to reporters from the *Denver Post* and *Time* magazine, he pinned the primary blame for unhealthy conditions in the mines on the AEC and charged that the federal government had failed to make its data on radiation hazards available to the states. The other governors eschewed such a belligerent position. They expressed concern about the Public Health Service's findings and emphasized their need for continued federal support and cooperation to carry out corrective measures. Woodruff reported "that the Governors and other state representatives at the meeting were made much more fully appreciative of the radon problem in the uranium mines and . . . the meeting helped to engender a sincere effort on their parts to establish programs designed to bring the hazard under control."[25]

Within a short time after the conference, several states took steps to reduce radiation risks for uranium miners. Despite the complaints that McNichols aired at the meeting, he initiated prompt action in Colorado. On 24 December 1960 Deputy Mine Commissioner G. A. Franz, who had sharply criticized the state health department a few months earlier for its comments on mine hazards, addressed a strongly worded letter to Colorado operators. He maintained that data compiled from physical examinations of miners before 1960 were "not of great significance," but the new information, particularly the sputum test results, was "alarming and a cause of great concern." He advised mine owners to analyze the effectiveness of their ventilating systems and announced that the state would enforce a limit of three hundred micromicrocuries per liter of air. "It is not an impossible problem," Franz declared, "and starting now it will not take too long to accomplish." In addition, the Colorado legislature appropriated funds so that the state Bureau of Mines could hire five mine inspectors and the state Public Health Department could employ a radiological consultant. The New Mexico Public Health Department developed plans to expand mine surveys, radiation-control efforts, and physical examinations of workers. Utah requested technical assistance from the U.S. Bureau of Mines to help operators lower radon levels, and South Dakota asked the U.S. Public Health Service to provide instruments needed to study mine conditions.[26]

Meanwhile, federal agencies, individually and collectively, continued to consider means by which they could promote mine safety. At the time of the conference with uranium-state governors, AEC chairman McCone took a personal interest in the problem. He requested legal opinions on whether the Commission could compel mine owners to observe health and safety requirements by invoking the Walsh-Healy Act or by refusing to purchase uranium from mines that failed to meet minimum standards. General Counsel Neil D. Naiden advised him that the AEC lacked clear authority to take such action and that trying to do so could create serious legal complications by being "construed as an attempt at informal blacklisting." The Department of Labor continued to ponder the applicability of Walsh-Healy to the mines. It concluded that the measure could be used in "captive mines"—those operated by uranium-processing mills with which the AEC had purchasing contracts. But it was less certain that "independent mines," where the worst problems usually existed, were subject to the act. The department initiated no enforcement proceedings in either case. The Public Health Service provided assistance to several states and kept monitoring miners' mortality rates. By May 1961, 4 more miners from the group of 907 that had worked underground for more than three years had died from lung cancer, bringing the total to 9 and helping confirm the trends already observed. The Federal Radiation Council began work on a report to establish radiation-protection guides for uranium mines, but progress remained slow.[27]

Although the Joint Committee on Atomic Energy took no action, formally or informally, to expand the federal role in uranium-mine safety, other congressional committees considered increasing the authority of the U.S. Bureau of Mines. Bills introduced in the House and Senate proposed that the Bureau of Mines be granted the power to inspect and report on mining conditions on a regular basis and on its own initiative rather than at the invitation of state officials or mine owners. The measure applied to all mineral mines, and its primary purpose was to reduce mine accidents. But in hearings on the bill in July 1961 the Select Subcommittee on Labor of the House Committee on Education and Labor also received testimony on radiation hazards in uranium mines from Public Health Service representatives. Labor spokesmen enthusiastically endorsed the bill. John Clark, president of the International Union of Mine, Mill and Smelter Workers, lamented federal inaction in enforcing compliance with uranium-mine standards and declared that "any reliance on the states for correction of these conditions would be futile." State officials and mining-company representatives took the opposite position; they objected to an extension of federal jurisdiction over traditional state functions. One industry spokesman denounced the Public Health Service's performance in compiling data on uranium-mine hazards as biased, inconsistent, unscientific, and secretive, the result of which was "to alarm the public needlessly." The Bureau of Mines also opposed the bill on the grounds that it was premature. Congress eventually passed a weakened version that directed the secretary of the interior to study and make recommendations for improving safety in all mining operations except coal and lignite. The act had no practical effect on radiation problems in uranium mines, but it did illustrate the political difficulties of significantly enlarging federal responsibility for mine regulation.[28]

In a high-level meeting on 1 August 1961, officials of the Department of Health, Education, and Welfare and the Atomic Energy Commission, including HEW secretary Abraham Ribicoff and AEC commissioner John S. Graham, discussed uranium-mine radiation hazards along with other problems of common concern. While they concluded that for the moment the best course of action was to encourage the states to enforce radiation regulations in the mines, they also agreed to tell the states that unless satisfactory progress in controlling radon levels was apparent by the following April, federal agencies would seek legislation to expand their regulatory authority. The conferees did not specify the nature or extent of the powers they might request. Graham, though hesitant to commit the Commission without consulting its other members, indicated that his agency would support legislation if it was necessary. In February 1962 the Public Health Service's Harold Magnuson, who as chief of the Division of Occupational Health had been deeply involved in uranium-mine issues, recommended against proposing federal legislation. He argued that since the 1960 conference with their governors, uranium-mining states had made "conscientious efforts" to enforce safety standards. They had substantially reduced radon concentrations in many mines and closed "high-hazard areas" until operators improved conditions. Furthermore, Colorado had established a precedent by awarding compensation to the widow of a miner who died from lung cancer, which would "have a salutary effect upon mine operators who have been dilatory in complying with regulations." Although problems remained to be solved, Magnuson contended that the states had demonstrated their willingness and ability to act effectively.[29] Magnuson's view prevailed, though one Public Health Service official argued in an internal memorandum that his own agency and the AEC had failed to act aggressively or responsibly to protect uranium miners from radiation. Bruce W. Maxwell of the Radiological Health Laboratory worried that "we may yet be the center of a national scandal based on our . . . lack of action." He faulted both the Public Health Service and the AEC for claiming a lack of authority for regulating the mines. "When large numbers of uranium miners die of lung cancer," Maxwell declared, "PHS will be asked what it did about the problem and the answer will have to be, 'Not much, we did too little too late.' . . . The only conclusion an objective observer can reach is that someone has abdicated his responsibility."[30]

In August 1963 the Public Health Service issued the melancholy news of its latest findings on cancer-mortality rates among uranium miners. Of 768 miners who had worked underground for more than five years, 11 had died from lung cancer. The figure was "10 times the number expected on the basis of death rates for all white males of comparable age living in the states included in the study." Although the press release did not say so, it gave reason to believe that an unusually high percentage of uranium miners with lengthy underground experience in poorly regulated conditions would continue to succumb to lung cancer.[31]

The 1963 announcement further confirmed patterns that state and federal health officials had strongly suspected and feared for many years. Yet at least until 1961 little action was taken to protect uranium miners from radiation hazards. Maxwell was correct in pointing out that miners suffered because "someone . . . abdicated his responsibility," but his indictment of the Public Health Service and the AEC too easily absolved the states. The states claimed primary jurisdiction over mine safety, and federal agencies accepted their position. Although the states insisted on retaining their regulatory authority, they exercised it fitfully and ineffectively. Contrary to McNichols's assertions in 1960, the states were informed about the nature and possible effects of the radiation problem in uranium mines, but they made only meager efforts to improve conditions until after the governors' meeting with concerned federal officials. Between the seven-state conference in 1955, where state health and mining authorities acknowledged the need to control radon levels, and 1961, when they finally began to enforce their regulations, radiation hazards in many mines worsened. The reasons for the states' failure to move promptly to improve the situation are unclear, but it apparently arose from a lack of awareness by key officials of how severe the problem was and from a desire to avoid imposing economic burdens on the mining industry. In any case, by the time the states acted, hundreds of miners had worked for several years in unhealthy conditions that significantly increased their susceptibility to lung cancer. Since the states took principal responsibility for regulating the uranium mines, they were primarily accountable for the failure to provide adequate protection to the miners.

Within the limitations of their statutory mandates, federal agencies did better. The Public Health Service compiled valuable information on the radon problem in the mines and gave useful advice on how to correct it. The Bureau of Mines also rendered important services in reporting on conditions in the mines it inspected. The AEC, despite some early concern that disclosures about mining hazards might adversely affect uranium supplies, cooperated with the Public Health Service's study of health risks to miners. It also demonstrated that radon levels could be controlled by its actions to reduce hazards in its leased mines, and it joined with other federal agencies in urging state governments to demand compliance with safety standards. As the sole purchaser of uranium, the AEC appeared to be in a strong position to impose its wishes on mine operators. Yet despite their recognition of the seriousness of the problem and McCone's interest in requiring corrective measures, agency officials consistently maintained that the AEC lacked regulatory authority over privately owned mines. The legislative histories of the 1946 and 1954 Atomic Energy Acts gave strong support to that argument, but the AEC might also have been influenced by other than strictly legalistic considerations. Although by 1957 the agency was no longer concerned about the adequacy of uranium supplies, it might have hesitated to press for a larger role in mine safety because of the political complications it would cause with the states and the additional responsibilities it would place on a staff already burdened with issues that seemed to be of greater consequence. Therefore, the AEC refrained from acting beyond the limits of authority that Congress clearly had given it.

In this case, as in so many others, the AEC would undoubtedly have responded to pressure from the Joint Committee. But the Joint Committee, despite expressions of concern by its members, took no action to legislate broader federal jurisdiction over privately owned mines or to informally prod the AEC to enforce corrective measures. In hearings in 1959, staff counsel David Toll suggested to Harold Price that the AEC might reinterpret the Atomic Energy Act to assume control over mine safety, but the committee never pushed for such an approach. The following year, staff executive director James T. Ramey wondered whether the AEC might encourage operators to improve conditions through price incentives or financial assistance for equipment; but again, the idea received little consideration. Toll and Ramey offered their proposals in passing, but if the Joint Committee had insisted, the AEC would surely have given them serious study and perhaps found ways to implement them effectively. In the absence of directives from the Joint Committee to reassess its position, the AEC maintained its long-standing legal stance.[32]

A key reason for congressional quiescence was the lack of persistent or persuasive spokesmen for the uranium miners. They were a relatively small and inarticulate group, and the risks they faced, however severe, were easily overlooked by the Joint Committee amid the press of other business. The radiation hazards of the mines did not cause a public outcry that might have drawn greater attention from the committee. Labor unions, though aware of and concerned about the problem, did not lobby aggressively for necessary improvements. Other than presenting predictable *pro forma* statements at congressional hearings, labor representatives gave little effective assistance to their constituents in the uranium mines. With no clamor from the public or the unions, the Joint Committee neither pressured the AEC informally nor broadened its mandate through legislation. The AEC confined its regulatory activity to areas where its jurisdiction unquestionably extended, and the states, at least until 1961, failed to exercise their authority. Bureaucratic passiveness on the part of the states and inertia on the part of the federal government impeded action on a problem that could have been greatly alleviated without unreasonable costs by application of technically feasible remedies.

The Atomic Energy Commission's authority to impose radiation standards in atomic industries other than uranium mines was clearly defined. It applied to any installation operating under an AEC contract or license. Before the 1954 Atomic Energy Act, the agency set safety requirements only for employees of its contractors, who numbered more than three hundred thousand people between 1945 and 1955.[33] The 1954 act expanded the AEC's responsibilities by requiring it to establish radiation standards for the growing numbers of workers in the privately owned nuclear facilities that it licensed. Soon after passage of the law, the agency began drafting regulations for licensees designed to protect employees and the general public from excessive radiation exposure.

In June 1955 the AEC's Division of Licensing submitted draft regulations of radiation-protection standards for review by the commissioners. The regulations included maximum permissible limits for occupational exposure to external and internal radiation that embodied the latest recommendations of the National Committee on Radiation Protection. They prescribed an allowable dose in critical tissue of 0.3 r per week from external sources and maximum permissible concentrations in air and water of a long list of internal emitters. The AEC, like the NCRP, did not assume that the levels represented a threshold below which harmful somatic effects would never occur. It believed that the standards provided a "substantial margin of safety" so that an individual exposed to radiation at or under the mandatory limits for a full working career was unlikely to suffer "appreciable bodily injury." But it could not guarantee "that a particular individual may not be harmed by exposure to radiation below the limits established in the regulation." The AEC also followed NCRP recommendations by setting a limit of one-tenth of the permissible occupational doses for minors under eighteen years of age and for all persons outside controlled areas (that is, areas in which the licensee restricted access). The agency made the distinction between occupational and nonoccupational exposure because of the "extra sensitivity of minors to radiation" and the enhanced possibility of genetic consequences if a segment of the general public absorbed radiation from an accident or malfunction in a licensed atomic facility.[34]

The draft regulations imposed other requirements on licensees. They specified permissible concentrations in air and water of radioactive effluents released to the environment during normal operations and prescribed conditions for disposing of small amounts of low-level radioactive waste. To safeguard workers and keep their exposure within allowable limits, the regulations directed that licensees train employees to use equipment properly and observe necessary precautions, post warning signs in radiation areas, and label containers of radioactive materials clearly. They further instructed licensees to monitor and maintain records showing the exposures of all individuals receiving more than one-quarter of the permissible level in any given week.[35]

The commissioners approved issuing the draft regulations for public comment, despite Libby's remark that he considered the NCRP's "approach to some practical problems to be unrealistically conservative." The proposed regulations drew "a considerable amount of comment and criticism" on wording, definitions, and procedures. In response, the

AEC made several relatively minor additions and deletions. But the main feature of the original draft—the numerical exposure limits—remained intact. After the Commission endorsed the revised version, the regulations took effect in February 1957.[36]

Although the AEC's radiation standards were designed to protect workers in atomic industries, labor representatives played an insignificant role in determining the final contents of the regulations. Labor spokesmen contributed few opinions on the draft proposals during the public-comment period. But labor's failure to influence the formulation of occupational standards in any important respects did not signify a lack of interest in atomic-energy issues. Labor organizations were vitally concerned with a broad range of questions and were often critical of the AEC. The legal intervention by three AFL-CIO unions in the Power Reactor Development Company case was the most notable but not the only instance in which labor took a strong and vocal position.

Andrew J. Biemiller, legislative representative for the AFL-CIO, aired a number of labor's concerns during Joint Committee on Atomic Energy hearings on the Price-Anderson indemnity bill in May 1956. He declared that a recent statement of Lewis Strauss "painted too rosy a picture of the safety precautions and the low level of accidents associated with the nuclear-science industries." Fearing that "the apparent good safety record at atomic energy installations may lull many into an unwise sense of security," Biemiller called for strong federal efforts to protect workers from radiation hazards. He suggested that the NCRP's recommended maximum permissible doses were too high and cited a recent paper by Professor Hoyt Whipple of the University of Rochester arguing that the limits should be lowered by a factor of ten in atomic-power plants. Biemiller further advised the Joint Committee that "top priority" should be given to providing fair compensation for workers who suffered radiation injuries, particularly since "existing state workmen's compensation legislation laws are largely inadequate for this purpose."[37]

The publication of the National Academy of Sciences report on the biological effects of radiation in June 1956, emphasizing the dangers of the growing use of peaceful atomic energy, reinforced labor's anxieties. Biemiller told the Joint Committee that the "implications of this report require, in our judgment, an immediate review of the regulations governing the operations of our total atomic energy program." He complained that while the Price-Anderson legislation would offer financial protection for reactor owners and the general public, the problems of workers exposed to radiation were not receiving enough attention. Biemiller's arguments won sympathy with Joint Committee staff counsel George Norris, Jr., and Congressman Melvin Price, then the chairman of the Subcommittee on Research and Development. Price suggested to Clinton Anderson in July 1956 that the committee undertake a comprehensive study of the problem of radiation injury, including the hazards of occupational exposure and the adequacy of workers'-compensation laws. "I believe that the Committee would want to be absolutely sure about the problems raised by radiation," he wrote, "before any more time passes and the program expands any further." The following spring, however, as the Joint Committee was preparing for its first series of fallout hearings, Price agreed that formal consideration of radiation risks for workers should be postponed "because we should see what the pure science hearings develop."[38]

By that time, a highly publicized accident in a Houston, Texas, laboratory had raised new concerns about occupational radiation hazards. The mishap occurred in the Nuclear Products Division of the New York–based M. W. Kellogg Company, a large industrial design and construction firm. Operating under an AEC license, the Nuclear Products Division used radioactive isotopes in the manufacture of a "Kel-Ray projector," which detected flaws in pipe welds. On 13 March 1957 Harold Northway, the laboratory's administrative manager, observed as Jackson McVey, the facility's assistant supervisor, opened by remote control a container of iridium-192 pellets. Because the pellets either were cut by the lathe that opened the container or had broken from unknown causes earlier, high levels of radiation contaminated the room atmosphere when the pellets were removed. As alarm bells sounded, a monitor showed concentrations of radioactivity in the air of greater than 500 r per hour. Northway left the lab immediately; McVey remained for a short time to move the damaged and undamaged pellets into a protective storage well, then scurried out of the room. He quickly showered and changed clothes. But both he and Northway failed to take elementary precautions, because they did not regard their exposure as particularly serious. Neither checked the amount of radiation they received by scanning their bodies or clothing with a personal monitor. Northway was wearing a business suit when the accident occurred, and McVey, even after shedding his protective clothing and respirator and showering, retained some radioactive particles on his skin, underwear, and shoes. As a result, both men unwittingly spread radiation out of the lab and into their homes.[39]

A few days after the accident, McVey reentered the contaminated lab and washed it down with soap and water. Radiation levels sharply decreased, but in the meantime some radioactive particles had filtered into other parts of the building. Northway and McVey reported the incident to Willard B. Converse, head of the Nuclear Products Division, on 19 March, but he did not learn of the degree of contamination until he visited the plant on 11 April. Ironically, Converse traveled to the Houston facility at that time to prepare to close it because it was unprofitable. He notified the AEC of the mishap on 19 April, eight days after he learned about it and more than five weeks after it occurred. The agency sent two inspectors to investigate the accident and suspended licenses for all of Kellogg's atomic operations until the inquiry was complete. At a meeting on 30 April the Commission received a preliminary report. Libby was appalled by the procedures used to open the container of pellets, wondering "who was the stupid man who thought he could machine that irradiated compact without breaking it?" Strauss was deeply troubled that Kellogg had not advised the AEC of the incident sooner, especially after he learned that the company had not disclosed a similar but less severe accident several months earlier. Since AEC regulations included no reporting requirements, Kellogg did not violate any rules by failing to inform the agency immediately on either occasion. The staff was in the process of drafting notification procedures in case of accidents, and Strauss urged that they be published soon. He was, he said, "terribly upset about this."[40]

On the day of the meeting the AEC notified the Joint Committee of the mishap. On 2 May it issued a press release announcing that it was investigating the "severe contamination" of the Kellogg lab and adding that two employees not only had received exposure of an undetermined extent but had spread radioactivity into their homes. Six days later the Commission approved an amendment to the radiation-protection regulations that spelled out reporting procedures for licensees in event of accidents. It required immediate notification of the AEC if any one of several situations occurred: exposure to an individual of more than 25 rems, release of radioactive materials in concentrations exceeding five thousand times the occupational limits, closing an operation for a week or more, or property damage of more than a hundred thousand dollars. In case of less serious mishaps, the regulations prescribed notification within twenty-four hours. They also directed licensees to inform the AEC within thirty days of any instance in which an individual received a radiation dose higher than the permissible levels. The agency made the new requirements effective immediately.[41]

Meanwhile, the AEC's Division of Inspection continued its investigation of the Kellogg accident. In its final report it attributed the contamination of the lab and exposure of the employees to two causes: the failure of Northway and McVey to observe company procedures for handling radioactive materials and monitoring the doses they received, and a lack of awareness on the part of plant managers and employees of the potential hazards involved in their work. "This incident illustrates pointedly," declared Division of Inspection director Curtis A. Nelson, "the truism that . . . substandard organization, discipline, and procedure substantially increases the probability of accident." He urged that such matters be given greater emphasis in reviewing future license applications. The AEC terminated Kellogg's license for the Houston facility while permitting the company to dispose of its inventory of radioactive materials from the lab. It also allowed the firm to resume use of isotopes in construction projects at other locations "after determining that no [radiation] hazards . . . would be incurred in the Construction Department continuing its work." Since Kellogg had planned to shut the Houston plant even before the accident occurred, it neither protested nor suffered appreciable losses from the AEC's withdrawal of the lab's license.[42]

The men involved in the accident, however, suffered grievously, not so much from radiation exposure as from financial and psychological stress. The day after the mishap, McVey visited a radiologist, who detected a slightly above-normal but not alarmingly high radiation count on his body and traces of radiation on his suit. About a month later, both McVey and Northway experienced nausea, vomiting, and extreme fatigue, and Northway developed two small blisters on his skin. McVey again consulted his radiologist, who again discovered radiation on his clothing and advised him to search his house for signs of contamination. When he checked his home with a Geiger counter, the results were shocking. Radiation showed up on the floors and walls, mattresses and bedding, rugs and furniture, the family car, and most of the clothing of McVey, his wife, and their three children. The counter ticked ominously when McVey held it to his five-year-old daughter's foot, but after a gentle washing of the skin with soap and water, the radioactivity disappeared. McVey was stricken by the realization that he had contaminated his home and family. Although he had changed clothes and showered after the accident, he had carried radioactive particles into his home on his body, underwear, shoes, and socks. The radiation had spread from normal movements and from laundering the contaminated clothing in the family's washing machine. Northway underwent a similar ordeal. Radioactive particles from his skin, shoes, and suit contaminated his home and exposed his wife, four-year-old son, and pet dog. "Every time I went to touch something," Mrs. Northway remarked sadly, "I wondered if it was contaminated." Fortunately, the levels of radiation found in the homes were low, and thorough physical examinations of McVey and Northway revealed no signs of internal radioactivity or serious injury. Although the health assessments were optimistic, they hardly relieved the guilt and anxiety that the two men felt.[43]

The Kellogg Company paid their medical expenses and reimbursed them for property damage, but Northway's and McVey's woes were compounded by the loss of their jobs. Their boss, Converse, terminated Northway with thirty days' notice when he visited the Houston lab on 11 April. Although McVey received a temporary reprieve, he too faced imminent unemployment. In both cases the dismissals came as a result of the company's decision to close the facility rather than as a consequence of the accident. The plight of the two families became even more painful after the AEC's public announcement of the incident on 2 May. Unintentionally, the press release suggested that the effects of the mishap were more serious than they actually turned out to be. It accurately described the contamination of the lab as "severe" and noted that two employees had been exposed to radiation of undetermined concentrations and had spread it outside the plant. But because the medical reports on Northway and McVey were not yet available, the press release could not balance that information with the more reassuring results of their physical examinations. The AEC did not disclose the names of the two men, but their identities quickly became known. The *Houston Post* ran front-page stories on the accident the two days following the AEC's announcement, making Northway and McVey unwilling celebrities. Their phones rang incessantly as friends and acquaintances called to express sympathy and to inquire as subtly as possible whether they might have been exposed to radiation in their contacts with the two families. Their concern was justified because the Northways and McVeys had unwittingly spread traces of radioactivity to the homes of a few of their friends. But the apprehensions exceeded reasonable proportions. Both families were dismayed when friends refused to shake hands or visit their homes.

Mrs. Northway revealed that her hairdresser asked whether her head was radioactive, a grocery-checkout clerk picked up her money with tissue paper, and her son was taunted and ostracized by schoolmates. In a feature story on the trials of the Northways and McVeys, *Look* magazine concluded that the entire episode caused a "kind of damage . . . which does not show up on radiation-measuring instruments and medical tests. It comes from fear and anxieties and disrupted family lives. It also comes from the dread that exposure to man-made radiation may produce results in future years that cannot be anticipated by current knowledge."[44]

The AEC informed the Joint Committee in May 1958 that it planned "no further action" in the Kellogg case, but the tribulations of the Northways and McVeys continued. After they filed claims under the Texas workers'-compensation laws, the state Industrial Accident Board ruled that Northway had not proved he had suffered compensable injury and ordered Kellogg's insurance company to pay McVey twenty-five dollars per week for not more than fifty weeks. Both men appealed the decision and eventually reached an out-of-court settlement for an undisclosed amount with the insurance carrier. Northway and McVey also sued Phillips Petroleum Company, the manufacturer of the irradiated pellets that had contaminated the lab, for $426,000, but a federal district court and later a federal court of appeals concluded that neither man had sustained any serious physical disorders from the accident. *Look* magazine told a different story in a 1960 article entitled "Sequel to Atomic Tragedy." It reported that neither Northway nor McVey had found employment since the mishap, that both men and Mrs. McVey had cataracts of the eye, and that Northway was suffering from cancer. Eighteen-year-old Eddie McVey worried that he could not have normal children. The article stirred several letters of inquiry from the Joint Committee and other members of Congress. In response to congressional interest and the demands of McVey's attorney, the AEC, while disclaiming any financial liability of the federal government for injuries of employees of a private company, agreed to pay for complete medical checkups of the McVey family at the Mayo Clinic in Rochester, Minnesota. Doctors at the clinic who conducted the examinations discovered no evidence of medical problems that could be attributed to radiation and, contrary to the *Look* story, reported that the McVeys were in good health.[45]

On a personal level, the lack of convincing evidence that Northway or McVey sustained permanent or severe pathological harm did not negate the mental anguish they experienced. In a broader sense, press accounts of the Kellogg accident, which occurred as concern about fallout from bomb testing was spreading, contributed to increasing public anxiety about the effects of radiation. The incident also generated more friction in the AEC's relations with organized labor, already strained by their conflicting positions in the PRDC litigation. In September 1957 two staff members of the Division of Civilian Application received a vivid sampling of labor's view of the mishap from Leo Goodman, a prominent spokesman for the AFL-CIO on atomic-energy issues. All were attending a conference on Industrial and Occupational Safety sponsored by the state of Pennsylvania. Goodman accused the AEC of withholding information on radiation accidents from the public and reporting them only when newspapers learned about them independently. He also suggested that the agency colluded with the Kellogg Company to prevent a public hearing on the incident and declared that the AEC was the "worst Federal Agency" in the government. The AFL-CIO supported the efforts of McVey and Northway to win compensation after the accident, and in a meeting with AEC officials and Joint Committee staff members in June 1960, Goodman repeated and extended his allegations against the agency. The AEC prepared a detailed rebuttal that satisfied the Joint Committee that, contrary to Goodman's charges, the agency had not departed from its own regulations, conspired with the Kellogg Company to suppress information on the mishap, acted irresponsibly by reissuing the firm's license to use radioisotopes in construction projects, or tried to "bamboozle" the jury that had dismissed Northway's and McVey's claims against Phillips Petroleum.[46]

Another important result of the Kellogg accident was the addition of reporting requirements to the AEC's radiation-protection regulations. In December 1957 General Manager Fields informed the Joint Committee that the AEC had received information on "28 abnormal situations, not all of which may be classified as incidents, under the existing regulations." None fell into the most serious category that required immediate notification. Noting that the AEC had issued approximately sixty-one hundred licenses, most for the use of radioisotopes, Fields observed that "inspection experience indicates that the vast majority of licensees are exercising serious and competent effort to meet their responsibility of protecting the health and safety of employees and the public." He added, however, that "there remains . . . much to be learned by licensees and the Commission in how to improve operational safety and further reduce the probability of and consequences of radiation incidents."[47]

Within a short time the AEC began to revise the maximum permissible limits in its regulations in accordance with the latest recommendations of the National Committee on Radiation Protection. In January 1957 the NCRP issued a preliminary statement that lowered its recommended whole-body permissible exposure to external radiation from 0.3 rem per week (or 15 rems per year) to 5 rems per year. A worker could still receive up to 15 rems in a given year and stay within allowable limits, however, as long as his average dose over an extended period did not exceed 5 rems per year. The NCRP stipulated that the accumulated maximum permissible dose should be no greater than five times the age of a radiation worker beyond age eighteen (it regarded the minimum age for employment in radiation industries as nineteen). Thus, using the formula $MPD = 5 (N - 18)$ where N was a person's age, a thirty-year-old worker was allowed a total accumulated dose of 60 rems over a twelve-year period but no more than 15 rems in a single one of those years. After considerable discussion the NCRP changed its recommended numerical limits in a final statement it released in April 1958. It retained the formula for computing permissible occupational doses based on an average of 5 rems per year, but it replaced its previous weekly limit with a quarterly level of 3 rems, allowing exposure in a single year of up to 12 rems. The NCRP emphasized, however, that the "allowance of a dose of 12 rems in any one year should not be encouraged as a part of routine operations; it should be regarded as an allowable but unusual condition." Furthermore, it applied "only when adequate past and current exposure records exist." In the absence of such records, the committee advised, a 5-rems-per-year limit should be used.[48]

The AEC incorporated the NCRP's recommendations into a draft of amended radiation-protection regulations that the Division of Licensing and Regulation submitted for Commission consideration in March 1959. The proposal adopted the 5-rems-per-year occupational limit for whole-body exposure to external radiation and one-tenth of that level for minors and persons outside controlled areas. It allowed licensees to use the NCRP formula for averaging maximum permissible dose [$MPD = 5 (N - 18)$] over a period of years if they had a complete record of an employee's past exposure. In that case, a worker could receive up to 3 rems per quarter or 12 per year. The AEC thought it "likely that a good many licensees will prefer to limit the occupational exposure of their employees to [a 5-rems-per-year] level rather than undertake the burden and expense of determining the permissible accumulated exposure." Although the NCRP was still considering changes in its recommendations for permissible concentrations of internal emitters, the AEC's draft, anticipating future NCRP action, reduced the allowable doses of radioisotopes that tended to settle in critical organs to one-third of the previous levels. Like the 1957 regulations, the AEC's amended version required licensees to keep records of employees' individual radiation exposures, and new provisions also directed that workers be notified regularly of their accumulated doses. As before, the AEC did not claim that the prescribed limits were absolutely safe, but it maintained that "based upon present knowledge and experience . . . exposure to radiation at levels permitted under the regulation for an indefinite period extending to a full lifetime is not likely to cause appreciable bodily injury."[49]

At a meeting on 6 April 1959 Harold Price outlined the proposed revisions in the regulations to the commissioners, who raised some questions but suggested no major changes. Chairman McCone and Commissioner Graham wondered why the staff had taken so long after the publication of the NCRP's new recommendations to complete its draft. Price responded that "if he could have anticipated a year ago the attention and concern which radiation and fallout are now receiving from Congress and the public, issuance of the regulation would have been accelerated." Because the NCRP had advised that its recommendations be implemented over a five-year period and because of the significance of the regulations, he added, the staff had proceeded "very deliberately." McCone also inquired about the effects the amended regulations might have on AEC and licensee operations. Staff attorney Robert Lowenstein replied by citing the importance of avoiding "the implication that safety regulations are designed to meet AEC program requirements." Commissioner Floberg supported him by declaring that "the Commission should ensure that safety standards are established without regard to the ease or convenience of working with radioactive materials." With little further discussion, the Commission approved publication of the draft for public comment.[50]

The AEC received comments on the proposed regulations from about 150 individuals and organizations, most of whom held licenses for medical, research, or industrial uses of radioactive materials. Fewer than thirty of those who submitted opinions commented on the changes in the maximum permissible doses for radiation workers. Most who addressed the issue protested the lowered limits on the grounds that no evidence existed showing that the previous levels were unsafe, that the standards should be issued as guidelines rather than mandatory rules, or that the reduced levels would create operational difficulties and impede the growth of the peaceful applications of atomic energy. Those complaints were not persuasive enough to cause the AEC to change the new permissible-exposure limits. Most of the comments dealt with administrative procedures in the proposed regulations. Many licensees strongly objected to supplying periodic reports to employees on their individual accumulated radiation exposure. Industry spokesmen worried that those requirements would incite excessive and undue anxieties among workers who did not understand the purpose or the content of the reports. As a result, the AEC revised the regulation by making licensees furnish the information only at the request of an employee. The agency also responded to organized labor's concerns expressed in three meetings between AEC officials and AFL-CIO representatives. The labor spokesmen generally agreed with the amended standards but urged that licensees be directed to post prominently a notice to workers briefly describing the nature of the AEC's regulations. The agency accepted their suggestion. By the time the public-comment period ended, President Eisenhower had established the Federal Radiation Council. Therefore, the AEC postponed final action on the regulations until the FRC made its recommendations to the president on radiation-protection standards in May 1960. The FRC's guidelines did not differ in any substantive way from the AEC's exposure limits and prompted no additional revisions in the regulations. The lengthy delay, however, generated increasing impatience on the part of the AFL-CIO, whose president, George Meany, complained to McCone that "thousands of workers . . . are now being deprived of the stronger protections over their health and safety on the job." The AEC finally issued the completed regulations in September 1960; they became effective on 1 January 1961.[51]

As the AEC was preparing the revised standards, the general problem of workers' radiation hazards was receiving the attention of the Joint Committee. In March 1959 it conducted the hearings on the issue it had postponed two years earlier. In six days of sessions the committee heard testimony from over forty witnesses on a broad range of subjects. The problem that generated the most comment and controversy was workers' compensation for employees of atomic industries. The purpose of workers'-compensation laws, which were a traditional responsibility of state governments, was to provide benefits to employees for losses in earning power caused by job-related disabilities. Because of the nature of injuries potentially caused by exposure to radiation, the adequacy and applicability of existing coverage in many cases were questionable. The greatest difficulty for a worker claiming compensation was establishing that an injury or disease resulted from radiation received on the job. A person who suffered cancer, leukemia, or genetic damage, for example, could not easily prove that the basic cause was occupational exposure to radiation rather than other factors. Even if that hurdle was overcome, the long latent period of radiation illnesses could prevent a worker from receiving compensation in states with time limitations for filing claims. Uncertainties also arose over whether an employer was entirely liable for radiation injuries to an employee who had worked for other companies, and whether provisions should be made to rehabilitate workers suffering from radiation-induced disorders who would have to find an entirely different occupation. Those issues were not unique in atomic-energy industries; they also applied to chemical workers, miners, and anyone who sustained occupational injuries that were not readily apparent. But they were important questions for labor spokesmen, health officials, and others concerned about protecting the interests of radiation workers.[52]

State workers'-compensation laws varied widely. Thirty-three states offered comprehensive coverage for occupational diseases, including those attributable to radiation, and twelve others provided partial coverage. Only nine states, however, defined time limitations on claims in such a way as to protect radiation workers fully. Most states stipulated that an application for compensation had to be filed within a few months after an injury or within one to three years after an employee's last exposure to radiation, conditions that excluded workers who might develop radiation-induced diseases only after a much longer period of time. Furthermore, only seven states had enacted detailed radiation-protection regulations and permissible exposure limits, which seemed likely to be a central consideration in judging an employee's claim for compensable injury from radiation. Earl F. Cheit, an economics professor at the University of California at Berkeley and an expert on workers' compensation, itemized the shortcomings in existing laws for the Joint Committee and stressed the importance of ensuring sufficient coverage for atomic workers. He commended the "excellent safety records of AEC contractors" but argued that the "safety record of licensees will not be as good." Citing the Kellogg Company incident as an example, Cheit predicted that accidents would multiply as more firms received licenses for atomic-energy operations. Not only was the number of people exposed to radiation increasing rapidly, but private firms seemed less likely than the AEC to observe strict safety precautions and install expensive equipment.[53]

Several AFL-CIO representatives who testified at the hearings called for federal workers'-compensation legislation to protect radiation workers from the inconsistencies and exclusions in state laws. "We . . . strongly urge the Congress to adopt a Federal workmen's compensation program for workers subjected to radiation hazards," declared Elwood D. Swisher, vice-president of the Oil, Chemical, and Atomic Workers International Union. "Not only have the several states so far failed to come to grips with this program, but we seriously doubt that they will be able to do so on any adequate basis." Spokesmen for state governments, atomic industries, and insurance companies disagreed. Harry A. Nelson, former director of the Wisconsin Department of Workmen's Compensation, observed that "there is great resistance to Federal usurpation of this field," and a representative of the Council of State Governments expressed confidence that the states would meet their obligations to radiation workers once they became fully aware of the problem. Two spokesmen for Liberty Mutual Insurance Company, the largest workers'-compensation carrier in the United States, also assured the committee that the states would take necessary action and denied that any emergency existed that required federal intervention. Other industry officials voiced similar sentiments. By the time the hearings ended, they had achieved the Joint Committee's primary purpose of gathering information on workers' radiation hazards and highlighting various opinions on how best to deal with the problem. The committee did not intend to devise legislation of its own, but hoped that the hearings would help spur action on both the state and federal level.[54]

The Council of State Governments, with the cooperation of the AEC, the U.S. Department of Labor, the International Association of Industrial Accident Boards and Commissions, and the National Association of Attorneys General, was already considering measures to improve coverage of occupational radiation-injuries in state workers'-compensation laws. In 1959, after reviewing existing legislation, the Council had recommended that states consider the adequacy of their programs on matters such as full coverage of occupational diseases, time limitations for filing claims, payment of benefits, and rehabilitation of injured workers. The following year, the Council established an Advisory Committee on Workmen's Compensation to prepare a model bill for the guidance of the states. Over a period of two years the advisory committee drafted proposals that it hoped would encourage better protection for workers suffering from job-related accidents or illnesses, including employees in atomic industries. Committee members Oscar Smith, director of the AEC's Division of Labor Relations, and Samuel Estep, professor of law at the University of Michigan, focused specifically on coverage for radiation workers. Both agreed that the most difficult issue was devising a fair system of compensation for diseases that might be radiation-induced but that were "nonspecific" in origin, such as cancer and leukemia. It was, observed Smith, a "somewhat insoluble complication." The conventional way to judge claims in such cases would be to use occupational-exposure records and the assessments of knowledgeable physicians, but that approach could "result in something short of full justice to both employees and employer." Estep suggested the establishment of a contingency fund to which both employees and employers would contribute and from which an employee could draw without having to prove that an illness was directly attributable to occupational radiation-exposure. But that idea "would seem to require a larger coverage base than most single states could provide."[55]

While the Council of State Governments was working on its proposed model bill for state action, labor unions and some members of Congress continued to insist that radiation workers would be assured of adequate protection only through federal legislation. In January 1960 the AFL-CIO submitted a draft bill for the consideration of the Joint Committee, but committee staff members were unenthusiastic. They doubted the constitutional authority of Congress to impose workers'-compensation requirements, particularly for injuries from radiation sources not covered by the 1954 Atomic Energy Act. Labor got a better response from the Select Subcommittee on Labor of the House Committee on Education and Labor, which in January 1962 began hearings on two bills to set up a federal workers'-compensation program for employees of atomic industries. The sponsors of the bills were subcommittee chairman Herbert Zelenko of New York and Melvin Price. Witnesses' comments on the proposals followed familiar patterns. Labor representatives, on the one hand, argued that federal legislation was necessary because many states still failed to provide sufficient coverage for radiation injuries. Spokesmen for the atomic industry, insurance companies, and the states, on the other hand, objected to federal intrusion into traditional state responsibilities. They contended that the states were making satisfactory progress in extending their programs to include radiation workers. They did not deny, however, that workers'-compensation laws in many states lacked full provisions for radiation illnesses.[56]

The AEC submitted statistics to the subcommittee showing very few radiation injuries or cases of overexposure among its contractors and licensees. It commented that the bills presented a "paradoxical situation, i.e. one of the safest industries in the Nation singled out for imposition of an unprecedented system of broad coverage of workers through Federal legislation." The agency acknowledged the deficiencies in state statutes but concluded that federal action was not warranted without further study. Secretary of Labor Arthur J. Goldberg, without either endorsing or opposing the bills, took a similar position. He agreed that workers'-compensation laws in many states were not adequate and promised to undertake a study, with the cooperation of other federal agencies, to prepare "sound recommendations" for the consideration of Congress. "We are faced with difficult issues which require the most constructive and imaginative approach we can devise, carefully worked out after a study of the whole problem," Goldberg declared. "There is no quick or easy solution, but it can and will be solved."[57]

Goldberg acted promptly on his proposal for a federal study. The Bureau of the Budget, which had approved the idea before Goldberg's congressional testimony, suggested to him that the Federal Radiation Council might be the logical agency to undertake the task. The FRC, however, indicated that it had no interest in the subject. The Department of Health, Education, and Welfare took the same position. The AEC was more receptive and agreed to work with the Labor Department to discuss and make recommendations on encouraging states to expand their workers'-compensation coverage, developing minimum and uniform national standards, ensuring the maintenance and retention of exposure records of employees, and devising a system of determining just compensation for diseases possibly but not definitely related to occupational radiation-exposure. The AEC also began an independent effort to fill voids in knowledge about the long-term biological effects of radiation, which was still based largely on extrapolations from animal experiments rather than on human health experience. It undertook a feasibility study to consider whether correlating lifetime health and mortality data with occupational radiation-exposure records of AEC and AEC-contractor employees would yield significant information. Such a survey could have broad implications in many aspects of radiation protection, including but not limited to workers' compensation. Neither the AEC–Labor Department study nor the AEC's proposed examination of relationships between radiation exposure and human health promised quick answers to questions about providing adequate workers' compensation to radiation workers. But at least they represented a serious attempt to deal with some of the most intractable facets of the problem.[58]

In the meantime, responsibility for workers' compensation remained with the states, whose uneven performance in providing sufficient coverage for radiation workers had prompted consideration of federal legislation. In some respects the arguments of both those who favored and those who disapproved a federal law were sound. The opponents, who contended that the states were making progress in extending their coverage and that no emergency existed that required federal action, pointed out that comparatively few cases of radiation injury or exposure exceeding permissible limits had occurred in atomic-energy installations. The AEC reported only three deaths caused by radiation between 1943 and 1960, two during the latter stages of the Manhattan Project and the other at Los Alamos in 1958. Statistics compiled for over 150,000 employees of AEC contractors during 1959 and 1960 showed that 94.5 percent received doses of less than 1 rem per year and 99.9 percent less than 5 rems per year. Between 1957 and 1960, 224 workers at facilities licensed by the AEC had received one-time exposures above permissible levels. The AEC was proud of the performance of the atomic industry, and labor unions and other supporters of a federal workers'-compensation law for radiation workers generally commended the past safety record of atomic installations. But they worried that as the use of atomic energy expanded, more accidents and cases of overexposure would inevitably take place. Therefore, they sought comprehensive workers'-compensation coverage to provide for future contingencies.[59]

Despite the remarkably good safety record of both AEC contractors and the private atomic industry, enough accidents and cases of serious overexposure occurred to give credence to labor's concerns. In May 1958, for example, a radiographer at a construction site in California lost the radiation source of an iridium-192 camera. Before the piece was located, thirteen persons were exposed and one worker received a whole-body dose of 82 rems. After investigating, the AEC concluded that "lack of training, inoperable survey instruments, ignorance of radiation safety procedures, the lack of adherence to construction specifications of the camera source plus the human element of taking short cuts whenever possible can, and usually does, lead to an accident." In January 1962, leakage of a sealed container of polonium 210 spread radiation throughout the Physics Building at the University of Alabama. After discovering the problem the university, which held an AEC license, closed the building and found that several individuals and their homes had been slightly contaminated. One AEC official sent to investigate the mishap suggested that a repetition of the public anxieties created by the Kellogg accident in Houston might easily have taken place but had been averted by the full and frank explanations the university, with AEC assistance, offered to the press. In October 1962 a radiographer in Fort Worth, Texas received a dose of between 24 and 30 rems from faulty equipment. The AEC reported numerous other radiation incidents, which, although mostly of minor consequence, underscored the fact that atomic workers could and did experience accidents resulting from a wide variety of causes.[60]

The most serious accident occurred in January 1961 at an AEC test reactor in Arco, Idaho, where three persons were killed. The reactor, known as SL–1, was built at the request of the Department of Defense, which had used it since 1958 to train military personnel in the operation and maintenance of nuclear reactors. Combustion Engineering, Inc. ran the facility under an AEC contract. On the night of 3 January, three military technicians, two from the army and one from the navy, were performing maintenance on the reactor's control rods in preparation for its restart after a temporary shutdown. Two of the men were certified operators and the other had completed his training course but had not yet taken his final examinations. Although the precise cause of the accident remained elusive even after lengthy investigation, a combination of design flaws, mechanical problems, and perhaps operator error led to the control rods being removed from the core too rapidly. The result was an explosion, probably precipitated by superheated steam that formed when the control rods were lifted, which blew the control rods out the top of the reactor vessel and killed two of the men instantly. The third died within two hours from massive head injuries. Even if the men had somehow survived the blast, they would have died from the high levels of radiation in the reactor building.[61]

An AEC internal board of inquiry that assessed the reasons for the accident found fault with several technical deficiencies and administrative procedures. It cited as a primary cause "the condition of the reactor core and the reactor control system [that] had deteriorated to such an extent that a prudent operator would not have allowed operation of the reactor to continue" without corrective measures. The panel also raised questions about the adequacy of Combustion Engineering's training programs and the procedures that permitted the victims of the accident to work on the reactor without supervision by the contractor or an operator present in the control room to monitor power level and reactivity. The board, however, did not limit its indictment to the contractor. It concluded that the AEC's own lack of clear organizational assignments to ensure the safety of the reactor and failure to provide continuing appraisals and inspections of its condition contributed significantly to the accident. "It is conceivable that clearer definition of these aspects of AEC staff responsibilities," the committee argued, "might also have prevented the SL–1 incident."[62]

Labor representatives expressed concern about the implications of the SL–1 tragedy not only for radiation workers but also for the general public. Two days after the accident, Walter Reuther declared that its occurrence graphically illustrated the strength of the AFL-CIO's position in the PRDC case. The AFL-CIO's own study of the causes of the SL–1 accident reached conclusions similar to those of the AEC's internal investigation. Gordon H. Freeman, president of the International Brotherhood of Electrical Workers, told the AEC that "the nuclear industry cannot be classed as a general or average risk industry *unless* standards, rules, regulations and carefully designed procedures . . . to protect the operating personnel and the general public are adopted and enforced." He added: "We know that had procedures been properly established and the facilities properly manned neither the Kellogg incident nor the SL–1 accident need have resulted in such chaos." In labor's view, the accident was a grim reminder of the continuing need to press for adequate protective measures and workers'-compensation coverage for the growing number of radiation workers.[63]

Overall, labor officials gave mixed reviews to the AEC's performance on issues of primary interest to them. Organized labor remained strongly favorable to expanding peaceful applications of atomic energy but insisted that the safety of radiation workers not be sacrificed to industrial progress. Union spokesmen disapproved of some of the AEC's regulatory programs and procedures. They objected to the state-agreements program on the grounds that the states were generally ill prepared to undertake even limited atomic-safety responsibilities. Furthermore, despite the reservations they held about the AEC, labor leaders feared that state governments would be even less responsive to their concerns. They urged that the AEC require states to provide adequate workers' compensation for radiation workers before they could enter the agreements program. Although labor spokesmen generally acknowledged that radiation-protection standards were necessarily imprecise and could not guarantee absolute protection to atomic workers, they remained displeased that the AEC had taken so long to issue the revised regulations that became effective in 1961. Leo Goodman, the most outspoken labor critic of the AEC, went further by denouncing the NCRP's recommendations as embodying "a concept of low morality" and by calling for the AEC "to establish more effective controls than the sheer wisdom of a philosophy of risk." Labor representatives wanted a "national radiation policy" for protection standards and workers' compensation but complained that they found instead confusion and drift. George H. R. Taylor, an economist with the AFL-CIO's Department of Research, told the Atomic Energy Law Committee of the Federal Bar Association in September 1963 that the unions' ultimate goal was "Federal establishment of minimum safe levels of radiation" in industry, medicine, and the environment. Despite the "generally favorable safety record of the Atomic Energy Commission's operations," he declared, "there are many administrative deficiencies in the field of radiation hazards control which we consistently call to the attention of the Commission and shall continue to do so in the most constructive way possible."[64]

The AEC took labor representatives' concerns seriously and implemented some of their proposals in its regulatory policies. But the agency necessarily acted as a broker for various interest groups, some of whom, particularly spokesmen for industry and for the states, held views that conflicted with those of labor. In attempting to placate different constituencies the AEC fulfilled only some of the requests of each. In revising the administrative requirements in the radiation-protection regulations, for example, it accepted suggestions from industry that made labor unhappy and some from labor that industry did not like. Some questions that labor raised about atomic safety simply were not answerable with the scientific knowledge and operating experience then available. This was true for the numerical occupational-exposure limits that the NCRP developed and the AEC adopted, and labor leaders generally accepted the fact that compliance with protection standards did not assure the complete absence of radiation risks for atomic workers. It was also true in the case of workers' compensation for employees exposed to radiation, an issue that generated considerable debate but defied easy resolution. As in so many areas of atomic safety and regulation, significant matters of concern to labor spokesmen could not be settled without further study and greater experience.

XII

RADIOACTIVE WASTE DISPOSAL: COMPLEXITIES AND CONTROVERSIES

The expanding use of atomic energy for peaceful purposes produced a growing quantity of radioactive waste materials. It also created rising concern within the Atomic Energy Commission and the scientific community, and ultimately among the general public, about safe disposal of those wastes. In approaching the problems of radioactive wastes generated by its licensees in the civilian uses of atomic energy, the AEC drew on the experience and knowledge it had gained from handling military wastes in its own installations. The agency maintained that it was managing dangerous high-level military wastes and discarding less hazardous low-level materials in ways that presented no threat to public health. It offered assurances that it would develop techniques for final disposal of high-level wastes from both defense-related and commercial activities in the foreseeable future. The AEC's assertions were not always convincing to an increasingly apprehensive public, however, and waste disposal became an emotional and controversial issue for a time during the late 1950s.

Radioactive wastes, whether in gaseous, liquid, or solid form, are inevitable by-products of atomic-energy operations. The difficulty of controlling radioactive wastes and the degree of hazard they pose vary according to their volume, the intensity of their radioactivity, the biological effects of specific radioisotopes present in them, and the half-lives of those radioisotopes. Generally, the radioisotopes in waste materials that caused the most concern were those with the longest

half-lives. The products of nuclear fission, for example, include strontium 90, with a half-life of twenty-eight years, and cesium 137, with a
half-life of thirty-three years, meaning that they remain radioactive for
hundreds of years or longer. Since the half-lives of radioisotopes are
fixed, their radioactivity diminishes only through natural decay at rates
that cannot be affected by temperature, pressure, or chemical changes.
The fundamental problem in waste management and disposal, therefore,
is preventing radioactive isotopes from escaping into the environment—
the air, water supply, or food chain—in sufficient concentrations to
threaten human health.[1]

In the late 1950s and early 1960s the Atomic Energy Commission focused its attention on liquid and solid wastes. By 1956 it regarded the
problems of gaseous wastes created in reactors, in fuel processing, and
in laboratory research as largely solved by the development of ventilation
and filtering systems. The agency defined liquid and solid wastes in
broad and necessarily imprecise categories on the basis either of their
level of radioactivity or of their potential biological effects. It considered
wastes to be "low-level" if their radioactivity measured in fractions of
one curie per gallon or if they gave off radiation of up to 50 milliroentgens
per hour that presented "no particular hazard to persons nearby." Low-
level wastes included solids such as chemical residues, contaminated
equipment, clothing, gloves, broken glassware, and carcasses of laboratory animals, and liquids used in uranium mills, in fuel fabrication,
and in reactor cooling. The AEC regarded wastes as "high-level" if their
radioactivity measured in the hundreds of curies per gallon or if they
emitted 2 r or more per hour so "as to materially reduce the time a
person can be near the radiating body." Most high-level wastes were
intensely radioactive liquids produced in the reprocessing of irradiated
reactor fuel. Intermediate-level wastes were those that fell between the
quantitative perimeters of the low-level and high-level categories.[2]

The AEC employed several methods for handling and disposing of
low- and intermediate-level liquid and solid wastes in its own operations.
It packaged solid materials within concrete fifty-five-gallon drums or in
concrete boxes. It buried most of the containers at its installations at Oak
Ridge, Hanford, Los Alamos, Arco, or Savannah River; it also dumped
solid wastes from Brookhaven National Laboratory and the University
of California Radiation Laboratories in the ocean. By 1960 the agency
had disposed of about twenty-three thousand drums at sites off the
Atlantic coast and about twenty-four thousand drums and concrete boxes

off the Pacific coast. For low and intermediate liquid wastes, which were relatively low in radioactivity but large in volume, the AEC used a strategy of "dilute and disperse." Most were treated to reduce their radioactivity by filtration, chemical precipitation, ion exchange, evaporation, and/or temporary storage and then released to adjacent waterways; some were packaged in drums for land burial or sea disposal. In 1957 the AEC estimated that its facilities were discharging a volume of more than eight billion gallons of low- and intermediate-level liquids annually. The agency was satisfied that its disposal of low- and intermediate-level solid and liquid wastes was safe and environmentally harmless.

The greatest sources of concern were high-level liquid wastes. They represented *"the* major waste problem . . . as measured by dollars, curies of radioactivity and potential health hazard," an AEC report declared in 1957. "All of the other kinds and categories of wastes, though significant, are several orders of magnitude less important." Since the techniques used for low-level wastes were not suitable for highly radioactive liquids, the AEC operated on a principle of "concentrate and contain." To keep high-level wastes, which were much smaller in volume than low-level liquids, from entering the environment, the agency placed them in large underground tanks, the life of which it estimated to be twenty years or more. In 1957 it was storing over sixty-two million gallons, most at the site of the plutonium production works at Hanford. Between 1953 and 1957, however, when adequate storage capacity was unavailable, the Hanford works discharged some high-level wastes directly to the ground. Military requirements clearly took precedence over environmental safeguards. The AEC made no mention of the release of high-level liquids that had received only limited treatment to reduce their radioactivity. Most high-level wastes remained in tanks, which allowed time for some of their radioactivity to dissipate. The AEC did not view tank storage as a final answer to the problem of high-level wastes and anticipated that satisfactory means of permanent disposal would be developed.[3]

At the same time that the AEC was seeking to resolve the technical aspects of waste disposal, it was attempting to assure the public that the problem was under control. In December 1949 the agency issued a public report outlining its waste-management practices. Despite the reservations of the Military Liaison Committee, which worried that the publication would furnish significant information on weapons programs, the Commission decided to release it "to dispel misconceptions and allay possible latent hysteria." The report described the nature and sources of radioactive wastes without emphasizing the difficulties they posed. It acknowledged that "improvement in control of wastes requires continued research and development work" and affirmed that "if the [atomic] industry is to expand, better means of isolating, concentrating, immobilizing, and controlling wastes will ultimately be required." But it gave few details on the existing uncertainties of waste disposal and only fleeting mention of the high-level liquids stored at Hanford. In general, the report provided an optimistic assessment by suggesting that with further research and experimentation waste problems would not prove to be unmanageable. Meanwhile, it declared, "the methods of safe handling used to date have successfully protected workers and the public."[4]

The prospects for rapid expansion in the peaceful uses of atomic energy after passage of the 1954 Atomic Energy Act intensified scientific and public concern about radioactive-waste disposal. In its 1956 report on the biological effects of radiation, the National Academy of Sciences commented that in dealing with atomic wastes, "past experience gives only a pale intimation of what is to come." It estimated that by the year 2000 the United States would accumulate 2.4 billion gallons of high-level liquid wastes, mostly from commercial reactors producing electricity. It called for expanded research to investigate the feasibility of proposed methods of "ultimate disposal." A number of popular magazines ran stories that made the same points in more dramatic terms. A 1955 article in *Collier's*, for example, explained the AEC's techniques for handling its "deadly broth of fission products." While praising the AEC's "remarkable safety record," it cautioned: "What makes the problem so serious is the fact that this radioactive garbage is bulking up at increasing rates—thousands of gallons every day. . . . So in the not-too-distant future, disposal of wastes will become a neighborhood matter." In 1957 *Newsweek* described about one-third of the growing volume of atomic wastes as "terrifyingly radioactive." It noted that scientists were seeking ways to dispose of high-level wastes safely but that no easy solutions were in sight. "We won't have a really serious problem in the U.S. until 2000," one marine biologist observed, "and I expect we'll have nice clean fusion power by then."[5]

Although the health hazards of radioactive wastes were the primary concern of those interested in expanding the uses of atomic energy, costs were also an important consideration. By the end of 1956 the AEC had invested about a hundred million dollars in waste facilities and was spending between three and five million dollars annually for treatment and disposal in its own installations. Tank construction and storage alone cost the agency from thirty cents to two dollars a gallon, depending on the nature of wastes being contained. Those amounts appeared to be a major obstacle to commercial atomic-power development because they were significantly higher than waste-disposal expenses in other industries. Clinton Anderson expressed a commonly held view when he told a constituent: "The main difficulty at present is not so much a technical one as it is the relatively high costs involved." Anderson and other atomic-power proponents predicted that the expense of waste management would decline proportionately as the atomic industry grew. They also hoped that employing chemical processes to extract radioisotopes that were potentially valuable would reduce the costs of waste disposal. Scientists were exploring the possibility of using cesium 137 in industrial radiography, strontium 90 in storage batteries, and other radioisotopes present in atomic wastes for a variety of medical, industrial, and agricultural purposes. If recovery of some portions of radioactive wastes for constructive applications proved feasible, it could help overcome the economic disadvantages that waste-disposal problems created for atomic progress. *Business Week*, while depicting waste management as a serious impediment "to reap[ing] the full benefits that can come from nuclear energy," also suggested that "today's waste may be tomorrow's bonanza."[6]

The difficulties that waste disposal raised for peaceful atomic development prompted the AEC to devote increased attention to the technical, economic, and public-relations aspects of the problem. One early step it took was to include conditions in its radiation-protection regulations for licensees disposing of small volumes of low-level waste. The regulations allowed discharge of radioactive waste material into public sewerage systems if it was "readily soluble or dispersible in water," did not exceed maximum permissible concentrations after dilution, and did not produce more than one curie per year of radioactivity. The regulations also permitted underground disposal of limited quantities of waste but restricted the number of burials to twelve per year in depths of at least four feet. All other waste-disposal procedures required specific AEC authorization.[7]

In March 1956 the Division of Reactor Development submitted a report to the Commission on the status of large-volume waste-disposal operations not covered by the regulations. It stated that "disposal of radio-active wastes is under control at all AEC installations" but predicted that "problems in cost and public relations may be expected to arise as the industry under private management advances toward populous areas." While maintaining that neither solid nor low-level liquid wastes posed serious technical difficulties, the staff pointed out that in both cases it was necessary to seek suitable locations where liquids could be safely dispersed in the environment and solids could be buried. Finding burial sites in the northeastern part of the country seemed particularly impor-tant because of the likelihood that many atomic facilities would be built there. Shipping solid wastes over long distances or dumping them at sea was undesirable because the costs were higher than for nearby land burial.[8]

High-level liquid wastes, of course, raised much more complicated questions. The staff report cited several possible approaches to safe ultimate disposal of high-level wastes that were being investigated and appeared promising. One was fixation of waste products in a solid, stable medium, such as clay, synthetic feldspar, or ceramic materials, to contain the radioactivity. The solid blocks might then be buried or stored per-manently without endangering the environment. A second possibility was discharging the high-level liquids directly into geologic formations that would keep the radioactive wastes from reaching water supplies or other natural resources. Among the kinds of sites being considered were salt beds and domes, deep basins of five thousand to fifteen thousand feet that were geologically isolated, and selected shale formations. A third proposal was to remove the long-lived isotopes, strontium 90 and cesium 137, from the high-level wastes. This would ease the difficulty of controlling the remaining isotopes, but it would not solve the problem of what to do with the strontium 90 and cesium 137. Finally, high-level liquids might conceivably be dumped in ocean waters, but the idea seemed less attractive than the others because of "lack of knowledge of pertinent oceanographic factors and complex technical problems and costs involved."[9]

Research on high-level waste disposal was still in the preliminary stages. The AEC was sponsoring projects at its own laboratories and several universities and working with the National Academy of Sciences, the U.S. Geological Survey, and other government agencies to gather and evaluate information on the problem. The staff expressed confidence "that practical, safe ultimate disposal systems will be developed." But it also suggested that technical issues were not the only waste-disposal problem that had to be resolved. Public relations were "an especially important consideration." As the atomic industry expanded and moved into populated areas, public concern about atomic safety generally and waste disposal specifically seemed likely to increase. Therefore, it was essential to cooperate closely with state and local government officials to explain the technical considerations involved in waste management and to secure their assistance in planning, siting, and assuring the safety of atomic-waste operations.[10]

The staff paper served as the basis for a publication on waste disposal that the AEC issued in November 1957. Although more frank than the 1949 report in citing the difficulties created by high-level liquid wastes, it presented similar assurances that safe and economical solutions would be found. The report tentatively suggested that fixation of high-level wastes in solid media offered "the best chances for technical success in the near future," though direct disposal in salt formations also appeared promising.[11]

A special study undertaken by the National Academy of Sciences reached the same conclusion about the prospects for eventually solving the problem of high-level wastes, though it reversed the order of preference for proposed approaches that the AEC report expressed. In early 1955, at the request of the AEC, the National Academy established a Committee on Waste Disposal as a part of its Division of Earth Sciences to examine the possibility of disposing of radioactive wastes on land. In a series of seminars, representatives of the AEC and the U.S. Geological Survey, industry spokesmen, and individual scientists exchanged views. The committee's final report, published in April 1957, declared that "radioactive waste can be disposed of safely in a variety of ways and at a large number of sites in the United States." It cautioned, however, that much research remained to be done "before any final conclusion is reached on any type of waste disposal," and added that "the hazard related to radio-waste is so great that no element of doubt should be allowed to exist regarding safety."[12]

In the committee's judgment, the most promising approach, at least in the short term, was to place high-level wastes in salt formations. This offered several advantages. The most significant was predicated on the belief that the existence of large salt deposits indicated that they had not been penetrated by water (otherwise they would not be there). The absence of water would prevent radioactive liquids placed in salt cavities from being carried into the environment. Furthermore, fissures in salt formations, unlike those in clay, shale, or granite quarries, would be "self-sealing," thus preventing leakage. And the two principal areas in the United States with large salt deposits, the north-central states and the southern states along the Gulf Coast, had low seismic activity and were level enough to facilitate underground access. The committee made clear, however, that several technical uncertainties about using salt formations for high-level waste disposal needed to be resolved. It expressed concern about the possibility that salt cavities might collapse and urged that research be done to determine the "size and shape of openings which can be relied upon to be structurally stable." Another problem was that radioactive wastes would continue to decay and generate heat, which could weaken the walls of salt formations and also produce hazardous radioactive vapors. Finally, transportation of high-level wastes from the installations where they were created to the site of ultimate disposal posed difficulties in terms of both safety and cost considerations.[13]

The committee report cited fixation of high-level wastes in stable solids as the second most promising approach to final disposal, presumably ranking it below use of salt formations because of the longer time it seemed likely to require to answer outstanding technical questions. The study also suggested that research on separation of strontium 90 and cesium 137 and on the possibility of disposal deep in porous substances such as sandstone be expanded. Although optimistic that solutions would eventually be devised, the committee pointed out the complexity and the variety of problems that had to be addressed before high-level wastes could be safely disposed of.[14]

Despite the widely acknowledged importance of developing safe and economical waste-disposal procedures for the growth of the atomic industry, it was not a top-priority issue within the AEC. No single unit in the agency was assigned overall responsibility for waste disposal. Although the Division of Reactor Development was most active in considering the question, the Divisions of Biology and Medicine, Industrial Development, Licensing and Regulation, and Production were also involved in specific aspects of the problem. In September 1957 Chairman Strauss asked General Manager Fields whether, in view of the possibility that "the waste disposal program could become a practical and political problem," it was appropriate "to formalize the planning and authority within the Commission for *waste disposal* standing alone." Fields responded that since waste management "involves many different scientific disciplines," it was "impracticable to concentrate . . . responsibility for it within one division or office." Instead he created a Waste Disposal Working Group to discuss the matter and coordinate the efforts of the various divisions of the agency concerned with it. The working group met for the first time in January 1958 and agreed on a series of tasks it should undertake. But it did little or nothing beyond its initial meeting and exerted no discernible impact on AEC consideration of waste problems. In October the Division of Reactor Development submitted a report to the Commission that made no mention of the Waste Disposal Working Group. The paper objected to proposed budget reductions for research on waste disposal and predicted that, with adequate support, full-scale field experiments on the feasibility of placing high-level wastes in salt formations and advanced pilot projects on fixation of wastes in solid media would be ready within five years. The Commission accepted the report's arguments and authorized the full amount requested, $4.5 million, for waste disposal research. But the fact that only the protests of the Division of Reactor Development averted a cut in funds further indicated that the agency did not attach highest priority or urgency to waste problems.[15]

The implications of the health hazards and costs of radioactive-waste disposal for atomic development concerned the Joint Committee on Atomic Energy. In late January and early February 1959 its Subcommittee on Radiation, chaired by Chet Holifield, held five days of hearings to gather and disseminate information on the subject. In an opening statement Holifield remarked that the interest of committee members and staff had grown after several witnesses had contended during the 1957 fallout hearings that the dangers of radioactive wastes would be more serious than those of fallout from weapons tests. He suggested that "the waste disposal problem may be just as neglected from a public standpoint, as fallout was in 1954," and hoped that "we will not require a series of incidents, such as the contamination of the . . . *Lucky Dragon,* . . . to focus public attention on the waste disposal problems."[16]

The testimony presented by a large number of experts and the papers included in the published proceedings of the hearings gave a comprehensive picture of the nature of the hazards of radioactive wastes, the procedures used to control waste materials, and the avenues being explored to resolve existing uncertainties, particularly with high-level liquids. The consensus of the witnesses, despite their acknowledgment of the difficulties involved, was that technical solutions for high-level waste disposal would be available, perhaps in the not-too-distant future. Joseph A. Lieberman, chief of the Environmental and Sanitary Engineering Branch of the AEC's Division of Reactor Development, predicted that within ten years "we will have alternate solutions to tank storage," though he added that "interim tank storage is always . . . going to be a part of this waste management situation." E. G. Struxness, director of the Waste Disposal Project at Oak Ridge National Laboratory, estimated that "development of disposal of liquid waste in salt . . . can be worked out in the next 2 or 3 years." He added: "It is not so much whether it can be done. It is just how to do it." The optimism that prevailed among the experts, both inside and outside the government, was tempered, however, by a few notes of caution. Abel Wolman, a respected member of the Advisory Committee on Reactor Safeguards and a professor of sanitary engineering at Johns Hopkins University, praised the AEC's handling of high-level wastes but expressed some doubts "that there is a final solution." He also suggested that as low-level wastes increased in volume, they could overwhelm the capacities of the environment for sufficient dilution and dispersal. Although disposal of high-level wastes in the ocean had never received serious consideration, D. W. Pritchard, director of Johns Hopkins's Chesapeake Bay Institute, voiced reservations about dumping even low-level wastes into the sea without a better understanding of the effects of radiation on marine life. In general, witnesses at the hearings stressed the need for careful supervision of all types of radioactive waste and agreed that devising solutions to outstanding problems was essential for the growth of the atomic industry.[17]

The hearings produced no startling revelations or controversy and attracted little public attention or press comment. But within a short time the prevailing public indifference to radioactive waste problems was shattered by a furor that arose over disposing of low-level wastes in ocean waters. Dumping of wastes into the sea had begun as early as 1946, and for over a decade the U.S. Navy had carried containers of low and intermediate wastes from AEC facilities to selected sites in the Atlantic and Pacific oceans. According to the AEC's "judgmental estimates" that it admitted could vary in either direction by a factor of ten, the radioactivity of the materials generally averaged about fifty to two hundred millicuries per drum, though in some instances it ranged as high as thirty curies per package. In addition, as of October 1958 the AEC had licensed six private firms to dispose of low-level wastes from hospitals, laboratories, and industrial operations. Although one licensee,

Crossroads Marine Disposal Corporation, had discarded wastes in relatively shallow coastal waters near Boston under a permit granted in 1952, the AEC, in accordance with recommendations made by the National Committee on Radiation Protection in 1954, began to require that disposal take place at sites with a depth of at least a thousand fathoms (six thousand feet). The agency was satisfied that its sea-disposal procedures created no public-health hazards in either case.[18]

The AEC received some indications of concern over the effects of disposing of wastes in ocean waters. One incident that attracted some press attention occurred in July 1957. During disposal of containers of radioactive sodium in the Atlantic Ocean, two drums remained afloat on the surface and finally sank only after being strafed by naval aircraft. Although the levels of radioactivity were too low to be hazardous, James Reston commented in the *New York Times* that "the incident points up one of the major problems arising from the increased use of radioactive materials" and warned that "careless disposal procedures can be as damaging to a community as fall-out from a nuclear weapon." In April 1958 the California legislature, citing the possibility that containers of waste materials might rupture before reaching bottom and the potential impact of ocean dumping on the fishing industry, requested that the AEC require that disposal take place in depths of at least two thousand fathoms in drums that would not break. An even stronger expression of public apprehension followed a license application by the Industrial Waste Disposal Corporation, a Houston chemical-waste disposal firm. In January 1958 the company requested AEC approval to collect low-level solid radioactive wastes, reinforce the drums it received with concrete, store them for a period not to exceed twenty-one months, and dump them 150 miles off the Texas coast at a depth of a thousand fathoms in the Gulf of Mexico. The proposed license would remain effective for two years and would limit Industrial Waste to dumping an aggregate of 240 curies and storing materials with a total of no more than 10 curies of radioactivity at one time. The announcement of the firm's proposal stirred considerable interest in the local area, particularly since, as Chet Holifield remarked, the people of Houston were "quite sensitive" to the possibility of accidents after the contamination of the M. W. Kellogg Company employees the previous year.[19]

At public hearings that AEC hearing examiner Samuel Jensch conducted in Houston in January 1959, five intervenors—the Sportsmen's Clubs of Texas, the counties of Harris and Nueces, the city of Corpus

Christi, and the Nueces County Navigation District—opposed issuing a license to Industrial Waste. They objected to transporting and storing radioactive materials in Houston and to disposing of wastes in the Gulf on the grounds that too little was known about the possible effects of dumping upon marine life. They also worried that water pressure would cause the drums containing the wastes to break. The intervenors argued that granting the license to the company could endanger the health of thousands of people who used Gulf waters for food supplies and recreation. On 29 May Jensch, supported by the evaluation of the agency "separated staff" working on the case, ruled in favor of issuing the license. He concluded that the waste-disposal services that Industrial Waste planned to provide were safe, feasible, and necessary, especially in view of the expanding use of radioactive materials in the Houston area by hospitals, laboratories, and industries. Jensch contended that allowing the firm to discard wastes in a regulated and systematic way was preferable to simply letting them accumulate at their place of origin. He denied that the low levels of radioactivity in the wastes that the company would be authorized to handle and dump represented a public-health hazard. Citing the opinions of scientists, the results of tests conducted at disposal sites in the Atlantic and Pacific oceans, and experience to date, the hearing examiner found that Industrial Waste's operations would neither "introduce any significant reactivity" nor "measurably affect the level of radioactivity already present" in the Gulf of Mexico. Even if the drums should rupture, the level of radioactivity was low enough to be dispersed to safe concentrations, especially since the proposed deposit of 240 curies over a period of two years . . . is infinitesimal in relation to the billions of curies of background radioactivity now in the Gulf." Unless the Commission elected to review the case, Jensch's decision would become effective in three weeks.[20]

The ruling triggered a storm of protests. The intervenors filed formal exceptions to Jensch's opinion and claimed that "once the precedent of sea disposal is established in the Gulf of Mexico it will soon become the radioactive dumping ground for the entire country." Several members of the Texas congressional delegation expressed strong support for their position, and Senator Lyndon Johnson asked the Joint Committee on Atomic Energy to look into the matter. Senator Ralph Yarborough was particularly outspoken. In a speech on the Senate floor before the hearing examiner's decision, he had voiced opposition to dumping wastes in the Gulf. A few days later he had met with members of the AEC staff, who

had assured him that Industrial Waste's operations would pose no significant hazards. They also promised to send him copies of reports on
ocean disposal and had given him the impression that the AEC would
take no action on the license application until he could study the material.
Before Yarborough received anything from the AEC, however, the hearing examiner issued his ruling. The senator was incensed. He accused
the agency of a "breach of faith" that "quite naturally impairs my trust
and confidence in the representatives of the Atomic Energy Commission." General Manager Luedecke sought with some success to soothe
Yarborough's anger by explaining the procedures of the hearing examiner and separated staff and assuring him that the staff members with
whom he met "would not intentionally leave the impression with you
that they could control the timing of . . . the decision."[21]

Other voices echoed the objections expressed by Texans. Senator Clair
Engle of California observed: "Questions have been raised regarding the
prevalence of this radioactive material in the atmosphere. Apparently
we are going to get it in the ocean as well." The Louisiana legislature
adopted a resolution opposing disposal of radioactive wastes in the Gulf
as "completely untenable" and a source of "great alarm." The government of Mexico informed the State Department of its deep concern over
the proposed dumping site. The U.S. embassy in Mexico City predicted
that a "violent adverse public reaction would result from approval of
the license," and the department urged that the AEC reject the
application.[22]

In view of the spirited public reaction, the AEC announced on 1 July
1959 that the Commission would review the hearing examiner's decision.
After holding hearings in January 1960 the Commission eventually settled the issue with a compromise. It granted Industrial Waste a license
to receive and store wastes but denied permission to dump them in the
Gulf of Mexico. Instead, the Commission authorized the firm to ship
the materials it collected to Oak Ridge or Arco, Idaho for land burial.
The AEC's primary reason for refusing to allow disposal in the Gulf was
the vehement opposition of Mexico. The agency accepted the State Department's advice that "granting of the license application would have
seriously harmful effects on our friendly relations with Mexico and with
the other countries of the hemisphere." Neither Industrial Waste nor
any intervenors objected to the AEC's final ruling.[23]

The hearing examiner's initial ruling on Industrial Waste's application
was only the first of a series of events in the summer of 1959 that created

widespread public concern over radioactive waste. On 21 June the National Academy of Sciences released a report on sea disposal of low-level wastes that amplified and extended the controversy. The AEC had requested a study of the feasibility of discarding wastes in coastal waters at depths of less than a thousand fathoms the previous year. It sought expert opinion on the subject because of the growing volumes of low-level wastes created in research, industrial, and medical activities and the high costs of transporting drums far from shore for disposal beyond the continental shelf. The National Academy's Committee on Oceanography established two working groups, one to explore the problem in the Atlantic Ocean and the Gulf of Mexico and the other in the Pacific Ocean. The scientists investigating the use of Atlantic and Gulf coastal areas completed this survey in early 1959, and their findings were those published in June. They identified twenty-eight places where safe disposal of low-level wastes seemed possible, conditioned on detailed study of any site that might be selected. They argued that even in water of approximately thirty fathoms, such materials, if disposed of properly and supervised carefully, would present no appreciable hazard to human health or the marine environment. The sites the report recommended included areas within 16 miles of Cape Cod, 10 miles of the Rhode Island coast, 22½ miles of Atlantic City, 22 miles of the North Carolina coast, 20 miles of Savannah, 2 miles of the Florida coast, 26 miles of the Louisiana coast, and 19 miles of the Texas coast. Many had formerly been used as dumping grounds for explosives.[24]

Whatever the scientific merits of the report, the timing of its publication, from the AEC's point of view, was lamentable. Appearing three weeks after the hearing examiner's provisional approval of Industrial Waste's proposal for dumping in the Gulf, it not only fueled the growing protests over the licensing case but inevitably linked the company's application with the National Academy of Sciences' tentative recommendations. Yarborough charged the AEC with "frantic haste" and argued that outstanding scientific questions about the effects of sea disposal should be answered. Other members of Congress expressed similar views. The AEC emphasized that none of the sites the National Academy survey designated would be used unless detailed scientific investigation of water circulation, marine life, and background-radiation levels confirmed the preliminary proposals. But those assurances were hardly sufficient to ease the anxieties the report generated. "After all, 'radioactivity' is a frightening word," the *Providence Journal* commented. "The prospect that quantities of radioactive waste may be dumped into the sea a few scant miles from [the coast] naturally evokes some concern."[25]

The concern was evident in a special hearing that Holifield's Subcommittee on Radiation held at the request of Senator John Pastore of Rhode Island, a senior member of the Joint Committee. Pastore wanted a hearing because of the "consternation" and "public apprehension" caused by the National Academy of Sciences study. Senators and congressmen from Texas, Florida, Rhode Island, and Massachusetts attacked the proposal to dispose of radioactive wastes in coastal waters. Several announced their support for a bill recently introduced by Representative Clark W. Thompson of Texas that would restrict dumping in the Gulf of Mexico to areas at least two hundred miles from shore in depths of a thousand fathoms or more in leakproof containers. Representative Charles E. Bennett of Florida submitted a bill with identical conditions for the Atlantic Ocean. The AEC opposed the legislation as overly rigid. General Manager Luedecke declared that they "would not permit us to continue to take into account the many varying, technical and scientific considerations involved." Furthermore, the agency did not require that containers "maintain their complete structural integrity" at a thousand fathoms because it believed that low-level wastes would be dispersed to a safe level even if the drums broke open. The chairman of the National Academy of Sciences' committee that prepared the report on disposal in coastal waters, Dayton E. Carritt of Johns Hopkins University, vigorously defended his group's recommendations. He denied that disposal in a thousand fathoms of water was necessarily safer than in shallower depths and reiterated that using coastal waters, if done with due care, would create no significant hazards. Carritt added: "I have heard no objections made by a reputable scientist to the basic approach . . . taken by our study group nor to the recommendations based upon our study."[26]

Pastore, punctuating his questions by slamming his hand on the table, grilled AEC officials who testified at the hearings. He wondered why the AEC would "retreat" from its policy of authorizing sea disposal only at depths of a thousand fathoms. Harold Price reaffirmed that the agency still retained that requirement and would not change it before consulting state and local government officials and holding public hearings. Representative William Bates of Massachusetts pursued a similar issue when he asked why, if disposal in coastal waters was not dangerous, the AEC was now making Crossroads Marine Disposal Corporation, which had been discarding low-level wastes in depths of 150 feet near Boston Harbor, discard its drums in a thousand fathoms. Price replied that the AEC did so "out of an overabundance of caution." During Carritt's testimony, Pastore explored the question of the psychological impact of dumping radioactive wastes near shore. Even if there was no scientific basis for fear, he suggested, "the suspicion alone would be enough to ruin the economic stability of the community." Holifield agreed that public anxieties could damage the fishing and tourist industries in areas close to the proposed dumping sites. Carritt explained that his committee had thought about the psychological reaction among the population but had no way of evaluating it. Holifield believed that at some point public perceptions had to be taken into consideration, but he also regretted that "all this excitement occurs just because of a few uninformed newspaper articles and editorials and a few hysterical people."[27]

Holifield and Pastore had ample reason for concern about public apprehension over hazards from radioactive waste. In addition to the objections raised to Industrial Waste's license application and the National Academy of Sciences' report, other incidents in the summer of 1959 both reflected and intensified public anxieties over waste disposal. A Fourth of July celebration at an Oregon beach was abruptly canceled when a barrel marked "Danger—AEC Radioactive Waste" washed ashore. It soon proved to be a hoax—the drum contained no radioactive materials—but not before sparking protests and drawing national attention.[28]

Of greater consequence was citizen opposition to licensing of waste-disposal operations in New England. Residents of New Britain, Connecticut organized a group known as People vs. Atomic Waste to challenge the proposal of a local firm, Walker Trucking Company, to store low-level wastes in their community. In March 1959 the company had received a license to collect wastes and hold them at a facility in Portland, Connecticut before disposing of them beyond the continental shelf in the Atlantic Ocean. A short time later, however, the town of Portland had passed a zoning ordinance that prohibited Walker Trucking from using the planned site. Therefore, the company asked the AEC to amend its license to permit collection and handling of atomic wastes in New Britain. The people of New Britain were unaware of Walker Trucking's intentions until a news reporter noticed an AEC announcement of public hearings. Once alerted, the citizens turned out in force to protest the application at hearings held in June. They also circulated a petition, signed by over three thousand people, objecting to storage of wastes in their city, and successfully appealed to the AEC to postpone action on the license application. After protracted hearings and legal proceedings, the AEC granted Walker Trucking permission to receive and store waste materials in New Britain in June 1961.[29]

As the controversy in New Britain was building, citizens of Cape Cod were also organizing to protest waste-disposal operations that they feared would affect them. On 11 August 1959 the AEC announced that unless it received a request for a formal hearing within fifteen days, it would issue a license to the U.S. Navy's Military Sea Transportation Service to discard packaged low-level solid wastes in a thousand fathoms of water at five sites, one of which was two hundred miles due east of Cape Cod. A group of Cape Cod residents wired the AEC to express their misgivings and within a short time formed the Lower Cape Cod Committee on Radioactive Waste Disposal. The committee urged the transfer of responsibility for waste disposal to the U.S. Public Health Service, and one of its members, a part-time journalist named Grace Des Champs, wrote a series of newspaper and magazine articles denouncing the AEC. She not only expressed grave concern about licensing the Military Sea Transportation Service but also accused the AEC of clandestinely allowing Crossroads Marine Disposal Corporation to dump wastes in coastal waters near Boston. Despite stories on the company's activities in *Newsweek* in 1957 and the *Saturday Evening Post* in 1958 and a lengthy discussion in the Joint Committee hearings, she insisted that information on the operation had been concealed from the public. Des Champs's charges received the editorial support of *The Nation,* which attacked the AEC for secrecy and "insolence" and asked: "Who could have guessed that for thirteen years the Atomic Energy Commission has been licensing the dumping of hot radioactive wastes in fifty fathoms of water twelve miles out of Boston Harbor?"[30]

The AEC responded by offering assurances that neither the coastal disposal carried out by Crossroads Marine nor the proposed deep-sea dumping in the Atlantic by the navy posed significant hazards. The Cape Cod committee remained unpersuaded and continued to call for assigning authority for handling radioactive wastes to the Public Health Service. Some people on Cape Cod seemed less concerned; one town selectman suggested that the controversy might have been averted if the AEC had announced that it planned to permit dumping "west of the Azores" rather than "east of Massachusetts." The agency deferred final action on the Military Sea Transportation Service's application, and as one writer noted: "The AEC must suspect that if it ever again comes close to the Cape Codders' territory, it is in for a rumble."[31]

One additional incident, though unrelated to questions about sea disposal, contributed to growing public anxieties about radioactive wastes during the summer of 1959. On 14 July the Public Health Service disclosed that the Vanadium Corporation of America's uranium-processing mill at Durango, Colorado had been discharging radioactive wastes into the Animas River that raised levels of radioactivity in the water far above permissible concentrations. The announcement denied that any immediate threat to public health existed and revealed that the company had agreed, after meeting with Public Health Service and AEC representatives, to take prompt measures to end the contamination. Nevertheless, the news stirred considerable alarm among people who depended on the Animas River for drinking-water. It also received national attention. A reporter asked Eisenhower about the matter at a press conference, and the president, though unaware of the problem, promised to look into it immediately. Several observers sharply criticized the AEC. Broadcaster Edward P. Morgan, for example, told his listeners on the ABC radio network that the agency had failed to carry out its responsibilities for protecting public health, and a Farmington, New Mexico physician declared at a town meeting that the AEC was the "real culprit" because it had been "lax" in regulating the Durango mill.[32]

AEC officials were dismayed by the public outcry over waste disposal, especially since it came in the wake of the fallout controversy in the spring of 1959 and while the Bureau of the Budget was still considering a reallocation of authority among federal agencies for radiation protection. McCone commented at a Commission meeting on 15 July that "he was seriously concerned about the growing volume of criticism AEC was receiving on the problem of radiation contamination." He and the other commissioners determined that the AEC needed an integrated organizational framework to administer its waste-disposal program, which had been tried without much success two years earlier. They also agreed that the agency should undertake a public-relations campaign to explain its waste-disposal procedures. This seemed advisable because the commissioners and the staff were convinced that apprehension over wastes had arisen largely because of "public misunderstandings concerning AEC policies." The AEC decided to conduct seminars in which agency officials would answer any questions, on the record and for attribution, that newsmen or members of the general public wished to ask about waste disposal. The first session was held in Boston in September 1959, and the AEC was so pleased with the response that it scheduled meetings with the same format in other locations.[33]

In addition to conducting public meetings, the AEC took other action to resolve issues that critics had raised about the safety of ocean dumping. It sponsored a survey of the disposal site near Boston Harbor used by Crossroads Marine Disposal Corporation until August 1959. Samples of water, sediments, and marine organisms collected by the U.S. Coast and Geodetic Survey and analyzed by the Public Health Service showed no radioactivity resulting from the company's operations. The AEC also initiated a series of experiments on the ability of drums used to package waste materials to withstand the impact of striking the ocean floor. Tests conducted in shallow water showed that the drums remained intact at velocities as high as fifteen miles per hour when they hit bottom. Those findings supplemented information from tests done in 1957 on the effects of water pressure on the containers. With few exceptions the barrels' structure and pressure-equalization features made them immune to pressure at depths of a thousand fathoms. The drums that broke open were those packed loosely enough to allow the formation of voids; consequently, the agency began to require that wastes be highly compressed in the containers to prevent voids. Even then, it acknowledged that some "drum failure" might occur, but it still maintained that the level of radioactivity released would not be hazardous.[34]

The AEC's findings did not end the controversy over sea disposal of radioactive wastes, though it continued at a distinctly lower level of intensity than was prevalent in the summer of 1959. Popular magazines and newspapers ran occasional articles on the subject, and Walter Cronkite discussed it briefly in his CBS television program "Twentieth Century." A series of incidents in Long Beach, California in early 1960 created a brief furor. The previous June, the AEC had issued a license to Coastwise Marine Disposal Company to collect, package, and store low-level wastes at a facility in Long Beach and dump them in a thousand fathoms in the Pacific Ocean. The license application had been uncontested. The company also secured approval from city authorities to conduct operations and paid a business-license fee, but for some reason never received the actual document. When the AEC made an inspection of Coastwise Marine's installation shortly after the firm began getting shipments of wastes, it discovered several violations of the terms of the license, including the absence of radiological survey equipment, lack of records on the radiation levels of the drums collected, unauthorized receipt of unpackaged wastes, and improper labeling of containers. The AEC demanded an explanation. Meanwhile, Long Beach officials had changed their minds about permitting the company to collect radioactive wastes in their city. They ordered Coastwise Marine to cease operations and sent the city police to block access to the firm's facilities. As a result, thirteen trucks carrying radioactive materials sat on city streets for several days. The head of the company, Robert Boswell, was formally charged with running a junk business without a city license. In the ensuing litigation, the California Superior Court ruled on 21 March 1960 that the city lacked authority to close Coastwise Marine because of the AEC's exclusive jurisdiction to protect against radiation hazards.[35]

Coastwise Marine's triumph was short-lived. Five days after the court's decision, an explosion occurred at the company's plant. The AEC and the city conducted investigations and found that it did not involve radioactive materials. But AEC inspectors concluded that Boswell "committed several falsehoods" when questioned about the incident. Boswell compounded his problems a short time later by accepting a shipment of wastes that included some drums with radiation levels that exceeded the limits authorized in his AEC license. Boswell's actions, along with the unsatisfactory explanations he offered for the earlier infractions, persuaded the AEC staff that he could not "be trusted to handle dangerous radioactive materials." In January 1961 the Commission revoked Coastwise Marine's license. The entire episode generated considerable media interest, though the seriousness of the matter was partially obscured by its comic-opera overtones.[36]

At a meeting on 20 June 1960 the Commission decided, at least for the time being, not to issue any new licenses for sea disposal of radioactive wastes. Although the commissioners were convinced that practices to date were safe, they expressed lingering concern about what happened to the drums after being dumped into the ocean. Furthermore, land burial seemed to offer an attractive alternative. Not only was it generally less expensive than sea disposal, but it seemed less likely to arouse public protests. McCone had suggested a few weeks earlier that "there would be little justification at the present time to press for ocean disposal sites in the face of strong public objection—despite the fact that such objections might be founded on emotional fears and not on technical facts."[37]

The uproar over sea disposal of low-level wastes was largely a result of growing public concern over radiation hazards. As one journalist observed, commenting on the protests over the Industrial Waste and Walker Trucking license applications: "Since American sensitivity to the dangers of radioactivity seems to be increasing, the outlook for more trouble of the same kind could not be brighter."[38] Critics of the AEC raised legitimate questions about the durability of the drums and about the uncertainties in scientific understanding of the sea and the effects of radiation on marine life. Their worries that acquiescence in the dumping of limited quantities of waste in areas near them would open the way for disposal of greater amounts at a later time were understandable, though premature. Many of the fears expressed about ocean dumping, however, were exaggerated out of proportion to the hazards involved. The volumes and the levels of radioactivity of the wastes discarded were small and, according to a consensus among scientific authorities and the results of tests conducted at disposal sites, did not contaminate the environment or pose a threat to human health. The National Academy of Sciences study on disposal in coastal waters, which generated sharp attacks, was a responsible effort instigated by the AEC to explore future solutions to a growing problem. It was only an advisory report, and had the AEC not sponsored it and similar surveys, the agency could have been fairly criticized for failing to seek possible ways to deal with radioactive waste. The distinctions between recommendations and policy and between the degrees of hazards from various kinds of radioactive materials were often lost in the clamor over ocean dumping.

The AEC had long recognized that radioactive-waste disposal involved important public-relations considerations, but it did not anticipate the intensity of the concern that became apparent in the summer of 1959. Agency officials voiced frustration when their explanations that they were proceeding cautiously and that ocean dumping was safe fell on deaf ears. Commissioner John Floberg complained during the Industrial Waste proceedings about "the damage already done to the rate of development of the peaceful uses of the atom by sensational exaggerations in the press and over the air," but he grudgingly concluded that it was sometimes necessary to take "extreme, even if not completely logical, measures to satisfy even unreasonable public doubts." Even then, as Pastore and Holifield had suggested during the Joint Committee hearings, it was not always possible to allay public anxieties. The reaction to sea-disposal operations was a vivid demonstration of public apprehension over any form of radiation, and it was hardly coincidental that the turmoil erupted at about the same time as the 1959 debate over fallout. By heightening public awareness of radiation hazards the fallout issue made people unlikely to welcome the prospect of radioactive materials in their backyard, even if the backyard was a thousand fathoms deep two hundred miles from shore. The fallout controversy also undermined the AEC's credibility, so that its assurances on waste disposal were less effective than they might otherwise have been. Moreover, sea disposal was particularly disturbing to many individuals, partly because the wastes were not recoverable and errors would be uncorrectable, but also because of a more philosophical belief in the sanctity of the sea. The noted writer E. B. White put it succinctly when he declared: "The sea doesn't belong to the Atomic Energy Commission, it belongs to me." Strong public opposition to ocean disposal was a major reason that the AEC decided to focus its efforts to handle the increasing inventories of low-level wastes on land burial. As one scholar observed in 1962: "Although the public's fears may be hypochondriacal, the AEC seems to prefer to encourage land burial rather than to arouse them further."[39]

The AEC discarded most of its low-level solid wastes in land-burial sites at its own installations, but it had issued no licenses for commercial burial operations. In December 1959 the staffs of the Divisions of Reactor Development and Licensing and Regulation prepared an analysis of land disposal for the Commission's consideration. They argued that both sea disposal and land burial were "safe and technically feasible," but land burial, except in certain situations, appeared to be cheaper and more convenient. The principal problems that had to be resolved were finding suitable sites and deciding whether the AEC should limit commercial operations to land owned by the federal or state governments. The agency had already rejected some license proposals for land disposal because of "the inability of applicants to assume long-term maintenance and control of the burial site." Since the materials would remain radioactive for hundreds of years, the staff was dubious about the capacity of private firms "to assure competent and responsible management of burial sites for the long periods of time over which the potential radioactivity hazard might extend." It proposed an amendment to the radiation-protection regulations stipulating that commercial land burial could only take place on government property.[40]

The staff recommended that the AEC encourage private firms to collect low-level wastes from licensees and bury them on federal or state lands that satisfied requirements of geology, hydrology, and meteorology. The need for action was particularly urgent in the northeastern states, where over twenty-five hundred licensees were already generating radioactive wastes. The staff estimated that a total of two hundred to three hundred acres would suffice to handle the wastes from licensees in the Northeast for the next twenty years. Until acceptable sites were located, selected, and prepared for operation, the staff advised that private waste-disposal companies be permitted to transport materials to Oak Ridge or Arco, Idaho for land burial in areas the AEC was using for that purpose. Mindful of the agency's experience with investigating potential sites for sea disposal, it also suggested that "site selection activities [for land burial] . . . be conducted with as little publicity as possible." Once a site was chosen, however, "appropriate and useful public relations activities [should] be undertaken . . . to help assure public acceptance."[41]

The Commission quickly approved the staff's recommendations, despite McCone's reservations that the AEC "could defend a position based upon a belief that a private entity could not establish as much perpetuity as a state or the Federal Government." The commissioners raised some questions about land disposal. McCone inquired about the chances that radioactive material might leach from the buried wastes into the earth and ultimately into rivers and streams. He received the staff's assurances that sites would be selected to prevent such an occurrence and would be kept under constant surveillance to guard against the possibility of contaminating the environment. The commissioners also requested more detailed information on the relative expense of sea disposal and land burial. The staff reported that sea disposal ran as high as $48.75 per fifty-five-gallon container while land burial of low-level wastes requiring no special protective shielding cost the AEC only $5.15 per drum. In May 1960 the AEC announced that on an interim basis it would accept packaged low-level solids from licensees at Oak Ridge and Arco and that it would charge 70 cents a cubic foot for burial of the wastes.[42]

The AEC's announcement elicited some complaints from waste-disposal companies that authorizing land burial at AEC facilities was an infringement of "private business rights." The agency planned to accept low-level wastes from licensees at its own installations only temporarily, however, and hoped that private firms would take over the function by establishing disposal sites on government-owned land. The response from private interests was hardly enthusiastic, but one company, Nuclear Engineering, which already held an AEC license for sea disposal in the Pacific Ocean, took prompt action. It applied for and in 1962 received an AEC license to operate a land-burial service on state-owned property near Beatty, Nevada. Nuclear Engineering also opened a burial facility on state land in Maxey Flats, Kentucky in 1963. Under the AEC's

state-agreements program, the state of Kentucky licensed that installation. In addition, the AEC in 1963 issued a construction permit to Nuclear
Fuel Services, Inc. and the New York State Atomic Research and Development Authority to build a spent-fuel processing plant on a 230-
acre state-owned tract thirty miles south of Buffalo. By reprocessing
irradiated fuel from commercial nuclear plants, the facility promised to
fill what the AEC had regarded as a "potential gap in a broadly based
commercial nuclear industry." Its operations would also include disposal
of low-level solid wastes and satisfy the need for a burial site in the
northeastern part of the country.[43]

In May 1963 the AEC decided to terminate its program of burying
low-level wastes from licensees at Oak Ridge or Arco. Nuclear Engineering requested that the agency withdraw from offering the use of its
sites, and the AEC, in light of its policy of not providing "Government-
owned facilities if and when commercial facilities are available to do the
job at a reasonable cost," agreed. Since Nuclear Engineering was operating two burial sites and the New York installation was expected to
begin receiving low-level wastes soon, the AEC did not want to compete
with private enterprise by continuing to accept materials from licensees.
The agency planned to ship some of its own packaged wastes to the
commercial burial sites. Although six firms were still authorized to dispose of materials at sea, more than 95 percent of low-level solid wastes
from both AEC and private sources were then buried on land.[44]

Meanwhile, the AEC was continuing to seek ways to dispose of the
most hazardous form of radioactive wastes, high-level liquids. Research
projects already under way received some additional incentive when in
1958 storage tanks at Hanford built during World War II showed signs
of deterioration. H. M. Parker, General Electric's manager of the Hanford
facility, told the Joint Committee during its 1959 waste-disposal hearings
that the estimated life of the tanks was "at least several decades." He
acknowledged that "we have had what might be described as suspicious
occurrences in these tanks," but he assured the committee that after
thorough investigation, "we have never detected a leak from any of
these tanks." The AEC made a similar assertion in its 1959 *Annual Report
to Congress*, which pointed out that "stored wastes are extremely cor-
rosive" but declared that "in more than a decade of tank storage at
Hanford no leaks have been detected." Unfortunately, the "suspicious
occurrences" later turned out to have been leaks of thousands of gallons
of high-level liquid wastes. In April 1963 P. H. Reinker, a General Electric
employee who supervised Hanford's chemical processing department,

admitted in Joint Committee hearings that 5 tanks of the 145 in use there had leaked. By that time, waste disposal had ceased to be a prominent public issue, and committee members did not pursue the matter or show much interest in Reinker's statement. The AEC did not believe that the leaks caused a public-health hazard because the tanks were two hundred feet above the water table and the dry sediments under them were capable of absorbing large volumes of liquid. Similar problems arose at Savannah River, where small quantities of high-level wastes seeped from a storage tank into the soil and groundwater in 1960. The leaks in tanks at Hanford and Savannah River underscored the need to find satisfactory ways of dealing with high-level liquid wastes.[45]

Research that the AEC was conducting or sponsoring on high-level wastes produced some significant advances. Of greatest immediate benefit was the development of techniques to reduce the volume of high-level wastes that required tank storage. At the Idaho installation, researchers converted high-level liquid wastes into powdery solids that could be isolated in steel containers. At Hanford, scientists devised methods of removing strontium 90 and cesium 137 from the liquid wastes and then decreasing the quantity of the remainder by evaporation. Those techniques alleviated the problem of storing large volumes of liquid wastes, but at the same time they made ultimate disposal of the sludge that remained in the Hanford tanks more complicated. The residual materials, the radioactivity of which was diminished by the separation of strontium 90 and cesium 137, would be more difficult to retrieve and transfer once a method of final disposal was developed. Although the AEC had previously regarded high-level liquid storage as a short-term interim approach, at least some authorities now suggested that storage of the sludge at Hanford might be satisfactory for an indefinite period. General Electric's Reinker told the Joint Committee in 1963 that "we consider that immobilization in our existing tanks represents an adequate and appropriate solution to the long-term waste management problem." In any event, the AEC still faced the task of seeking a permanent solution for disposing of the strontium 90 and cesium 137 that was separated at Hanford, the powdery solids at Idaho, and other high-level wastes from its own and commercial operations. Experiments on fixation of fission products in inert clay, glass, and ceramic materials were encouraging, and the agency was exploring the feasibility of direct disposal in salt cavities by conducting preliminary field investigations in a salt mine in Kansas.[46]

The AEC believed that it was making good progress toward finding satisfactory means to dispose of high-level wastes and that the prospects for a permanent solution were promising. It was annoyed, therefore, by criticism from the Waste Disposal Committee of the National Academy of Sciences' Division of Earth Sciences, the group that had prepared the 1957 report suggesting that salt formations were the most promising repositories for high-level wastes. In June 1960 the committee's chairman, H. H. Hess, a Princeton University geologist, informed McCone of the group's concern over the existing and future status of high-level wastes. He expressed the committee's uneasiness over the fact that AEC installations were not located at sites where disposal of their wastes was geologically possible, and over the failure to develop techniques for ultimate disposal of high-level wastes that would keep them "completely isolated from all living things for the period during which they are dangerous." The committee thought it "urgent" that waste-disposal facilities be established in suitable geologic formations and recommended that plans for safe disposal of wastes be a prerequisite for AEC approval of sites for any atomic installations.[47]

The AEC found Hess's letter objectionable on several counts. He made no mention of the potential for fixation of high-level wastes in inert, solid form, an approach the agency regarded as "a major possibility" that was "farthest advanced in development." While agreeing that existing AEC facilities were not located where high-level wastes could be deposited in geologic formations, the AEC insisted that its storage tanks provided a satisfactory method of interim management until proven techniques for ultimate disposal were developed. The agency rejected Hess's implication that waste disposal would be safe only if it allowed zero radioactivity to reach the environment. It maintained that such a requirement would ignore the findings and recommendations of the National Committee on Radiation Protection, the International Commission on Radiological Protection, and other scientific groups, and "would make any atomic energy activity virtually impossible." The AEC concurred on the need to consider waste-disposal problems carefully when evaluating license applications and pointed out that it was already doing so. Finally, although it planned to pursue solutions to high-level waste disposal "vigorously," the agency believed that a crash program was "neither desirable nor required." After lengthy deliberation by the staff and commissioners, the AEC replied to Hess in a letter that only partially obscured its impatience and irritation with the committee's observations.[48]

Despite the differences of views apparent in the correspondence between the committee and the AEC, neither indicated any serious doubts that safe methods for disposing high-level wastes would be developed. The prevailing opinion within the agency and among scientific experts in the late 1950s and early 1960s was that the problems of high-level wastes could be solved. The major questions seemed to be how soon the breakthrough would occur and what technique, or combination of various procedures, was the best option. The AEC investigated a number of approaches, but it saw little reason to proceed with great haste or urgency. It seemed better to explore carefully the possible advantages and disadvantages of all alternatives than to increase the chances for errors by moving too rapidly. Since few power reactors were yet in operation and the agency believed that its storage of high-level wastes at its own installations was satisfactory for the time being, policy decisions on high-level wastes could wait until outstanding technical questions were answered. The AEC had already made progress in some areas and expected that other issues would be settled in the near future.

The AEC acknowledged the importance of eventually developing means of safe disposal of radioactive wastes, both in terms of the growth of the atomic industry and in terms of public safety. But it did not attach high priority to the issue. Despite the periodic requests of Strauss, McCone, and other key officials, the agency never effectively centralized or coordinated its internal organization to focus specifically on waste. As long as the problems of high-level wastes appeared to be steadily approaching resolution and the technical difficulties of low-level materials were regarded as negligible, the need for administrative changes did not seem pressing enough to bring about action.

Even if the technical and administrative questions relating to waste disposal were settled, the AEC faced a major challenge in winning public acceptance for any solutions that were devised for high-level wastes. The public furor in the summer of 1959 arose over disposal of low-level materials. Although the AEC acknowledged that low-level wastes could be hazardous if not properly controlled, it was convinced that its procedures for ocean dumping posed no appreciable dangers to public health and the environment. But public fears over low-level disposal represented an unmistakable sign of widespread anxiety about radioactive materials. If the public was so concerned about relatively harmless low-level wastes, it was likely to show even greater alarm over much more hazardous high-level wastes.

The AEC was aware of the problem. A 1960 staff paper noted: "The sensitive and serious public relations implications of radioactive waste management will continue to prevail."[49] But neither that paper nor any others offered suggestions on how to allay public apprehension, perhaps because no obvious approaches were available. Assuming that the AEC developed methods for high-level disposal that were technically sound, it had to tread a fine line between informing the public about what it planned to do and preventing an outcry of consternation and fear. The controversy over ocean dumping demonstrated how difficult that would be. In the absence of ideas about how to deal with the problem, the AEC could only hope that by the time it was ready to apply techniques for disposing of high-level wastes, the public would be more receptive. From that perspective, the AEC's failure to detect immediately the problem of tank leakage at Hanford and take prompt action to correct it was particularly unfortunate because it could (and later did) raise questions about both the agency's competence and its credibility.

The one irrefutable certainty about high-level wastes was that they would continue to accumulate as atomic development proceeded and more power reactors began operating. It was imperative, therefore, both to find viable technical means to dispose of the increasing quantities of waste and to gain public acceptance of any site that might be selected for ultimate disposal. The experience of the late 1950s and early 1960s suggested that securing public approval, or at least acquiescence, would be the more difficult of the two problems.

XIII

IMPROVING THE REGULATORY PROCESS

The AEC's regulatory organization and licensing procedures underwent several major changes with significant policy implications between 1957 and 1962. Broadly viewed, the changes reflected the agency's licensing experience and aimed to meet two objectives: to increase public confidence both in the organization and in its system of licensing power reactors while at the same time providing an efficient regulatory process capable of handling the anticipated growth in atomic power. In addition, the reorganizations not only constituted another chapter in the continuing executive-legislative struggle between the AEC and the Joint Committee but also revealed internal staff differences over agency governance. Once the changes were in place, only future experience disclosed the extent to which they accomplished the stated goals; in any event, the alterations established the regulatory organization that remained basically intact for the remaining life of the Atomic Energy Commission.

One of the Joint Committee's primary concerns about the AEC regulatory system stemmed from the 1956 PRDC controversy. At that time committee members, especially Senator Anderson, questioned whether the regulatory functions of the Commission should not be separated from the promotional and operational responsibilities. The 1957 Joint Committee staff study prepared by David Toll suggested several possible reorganization approaches but reached no conclusion except to note that arguments against a separate regulatory agency were strong at that stage of atomic-power development. But the study recommended that the separation idea be analyzed further. This conclusion arose in part from knowledge that the AEC had also reviewed its internal organization. It had reported to the Joint Committee in January 1957 that it was considering reorganizing the Division of Civilian Application. Consequently, the Price-Anderson Act, passed in the late summer of 1957, was silent on regulatory organization, although it explicitly dealt with several other regulatory issues raised during consideration of the bill.[1]

In the aftermath of the PRDC controversy, the Commission recognized the need to realign the Civilian Application Division in order to develop stronger public confidence in its regulatory and licensing functions. To assist this process, General Counsel William Mitchell and Civilian Application director Harold Price presented a paper on reorganization to the commissioners in December 1956. They thought that some system should be devised whereby the regulators could continue to draw on the development side of the agency for specialized technical competence without undermining their independence or objectivity in assessing safety issues. Mitchell and Price suggested abolishing the Civilian Application Division, which was responsible for all aspects of nonmilitary uses of atomic energy, and creating a Division of Licensing and Regulation to perform only specific safety-related functions. The developmental functions currently within Civilian Application would be transferred to other AEC organizational units or to a new Office of Industrial Development. The Mitchell-Price plan proposed that the new division report to the general manager, just as Price was doing as head of Civilian Application. For Commission consideration, however, they also posed an alternate plan in which Licensing and Regulation would report directly to the Commission rather than to the general manager, thus separating regulatory questions even more completely at the staff level. Because it greatly increased administrative overhead, however, Mitchell and Price downplayed the alternate plan.[2]

The commissioners initially deferred a decision on the Mitchell-Price package, but when they took up the matter again in May 1957, Chairman Strauss wanted several other alternatives investigated. In April the Joint Committee had released the Toll study on regulatory organization that discussed the possibility of creating an internal licensing board with adjudicatory authority. The board's three members would be appointed by the president with the consent of the Senate. The panel would possess final adjudicatory authority in licensing cases, but rule-making would remain the responsibility of the Commission. Strauss wanted the staff to consider that arrangement and also suggested other possibilities for further analysis, such as a panel of commissioners for regulatory hearings or a bureau of regulation within the agency. Even though Strauss wanted all possible options researched before the Commission reached a decision, he and his colleagues still opposed a separate regulatory agency such as the Joint Committee had originally proposed.[3]

The subsequent staff report presented the advantages and disadvantages of each plan requested by Strauss, but showed little inclination toward reducing established bureaucratic authority vested in the general manager. The report revealed rather clearly how the agency paper process worked. The ideas presented were the ones the general manager advocated. In discussing each of the alternatives the report emphasized the merits of the organizational concept of "singleness of administration" under the general manager, which outweighed any advantages gained through the other plans. The report, for example, declared the Joint Committee's licensing-board idea unworkable. In effect, the staff argued, the plan created an independent group within the agency because it would exercise final authority in adjudicatory matters. The staff suggested further that even informal contact between the board and the regular agency staff would not substitute for an "integrated program under common leadership of the Commissioners."[4]

The staff report considered an adjudicatory board appointed by and reporting directly to the Commission. On the one hand, this plan offered certain advantages over the Joint Committee's proposal. The board would be a more integral part of the agency, and the Commission would continue to be the single federal agency responsible for the entire atomic-energy program. Furthermore, the report noted how the board concept provided a group judgment in facility-licensing cases at a level below the Commission that possibly would generate more public confidence in the licensing program. On the other hand, the staff report emphasized that those advantages were outweighed by the problems that might develop in coordination of programs and administrative matters that were currently directed by the general manager. The staff argued that such a plan would be less efficient.[5]

The report also evaluated placing all regulatory functions under one office reporting directly to the Commission such as Mitchell and Price had proposed earlier. And just as Mitchell and Price had done, the staff emphasized that such an arrangement would undermine the traditional AEC method of operation in which the general manager was responsible for supervision and control of all agency activities. Such a plan, the report reasoned, would mean the agency would have two principal administrative officers, which would then require the Commission itself to coordinate the activities of the parallel subordinate organizations. Moreover, it would lead to much duplication of supporting staff services. Like the two board plans, the staff considered this one unworkable.[6]

These considerations ultimately led back to the original Mitchell-Price plan that favored abolishing the Division of Civilian Application and placing all the regulatory functions in a new Division of Licensing and Regulation reporting to the general manager. This reorganization, the report stressed, would continue the singleness-of-administration concept, would probably satisfy the Joint Committee, and could be accomplished immediately. With little discussion the Commission approved the plan on 30 October 1957. The realignment took effect in December.[7]

In 1959 and 1960 another shake-up occurred that affected some regulatory functions that had not previously been a part of the Division of Licensing and Regulation. An ongoing agency study of the overall AEC organization brought about this realignment, but it was primarily influenced by two events: congressional enactment of the amendment providing for a state role in nuclear regulation and President Eisenhower's creation of the Federal Radiation Council. The 1959 amendment to the Atomic Energy Act necessitated an agency focal point to furnish technical assistance to help agreement states carry out their responsibilities for radiation protection and to administer the transfer of specified AEC regulatory responsibilities to those states. The presidential executive order establishing the Federal Radiation Council likewise required an agency contact point for cooperation with the new organization in the formulation of radiation-protection standards.[8]

The Commission organized a new Office of Health and Safety to perform those duties. Staff members of the unit served on the working groups of the Federal Radiation Council and maintained liaison with outside scientific groups that dealt with radiation protection, such as the National Committee on Radiation Protection and the National Academy of Sciences. Furthermore, the office integrated various AEC staff efforts on health and safety that had been dispersed. It acted as a clearinghouse on safety information within the agency and evaluated field health and safety programs. The office's state relations branch reviewed proposed state regulations, consulted with state officials on special problems such as waste disposal, provided advice on establishment of state regulatory programs, and strove to encourage states to develop uniform radiation-protection standards.[9]

Prior to 1960 the Division of Inspection surveyed and reported on licensed activities. The 1954 act had established the division as the functional equivalent of an inspector general's office in a branch of the armed forces. It gathered information to determine whether contractors, licensees, and AEC employees were complying with the law and AEC regulations. With the growth of the licensing program in the late 1950s the Commission, recognizing the need for a separate unit that dealt solely with inspection of licensed activities, set up the Division of Compliance. At first the division was not clearly organized because field inspections continued to be carried out by personnel working under the several AEC field-operations offices rather than directly for the Division of Compliance. Nevertheless, establishment of the unit symbolized the need for a program within the regulatory organization to monitor licensed activities. Subsequent organizational changes eventually created a self-sustaining inspection-and-enforcement office.[10]

To coordinate the three regulatory units, the Division of Compliance, the Office of Health and Safety, and the Division of Licensing and Regulation, the Commission established in November 1959 a new position of assistant general manager for regulation and safety. Chairman McCone told the Joint Committee in early 1960 that creation of the new post acknowledged the growing importance of regulatory activities. Under the general manager, several assistant general managers were responsible for various program areas. The assistant general manager for research and industrial development, for example, supervised the separate Divisions of Research, Biology and Medicine, and Reactor Development, and the Office of Isotopes Development. With the installation of the Office of Health and Safety and the proposed Division of Compliance it seemed appropriate that the overall regulatory and safety program be given equal organizational status with the other assistant-general-manager offices.[11]

While the creation of the assistant general manager for regulation and safety may have symbolically increased the stature of the regulatory program within the agency, from a practical standpoint it stacked an additional bureaucratic layer between the regulatory staff and the Commission. Former Bureau of the Budget official William F. Finan, appointed as the first (and, as it turned out, the only) assistant general manager for regulation and safety, had only limited authority. He served principally as a coordinator and reviewer of the functions of the three units reporting to his office. For example, the new organization placed

Harold Price, who continued to head the Division of Licensing and Regulation, in a peculiar situation. He had to seek the concurrence of Finan before taking an issue to the general manager or to the Commission, but he still retained delegated authority from the general manager to take licensing actions.[12]

Even as McCone told the Joint Committee of Finan's appointment in April 1960, the chairman indicated the new regulatory organization probably would be temporary. Disclosing that over the next several months his staff would study the regulatory and licensing organization and procedures, he promised recommendations to the Joint Committee. While McCone would not say whether further realignments might be in the offing, he emphasized that the agency was at a point in time where "we must improve our machinery for doing this job."[13]

Regulatory organization was only part of the process demanding reconsideration by the end of 1960. The technical-review and hearing format underwent significant change between 1957 and 1960, mostly as a result of the 1957 amendments incorporated in the Price-Anderson Act. By 1960 the cumulative result raised questions about both the efficiency and the integrity of licensing procedures during that period.

The early informal phases of the licensing process for power and test reactors remained untouched by the Price-Anderson amendments. Well before an official application was submitted to the AEC, the applicant and the reactor vendor usually met informally with both the licensing staff and members of the Safeguards Committee to solicit early unofficial opinions on site requirements for the type of reactor contemplated. In order to obtain even a qualified opinion from the agency at this stage of the process, the applicant had to provide a preliminary description of the reactor, the levels of radiation that might be anticipated in both normal and accident situations, and essential information about site topography, population distribution, use of land around the site, and any significant meteorological, hydrological, geological, and seismological conditions. The early meetings also provided the applicant with guidance in filing its formal application for a construction permit.[14]

From the safety standpoint, the important part of the formal application was the hazards-summary report. The applicant prepared an analysis that described the kinds of accidents that seemed credible for the particular reactor, the precautions devised to prevent such mishaps, and the possible consequences of the various calamities. Using this report, the Hazards Evaluation Branch in the Licensing and Regulation Division performed its technical assessment. One or two members of the small technical staff were given responsibility for an individual project.[15]

By 1960 Price had split the technical review unit into two branches, the Research and Power Reactor Safety Branch and the Test and Power Reactor Safety Branch. Both reported to Clifford Beck, Price's assistant director for nuclear facilities safety. Still small, but adequate for the number of applications received (one branch had eight engineers, the other five engineers and two physicists), the two units were assigned projects by reactor type. The Research and Power Reactor Safety Branch handled applications for boiling-water, pressurized-light-water, organic-moderated, research-training, and graphite-production reactors. The Test and Power Reactor Safety Branch analyzed sodium-cooled and gas-cooled reactors, all test reactors, and heavy-water production reactors. As it had done in the past, the staff also drew on the technical skills of people in the fields of meteorology, seismology, biology, and medicine who worked in other branches of the AEC or who were hired as consultants. But responsibility for evaluating each application still rested with the one or two assigned branch staff members.[16]

In due time the case-by-case staff evaluation resulted in a formal written analysis that contained a summary description of the facility and an assessment of the significant safety issues involved. In making this analysis the staff often held a number of informal discussions with the applicant and the vendor to clarify information and to assure that all the necessary data had been included in the applicant's hazards-summary report. In addition, the staff consulted with members of the Safeguards Committee, which also received a copy of the application and concurrently conducted its own independent review. The completed staff report also was submitted to the Safeguards Committee before it scheduled its final meeting to consider the application. Although after 1957 the staff report formed the basis for agency testimony at the public hearing, the document itself was regarded as an internal agency report and was not part of the public record. Those procedures generally had been followed since the early days of licensing. The 1957 amendments did not affect the process to this point.[17]

The Price-Anderson legislation, however, legally required the Safeguards Committee to review and prepare for the Commission a public report on each reactor application. Written in executive session after the committee had conducted its own extensive review of each project, the public reports generally were not intended to duplicate the ones prepared by the licensing staff. Rather, they were simply a summary of the Committee's collegial conclusions. In letter form to the Commission, the Safeguards Committee reports reflected the difficulty of reconciling for public consumption the sometimes conflicting opinions of ten to fifteen experts in the fields of science and engineering. In other words, the careful work and thought that the Safeguards Committee put into every application analysis was not necessarily demonstrated in the rather bland letters that usually lacked both comprehensiveness and detail. Nonetheless, the public reports were highly regarded by members of the Joint Committee on Atomic Energy and that segment of the public concerned with atomic energy because of the independence of the committee and the prestige of its individual members. Although the Safeguards Committee's status was only advisory under the Price-Anderson amendment, most outsiders considered the committee as the ultimate technical-review authority responsible for protecting the public from reactor hazards.[18]

Another part of the Price-Anderson Act substantially altered an important portion of the licensing process. Before passage of the 1957 amendment requiring that public hearings be held prior to the licensing of power and test reactors, the AEC held no hearings unless requested by a third party. In the wake of the PRDC turmoil, the agency in December 1956 adopted the procedure of notifying the public that it was planning to issue a license and would do so unless a party requested a hearing. But after the Joint Committee imposed mandatory hearing requirements in September 1957, the agency followed the exact letter and spirit as well as the legislative history of the statute and held formal hearings on every application. It caused one legal scholar to complain later that the agency was afflicted with a "bad case of dueprocessitis." By 1961 the AEC's procedures incurred harsh criticism from both the industrial and legal communities and once again stirred the Joint Committee to review the licensing process.[19]

With the exception of the PRDC case, in which intervention occurred prior to the mandatory-hearing requirement, all reactor applications between September 1957 and the summer of 1962 were uncontested by members of the public. Typically, any differences on major technical issues between the applicant and the regulatory staff or the Safeguards Committee had been ironed out in the informal review performed before a case came before the hearing examiner. An applicant would not go to a hearing if any outstanding safety question had not been resolved by the previous technical reviews. In other words, the parties at an uncontested hearing—the AEC staff and the applicant—were already in agree-ment that a favorable decision should be made. Unless a third-party intervention occurred, the mandatory hearing would be a *pro forma* pro-ceeding to establish a public record on agreements already reached.

As the legislative history of the 1957 requirement showed, the Joint Committee believed reactor-safety issues were important enough that an automatic opportunity should be provided for the public to attend and observe the discussion at an open hearing. Requiring the staff and the applicant to present their views in laymen's terms in public would help build public confidence in the safety of reactors, the Joint Committee hoped. The legislators also thought that the preparation for such hear-ings might force the AEC and applicants to view in a different perspective some safety problems that had been previously considered. In this way they could become aware of a need to reexamine some facet of an issue.[20]

In theory the Joint Committee goals for informal mandatory hearings seemed easy to accomplish, but in practice the AEC embarked on a formal public-hearing process. This took several forms, the most con-spicuous of which were the formal legal separation of the licensing staff from the hearing examiners and the commissioners once a case reached the hearing stage, adoption of an *ex parte* rule, and reliance by the hearing examiners on strict formal procedures of examination and cross-exam-ination of witnesses at the hearings. Those steps were carried out within the provisions of the Administrative Procedure Act of 1946, which pro-vided guidance for federal regulatory agencies.

The separated-staff procedure, used initially by the agency in the 1956 PRDC case, was formally established in 1957 after the mandatory-hearing requirement went into effect. The staff to be separated consisted of Price's Division of Licensing and Regulation, the Division of Compliance, attorneys from the general counsel's office assigned to Price's staff for a particular case, and other specifically designated AEC staff members who might be required to assist in the agency presentation at a hearing. All were separated at the time of the issuance of the notice of a hearing and continued as a separated staff during the entire course of the pro-ceeding. Those separated could not discuss the merits of a case with the hearing examiner or with the Commission except on the public record. For its advice on any particular case the Commission had to rely on other members of the general counsel's staff and personnel from various nonseparated AEC divisions.[21]

In addition, the Commission in late 1959 approved an agency rule change that restricted *ex parte* communications with people outside the agency. (The term *ex parte* refers to communications made to a decision-maker by only one side in a proceeding, without notice having been given to other parties.) The rule was prompted by a number of court decisions in 1959 in which licensing decisions of other agencies—particularly the Federal Communications Commission—were reversed because of *ex parte* communications from outsiders to agency decision-makers. The new AEC regulation sought to protect the Commission from charges of conflict of interest by prohibiting oral or written communications involving any adjudicatory proceeding unless they were placed in the public record. Nonetheless, the rules recognized the Commission's dual functions. Promotional tasks were unaffected as long as substantive matters about a pending regulatory proceeding were not discussed off the record.[22]

The mandatory-hearing requirement obligated the Commission to obtain its own hearing examiner. At the PRDC hearing, which occurred prior to the 1957 amendment, the agency had borrowed examiner Jay Kyle from the Federal Communications Commission to preside. Kyle certified the record to the Commission, which in turn issued the decision. That arrangement was no longer workable under the new procedures, so in 1958 the Commission established an Office of Hearing Examiners and appointed Samuel W. Jensch, an experienced and certified hearing examiner with the Federal Power Commission, as the chief hearing examiner. The sole presiding officer until July 1960, Jensch prepared hearing calendars, fixed times and places for hearings, presided over the mandatory sessions, and issued initial decisions. With the hearing caseload increasing, the Commission in mid-1960 appointed a second presiding officer, J. D. Bond, like Jensch an experienced hearing examiner. He came from the Federal Communications Commission.[23]

Although the Office of Hearing Examiners was separated from the AEC staff as well as the Commission, Jensch and Bond applied administrative-law procedures and made decisions that contributed changes to the agency's rules of practice. Since a favorable decision was needed from the hearing examiner to authorize Harold Price to issue a license, there was no question that Jensch and Bond would influence the process. Both hearing examiners, moreover, were dedicated to the concept of fair procedures and decisions based on a complete record. This eventually resulted in considerable Joint Committee and industry attention to the hearing phase and overshadowed the technical staff and Safeguards

Committee reviews where the bulk of the agency's regulatory technical resources was located.

The uncontested nature of the mandatory hearing placed a heavy burden on the AEC's hearing examiners. No other federal agency had to make comparable licensing decisions that involved the potential for catastrophic accidents. In most licensing cases conducted by other federal agencies, the hearing examiner's task amounted to adjudicating between competing private economic interests and determining which party would best serve the public interest. In contrast, the primary concern of the uncontested AEC hearing was to determine, for the public record, that public health and safety would be safeguarded. As originally anticipated and subsequently carried out after 1955, the licensing process involved internal technical-staff and Safeguards Committee reviews that determined whether the public health and safety requirements had been met. When the Joint Committee established the hearing requirement, it meant to publicize those reviews as well as to allow for public education and participation. In other words, the Joint Committee wanted to ensure that important AEC decisions would be made publicly. In practice, the Commission instructed the hearing examiner to issue initial decisions that became final in twenty days, unless one of the parties appealed to the Commission or the Commission elected on its own motion to review an initial decision. Considering his decision-making responsibility in the context of the possible threat to public health and safety naturally made the examiner want to assure himself that the facility under examination would be safe. What evolved was that the hearing examiner assumed an adversarial role as a *de facto* public defender. Although legally trained, Jensch and Bond lacked technical competence in reactor science and engineering, making it difficult for them to conduct a meaningful review of safety factors. In addition, they were barred from off-the-record consultation with the staff because of the separated-staff procedure. In assuming what rightfully was their role, the hearing examiners relied on their own knowledge of administrative procedure to satisfy themselves that health and safety could be reasonably assured. This method contributed to the formalization, judicialization, and, to a lesser extent, the length of the licensing process.[24]

The process evolved through a number of cases between 1957 and 1961 that provided the foundation for further reform. The first hearings held after passage of the amendment were brief. Most of the evidence submitted was in written form following the recommendations of the

Commission's rules of practice. But at later hearings the examiner began to require more time-consuming and formalized oral testimony by both staff and applicant. In large measure, this allowed the examiner to assume his adversarial role and question the staff and applicant witnesses, ostensibly gaining for himself a better understanding of the complex safety considerations in each case. This procedure also appeared as a logical outgrowth of the role he undertook as a public defender in the uncontested cases. While the examiner's actions could be seen as a means of compiling a complete public record, as well as assuring himself that the facility under review presented no undue risk to the public health and safety, many observers viewed it as inconsistent with the idea of an uncontested hearing.[25]

Considering the novelty of the mandatory uncontested hearing combined with the pioneering nature of the cases, the total number of days of hearings was not excessive. In February 1961 the AEC reported that there had been no instance in which more than three days of hearings were required prior to issuance of a construction permit. In several cases only one day was required. The number of days of hearings for issuance of operating licenses ranged from one to eight. The Yankee Atomic Electric Company's reactor, the first to go to a hearing for both a construction permit and an operating license, required a total of eight days for both phases. So the actual number of hearing days gave little support to later complaints about the unseemly length of the hearing process.[26]

But hidden behind those numbers lay increased time between hearings that was necessary either to prepare for the formalities or to resolve issues that were raised during the hearing. For example, the tendency of the hearing examiner to require that a hearing record not be closed until all matters related to safety were introduced in the formal proceedings increased the license-processing time. Yankee Atomic's operating license illustrated this point. Yankee submitted two amendments to its final license that proposed several minor changes in the design of the reactor after the Safeguards Committee had reported favorably on the operating license in the spring of 1960. Although staff testimony at the subsequent hearing on the license indicated that the amendments would have no effect on the safety of the reactor, presiding officer Jensch recessed the hearing on the grounds that the matter could not be decided until the Safeguards Committee reviewed and reported on the two outstanding amendments. A forty-five-day delay resulted. This example, which was not an isolated one, underscored two characteristics in the evolving hearing process. First, Jensch's emphasis on continued hearings even on matters that the technical staff cited as involving no significant new hazards delayed final decisions. In addition, it usurped not only the licensing staff's time but also the rather limited services of the part-time Safeguards Committee. Second, the Yankee Atomic case illustrated the difficulties that technical decisions imposed on the hearing examiner. Aware of the gravity of his responsibilities, conscientious in his exercise of authority, and lacking easy access to technically qualified advisers, Jensch elected in such situations to refer the matter back to technical experts.[27]

The need for hearings on amendments to both construction permits and operating licenses was an important question confronting the AEC during this time. The legislative history of the mandatory-hearing requirement had been silent on the amendment matter. The law clearly contemplated at least two hearings, one each at the construction-permit and operating-license stages. But the evolving nature of atomic technology dictated revisions in design as a reactor facility moved from its construction phase to operation. Those changes, incorporated as amendments to permits and licenses, posed a practical legal problem for the agency. If mandatory hearings were held only on construction permits and operating licenses and not on amendments, what would prevent an applicant from withholding "difficult" issues from an application for a construction permit that was subject to a hearing and later introduce them as amendments to the application? Yet if each minor amendment or even groups of amendments were reviewed by the AEC staff and the Safeguards Committee and then scheduled for a hearing, the ensuing delay would be burdensome and costly to both the applicant and the agency. Lacking any clear guidance from the legislative history, the AEC legal staff interpreted the 1957 law to mean that all amendments had to be not only reviewed but also scheduled for public hearing. This procedure eventually evoked complaints from applicants and from the Joint Committee that the regulators were overreacting to the 1957 requirement.[28]

By the time that dissatisfaction over delays in uncontested cases was becoming increasingly evident in 1960, the AEC had begun to develop procedures to deal more expeditiously with some of the routine license amendments. In the summer of that year the General Electric Company requested Commission review of an operating-license decision by hearing examiner Jensch on its Vallecitos, California boiling-water experimental power reactor. Jensch had approved an amendment but directed that the revised license contain certain restrictions regarding General Electric's future applications. General Electric protested that the restrictions, requiring the company not to change or modify "design or performance specifications or operating limits or procedures" without Commission authorization, threatened to impede progress on its project.[29]

Prior to the Commission's October 1960 hearing on the requested review, the licensing staff, after consultation with General Electric engineers, filed a revised form of the license. It incorporated redrafted technical specifications and eliminated many that did not have an effect on safety. In its subsequent memorandum and order of 2 November, the Commission acknowledged those changes and stated that General Electric in the future could initiate changes "within the parameters of the technical specifications, provided that no unreviewed safety question is involved." In doubtful cases the company could not proceed but had to refer the changes to the director of the Division of Licensing and Regulation. If the director found that the proposals presented no significant new hazards questions, he could authorize the change. If the director found a significant new safety consideration, however, he was required to refer the matter to the Safeguards Committee and schedule a hearing on the amendment.[30]

The Vallecitos case was important as precedent for other cases. Later codified as a regulation, it reduced the time consumed by hearings. Furthermore, it placed greater reliance on the technically qualified licensing staff than on the hearing examiner for determination of safety matters in the licensing process.[31]

The agency still faced the cumbersome task of conducting public hearings at the construction-permit and operating-license phases of a power-reactor licensing proceeding. Moreover, the Commission continued to follow its own interpretation of the 1957 law and held mandatory hearings on many significant license amendments. While some efforts had been made even in this early stage to speed licensing, the process remained so laborious that it greatly bothered the Commission, private industry, and the Joint Committee. In April 1960, even before the Vallecitos decision, Chairman McCone told the Joint Committee that his agency planned on intensive examination of its regulatory program.[32]

The subsequent agency study consisted of two parts. The first, a lengthy factual report, "The Regulatory Program of the Atomic Energy Commission," contained a wealth of information on the procedures and organization of the regulatory side of the agency. A special section described all reactor cases heard to that time. The Joint Committee published it in 1960. The second part of the study, "A Report on the Regulatory Program of the Atomic Energy Commission," was completed in early 1961 and included the agency's recommendations to the Joint Committee for improving the existing regulatory organization and procedures. While the first part was the product of many people on the agency staff, the second part was completed under the close supervision of Commissioner Loren K. Olson.[33]

Olson's strong interest in the regulatory program stemmed from his previous staff position as general counsel of the AEC. The son of a Wisconsin farmer, Olson was trained at the University of Wisconsin Law School and served in the navy in World War II. For six years after the war, he worked with the navy in liquidating its war-loans program before entering private practice in Washington, D.C. in 1951. The Commission appointed him general counsel in 1958, replacing William Mitchell. In that job Olson quickly developed a reputation among his colleagues for thoroughness and persistence. He took particular interest in administrative procedures and followed the developing regulatory program carefully. In May 1960, when a vacancy occurred on the Commission after the resignation of John Floberg, President Eisenhower nominated Olson to fill Floberg's two-year unexpired term. As a commissioner, Olson supervised the regulatory study, and the report bore his imprimatur. Because of his involvement in this work Olson became the main AEC spokesman on regulatory matters.[34]

Referred to as the "Olson report" by AEC insiders, the "Report on the Regulatory Program of the Atomic Energy Commission" clearly outlined the agency's position in a number of areas. One proposal described in the report, however, created a spirited internal argument before finally being approved in February 1961. After his lengthy study of the situation, Olson urged further separation of the regulatory and promotional functions of the agency, this time at the Commission level. He suggested a reorganization that would eliminate the system that required the regulatory and licensing arm to report to the general manager through the assistant general manager. Instead he proposed a new position of director of regulation who would be responsible solely to the Commission. All the functions of the Division of Licensing and Regulation, Office of Health and Safety, and Division of Compliance would report to the new director. Undeniably a significant break with the past, the change would subvert the long-held "singleness of administration" concept under the general manager. Olson succinctly substantiated his reasoning on the need for change. He cited thirteen officers presently reporting to the general manager, indicating the wide variety of activities the chief executive officer supervised. As a result, the general manager was no longer in a position to "devote to the regulatory function the informed and effective attention it requires." In principle, Olson wrote, it was unwise to have the regulators supervised by senior staff who had operational and promotional responsibilities. Furthermore, he believed it particularly important that communications between the Commission and the regulators "should be frequent, free, and informed, and more direct than at present." Equally important, but for obvious reasons not in the report, the Commission recognized that if it did not initiate such an organizational change internally, the Joint Committee might impose a less desirable reorganization by legislative action, perhaps even separate promotional and regulatory agencies.[35]

Although the Olson report proposals received backing by the other commissioners, the idea for making the director of regulation report to the Commission rankled General Manager A. R. Luedecke, his assistant, Dwight Ink, and William Finan, the assistant general manager for regulation and safety. The Commission tentatively approved the report on 5 January, but it reserved a final decision until the general manager could comment at a later meeting.[36]

At a meeting in late January, Luedecke told the Commission that although he realized the reorganization decision was final for all practical purposes, he wanted his dissent known. He agreed in principle with separation of the functions, he said, but the proposed degree of separation bothered him. Luedecke believed the steps taken over the previous three years to accentuate the functional separation showed that the agency was moving in the right direction. To go further and make the director of regulation responsible directly to the Commission was premature, he thought.[37]

In an earlier memorandum Luedecke had outlined for the commissioners his arguments against a separate director of regulation. He cited all the familiar points the Commission itself had used in its previous discussions on the issue with the Joint Committee: coordination burdens on the Commission, creation of administrative red tape, duplication of staff support functions, and organizational problems regarding the inspection staff. Only after those difficulties had been resolved, the general manager wrote, should the Commission separate the functions completely. Backing up Luedecke at the meeting, Ink and Finan reiterated the same arguments. Olson parried each one, concluding that the general manager's points merely concerned the application of "general principles of separation and did not affect the validity of the concept." No minds were changed as a result of the discussion. The Commission formally approved the proposal the next day. Implementation occurred in mid-March 1961. The Commission appointed Harold Price director of regulation.[38]

The AEC's organizational changes disturbed the Bureau of the Budget staff, which was in the process of developing its own government-wide reorganization program for the Kennedy administration. One major organizational issue the Bureau was considering entailed the possibility of converting the AEC from a commission to an agency headed by a single administrator. The Bureau staff had tentatively concluded that a single-headed atomic agency would be more efficient and more responsive to executive leadership. Although it recognized that such a change would be controversial and had reached no decisions at the time of the AEC regulatory reorganization, the staff thought the AEC's own changes might preempt its own more far-reaching options. The Bureau staff further concluded that making the director of regulation report directly to the Commission would "further emphasize the role of the five-man Commission in the regulatory area, and because of the unwarranted tradition that economic regulatory functions must necessarily be performed by multi-headed bodies, would therefore tend to perpetuate the continued existence of the Commission to regulate safety." Increased Commission involvement in the regulatory process would make it more difficult to convert to a single administrator if President Kennedy wanted to do so.[39]

Speculation on opposition to the idea of a single administrator centered on the Commission and the Joint Committee. The Bureau staff believed the Commission would be opposed on three grounds: because its own existence would be at stake, because it was convinced of the basic utility of the commission form, and because of the widespread assumption that "regulatory functions (including those involving atomic energy) can most appropriately be exercised by multi-headed bodies" (Commissioner Olson bluntly expressed this view to Budget officials when he delivered the AEC report). While the Bureau staff concluded that Joint Committee opposition would be based in part on similar reasons, the "most important (though unstated) reason would probably be the threat posed by such a reorganization to the Joint Committee's control of the Commission." Although the Bureau elected not to open discussion with the Commission on the issue at the time, it alerted AEC chairman Seaborg to its thinking on the matter.[40]

Even though the most important part of the Olson report dealt with the AEC's regulatory reorganization, it also made legislative recommendations to the Joint Committee about the hearing process. In addition, the report defended its use of hearing examiners against the ever-present Joint Committee idea for a three-man licensing board. The board concept had been raised again as the Joint Committee staff prepared its own study of the AEC regulatory structure. In August 1960 Joint Committee staff director Ramey, concerned about the lengthy and detailed requirements of the AEC's regulatory program, had assigned David Toll to update his earlier work on the regulatory process. Ramey wanted the study completed by the spring of 1961 so that the Joint Committee could hold hearings on both the AEC's and its own recommendations.[41]

The Olson report recommended legislative changes affecting the hearing process but opposed a licensing board. It built on the previous three-year record in developing a workable licensing process. It admitted that further refinements were needed, but emphasized that they could be accomplished through rule-making and minor legislative amendments. On the mandatory-hearing requirement, for example, the report suggested that the Joint Committee might amend the law to permit the Commission to dispense with a mandatory hearing at the operating-license stage if a particular reactor presented no substantial novel safety questions. This would eliminate the expense and delay caused by the double hearing requirement under the existing law. Likewise, the report contended that considerable time could be saved if the Safeguards Committee could be relieved of its responsibility to review and report publicly on every licensed power and test reactor. The report argued that the committee should be concerned with broad principles of safety rather than with the comprehensive review of specific problems of individual reactors. The agency observed that its hazards-evaluation staff was rapidly gaining maturity and was approaching the time when it could obviate the need for the Safeguards Committee's case-by-case review of each reactor application.[42]

Those recommendations were set in the context of the agency's progressive development of the licensing process. Consequently, the AEC argued against any fundamental change in the composition of the agency that had been suggested by either separation into two new agencies or creation of a licensing board. The Olson report stated that use of a hearing examiner offered a more economical, flexible, and expeditious method than hearings before a board. It saw no advantage of a board composed of technical experts and lawyers since the function of a hearing examiner was to "receive, marshal, and evaluate, not to supplement or qualify, the evidence." The key question the report posed was whether the present system could properly evaluate the merits of a planned reactor. The technical expertise of the presiding officer was irrelevant to the normal judicial function of the hearing examiner, which was to decide on the basis of the record. As a lawyer himself, Olson believed that such decisions required legal, not technical, skills. Even if the intended board's decisions were reviewed by the Commission, the AEC insisted that the panel's functions would simply substitute for those of the present hearing examiners while imposing substantial disadvantages of inflexibility, delay, and loss of economy.[43]

The AEC report, therefore, did not address the issue of technical review by either the hearing examiner or a board since in the agency's thinking that was not a fundamental issue. The Joint Committee staff, however, disagreed in its March 1961 report. After spending six months holding discussions with applicants, intervenors, AEC staff members, and Safeguards Committee members, as well as reviewing reactor-licensing case histories, the Joint Committee staff identified the "lack of a technically qualified body to review the staff determinations" as the most serious shortcoming in licensing atomic reactors. It agreed in part with the AEC report that the current Safeguards Committee review should be limited to "important or novel safety questions" because of the limitations on its time. But this only seemed to intensify the need for a full-time technical body to review the regulatory staff's findings. The AEC solution—continuation of the present organization with only minor organizational and procedural changes—failed to address this "really significant" problem.[44]

If the proposed AEC changes would not solve the technical-review problem, the idea of complete separation of promotional and regulatory responsibilities offered a possible alternative. An independent, year-long examination of the licensing process based on agency records had been completed by former AEC attorneys William Berman and Lee Hydeman under the auspices of the University of Michigan Law School. Published in March 1961, it received considerable attention from the Joint Committee staff, and key sections of the study were included in the Joint Committee's background print on "Improving the AEC Regulatory Process." President Kennedy was even questioned about it at a press conference. Berman and Hydeman concluded that separation was the only acceptable course. Kennedy noted his disagreement, stating that he thought there was a "fair balance today" between development and regulation. The Joint Committee's final staff report concurred with the AEC. It considered the Berman-Hydeman concept as too extreme a solution because of the early stage of atomic development. Instead the Joint Committee staff suggested a compromise based on its proposal for an internal "Atomic Safety and Licensing Board."[45]

The idea, of course, was not new. The staff had suggested a separate independent three-member board in 1957, but the Joint Committee decided at the time that it was not necessary. Its 1961 staff report, however, gave a more detailed explanation of how the board would be composed and how it would operate.[46]

The full-time board would be appointed by the president for staggered five- or six-year terms. Two members would be technically qualified in "fields of science or engineering relevant to safety," and the Joint Committee staff suggested that the third member be "knowledgeable in the conduct of administrative proceedings." It would operate internally within the agency, aided by its own small staff and by legal and technical assistance from other AEC divisions. The Joint Committee staff concluded that granting the board final licensing authority not subject to Commission review, and a role in the development of regulatory rules and standards over which the Commission would retain final authority, would result in the best performance of the AEC licensing function over the next ten years.[47]

The board would review all privately owned and government-owned reactors, and its decisions would be public except in the case of government-owned military or production reactors. The panel would also have jurisdiction over materials licenses. The Joint Committee staff was not clear about what the board's functions should be in the rule-making area. It expected that the board's recommendations to the Commission would grow naturally out of its handling of specific licensing cases. As it gained experience, the staff foresaw the board reviewing and proposing regulations "of general applicability governing not only licensing but also radiation safety generally."[48]

Relations between the board and other parts of the AEC concerned the Joint Committee staff. It hoped the Commission and the board would establish informal communications to resolve any jurisdictional problems. More important were the relationships between the board on the one hand and the Licensing Division and the Advisory Committee on Reactor Safeguards on the other. The Licensing Division would represent the agency before the board in all cases, so the board members would have to avoid participation before a case was scheduled for hearing. The Joint Committee staff anticipated the eventual development of rules governing such questions as whether a particular safety issue should be referred to the Safeguards Committee before a hearing or whether amendments to a license might require a further hearing. A major benefit coming from the creation of the board would be to free the Safeguards Committee from review of routine cases. But the Joint Committee staff believed the Safeguards Committee should continue to have authority to examine matters that raised important or novel safety questions.[49]

The Joint Committee staff believed that the creation of a full-time, technically qualified group to evaluate AEC staff work would be an important contribution. Its report admitted that no board could have all the knowledge of pure and applied science that was relevant to a reactor-safety decision, but it believed that such an organization should be established because "sound scientific training and experience in one field can enable its possessor to appreciate the problems of another field and equip him to evaluate evidence, experiment, and opinion bearing on those problems."[50]

The three positions taken by the different studies formed the basis for comments solicited by the Joint Committee before it scheduled hearings in the late spring of 1961. The committee wrote to industrial leaders as well as university professors with expertise in administrative law and asked for their views on the new AEC organization, the Berman-Hydeman proposal for a separate agency, and the Joint Committee staff's proposal for a licensing board. It received thirty-three replies.[51]

The responses were mixed, but most favored both the regulatory reorganization of the AEC and the Joint Committee's idea for a licensing board. There was little support for a separate agency. Particularly significant on the board question were favorable comments from the Safeguards Committee and the Atomic Industrial Forum. Additional backing came from James Campbell, president of Consumers Power Company; W. Kenneth Davis of Bechtel; J. Forrester Davison of George Washington University Law School; R. L. Doan, manager of the Atomic Energy

Division within Phillips Petroleum; Alexander Grendon, the coordinator for the State of California Office of Atomic Energy Development and Radiation Protection; Murray Joslin of Commonwealth Edison; Philip Sporn, representing the American Electric Power Service Corporation; and Charles Weaver, vice-president at Westinghouse. A consensus of replies also generally held that the mandatory-hearing requirement should be relaxed in uncontested cases and that the law should be amended to permit more discretion in referrals to the Safeguards Committee.[52]

Drafts of Commission testimony for the upcoming hearings, particularly that of Commissioner Olson, relied on those parts of the comments that supported agency arguments against a licensing board. When the drafts were forwarded to the Bureau of the Budget for its customary review, it stirred Bureau interest once again in the single-administrator issue. Since commenting earlier on the AEC regulatory report, the Bureau staff had reviewed the Joint Committee staff report and had liked the licensing-board idea "because it would be easier to bridge to the later step of replacing the 5-man Commission with a single head." The Bureau had also received indications that some members of the Joint Committee might be willing to go along with a single-administrator reorganization, and the Bureau staff knew that the concept had been circulating in congressional circles. In addition, the Berman-Hydeman study had recommended a single head for the separate promotional agency it espoused, with a three-man board for the regulatory agency. And even the Joint Committee staff study had introduced its proposal for a licensing board with the statement that its plan was "compatible with the continuance of a five-man Commission, with a reduction in the Commission's number to three, or with the substitution of an Administrator for the Commission." But now the AEC testimony against the licensing-board proposal worried the Budget office because if the Commission was successful in arguing that its recent reorganization was all that was necessary, any subsequent move toward a single administrator by the executive branch would be difficult to achieve.[53]

The main problem confronting both the Budget staff and presidential aides appeared to be a lack of consensus among several top presidential advisers on the single-administrator issue, including Seaborg; David Bell, the head of the Budget Bureau; Jerome Wiesner, the president's science adviser; and James Landis, a legal scholar and expert in administrative law and now Kennedy's special assistant on regulatory matters. In the absence of agreement on the matter, William Carey, the Budget

Bureau's executive assistant director, told presidential aide Frederick Dutton that the AEC had to be "given the green light to state its case" in the Joint Committee hearings. But he cautioned that the single-administrator issue was still pending and that the administration should therefore remain neutral on the AEC testimony.[54]

The Joint Committee held two days of hearings on the regulatory process in June 1961. The bulk of the testimony added little to the record already compiled in the Joint Committee prints that served as a basis for the hearings. Private witnesses, for example, echoed what they had supplied earlier in their written views. Commissioner Olson's appearance, however, paved the way for compromise on the licensing-board proposal. Continuing as the lead commissioner on regulatory matters, Olson initially argued against the concept, stating the familiar reasons why the AEC should be allowed to continue the licensing process it was slowly developing. Olson admitted to the lawmakers that the Commission had probably reacted overzealously in carrying out the demands of the 1957 Price-Anderson amendments. But the accumulation of agency licensing experience combined with the previous year's studies had allowed the agency to gain a better understanding of the problem. This had resulted in a needed reorganization as well as in pointing out useful ways to streamline the licensing process. In addition, Olson thought the Joint Committee, after studying the three reports, should conclude that the mandatory-hearing requirement ought to be modified. It had accomplished its purposes since 1957, and relaxation now would make possible a reduction in the number of hearings "without prejudice to the public's right of access to full and timely information; and without prejudice to any interested party's right and opportunity to intervene." Such a change, Olson noted, would also allow the agency flexibility in referring cases to the Safeguards Committee. In his thinking, this revision of the law was all that was needed. "The conclusions the Commission has reached," he told the Joint Committee, "are not dramatic. We do not believe we have a situation calling for drastic departure from well-proven administrative procedures."[55]

In the discussion following Olson's statement, Chet Holifield, who had assumed the chairmanship of the Joint Committee, asked him to clarify the nature of the review the Commission itself gave each decision rendered by the hearing examiner. Olson indicated that Commission review was both procedural and substantive. Staff director Ramey moved the discussion to the hearing examiner's level. "The focus of all this is the technical problem of safety," he said. "The hearing examiner is not a technical man. Does he go into the substance?" Replying that the examiner based his decision "upon the record on the ultimate question of safety," Olson stated that the examiner had a broader function than just being "a notary taking a deposition." But Olson emphasized that more than technical expertise went into a decision. Broad legal policy was a part of the decision process that the hearing examiner was equipped to handle.[56]

Pressing Olson further on the hearing examiner's technical qualifications, Ramey disclosed that he had heard a rumor that the AEC's examiner had a technical adviser. Olson confirmed the rumor as fact, explaining that the Commission decided to "give him a law clerk, so to speak, with a technical background who can go through the testimony, the narrative testimony, the application, so the examiner could discuss it with some technical competence." Half-humorously, Ramey commented, "What if you gave him one more technical assistant and called it a Board?" Though somewhat taken aback, Olson saw room for compromise.

> Olson: I think that has a lot of merit. I think that has a lot of merit provided you would not clothe it with complete independence of authority and make it separate but within the Commission. I think that has a lot of merit.
> Ramey: So you have a little board there. Then the other thing that has happened since the committee's staff report was that the Commission established this rule of a certiorari procedure so that the decision of your hearing examiner, or if you went to your hearing examiner and two technical assistants, is final so far as the applicant is concerned.
> Olson: Subject to our right to review on our own motion.
> Ramey: Subject to the right of the Commission if it so determines to review. There is no right by the applicant, as such, to have a further review. All he can do is go to court; is that correct?
> Olson: Yes, that is right.
> Ramey: So in a sense you have limited your review.
> Olson: We have limited the right to review but not our right of review. I think there is a lot of merit to the suggestion that Mr. Ramey has just made to have a Board like this, provided it still was under the single authority of the Commission. I would say that whether I was on the Commission or not. I think there is some advantage to this unitary command in the whole atomic energy program.[57]

Holifield, noting that the other members of the Commission were present at the hearing, asked whether Olson's statement represented their viewpoints. All agreed.[58]

Later that same day, Olson participated in a panel discussion that closed the hearings before the Joint Committee. Also included on the panel were two prominent specialists in administrative law, Kenneth Culp Davis of the University of Minnesota Law School and David Cavers from the Harvard Law School. The latter was also a consultant to the Joint Committee. Lee Hydeman, coauthor of the Berman-Hydeman study, and Theos J. Thompson of MIT and the Reactor Safeguards Committee rounded out the panel. All gave their different perspectives on the regulatory problem; Olson's comments, however, indicated he had thought more about his morning exchange with Ramey. He submitted that the "hybrid of the licensing board concept" which had surfaced that morning was something that no one had adequately explored. It had more potential than anything else that had been proposed, he said. Although the original concept of an independent board suggested in the Joint Committee staff study would "breed a lot of trouble," Olson concluded that he would prefer to see modifications of the board idea which would continue the "unitary command of the atomic energy program." Ramey acknowledged the possibility of compromise.[59]

In several meetings in July and August the Joint Committee and the agency staffs worked out a compromise. They prepared amendments to relax the mandatory-hearing requirement, to provide more flexibility in the scope of review required by the Safeguards Committee, and to establish a licensing board. The first two matters were easily agreed upon since they represented the consensus at the hearings. A mandatory hearing would be held at the construction-permit phase, but the Commission could later issue an operating license without a hearing as long as it gave a thirty-day notice. An additional sentence regarding amendments to either construction permits or operating licenses, which reflected the earlier action taken by the AEC in the Vallecitos reactor case, allowed the Commission to dispense with any notice as long as it determined that the amendment involved "no significant hazards consideration."[60]

The AEC and Joint Committee staffs also easily agreed on revised language for referrals to the Safeguards Committee. It gave the Commission discretion on requiring Safeguards Committee review on amendments to a construction permit or to an operating license, though the committee would continue to review the initial construction permit and operating license for each facility. In working out this matter, the agency told the Joint Committee it would continue to submit all documents filed by an applicant to the Safeguards Committee and indicated that the AEC staff would seek the Safeguards Committee's advice on the items in which formal referral for review and report did not seem necessary.[61]

Creating the Atomic Safety and Licensing Board, however, involved intense negotiations. Both the AEC and the Joint Committee backed away from their original positions to reach agreement. The agency initially suggested that the Commission be allowed, by regulation or order, to designate "two or more persons to serve with a duly appointed hearing examiner as a board to conduct hearings and render a decision." It did not expect the board to function as a full-time body, but envisioned it operating on an *ad hoc* basis for individual cases. Furthermore, the AEC wanted the flexibility to use either a hearing examiner or a three-man board. The Joint Committee maintained that the AEC was not willing to go far enough. The legislators agreed with their staff study that a hearing examiner without technical training should not make the initial decision in licensing cases by himself. While they thought the Commission might try the board idea on an *ad hoc* basis, they hoped it eventually would evolve into a permanent organization. The Joint Committee found the use of the hearing examiner as the administrative-law expert on the board acceptable, but it insisted that "outside people" should also be involved. Moreover, it demanded that the technically trained board members "should be persons of the caliber of the Safeguards Committee."[62]

To gain agreement on establishing a permanent board, the Joint Committee gave in to the Commission on the critical matter of the board's independence. The Commission, rather than the president, would appoint the board members. And the Joint Committee consented to allow Commission review of the board's decisions. Thus the Joint Committee backed off from its own staff-report recommendation and accepted instead the arrangement on which Olson and Ramey had concurred at the June hearing.[63]

The Joint Committee also broadened the role the board might play in the overall regulatory process. Olson had criticized the separate-licensing-board proposal because it would divorce adjudication from rule-making, with authority for the latter retained by the Commission. After further staff discussions the Joint Committee allowed the Commission to utilize the board for "other regulatory functions," thus providing both the Commission and the board a wide range of flexibility.[64]

Holifield and Pastore introduced identical bills on 15 August incorporating the compromises. Ramey observed privately that the agreement with the AEC was "not all that we wanted," but it was "nevertheless a first step and it may be best to use the Board initially on a trial basis." A week later, he reported with disappointment to consultant David Cavers that Joint Committee reception of the measure was "not enthusiastic." The legislators decided to defer action pending further study, which meant no decision in the 1961 session.[65]

The Joint Committee reconsidered the issue in the following session of Congress, opening with a day of hearings on the bills in April 1962. Olson, again the main Commission representative at the hearing, recommended a change in language authorizing the agency to establish boards as needed instead of having a single board. He also suggested some minor clarifying legal language to make the boards fit the requirements of the Administrative Procedure Act. Both changes met no opposition from the Joint Committee, and clean bills introduced at the end of June reflected Olson's recommendations. The revised bills added a sentence that the agency could appoint a panel of qualified people from which board members might be selected. With no debate Congress passed the measure on 29 August.[66]

While the 1962 legislative reforms to the licensing process were being negotiated, President Kennedy accepted Glenn Seaborg's suggestion that the AEC undertake a new study of the civilian atomic-power program. Budget Bureau director David Bell saw this as an opportunity to reconsider the idea of an AEC reorganization, which had remained in limbo for the past year. Bell had in hand a new draft reorganization plan for the AEC that his staff had readied. It called for an Atomic Energy Administration with a single administrator. All current functions of the AEC, including regulation and licensing, would be transferred to the new agency. In a memorandum of 3 May to Kennedy, Bell wrote that the "original reason for establishing the commission—the feeling that this awesome new power should not be entrusted to normal Executive Branch arrangements—[had] passed." He thought the time opportune to move toward a single administrator for atomic energy. Until recently, he told Kennedy, it was difficult to approach the reorganization subject without stirring up old controversies. But he sensed that new conditions now prevailed that might permit a reorganization. Contacts with prominent Democratic members of the Joint Committee—Holifield, Pastore, and Jackson—indicated that they might support a change. Furthermore, Bell received a report indicating that all five commissioners would agree, and cited Loren Olson as "actively campaigning for it." The possibility was further enhanced by the fact that Commissioners Olson and John Graham completed their terms in 1962.[67]

On the basis of his favorable assessment, Bell suggested proceeding by legislation rather than by a reorganization plan imposed by the president in order "to avoid cheap opposition arguments about 'centralization of control.'" Either Kennedy or the Joint Committee could initiate the move. Tactically, Bell suggested that Kennedy invite Holifield to the White House to talk about methods to achieve the most effective atomic-energy program for the 1960s and 1970s, and follow it with a letter to the Joint Committee. This, Bell thought, would pave the way for Holifield "to surface the matter" with the Joint Committee, which had already announced its intention to review the organizational changes made over the previous year by the AEC. Bell believed, therefore, that the president and the Joint Committee Democrats were in a strong position to make the change. He urged that the timing be planned to produce final legislative action in the spring of 1963. In the meantime, the two new members of the Commission could be appointed with the understanding "either that they will have temporary appointments or that they will be given other jobs if the Commission form is altered." Bell noted that three of Kennedy's close advisers—Theodore Sorenson, McGeorge Bundy, and Ralph Dungan—concurred in his plan.[68]

Bell based his strategy on the assumption that both the Commission and Holifield would cooperate. He apparently already had communicated with the Commission because he noted in his memo to Kennedy that he thought it would be possible to "get a letter from the present Commission proposing or urging a change in organizational form." In fact, on the following day, 4 May, Olson sent such a letter to Seaborg for his comments. The letter's first line summarized everything Bell wanted: "The Commission has carefully considered its statutory form of organization and has come to the unanimous conclusion that the present five-man Commission should be replaced by a single administrator." A short paragraph gave the rationale for the decision, maintaining that with the passage of time the initial concern over the concentration of power in a single individual had become relatively less important than the need for an organizational mechanism which would accelerate the decision-making process. Without a formal meeting, the other commissioners approved the final version of the letter. It also included a separate statement by Commissioner Graham, who concurred in the decision but wanted it conditioned on other statutory changes relating to the functions of the Military Liaison Committee. The letter asked Bell to designate someone to work with the AEC to draft the necessary implementing legislation.[69]

This document, remarkable because of the unusual phenomenon of a government body recommending its own demise, reflected the new administration's evolving view of the AEC. Early in his presidency, Kennedy expressed dissatisfaction with the commission form and indicated he favored a single executive. Commissioner Graham, in his letter attached to the recommendation, provided one of the most telling reasons why the Commission favored its own abolition. He described the production and possession of atomic weapons as the predominant basis for initially vesting trust in a multiheaded commission. Throughout the 1950s, however, the possession of atomic weapons was transferred under presidential directives to the armed forces, leaving the AEC with only the task of producing weapons. This changed situation, Graham noted, had made the Commission "not significantly different from that of any major industrial contractor supplying munitions to the armed forces." Thus the original concept of civilian control of atomic weapons vested in the AEC had diminished with the passage of time. This reduced the necessity for a multiheaded body to make awesome decisions on controlling atomic weapons. In its place was needed a more streamlined decision-making process.[70]

Whether the other commissioners accepted Graham's reasoning is unclear. But Bell, certain of Seaborg's backing and aware that Olson and Graham, both supporters of a single executive, would be leaving the Commission soon, pressured the commissioners for their support on the reorganization. The other two commissioners, Robert Wilson and Leland Haworth, undoubtedly saw no personal or institutional benefit in being relegated to the minority on the question. In addition, the fact that the decision was reached in private among the commissioners minimized any internal agency objections they might have received from top-level career officials. In other words, the strongest pressure the Commission received came from the White House through the Budget Bureau.[71]

Holifield's cooperation, which was critical to the success of the plan, was not so easily obtained. The Joint Committee chairman had requested a meeting with Kennedy on the power program, particularly about an AEC request for a supplemental appropriation. Mindful of Bell's suggestion to gain agreement from Holifield on the single-administrator issue, the president met with the congressman on 14 May. Holifield, though, did not like the idea. Through a press release the following day, the congressman tersely announced that it was too late in the session to hold hearings on the single-administrator matter. The motive for his delay was the threat that the proposed reorganization might pose to the position the Joint Committee had established over the years toward the executive branch. A single administrator would tend to decrease Joint Committee control over the agency while it would conversely readjust the balance of power in favor of the White House. Most observers saw Holifield's views on the single-administrator issue as based on his concern with maintaining committee leverage over the Commission.[72]

Later events reinforced this impression. Olson left the Commission when his term expired at the end of June 1962. In his place Kennedy nominated James Ramey, the Joint Committee choice for the job and a close adviser to Holifield and Anderson, as staff executive director. Ramey assumed his post on 31 August. After the appointment of Columbia University law professor John Palfrey to fill the vacancy created by the resignation of John Graham in the summer of 1962, the Commission decided to study the agency organization and informally appointed a group of three consultants in the fall of 1962 to review the single-administrator issue. They recommended that the Commission support such a change.[73]

One of the Commission's consultants, political scientist Richard Neustadt, assessed the Joint Committee's stake in the issue for Elmer Staats, the deputy director of the Budget Bureau. Neustadt conceded that the argument for a single administrator was very strong in terms of operational effectiveness, organizational neatness, and administrative convenience within the executive branch. But he thought those reasons were overshadowed by the executive-legislative power issue. He told Staats that both the Joint Committee staff and its key members saw an advantage in the five-man Commission because they could better exert detailed control over the AEC's administrative decisions than if there were a single administrator. The Joint Committee was well aware, Neustadt wrote, "that a five-man Commission speaks with a blurred voice and a relatively weak one. To put it more bluntly," Neustadt added, "if the current chairman's voice is blurred by virtue of Commission structure, they [the Joint Committee] think that a good thing." On the basis of this analysis, he questioned whether the Kennedy administration should pursue the single-administrator issue. Moreover, after Holifield's cool response to the reorganization idea the previous spring, the White House undertook no major initiative on the issue. By January 1963 Senator Pastore, who had assumed the Joint Committee chair from Holifield, told an interviewer that "most of the steam is gone from the drive for AEC reorganization." Unless the president raised the issue, Pastore said he would not pursue it. After all, the Joint Committee had not only a collegial body at the AEC that it favored but also at least one strong and friendly member in Ramey.[74]

The Commission moved quickly to implement the new amendments to the Atomic Energy Act on the licensing process. Senior officials from several AEC offices developed a list of potential members for the Atomic Safety and Licensing Boards. Fifteen individuals finally agreed to serve. The three full-time agency hearing examiners provided the core for the nontechnical administrative-law group. In addition, Arthur Murphy, a New York attorney well known in administrative-law circles, accepted part-time membership. The technical members on the initial panel included Dixon Callihan, associate director of the Neutron Physics Division at Oak Ridge; Richard L. Doan, former Safeguards Committee member; retired chemical engineer R. M. Evans, who had served at Hanford and Savannah River for the E. I. Du Pont Company; Eugene Grenling, a Duke University physicist; Patrick Howe, a health physicist who headed the health chemical department at the Lawrence Radiation Laboratory; physicist Albert Kirschbaum, also at the Lawrence laboratory; Warren Nyer, physicist and manager of the reactor projects branch for Phillips Petroleum at Idaho Falls; Hugh Paxton from the Los Alamos laboratory; Thomas Pigford, head of the nuclear engineering department at Berkeley; Lawrence Quarles, a physicist and dean of the engineering school at the University of Virginia; and Abel Wolman of Johns Hopkins and a former member of the Safeguards Committee.[75]

The Commission met with several of its appointees in November 1962 and outlined what the duties of the board would be. Commissioner Ramey discussed the functions of the board at some length, showing his strong interest in implementing the organization he had played a role in creating. Ramey hoped the regulatory process would be improved and predicted that the board's experiences would result in further refinement of the process. Samuel Jensch, who had several years of experience presiding over reactor-licensing cases, told the gathering that the use of such boards was important not only to the AEC but also to other government regulatory agencies. The Federal Power Commission and the Federal Trade Commission, he said, were finding the regulatory process extremely complex, and the AEC had now taken the lead among government regulatory agencies in combining technology and administrative practice into the licensing process. Ramey interjected that the intent of Congress was that the AEC board would provide a combination of legal due process and technical judgment. He noted that the Commission would informally review all decisions of the board.[76]

With the board operating by the end of 1962, only time could provide a basis for judgment on whether the regulatory process had been substantively reformed. One other change occurred, however, that gave a degree of separation that symbolized the evolution of the regulatory operations of the AEC. In June 1963 the regulatory staff physically moved from the sprawling pastoral Germantown, Maryland AEC building complex to an office building in Bethesda, Maryland. Although shortage of office space at Germantown necessitated the move, the actual physical separation of the regulatory staff from the developmental and operational staff signaled the agency's effort to maintain both elements within its organization while at the same time providing a modicum of distinction.[77]

The regulatory and licensing changes that occurred between passage of the Price-Anderson amendments in 1957 and the creation of the Atomic Safety and Licensing Boards in 1962 were meant to accomplish several things. The Joint Committee wanted greater public confidence in the AEC procedures for ensuring that new atomic-power reactors did not present an unreasonable risk to the health and safety of the public. From its position the committee believed that this would be best accomplished by strengthening the technical review of reactor proposals in full view of the public. The amendments it developed to existing atomic law— mandatory hearings, public reports from the Safeguards Committee, and technical review and decisions by licensing boards—all pointed in that direction.

The agency also realized the importance of public acceptance of its regulatory decisions. Recognizing that the PRDC case had damaged its image, the Commission sought to establish procedures that would enhance public confidence in its regulatory actions. Reorganization of the regulatory staff, at first divesting it of all promotional functions and later placing it directly under Commission control, reduced somewhat the inherent conflict of interest the agency had been assigned in 1954. Internally, the AEC slowly built its technical-licensing staff. It believed that the technical review furnished by its experts and the Advisory Committee on Reactor Safeguards provided an adequate means to ensure the safety of atomic facilities.

To guarantee due process in its procedures, the Commission also took what it considered necessary steps. The use of separated staff in each licensing case, adoption of an *ex parte* rule, and use of formal procedures by agency hearing examiners in the mandatory hearings were all arguably necessary to achieve due process in the Commission's licensing procedures. But its rigid application of the ambiguous legislative history of the 1957 amendments, particularly through its use of the mandatory hearing in amendments to construction permits and operating licenses, soon raised questions whether the ends achieved justified the lengthening time each case was taking. Those circumstances prompted the Joint Committee to reform the regulatory process once again.

The basic issue to be resolved boiled down to the question of how to combine due process with adequate technical review in a procedure that would meet safety concerns expeditiously. The Joint Committee particularly regarded this as a problem that would become more acute in the future as more reactor applications came before the AEC. The agency believed that the 1957 amendments left it little choice but to apply the mandatory-hearing requirement as it did. But it maintained that it could, through modification of the hearing format and procedures, streamline the process without further major legislation. And as it developed more technical standards and criteria, the Commission asserted that it could speed up the time to reach decisions.

The Joint Committee disagreed. It argued that the AEC's emphasis on procedural fairness and making a suitable record for judicial review would not solve the main difficulty of licensing atomic reactors. Its 1961 staff report noted that "where the safety of many people and the future of a potentially great industry are at stake, a reactor licensing review that reaches the wrong result is not satisfactory simply because it satisfies due process." Although the legislators supposed that the AEC's tinkering with the legal process as it accumulated experience in reactor cases would help the problem, they worried about the lack of technical expertise at the formal-decision level. The Joint Committee's solution called for an independent and technically qualified licensing board operating within the agency that could both develop a formal public record and make decisions in a licensing case. It wanted a technically qualified board available to rule promptly on questions submitted by the staff as to whether particular safety matters should be referred to the Safeguards Committee before a hearing was held. Furthermore, a board would be able to rule on whether amendments to an application would require further hearings. This, the Joint Committee believed, would streamline the process and eliminate the delays caused by the hearing examiner's formal procedure, which often referred all doubtful safety questions to the Safeguards Committee before the record was completed and a decision reached. The oversight committee's staff report noted that the board could "pass on [safety] questions which merited urgent attention." It could "dispose of its business without requiring as many legal steps as at present and with shorter intervals between them."[78] Legislation created the technical board in 1962, but not before the Joint Committee compromised on the board's independence. The new law allowed the Commission to select the board members and to review the board's decisions.

In the backs of the minds of most participants in this evolving question of licensing reform lay the issue of eventually dividing regulatory and developmental functions into two separate agencies. They realized that if reforms could not resolve the inherent conflict of interest within the framework of the present organization, separation might become necessary.

XIV

WATERSHED: THE 1962 REPORT
TO THE PRESIDENT

At the same time that its regulatory program reached a new level of maturity with the enactment of licensing reforms, the AEC perceived the atomic-power industry as poised on the threshold of becoming economically competitive with other means of electrical production. In November 1962 the agency issued a milestone document, "Civilian Nuclear Power—A Report to the President," that enunciated strong faith in the future of nuclear power. It represented a turning point by marking the conclusion of the early developmental stage of atomic power even as it heralded a new phase of rapid expansion for the industry. Yet despite the report's optimism, it came at a time when White House interest in and federal funds for atomic development were declining, a source of concern within both the AEC and the Joint Committee on Atomic Energy.

The victory of John F. Kennedy in November 1960 raised the hopes of Democratic members of the Joint Committee for new emphasis on atomic power. Both Senator Anderson and Congressman Holifield had been instrumental in inserting planks dealing with atomic energy in the party's campaign platform. They included such items as calling for a "truly nonpartisan and vigorous administration" of the atomic-power program, the development of "various promising experimental and prototype atomic power plants which show promise," and "increasing support for longer-range projects at the frontiers of atomic energy application." Shortly after the election, Anderson wrote to the president-elect in response to Kennedy's request for budget suggestions on the atomic-power program. Anderson argued that the AEC lacked vigor and direction, and although he maintained that in the past year the agency had recognized the need for more aggressive leadership, he thought it "had not been translated very effectively into action."[1]

This was particularly true in the power-reactor program, Anderson observed, which seemed to be languishing on "dead center." Many of the projects started several years before had been delayed because of technical and financial problems. He told the president-elect that AEC bureaucratic ineptitude had slowed several projects that had been added to the program by the Joint Committee in 1959. Although Anderson cautioned against coming out with detailed atomic-power proposals in the "next month or two," he hoped for a more dynamic program over a longer period of time.[2]

Holifield, the new chairman of the Joint Committee, wasted little time in setting forth for Kennedy some of the problems he saw in the program. In lengthy "Notes for President Kennedy" he submitted in February 1961, he echoed Anderson's complaints. He was deeply disturbed that the authorizations for the power-demonstration program from 1958 through proposed fiscal year 1962 showed a sharp downward trend. In addition, Holifield listed several specifically authorized government-sponsored power-reactor experimental projects that had not been started. He blamed the "Strauss-McCone resistance to a vigorous atomic power program under Federal funding and direction" as the reason why the nation was "far from the goal of economic power through fission." He declared that if such an achievement was to continue to be a vital national goal, a complete revision of planning, funding, and technical administrative direction should be ordered by the president.[3]

Although Kennedy placed a strong advocate of atomic development at the head of the AEC in the person of Glenn Seaborg, the president did not give atomic power the high priority in his budget that Holifield and other members of the Joint Committee expected. The administration approved the fiscal year 1962 and 1963 budgets with only small funds for reactor programs, which suffered from the emphasis placed on space and defense outlays. Indeed, a Bureau of the Budget analysis in 1962 noted that "atomic power has been clearly replaced as the Nation's principal domestic technological goal by the exploration of outer space."[4]

Faced with tighter budget restrictions for promotional efforts, the AEC sought ways to arrest the trend and came up with the idea of a study of the civilian power program. Seaborg laid the groundwork for such a review in a speech to a joint meeting of the Atomic Industrial Forum and the American Nuclear Society in November 1961. He offered an ambitious goal for atomic power, reminding his audience that the AEC had established two objectives in 1958. The short-range one was to make large atomic-power plants competitive with fossil plants in high-cost fuel areas by 1968. The long-range objective was to broaden the areas of the country that would benefit from atomic power. He believed that the industry had proven that light-water reactor technology could meet the short-range goal. Seaborg singled out the fast-neutron reactor system as the most promising design to accomplish the long-range goal. He cited the system's advantages of high temperatures and long fuel life in addition to the "attractive possibility of breeding" as reasons for development. He stressed the importance of the long-range objective within the perspective of the nation's continued growth in demand for electrical power coupled with the exhaustibility of its oil and gas reserves.[5]

Although Seaborg optimistically outlined the future of atomic power, he realized that budget constraints and other priorities of the administration required him to seek broader support for his position. He told the assembled nuclear groups that more extensive government assistance for power-reactor development did not appear likely at that time. Consequently, the industry had to accept the challenge of the goals and "move forward with power plant construction adequate to the task of demonstrating economic power in high fuel cost areas of the country."[6]

A short time later the AEC chairman acted to increase presidential support for the atomic-power program. In December 1961 Seaborg's staff started developing a draft statement that the president might use at one of his press conferences. Seaborg's idea was to have Kennedy emphasize the need to construct prototype and demonstration reactors that employed promising new concepts. In this way the AEC could claim presidential backing for its long-range goals for atomic power, including advanced reactor designs such as the breeder.[7]

The statement that Seaborg sent to the Bureau of the Budget in late January 1962 for transmission to Kennedy added a new twist not included in earlier drafts. More than simply a statement on atomic power, it included a presidential request that the AEC "take a new and hard look" at the role of atomic energy in the nation's economy and make recommendations for a possible program to be sponsored by the government. In the covering letter to the president, Seaborg suggested that the statement was not intended as a prelude to restoration of fiscal-year 1963 budget funds for prototype construction but rather as a means to improve the agency's and the administration's posture in the Joint Committee's upcoming "202" hearings. Seaborg cautioned the president that since the 1963 budget greatly reduced construction outlays in comparison with earlier years, it would "undoubtedly be the subject of extensive inquiry by the Joint Committee." He further indicated that the proposed statement did not commit Kennedy to "any course of action" other than directing the AEC to study the problem, although there would be the "implication that some affirmative Federal action would follow."[8]

Reactions to Seaborg's proposal varied within the executive office staff. The Budget Bureau viewed it as an attempt to "protect the President (and AEC) in such a way that specific forward-looking actions could be taken at this time without a commitment of public funds now." Kennedy's science adviser, Jerome Wiesner, took a dimmer view of the proposal. Wiesner mentioned it to the president, who initially did "not feel strongly" about it one way or the other. Wiesner indicated that if such a study was to be useful, it should consider the need for atomic power within the broad context of energy supplies from all sources.[9]

While Seaborg's request was being discussed within the administration, a strong impetus for clarification of the president's position on the civilian power program came once again from the Joint Committee. On 13 February Holifield wrote to Kennedy and complained that "this Administration will be vulnerable when it can be shown that it is de-emphasizing atomic power development more than the previous Eisenhower Administration." He commented that the power program was at the stage "where we really need to begin some practical demonstrations" and pointed out that "we have invested almost a billion dollars in atomic power development and have only a relatively short way to go to achieve economic nuclear power." Holifield believed it imperative that the administration continue supporting development through the prototype stage and complained that "the downgrading by this Administration of the atomic power program has gone much too far." At only a relatively small cost, Holifield argued, "one of the great achievements during your term of office could be the achievement of economic competitive kilowatts from fission."[10]

Not wishing to alienate the Joint Committee, particularly the Democratic members who had always advocated a stronger federal role in the atomic-power program, Kennedy decided to accept the AEC's recommendation for a study of the problem. He hoped it would placate Holifield. On 17 March 1962 the president sent a publicly released letter to Seaborg, directing him to study the atomic-power development program in the "light of the Nation's prospective energy needs and resources and advances in alternate means for power generation." Kennedy made no commitments, but merely instructed Seaborg to make recommendations on steps to assure the development and construction of projects, "including the construction of necessary prototypes." He asked for the AEC report by 1 September 1962.[11]

The president's letter received unexpectedly strong criticism from the Joint Committee, where it became the first item of business at the opening session of the "202" hearing on 20 March 1962. The attack was bipartisan, led by Democrats Holifield, Anderson, and Price, and Republican Craig Hosmer. Holifield informed Seaborg and the other AEC commissioners that in light of the president's statement he was releasing to the public a letter he had sent to the AEC chairman on 15 March. Similar to a letter he had written to President Kennedy on 13 February (several sections were verbatim extractions), the latest Holifield statement strongly criticized the atomic-power program. This message was loaded with statistics and facts that Holifield said showed the "present decline in new starts and the inadequacy of the Commission's civilian power program." Anderson asked whether Kennedy's letter to Seaborg requesting the study had been in response to Holifield's complaints. Seaborg told the disbelieving senator that there was no relationship. Obviously dubious about the value of the study, the Joint Committee kept Seaborg on the defensive.[12]

Holifield followed up the barrage of criticism the next day with another blistering letter to Seaborg (the Budget Bureau viewed it as an attempt to "embarrass and ridicule the President"). Listing past studies on the power-reactor program, Holifield asked what had happened to make yet another one necessary. Furthermore, he wanted to know whether the study would "promote the development of nuclear power in this year and next where a hiatus now exists." The president, too, was subjected to criticism. Craig Hosmer wrote what budget director David Bell privately called an "ill-mannered" letter to Kennedy on 8 April, questioning the need for the AEC study. Citing the reduced budget for the power-reactor program, he charged that "study papers do not produce nuclear kilowatts—only hardware will do it." What needed to be done, Hosmer wrote, "is already clear and requires no study." He urged the president to "abandon the 'no nuclear power program' and get on with the business of achieving economic nuclear power in this country."[13]

The criticism placed Seaborg in an awkward position. He agreed with the Joint Committee that the power program should be pushed, but he had to defend the administration's position. He informed Holifield that the study would move ahead rapidly so that its "conclusions can be reflected in budget planning for fiscal year 1964." He assured the Joint Committee chairman that the project was "not just another study." Not only had he asked Commissioners Leland J. Haworth and Robert E. Wilson to direct it, but the project would receive his personal attention.[14]

Wilson and Haworth were well qualified to direct the project. Wilson had been on the Commission since early 1960. He had retired in 1958 as chairman of the board and chief executive officer of the Standard Oil Company of Indiana. As a research-oriented chemical engineer, Wilson had served on various advisory committees to the AEC from the beginning of the agency in 1947. Particularly significant for this assignment was the fact that he had been a member of the 1958 Ad Hoc Advisory Committee on Reactor Policies and Programs that had submitted one of the previous studies cited by the Joint Committee. Haworth had been appointed to the Commission by Kennedy in 1961. He came to Washington from the directorship of the Brookhaven National Laboratory, where as a specialist in nuclear physics and electronics he had engaged in both research and administration. Although the two commissioners codirected the study, Haworth was the key architect of the final report.

Seaborg wanted to be sure the study was more than a rehash of previous reports. He ordered that the project be completed by 1 July 1962 so that the Commission's 1964 fiscal-year budget considerations could reflect its conclusions. Consequently, he insisted that the study include a "series of practical recommendations with immediate technical programmatic steps." Seaborg's own ideas were incorporated into the directive. He wanted the investigators to "consider the immediate short-range objectives of breeder reactors together with the long-term utilization of nuclear fuels in breeder reactors." And the study of the overall reactor program had to be set in the context of "national raw materials requirements" as well as taking into account such AEC concerns as reactor siting and public health and safety.[15]

Seaborg also directed that the AEC report should be coordinated with two related studies the president had mentioned in his letter. One was a National Academy of Sciences survey on development and preservation of the country's natural resources. The other was a report the Federal Power Commission was just beginning on the long-range power requirements of the nation.[16]

With such a tight schedule, Haworth and Wilson, assisted by Reactor Development Division director Frank Pittman, set up a series of meetings with representatives of both industry and government to gather the needed information. Various reports and studies supplemented the meetings. Particularly important were a draft report on energy resources prepared by the National Academy of Sciences and a report by the Interior Department energy-policy staff on supplies, costs, and uses of fossil fuels. Both of those works drew on a 1960 study done by the U.S. Geological Survey on the nation's coal reserves. The reports as well as further meetings with the staffs of those agencies provided the broad energy context within which Haworth placed nuclear power.[17]

The AEC sent its draft report to the Bureau of the Budget in mid-September. Initial reviews by the Bureau staff and by the President's Science Advisory Committee indicated concern over the report's emphasis on the urgency of the need for atomic power. Wiesner, who had always been lukewarm on the idea of such a report, was particularly outspoken in expressing this view. Budget director Bell decided to circulate the report to the State and Interior departments and to the Federal Power Commission for their reactions before making a decision on disposition of the document. After he discussed the report with Haworth and Wilson, the AEC redrafted and resubmitted it. The new draft incorporated a somewhat changed tone, but the conclusions remained essentially the same as in the September version. The president released it on 20 November, nearly three months after its deadline.[18]

The first part of the report analyzed the nation's fossil-fuel reserves in some detail, estimated the growth of energy consumption, and related them to the need for development of nuclear energy. It maintained that fossil fuels supplying most of the energy in the United States would be exhausted in the not-too-distant future. Using different combinations of energy estimates, the report predicted that low-cost readily available domestic supplies would be depleted in 75 to 100 years and total supplies in 150 to 200 years.

When viewed in a worldwide context, the long-range projections were even more disturbing. Based on those dreary estimates, the report's first conclusion was not surprising. It recommended supplementing diminishing fossil fuels where technically satisfactory and reasonably economic substitutes could be made on a significant scale. This would conserve fossil resources so that they could be applied in other ways.[19]

In spite of certain limitations, the report suggested, nuclear energy appeared as the feasible way to supplement and conserve fossil fuels. Thus far, the argument was not new. Earlier advocates of atomic-power development had advanced the same views. The AEC did, however, add some new considerations. First of all, the report contended that nuclear power had progressed to a point where light-water technology was "on the threshold of being competitive with conventional power in the highest fuel cost areas." Furthermore, the report concluded that with further cost reductions, nuclear power could "increasingly reduce the inter-area differential in power generation costs and eventually place the entire country on an equal basis." Even more significant for the long term, however, was the AEC's argument about uranium 235, the isotope used to fuel the existing light-water reactors.[20]

Uranium 235 is the readily fissionable material found in nature. It constitutes only 0.7 percent of natural uranium. The report contended that if this small percentage was the only potential source of fissionable material, the contribution of atomic power would scarcely be worth the costs of development. Although light-water reactors utilizing uranium 235 satisfied short-term needs, other technical developments were necessary to take advantage of the vast quantities of remaining uranium. The fertile isotopes—uranium 238, which constituted the rest of natural uranium, and thorium 232, which constituted practically all natural thorium—could be converted in large amounts to fissionable plutonium 239 and uranium 233. Consequently, a successful breeder-reactor program would make available as potential fuel all supplies of uranium and thorium instead of only the small percentage of uranium 235. Over the long term, then, fuel supplies would be almost limitless. Even more important, the report maintained, this would lead to the conservation of the exhaustible fossil fuels. In this sense, the document concluded, "nuclear energy can and should make an important and, eventually, a vital contribution toward meeting our long-term energy requirements."[21]

Competitive nuclear power had always been the goal of both the industry and the AEC. The report did not change that goal. But by insisting that nuclear power was "on the threshold of economic competitiveness" and concluding that "relatively modest assistance by the AEC will assure crossing that threshold," the report looked beyond the current program toward a new phase of nuclear technology. In doing this it predicted that nuclear power might contribute up to half of the generating capacity of the country by the year 2000.[22]

There were practical implications for the AEC in taking an optimistic long-range view. As nuclear power moved toward full-scale utilization of breeder technology, the role of the government would continue. AEC laboratories would do the research and development, and the government would construct experimental reactors. The report envisioned construction of seven or eight power-producing prototype reactors over the following dozen years largely financed by the AEC. The AEC's long-range analysis of the need for nuclear power suggested none too subtly a corresponding need for an increased budget for the agency.[23]

The AEC acknowledged some reason for caution amidst its optimistic assessment of the proposals for nuclear power. Safety problems related to the design of some reactor components and uncertainties about siting could affect reactor economics. Until enough operating experience had been accumulated to permit statistical evaluations of safety-related functions, reactors had to be "fairly far removed" from population centers, thus increasing transmission costs. The report also mentioned waste management as an important safety issue that needed to be resolved. "Aside from the central reactor development program proper," the report noted, "no other phase of the entire program is more important than that of waste disposal."[24]

Licensing and regulation also were key considerations if the future reactor program was to be successful. The report outlined the steps recently taken to reform the licensing process. Future improvements would include efforts to reduce the number of technical reviews. Standardization of reactor designs would also greatly facilitate the process, the report declared, and help to reduce costs.[25]

The AEC's report was partly an attempt to soothe critics, especially ever-skeptical members of the Joint Committee, who charged that progress was too sluggish. At the same time it was a promotional paean designed to win additional backing for development efforts. This seemed particularly important to the AEC because of the tepid support of the Kennedy administration for an aggressive atomic-power program. The AEC's goal of encouraging the growth of a mature, economically competitive nuclear-power industry was the same as it had been since the 1954 Atomic Energy Act. But the reasons the agency cited for fostering atomic development had undergone a shift in emphasis by 1962. During the Eisenhower administration the need for new energy sources had been viewed as an important but long-range objective. The urgency that infused peaceful atomic-power programs arose from a desire to maintain world leadership and prestige, a concern that the president, the AEC, the Joint Committee, and presumably the American people shared. Under Kennedy, however, the struggle to impress the world and outstrip the Soviet Union in scientific achievement moved away from the field of atomic energy. The AEC, therefore, stressed the future energy requirements of the United States and the world as the major incentive for continued atomic progress and played down the significance of international considerations.

Widespread press comments on the report were generally favorable and supported its call for an expanded atomic-power program.[26] Joint Committee members also voiced agreement with the report's conclusions but registered some doubts about its impact. Senator Pastore, scheduled to assume the committee's chairmanship in January 1963, observed that it reflected "what the attitude of the Joint Committee on Atomic Energy has been. It ought to be subscribed to by the administration, by Congress, and by industry." Holifield noted that it was the first time the government had set out a long-range program coordinated with other forms of energy. He cautioned, however, that it was "worthless unless there is acceptance by the Administration of the need to implement it."[27]

President Kennedy had released the report without endorsing it. His advisers reported to him that the document was deficient in two major respects. It overstated the urgency of further large government expenditures on research and development, thus reading "more like a promotional document than the 'hard look' you requested." Furthermore, they considered the report one-sided because, for example, it did not consider benefits from a substantial research-and-development program in the conventional-power field. McGeorge Bundy wrote to Seaborg to acknowledge receipt of the report for the president and noted that it would be useful when placed "side by side with results of other studies now underway on the nonnuclear side of the national energy picture." The administration's disappointment that the AEC study failed to fully consider atomic energy in the context of total energy supplies was underscored in February 1963 when Kennedy created an Interdepartmental Energy Study Group, which included the chairman of the AEC. He wanted it to make a comprehensive study of the nation's total energy resources in order to determine the most effective allocation of research-and-development funds. The president sought a broader view, which he said the "Commission considered inappropriate to cover in its report," of the effects of major research on the economics of nonnuclear energy sources.[28]

The same assessment had come earlier from an outspoken and influential industry spokesman, Philip Sporn. In a long analysis of the report that he submitted to Commissioner Wilson, Sporn wrote that although it was a commendable effort, the length of time permitted to conduct the study could not appraise the technological developments in nonnuclear areas. Such an effort, he said, would be strongly in the national interest.

> By concentrating on nuclear energy the Report ends up recommending a program which makes nuclear energy almost a special end in itself. It does not adequately relate nuclear energy to the total energy situation. For example, even if electric energy in the year 2000 should account for 50 per cent of total energy use, and nuclear energy for 50 per cent of that, it would mean that 75 per cent of our total energy needs would still have to be satisfied by fossil fuels. But it may very well be that in the light of the fact that nuclear energy is already on the threshold of competitiveness in the high-cost fuel areas of the United States fossil fuels should receive far more attention than nuclear energy.

Sporn's misgivings about the report's projections made him question its emphasis on an urgent need for breeder reactors. He thought that evolution to the breeder lay in improving promising types of converter reactors rather than in the early construction of breeder prototypes.[29]

Another critic of the report was former AEC chairman David Lilienthal. As part of a series of lectures at Princeton University in February 1963, he reflected on the course of atomic development since he helped foster it in the late 1940s. Like Sporn, he regretted that atomic power occupied a special category rather than assuming a more modest position in the mainstream of America's total energy policies and political affairs. Lilienthal attributed atomic energy's unique status to the elevated claims that were advanced about its potential blessings, arising from the conviction that "this great new source of energy for mankind could produce results as dramatically and decisively beneficial to man as the bomb was dramatically destructive." But the inflated expectations for the atom's peaceful uses inevitably failed to materialize. Lilienthal argued that the objectives for atomic power had diminished from profoundly improving the world to simply producing electricity that was competitive in cost with fossil fuels. He criticized the AEC report to the president for overstating the need for atomic power and for understating the fact that, even if it were cost-competitive, it differed significantly from other forms of energy because of the hazards of radiation. While acknowledging its potential as an important energy source in the future, Lilienthal suggested that "we should stop trying to force-feed atomic energy."[30]

Despite the mixed response it received, the AEC's 1962 report represented a milestone in the early history of nuclear development. It was justified in pointing out that private firms, with government encouragement, had made impressive progress in building an atomic-power industry in the short time since the 1954 Atomic Energy Act had opened the technology to private enterprise. Six sizable reactors ranging from 50 to 265 megawatts electric were operating, seven more prototype plants were expected to be completed by the end of 1963, and several others were under construction. The AEC contended that experience to date and projections for future growth indicated that the nuclear-power industry was on the verge of maturity, both economically and technologically. The agency believed, furthermore, that the procedures and rules it had formulated since 1955 gave it the ability to license and regulate safely new reactors constructed in the future. Not only was the 1962 report a springboard to the future, it also marked an end to the early developmental phase of the atomic-power industry.

The 1962 report underscored the AEC's customary emphasis on promotional rather than regulatory issues. Although it labeled safety as "an overriding consideration," it focused on the advantages of and need for further atomic-power development. Regulatory problems such as siting and waste disposal received only brief discussion. A similar assignment of priorities had characterized the AEC's civilian programs since the 1954 Atomic Energy Act. The allocation of time, attention, and resources had clearly accentuated developmental efforts rather than regulatory matters.

The precedence the AEC gave to developmental programs resulted from a number of considerations. The 1954 act made it a national policy to encourage the widespread use of atomic energy for peaceful purposes; but private industry, despite its interest in the potential of nuclear power, was often hesitant to undertake the risks of development. Because initial costs were high, immediate profits were unlikely, and the technology was hazardous, few companies were eager to invest heavily in nuclear power until existing economic and technical uncertainties were resolved. Therefore, the AEC felt obliged to cajole, induce, or persuade private interests to participate in atomic development. This seemed particularly urgent because of the intense pressure the Joint Committee placed on the agency to speed progress and its persistent threat to require the AEC to construct plants if private firms failed to act promptly. The AEC and the Joint Committee agreed on the objective of spurring the rapid growth of atomic power, but they frequently clashed on the best means to accomplish that goal. The Gore-Holifield bill and other Joint Committee initiatives that the AEC opposed helped goad the agency to vigorously promote private atomic development.

In addition, the AEC recognized that progress toward atomic power would not occur without public support. A part of its promotional program, therefore, was intended to secure public acceptance of constructive atomic applications. Following the lead of Eisenhower's 1953 Atoms-for-Peace speech, the agency also sought to dissociate the peaceful from the destructive uses of atomic energy. In a 1955 *Reader's Digest* article, Lewis Strauss articulated the prevalent attitude of the AEC by attempting to dispel fears that "atomic discoveries of recent years [were] part of a nightmare that disrupts the peaceful dreams of civilized man." His own belief, he added, was that "knowledge of the atom is intended by the Creator for the service and not the destruction of mankind."[31]

Political considerations and public attitudes were not the only reasons for the AEC's emphasis on atomic-energy development. During the 1950s, atomic energy was widely regarded as a glamorous technology that could provide dramatic benefits in medicine, agriculture, and industry as well as electrical generation. By encouraging the various uses of the peaceful atom, the agency could fulfill the objectives of the 1954 act. It would enhance America's international prestige and demonstrate the salutary dimensions of atomic energy. The fruits of developmental efforts, unlike those of regulatory programs, were tangible and measurable. Gleaming reactor buildings, tabulations of kilowatts produced, and growing lists of isotope users could be pointed to with pride as evidence that the AEC was carrying out its mandate.

Atomic regulation, by contrast, was largely invisible, intangible, and undramatic. Simply because protection of the public health and safety was the basic principle of regulation, it generated little of the glamor of development. Only in a negative sense—in the event of an accident— would it become dramatic. Safety questions were largely a matter of judgment rather than something concrete or quantifiable, and AEC officials found it easier to assume that such issues had been or would be satisfactorily resolved than to assume that reactors would be built. When it issued a construction permit for the PRDC fast-breeder reactor, for example, the Commission's vision of an advanced-technology plant that showed the effectiveness of its Power Demonstration Reactor Program

outweighed the reservations of its Advisory Committee on Reactor Safeguards. Though aware of the implications that safety questions posed
to development of the technology, the AEC believed that nuclear science,
in due time, would provide the answers to any outstanding problems.
In other words, the desire for tangible signs of progress was more compelling than the commitment to first resolving more ethereal safety issues.

Members of the Commission devoted more attention to weapons and
developmental programs than to regulatory matters. In late 1960, for
example, the commissioners estimated that they spent from one-sixth
to one-third of their time on regulatory work.[32] Except for the PRDC
construction permit, regulatory issues rarely generated controversy or
dissension among the commissioners. The staff resolved most questions,
and although commissioners sometimes requested further information
or clarification, they usually endorsed staff regulatory proposals promptly.
Consequently, regulatory programs and procedures did not dramatically
change as new commissioners or chairmen took office between 1954 and
1963. More often, shifts that did occur were due to outside influences,
such as pressure from the Joint Committee or, in the case of radiation-
protection standards, because of revised recommendations of the National Committee on Radiation Protection.

The AEC's emphasis on developing atomic energy and the relatively
limited participation by commissioners in regulatory issues did not mean
that the agency was inattentive to safety concerns. The AEC took its
mandate to protect public health and safety seriously. The regulations
the staff began to draft shortly after passage of the 1954 act reflected
careful consideration of the best scientific information and judgment
available at the time. The AEC recognized and publicly acknowledged
the possibility of accidents in such a new and rapidly changing technology, ranging from overexposure of an individual radiation worker to
a runaway reactor that could threaten the health and safety of large
numbers of people. The agency never offered absolute assurances that
such incidents would not occur, although it constantly maintained that
its safety requirements reduced their likelihood to a minimum. It regarded the chances of a major reactor accident as extremely remote, a
view with which most experts outside the government concurred.

The AEC's outlook on health and safety issues was based partly on
experiences in atomic-energy operations since the Manhattan Project.
With the exception of the failure to protect uranium miners adequately,
both government and private nuclear facilities compiled an excellent

safety record. Despite the dangers inherent in working with radioactive materials and a novel technology, the performance of atomic enterprises compared favorably with that of other hazardous industries. The serious accidents that did occur, such as the SL–1 tragedy and the contamination of the M. W. Kellogg plant in Houston, generated concern within the AEC and prompted corrective measures to prevent similar mishaps. But the agency regarded those and less severe accidents as aberrations rather than harbingers of future problems. They did not suggest a need for a fundamental reassessment of the assumptions underlying the regulatory system.

Developmental considerations also heavily influenced the agency's position on health and safety matters. The 1954 act created a built-in conflict of interest by inextricably linking regulatory and developmental functions. On the one hand, if efforts to encourage atomic development were unproductive, the scope of the regulatory program would be correspondingly diminished. On the other hand, the AEC was acutely aware that a severe accident would hinder or even end the prospects for atomic progress, and therefore an effective regulatory program was essential for growth. Agency officials were concerned, however, that regulations that were too restrictive or inflexible would impede development. The principal thrust of the regulatory program was to protect the health and safety of radiation workers and the general public without placing undue burdens on the atomic industry.

The inherent difficulty of achieving a balance between necessary and excessive regulation was compounded by the lack of operating experience with reactors and the many scientific uncertainties about atomic energy and radiation. In the case of radiation-protection regulations, the AEC drew on a broad consensus of scientific opinion. Although experts acknowledged that important questions about the biological effects of radiation were unresolved, the permissible-exposure limits were imposed with little deliberation about their operational implications. The AEC accepted the NCRP's judgment that its recommendations provided adequate protection to workers without placing unreasonable demands on industry. Regulations for power reactors were more difficult to draft because, as the WASH–740 study on the probability and consequences of accidents vividly demonstrated, many aspects of reactor safety were largely theoretical. There were too many unknowns to enable the agency to devise definitive rules. In cases where scientific consensus, empirical evidence, or operating experience was lacking or very limited, the in-

terests of industry and the promotional concerns of the AEC were particularly influential. In drafting site criteria, for example, industry's
insistence on the need to locate plants close to population centers and
assurances that safety problems could be mitigated by engineered safety
features played a vital part in persuading the AEC to endorse industry's
position. The development of the site criteria underscored industry's
fear that rigid requirements would undermine atomic growth. The AEC
always emphasized that its paramount concern in the civilian atomic
program was safety, and it made a concerted effort to devise and implement effective regulations. But its judgment on safety could not be
divorced from developmental considerations. This did not mean that it
viewed developmental programs as more important than regulatory policies, but only that the need to encourage atomic progress seemed more
immediate.

The AEC, at the same time that it was acclaiming the benefits of
peaceful atomic energy in a plethora of articles, pamphlets, speeches,
and films, sought to assure the public that nuclear-power development
was proceeding with due regard for health and safety. In some respects
the effort was successful; between 1954 and 1962 there was little evidence
of public opposition to atomic power for electrical production or uneasiness about its safety. With the exception of objections that a proposed
power station on the California coast would destroy the natural beauty
of the area, no citizens groups formed to protest the construction of
plants. Only in the PRDC case did outside organizations intervene in
the licensing process. The only public-opinion poll taken during this
period on atomic power showed in February 1956 that 69 percent of
those surveyed had "no fear" of having a plant located in their community; only 20 percent were fearful.[33] Neither the public nor the news
media demonstrated sustained interest in issues relating to the safety
of peaceful atomic energy.

The Joint Committee provided the only day-to-day scrutiny of the
AEC's regulatory program. It alone forced the agency to review constantly its statutory conflict of interest between regulation and development. Although the committee accepted the AEC's argument that
regulatory functions should not be vested in a separate agency during
the early stages of atomic development, it indicated, and the AEC generally concurred, that at some later time a separation between regulatory
and developmental responsibilities would be desirable. The AEC and
the Joint Committee agreed on the ends of regulatory policies, but they
frequently clashed over the best means to protect public health and

safety, particularly on internal regulatory organization and the licensing process. The Joint Committee wanted to build public confidence in AEC licensing procedures, and it believed the best way to accomplish this goal was by strengthening the technical review of power-reactor applications in full view of the public. It amended the 1954 act—requiring mandatory public hearings, public reports from the Safeguards Committee, and technical reviews and decisions by highly qualified licensing boards—to achieve this purpose.

The agency disagreed but went along with the amendments. It also sought, through measures at its disposal, to improve public confidence in its regulatory program. On several occasions it reorganized the regulatory staff, first divesting it of all developmental functions and then placing it directly under the Commission. It slowly built its technical licensing staff. It used a separated staff in each licensing case, adopted an *ex parte* rule, and used formal procedures at the hearings in an attempt to ensure due process in its licensing program and fit highly technical issues into the government's traditional administrative legal framework. Whether the substantial amount of time and effort that went into those undertakings achieved its purpose is questionable. Certainly the issue was significant for the Joint Committee, the AEC, and the industry. But in the short term it was hardly comprehensible, noticeable, or meaningful to the public or to the press.

Although the public showed little concern about the safety implications of atomic power, it became increasingly apprehensive and knowledgeable about the hazards of radiation. Issues arising mostly from the AEC's responsibilities for atomic-weapons testing and to a lesser degree for the development of nuclear power indirectly undermined the agency's attempts to inspire public confidence in its regulatory programs. The PRDC case generated only sporadic news coverage, and its impact on public perceptions is difficult to assess. The controversy, however, unquestionably raised doubts in the minds of Joint Committee members, labor unions, and some public-health officials about the AEC's ability to balance its developmental and regulatory responsibilities. The 1959 report of the National Advisory Committee on Radiation to the surgeon general did not specifically cite the PRDC decision, but it emphasized the conflict of interest inherent in assigning both functions to a single agency. The report contributed to the growing reservations about the AEC's performance in protecting public health and safety that were so prevalent by the spring of 1959.

The fallout debate, more than any other issue, impaired public trust in and damaged the public image of the AEC. The diminished credibility of the agency's assurances that fallout from weapons testing created no major health hazards resulted in a decline of confidence in the agency's regulatory programs. This was evident, for example, in the statements of some state health officials who wanted the states to be granted a larger role in nuclear regulation. The weakened public trust in the AEC was even more apparent in the uproar over ocean disposal of low-level radioactive wastes in mid-1959.

Although AEC officials believed that public apprehension over radiation hazards often was based on misunderstanding or misinformation, the agency was attentive to public concerns. It decided to stop issuing licenses for ocean dumping of low-level wastes in 1960 largely because of the public outcry. The AEC was less malleable on the fallout question because of its possible ramifications for the weapons program, but it still sponsored research and released a great deal of scientific information on the subject. The American people were but one constituency that influenced the AEC on regulatory matters. Industry groups exerted the greatest impact among organizations outside the federal government, most directly on indemnity and siting. Labor unions played an important role in some safety issues, not only by intervening in the PRDC case but also in procedural aspects of the radiation-protection regulations and the efforts to devise adequate workers'-compensation laws for employees of atomic industries. Scientific organizations, particularly the NCRP and the National Academy of Sciences, contributed expert advice and judgment on vital regulatory problems. The positions of state governments were instrumental in the establishment of the agreements program and on matters such as uranium-mining hazards, workers' compensation, and land burial of low-level radioactive wastes.

In addition, the AEC was responsible to both the executive and legislative branches of the federal government. Neither Eisenhower nor Kennedy took much interest in regulatory affairs, but their views were pivotal in defining the political atmosphere in which atomic development proceeded. Furthermore, Eisenhower's creation of the Federal Radiation Council affected the regulatory program of the AEC, though to a limited degree, by making the agency answerable to another bureaucratic layer and considering questions of concern to the AEC. Above all, the Joint Committee exerted direct and frequently decisive influence over the agency's regulatory activities. Despite their agreement on the twin objectives of encouraging the development of atomic power and safeguarding public health and safety, the committee and the agency frequently diverged on the specifics of how best to attain those goals. In several instances the Joint Committee imposed its will on a reluctant and resistant AEC. In sum, despite the substantial size, power, prestige, funding, and expertise the AEC commanded, it was not free to act independently, at least on matters in which other agencies and organizations or the public took an interest. The AEC did not operate in a political vacuum and often had to modify its own preferences on regulatory questions in the face of outside pressures. In cases where the views of different constituencies conflicted, the AEC had to try to compromise various points of view or risk antagonizing a group whose wishes were not satisfied. As a result, the regulatory program as it had evolved by 1962 was a hybrid embodying the positions of many different interests, though those that were most intimately involved—the AEC itself, the Joint Committee, and industry—were generally most influential.

The 1954 Atomic Energy Act established the national goal of developing the widespread use of atomic energy for peaceful purposes and charged the AEC with the task of encouraging the growth of nuclear power for electrical generation. By 1962 the primary motives behind the drive for rapid development of atomic power had been superseded by other concerns or had proved illusory. The Kennedy administration sought to assert world leadership and win international prestige through the space race rather than through the quest for economical atomic kilowatts. The hope, so prominent in the 1950s, that the peaceful atom would counterbalance the destructive power of nuclear weapons by providing spectacular benefits for all mankind had dimmed. As David Lilienthal observed in his 1963 lecture at Princeton University: "The peaceful atom has not ushered in a 'new world' but has rather become a part, a minor part, of the old one."[34] Concern about future energy supplies had been an important long-range consideration in pushing for atomic development in 1953, and it continued to be so a decade later. But in an era when alternative energy sources were cheap and abundant, the prospect that atomic power would be vital in meeting future energy demands was not enough in itself to give a sense of urgency to the atomic-power program.

By 1963 the future of atomic development hinged less on the decline in importance of its original motivations than on the momentum that the program had acquired. By that time the AEC and the Joint Committee for political reasons, and the atomic industry for economic reasons, had a vital stake in the continued growth of atomic power. Utilities that had invested in the technology favored further development to make it more competitive economically. Vendors of components wanted to maintain and enlarge their markets. Bureaucratic considerations such as budget outlays, prestige, and affirmation of the value of the achievements already made prompted the AEC to press for greater progress. Similar impulses moved the Joint Committee, which despite its policy disputes with the AEC had a vested interest in atomic growth. Committee members became increasingly sensitive to criticisms of the atomic-power program. In April 1963, for example, the Joint Committee subjected Lilienthal to a hostile grilling for his skeptical review of peaceful atomic applications in his Princeton University lecture. Chet Holifield remarked privately to the former AEC chairman: "You have hurt the program, hurt it badly."[35] The advocacy of the AEC, the Joint Committee, and the nuclear industry spurred atomic development even after its original broad purposes had largely faded from view. Although the AEC set up its regulatory structure and requirements in the embryonic stages of the peaceful atomic program and although many questions remained to be resolved, agency officials felt confident that they were prepared to ensure the safety of an expanding industry and a sophisticated technology.

Appendix 1
GLOSSARY OF ORGANIZATIONS AND ACRONYMS

Advisory Committee on Reactor Safeguards (referred to in the text as the "Safe-guards Committee")—Panel of outside experts established by the AEC in 1953 to provide an independent review of the safety aspects of nuclear reactors. Congress made it a statutory body in 1957.

Advisory Committee of State Officials—Panel of representatives of twelve states established by the AEC in 1955 for consultation on issues related to federal-state relations in nuclear regulation.

Advisory Committee on X-Ray and Radium Protection—Established in 1929 by professional societies and X-ray equipment manufacturers in the United States to provide information and recommendations on radiation protection. It was renamed the National Committee on Radiation Protection in 1946.

Atomic Industrial Forum—Private organization founded in 1953 to promote industrial development of atomic energy.

Atomic Power Development Associates (APDA)—A nonprofit technical consortium organized by the Detroit Edison Company to design and conduct research on a commercial fast-breeder reactor.

Atomic Safety and Licensing Boards—Three-member panels established by Congress in 1962 to conduct hearings and make decisions on issuing reactor licenses. The boards were appointed by the Commission, which retained authority to review and overrule their licensing decisions.

Committee on Waste Disposal—Panel established by the National Academy of Sciences in 1955 to study disposal of radioactive wastes on land. It issued a report in 1957 suggesting that salt formations offered the most promising solution to the problem of high-level wastes.

Federal Radiation Council (FRC)—Created by executive order in August 1959 to advise the president and executive agencies on radiation-protection standards and regulations. Originally composed of the secretaries of defense, commerce, and health, education, and welfare and the chairman of the AEC. Congress added the secretary of labor and made the Council a statutory body in September 1959.

Industrial Advisory Group—Committee of industry representatives established by the AEC in 1947 to explore the commercial potential of nuclear energy.

Industrial Committee on Reactor Location Problems—Panel of industrial and scientific representatives established by the AEC in 1950 to review reactor-siting questions. Its functions were assumed in 1953 by the Advisory Committee on Reactor Safeguards.

International Commission on Radiological Protection (ICRP)—Panel composed of scientists from different countries that studied and made recommendations on "maximum permissible doses" of radiation.

International X-Ray and Radium Protection Committee—Organized by the Second International Congress of Radiology in 1928 to provide information and guidance on radiation protection. In 1950 it was expanded and reorganized under a new name, the International Commission on Radiological Protection.

Joint Federal-State Action Committee—Task force appointed by the president and the chairman of the National Conference of Governors in 1957 to study federal-state relations on a variety of issues, including atomic energy.

National Advisory Committee on Radiation—Panel created by the surgeon general of the United States in 1958 to recommend means for establishing a comprehensive program to cover all aspects of radiation protection.

National Committee on Radiation Protection (NCRP)—American committee of scientific authorities that published recommendations on maximum permissible exposure to radiation.

Power Reactor Development Company (PRDC)—Consortium of utilities headed by the Detroit Edison Company formed to construct, own, and operate a commercial fast-breeder reactor at Lagoona Beach, Michigan.

Reactor Safeguard Committee—Advisory panel of outside experts established by the AEC in 1947 to evaluate safety aspects of reactors. Its functions were assumed in 1953 by the Advisory Committee on Reactor Safeguards.

Regional Advisory Committee on Nuclear Energy—Established by the Southern Governors' Conference in 1957 to promote atomic development, provide technical advice, and encourage the adoption of radiation-protection regulations in the southern states.

Appendix 2

CHRONOLOGY OF REGULATORY HISTORY

DATE	EVENT
16 July 1945:	First atomic device, "Trinity," detonated at Alamogordo, New Mexico by the Manhattan Engineer District of the Army Corps of Engineers (Manhattan Project).
6 August 1945:	First atomic bomb, "Little Boy," dropped on Hiroshima, Japan.
9 August 1945:	Atomic bomb, "Fat Man," dropped on Nagasaki, Japan.
1 August 1946:	Atomic Energy Act of 1946 became law. Established the Atomic Energy Commission (AEC) and transferred Manhattan Project's programs and facilities to the five-member civilian commission.
1 January 1947:	AEC officially began operations under Chairman David E. Lilienthal.
June 1947:	Reactor Safeguard Committee established to advise the Commission on the hazards of reactor operation.
20 October 1947:	Industrial Advisory Group appointed to investigate peaceful uses of atomic energy.
5 August 1948:	AEC established a Division of Reactor Development.
31 January 1950:	President Truman announced program to develop the thermonuclear bomb.
November 1950:	AEC established the Industrial Committee on Reactor Location Problems to review reactor-siting questions.
20 December 1951:	First generation of electrical power from a nuclear reactor at AEC's reactor-testing center in Arco, Idaho.
20 March 1953:	National Committee on Radiation Protection (NCRP) published recommendations on maximum permissible amounts of radioisotopes in the human body and maximum permissible concentrations in air and water.

2 July 1953:	Lewis L. Strauss became chairman of AEC.
9 August 1953:	AEC merged the Reactor Safeguard Committee and the Industrial Committee on Reactor Location Problems into the Advisory Committee on Reactor Safeguards (Safeguards Committee).
8 December 1953:	President Eisenhower delivered "Atoms for Peace" speech before the United Nations.
24 January 1954:	Navy launched the first atomic-powered submarine, *U.S.S. Nautilus.*
February–May 1954:	AEC detonated six test weapons at the Marshall Islands. The largest detonation on 1 March contaminated a Japanese fishing vessel, *Lucky Dragon.*
14 March 1954:	AEC and Duquesne Light Company negotiated agreement to construct jointly a pressurized-water reactor demonstration facility at Shippingport, Pennsylvania.
30 August 1954:	Atomic Energy Act of 1954 became law. AEC assigned expanded regulatory responsibilities.
24 September 1954:	NCRP published recommendations on maximum permissible doses of radiation from external sources.
10 January 1955:	AEC announced Power Demonstration Reactor Program, under which government and industry would cooperate in construction and operation of experimental power reactors.
15 February 1955:	AEC released report on "Effects of High-Yield Nuclear Explosions."
22–23 February 1955:	Seven-state Uranium Mining Conference on Health Hazards established "working levels" of radon and radon daughters in uranium mines.
30 March 1955:	AEC created Division of Licensing and named Harold L. Price director.
8 April 1955:	Reactor Hazards Evaluation Staff established in the Office of the General Manager.
8 June 1955:	AEC established the Division of Civilian Application to administer licensing and regulation functions. Harold Price named director.
6 November 1955:	Reactor Hazards Evaluation Staff transferred to the Division of Civilian Application.
1955–1957:	AEC issued several new regulations dealing with nuclear power under Title 10 of the *Code of Federal Regulations.*
6 January 1956:	Power Reactor Development Company (PRDC) applied to the AEC for a construction permit to build a commercial fast-breeder reactor in Lagoona Beach, Michigan.

4 May 1956:	AEC issued first construction permits for two large-scale nuclear power facilities—Consolidated Edison's Indian Point plant and Commonwealth Edison's Dresden reactor.
6 June 1956:	Safeguards Committee sent cautionary letter to the Commission on the PRDC reactor.
12 June 1956:	National Academy of Sciences issued report on "The Biological Effects of Atomic Radiation."
4 August 1956:	AEC issued construction permit for the PRDC reactor.
31 August 1956:	AFL-CIO unions petitioned the AEC for a hearing on the PRDC construction permit.
September 1956:	Joint Committee on Atomic Energy staff began study of AEC licensing procedures and regulatory organization.
8 October 1956:	AEC granted the unions' request for a hearing.
8 January 1957:	PRDC hearing opened in Washington, D.C. Continued until 7 August 1957.
13 March 1957:	Radiation exposure accident occurred at M. W. Kellogg Company plant in Houston, Texas.
21 March 1957:	On the basis of Joint Committee staff study, Senator Anderson introduced an amendment to give Safeguards Committee statutory status and to require mandatory hearings on specified facility licenses.
22 March 1957:	AEC completed WASH–740, "Theoretical Possibilities and Consequences of Major Accidents in Large Nuclear Power Plants."
27 May–7 June 1957:	Joint Committee held hearings on the "Nature of Radioactive Fallout and Its Effects on Man."
2 September 1957:	Price-Anderson amendment to 1954 Atomic Energy Act became law. Provided government indemnity in event of major reactor accident. Also incorporated Senator Anderson's changes in licensing procedures. Safeguards Committee made a statutory body.
26 December 1957:	Division of Civilian Application abolished. Regulatory functions transferred to Division of Licensing and Regulation, promotional functions assigned to Office of Industrial Development.
13 January 1958:	Industrial Waste Corporation applied for a license to dispose of low-level radioactive waste in the Gulf of Mexico.
15 April 1958:	NCRP published revised recommendations on maximum permissible doses of radiation from external sources.
14 July 1958:	John A. McCone became chairman of AEC.
1 August 1958:	AEC established an Office of Hearing Examiners.

22 August 1958:   President Eisenhower announced a moratorium on U.S. nuclear-weapons tests.

10 December 1958:   AEC issued initial decision in PRDC case reaffirming approval of the construction permit.

28 January 1959:   AEC proposed bill to the Joint Committee giving states some jurisdiction in safeguarding public health and safety.

26 March 1959:   Surgeon general's National Advisory Committee on Radiation recommended that primary authority for radiation safety be vested in the U.S. Public Health Service.

23 April 1959:   AEC issued for public comment revised radiation-protection regulations.

28 April 1959:   AEC issued for public comment rule-making proposal on reactor-site criteria.

5–8 May 1959:   Joint Committee held hearings on "Fallout from Nuclear Weapons Tests."

26 May 1959:   AEC issued final decision in PRDC case to continue the construction permit.

29 May 1959:   AEC hearing examiner ruled in favor of issuing a license to the Industrial Waste Corporation.

21 June 1959:   Committee on Oceanography of the National Academy of Sciences released its report on sea disposal of radioactive wastes.

25 July 1959:   AFL-CIO unions petitioned for review of AEC decision in the PRDC case before the United States Court of Appeals for the District of Columbia.

14 August 1959:   President Eisenhower created the Federal Radiation Council to provide guidance to agencies on radiological health protection.

September 1959:   AEC withdrew its reactor-siting rule-making proposal after receiving adverse comments.

12 September 1959:   Office of Health and Safety established.

23 September 1959:   Amendment to the 1954 Atomic Energy Act enacted authorizing AEC to enter into agreements with states allowing them to assume specified regulatory responsibilities.

28 September 1959:   AEC issued an operating license to the Commonwealth Edison Dresden facility, the first large-scale privately owned plant to receive a license to operate.

13 November 1959:   Position of Assistant General Manager for Regulation and Safety established. Responsible for Division of Licensing and Regulation, Office of Health and Safety, and newly created Division of Compliance.

January 1960– April 1962:	AEC reviewed Industrial Waste Corporation decision. Decided not to allow the company to dispose of wastes in the Gulf of Mexico but rather to require them to be shipped for land burial at AEC installations.
13 May 1960:	Federal Radiation Council submitted radiation-protection guidelines. Promptly approved by President Eisenhower.
10 June 1960:	United States Court of Appeals for the District of Columbia declared the PRDC construction permit illegal.
19 November 1960:	United States Supreme Court granted AEC and PRDC a review of the decision by the Court of Appeals.
15–16 December 1960:	Meeting held of federal officials and governors of uranium-mining states on radiation hazards in mines.
1 January 1961:	Revised radiation-protection regulations became effective.
3 January 1961:	SL-1 test reactor accident at Arco, Idaho killed three technicians.
February 1961:	AEC issued "Report on the Regulatory Program of the Atomic Energy Commission" that recommended regulatory offices report directly to the commissioners.
1 March 1961:	Glenn T. Seaborg became chairman of AEC.
16 March 1961:	Position of Assistant General Manager for Regulation and Safety abolished. New position established, Director of Regulation, that reported to the commissioners. Incorporated all regulatory and licensing functions.
12 June 1961:	United States Supreme Court, in a seven-to-two vote, upheld the AEC in the PRDC case.
20 September 1961:	President Kennedy approved Federal Radiation Council's proposal to change guidelines for population exposure to strontium 89, strontium 90, iodine 131, and radium 226. AEC subsequently modified its regulations.
8 February 1962:	State of Kentucky became first to enter state-agreements program under the 1959 amendment.
1 June 1962:	AEC published revised reactor-site criteria effective 30 June 1962. Federal Radiation Council released report, "Health Implications of Fallout from Nuclear Weapons Testing through 1961."
29 August 1962:	Amendment to the 1954 Atomic Energy Act created Atomic Safety and Licensing Boards to hold hearings in reactor-licensing cases.
20 November 1962:	AEC issued "Civilian Nuclear Power—A Report to the President."
5 August 1963:	Limited Test Ban Treaty signed by the United States, Great Britain, and the Soviet Union. Banned nuclear tests in the oceans, in the atmosphere, and in outer space.

NOTES

For a detailed explanation of the primary source materials cited in the notes, see the Select Bibliographic Essay. Citations in the form "Lewis L. Strauss to Dwight D. Eisenhower, 18 Mar. 1955" refer to correspondence and memoranda.

I. TOWARD THE PEACEFUL ATOM

1. Jack G. Shaheen, ed., *Nuclear War Films* (Carbondale: Southern Illinois University Press, 1978) pp. 3–10; John Hersey, "Hiroshima," *New Yorker*, 31 Aug. 1946, pp. 15–26; John Hersey, *Hiroshima* (New York: Alfred A. Knopf, 1946); David V. Bradley, "No Place to Hide," *Atlantic Monthly*, Oct. 1948, pp. 25–32; Nov. 1948, pp. 28–34; Dec. 1948, pp. 65–70; David V. Bradley, *No Place to Hide* (Boston: Little, Brown and Co., 1948).

2. *Congressional Record*, 79th Cong., 2d sess., 1946, p. 6094; U.S. Senate, Special Committee on Atomic Energy, *Hearings on Atomic Energy Pursuant to S. Res. 179*, 79th Cong., 1st sess., 1945, p. 339; "For the Future," *Newsweek*, 20 Aug. 1945, pp. 59–60.

3. Atomic Energy Act of 1946 (Public Law 585, 79th Cong.), *United States Statutes at Large* 60:755 (chap. 724); all documents pertaining to the 1946 act are compiled in *Legislative History of the Atomic Energy Act of 1946*, comp. James D. Nuse, 3 vols. (Washington: U.S. Atomic Energy Commission, 1965). The best overall account is Richard G. Hewlett and Oscar E. Anderson, Jr., *A History of the United States Atomic Energy Commission*, vol. 1, *The New World, 1939–1946* (University Park: Pennsylvania State University Press, 1962), chaps. 13 and 14. See also Byron S. Miller, "A Law Is Passed: The Atomic Energy Act of 1946," *University of Chicago Law Review* 15 (Summer 1948), 799–821, and James R. Newman and Byron S. Miller, *The Control of Atomic Energy: A Study of Its Social, Economic, and Political Implications* (New York: Whittlesey House, 1948).

4. Richard G. Hewlett and Francis Duncan, *A History of the United States Atomic Energy Commission*, vol. 2, *Atomic Shield, 1947–1952* (University Park: Pennsylvania State University Press, 1969), chaps. 1–3.

5. Atomic Energy Act of 1946 § 2; Hewlett and Anderson, *New World*, p. 511.

6. U.S. Congress, Joint Committee on Atomic Energy (JCAE), *Hearings on the Confirmation of the Atomic Energy Commission and the General Manager*, 80th Cong., 1st sess., 1947.

7. Lewis L. Strauss, *Men and Decisions* (Garden City, N.Y.: Doubleday and Co., 1962), pp. 1–230; Hewlett and Duncan, *Atomic Shield*, pp. 130–131, 380–409; Warren Unna, "Dissension in the AEC," *Atlantic Monthly*, May 1957, pp. 36–41. The 1946 law established the General Advisory Committee, composed of nine civilian members appointed by the president to give assistance to the agency on scientific and technical matters. The GAC significantly influenced Commission policy down to the 1960s.

8. Hewlett and Anderson, *New World*, pp. 638–641.

9. Details of the transition period are discussed fully in Hewlett and Anderson, *New World*, pp. 620–655. A brief overview is in Corbin Allardice and Edward Trapnell, *The Atomic Energy Commission* (New York: Praeger Publishers, 1974), pp. 33–35.

10. Hewlett and Anderson, *New World*, pp. 640–641, 649; Richard G. Hewlett, "Nuclear Power in the Public Interest: The Atomic Energy Act of 1954," unpublished paper presented at the Ninety-second Annual Meeting of the American Historical Association, Dec. 1977, pp. 6–8; Richard A. Tybout, *Government Contracting in Atomic Energy* (Ann Arbor: University of Michigan Press, 1956), pp. 51–87; Harold Orlans, *Contracting for Atoms* (Washington: Brookings Institution, 1967), pp. 211–212.

11. Atomic Energy Act of 1946 § 2(a)(4).

12. Hewlett and Duncan, *Atomic Shield*, pp. 20–21, 42.

13. Richard O. Niehoff, "Organization and Administration of the United States Atomic Energy Commission," *Public Administration Review* 8 (Spring 1948), 91–102.

14. Ibid., pp. 99–100; Allardice and Trapnell, *Atomic Energy Commission*, p. 64.

15. Niehoff, "Organization and Administration," pp. 94–98.

16. Hewlett and Anderson, *New World*, pp. 115–141, 624–625; Allardice and Trapnell, *Atomic Energy Commission*, pp. 16–17; Richard G. Hewlett and Francis Duncan, *Nuclear Navy, 1946–1962* (Chicago: University of Chicago Press, 1974), pp. 29, 35; Hewlett and Duncan, *Atomic Shield*, pp. 105–106, 120.

17. Hewlett and Anderson, *New World*, pp. 212–226, 302–310, 629; Allardice and Trapnell, *Atomic Energy Commission*, pp. 16–17.

18. Hewlett and Anderson, *New World*, pp. 227–254, 310–316, 374–376, 625, 626, 631–633; Allardice and Trapnell, *Atomic Energy Commission*, pp. 17–18.

19. Hewlett and Anderson, *New World*, pp. 634, 636, 645; Hewlett and Duncan, *Atomic Shield*, pp. 185–186, 417–419, 210–211, 495–496; Allardice and Trapnell, *Atomic Energy Commission*, pp. 18–19.

20. Hewlett and Duncan, *Atomic Shield*, p. 317–318, 224–225; Allardice and Trapnell, *Atomic Energy Commission*, p. 20.

21. Hewlett and Duncan, *Atomic Shield*, pp. 430–431, 531–532, 586; Allardice and Trapnell, *Atomic Energy Commission*, pp. 17, 20.

22. *Confidential Committee Print*, no. 4, 27 Mar. 1946, in *Legislative History of the Atomic Energy Act of 1946*; JCAE, committee print, *Current Membership of the Joint Committee on Atomic Energy*, 94th Cong., 2d sess., p. 3 (hereafter cited as JCAE print, *Current Membership*).

23. *Confidential Committee Print*, no. 4, 27 Mar. 1946.

24. JCAE print, *Current Membership*, pp. 3–5; Harold P. Green and Alan Rosenthal, *Government of the Atom* (New York: Atherton Press, 1963), pp. 1–20.

25. Hewlett and Anderson, *New World*, p. 627; John F. Hogerton, "The Arrival of Nuclear Power," *Scientific American*, Feb. 1968, p. 21; Atomic Energy Act of 1946 § 1.

26. Hewlett and Duncan, *Atomic Shield*, pp. 100–101; Frank G. Dawson, *Nuclear Power, Development and Management of a Technology* (Seattle: University of Washington Press, 1976), pp. 31–32.

27. In reactor technology the terms "primary coolant" and "secondary coolant" are commonly used. The first refers to the fluid that cools the reactor core; the second refers to the working fluid (usually water) used in converting the heat (which is absorbed from the primary coolant through a heat exchanger) to electricity. A third term, "intermediate coolant," refers to the use of a heat-exchange medium that is interposed between the primary and secondary coolants, as in sodium-cooled reactors.

28. Hewlett and Duncan, *Atomic Shield*, pp. 29–30.

29. Ibid., pp. 195–200.

30. Ibid., pp. 204–216; Dawson, *Nuclear Power*, pp. 38–40.

31. David E. Lilienthal, speech to the Economic Club, Detroit, 6 Oct. 1947, Development of Atomic Power File, Atomic Energy Commission Records, Department of Energy, Germantown, Maryland; AEC press release, 6 Oct. 1947, Atomic Energy Commission Records, Nuclear Regulatory Commission, Washington, D.C. When the AEC was disbanded in 1975, the records of the agency were divided functionally between its two successor agencies: the Nuclear Regulatory Commission and the Energy Research and Development Administration; the latter subsequently became part of the Department of Energy. AEC records that are located in the Department of Energy are designated AEC/DOE and those located in the Nuclear Regulatory Commission are designated AEC/NRC.

32. Report of Industrial Advisory Group, 15 Dec. 1948, Development of Atomic Power File, AEC/DOE.

33. Hewlett and Duncan, *Atomic Shield*, pp. 435–436.

34. David E. Lilienthal, "Free the Atom," *Collier's*, 17 June 1950, pp. 13–14.

35. Charles A. Thomas, proposal for industrial development of atomic power, enclosure, Thomas to Sumner Pike, 20 June 1950, J. W. Parker to Gordon Dean, 11 Dec. 1950, Development of Atomic Power File, Commission Meeting (CM) 510 (20 Dec. 1950), AEC/DOE; Hewlett and Duncan, *Atomic Shield*, pp. 437–438.

36. AEC press release, 28 Jan. 1951, AEC/NRC.

37. Report of Commonwealth Edison, 23 Jan. 1952; report of Bechtel/ Pacific Gas and Electric, 4 Jan. 1952, AEC/DOE; AEC press release, 6 Apr. 1952, AEC/NRC.

38. Monsanto Chemical Company/Union Electric Company, "Plutonium-Power Reactor Feasibility Study"; Dow Chemical Company/Detroit Edison Company, "Study of Materials and Power Producing Reactors"; Commonwealth Edison Company/Public Service Company, "Report on Power Generation Using Nuclear Energy"; Pacific Gas and Electric Company/Bechtel Corporation, "Industrial Reactor Study," Development of Atomic Power File, AEC/DOE.

39. JCAE, committee print, *Atomic Power and Private Enterprise*, 82d Cong., 2d sess., 1952.

40. JCAE, *Hearings on Atomic Power Development and Private Enterprise*, 83d Cong., 1st sess., 1953, pp. 5–13, 562–567, 570, 571.

41. JCAE, *Hearings on Atomic Power Development*, pp. 5–13, 562–567; Richard G. Hewlett and Jack M. Holl, "Atoms for Peace and War," draft, chap. 2, Department of Energy History Division. This volume will cover the AEC's military and industrial development activities during the Eisenhower administration. We are grateful to Messrs. Hewlett and Holl for allowing us to read draft chapters of this manuscript.

42. Dawson, *Nuclear Power*, pp. 42–43; Robert Perry et al., *Development and Commercialization of the Light Water Reactor, 1946–1976* (Santa Monica, Calif.: Rand Corporation, 1977), pp. 6–7. The best account of the Shippingport project is in Hewlett and Duncan, *Nuclear Navy, 1946–1962*, pp. 228–254.

43. Craufurd D. Goodwin, "The Truman Administration: Toward a National Energy Policy," in *Energy Policy in Perspective*, ed. Craufurd D. Goodwin (Washington: Brookings Institution, 1981), pp. 53–56, 199; JCAE, *Hearings on Atomic Power Development*, pp. 9, 167, 248, 347, 360–361, 563.

44. JCAE, *Hearings on Atomic Power Development*, pp. 6, 58, 63–65, 167, 575, 617; Thomas E. Murray, speech, "Far More Important Than War," 22 Oct. 1953, Walter Reuther Papers, Archives of Labor History and Urban Affairs, Wayne State University, Detroit; Chet Holifield, speech to National Industrial Conference Board, 29 Oct. 1953, Box 79, Chet Holifield Papers, University of Southern California, Los Angeles.

45. JCAE, *Hearings on Atomic Power Development*, p. 4; Robert A. Divine, *Eisenhower and the Cold War* (New York: Oxford University Press, 1981), pp. 110–114; Thomas F. Soapes, "A Cold Warrior Seeks Peace: Eisenhower's Strategy for Nuclear Disarmament," *Diplomatic History* 4 (Winter 1980), 57–71.

46. *The Public Papers of Dwight D. Eisenhower, 1953* (Washington: Government Printing Office, 1960), pp. 813–822; Soapes, "Cold Warrior Seeks Peace," p. 63.

47. *Congressional Record*, 83d Cong., 2d sess., 1954, pp. 1921–1924.

48. AEC 615/8 (11 May 1953), AEC 615/9 (21 May 1953), CM 930 (21 Oct. 1953),

AEC/DOE; AEC 615/22 (14 Oct. 1953), AEC/NRC; Hewlett and Holl, "Atoms for Peace and War," draft, chap. 5, Department of Energy History Division.

49. Allardice and Trapnell, *Atomic Energy Commission*, p. 44; *Congressional Record*, 83d Cong., 2d sess., 1954, pp. 11655–11656; Green and Rosenthal, *Government of the Atom*, pp. 124–125; Hewlett and Holl, "Atoms for Peace and War," draft, chap. 5, DOE History Division.

50. JCAE, transcripts of hearings, AEC/DOE; JCAE, *Hearings on S. 3323 and H.R. 8862 to Amend the Atomic Energy Act of 1946*, 83d Cong., 2d sess., 1954. All public documents pertaining to the 1954 act are compiled in *Legislative History of the Atomic Energy Act of 1954, Public Law 703, 83rd Congress*, comp. Madeleine W. Losee, 3 vols. (Washington: U.S. Atomic Energy Commission, 1955).

51. Unna, "Dissension in the AEC," pp. 36–41; Richard G. Hewlett, "Thomas Edward Murray," in *Dictionary of American Biography, Supplement Seven, 1961–1965*, ed. John A. Garraty (New York: Charles Scribner's Sons, 1981), pp. 564–565.

52. JCAE, transcript of hearing, 3 May 1954, pp. 84–85, AEC/DOE.

53. Ibid., pp. 89–92, 105–120; JCAE, *Hearings on S. 3323*, 83d Cong., 2d sess., 1954, pp. 805–829; H.R. 9757, "A Bill to Amend the Atomic Energy Act of 1946," 83d Cong., 2d sess., 1954.

54. JCAE, transcript of hearing, 4 May 1954, AEC/DOE, pp. 315–316, 352–374; *Hearings on S. 3323*, 83d Cong., 2d sess., 1954, pp. 25–46, 58–60, 225–226, 306–318, 326–329, 375–378; H.R. 9757, S. 3690, "A Bill to Amend the Atomic Energy Act of 1946," 83d Cong., 2d sess., 1954.

55. JCAE, transcript of hearing, 4 May 1954, AEC/DOE, pp. 316, 375–378; *Hearings on S. 3323*, 83d Cong., 2d sess., 1954, pp. 61, 92, 172, 177, 218, 221, 271–274, 306–312, 334–337, 401, 441, 467; H.R. 9757, S. 3690, 83d Cong., 2d sess., 1954.

56. *Congressional Record*, 83d Cong., 2d sess., 1954, p. 5236; JCAE, *Hearings on S. 3323*, 83d Cong., 2d sess., 1954, pp. 75–77.

57. JCAE, *Hearings on S. 3323*, pp. 92, 335.

58. *Congressional Record*, 83d Cong., 2d sess., 1954, pp. 1921–1924.

59. Atomic Energy Act of 1954, chaps. 1, 6, 7, 8, 10.

60. U.S. Congress, S. Rept. 1699, 83d Cong., 2d sess., 1954, p. 3; H. Rept. 2181, 83d Cong., 2d sess., 1954, p. 3; S. Rept. 1211, 79th Cong., 2d sess., 1946, p. 28; Atomic Energy Act of 1946 § 12(a)(2); Atomic Energy Act of 1954 § 161b.

61. H.R. 9757, 30 June 1954; S. 3690, 30 June 1954, *Congressional Record*, 83d Cong., 2d sess., 1954, pp. 10960–10972, 14603–14606, 14852–14873; *United States Statutes at Large* 68:919 (chap. 1073). Codified in Title 42, *United States Code* §§ 2011 ff.

II. THE PRINCIPLES OF RADIATION PROTECTION

1. Jack Schubert and Ralph E. Lapp, *Radiation: What It Is and How It Affects You* (New York: Viking Press, 1957), pp. 12–20; Lawrence Badash, *Radioactivity in America: Growth and Decay of a Science* (Baltimore: Johns Hopkins University Press, 1979), pp. 9–32.

2. Schubert and Lapp, *Radiation*, pp. 12–20; Isaac Asimov and Theodosius Dobzhansky, *The Genetic Effects of Radiation* (Washington: U.S. Atomic Energy Commission, 1966); *Atomic Energy Basics* (Washington: U.S. Atomic Energy Commission, 1970); Robert S. Stone, "The Concept of a Maximum Permissible Exposure," *Radiology* 58 (May 1952), 639–660.

3. Schubert and Lapp, *Radiation*, p. 18; Lauriston S. Taylor, *Organization for Radiation Protection: The Operations of the ICRP and NCRP, 1928–1974* (Springfield, Va.: National Technical Information Service, 1979), pp. 1–001 to 4–001; Lauriston S. Taylor, *Radiation Protection Standards* (Cleveland: CRC Press, 1971), pp. 9–20; Daniel Paul Serwer, "The Rise of Radiation Protection: Science, Medicine, and Technology in Society, 1896–1935" (Ph.D. diss., Princeton University, 1977), pp. viii–ix, 38–44, 68–70, 174–181.

4. Taylor, *Organization for Radiation Protection*, pp. 4–012 to 4–025; Taylor, *Radiation Protection Standards*, pp. 13–19. In specific terms, the roentgen unit was a measure of "the quantity of gamma or x-rays required to produce ions carrying 1 electrostatic unit of electricity in 1 cubic centimeter of dry air under standard conditions." It did not measure other forms of radiation, such as alpha or beta particles. Although often used to measure the amount of radiation absorbed by human tissue, it was not technically applicable for that purpose. John F. Hoerton, *The Atomic Energy Deskbook* (New York: Reinhold Publishing Corp., 1963), pp. 430, 486.

5. Taylor, *Organization for Radiation Protection*, pp. 4–012 to 4–021; Taylor, *Radiation Protection Standards*, pp. 9–19; Stone, "Concept of a Maximum Permissible Exposure," p. 642; Lauriston S. Taylor, "The Development of Radiation Protection Standards (1925–1940)," *Health Physics* 41 (Aug. 1981), 227–232.

6. Schubert and Lapp, *Radiation*, pp. 108–116; Daniel Lang, "A Most Valuable Accident," *New Yorker*, 2 May 1959, pp. 49–64; Robley D. Evans, "Inception of Standards for Internal Emitters, Radon and Radium," *Health Physics* 41 (Sept. 1981), 437–448; Taylor, *Radiation Protection Standards*, pp. 19–20.

7. Ronald L. Kathren, "Historical Development of Radiation Measurement and Protection" in *CRC Handbook of Radiation Measurement and Protection*, ed. Allen Brodsky, Section A, vol. 1 (West Palm Beach, Fla.: CRC Press, 1978), pp. 43–50; T. J. Thompson, "Accidents and Destructive Tests," in *The Technology of Nuclear Reactor Safety: Reactor Physics and Control*, ed. T. J. Thompson and J. G. Beckerley, 2 vols. (Cambridge: MIT Press, 1964, 1973), 1:609–610; Barton C. Hacker, "Elements of Controversy: A History of Radiation Safety in the

Nuclear Weapons Test Program," draft, chaps. 1–2. We are grateful to Dr. Hacker for allowing us to read his material in draft form.

8. Taylor, *Organization for Radiation Protection*, pp. 7–001 to 7–007; Taylor, *Radiation Protection Standards*, pp. 23–24.

9. Taylor, *Organization for Radiation Protection*, pp. 7–008 to 7–010, 7–016, 7–032.

10. Stone, "Concept of Maximum Permissible Exposure," pp. 642–644; Schubert and Lapp, *Radiation*, chap. 9; Taylor, *Radiation Protection Standards*, pp. 22, 35; National Committee on Radiation Protection, *Permissible Dose from External Sources of Ionizing Radiation*, National Bureau of Standards, Handbook 59 (Washington, 1954), pp. 1–2, 17–19, 26–27.

11. Taylor, *Radiation Protection Standards*, pp. 24–25; NCRP, *Permissible Dose from External Sources*, pp. 61–73.

12. Taylor, *Radiation Protection Standards*, pp. 28–30; Taylor, *Organization for Radiation Protection*, pp. 7–001, 7–123; Schubert and Lapp, *Radiation*, pp. 120–122; National Committee on Radiation Protection, *Maximum Permissible Amounts of Radioisotopes in the Human Body and Maximum Permissible Concentrations in Air and Water*, National Bureau of Standards, Handbook 52 (Washington, 1953).

13. Taylor, *Organization for Radiation Protection*, pp. 7–087, 7–235; Taylor, *Radiation Protection Standards*, pp. 37–40; NCRP, *Permissible Dose from External Sources*, pp. 55–57.

14. Schubert and Lapp, *Radiation*, pp. 88–107, 112, 154–180; "Now There's a Warning about Too Much X Ray," *U.S. News and World Report*, 22 June 1956, pp. 63–64; Jack G. Shaheen, ed., *Nuclear War Films* (Carbondale: Southern Illinois University Press, 1978), pp. 3–25.

15. AEC 604/3 (4 Nov. 1953), AEC/DOE; U.S. Congress, House Committee on Interstate and Foreign Commerce, *The Forgotten Guinea Pigs: A Report of Health Effects of Low-Level Radiation Sustained as a Result of the Nuclear Weapons Testing Program Conducted by the United States Government*, 96th Cong., 2d sess., 1980, pp. 3–13; *New York Times*, 20 May 1953, p. 8, 25 May 1953, p. 21, 17 Jan. 1954, p. 46; *Las Vegas Sun*, 20 May 1953, p. 1.

16. Robert A. Divine, *Blowing on the Wind: The Nuclear Test Ban Debate, 1954–1960* (New York: Oxford University Press, 1978), pp. 1–35; Schubert and Lapp, *Radiation*, pp. 218–228; "Where Now, World?" *Newsweek*, 29 Mar. 1954, 19–23.

17. Howard Brown to Roy Snapp, 22 Oct. 1953, Box 3363, Organization and Management–11 (Project Gabriel 1953), Division of Biology and Medicine Files, AEC/DOE; "A Report by the United States Atomic Energy Commission on the Effects of High-Yield Nuclear Explosions," 15 Feb. 1955 (Fallout File), Lewis L. Strauss Papers, Herbert Hoover Library, West Branch, Iowa.

18. "Report . . . on the Effects of High-Yield Nuclear Explosions," memoranda for the files, 10 Dec. 1954, 7 Feb. 1955 (Fallout File), Strauss Papers; "How Fatal Is the Fall-Out?" *Time*, 22 Nov. 1954, pp. 79–81; Lewis L. Strauss to Dwight D.

Eisenhower, 10 Dec. 1954, Administrative Series, Ann Whitman File, Dwight D. Eisenhower Papers, Dwight D. Eisenhower Library, Abilene, Kansas; Divine, *Blowing on the Wind,* pp. 36–38.

19. Michael Straight, "The Ten-Month Silence," *New Republic,* 7 Mar. 1955, pp. 8–11; *Chicago Sun-Times,* 16–20 Jan. 1955; Divine, *Blowing on the Wind,* pp. 38–47, 65.

20. Lewis L. Strauss to Dwight D. Eisenhower, 18 Mar. 1955, Administrative Series, Ann Whitman Files, Eisenhower Papers; Strauss to Curtis A. Nelson, 28 Mar. 1959 (Fallout File), Strauss Papers; W. F. Libby to M. Stanley Livingston, 9 May 1955 (Sunshine—Miscellaneous), Office Files of W. F. Libby, Linus Pauling to W. F. Libby, 6 May 1955, AEC 604/8 (12 May 1955), CM 1065 (14 Mar. 1955), AEC/DOE; National Academy of Sciences press release, 8 Apr. 1955, General Correspondence (Radiation—General), Joint Committee on Atomic Energy Papers, Record Group 128 (Records of the Joint Committees of Congress), National Archives, Washington, D.C.; *The Biological Effects of Atomic Radiation: A Report to the Public* (Washington: National Academy of Sciences–National Research Council, 1956), pp. 33–40; Lewis L. Strauss, *Men and Decisions* (Garden City, N.Y.: Doubleday and Co., 1962), pp. 414–415; Divine, *Blowing on the Wind,* pp. 47–57.

21. *The Biological Effects of Atomic Radiation: A Report to the Public,* pp. 2–6, 25; *The Biological Effects of Atomic Radiation: Summary Reports* (Washington: National Academy of Sciences–National Research Council, 1956), pp. 68–70.

22. *Report to the Public,* pp. 14–20; *Summary Reports,* pp. 3–30.

23. *Report to the Public,* pp. 8, 30–32; *Summary Reports,* pp. 30, 60, 101–108.

24. *Report to the Public,* pp. 2, 26–27, 32; *Summary Reports,* p. 34.

25. Charles L. Dunham to W. F. Libby, 7 June 1956 (National Academy of Sciences Correspondence), Libby Office Files, AEC 604/20 (18 July 1956), 604/21 (7 Aug. 1956), AEC/DOE; C. Auerbach, "Biological Hazards of Nuclear and Other Radiations," *Nature* 178 (1 Sept. 1956), 453–454; "Now There's a Warning about Too Much X Ray," *U.S. News and World Report,* p. 70.

26. H. J. Muller, "Race Poisoning by Radiation," *Saturday Review,* 9 June 1956, pp. 9–11, 37–39; Robert W. Miller, "Safeguarding Children from Radiation Risks," *Children* 3 (Nov.-Dec. 1956), 203–207; "Atomic Radiation: The r's Are Coming," *Time,* 25 June 1956, pp. 64–65; Frank Cotter to Mr. Price, 14 June 1956, General Correspondence (Fallout), JCAE Papers; *Washington Post,* 14 June 1956, p. 14; *New York Times,* 14 June 1956, p. 32; *Detroit News,* 14 June 1956, p. 38; *Chicago Sun-Times,* 13 June 1956, p. 4; *Las Vegas Sun,* 13 June 1956, p. 1; *Seattle Post-Intelligencer,* 13 June 1956, p. 1; "The Truth about the X-ray Scare," *This Week,* 23 Feb. 1958, pp. 8–9.

27. W. F. Libby to Otis Lee Wiese, 20 Dec. 1956 (Sunshine—Public Information Program), Libby Office Files, CM 1256 (19 Dec. 1956), AEC/DOE; Morse Salisbury to Everett Holles, 31 Oct. 1956 (Fallout File), Strauss Papers; Pare Lorentz, "The Fight for Survival," *McCall's,* Jan. 1957, pp. 29, 73–74.

28. Divine, *Blowing on the Wind,* pp. 84–112.

29. Linus Pauling to Dwight D. Eisenhower, 4 June 1957, Official File 108-A; Lewis Strauss to Dwight D. Eisenhower, 23 July 1957, Administrative Series, Ann Whitman File, Eisenhower Papers; "Memo as provided to President for his press conference on 6–5–57," n.d. (Eisenhower, Dwight D. File), Strauss Papers; Hazel Gaudet Erskine, "The Polls: Atomic Weapons and Nuclear Energy," *Public Opinion Quarterly* 27 (Summer 1963), 163, 188; Eugene J. Rosi, "Mass and Attentive Opinion on Nuclear Weapons Tests and Fallout, 1954–1963," *Public Opinion Quarterly* 29 (Summer 1965), 208–297; Divine, *Blowing on the Wind*, pp. 113–142.

30. C. L. Dunham to K. E. Fields, 8 Apr. 1957, Medicine, Health, and Safety-3, vol. 3–Radiation, AEC/DOE; Chet Holifield to Carl T. Durham, 13 May 1957, File 1425, Carl T. Durham Papers, Southern Historical Collection, University of North Carolina Library, Chapel Hill; memorandum for the files, 31 July 1956 (Holifield, Chet File), Strauss Papers; Warren Unna, "Holifield of California," *Atlantic Monthly*, Apr. 1960, pp. 79–82; *New York Times*, 24 Aug. 1959, p. 14; *Current Biography Yearbook: 1955* (New York: H. W. Wilson Co., 1955), pp. 287–289.

31. Joint Committee on Atomic Energy, *Hearings on the Nature of Radioactive Fallout and Its Effects on Man*, 85th Cong., 1st sess., 1957, pp. 691, 955–1008.

32. Ibid., pp. 141–170, 1211–1217, 1227–1241, 1392.

33. Ibid., pp. 578, 1038–1040, 1046, 1057, 1086, 1241, 1323.

34. Ibid., pp. 1243–1249, 1279; Divine, *Blowing on the Wind*, p. 38.

35. JCAE, *Hearings on Fallout*, 1957, pp. 1045–1047, 1287–1300.

36. "The Philosophers' Stone," *Time*, 15 Aug. 1955, pp. 46–50; *Current Biography Yearbook: 1954* (New York: H. W. Wilson Co., 1954), pp. 406–407; CM 1062 (23 Feb. 1955), AEC/DOE.

37. JCAE, *Hearings on Fallout*, 1957, pp. 1208–1210, 1222–1227, 1232–1235, 1315–1316, 1373–1374.

38. Joint Committee on Atomic Energy, *Hearings on Fallout from Nuclear Weapons Tests*, 86th Cong., 1st sess., 1959, p. 15; Lewis Strauss to K. E. Fields, 10 July 1957 (Fields, Gen. Kenneth E. File), Strauss Papers; Charles O. Porter et al. to Dwight D. Eisenhower, 7 June 1957, Official File 108-A, George H. Clark to Dwight D. Eisenhower, 6 Aug. 1957, Thomas P. Lowry to Dwight D. Eisenhower, 21 Oct. 1957, Official File 108, Eisenhower Papers; *Congressional Record*, 85th Cong., 1st sess., 1957, p. A4354; *New York Times*, 17 June 1957, p. 22.

39. Chet Holifield, "Who Should Judge the Atom?" *Saturday Review*, 3 Aug. 1957, pp. 34–37; Divine, *Blowing on the Wind*, pp. 143–169.

40. JCAE, *Hearings on Fallout*, 1957, pp. 805–809, 852; Taylor, *Radiation Protection Standards*, pp. 47–49.

41. JCAE, *Hearings on Fallout*, 1957, pp. 813–819, 827–831; and *Hearings on Employee Radiation Hazards and Workmen's Compensation*, 86th Cong., 1st sess., 1959, pp. 37–40; Taylor, *Radiation Protection Standards*, pp. 49–50; Taylor, *Organization for Radiation Protection*, p. 8–061. For additional details see chap. 11.

42. JCAE, *Hearings on Fallout*, 1957, pp. 778–794, 807–810, 1062; and *Hearings*

on *Employee Radiation Hazards*, 1959, p. 42; Taylor, *Radiation Protection Standards*, pp. 47–50; Taylor, *Organization for Radiation Protection*, pp. 8–068 to 8–072, 8–079, 8–082; *Washington Post*, 2 June 1956, p. 1.

43. *Eighth Semiannual Report of the Atomic Energy Commission*, July 1950, pp. 10–19; AEC 841 (23 June 1955), AEC/DOE.

44. AEC 841, 841/3 (28 Nov. 1956), AEC/DOE; AEC 985 (9 Oct. 1957), AEC-R 8 (17 Dec. 1956), AEC-R 8/4 (19 Mar. 1959), AEC-R 8/7 (13 July 1960), AEC/NRC. See also chap. 11.

45. Lewis L. Strauss to Willard F. Libby, 4 June 1956, Libby to Strauss, 6 June 1956 (National Academy of Sciences Correspondence), Libby Office Files, AEC/DOE.

46. JCAE, *Hearings on Fallout*, 1957, p. 19.

47. See, for example, Holifield, "Who Should Judge the Atom?" p. 37; *New York Times*, 2 Sept. 1957, p. 2.

III. THE STRUCTURE OF ATOMIC REGULATION

1. Atomic Energy Act of 1954 (Public Law 703, 83d Cong.), *United States Statutes at Large* 68:919 (chap. 1073). The government owned all special nuclear material until 1964 when the act was amended to allow private ownership.

2. Atomic Energy Act of 1954 §§ 2, 3, 11, 53, 81, 103, 104, 161.

3. CM 1085 (8 June 1955), Joint Committee on Atomic Energy, transcript of hearing, 3 May 1954, pp. 135–136, AEC/DOE.

4. Richard G. Hewlett and Francis Duncan, *A History of the United States Atomic Energy Commission*, vol. 2, *Atomic Shield, 1947–1952* (University Park: Pennsylvania State University Press, 1969), pp. 186–187; "The Evolving Role of the Advisory Committee on Reactor Safeguards," 11 Mar. 1974, Advisory Committee on Reactor Safeguards (ACRS) File, AEC/NRC; Edward Teller and Allen Brown, *The Legacy of Hiroshima* (Westport, Conn.: Greenwood Press, 1975), p. 102; CM 222 (8 Dec. 1948), CM 225 (15 Dec. 1948), CM 352 (11 Jan. 1950), AEC/DOE. Early members of the Safeguard Committee included John A. Wheeler, physicist at Princeton; Joseph W. Kennedy, chemist at Washington University in St. Louis; Manson Benedict, chemical engineer with Hydrocarbon Research, Inc.; Benjamin Holzman, meteorologist and head of geophysical sciences in the Air Force Office of Research and Development; and Abel Wolman, professor of sanitary engineering at Johns Hopkins. See AEC report, WASH-3 (rev.), "Summary Report of Reactor Safeguard Committee," 31 Mar. 1950, AEC/NRC.

5. CM 499 (27 Nov. 1950), CM 855 (25 Apr. 1953), AEC 661 (2 July 1953), CM 844 (7 July 1953), report to AEC of 17th meeting of the Reactor Safeguard Committee, 27 Aug. 1952, AEC/DOE; AEC press release, 9 Aug. 1953, "The Evolving Role of the Advisory Committee on Reactor Safeguards," AEC/NRC.

6. Teller and Brown, *The Legacy of Hiroshima*, p. 104.

7. Ibid.; Edward Teller, *Energy From Heaven and Earth* (San Francisco: W. H.

Freeman and Co., 1979), p. 158. Also see AEC report, WASH-3 (rev.), AEC/NRC.

8. Bulletin GM-RVD-2, "Reactor Safety Determination," 1 Oct. 1951; revised as Appendix A to AEC 661, AEC/NRC.

9. Ibid.

10. Ibid.

11. Ibid.

12. Joint Committee on Atomic Energy, *Hearings on Development, Growth and State of the Atomic Energy Industry*, 84th Cong., 1st sess., 1955 (hereafter called JCAE, *"202" Hearings*).

13. AEC 661/4 (15 Apr. 1955), AEC/NRC.

14. CM 1067 (18 Apr. 1955), AEC/DOE.

15. AEC 661/4, AEC/NRC.

16. CM 1067, AEC/DOE.

17. AEC 804/3 (26 Sept. 1955), AEC/NRC.

18. AEC 23/14 (13 Sept. 1954), AEC/NRC; Hewlett and Duncan, *Atomic Shield*, pp. 252–253.

19. AEC press releases, 22 Oct. 1954, 30 Mar. 1955, AEC/NRC. Price headed the AEC regulatory function until his retirement in 1971.

20. AEC 804 (16 Mar. 1955), CM 1068 (22 Mar. 1955), CM 1085 (8 June 1955), CM 1089 (14 June 1955), AEC/DOE; AEC 804/1 (18 May 1955), AEC/NRC.

21. AEC 804/1, AEC/NRC; JCAE, *"202" Hearings*, 84th Cong., 1st sess., 1955.

22. AEC 804/1, AEC/NRC.

23. Ibid.; CM 1085, AEC/DOE.

24. Ibid.

25. AEC 804/1, AEC/NRC.

26. AEC Organization Chart, Division of Civilian Application, 1 Jan. 1956, AEC/NRC.

27. AEC Announcement 382, 23 Nov. 1955, Announcement 383, 23 Nov. 1955, AEC Organization Chart, Division of Civilian Application, 1 Dec. 1956, AEC/DOE; AEC press release, 11 July 1954, AEC/NRC.

28. Memorandum, K. E. Fields to managers of operations, 14 Oct. 1955, Organization and Management–2 (Civilian Application), AEC/DOE; AEC press release, 17 June 1955, AEC/NRC.

29. Minutes of agenda planning session, 30 Mar. 1956, Lewis Strauss to Carroll A. Hochwalt, 25 July 1956, AEC Announcement 474, 31 July 1956, AEC/DOE.

30. Minutes of agenda planning session, 30 Mar. 1956, AEC/DOE; AEC press releases, 3 Apr. 1956, 20 Oct. 1955, AEC/NRC.

31. AEC 23/14, AEC/NRC; CM 1024 (14 Sept. 1954), AEC/DOE.

32. Atomic Energy Act of 1954 § 104; JCAE, *"202" Hearings*, 84th Cong., 1st sess., 1955, pp. 55–59, 84th Cong., 2d sess., 1956, p. 6

33. Atomic Energy Act of 1954 §§ 102, 103. AEC to JCAE, 18 Nov. 1955, printed

in JCAE, committee print, *Background Material for the Report of the Panel on the Impact of the Peaceful Uses of Atomic Energy*, 84th Cong., 2d sess., 1956, pp. 645–646; JCAE, *"202" Hearings*, 84th Cong., 2d sess., 1956, p. 394.

34. Atomic Energy Act of 1954 § 104; Joint Committee on Atomic Energy, transcript of hearing, 4 May 1954, pp. 318–319, AEC/DOE.

35. Atomic Energy Act of 1954 §§ 103, 104, 182.

36. Ibid. § 185. For an early discussion on the health and safety aspects of the 1954 law, see Harold P. Green, "The Law of Reactor Safety," *Vanderbilt Law Review* 12 (Dec. 1958), 115–144.

37. CM 1061 (23 Feb. 1955), AEC/DOE.

38. AEC 23/15 (13 Dec. 1954), AEC/NRC; CM 1044 (21 Dec. 1954), AEC/DOE.

39. AEC 23/15, AEC/NRC; memoranda, Nichols to the Commission, 7, 25 Jan., 9, 27 Feb. 1955, PFC-1, AEC/DOE. Representatives, by groups, were:

Utilities: E. Parks Baker, Seminole Electric Cooperative, Inc.; James B. Black, Pacific Gas and Electric Company; Philip A. Fleger, Duquesne Light Company; Willis Gale, Commonwealth Edison Company; George M. Gadsby, Utah Power and Light Company; Donald S. Kennedy, Oklahoma Gas and Electric Company; Charles E. Oakes, Pennsylvania Power and Light Company; Arthur Prager, Public Service Company of New Mexico; Paul J. Raver, City of Seattle Department of Lighting; Ray L. Schact, Consumers Public Power District; Herbert J. Scholz, Southern Services, Inc.; Hudson R. Searing, Consolidated Edison Company; Philip Sporn, American Gas and Electric Company; H. D. Vogel, Tennessee Valley Authority; William Webster, New England Electric System.

Vendors: Walter B. Smith, American Machine and Foundry Company; R. S. Stevenson, Allis-Chalmers Manufacturing Company; Walter Kingston, Sylvania Electric Products, Inc.; D. Raymond McNeal, Anadale Company; Francis K. McCune, General Electric Company; A. C. Monteith, Westinghouse Electric Corporation; Broderick Haskell, Combustion Engineering, Inc.; Perry T. Egbert, American Locomotive Company; J. S. Fluor, Fluor Corporation Limited; George J. Wacholz, Minnesota Mining and Manufacturing Company; G. J. Keady, Sharples Corporation; J. W. Landis, Babcock and Wilcox Company; John Cartinhour, Foster Wheeler Corporation; Frederick Hayes Warren, General Dynamics Corporation.

Chemicals Industry: Kenneth C. Towe, American Cyanamid Company; Raymond F. Evans, Diamond Alkali Company; Mark E. Putnam, Dow Chemical Company; Crawford H. Greenewalt, E. I. Du Pont de Nemours and Company; Joseph Fistere, Mallinckrodt Chemical Works; Charles A. Thomas, Monsanto Chemical Company; Kenneth Rush, Union Carbide and Carbon Corporation; J. Carlton Ward, Jr., Vitro Corporation of America; J. C. Franklin, General Analine and Film Corporation; Charles Rogers Linsay III, Linsay Chemical Company; Kenneth Aldred Spencer, Spencer Chemical Company.

Research Organizations: Clyde E. Williams, Battelle Memorial Institute; Shields

Warren, New England Deaconness Hospital; Clifford K. Beck, North Carolina State College; Bruce S. Old, Nuclear Metals, Inc.; Karl P. Cohen, Walter Kidde Nuclear Laboratories, Inc.; James H. Jensen, Iowa State College; Andrew H. Dowdy, University of California at Los Angeles; George Granger Brown, University of Michigan; John R. Menke, Nuclear Development Associates, Inc.; William M. Breazeale, Pennsylvania State University; C. P. Rhoads, Sloan Kettering Institute for Cancer Research; Elvin C. Stakman, University of Minnesota.

40. JCAE, "202" Hearings, 84th Cong., 1st sess., 1955, p. 57.

41. Ibid.

42. AEC 23/16 (22 Dec. 1954), AEC/DOE.

43. Ibid.

44. Ibid.

45. Ibid., CM 1061, AEC 23/22 (30 Mar. 1955), AEC/DOE.

46. CM 1159 (21 Dec. 1955), CM 1073 (6 Apr. 1955), AEC 23/34 (16 Dec. 1955), AEC/DOE; Harold L. Price, "The Civilian Application Program," in Proceedings of a Meeting of the Atomic Industrial Forum on Commercial and International Developments in Atomic Energy (New York: Atomic Industrial Forum, 1955); AEC 23/22, AEC press release, 18 Jan. 1956, AEC/NRC.

47. AEC 23/34, AEC/DOE; JCAE, "202" Hearings, 84th Cong., 2d sess., 1956, p. 108; Green, "The Law of Reactor Safety," p. 124 n. 37.

48. CM 1061, CM 1159, AEC 23/34, AEC/DOE.

49. AEC 23/34, AEC/DOE.

50. JCAE, Hearings on Government Indemnity for Private Licensees and AEC Contractors against Reactor Hazards, 84th Cong., 2d sess., 1956, pp. 63–64.

51. See John G. Palfrey, "Atomic Energy: A New Experiment in Government-Industry Relations," Columbia Law Review, Mar. 1956, pp. 367–392.

52. AEC press release, 10 Jan. 1955, Lewis Strauss, speech to National Association of Science Writers, 16 Sept. 1954, AEC/NRC; JCAE, "202" Hearings, 1956, pp. 45–48; Profit Perspectives in Atomic Energy: Problems and Opportunities (New York: American Management Association, 1957), pp. 175–176.

53. AEC 771/1 (17 Dec. 1954), AEC/NRC; CM 1049 (21 Dec. 1954), CM 1052 (5 Jan. 1955), AEC 777 (13 Dec. 1954), AEC/DOE.

54. Frank G. Dawson, Nuclear Power, Development and Management of a Technology (Seattle: University of Washington Press, 1976), pp. 93–98; AEC press release, 10 Jan. 1955, AEC/NRC.

55. Wendy Allen, Nuclear Reactors for Generating Electricity: U.S. Development from 1946 to 1963 (Santa Monica, Calif.: Rand Corporation, 1977), pp. 42–44; Kendall Birr, Pioneering in Industrial Research: The Story of the General Electric Research Laboratory (Washington: Public Affairs Press, 1957); George Wise, "A New Role for Professional Scientists in Industry: Industrial Research at General Electric, 1900–1916," Technology and Culture 21 (July 1980), 408–429; Richard G. Hewlett and Francis Duncan, Nuclear Navy, 1946–1962 (Chicago: University of Chicago

Press, 1974), pp. 38–40, 109–117, 272–276; "Atomic Energy: The Powerhouse," *Time*, 12 Jan. 1959, p. 75; R. B. Richards, "Boiling Water Reactors," Oct. 1959, General Correspondence (General Electric Company), Joint Committee on Atomic Energy Papers, Record Group 128 (Records of the Joint Committees of Congress), National Archives, Washington, D.C.; AEC Docket no. 50-70, Vallecitos Boiling Water Reactor, General Electric Company, AEC Docket no. 50-10, Dresden Nuclear Power Station, Unit 1, Commonwealth Edison Company, AEC/NRC.

56. Allen, *Nuclear Reactors for Generating Electricity*, pp. 39–52. See below, chaps. 5–6.

57. Philip L. Cantelon, "Engineers and Alchemists: Electricity from Nuclear Energy," draft of unpublished paper in progress, pp. 10–12; AEC Docket no. 50-3, Consolidated Edison Indian Point, AEC/NRC.

58. AEC press release, 21 Sept. 1955, AEC/NRC; Allen, *Nuclear Reactors for Generating Electricity*, pp. 54–55.

59. Harold P. Green, "The Strange Case of Nuclear Power," *Federal Bar Journal* 17 (April-June 1957), 112; Dawson, *Nuclear Power*, pp. 98–100.

60. AEC press releases, 7 Jan. 1957, 23 Aug. 1962, AEC/NRC; Green, "Strange Case of Nuclear Power," p. 118; Allen, *Nuclear Reactors for Generating Electricity*, pp. 67–74.

61. Atomic Energy Act of 1954 §§ 51, 52, 53, 57.

62. AEC 784/2 (30 Mar. 1955), AEC/NRC.

63. AEC 784 (28 Jan. 1955), CM 1060 (2 Feb. 1955), AEC/DOE.

64. AEC 784/2, AEC/NRC; CM 1061, CM 1072 (6 Apr. 1955), AEC/DOE.

65. Ibid.

66. Joint Committee on Atomic Energy, transcript of hearing, 4 May 1954, pp. 344–348, CM 1060 (11 Feb. 1955), AEC/DOE; AEC 786 (7 Feb. 1955), AEC/NRC.

67. AEC 786/1 (30 Mar. 1955), AEC/NRC; CM 1073, AEC/DOE.

68. AEC 786/2 (23 May 1955), AEC/NRC; CM 1085, AEC/DOE.

69. JCAE, committee print, *A Study of AEC Procedures and Organization in the Licensing of Reactor Facilities*, 85th Cong., 1st sess., 1957, pp. 106–107.

70. Ibid., p. 107.

71. Title 10, *Code of Federal Regulations*, part 2; "Procedures and Considerations Governing the Review of and Actions Taken on Applications for Class 104 Licenses Relating to Power Reactors," in JCAE, *A Study of AEC Procedures*, pp. 101–102.

72. JCAE, *A Study of AEC Procedures*, pp. 102–103.

73. "Division of Civilian Application Responsibilities and Objectives with Respect to Reactor Hazards," in JCAE, *A Study of AEC Procedures*, pp. 107–108; JCAE, *Hearings on Government Indemnity and Reactor Safety*, 85th Cong., 1st sess., 1957, p. 53.

74. JCAE, *A Study of AEC Procedures*, p. 106; C. Rogers McCullough, "Reactor Safety," *Nucleonics*, Sept. 1957, p. 136.

75. JCAE, *Hearings on Government Indemnity and Reactor Safety*, 1957, p. 54.

76. Ibid., pp. 47–53; Richard G. Hewlett, "The Experimental Breeder Reactor No. 1: The Life Story of a Nuclear Reactor," unpublished manuscript, History Division, DOE.

77. JCAE, *A Study of AEC Procedures*, pp. 9–10.

78. Ibid., pp. 103–104.

79. 10 C.F.R. 50.35; CM 1061, CM 1073, AEC/DOE.

80. Section 2.790 of the Commission's rules of practice stated, "The Commission may withhold any document or part thereof from public inspection if disclosure of its contents is not required in the public interest and would adversely affect the interest of the person concerned." See AEC 23/28 (7 July 1955), AEC 23/35 (6 Jan. 1956), AEC press release, 6 Feb. 1956, AEC/NRC. See also Green, "Law of Reactor Safety," p. 130.

81. AEC 23/28, AEC 23/35, AEC press release, 3 Feb. 1956, AEC/NRC; CM 1107 (21 July 1955), CM 1163 (11 Jan. 1956), AEC/DOE.

82. "Conversion of the Construction Permit to a License Authorizing Operation of the Facility," in JCAE, *A Study of AEC Procedures*, pp. 104–105.

83. CM 1061, AEC/DOE.

IV. INSURING AGAINST CATASTROPHE: PRICE-ANDERSON

1. U.S. Congress, Joint Committee on Atomic Energy, *Hearings on S. 3323 and H.R. 8862 to Amend the Atomic Energy Act of 1946*, 83d Cong., 2d sess., 1954, pp. 334–335.

2. Ibid.

3. Atomic Energy Act of 1954 § 53(e)(8).

4. Memoranda, Norris to Corbin Allardice, 9 Dec. 1954, 25 Jan. 1955, General Correspondence (AEC—Insurance—General), Joint Committee on Atomic Energy (JCAE) Papers, Record Group 128 (Records of the Joint Committees of Congress), National Archives; JCAE, *Hearings on Development, Growth, and State of the Atomic Energy Industry*, 84th Cong., 1st sess., 1955, pp. 8, 59, 68–69, 186–187 (hereafter called JCAE, *"202" Hearings.*)

5. JCAE, *"202" Hearings*, 1955, p. 69.

6. Ibid., pp. 247–258.

7. Ibid., pp. 388–389, 549.

8. Ibid., pp. 403–404.

9. Ibid., pp. 493, 498–499.

10. Description of the meetings and their participants are included in "Insurance of Reactor Operations," a Joint Committee staff study written by George Norris, in JCAE, *Background Material for the Report of the Impact of the Peaceful Uses*

of Atomic Energy, 84th Cong., 2d sess., 1956, pp. 611–613; H. M. Parker and J. W. Healy, "Environmental Effects of a Major Reactor Disaster," *Proceedings of the International Conference on the Peaceful Uses of Atomic Energy,* vol. 13 (New York: United Nations, 1956), pp. 106–109; C. R. Williams, "Insurance for Reactors," ibid., pp. 54–58.

11. Memorandum, Don S. Burrows to Kenneth D. Nichols, 21 Jan. 1955, in AEC 785/1 (1 Feb. 1955), AEC 785/2 (1 Apr. 1955), AEC 785/3 (7 June 1955), CM 1093 (28 June 1955), AEC/DOE; AEC press releases, 15 Mar. 1955, 13 July 1955, AEC 785/5 (20 June 1955), AEC/NRC. The Insurance Study Group's members were: K. E. Black, president, Home Insurance Company; Donald H. Burr, secretary, Aetna Casualty and Surety Company; Percy Chubb, president, Federal Insurance Company; Charles J. Haugh, vice-president, Travelers Insurance Company; Manning W. Heard, general counsel, Hartford Accident and Indemnity Company; A. B. Jackson, president, St. Paul Fire and Marine Insurance Company; H. C. Jones, president, Arkwright Mutual Fire Insurance Company; A. L. Paperfuss, vice-president, Employers Mutual Liability Insurance Company of Wisconsin; M. B. Weber, vice-president, Lumbermens Mutual Casualty Company; and H. W. Yount, vice-president, Liberty Mutual Insurance Company.

12. AEC press release, 13 July 1955, AEC/NRC. This press release included the "Preliminary Report of Insurance Study Groups."

13. Ibid.

14. Ibid.

15. CM 1093 (28 June 1955), AEC/DOE; AEC 785/6 (8 Aug. 1955), AEC/NRC. Letters were sent to the following probable operators: Detroit Edison, Yankee Electric Company, Consumers Public Power District, Consolidated Edison of New York, Commonwealth Edison; and to the following vendors: North American Aviation, AMF Atomics, Babcock and Wilcox, General Electric, and Westinghouse.

16. Responses appended to AEC 785/8 (17 Feb. 1956), AEC/NRC.

17. AEC 785/7 (23 Dec. 1955), CM 1149 (16 Nov. 1955), AEC/DOE.

18. Norris, "Insurance of Reactor Operations" in *Background Material,* pp. 613–614; *Financial Protection against Atomic Hazards* (New York: Atomic Industrial Forum, 1957), pp. 33–34.

19. George Norris to Robert McKinney, 28 Nov. 1955, Box 800, Norris to Clinton P. Anderson, 3, 12 Jan., 3 Mar. 1956, Box 797, Clinton P. Anderson Papers, Library of Congress; Willard F. Libby to Melvin Price, 24 Feb. 1956, General Correspondence (Insurance—Seminar, 1956), "Staff Memorandum on Insurance Problems," 2 Dec. 1955 (Indemnity), JCAE Papers; AEC 785/8, AEC/NRC.

20. Libby to Price, 24 Feb. 1956, JCAE Papers; AEC 785/8, AEC/NRC; AEC 785/10 (14 Mar. 1956), AEC/DOE.

21. JCAE, Committee Print, *Peaceful Uses of Atomic Energy, Report of the Panel on the Impact of the Peaceful Uses of Atomic Energy*, 84th Cong., 2d sess., 1956, pp. v, 126–128.

22. AEC 785/8, AEC/NRC.

23. Ibid.

24. JCAE, *"202" Hearings*, 84th Cong., 2d sess., 1956, pp. 111–114.

25. Clinton P. Anderson, *Outsider in the Senate: Senator Clinton P. Anderson's Memoirs* (New York: World Publishing Co., 1970), pp. 3–178; "The Strauss Affair," *Time*, 15 June 1959, pp. 21–25; Lewis L. Strauss, memorandum for the files, 7 Apr. 1958 (Eisenhower, Dwight D. File), Lewis L. Strauss Papers, Herbert Hoover Library, West Branch, Iowa.

26. JCAE, *"202" Hearings*, 1956, pp. 239–241, 252, 527–528.

27. Ibid., pp. 252–253; George Norris to Clinton Anderson, 17, 27 Feb., 1 Mar. 1956, General Correspondence (Indemnity), Norris to Anderson, 6 Mar. 1956 (Insurance—Seminar, 1956), JCAE Papers; Norris to Anderson, 1 Mar. 1956, Frank Cotter to Anderson, 5 Mar. 1956, JCAE press release, 14 Mar. 1956, Box 797, Anderson Papers.

28. H.R. 9701, 1 Mar. 1956; H.R. 9802, 7 Mar. 1956, 84th Cong., 2d sess.; William F. Kennedy to W. Sterling Cole, 4 Apr. 1956, Box 38, W. Sterling Cole Papers, accession no. 28, Department of Manuscripts and University Archives, Cornell University, Ithaca, New York.

29. "Preliminary Report on Financial Protection against Atomic Hazards," Mar. 1956, General Correspondence (Insurance—Seminar, 1956), JCAE Papers (hereafter cited as "Preliminary Report").

30. George Norris to Clinton P. Anderson, 28 Feb. 1956, General Correspondence (Indemnity), John M. Kernochan to Members of Advisory Seminar, n.d. (Insurance—Seminar, 1956), JCAE Papers.

31. "Preliminary Report," p. 2, JCAE Papers.

32. Ibid., pp. 3–23.

33. Ibid., pp. 16–17, 23.

34. Ibid., pp. 24–37.

35. JCAE press release, 14 Mar. 1956, George Norris to Clinton P. Anderson, 6 Mar. 1956, Anderson to Lewis L. Strauss, 7 Mar. 1956, statement of the Atomic Energy Commission before the Joint Committee on Atomic Energy Seminar, 15 Mar. 1956, General Correspondence (Insurance—Seminar, 1956), JCAE Papers; CM 1185 (14 Mar. 1956), AEC/DOE; AEC 785/11 (14 Mar. 1956), AEC/NRC.

36. Manning W. Heard to Clinton P. Anderson, 28 Mar. 1956, Ambrose Kelly to Anderson, 29 Mar. 1956, Kenneth E. Black to Anderson, 2 Apr. 1956, George Norris to James T. Ramey, 7 May 1956, Box 797, Anderson Papers; AEC 785/12 (30 Apr. 1956), AEC/NRC; Stoddard W. Stevens to Anderson, 30 Mar. 1956, General Correspondence (Indemnity), JCAE Papers.

37. Statement of the Atomic Energy Commission before the Joint Committee on Atomic Energy Seminar, 15 Mar. 1956, CM 1185, 14 Mar. 1956, informal meeting, 26 Mar. 1956, all in AEC 785/12, AEC/NRC.

38. AEC 785/12, AEC/NRC; George Norris to James T. Ramey, 7 May 1956, Box 797, Anderson Papers; S. 3929, 84th Cong., 2d sess., 1956.

39. JCAE, *Hearings on Government Indemnity for Private Licensees and AEC Contractors against Reactor Hazards*, 84th Cong., 2d sess., 1956, pp. 120–122 (hereafter called JCAE, *Indemnity Hearings*).

40. AEC 785/12, AEC/NRC.

41. Ibid.

42. Ibid.

43. Ibid.

44. Ibid.

45. Ibid.; CM 1198 (14 May 1956), AEC/DOE.

46. CM 1198, AEC/DOE.

47. Staff memorandum from R. W. Cook, 2 May 1956, staff memorandum from Robert E. Hollingsworth, 2 May 1956, Budget-12 (Insurance), AEC/DOE; H.R. 11242, 84th Cong., 2d sess., 1956; JCAE *Indemnity Hearings*, pp. 1–99.

48. JCAE, *Indemnity Hearings*, pp. 10–11.

49. Ibid., pp. 14–17; for insurance-industry opposition to government reinsurance, see pp. 164–170, 172, 206, 237–239, 244–246, 348–349, 355, 374.

50. Ibid., pp. 88–89.

51. Ibid., pp. 40, 43–44.

52. Ibid., pp. 46–50.

53. Ibid., p. 51.

54. Ibid., p. 52; memorandum from R. W. Cook, 2 May 1956, Budget-12 (Insurance), AEC/DOE.

55. JCAE, *Indemnity Hearings*, pp. 52–53.

56. Ibid., pp. 53–54.

57. Ibid., p. 54.

58. Ibid., p. 376; Energy Research and Development Administration, *Nuclear Reactors Built, Being Built, or Planned in the United States as of Dec. 31, 1976* (Oak Ridge, Tenn.: ERDA Technical Information Center, 1977).

59. JCAE, *Indemnity Hearings*, pp. 60–69.

60. S. 3929, 25 May 1956, H.R. 11523, 29 May 1956, 84th Cong., 2d sess. Minor revisions were incorporated before the Joint Committee reported the bills. The revised measures were S. 4112 and H.R. 12050.

61. JCAE, *Indemnity Hearings;* Ramey to Fields, 29 May 1956, attached to AEC 785/14 (1 June 1956), CM 1206 (4 June 1956), AEC/DOE.

62. AEC 785/14, CM 1206, AEC/DOE.

63. JCAE, *Indemnity Hearings*, pp. 313–324.

64. Ibid., pp. 317–319.

65. U.S. Congress, S. Rept. 2298, H. Rept. 2531, 84th Cong., 2d sess., 1956.

66. "Separate Views of Representative Holifield" attached to H. Rept. 2531.

67. JCAE, *Hearings of Proposed Legislation for Accelerating Civilian Reactor Program*, 84th Cong., 2d sess., 1956, and *Hearing on a Bill Providing for a Civilian Atomic Power Acceleration Program*, 84th Cong., 2d sess., 1956; U.S. Congress, S. Rept. 2390, 84th Cong., 2d sess., 1956; Chet Holifield to Kyle Palmer, 29 Oct. 1958, Box 41 (Atomic Energy, 1956–1960 Misc.), Chet Holifield Papers, University of Southern California, Los Angeles; Virginia Walker, note for Sterling Cole, 29 June 1956, Lewis Strauss to Cole, 19 July 1956 (Cole, Sterling File), Strauss Papers; Percevil Brundage to Gerald D. Morgan, 6 July 1956, Official File 108-H, Dwight D. Eisenhower Papers, Dwight D. Eisenhower Library, Abilene, Kansas; Melvin Price, speech attached to JCAE press release, 25 Sept. 1956, General Correspondence (Committee General), JCAE Papers; Harold P. Green and Alan Rosenthal, *Government of the Atom* (New York: Atherton Press, 1963), pp. 15–16, 134–138.

68. Strauss to W. B. Persons, 16 July 1956, Official File 61, Eisenhower Papers; Strauss, memorandum for files, 31 Dec. 1956 (Eisenhower, Dwight D. File), Strauss Papers.

69. Green and Rosenthal, *Government of the Atom*, p. 153; *Congressional Record*, 84th Cong., 2d sess., 1956, pp. 12452–12469.

70. *New York Times*, 18 July 1956, p. 15; Green and Rosenthal, *Government of the Atom*, p. 154.

71. *Congressional Record*, 84th Cong., 2d sess., 1956, pp. 14246–14248, 14281.

72. Ibid., pp. 14271–14287; William Mitchell to Strauss with attachment, 22 July 1956 (Cole, Sterling File), Strauss Papers.

73. Strauss, memorandum for files, 25 July 1956 (Eisenhower, Dwight D. File), Strauss Papers.

74. Ibid.; Green and Rosenthal, *Government of the Atom*, p. 152; *Congressional Record*, 84th Cong., 2d sess., 1956, pp. 14565, 15199; James T. Ramey to C. F. J. Harrington, 28 July 1956, General Correspondence (AEC Legislation-Insurance), JCAE Papers.

V. THE POWER REACTOR DEVELOPMENT COMPANY CONTROVERSY

1. For the PRDC facility see John G. Fuller, *We Almost Lost Detroit* (New York: Reader's Digest Press, 1975), an antinuclear view; and E. Pauline Alexanderson, ed., *Fermi-1: New Age for Nuclear Power* (LaGrange Park, Ill.: American Nuclear Society, 1979), a collection of accounts by people associated with PRDC.

2. Fuller, *We Almost Lost Detroit*, pp. 7–8; U.S. Congress, Joint Committee on Atomic Energy, *Hearings on Atomic Power Development and Private Enterprise*, 83d Cong., 1st sess., 1953, pp. 134–166, and *Hearings on S. 3323 and H.R. 8862 to Amend the Atomic Energy Act of 1946*, 83d Cong., 2d sess., 1954, pp. 73–91.

3. Members of the PRDC were large and nationally known: Allis-Chalmers Manufacturing, Babcock and Wilcox, Burroughs Corporation, Central Hudson Gas and Electric, Cincinnati Gas and Electric, Columbus and Southern Ohio Electric, Combustion Engineering, Consumers Power Company, Delaware Power and Light, Detroit Edison, Fruehauf Trailer Corporation, Holley Carburetor Company, Iowa and Illinois Gas and Electric, Long Island Lighting, Philadelphia Electric, Potomac Electric Power, Rochester Gas and Electric, Southern Services, Inc., Toledo Edison Company, Westinghouse Electric, Wisconsin Electric Power. Articles of Incorporation, PRDC, 30 Aug. 1955, Exhibit 3 to Application for License, 6 Jan. 1956, AEC Docket no. 50-16, PRDC, AEC/NRC.

4. AEC 777/11 (30 June 1955), AEC/DOE; AEC press releases, 8 Aug. 1955, 4 Aug. 1956, 26 Mar. 1957, AEC/NRC.

5. Only a breeder reactor generates as much fuel as or more than it consumes. If the generation of new fissionable material occurs at a slower rate than the consumption of fissionable material, the reactor is termed a "converter."

6. Atomic Power Development Associates, APDA-108, "Description of Developmental Fast Neutron Breeder Power Reactor Plant" (1 Sept. 1955), Advisory Committee on Reactor Safeguards (ACRS) File, AEC/NRC.

7. Ibid.; W. J. McCarthy, Jr., "Some Inherent and Design Safety Features of the ADPA Fast Breeder Reactor," n.d., ACRS File, AEC/NRC; Alfred Amorosi, "Concept and Design," in Fermi-1, ed. Alexanderson, pp. 131–162.

8. Appendix B to AEC 331/114 (30 July 1956), report of Subcommittee of Advisory Committee on Reactor Safeguards on Detroit Edison Reactor, 20 Apr. 1955, Annex A to Appendix B to AEC 331/114, AEC/DOE.

9. C. R. McCullough to K. E. Fields, 29 July 1955, ACRS File, AEC/NRC.

10. Richard G. Hewlett, "The Experimental Breeder Reactor No. 1: The Life Story of a Nuclear Reactor," unpublished paper, Mar. 1974, DOE History Division; U.S. Atomic Energy Commission, Sixteenth Semiannual Report of the Atomic Energy Commission (July 1954), pp. 25–26; U.S. Atomic Energy Commission, Major Activities in the Atomic Energy Programs, July-December 1955 (Jan. 1956), pp. 43–44.

11. U.S. Atomic Energy Commission, Major Activities in the Atomic Energy Program, January-June 1956, pp. 45–47; minutes of meeting of Subcommittee of Advisory Committee on Reactor Safeguards, 20 Mar. 1956, Annex G to Appendix B to AEC 331/114, AEC/DOE; Fuller, We Almost Lost Detroit, pp. 33–35; John F. Hogerton, The Atomic Energy Deskbook (New York: Reinhold Publishing Corp., 1963), p. 157.

12. AEC Docket no. 50-16, PRDC, AEC/NRC.

13. Appendix B to AEC 331/114, minutes of meeting of Subcommittee of Advisory Committee on Reactor Safeguards on Detroit Edison (APDA-PRDC), 20 Mar. 1956, Annex C to Appendix B to AEC 331/114, AEC/DOE.

14. Ibid.

15. Ibid.

16. Application for License, PRDC, 6 Jan. 1956, AEC Docket no. 50-16, PRDC, AEC/NRC.

17. Fuller, *We Almost Lost Detroit,* pp. 41–44; C. R. McCullough to K. E. Fields, 6 June 1956, ACRS File, AEC/NRC.

18. McCullough to Fields, 6 June 1956, ACRS File, AEC/NRC.

19. Ibid.

20. Ibid.

21. Ibid.

22. Ibid.

23. Ibid.

24. Harvey Brooks to C. R. McCullough, 17 June 1956, minutes of meeting of PRDC Fast Breeder Reactor Subcommittee with AEC staff members, 21 June 1956, B. John Garrick to Harold Price re ACRS recommendations on PRDC reactor—record of discussion, ACRS File, AEC/NRC.

25. Harvey Brooks to Harold Price, 23 June 1956, ACRS File, AEC/NRC.

26. Harvey Brooks to J. Z. Holland, 4 July 1956, Annex E to Appendix B to AEC 331/114, AEC/DOE.

27. Strauss, memorandum for file, 14 Jan. 1955 (Benedict, Manson File), memorandum for file, fall 1956 (Eisenhower, Dwight D. File), memorandum for chairman, 15 Aug. 1957 (Dissents File), memorandum for file, 27 June 1957 (Cole, Sterling File), Lewis L. Strauss Papers, Herbert Hoover Library, West Branch, Iowa; Robert Gray to Sherman Adams re Thomas Murray, 17 May 1957, Official File 61, Murray to Eisenhower, 22 May 1957, Official File 108, Dwight D. Eisenhower Papers, Dwight D. Eisenhower Library, Abilene, Kansas.

28. U.S. Congress, House Committee on Appropriations, Subcommittee on Public Works Appropriations, *Hearings on Second Supplemental Appropriation Bill, 19757, Investigation of Atomic Electric Power,* 84th Cong., 2d sess., 1956 (hereafter called House Appropriations, *Hearings on Second Supplemental*).

29. Ibid., pp. 174–175.

30. Walker Cisler to Lewis Strauss, 1 May 1956, Industrial Research and Application–6, AEC/DOE; Clinton P. Anderson, *Outsider in the Senate: Senator Clinton Anderson's Memoirs* (New York: World Publishing Co., 1970), p. 159.

31. House Appropriations, *Hearings on Second Supplemental,* pp. 225–227.

32. Anderson, *Outsider in the Senate,* p. 159.

33. CM 1213 (10 July 1956), AEC/DOE; the Anderson letter is printed in JCAE, committee print, *A Study of AEC Procedures and Organization in the Licensing of Reactor Facilities,* 85th Cong., 1st sess., 1957, p. 117 (hereafter cited as JCAE print, *A Study of AEC Procedures*).

34. CM 1214 (11 July 1956), AEC/DOE. Previous examples of Joint Committee requests for information are in Green and Rosenthal, *Government of the Atom,* pp. 94–96.

35. CM 1214, AEC/DOE.

36. Ibid.

37. Ibid.

38. Ibid.

39. Ibid.; the Commission letter is printed in JCAE print, *A Study of AEC Procedures*, pp. 117–118.

40. JCAE print, *A Study of AEC Procedures*, pp. 118–121.

41. Minutes of Atomic Energy Study Committee meeting, 16 July 1956, G. Mennen Williams to Strauss, 16 July 1956, Box 173, G. Mennen Williams Papers, Michigan Historical Collections, Bentley Historical Library, University of Michigan, Ann Arbor.

42. K. E. Fields to Williams, 17 July 1956, Box 173, Williams Papers.

43. CM 1217 (18 July 1956), CM 1220 (1 Aug. 1956), AEC/DOE.

44. JCAE, *A Study of AEC Procedures*, p. 121.

45. Robert W. Hartwell to Price, 11 July 1956, with enclosure, "Amendment No. 2 to Application for License under Atomic Energy Act of 1954," Exhibit X to Application for License, AEC Docket no. 50-16, PRDC, AEC/NRC.

46. Appendix B to AEC 331/114, AEC/DOE.

47. Ibid.

48. Ibid.

49. Ibid.

50. AEC 331/114, AEC/DOE.

51. CM 1221 (2 Aug. 1956), AEC/DOE.

52. Ibid., McCullough to members of Safeguards Committee, 8 Aug. 1956, ACRS File, AEC/NRC.

53. CM 1221, AEC/DOE.

54. *Congressional Record*, 84th Cong., 2d sess., 1956, p. 14285.

55. CM 1221, AEC/DOE; AEC press release, 5 Aug. 1956, AEC/NRC.

56. Clinton P. Anderson, press release, 4 Aug. 1956, General Correspondence (Power Reactor Development Company), Joint Committee on Atomic Energy (JCAE) Papers, Record Group 128 (Records of the Joint Committees of Congress), National Archives.

57. Holifield, press release, 4 Aug. 1956, Holifield to G. Mennen Williams, 4 Aug. 1956, Holifield to Eisenhower, 4 Aug. 1956, General Correspondence (Power Reactor Development Company), JCAE Papers; White House route slip to Strauss, 6 Aug. 1956, Strauss to Bryce Harlow, 9 Aug. 1956, Harlow to Holifield, 13 Aug. 1956, Official File 108-H, Eisenhower Papers.

VI. THE PRDC IN COURT

1. James L. Morrisson and B. John Garrick, "What We Learned from the PRDC Case," *Nucleonics* 17 (July 1959), 60–63; Petitions for Intervention and Requests for Formal Hearing before the United States Atomic Energy Commission, from

International Union of Electrical, Radio and Machine Workers; International Union, United Paperworkers of America; International Union, United Automobile, Aircraft and Agricultural Implement Workers of America, AFL-CIO, 31 Aug. 1956, AEC Docket no. 50-16, PRDC, AEC/NRC (hereafter cited as Petitions for Intervention).

2. U.S. Congress, Joint Committee on Atomic Energy, *Hearings on S. 3323 and H.R. 8862 to Amend the Atomic Energy Act of 1946*, 83d Cong., 2d sess., 1954, pp. 269–301, 486–515; JCAE, committee print, *Peaceful Uses of Atomic Energy*, 84th Cong., 2d sess., 1956, pp. 501–508; JCAE, *Hearings on Development, Growth and State of the Atomic Energy Industry*, 84th Cong., 2d sess., 1956, pp. 268–282; Wendy Allen, *Nuclear Reactors for Generating Electricity: U.S. Development from 1946 to 1963* (Santa Monica, Calif.: Rand Corporation, 1977), pp. 54–66.

3. Chet Holifield, press release, 4 Aug. 1956, General Correspondence (AEC— Facility Licensing), Holifield to G. Mennen Williams, 4 Aug. 1956 (Power Reactor Development Company), Joint Committee on Atomic Energy Papers (JCAE), RG 128 (Records of the Joint Committees of Congress), National Archives; Leo Goodman to Antony Tashnic, 10 Aug. 1956, John H. McCarthy to G. Mennen Williams, 21 Aug. 1956, Box 173, G. Mennen Williams Papers, Michigan Historical Collections, Bentley Historical Library, University of Michigan, Ann Arbor; Raymond Moley, "Lagoona Controversy," *Newsweek*, 11 Nov. 1957, p. 128; interview with Leo Goodman, Washington, D.C., 15 Mar. 1982; Clinton P. Anderson, speech before the Second Annual Convention of the New Mexico State AFL-CIO, 26 Oct. 1957, Box 963, Clinton P. Anderson Papers, Library of Congress.

4. Donald Montgomery to Walter P. Reuther, 22 Aug. 1956, Social Issues Series (Atomic Energy, 1956), transcript of interview with Walter P. Reuther on Proposed Atomic Power Reactor at Monroe, Michigan, 23 Sept. 1956 (Atomic Energy—Detroit Edison Reactor Case, 1956), Walter P. Reuther Papers, Archives of Labor History and Urban Affairs, Wayne State University, Detroit, Michigan.

5. Ibid.

6. AEC 23/28 (7 July 1955), AEC 23/35 (6 Jan. 1956), AEC press release, 3 Feb. 1956, AEC/NRC; CM 1107 (21 July 1955), CM 1163 (11 Jan. 1956), AEC/DOE; interview with Robert Lowenstein, Washington, D.C., 27 Mar. 1979.

7. AEC 23/28, AEC/NRC; 10 C.F.R. 2.102.

8. AEC 23/28, AEC/NRC.

9. Petitions for Intervention; Power Reactor Development Company Answer to Petition of International Union of Electrical, Radio and Machine Workers, AFL-CIO, Jarvis B. Carey, Al Hartnett and James Douglas Insofar As Said Petition Relates to a Request for Leave to Intervene and for Suspension of the Construction Permit Issued to Power Reactor Development Company on August 4, 1956, 14 Sept. 1956, AEC Docket no. 50-16, PRDC, AEC/NRC.

10. Commission Meeting—Regulatory Proceedings, no. 1, 26 Sept. 1956 (hereafter designated as CM-Reg. followed by meeting number and date), AEC/NRC.

11. Ibid., AEC-R 1/1 (25 Sept. 1956), AEC/NRC.

12. Ibid., AEC-R 1/2 (27 Sept. 1956), CM-Reg. no. 2 (28 Sept. 1956), AEC/NRC.

13. AEC-R 1/6 (8 Oct. 1956), Notice of Hearing Order and Memoranda, 8 Oct. 1956, Docket no. 50-16, PRDC, CM-Reg. no 2, CM-Reg. no. 5 (8 Oct. 1956), AEC/NRC.

14. Petitions for Intervention, AEC Docket no. 50-16, PRDC, CM-Reg. no. 4 (4 Oct. 1956), CM-Reg. no 5, AEC-R 1/6, Lewis Strauss to commissioners and general manager with revised letter, 9 Oct. 1956, Industrial Research and Application–6 (Reg. Power Reactor Development Company), AEC/NRC.

15. Wire Service Dispatch read by Mr. Strauss at Meeting 1233 on October 11, 1956, Industrial Research and Application–6 (Reg. Power Reactor Development Company), AEC/NRC. The Joint Committee Investigation is discussed in chap. 7.

16. AEC-R 1/6, CM-Reg. no. 5, Notice of Hearing Order and Memoranda, 8 Oct. 1956, Docket no. 50-16, PRDC, AEC/NRC.

17. "Position of AEC Staff at the Hearing," n.d., CM-Reg. no. 5, W. B. McCool to W. Mitchell and H. L. Price, 10 Oct. 1956, Industrial Research and Application–6 (Power Reactor Development Company), AEC/NRC.

18. AEC-R 1/8 (18 Oct. 1956), AEC/NRC.

19. CM-Reg. no. 7 (18 Oct. 1956), AEC-R 1/26 (4 Dec. 1956), K. E. Fields to managers of operations: "The Separated Staff and Their Functions," 3 Dec. 1956, attached to AEC-R 1/26, AEC/NRC. Other members assigned to the separated staff included Clifford K. Beck, B. John Garrick, Lyall E. Johnson, Edward Bruenkant, William C. Woods, Charles F. Knesel, Milford K. Kellogg, Earl F. Lane, and Lee M. Hydeman.

20. Notice of Hearing Order and Memoranda, 8 Oct. 1956, Motion for Reconsideration and Suspension of "Conditional" Construction Permit, 18 Oct. 1956, Memorandum for the Staff of Intervenors' Motion for Reconsideration and Suspension of "Conditional" Construction Permit, 25 Oct. 1956, Motion to Amend Specification of Issues, 2 Nov. 1956, Intervenors' Motion for Access to Certain Restricted Data, 21 Nov. 1956, Intervenors' Memorandum in Support of Motion for Access to Certain Restricted Data, 30 Nov. 1956, On Motions Order and Memorandum, 21 Dec. 1956, Docket no. 50-16, PRDC, CM-Reg. no. 12 (12 Dec. 1956), AEC/NRC.

21. Answer of Intervenors, 19 Oct. 1956, On Motions Order and Memorandum, 21 Dec. 1956, AEC/NRC.

22. *Washington Post*, 2 Jan. 1957, p. 2; Summary of Case Regarding PRDC Atomic Power Reactor at Lagoona Beach, Michigan, 13 Aug. 1957, Box 803, Anderson Papers; interview with Leo Goodman, 15 Mar. 1982.

23. AEC-R 1/22 (23 Nov. 1956), AEC-R 1/21 (26 Nov. 1956), AEC-R 1/25 (4 Dec. 1956), AEC-R 1/30 (4 Jan. 1957), AEC-R 1/34 (15 Jan. 1957), AEC/NRC.

24. *New York Times,* 1 Jan. 1957, p. 3; AEC-R 1/47 (19 Feb. 1957), AEC-R 1/48 (4 Mar. 1957), Commission agenda planning session, 1 Mar. 1957, CM-Reg. no. 16 (4 Mar. 1957), AEC/NRC.

25. Order and Memorandum on Motion for Unrestricted Access to Restricted Data, 5 Mar. 1957, Docket no. 50-16, PRDC, AEC/NRC.

26. Ibid.

27. Ibid.

28. *Washington Post,* 9 Jan. 1957, p. B5; *Detroit News,* 9 Jan. 1957, p. 1; James T. Ramey to Joint Committee on Atomic Energy, 12 Jan. 1957, General Correspondence (Power Reactor Development Company), JCAE Papers; transcript of hearing, 8 Jan.–7 Aug. 1957, pp. 1–3919; narrative testimonies, pp. 3920–4401, certified record transcript, Docket no. 50-16, PRDC, AEC/NRC.

29. *Wall Street Journal,* 8 Jan. 1957, p. 14; *Washington Star,* 9 Jan. 1957, p. A6; *Detroit News,* 6 Mar. 1957, p. 50, 1 Aug. 1957, p. 8; Morrisson and Garrick, "What We Learned from the PRDC Case," pp. 60–63; UAW press release, 6 Jan. 1957, General Correspondence (Power Reactor Development Company), JCAE Papers.

30. Transcript of hearing, 8 Jan. 1957, pp. 26–27, narrative testimony of Hans Bethe, Norman Hilberry, W. Kenneth Davis, Walter J. McCarthy, Alfred Amorosi, pp. 3950–4240, certified record transcript, Docket no. 50-16, PRDC, AEC/NRC.

31. Hans Bethe, "Reactor Safety and Oscillator Tests," 15 Oct. 1956, APDA-117, Exhibit 31, narrative testimony of Bethe, pp. 55, 58, certified record transcript, transcript of hearing, 14 Mar. 1957, p. 1325, Docket no. 50-16, PRDC, AEC/NRC.

32. Narrative testimony of Manson Benedict, pp. 4361, 4364, certified record transcript, Docket no. 50-16, PRDC, AEC/NRC.

33. Transcript of hearing, 20 May 1957, pp. 2908–2940, 21 May 1957, pp. 2950–2959, 10 June 1957, pp. 3131–3132, 17 June 1957, pp. 3270–3276, 3280–3281, Docket no. 50-16, PRDC, AEC/NRC.

34. PRDC construction permit in AEC press release, 4 Aug. 1956, AEC/NRC.

35. Narrative testimony of Ernest R. Acker, pp. 3920–3949; certified record transcript; transcript of hearing, 4–8 Mar. 1957, pp. 260–916, Docket no. 50-16, PRDC, AEC/NRC; "Summary of Case Regarding PRDC Atomic Power Reactor at Lagoona Beach, Michigan," 13 Aug. 1957, Box 803, Anderson Papers.

36. Transcript of hearing, 4 Mar. 1957, pp. 314–315, Docket no. 50-16, PRDC, AEC/NRC.

37. Ibid., p. 346.

38. Post-hearing Brief of Intervenors with Proposed Findings and Conclusions, n.d., pp. 52–53, Docket no. 50-16, PRDC, AEC/NRC.

39. AEC press release, 26 Mar. 1957, AEC/NRC; *New York Times,* 27 Mar. 1957, p. 62; "Schizophrenia," *Newsweek,* 26 June 1961, p. 84.

40. AEC press release, 26 Mar. 1957, AEC/NRC.

41. JCAE, *Hearings on Authorizing Appropriations for the Atomic Energy Commission*, 85th Cong., 1st sess., 1957, pp. 19–20.

42. Ibid., pp. 597–617.

43. Ibid., pp. 619, 627.

44. Ibid., p. 612; *New York Times*, 31 July 1957, p. 1; U.S. Congress, H. Rept. 978, *Authorizing Appropriations for the Atomic Energy Commission*, 85th Cong., 1st sess., 1957, pp. 19–20.

45. Lewis Strauss to Sterling Cole, 3 Aug. 1957, printed in *Congressional Record*, 85th Cong., 1st sess., 1957, pp. A 6319–6321. The authorization bill became embroiled in the chronic public-versus-private-power debate before final passage on 21 August 1957. The law provided further compromise on fast-breeder reactor funds. It restored $4.3 million in the authorization, but only $1.5 million could be spent in the current fiscal year, and only for research and development in AEC laboratories on fast-breeder technology. The AEC-PRDC contract remained in abeyance. Public Law 85-162, *United States Statutes at Large* 71:403.

46. Transcript of hearing, 7 Aug. 1957, pp. 3906–3912, Motion to Disqualify Chairman of the Atomic Energy Commission, 9 Oct. 1957, Docket no. 50-16, PRDC, AEC/NRC.

47. "The Dissenter," *Time*, 6 May 1957, p. 24.

48. CM-Reg. no. 25 (27 Nov. 1957), AEC/NRC.

49. CM 1329 (1 Jan. 1958), CM 1331 (5 Feb. 1958), CM 1335 (17 Feb. 1958), CM 1350 (2 Apr. 1958), CM 1358 (17 Apr. 1958), AEC/DOE; CM-Reg. no. 26 (11 Dec. 1957), Order for Hearing, 18 Apr. 1958, Docket no. 50-16, PRDC, L. K. Olson to W. B. McCool, 2 June 1958, Industrial Research and Application–6 (Reg. Power Reactor Development Company), AEC-R 1/85 (23 June 1958), AEC/NRC.

50. Benjamin Sigal to John A. McCone, 30 Aug. 1958, in AEC-R 1/87 (8 Sept. 1958), AEC/NRC.

51. AEC-R 1/88 (9 Dec. 1958), CM-Reg. no. 32 (10 Dec. 1958), Opinion and Initial Decision, Power Reactor Development Company, 10 Dec. 1958, Docket no. 50-16, PRDC, AEC/NRC.

52. Opinion and Initial Decision, 10 Dec. 1958, Docket no. 50-16, PRDC, AEC/NRC.

53. Ibid.

54. CM-Reg. no. 35 (6 Jan. 1959), Intervenors' Exceptions to Opinion and Initial Decision, with Supporting Brief, 14 Jan. 1959, Reply for AEC Staff to Intervenors' Exceptions to Opinion and Initial Decision, 5 Feb. 1959, Applicant's Brief in Opposition to Intervenors' Exceptions to Initial Decision, 5 Feb. 1959, Docket no. 50-16, PRDC, AEC/NRC.

55. Intervenors' Exception and Brief, pp. 10–11, Docket no. 50-16, PRDC, AEC/NRC.

56. Ibid., pp. 11, 13–14.

57. Ibid., pp. 15–16.

58. Reply for AEC Staff, pp. 2–3, Docket no. 50-16, PRDC, AEC/NRC.

59. CM 1501 (1 May 1959), AEC/DOE; AEC-R 1/101 (25 May 1959), CM-Reg. no. 46 (26 May 1959), AEC/NRC.

60. Opinion and Final Decision, 26 May 1959, p. 2, Docket no. 50-16, PRDC, AEC/NRC.

61. Ibid., pp. 7–77.

62. Ibid., pp. 20–23.

63. Ibid., pp. 24–25.

64. Ibid., pp. 88, 90, 91.

65. UAW press conference, 9 Jan. 1957, Social Issues Series (Atomic Energy), Reuther Papers; Anderson, speech, 26 Oct. 1957, Box 963, Anderson Papers; L. K. Olson to commissioners, "Meeting with APDA-PRDC Representatives," 17 June 1959, Industrial Research and Application–6 (Reg. Power Reactor Development Company), U.S. Court of Appeals, District of Columbia, Amended Petition for Review of an Order of the Atomic Energy Commission, 25 July 1959, Docket no. 50-16, PRDC, AEC/NRC.

66. U.S. Court of Appeals for the District of Columbia, *International Union of Electrical, Radio and Machine Workers, AFL-CIO, et al., Petitioners, v. United States of America and Atomic Energy Commission, Respondents; Power Reactor Development Company and State of Michigan, Intervenors,* no. 1524; Brief for Petitioners, on Petition to Review and Set Aside an Order of the Atomic Energy Commission, 23 Dec. 1959, pp. 12–13, 14–31.

67. U.S. Court of Appeals for the District of Columbia, *International Union of Electrical, Radio and Machine Workers, AFL-CIO, et al., Petitioners, v. United States of America and Atomic Energy Commission, Respondents; Power Reactor Development Company and State of Michigan, Intervenors,* no. 15271; Brief for Respondents, on Petition to Review and Set Aside an Order of the Atomic Energy Commission, 1 Feb. 1960, pp. 24–39.

68. *International Union of Electrical, Radio, and Machine Workers, AFL-CIO; United Automobile, Aircraft and Agricultural Implement Workers of America; and United Papermakers and Paperworkers, Petitioners, v. United States of America and Atomic Energy Commission, Respondents; Power Reactor Development Company, State of Michigan, Intervenors,* 280 F.2d 645 (D.C. Cir. 1960).

69. 280 F.2d 647–649.

70. Ibid., pp. 649–650.

71. Ibid., pp. 650–651.

72. Ibid., pp. 651–652.

73. Ibid., pp. 652–654.

74. *New York Times,* 11 June 1960, p. 1, 12 June 1960, p. 27; "Roadblock to Progress," *Time,* 20 June 1960, p. 78.

75. CM-Reg. no. 69 (13 June 1960), Howard Brown, memorandum to files, 15 June 1960, Industrial Research and Application–6 (Power Reactor Develop-

ment Company), Respondents' Petition for Rehearing en Banc, June 1960, U.S. Court of Appeals for the District of Columbia, Order Denying Petition of Respondents for Rehearing en Banc, 25 July 1960, Docket no. 50-16, PRDC, AEC press release, 26 July 1960, John S. Graham to William P. Rogers, 28 July 1960, Industrial Research and Application–6 (Reg. Power Reactor Development Company), AEC/NRC; CM 1638 (26 July 1960), AEC/DOE; *Power Reactor Development Company, Petitioner, v. International Union of Electrical, Radio and Machine Workers, AFL-CIO, et al.*, and *United States et al., Petitioners, v. International Union of Electrical, Radio and Machine Workers, AFL-CIO, et al.* 364 U.S. 889 (1960).

76. *Power Reactor Development Company and United States v. International Union of Electrical, Radio and Machine Workers, et al.*, 364 U.S. 889 (1960).

77. U.S. Supreme Court, *United States of America and Atomic Energy Commission, Petitioners, v. International Union of Electrical, Radio and Machine Workers, AFL-CIO, et al., Respondents*, no. 454, Brief for Petitioners on Writ of Certiorari to the United States Court of Appeals for the District of Columbia, 11 Feb. 1961, pp. 33–90.

78. U.S. Supreme Court, *Power Reactor Development Company, Petitioner, v. International Union of Electrical, Radio and Machine Workers, AFL-CIO, et al., Respondents*, and *United States of America and Atomic Energy Commission, Petitioners, v. International Union of Electrical, Radio and Machine Workers, AFL-CIO, et al., Respondents*, no. 315 and no. 454, Brief for Respondents on Writs of Certiorari to the United States Court of Appeals for the District of Columbia Circuit, 29 Mar. 1961, pp. 28–90.

79. Clinton P. Anderson to Archibald Cox, 3 May 1961, Box 835, Anderson Papers.

80. Archibald Cox to Clinton Anderson, 1 June 1961, Box 835, Anderson Papers.

81. Ibid.

82. *Power Reactor Development Company, Petitioner, v. International Union of Electrical, Radio and Machine Workers, AFL-CIO, et al.* (no. 315) and *United States et al., Petitioners, v. International Union of Electrical, Radio and Machine Workers, AFL-CIO, et al.* (no. 454), 367 U.S. 403–406.

83. Ibid., pp. 406–408.

84. Ibid., pp. 408–409.

85. Ibid., pp. 409–410.

86. Ibid., pp. 410–414.

87. Ibid., pp. 416–419.

88. Cox to Anderson, 1 June 1961, Anderson Papers.

89. CM 1749 (12 June 1961), AEC/DOE.

90. *New York Times*, 13 June 1961, p. 1.

VII. LICENSING REFORM AND PRICE-ANDERSON

1. Joint Committee press release, 4 Aug. 1956, Clinton P. Anderson to Lewis L. Strauss, 9 Aug. 1956, General Correspondence (AEC—Procedure and Or-

ganization in Licensing of Reactor Facilities), Joint Committee on Atomic Energy (JCAE) Papers, RG 128 (Records of the Joint Committees of Congress), National Archives.

2. U.S. Congress, Joint Committee on Atomic Energy, committee print, *A Study of AEC Procedures and Organization in the Licensing of Reactor Facilities*, 85th Cong., 1st sess., 1957, p. 2 (hereafter cited as JCAE print, *A Study of AEC Procedures*); David Toll to James Ramey, 30 Aug., 5, 6, 7 Sept. 1956, General Correspondence (AEC—Procedure and Organization in Licensing of Reactor Facilities), JCAE Papers.

3. David Toll to James Ramey, 11, 26 Sept., 3 Oct. 1956, Ramey to Clinton P. Anderson, 11 Oct. 1956, General Correspondence (AEC—Procedure and Organization in Licensing of Reactor Facilities), JCAE Papers.

4. Toll to Ramey, 9 Oct. 1956, General Correspondence (AEC—Procedure and Organization in Licensing of Reactor Facilities), JCAE Papers.

5. Ibid.; K. E. Fields to Ramey, 9, 17 Oct. 1956, with enclosures, reproduced in JCAE print, *A Study of AEC Procedures*, pp. 100–108, 136–168.

6. Ramey to Anderson, 11 Oct. 1956, Anderson to Strauss, 16 Oct. 1956, General Correspondence (AEC—Procedure and Organization in Licensing of Reactor Facilities), JCAE Papers.

7. AEC-R 4 (15 Oct. 1956), AEC/NRC.

8. Ibid., CM-Reg. no. 6 (17 Oct. 1956), AEC/NRC.

9. CM-Reg. no. 6, AEC/NRC.

10. Ibid., CM-Reg. no. 9 (31 Oct. 1956), AEC/NRC.

11. Summary of Meeting between Members of JCAE Staff and AEC Staff on November 19, 1956 at AEC, 24 Nov. 1956, William Mitchell to James Ramey, 15 Nov. 1956, Box 813, Clinton P. Anderson Papers, Library of Congress.

12. "Summary of Meeting, November 19, 1956," Ramey to members of the Joint Committee, Nov. 1956, Box 813, Anderson Papers.

13. Draft letter, Anderson to Strauss, 23 Nov. 1956, General Correspondence (AEC—Procedure and Organization in Licensing of Reactor Facilities), JCAE Papers; Ramey to Anderson, 17 Dec. 1956, Box 813, Anderson Papers.

14. CM 1246 and 1247 (14 Nov. 1956), AEC/DOE.

15. CM 1247, AEC/DOE.

16. Bryan F. LaPlant to R. E. Hollingsworth, 20 Nov. 1956, in AEC 496/32 (29 Nov. 1956), AEC/DOE.

17. AEC 734/18 (28 Nov. 1956), CM 1250 (28 Nov. 1956), AEC/DOE.

18. CM 1250, AEC/DOE.

19. Ibid.

20. CM 1251 (4 Dec. 1956), AEC/DOE.

21. Strauss to Anderson, 2 Jan. 1957, General Correspondence (AEC—Procedure and Organization in Licensing of Reactor Facilities), JCAE Papers.

22. AEC-R 2/1 (7 Dec. 1956), AEC/NRC.

23. Ibid.

24. Ibid.

25. Ibid.; *Workshops on Legal Problems of Atomic Energy* (Ann Arbor: University of Michigan Law School, 1956).

26. AEC-R 2/1, AEC/NRC.

27. Ibid.

28. Ibid., CM-Reg. no. 12 (12 Dec. 1956), AEC/NRC.

29. AEC-R 5/1 (7 Dec. 1956), AEC-R 7 (7 Dec. 1956), AEC-R 7/1 (12 Dec. 1956), CM-Reg. no. 12, AEC/NRC. The notice on the AMF reactor was published in the *Federal Register* on 29 December 1956 and the Westinghouse reactor notice on 5 January 1957. See AEC press releases, 28 Dec. 1956, 4 Jan. 1957, AEC/NRC.

30. Strauss to Anderson, 4 Jan. 1957, reproduced in JCAE print, *A Study of AEC Procedures*, pp. 109–110.

31. Anderson to Strauss, 9 Aug. 1956, General Correspondence (AEC—Procedure and Organization in Licensing of Reactor Facilities), JCAE Papers; Appendix A to AEC 948 (17 Dec. 1956), Wayne P. Brobeck to Harold Price, 27 Nov. 1956, Appendix A to AEC 948/1 (20 Dec. 1956), AEC/NRC.

32. Appendix A to AEC 948, AEC/NRC.

33. Ibid.

34. Ibid.

35. Ibid.

36. Ibid.

37. Ibid.

38. Ibid., AEC 948/1, AEC/NRC; CM 1257 (20 Dec. 1956), CM 1258 (3 Jan. 1957), AEC/DOE.

39. Strauss to Anderson, 4 Jan. 1957, reproduced in JCAE print, *A Study of AEC Procedures*, pp. 108–109.

40. AEC Licensing Procedures and Organization, n.d., Toll to Ramey, 4 Mar., 4 Apr. 1957, General Correspondence (AEC—Procedure and Organization in Licensing of Reactor Facilities), JCAE Papers; JCAE print, *A Study of AEC Procedures;* S. 1684, 85th Cong., 1st sess., 1957.

41. JCAE print, *A Study of AEC Procedures*, pp. v–vi.

42. Ibid., pp. 9–10.

43. Ibid., pp. 17–25.

44. Ibid., pp. 32–35.

45. Ibid., pp. 37–48.

46. S. 1684, 85th Cong., 1st sess., 1957; *Congressional Record*, 85th Cong., 1st sess., 1957, pp. 4093–4094.

47. JCAE press release, 12 Mar. 1957, Durham to Strauss, 12 Mar. 1957, letter from Ramey, 22 Mar. 1957, printed in JCAE, *Hearings on Government Indemnity and Reactor Safety*, 85th Cong., 1st sess., 1957, pp. 2–3, 8.

48. CM 1205 (1 June 1956), Anderson to K. E. Fields, 6 July 1956, attached to AEC 943 (7 Nov. 1956), AEC/DOE; "Separate Views of Representative Holifield,"

attached to H. Rept. 2531, 84th Cong., 2d sess., 1956; Melvin Price, speech, Chicago, 25 Sept. 1956, attached to JCAE press release, 25 Sept. 1956, General Correspondence (Press Releases), JCAE Papers.

49. Frank Pittman to K. E. Fields, 14 Aug. 1956 attached to AEC 943, AEC/DOE.

50. Ibid.

51. Harold Price to K. E. Fields, 18 Oct. 1956, attached to AEC 943, AEC/DOE.

52. CM 1221 (2 Aug. 1956), Thomas Murray to Lewis Strauss, 11 Sept. 1956, attached to AEC 785/17 (26 Dec. 1956), AEC 941/2 (30 Nov. 1956), AEC 785/18 (10 Jan. 1957), CM 1260 (16 Jan. 1957), AEC/DOE.

53. Strauss, memorandum for files, 31 Dec. 1956 (Eisenhower, Dwight D. File), Lewis Strauss Papers, Herbert Hoover Library, West Branch, Iowa.

54. Clinton P. Anderson, speech to Dallas Rotary Club, 21 Nov. 1956, General Correspondence (Committee General), T. Brown to James Ramey, 13 Dec. 1956 (Indemnity), JCAE Papers; H.R. 1981, 85th Cong., 1st sess., 1957; S. 715, 85th Cong., 1st sess., 1957; JCAE, *Indemnity and Reactor Safety Hearings*, pp. 1–8.

55. AEC 785/19 (13 Mar. 1957), Appendix B to AEC 785/21 (18 Mar. 1957), AEC/DOE.

56. JCAE, *Indemnity and Reactor Safety Hearings*, p. 46.

57. AEC 785/19, AEC/DOE.

58. Appendix B to AEC 785/21, AEC/DOE.

59. Fields to the commissioners, 15 Mar. 1957, Medicine, Health, and Safety-3, AEC/DOE WASH-740, "Theoretical Possibilities and Consequences of Major Accidents in Large Nuclear Power Plants," Mar. 1957, AEC/NRC.

60. WASH-740, p. 1.

61. Ibid., p. 2.

62. Ibid., p. 3.

63. Ibid., pp. 4–5.

64. Ibid., pp. 5–6.

65. Ibid., p. 6.

66. Ibid., pp. 7–8, 25–26.

67. Ibid., p. 10.

68. Ibid., pp. 11–14, 81–85, 97–105.

69. CM 1271 (20 Mar. 1957), AEC/DOE.

70. JCAE, *Indemnity and Reactor Safety Hearings*, 1957, pp. 11–13.

71. Ibid., pp. 144–157.

72. Ibid., pp. 81–288.

73. Ibid., pp. 115–116, 126–130, 160–161, 258–268.

74. Memorandum with letter enclosures, Ramey to Joint Committee members, 13 Apr. 1957, Anderson, speech to American Management Association, 9 May 1957, Box 813, Anderson Papers.

75. Joint Committee press release, 2 May 1957, General Correspondence (AEC—

Procedure and Organization in Licensing of Reactor Facilities), JCAE Papers; S. 2051, H.R. 7383, 85th Cong., 1st sess., 1957; U.S. Congress, H. Rept. 435, 85th Cong., 1st sess., 1957, pp. 35–40.

76. Ramey to Fields, 20 May 1957, Budget-12, AEC 785/28 (21 May 1957), AEC/DOE.

77. CM 1283 (21 May 1957), Strauss to Durham, 5 June 1957, Fields to Ramey, 5 June 1957, in AEC 785/29 (11 June 1957), AEC/DOE.

78. *Congressional Record*, 85th Cong., 1st sess., 1957, pp. 10714–10718, 10722–10725; Chet Holifield to Wright Patman, 14 June 1957, Box 41 (Atomic Energy, 1956–60, Misc.), Chet Holifield Papers, University of Southern California, Los Angeles.

79. *Congressional Record*, 85th Cong., 1st sess., 1957, pp. 10714–10718, 10722–10725.

80. Ibid., p. A 7488; Strauss to Eisenhower, 27 Aug. 1957, Official File 61, Eisenhower Papers; Francis McCune to Carl Durham, 5 Sept. 1957, General Correspondence (AEC Legislation—Insurance, June 1957–Aug. 1958), JCAE Papers.

VIII. STANDARDS DEVELOPMENT: THE REACTOR-SITE CRITERIA

1. U.S. Congress, Joint Committee on Atomic Energy, *Hearings on Development, Growth, and State of the Atomic Energy Industry*, 84th Cong., 2d sess., 1956, pp. 133, 173 (hereafter called JCAE, *"202" Hearings*); JCAE, *Hearings on Government Indemnity for Private Licensees and AEC Contractors against Reactor Hazards*, 84th Cong., 2d sess., 1956, p. 62 (hereafter called JCAE, *Indemnity Hearings*). For continuing comment on the difficulty in establishing standards and criteria, see JCAE, *"202" Hearings*, 85th Cong., 1st sess., 1957, pp. 146–147; JCAE, *Hearings on Governmental Indemnity and Reactor Safety*, 85th Cong., 1st sess., 1957, p. 54; JCAE, *"202" Hearings*, 85th Cong., 2d sess., 1958, pp. 117–118; JCAE, *Hearings on Operation of AEC Indemnity Act*, 85th Cong., 2d sess., 1958, pp. 51–53; JCAE, committee print, *AEC Report on Indemnity Act and Advisory Committee on Reactor Safeguards*, 86th Cong., 1st sess., 1959, pp. 22, 60.

2. J. H. Harlow, "The ASME Boiler and Pressure Vessel Code: How the Code Originated," *Mechanical Engineering* 81 (July 1959), 56–58.

3. Nunzio J. Palladino, "Mechanical Design of Components for Reactor Systems," in *The Technology of Nuclear Reactor Safety*, ed. T. J. Thompson and J. G. Beckerley, 2 vols. (Cambridge: MIT Press, 1964, 1973), 2:111.

4. Ibid., pp. 112–113; JCAE, *"202" Hearings*, 1956, p. 173; JCAE, *Indemnity Hearings*, 1956, pp. 62–63.

5. Richard G. Hewlett and Francis Duncan, *A History of the United States Atomic Energy Commission*, vol. 2, *Atomic Shield, 1947–1952* (University Park: Pennsylvania State University Press, 1969), p. 196; Appendix A, "Estimate of Radiation From Cloud Containing All of a Reactor's Fission Products," in AEC report,

WASH-3 (rev.), "Summary Report of Reactor Safeguard Committee," 31 Mar. 1950, AEC/NRC.

6. Summary Report of Reactor Safeguard Committee, 31 Mar. 1950, AEC/NRC.

7. Charles R. Russell, *Reactor Safeguards* (New York: Pergamon Press, 1962), pp. 98–101; T. J. Thompson and C. Rogers McCullough, "The Concepts of Reactor Containment," in *Technology of Nuclear Reactor Safety*, ed. Thompson and Beckerley, 2:755–756.

8. JCAE, *"202" Hearings*, 1956, pp. 172–174.

9. Bourke Hickenlooper to Rogers McCullough, 15 Feb. 1956, ACRS File, AEC/NRC.

10. Willard Libby to Bourke Hickenlooper, 14 Mar. 1956, ACRS File, AEC/NRC.

11. Ibid.

12. Minutes of 2d Reactor Safeguards Committee meeting, 1–3 Nov. 1957, ACRS File, AEC/NRC. An excellent discussion of early reactor siting from the point of view of a Safeguards Committee member is in David Okrent, *Nuclear Safety: The History of the Regulatory Process* (Madison: University of Wisconsin Press, 1981), pp. 12–56.

13. Minutes of 9th Reactor Safeguards Committee meeting, 4–5 Aug. 1958, ACRS File, AEC/NRC; AEC 842/18 (2 Oct. 1958), AEC/DOE.

14. AEC 842/18, CM 1411 (10 Oct. 1958), AEC/DOE; minutes of 10th Reactor Safeguards Committee meeting, 15–17 Oct. 1958, ACRS File, AEC/NRC.

15. 10th Reactor Safeguards Committee meeting, 15–17 Oct. 1958, AEC/NRC.

16. Minutes of Subcommittee on Site Selection Criteria, 26 Nov. 1958, ACRS File, AEC/NRC.

17. Ibid., C. Rogers McCullough to John A. McCone, 17 Dec. 1958, ACRS File, AEC/NRC; McCullough to McCone, 15 Dec. 1958 in AEC 842/19 (23 Dec. 1958), AEC/DOE.

18. McCullough to McCone, 15 Dec. 1958 in AEC 842/19, AEC/DOE.

19. Ibid.

20. Minutes of 13th Reactor Safeguards Committee meeting, 8–10 Jan. 1959, ACRS File, AEC/NRC.

21. Minutes of Environmental Subcommittee, 18 Feb. 1959, minutes of 14th Reactor Safeguards Committee meeting, 12–14 Mar. 1959, ACRS File, AEC-R 2/7 (24 Apr. 1959), AEC/NRC.

22. 14th Reactor Safeguards Committee meeting, 12–14 Mar. 1959, AEC-R 2/7, AEC/NRC.

23. CM-Reg. no. 44 (28 Apr. 1959), AEC/NRC.

24. Chet Holifield to Clement Miller, 13 July 1959, Box 41 (Atomic Energy, 1956–1960, Misc.), Chet Holifield Papers, University of Southern California, Los Angeles; CM-Reg. no. 48 (19 June 1959), Reactions to the AEC's Proposed Reactor Site Rule-Making, Appendix B to AEC-R 2/20 (10 Dec. 1960), AEC/NRC.

25. Harold Price to A. R. Luedecke, 31 Aug. 1959 in AEC-R 2/9 (17 Sept. 1959), Appendix B to AEC-R 2/20, AEC/NRC.

26. Price to Luedecke, 31 Aug. 1959, AEC/NRC; JCAE, *"202" Hearings,* 86th Cong., 2d sess., 1960, pp. 110–111.

27. Rogers McCullough to John A. McCone, 16 Nov. 1959, A. R. Luedecke to commissioners, 9 Nov. 1960, Appendix A to AEC-R 2/21 (13 Dec. 1960), AEC/NRC.

28. JCAE, *Hearings on Indemnity and Reactor Safety,* 86th Cong., 2d sess., 1960, pp. 196–204. See also Leslie Silverman to John McCone, 14 Mar. 1960, ACRS File, AEC/NRC.

29. JCAE, *Hearings on Indemnity,* 1960, pp. 222–223, 240–241.

30. Ibid., p. 232; Oliver Townsend to Chet Holifield, 9 Nov. 1960, in AEC-R 2/17 (23 Nov. 1960), AEC/NRC.

31. Minutes of Environmental Subcommittee meeting, 8 Apr., 23 Aug. 1960, minutes of 25th Reactor Safeguards Committee meeting, 5–7 May 1960, minutes of 28th Reactor Safeguards Committee meeting, 22–24 Sept. 1960, ACRS File, AEC/NRC.

32. Clifford K. Beck, "Safety Factors to Be Considered in Reactor Siting," paper presented at Sixth International Congress and Exhibition of Electronics and Atomic Energy, June 1959, Rome, Italy, Technical Information Document (TID)–7579 (U.S. Atomic Energy Commission, Oct. 1959); Appendix A to AEC-R 2/19 (10 Dec. 1960), AEC/NRC.

33. Appendix A to AEC-R 2/19, AEC/NRC.

34. Environmental Subcommittee meetings, 8 Apr., 23 Aug. 1960, 25th Reactor Safeguards Committee meeting, 5–7 May 1960, ACRS File, Appendix B to AEC-R 2/19, AEC/NRC.

35. Appendix B to AEC-R 2/19, AEC/NRC.

36. Environmental Subcommittee meeting, 23 Aug. 1960, 28th Reactor Safeguards Committee meeting, 22–24 Sept. 1960, ACRS File, draft criteria, 20 Sept. 1960 in AEC-R 2/22 (10 Dec. 1960), AEC/NRC. According to the NCRP guidelines, the 25-rem once-in-a-lifetime exposure need not be included in the determination of the radiation status of the person exposed. See JCAE, *Hearings on Employee Radiation Hazards and Workmen's Compensation,* 86th Cong., 1st sess., 1959, p. 39.

37. Draft criteria, 20 Sept. 1960, Appendix A to AEC-R 2/19, AEC/NRC.

38. Appendix A to AEC-R 2/19, AEC/NRC.

39. Appendixes A and B to AEC-R 2/19, AEC/NRC.

40. Leslie Silverman to John McCone, 26 Sept. 1960 in Appendix C-1 to AEC-R 2/19, report of Ad Hoc Committee on Reactor Safety Criteria, 29 Sept. 1960, in AEC-R 2/21, AEC/NRC.

41. Report on Reactor Safety Criteria, AEC/NRC.

42. Silverman to McCone, 22 Oct. 1960, Appendix C-2 to AEC-R 2/19, AEC/NRC.

43. Ibid.

44. AEC-R 2/19, AEC-R 2/21, AEC-R 2/23 (16 Dec. 1960), CM-Reg. no. 86 (16 Dec. 1960), CM 1683 (22 Dec. 1960), AEC/NRC.

45. CM-Reg. no. 86, CM 1683, AEC/NRC.

46. Ibid.

47. Minutes of 31st Reactor Safeguards Committee meeting, 12, 14 Jan. 1961, ACRS File, AEC/NRC.

48. Ibid.

49. Ibid.

50. AEC-R 2/24 (27 Jan. 1961), minutes of special meeting of Reactor Safeguards Committee, 28 Jan. 1961, ACRS File, AEC/NRC.

51. AEC-R 2/24, AEC/NRC.

52. Special Reactor Safeguards Committee meeting, 28 Jan. 1961, ACRS Files, AEC-R 2/24, AEC-R 2/25 (30 Jan. 1961), CM-Reg. no. 90 (31 Jan. 1961), CM-Reg. no. 91 (1 Feb. 1961), AEC/NRC.

53. JCAE, "202" Hearings, 87th Cong., 1st sess., 1961, pp. 518–519; James T. Ramey to A. R. Luedecke, 8 Mar. 1961, Price to Ramey, 20 Mar. 1961, in AEC-R 2/28 (29 Mar. 1961), AEC/NRC.

54. Appendix G to AEC-R 2/39 (23 Feb. 1962), AEC/NRC.

55. Oak Ridge National Laboratory comments, ibid. For details on the Federal Radiation Council, see chap. 9.

56. Minutes of 32d Reactor Safeguards Committee meeting, 2–4 Mar. 1961, ACRS File, AEC/NRC.

57. Appendix G to AEC-R 2/39, AEC/NRC.

58. Ibid.

59. Ibid.

60. Clifford Beck, memorandum to the files, 3 Apr. 1961, minutes of 33d Reactor Safeguards Committee meeting, 6–8 Apr. 1961, ACRS Files, AEC/NRC.

61. Minutes of 33d Reactor Safeguards Committee meeting, ACRS Files, W. Kenneth Davis to Price, with enclosed redraft of site criteria, 6 June 1961, in AEC-R 2/32 (8 June 1961), AEC/NRC.

62. AEC-R 2/32, W. B. McCool, memorandum to the file, re 31 July 1961 meeting with Atomic Industrial Forum Committee on Reactor Safety, 3 Aug. 1961, Production Facilities Control 1–1, AEC-R 2/33 (16 Aug. 1961), Appendix G to AEC-R 2/39, AEC/NRC.

63. CM-Reg. no. 118 (26 Oct. 1961), Beck, speech to joint meeting of Atomic Industrial Forum and the American Nuclear Society, 7 Nov. 1961, in AEC 973/60 (29 Nov. 1961), Beck, speech to U.S.-Japan Atomic Industrial Forums, 7 Dec. 1961, AEC press release, 7 Dec. 1961, AEC/NRC.

64. Appendixes B and C to AEC-R 2/39, AEC-R 2/32, AEC/NRC.

65. Appendixes A and C to AEC-R 2/39, AEC/NRC.

66. Ibid.

67. Ibid.

68. Ibid.

69. Ibid.

70. Minutes of Environmental Subcommittee, 29 Nov. 1961, minutes of 38th Reactor Safeguards Committee meeting, 7–9 Dec. 1961, ACRS File, AEC-R 2/39, CM-Reg. no. 131 (23 Mar. 1962), AEC/NRC; *Federal Register*, 1 June 1962.

71. Appendix G to AEC-R 2/39, AEC/NRC.

72. Ibid.; Appendix A to AEC-R 2/7, AEC/NRC.

73. Appendix A to AEC-R 2/39, AEC/NRC.

IX. THE POLITICS OF RADIATION PROTECTION

1. "Atom Fallout . . . How Bad It Is . . . What We Can Do about It Now," *Newsweek*, 6 Apr. 1959, pp. 36–38; Robert A. Divine, *Blowing on the Wind: The Nuclear Test Ban Debate, 1954–1960* (New York: Oxford University Press, 1978), pp. 182–187, 195–206, 213–240, 262–264.

2. Joint Committee on Atomic Energy, *Hearings on AEC Authorizing Legislation, Fiscal Year 1960*, 86th Cong., 1st sess., 1959, pp. 190–197; *New York Times*, 14 Mar. 1959, p. 1.

3. "Atom Fallout," *Newsweek*, p. 36; "The Debate Is Over," *Saturday Review*, 4 Apr. 1959, p. 26; *New York Times*, 1 Mar. 1959, p. 51; *Congressional Record*, 86th Cong., 1st sess., 1959, p. 4881.

4. "Why All the Talk about Fall-Out Now," *U.S. News and World Report*, 6 Apr. 1959, p. 48; *Congressional Record*, 86th Cong., 1st sess., 1959, pp. 4875–4878.

5. *Congressional Record*, 86th Cong., 1st sess., 1959, pp. 4875–4880; JCAE, *Hearings on AEC Authorizing Legislation*, 1959, pp. 314–324; *New York Times*, 22 Mar. 1959, p. 1, 24 Mar. 1959, p. 11; "Slight Miscalculation," *Commonweal*, 10 Apr. 1959, p. 45; "Fallout Report Stirs AEC Foes," *Business Week*, 28 Mar. 1959, pp. 33–34.

6. Pre–press-conference notes, 26 Mar. 1958, DDE Diary Series, Lewis Strauss to Dwight D. Eisenhower, 31 Mar. 1958, Administrative Series, Ann Whitman File, Dwight D. Eisenhower Papers, Dwight D. Eisenhower Library; Charles J. V. Murphy, "Mr. McCone Arrives in Washington," *Fortune*, Aug. 1958, pp. 112–114; "The AEC's 'Quiet Dynamo,'" *Newsweek*, 14 July 1958, p. 52.

7. JCAE, *Hearings on AEC Authorizing Legislation*, 1959, pp. 311–314; memorandum for the general manager, 27 Mar. 1959, File 2261 (Radiation and Fallout), Office Files of John A. McCone, AEC/DOE.

In March 1960 the general manager reported that after a review of 100,000 documents relating to fallout, the agency had found 180 that had not been previously released in full or part. Of those, 23 remained classified because they contained sensitive information on weapons. A. R. Luedecke to the commissioners, 3 Mar. 1960, File 2266, Organization and Management (O&M)–12-1 (HEW), McCone Office Files.

8. Statement by the president, 25 Mar. 1959, Official File 108-I, Eisenhower Papers; National Academy of Sciences press release, 24 Mar. 1959, File 2261 (Radiation and Fallout), McCone Office Files; Divine, *Blowing on the Wind*, p. 269.

9. *New York Times*, 27 Mar. 1959, p. 1; Russell H. Morgan, "Progress toward a Comprehensive Program in Radiation Safety," *American Journal of Roentgenology, Radium Therapy and Nuclear Medicine* 79 (Feb. 1958), 349–351; Department of Health, Education, and Welfare press release, 12 Feb. 1958, File 189, U.S. Public Health Service Records, Division of Radiological Health, U.S. Public Health Service, Rockville, Maryland. In the preparation of a 1979 report, "Effects of Nuclear Weapons Testing on Health," the Public Health Service collected a large body of records relating to its role in radiological safety. They are available on microfilm for public examination.

10. Transcript of first meeting of the National Advisory Committee on Radiation, 13 Mar. 1958, File 193, "Report to the Surgeon-General on the Regulation of Radiation Safety in the United States" (draft), Oct. 1958, File 189, Public Health Service Records.

11. Transcript of proceedings of National Advisory Committee on Radiation, 2 Mar. 1959, File 192, Public Health Service Records; statement by Arthur S. Flemming, 16 Mar. 1959, Official File 108-I, Eisenhower Papers; JCAE, *Hearings on Employee Radiation Hazards and Workmen's Compensation*, 86th Cong., 1st sess., 1959, pp. 111–119. For a different view of the advisory committee's deliberations, written before much documentation was available, see Michael Goodman, "National Radiation Health Standards: A Study in Scientific Decision Making," *Atomic Energy Law Journal* 6 (Fall 1964), 217–273.

12. Francis J. Weber to David E. Price, 11 Mar. 1959, File 189, Public Health Service Records; *Congressional Record*, 86th Cong., 1st sess., 1959, pp. 4881, 5485, 5528, 5703, 5867; "The Bias of the AEC," *Nation* 188 (9 May 1959), 417; *New York Times*, 8 Mar. 1959, p. 32, 27 Mar. 1959, p. 1, 14 Apr. 1959, p. 8; *Washington Post*, 17 Mar. 1959, p. 14, 22 Mar. 1959, p. E5, 27 Mar. 1959, p. 1, 29 Mar. 1959, p. E4; *Rocky Mountain News*, 29 Mar. 1959, p. 28; *Denver Post*, 2 Apr. 1959, p. 26; *St. Louis Post-Dispatch*, 27 Mar. 1959, p. 1.

13. John D. Porterfield to Arthur S. Flemming, 12 May 1959, File 189, Public Health Service Records; Elmer B. Staats to Robert E. Merriam, 11 Apr. 1959, Official File 108-I, Eisenhower Papers; *Nucleonics* 17 (May 1959), 27; *New York Times*, 4 Apr. 1959, p. 1; *St. Louis Post-Dispatch*, 29 Mar. 1959, sec. 2, p. 1; interview with Lauriston S. Taylor, Bethesda, Maryland, 8 Oct. 1981.

14. Arthur S. Flemming to General Goodpaster, 22 Aug. 1958, Office of Staff Secretary Files, Eisenhower Papers; M. Allen Pond to the surgeon general and commissioner of food and drugs, 10 Dec. 1958, File 2372, Clinton C. Powell to the surgeon general, 2 Mar. 1959, File 2369, Public Health Service Records; Lauriston S. Taylor, *Organization for Radiation Protection: The Operations of the ICRP*

and NCRP, 1928–1974 (Springfield, Va.: National Technical Information Service, 1979), pp. 8–162 to 8–169.

15. *Washington Post*, 25 Apr. 1959, p. 1; *New York Times*, 28 Apr. 1959, p. 34; *Science* 129 (29 May 1959), 1473–1474; Charles L. Dunham to Dwight Ink, 28 Apr. 1959, File 2261 (Radiation and Fallout), McCone Office Files, AEC/DOE; Lauriston S. Taylor to Chet Holifield, 30 Apr. 1959, Box 43 (Radiation Effects), Chet Holifield Papers, University of Southern California, Los Angeles.

16. A study of public opinion in the early 1960s suggested that disagreement among experts contributed to anxiety about fallout hazards. See Sidney Kraus, Reuben Mehling, and Elaine El-Assal, "Mass Media and the Fallout Controversy," *Public Opinion Quarterly* 27 (Summer 1963), 191–205.

17. Chet Holifield to Charles Porter, 24 Apr. 1958, Holifield to George M. Ewing, 19 May 1959, Holifield to J. E. Miller, 1 July 1959, transcript of Holifield interview on "Face the Nation," 3 May 1959, Box 41 (Atomic Energy 1956–60 Misc.), Holifield Papers; Divine, *Blowing on the Wind*, pp. 271–277.

18. JCAE, *Hearings on Fallout*, 1959, pp. 11–23, 770–778, 882–898, 1825–1828; "Problem of Fallout," *Time*, 18 May 1959, p. 59.

19. Russell H. Morgan to LeRoy Burney, 19 Jan. 1959, File 189, Public Health Service Records; JCAE, *Hearings on Fallout*, 1959, pp. 1608–1609, 1956–1958.

20. JCAE, *Hearings on Fallout*, 1959, pp. 930–931, 1787–1812, 2139–2140.

21. Bureau of the Budget paper on organizational responsibilities for radiation protection, 28 May 1959, attachment to memorandum for the files of John A. McCone, 29 May 1959, File 2265 (Federal Radiation Council), McCone Office Files, AEC/DOE.

22. Ibid.

23. Memorandum for the files of John A. McCone, 29 May 1959, McCone Office Files, AEC/DOE; Elmer B. Staats, memorandum for the president, 31 July 1959, Official File 360, Eisenhower Papers; William F. Finan to Elmer B. Staats, 8 July 1959, File R5-7, Series 52.1, Record Group 51 (Records of the Bureau of the Budget), National Archives.

24. Staats, memorandum for the president, 31 July 1959, White House press releases, 14, 22 Aug. 1959, Official File 360, Eisenhower Papers; W. L. Oakley to the general manager, 19 Aug. 1959, O&M-7 (Federal Radiation Council), AEC/DOE; JCAE, *Hearings on Federal-State Relationships in the Atomic Energy Field*, 86th Cong., 1st sess., 1959, pp. 497–503.

25. Transcript of proceedings, National Advisory Committee on Radiation, 28 Sept. 1959, File 191, Clinton Powell to the surgeon general, 18 Nov. 1959, File 195, Public Health Service Records; Forrest Western to James T. Ramey, 17 Nov. 1959, General Correspondence (Fallout), Joint Committee on Atomic Energy Papers, Record Group 128, National Archives; A. R. Luedecke to John A. McCone, 29 Feb. 1960, Medicine, Health, and Safety–3 (vol. 2—Radiation), AEC/DOE; Divine, *Blowing on the Wind*, pp. 277–278.

26. *New York Times*, 21 Jan. 1960, p. 9, 28 Apr. 1960, p. 11, 21 Sept. 1960, p. 4, 19 Dec. 1960, p. 25; "Fallout: The Facts Are Brighter," *Newsweek*, 18 Apr. 1960, p. 68; "Fallout Nearly All Gone," *Science News Letter* 78 (2 July 1960), 2; *The Biological Effects of Atomic Radiation: A Report to the Public, 1960* (Washington: National Academy of Sciences–National Research Council, 1960), pp. 1–12.

27. Minutes of Federal Radiation Council meetings, 9 Sept. 1959, File 6232, 13 Apr. 1960, File 50, Public Health Service Records; JCAE, *Hearings on Radiation Protection Criteria and Standards: Their Basis and Use*, 86th Cong., 2d sess., 1960, pp. 614–663; George B. Kistiakowsky, *A Scientist at the White House: The Private Diary of President Eisenhower's Special Assistant for Science and Technology* (Cambridge: Harvard University Press, 1976), p. 302.

28. JCAE, *Hearings on Radiation Standards, Including Fallout*, 87th Cong., 2d sess., 1962, pp. 555–579; AEC-R 8/16 (4 Oct. 1962), AEC-R 8/20 (7 Oct. 1964), AEC/NRC; minutes of Federal Radiation Council meeting, 11 Jan. 1961, File 41, Public Health Service Records.

29. JCAE, *Hearings on Radiation Protection Criteria and Standards*, 1960, pp. 98–106, 116–117, 138–145, 190–191, 448, 528–533, 543–544; JCAE, *Radiation Protection Criteria and Standards: Their Basis and Use, Summary-Analysis of Hearings*, 86th Cong., 2d sess., 1960, pp. 5–6, 34–40; Donald R. Chadwick to James T. Ramey, 18 Nov. 1959, General File 239, Eisenhower Papers.

30. JCAE, *Hearings on Radiation Protection Criteria and Standards*, 1960, pp. 52, 114–115, 474–475.

31. *New York Times*, 6 Sept. 1961, p. 1, 3 Nov. 1961, p. 1, 9 Nov. 1961, p. 3; "Testing," *Time*, 10 Nov. 1961, pp. 21–25; Glenn T. Seaborg, *Kennedy, Khrushchev, and the Test Ban* (Berkeley, Los Angeles, London: University of California Press, 1981), pp. 31–32.

32. JCAE, *Hearings on Radiation Standards*, 1962, pp. 111–113, 855–858; "Iodine-131 in Fallout: A Public Health Problem," *Consumer Reports* 27 (Sept. 1962), 446–447.

33. JCAE, *Hearings on Radiation Standards*, 1962, pp. 111–116, 859; "Iodine-131 in Fallout," *Consumer Reports*, p. 447; Transcript of proceedings, Public Health Service meeting with state health officers, 26 Oct. 1961, File 144, Public Health Service Records; American Medical Association news release, 29 Sept. 1961, General Correspondence (Fallout), JCAE Papers; Hazel Gaudet Erskine, "The Polls: Atomic Weapons and Nuclear Energy," *Public Opinion Quarterly* 27 (Summer 1963), 188.

34. Donald R. Chadwick to David King, 22 Jan. 1962, File 9, Public Health Service Records; David Lawrence, "The 'Fallout' Scare," *U.S. News and World Report*, 13 Nov. 1961, p. 144; "Give Us the Truth about Fallout!" *Christian Century* 78 (22 Nov. 1961), 1387–1388; *New York Times*, 24 Jan. 1962, p. 1.

35. Erskine, "Atomic Weapons and Nuclear Energy," p. 186; Clinton P. Anderson, press release, 1 Nov. 1961, Anderson to I. Murray Berkovits, 16 Feb.

1962, Box 835, Clinton P. Anderson Papers, Library of Congress; Theodore C. Sorenson, *Kennedy* (New York: Harper and Row, 1965), pp. 617–623; Arthur M. Schlesinger, Jr., *A Thousand Days: John F. Kennedy in the White House* (Boston: Houghton Mifflin Co., 1965), pp. 454–455.

36. George A. W. Boehm, "The AEC Gets a Different Kind of Scientist," *Fortune,* Apr. 1961, pp. 158–160; "Seaborg's AEC: Atoms for War or Peace," *Newsweek,* 16 Oct. 1961, pp. 63–68; "Glenn Seaborg: From Californium to the AEC," *Time,* 10 Nov. 1961, p. 23; Seaborg, *Kennedy, Khrushchev, and the Test Ban,* pp. 112–115.

37. *New York Times,* 3 Mar. 1962, p. 1; Erskine, "Atomic Weapons and Nuclear Energy," p. 186; Sorensen, *Kennedy,* pp. 623–624.

38. Federal Radiation Council, memorandum for the president, 18 May 1962, File 44, Public Health Service Records; JCAE, *Hearings on Radiation Standards, Including Fallout,* 87th Cong., 2d sess., 1962, pp. 835–852; *New York Times,* 2 June 1962, p. 1; "110 Babies," *Newsweek,* 11 June 1962, p. 62.

39. Paul B. Dague to Abraham A. Ribicoff, 1 June 1962, William W. Scranton to Abraham A. Ribicoff, 5 June 1962, File 9, Public Health Service Records; Public Health Service press release, 24 May 1962, Box 839, Anderson Papers; *New York Times,* 31 May 1962, p. 17, 10 June 1962, p. E12; William E. Boggs, "Fallout Isn't All That Dangerous," *New Republic,* 18 June 1962, p. 8; *Congressional Record,* 87th Cong., 2d sess., 1962, p. 10917.

40. James S. Ayars to Everett Dirksen, 4 May 1962, Jim G. Akin to Everett Dirksen, 31 May 1962, File 9, Russell H. Morgan to John H. Barr, 2 May 1962, John D. Porterfield to the secretary, 18 May 1962, File 141, transcript of proceedings, National Advisory Committee on Radiation, 9 Oct. 1962, File 143, Public Health Service Records; *New York Times,* 3 May 1962, p. 10; *Washington Post,* 2 June 1962, p. 1; JCAE, *Hearings on Radiation Standards,* 1962, pp. 369–379.

41. JCAE, *Hearings on Radiation Standards,* 1962, pp. 590–602.

42. Ibid.

43. Gordon M. Dunning to Dwight A. Ink, 25 July 1962, Dunning to Ink, 3 Aug. 1962, Dunning to Ink, 17 Aug. 1962, File 3286 (Fallout—Iodine 131), Biology and Medicine (B&M)–4, AEC/DOE; *Salt Lake Tribune,* 1 Aug. 1962, p. 17, 2 Aug. 1962, p. B-1, 3 Aug. 1962, p. B-1, 8 Aug. 1962, p. 19; *Deseret News* (Salt Lake City), 7 Aug. 1962, p. B-1.

44. Luther L. Terry to Hubert H. Humphrey, 31 Aug. 1962, Terry to Humphrey, 13 Sept. 1962, File 9, transcript of proceedings, National Advisory Committee on Radiation, 9 Oct. 1962, File 143, Public Health Service Records; *New York Times,* 19 Aug. 1962, p. 88; *Minneapolis Star,* 27 Aug. 1962, p. 3A; minutes of Federal Radiation Council meeting, 29 Aug. 1962, File 3381 (Federal Radiation Council), B&M–4, AEC/DOE.

45. Office of Radiation Standards, "Documentation of FRC Guidance Related to the I–131 Problem," 14 June 1962, File 3381, B&M–4, AEC/DOE; JCAE, *Hearings*

on Radiation Standards, 1962, pp. 417–419, 582–587, 977–978; Jerome B. Wiesner, memoranda for the president, 20, 26 June 1962, President's Office Files (Office of Science and Technology), John F. Kennedy Papers, John F. Kennedy Library, Boston, Massachusetts.

46. Transcript of proceedings, National Advisory Committee on Radiation, 9 Oct. 1962, File 143, Public Health Service Records; "Selected Notes on Atomic Energy Prepared for the President of the United States," March 1963, President's Office Files (Nuclear Testing, 1962–63), Kennedy Papers; JCAE, *Hearings on Radiation Standards*, 1962, pp. 587–588; Ralph Caplan, "We Have No Fallout Policy," *Nation* 195 (13 Oct. 1962), 219–221; *Washington Post*, 17 Oct. 1962, p. B-6.

47. *Congressional Record*, 87th Cong., 2d sess., 1962, pp. 18424–18429.

48. For other Republican criticism of the Kennedy administration, see, for example, ibid., pp. 17986–17987, A6810.

49. Harold Knapp to Charles L. Dunham, 13 Sept. 1962, Charles Dunham to A. R. Luedecke, 1 Oct. 1962, Knapp File (July 1962–May 1963), Division of Biology and Medicine, Charles L. Dunham to A. R. Luedecke, 13 Aug. 1963, Knapp Report—Iodine 131, Office of the General Manager, AEC/DOE; Richard G. Hewlett, "Nuclear Weapon Testing and Studies Related to Health Effects: An Historical Summary," in *Consideration of Three Proposals to Conduct Research on Possible Health Effects of Radiation from Nuclear Weapons Testing* (Washington: National Institutes of Health, 1980).

50. Harold A. Knapp to Spofford G. English, 6 June 1963, Gordon M. Dunning to N. H. Woodruff, 14 June 1963, Research and Development (R&D) (General)—Dr. Harold Knapp, Files of the Office of the General Manager, AEC/DOE.

51. Memorandum to Dr. Haworth on telephone conversation with Dr. Knapp, 24 June 1963, Fallout-Knapp Paper, Office Files of Leland J. Haworth, Oliver R. Placak to Wright Langham, 27 June 1963, Wright Langham to John Totter, 31 July 1963, Knapp File (June 1963–January 1964), Division of Biology and Medicine, C. L. Dunham to A. R. Luedecke, 13 Aug. 1963, Knapp Report—Iodine 131, Duncan Clark to A. R. Luedecke, 24 Dec. 1963, R&D (Gen)—Dr. Harold Knapp, Office of the General Manager, AEC/DOE; JCAE, *Hearings on Fallout, Radiation Standards, and Countermeasures*, 88th Cong., 1st sess., 1963, pp. 914–1078.

52. JCAE, *Hearings on Fallout*, 1963, pp. 337–338, 347–351; AEC 604/71 (14 Jan. 1963), AEC 604/73 (8 Feb. 1963), AEC 604/75 (14 Mar. 1963), AEC/NRC.

53. JCAE, *Hearings on Fallout*, 1963, pp. 536–563, 607–672; *New York Times*, 2 Oct. 1963, p. 19; Hewlett, "Nuclear Weapon Testing and Studies Related to Health Effects."

54. *Washington Post*, 21 Aug. 1963, p. 16; *New York Times*, 22 Aug. 1963, p. 12, 10 Nov. 1963, p. 40; *St. Louis Post-Dispatch*, 22 Aug. 1963, p. 6; *Los Angeles Times*, 21 Aug. 1963, p. 2; *Salt Lake Tribune*, 22 Aug. 1963, p. 1; "'I Can Look My Children In The Eye Again,'" *Newsweek*, 12 Aug. 1963, p. 16.

55. Erskine, "Atomic Weapons and Nuclear Energy," p. 188; "Is 'Fallout' a False Scare?" *U.S. News and World Report*, 27 Nov. 1961, p. 72.

56. Saul J. Harris, "State and Local Regulation of Radiation," *A.M.A. Archives of Industrial Health* 19 (Mar. 1959), 302.

57. "110 Babies," *Newsweek*, p. 62.

X. THE STATES AND ATOMIC REGULATION

1. George Norris, Jr. to David Toll, 17 Apr. 1956, General Correspondence (AEC—Licensing Regulations with States), Clinton P. Anderson to Frank Norton, 12 June 1956 (Indemnity), Joint Committee on Atomic Energy (JCAE) Papers, Record Group 128 (Records of the Joint Committees of Congress), National Archives.

2. Alfred C. Neal to Sherman Adams, 18 Feb. 1953, Jesse J. Friedman to Charles F. Honeywell, 21 Feb. 1953, Sinclair Weeks to Sherman Adams, 13 Mar. 1953, Official File 108, Dwight D. Eisenhower Papers, Dwight D. Eisenhower Library, Abilene, Kansas; *Atomic Energy and New England: The Report of the New England Committee on Atomic Energy to the New England Governors' Conference* (Cambridge: MIT Press, 1955); William A. W. Krebs, Jr., "What Are You Doing about Atomic Development?" *State Government* 29 (May 1956), 79 ff.; Douglas H. Parker, "The Need for State Atomic Energy Programs in the West," *Rocky Mountain Law Review* 29 (Apr. 1957), 296–366.

3. *Implications of Atomic Energy for Texas*, Staff Research Report to the Texas Legislative Council, no. 53-8, May 1955; Frank Norton to Clinton P. Anderson, 15 June 1956, General Correspondence (AEC—Licensing Regulations with States), Frank Norton to David R. Toll, 2 Nov. 1956 (Cooperation with States), JCAE Papers; Frank Norton, speech, "Report on Texas Committee on Atomic Energy," May 1956, Box 40, E. Blythe Stason Papers, Michigan Historical Collections, Bentley Historical Library, University of Michigan, Ann Arbor.

4. LeRoy Collins, speeches, 20 Oct. 1955, 25 Jan. 1956, General Correspondence (Southern Regional Education Board), JCAE Papers; LeRoy Collins, "The Importance of Nuclear Energy to the South," in *Prospects for Atomic Energy in the South* (New York: Atomic Industrial Forum, 1956), pp. 27–34.

5. Southern Regional Education Board, "The Place of Nuclear Energy in the South's Future," typescript (1956), General Correspondence (Southern Regional Education Board), JCAE Papers; Southern Regional Education Board, *Role of Atomic Energy in the South* (Atlanta, 1956).

6. Norton, "Report on Texas Committee," G. Mennen Williams to E. Blythe Stason, 24 Aug. 1955, Box 40, Stason Papers; *Proceedings of the Governors' Conference, 1956* (Chicago, 1956), pp. 138–139; *Forum Memo* (newsletter of the Atomic Industrial Forum), Dec. 1955, pp. 14–15.

7. *Atomic Energy and New England*, pp. 31–32; "The Place of Nuclear Energy in the South's Future," pp. 1–23; *Proceedings of the Governors' Conference, 1956,*

pp. 138, 174–175; Redding S. Sugg, Jr., ed., *Nuclear Energy in the South* (Baton Rouge: Louisiana State University Press, 1957); minutes of Michigan Atomic Energy Study Committee meeting, 2 Mar. 1955, Box 173, G. Mennen Williams Papers, Michigan Historical Collections.

8. Texas Committee on Atomic Energy, "Informal Report of Activities," 1956, General Correspondence (AEC—Licensing Regulations with States), JCAE Papers; report of Atomic Energy Study Committee to Governor Williams, n.d., Box 40, Stason Papers.

9. Krebs, "What Are You Doing about Atomic Development?" pp. 79–81; J. Raymond Dyer, "The Role of the States in the Power Reactor Program," *Public Utilities Fortnightly* 58 (8 Nov. 1956), 781–788; John H. McCarthy to G. Mennen Williams, 21 June 1956, Box 173, Williams Papers.

10. *Forum Memo*, Aug. 1955, pp. 13–14; summary of proceedings, Conference of State Representatives on the AEC Licensing Program, 13–14 July 1955, Box 144, Williams Papers; CM 1073 (6 Apr. 1955), CM 1092 (22 June 1955), AEC 23/25 (27 Apr. 1955), AEC/DOE.

11. CM 1123 (15 Sept. 1955), AEC 865 (9 Sept. 1955), 865/1 (2 Mar. 1956), AEC/DOE; memorandum from Albert E. Heustis to all state health officers, 9 Apr. 1956, Box 173, Williams Papers; Goodwin Knight to Thomas H. Kuchel, 5 Apr. 1956, General Correspondence (Cooperation with States), JCAE Papers.

12. Minutes of Atomic Energy Study Committee meeting, 16 July 1956, G. Mennen Williams to Lewis L. Strauss, 16 July 1956, Box 173, Williams Papers.

13. K. E. Fields to G. Mennen Williams, 17 July 1956, Lawrence L. Farrell to Lewis L. Strauss, 18 July 1956, G. Mennen Williams to John H. McCarthy, 20 July 1956, Clinton P. Anderson to G. Mennen Williams, 3 Aug. 1956, Box 173, Williams Papers.

14. AEC/957 (15 Feb. 1957), AEC/DOE; George Norris, Jr. to Senator Anderson and Congressman Durham, 14 Feb. 1956, General Correspondence (AEC Licensing Regulations with States), George Norris, Jr. to James T. Ramey, 18 Dec. 1956 (Cooperation with States), Clinton P. Anderson, speech, 21 Nov. 1956 (Committee—Active Members, Anderson), JCAE Papers; Doyle Kline to Senator Anderson, 10 July 1956, Box 795, Clinton P. Anderson Papers, Library of Congress.

15. AEC 957, 957/1 (31 May 1957), CM 1266 (20 Feb. 1957), AEC/DOE; Curtis A. Nelson, speech, 2 Feb. 1957, Box 42, Stason Papers.

16. AEC 957, AEC/DOE.

17. AEC 957, 957/1, 957/2 (2 July 1957), CM 1289 (5 June 1957), AEC/DOE; Lewis L. Strauss to Carl T. Durham, 21 June 1957, Box 603, Anderson Papers.

18. *Summary of Conference on the States and Atomic Energy Development* (Chicago: Council of State Governments, 1957); AEC 957/1, AEC/DOE; Military Division to Roger Jones, 19 June 1957, "A.E.C. *Draft* Material," 19 June 1957, Atomic Energy File, Douglas R. Price Papers, Eisenhower Library.

19. *Summary of Conference on the States and Atomic Energy Development*, pp. 13–

15, 23–25; JCAE, *Selected Materials on Federal-State Cooperation in the Atomic Energy Field*, 86th Cong., 1st sess., 1959, pp. 154–157.

20. *Summary of Conference on the States and Atomic Energy Development*, pp. 19, 24–25; JCAE, *Selected Materials*, pp. 151–154; K. E. Fields to Frank Bane, 20 Feb. 1957, General Correspondence (Cooperation with States), JCAE Papers; Clinton P. Anderson to Allyn Donnelly, 19 Dec. 1958, Box 803, Anderson Papers.

21. JCAE, *Selected Materials*, pp. 4–5; Saul J. Harris, ed. and comp., *State Activities in Atomic Energy* (New York: Atomic Industrial Forum, 1958); W. A. McAdams, speech, "Laws, Codes and Standards in the Nuclear Field," 17 Apr. 1958, General Correspondence (Radiation Standards for Protection), JCAE Papers.

22. G. O. Robinson to Carl T. Durham, 14 June 1957, R. M. Cooper to Clinton P. Anderson, 10 July 1957, General Correspondence (Cooperation with States), Regional Advisory Council on Nuclear Energy, "A Progress Report," 25 Sept. 1957 (Southern Governors' Conference), JCAE Papers; "Pattern for Atomic Progress in the South," 22 Sept. 1958, Box 236, Williams Papers; *Christian Science Monitor*, 13 Nov. 1958, p. 6. See also J. Samuel Walker, "The South and Nuclear Energy, 1954–62," *Prologue* 13 (Fall 1981), 174–191.

23. National Committee on Radiation Protection, *Regulation of Radiation Exposure by Legislative Means*, National Bureau of Standards, Handbook 61 (Washington, 1955); George T. Frampton, "Radiation Exposure: The Need for a National Policy," *Stanford Law Review* 10 (Dec. 1957), 7–52; JCAE, *Selected Materials*, pp. 5–6; William C. Ellet, *State Control and Administration of Atomic Radiation* (Iowa City: Institute of Public Affairs of the State University of Iowa, 1957); William H. Berman and Lee M. Hydeman, "State Responsibilities in the Atomic Energy Field," *State Government* 32 (Spring 1959), 114–120; *Minneapolis Star*, 17 Nov. 1958, p. 6.

24. Charles Robbins, "Community Relations for Atomic Energy," in *The Impact of the Peaceful Uses of Atomic Energy on State and Local Government* (New York: Atomic Industrial Forum, 1959), p. 35; William A. W. Krebs, Jr., "Federal-State Relations in Atomic Energy—1958," in *Management and Atomic Energy, 1958* (New York: Atomic Industrial Forum, 1958), pp. 159–165; Chamber of Commerce of the United States of America, "Policy on Atomic Energy" (mimeograph), File 1509, Carl T. Durham Papers, Southern Historical Collection, University of North Carolina Library, Chapel Hill.

25. Krebs, "Federal-State Relations," pp. 161–165; McAdams, speech, "Laws, Codes and Standards," JCAE Papers; JCAE, *Selected Materials*, pp. 342–345, 359–362.

26. Dwight D. Eisenhower to Swede Hazlett, 24 June 1957, DDE Diary Series, Ann Whitman File, Eisenhower Papers; *Final Report of the Joint Federal-State Action Committee* (Washington: Government Printing Office, 1960); *Congressional Record*, 86th Cong., 1st sess., 1959, p. 825; AEC 957/3 (24 Jan. 1958), 957/4 (14 Mar. 1958), AEC/DOE.

27. JCAE, *Hearings on Employee Radiation Hazards and Workmen's Compensation,* 86th Cong., 1st sess., 1959, pp. 111–119, *Congressional Record,* 86th Cong., 1st sess., 1959, p. 4881.

28. AEC 957/8 (28 Jan. 1959), AEC/NRC.

29. JCAE, *Selected Materials,* pp. 24–29; AEC press release, 10 Nov. 1958, AEC/NRC.

30. JCAE, *Selected Materials,* pp. 26–34; AEC 957/8, AEC/NRC.

31. Ibid.

32. Albert E. Heustis to the Governor's Atomic Energy Study Committee, 31 Mar. 1959, Box 268, Williams Papers.

33. JCAE, *Hearings on Federal-State Relationships in the Atomic Energy Field,* 86th Cong., 1st sess., 1959.

34. Ibid.; Clinton P. Anderson to John A. McCone, 29 May 1959, General Correspondence (Cooperation with States), JCAE Papers.

35. JCAE, *Hearings on Federal-State Relationships,* pp. 485–488; Senate Calendar no. 896, Report no. 870, 1 Sept. 1959, Box 629, Anderson Papers; William F. Finan to Elmer B. Staats, 8 July 1959, File R5-7 Series 52.1, Record Group 51 (Records of the Bureau of the Budget), National Archives.

36. Clinton P. Anderson to James T. Ramey, 30 July 1959, Box 832, Anderson Papers; *Congressional Record,* 86th Cong., 1st sess., 1959, pp. 19042–19046, 19170, 19690.

37. AEC 957/12 (12 Feb. 1960), AEC/NRC.

38. Ibid.

39. AEC 957/16 (3 Jan. 1961), AEC/NRC; John A. McCone to Dwight D. Eisenhower, 7 Apr. 1960, Leg-7 (Federal-State Relationships), Office Files of John A. McCone, AEC/DOE.

40. AEC 957/16, AEC-R 70/2 (5 Aug. 1961), AEC/NRC; JCAE, *Hearings on Radiation Protection Criteria and Standards: Their Basis and Use,* 86th Cong., 2d sess., 1960, pp. 150, 164–165.

41. AEC 957/16, AEC/NRC; Jerome Maslowski to Nicholas V. Olds, 21 Sept. 1960, Box 297, Williams Papers; *Forum Memo,* Jan. 1960, p. 22; Samuel D. Estep and Martin Adelman, "State Control of Radiation Hazards: An Intergovernmental Relations Problem," *Michigan Law Review* 60 (Nov. 1961), 41–80.

42. AEC-R 70 (8 Mar. 1961), AEC-R 70/2, AEC/NRC; JCAE, *Hearings on Radiation Protection Criteria and Standards,* 1960, p. 165.

43. AEC-R 70/2, AEC/NRC.

44. AEC-R 70/6 (2 Oct. 1961), AEC-R 70/12 (26 Oct. 1961), AEC/NRC.

45. AEC-R 70/9 (12 Oct. 1961), AEC-R 70/14 (4 Dec. 1961), AEC-R 70/16 (15 Jan. 1962), AEC-R 70/20 (2 Apr. 1962), AEC/NRC.

46. AEC-R 70/20, AEC/NRC; James N. Neel, Jr., "The Atomic Energy Commission's Federal-State Program and Its Impact on the Utilization of Nuclear Materials in Kentucky," *Atomic Energy Law Journal* 6 (Fall 1964), 274–287.

47. U.S. Nuclear Regulatory Commission, "Final Task Force Report on the Agreement States Program," NUREG-0388 (1977), p. A-53; AEC-R 88/4 (23 Feb. 1962), AEC/NRC; Southern Interstate Nuclear Board, *The Atom in the South: Story of Leadership and Achievement* (report to the Southern Governors' Conference, 1962).

48. William H. Berman and Lee M. Hydeman, *Federal and State Responsibilities for Radiation Protection: The Need for Federal Legislation* (Ann Arbor: University of Michigan Atomic Energy Research Project, 1959), pp. 66–69.

49. Transcript of proceedings, National Advisory Committee on Radiation, 2 Mar. 1959, File 192, U.S. Public Health Service Records, Division of Radiological Health, U.S. Public Health Service, Rockville, Maryland.

XI. WORKERS AND RADIATION HAZARDS

1. Richard G. Hewlett and Francis Duncan, *A History of the United States Atomic Energy Commission*, vol. 2, *Atomic Shield, 1947–1952* (University Park: Pennsylvania State University Press, 1969), pp. 147–149, 173, 426, 551; Larry L. Meyer, "U-Boom on the Colorado Plateau," *American Heritage*, June/July 1981, pp. 74–79; AEC press release, 10 Apr. 1948, AEC/NRC; Joint Committee on Atomic Energy, *Hearings on Problems of the Uranium Mining and Milling Industry*, 85th Cong., 2d sess., 1958, pp. 38–40.

2. Meyer, "U-Boom on the Colorado Plateau," pp. 75–79; JCAE, *Hearings on Mining and Milling Industry*, 1958, pp. 287–289.

3. Hewlett and Duncan, *Atomic Shield*, pp. 148–149; JCAE, *Hearings on Mining and Milling Industry*, 1958, pp. 289–292.

4. S. E. Miller, D. A. Holaday, and H. N. Doyle, "Health Protection of Uranium Miners and Millers," in *Proceedings of the International Conference on the Peaceful Uses of Atomic Energy* (New York: United Nations, 1956), pp. 242–247; Federal Radiation Council, "Background Material for the Development of Radiation Standards for Uranium Mining," draft, 1 Nov. 1962, File 3381, Biology and Medicine (B&M)–4, AEC/DOE; William F. Bale, "Memorandum to the Files, March 14, 1951: Hazards Associated with Radon and Thoron," *Health Physics* 38 (June 1980), 1061–1066, and John H. Harley, "Sampling and Measurement of Airborne Daughter Products of Radon," ibid., pp. 1067–1074.

5. Egon Lorenz, "Radioactivity and Lung Cancer: A Critical Review of Lung Cancer in the Miners of Schneeberg and Joachimsthal," *Journal of the National Cancer Institute* 5 (Aug. 1944), 1–15; Sigismund Peller, "Lung Cancer among Mine Workers in Joachimsthal," *Human Biology* 11 (Feb. 1939), 130–143; Miller, Holaday, and Doyle, "Health Protection of Uranium Miners and Millers," p. 242; Bale, "Memorandum to the Files," pp. 1063–1065; Harley, "Sampling and Measurement of Airborne Daughter Products of Radon," p. 1071.

6. *Congressional Record*, 79th Cong., 2d sess., 1946, pp. 6078–6085; AEC 544/6 (12 Apr. 1960), AEC/NRC.

7. Federal Radiation Council, "Background Material for the Development of Radiation Standards for Uranium Mining," preliminary draft, 21 July 1961, File 3380, FRC, "Background Material . . . for Uranium Mining," draft, 1 Nov. 1962, File 3381, B&M-4, AEC/DOE.

8. Henry N. Doyle, "Uranium Mining and Milling: A Current Study," *Occupational Health* 13 (Mar. 1953), 37, 46; AEC 544 (4 Apr. 1952), AEC/DOE; Miller, Holaday, and Doyle, "Health Protection of Uranium Miners and Millers," pp. 242–243.

9. AEC 544, AEC 544/1 (14 July 1953), AEC/DOE; Miller, Holaday, and Doyle, "Health Protection of Uranium Miners and Millers," pp. 243–245.

10. *Proceedings of Seven-State Uranium Mining Conference on Health Hazards* (Salt Lake City: Industrial Commission of Utah, 1955), pp. 1–3, 70–72, 92–93, 96.

11. Ibid., pp. 66–69, 85.

12. Ibid., pp. 53, 55, 66, 74–75, 84–93; *Science News Letter* 67 (30 Apr. 1955), 277.

13. L. E. Burney to Charles L. Dunham, 27 Oct. 1958, File 1634, Public Health Service Records, Division of Radiological Health, U.S. Public Health Service, Rockville, Maryland.

14. AEC 544/2 (8 Dec. 1958), AEC 544/5 (17 Feb. 1960), AEC/NRC; L. K. Olson to Charles L. Dunham, 11 Mar. 1959, Medicine, Health, and Safety (MH&S)–11 (Uranium Mining, vol. 1), AEC/DOE.

15. AEC 544/5, AEC/NRC; Arthur J. Goldberg to Wayne Aspinall, 18 Sept. 1961, General Correspondence (Source Materials—Uranium), Joint Committee on Atomic Energy Papers, Record Group 128, National Archives.

16. AEC 544/5, AEC/NRC; M. Allen Pond to Arthur Flemming, 15 Nov. 1960, File 1632, Public Health Service Records.

17. JCAE, *Hearings on Employee Radiation Hazards and Workmen's Compensation*, 86th Cong., 1st sess., 1959, pp. 190–204, 282, 577–578, 587; JCAE, *Hearings on Radiation Protection Criteria and Standards: Their Basis and Use*, 86th Cong., 2d sess., 1960, pp. 103–104, 353–361, 430–433; *Denver Post*, 16 Mar. 1959, p. 15.

18. JCAE, *Hearings on Radiation Protection Criteria*, pp. 364–367; H. L. Price to John T. Conway, 24 Oct. 1963, Edward J. Bauer to the files, 1 Oct. 1963, General Correspondence (Source Materials—Uranium), JCAE Papers.

19. AEC 544/3 (13 July 1959), AEC press release, 30 July 1959, AEC/NRC; "Public Health Service Activities re Water Pollution Caused by Radioactive Wastes," 20 July 1959, File 1634, Public Health Service Records.

20. AEC 544/3, AEC press releases, 30 July, 10 Nov. 1959, AEC/NRC; A. R. Luedecke to Robert W. Kastenmeier, 5 Dec. 1959, General Correspondence (Source Materials—Uranium), JCAE Papers; "Public Health Service Activities re Water Pollution," Public Health Service Records; JCAE, *Hearings on Radiation Protection Criteria*, pp. 364–367.

21. AEC 544/6, 544/8 (24 June 1960), AEC/NRC; A. R. Luedecke to Clinton P.

Anderson, 12 Feb. 1960, General Correspondence (Source Materials—Uranium), JCAE Papers.

22. Royce A. Hardy to Clinton P. Anderson, 11 Sept. 1958, General Correspondence (Cooperation with States), JCAE Papers; Louis S. Gerber to Chief, Division of Radiological Health, 14 Oct. 1960, File 1632, Public Health Service Records; *Denver Post*, 12 May 1960, p. 12, 26 May 1960, p. 3.

23. Pond to Flemming, 15 Nov. 1960, File 1632, Public Health Service Records; AEC 544/11 (6 Dec. 1960), AEC/NRC.

24. Nathan H. Woodruff to A. R. Luedecke, 23 Dec. 1960, MH&S-11 (Uranium Miners, vol. 1), AEC/DOE; JCAE, *Hearings on Radiation Exposure of Uranium Miners*, 90th Cong., 1st sess., 1967, pp. 902–910.

25. Woodruff to Luedecke, 23 Dec. 1960, Duncan Clark to Luedecke, 28 Dec. 1960, MH&S-11 (Uranium Miners, vol. 1); AEC/DOE; JCAE, *Hearings on Radiation Exposure of Uranium Miners*, p. 910; "Uranium Miners' Cancer," *Time*, 26 Dec. 1960, p. 33; *Denver Post*, 16 Dec. 1960, p. 13.

26. AEC 544/12 (13 Jan. 1961), AEC/NRC; AEC 544/14 (18 May 1961), AEC/DOE; Simon P. Abrahams to chief, Division of Radiological Health, 8 Feb. 1961, File 29, Public Health Service Records.

27. Howard C. Brown, memoranda for the general manager, 20 Dec. 1960, 5 Jan. 1961, Neil D. Naiden to Howard C. Brown, 18 Jan. 1961, Neil D. Naiden to the commissioners, 28 June 1961, MH&S-11, AEC/DOE; Simon Abrahams to the files, 1 May 1961, File 29, minutes of Federal Radiation Council Working Group, 4, 18, 25, 31 Jan. 1961, File 41, Federal Radiation Council, memorandum for the president, 18 Jan. 1961, minutes of Federal Radiation Council, 17 May 1961, File 43, Public Health Service Records.

28. U.S. Congress, House Committee on Education and Labor, *Hearings on Mine Safety (Metallic and Nonmetallic Mines)*, 87th Cong., 1st sess., 1961, pp. 32–33, 124–132, 172, 318–324; Attachment E to Harold J. Magnuson to assistant surgeon general for operations, 13 Feb. 1962, File 29, Public Health Service Records.

29. Magnuson to assistant surgeon general, 13 Feb. 1962, File 29, draft notes prepared by James G. Terrill on Atomic Energy Commission–Department of Health, Education, and Welfare Meeting, 1 Aug. 1961, File 1133, Public Health Service Records; John S. Graham to W. B. McCool, 14 Sept. 1961, Federal Radiation Council Formal Correspondence, Office Files of Leland J. Haworth, AEC/DOE.

30. B. W. Maxwell to J. C. Terrill, Jr., 4 Mar. 1962, File 29, Public Health Service Records.

31. Department of Health, Education, and Welfare press release, 26 Aug. 1963, General Correspondence (Source Materials—Uranium), JCAE Papers; Joseph K. Wagoner et al., "Mortality Patterns among United States Uranium Miners and Millers, 1950 through 1962," *Atomic Energy Law Journal* 6 (Spring 1964), 1–13.

32. JCAE, *Hearings on Employee Radiation Hazards*, 1959, p. 282; JCAE, *Hearings on Radiation Protection Criteria*, 1960, p. 431. Leo Goodman, a major spokesman for the AFL-CIO on atomic-energy issues, has asserted that the Joint Committee failed to take action because Congressman Wayne Aspinall of Colorado, a committee member, strongly objected. His colleagues went along in return for Aspinall's support on other matters. Goodman's argument is plausible but impossible to substantiate from available documentation. Interview with Leo Goodman, Washington, D.C., 15 Mar. 1982.

33. U.S. Atomic Energy Commission, "A Summary of Accidents and Incidents Involving Radiation in Atomic Energy Activities, June 1945 through December 1955," Technical Information Document (TID)–5360, p. iv.

34. AEC 841 (23 June 1955), AEC/DOE. For discussion of the background of the regulations, see chap. 2.

35. AEC 841, AEC/DOE.

36. AEC 841/2 (2 Mar. 1956), 841/3 (28 Nov. 1956), AEC/DOE; AEC-R 8 (17 Dec. 1956), AEC press release, 25 Jan. 1957, AEC/NRC.

37. JCAE, *Hearings on Governmental Indemnity for Private Licensees and AEC Contractors against Reactor Hazards*, 84th Cong., 2d sess., 1956, pp. 306–312.

38. Ibid., pp. 356–373; George Norris, Jr. to Mr. Price, 6 July 1956, Melvin Price to Clinton P. Anderson, 25 July 1956, General Correspondence (Indemnity), George Norris, Jr. to James T. Ramey, 20 May 1957 (Radiation—Health and Safety), JCAE Papers.

39. AEC 290/15 (3 May 1957), AEC/DOE; United States Court of Appeals for the Fifth Circuit, *Jackson E. McVey and H. E. Northway vs. Phillips Petroleum Company*, 10 Mar. 1961, General Correspondence (Nuclear Accidents—M. W. Kellogg), JCAE Papers; Joseph P. Blank, "Atomic Tragedy in Texas," *Look*, 3 Sept. 1957, pp. 25–29.

40. AEC 290/15, CM 1278 (30 Apr. 1957), AEC/DOE; Blank, "Atomic Tragedy," p. 27; "AEC Statement on Allegations Regarding M. W. Kellogg Co. Incident," enclosure with A. R. Luedecke to James T. Ramey, 14 June 1960, General Correspondence (Nuclear Accidents—M. W. Kellogg), JCAE Papers.

41. AEC 290/15, AEC/DOE; AEC-R 8/1 (7 May 1957), AEC press releases, 2, 11 May 1957, AEC/NRC.

42. AEC 981 (18 Sept. 1957), AEC/DOE; AEC press release, 6 Nov. 1957, AEC/NRC.

43. AEC 290/16 (24 May 1957), AEC/DOE; Blank, "Atomic Tragedy," pp. 26–29.

44. AEC press release, 2 May 1957, AEC/NRC; Blank, "Atomic Tragedy," pp. 26–29; *Houston Post*, 3 May 1957, p. 1, 4 May 1957, p. 1; "Plague of Iridium 192," *Time*, 13 May 1957, p. 79; "'Lepers' of Our Times," *Newsweek*, 13 May 1957, p. 36.

45. Lewis Strauss to Carl T. Durham, 2 May 1958, H. L. Price to James T.

Ramey, 20 May 1960, Dwight Ink to Chet Holifield, 28 Feb. 1961, James T. Ramey to all committee members, 7 Mar. 1961, Dwight Ink to Lyndon B. Johnson, 5 Feb. 1963, *McVey and Northway vs. Phillips Petroleum*, 10 Mar. 1961, General Correspondence (Nuclear Accidents—M. W. Kellogg), JCAE Papers; AEC 981/22 (21 Oct. 1960), 981/23 (8 Nov. 1960), 981/24 (29 Nov. 1960), 981/26 (19 Dec. 1960), AEC/NRC; "Sequel to Atomic Tragedy," *Look*, 12 Apr. 1960, pp. 23–30.

46. AEC 981/1 (2 Oct. 1957), AEC/DOE; "AEC Statement on Allegations Regarding M. W. Kellogg Co. Incident," "Notice to the Press," 18 June 1960, General Correspondence (Nuclear Accidents—M. W. Kellogg), JCAE Papers.

47. AEC 981/4 (13 Dec. 1957), AEC/NRC.

48. Lauriston S. Taylor, *Organization for Radiation Protection: The Operations of the ICRP and NCRP, 1928–1974* (Springfield, Va.: National Technical Information Service, 1979), pp. 8–061 to 8–154; JCAE, *Hearings on Employee Radiation Hazards*, pp. 37–40.

49. AEC-R 8/4 (19 Mar. 1959), AEC/NRC.

50. CM-Reg. no. 42 (6 Apr. 1959), AEC/NRC.

51. George Meany to John McCone, 25 Aug. 1960, AEC-R 8/7 (13 July 1960), AEC 957/14 (16 Sept. 1960), AEC/NRC.

52. JCAE, *Hearings on Employee Radiation Hazards*, pp. 399–407; Bruce A. Greene, "Workmen's Compensation Aspects of the Peaceful Uses of Atomic Energy," *Proceedings of the International Conference on the Peaceful Uses of Atomic Energy*, vol. 13 (New York: United Nations, 1956), pp. 59–62.

53. JCAE, *Hearings on Employee Radiation Hazards*, pp. 384–420.

54. Ibid., pp. 415–468, 518–527, 542–570, 579–585, 620–666; JCAE, *Employee Radiation Hazards and Workmen's Compensation: Summary-Analysis of Hearings*, 86th Cong., 1st sess., 1959, pp. 1–2, 15–16.

55. AEC 985/9 (20 June 1962), AEC/NRC; U.S. Congress, House Committee on Education and Labor, *Hearings on Radiation Workers Compensation Act*, 87th Cong., 2d sess., 1962, pp. 316–317.

56. House Committee on Education and Labor, *Hearings on Radiation Workers Compensation Act*, pp. 1–2, 88–101, 152–156, 166–167, 180–186, 205–229, 316–319; David R. Toll to Clinton P. Anderson, 26 Jan. 1960, Box 818, Clinton P. Anderson Papers, Library of Congress.

57. House Committee on Education and Labor, *Hearings on Radiation Workers Compensation Act*, pp. 2–7, 74–77.

58. Stephen N. Shulman to Timothy J. Reardon, 30 Jan. 1962, William D. Carey to Mr. Reardon, 9 Feb. 1962, Stephen N. Shulman to T. J. Reardon, 15 Feb. 1962, William D. Carey to Mr. Reardon, 2 Mar. 1962, White House Central Files (HE6—Radiological Health), John F. Kennedy Papers, John F. Kennedy Library, Boston, Massachusetts; AEC 503/4 (13 June 1962), AEC 503/6 (19 Nov. 1963), AEC 1136 (27 June 1963), AEC/NRC.

59. House Committee on Education and Labor, *Hearings on Radiation Workers Compensation Act*, pp. 74–77; T. J. Thompson, "Accidents and Destructive Tests,"

in *The Technology of Nuclear Reactor Safety*, ed. T. J. Thompson and J. G. Beckerley, 2 vols. (Cambridge: MIT Press, 1964, 1973), 1:608–612.

60. AEC-R 36/2 (31 July 1958), AEC-R 74/11 (31 Jan. 1962), AEC-R 74/12 (8 Feb. 1962), AEC-R 74/14 (27 Feb. 1962), AEC-R 74/22 (28 Jan. 1963), AEC/NRC.

61. JCAE, *SL-1 Accident: Atomic Energy Commission Investigation Board Report*, 87th Cong., 1st sess., 1961, pp. 2–39; JCAE, *Hearings on Radiation Safety and Regulation*, 87th Cong., 1st sess., 1961, pp. 69–181; House Committee on Education and Labor, *Hearings on Radiation Workers Compensation Act*, p. 74.

62. JCAE, *SL-1 Accident*, pp. v–x; JCAE, *Hearings on Radiation Safety and Regulation*, 1961, pp. 69–71.

63. JCAE, *Hearings on Radiation Safety and Regulation*, 1961, pp. 115–184, 397–418; AEC 1066/3 (1 Mar. 1961), AEC/NRC.

64. George Meany to John F. Kennedy, 28 Mar. 1962, White House Central Files (AT—Atomic Energy), Kennedy Papers; AEC 675/13 (29 Oct. 1963), AEC/NRC; Leo Goodman, "The Need for Trade Union Action to Revise Regulations Covering Occupational Radiation Hazards," *Atomic Energy Law Journal* 5 (Winter 1963), 261–268; JCAE, *Hearings on Radiation Protection Criteria and Standards*, pp. 544–565.

XII. RADIOACTIVE WASTE DISPOSAL: COMPLEXITIES AND CONTROVERSIES

1. Charles H. Fox, *Radioactive Wastes* (Washington: U.S. Atomic Energy Commission, 1965), pp. 3–14; C. B. Amphlett, *Treatment and Disposal of Radioactive Wastes* (New York: Pergamon Press, 1962), pp. 1–12; Alton Frye, *The Hazards of Atomic Wastes: Perspectives and Proposals on Oceanic Disposal* (Washington: Public Affairs Press, 1962), pp. 6–10.

2. Fox, *Radioactive Wastes*, pp. 11–20; AEC 180/5 (30 Mar. 1956), AEC/NRC; AEC 180/6 (14 June 1957), Joseph A. Lieberman, speech, 27 Jan. 1960, Materials–12 (Waste Processing and Disposal, vol. 1), AEC/DOE.

3. Fox, *Radioactive Wastes*, pp. 14–29; AEC 180/5, AEC/NRC; AEC 180/6, Lieberman, speech, 27 Jan. 1960, AEC/DOE; "Status Report on Handling and Disposal of Radioactive Wastes in the AEC Program" (WASH-742) (Washington: U.S. Atomic Energy Commission, 1957), p. 3; U.S. Nuclear Regulatory Commission, *Regulation of Federal Radioactive Waste Activities* (NUREG-0527), 1979.

4. U.S. Atomic Energy Commission, *Handling Radioactive Wastes in the Atomic Energy Program* (Washington: Government Printing Office, 1949); AEC 180/1 (17 Oct. 1949), AEC/DOE; AEC press release, 9 Dec. 1949, AEC/NRC.

5. *The Biological Effects of Radiation: A Report to the Public* (Washington: National Academy of Sciences–National Research Council, 1956), pp. 30–31; Robert De Roos, "What Are We Doing about Our Deadly Atomic Garbage?" *Collier's*, 20 Aug. 1955, pp. 28–34; "Death-Dealing Debris," *Newsweek*, 15 July 1957, pp. 96–98.

6. AEC 180/5, AEC/NRC; AEC 180/6, AEC/DOE; Clinton P. Anderson to Helen

S. Eaton, 8 Mar. 1956, General Correspondence (Waste Disposal), Joint Committee on Atomic Energy Papers, Record Group 128, National Archives; Arthur E. Gorman, "Environmental Aspects of the Atomic Energy Industry," in *Proceedings of the International Conference on the Peaceful Uses of Atomic Energy*, vol. 13 (New York: United Nations, 1956), pp. 298–303; "'Hot Stuff': Big Hurdle for Atomic Power," *Business Week*, 23 July 1955, pp. 72–77; "Reactor Ashes Precious," *Science News Letter*, 68 (27 Aug. 1955), 131–132; De Roos, "Atomic Garbage," p. 34.

7. AEC 841 (23 June 1955), AEC/DOE; AEC press release, 25 Jan. 1957, AEC/NRC.

8. AEC 180/5, AEC/NRC.

9. Ibid.

10. Ibid.

11. "Status Report . . . on Radioactive Wastes" (WASH-742), pp. 3, 21–27; Morse Salisbury to James T. Ramey, 5 Nov. 1957, General Correspondence (Waste Disposal), JCAE Papers.

12. *The Disposal of Radioactive Waste on Land* (Washington: National Academy of Sciences–National Research Council, 1957), pp. 2–3.

13. Ibid., pp. 3–4, 92–139.

14. Ibid., pp. 1–7.

15. Lewis Strauss to general manager, 13 Sept. 1957, K. E. Fields to Mr. Strauss, 6 Dec. 1957 (Fields, Gen. Kenneth E. File), Lewis Strauss Papers, Herbert Hoover Library, West Branch, Iowa; AEC 719/20 (3 Apr. 1958), AEC/NRC; AEC 180/8 (6 Oct. 1958), AEC/DOE.

16. Joint Committee on Atomic Energy, *Hearings on Industrial Radioactive Waste Disposal*, 86th Cong., 1st sess., 1959, p. 1.

17. Ibid., pp. 7–22, 1271–1277, 2086, 2427, 3028.

18. Ibid., pp. 2993–3026; Arnold B. Joseph, *United States Sea Disposal Operations: A Summary to December 1956* (WASH-734) (Washington: U.S. Atomic Energy Commission, 1957), pp. 1–6; "Disposal of Radioactive Wastes in the Ocean," statement of U.S. Atomic Energy Commission to the state of California, 20 Oct. 1958, General Correspondence (Waste Disposal), JCAE Papers; John Kobler, "Gangway for the Atomic Garbage Man!" *Saturday Evening Post*, 25 Jan. 1958, pp. 36, 73; "Death-Dealing Debris," *Newsweek*, p. 96.

19. JCAE, *Hearings on Industrial Radioactive Waste Disposal*, p. 1000; AEC-R 35/1 (8 May 1958), AEC-R 35/4 (18 Sept. 1958), AEC-R 42 (7 Jan. 1959), AEC-R 42/8 (3 Apr. 1959), AEC-R 42/9 (2 June 1959), AEC/NRC; AEC 180/7 (2 Oct. 1957), AEC/DOE; *New York Times*, 16 July 1957, p. 3.

20. AEC-R 42/8, AEC-R 42/9, AEC/NRC.

21. AEC-R 42/10 (16 June 1959), AEC/NRC; Lyndon B. Johnson to Clinton P. Anderson, 15 June 1959, General Correspondence (Waste Disposal), JCAE Papers; H. L. Price to Dwight A. Ink, 16 June 1959, H. L. Price to George E. Reedy,

18 June 1959, A. R. Luedecke to Ralph W. Yarborough, 18 June 1959, A. R. Luedecke to Clinton P. Anderson, 26 June 1959, File 2261 (Radioactive Waste and Waste Disposal), Office Files of John A. McCone, AEC/DOE; *Congressional Record*, 86th Cong., 1st sess., 1959, pp. 8256–8258, 10507–10510, 12658; *Washington Post*, 16 May 1959, p. 1.

22. AEC-R 42/15 (30 June 1959), AEC/NRC; Price to Ink, 16 June 1959, Clark C. Vogel to the commissioners, 10 Aug. 1959, File 2261, McCone Office Files, AEC/DOE; *Congressional Record*, 86th Cong., 1st sess., 1959, p. 10508.

23. AEC-R 42/29 (23 Apr. 1962), AEC/NRC; A. A. Wells to Chairman McCone, 5 Oct. 1959, Philip J. Farley to Algie A. Wells, 25 Aug. 1959, Box 2247 (Waste Disposal), Office Files of John F. Floberg, AEC/DOE.

24. *Radioactive Waste Disposal into Atlantic and Gulf Coastal Waters* (Washington: National Academy of Sciences–National Research Council, 1959); National Academy of Sciences–National Research Council press release, 21 June 1959, General Correspondence (Waste Disposal), JCAE Papers.

25. A. R. Luedecke to Bob Casey, 2 July 1959, John A. McCone to Theodore Francis Green, 29 July 1959, File 2261, McCone Office Files, AEC/DOE; *Houston Post*, 21 June 1959, p. 9; *New York Times*, 21 June 1959, p. 41; *Providence Journal*, 19 July 1959, p. 29.

26. John Pastore to Clinton P. Anderson, 19 July 1959, Box 818, Clinton P. Anderson Papers, Library of Congress; JCAE, *Hearings on Industrial Radioactive Waste Disposal*, pp. 3060–3074, 3096–3100, 3111, 3125–3128, 3135–3136.

27. JCAE, *Hearings on Industrial Radioactive Waste Disposal*, pp. 3075–3085, 3101–3108, 3123–3124; *Providence Journal*, 30 July 1959, p. 7.

28. *Congressional Record*, 86th Cong., 1st sess., 1959, p. 12658; Wesley S. Griswold, "Getting Rid of Radioactive Rubbish," *Popular Science*, Sept. 1960, p. 260; AEC press release, 8 July 1959, AEC/NRC; *Wall Street Journal*, 18 Feb. 1960, p. 1.

29. AEC-R 39/22 (25 May 1959), AEC-R 39/34 (13 June 1961), AEC/NRC; Gerald McCourt, "Test Case on Atomic Waste," *Nation* 189 (1 Aug. 1959), 43–45; JCAE, *Hearings on Industrial Radioactive Waste Disposal*, p. 3095.

30. AEC press release, 11 Aug. 1959, AEC/NRC; telegram to AEC from residents of Cape Cod, 24 Aug. 1959, Ned Lehac to John F. Kennedy, 14 Oct. 1959, General Correspondence (Waste Disposal), JCAE Papers; E. J. Kahn, Jr., "The Government and the People," *New Yorker*, 15 Oct. 1960, pp. 104–124; Grace Des Champs, "'Hot' Dumping Off Boston," and editorial, "The Public Be Damned," *Nation* 189 (19 Sept. 1959), 142–146; "Death-Dealing Debris," *Newsweek*, p. 96; Kobler, "Atomic Garbage Man," pp. 36, 73; *Boston Globe*, 30 Aug. 1959, p. 40.

31. Kahn, "Government and the People," pp. 106–119; "Sea Disposal of Atomic Wastes," *Bulletin of the Atomic Scientists* 16 (Apr. 1960), 141; H. L. Price to Bernard Hartley, 16 Sept. 1959, Docket no. 27-19, AEC/NRC.

32. Radio Reports, Inc., transcript of Edward P. Morgan broadcast, 15 July

1959, File 2261, McCone Office Files, AEC/DOE; John A. McCone to Dwight D. Eisenhower, 24 July 1959, Administrative Series, Ann Whitman File, Dwight D. Eisenhower Papers, Dwight D. Eisenhower Library; Clinton P. Anderson to Paul K. Greening, 31 July 1959, Anderson to Mrs. L. B. Hall, 3 Aug. 1959, Anderson to Stewart F. Loeb, 8 Aug. 1959, Anderson to Mr. and Mrs. J. R. Bernard, 16 Sept. 1959, clipping from *Farmington Times*, 24 July 1959, Box 174, Anderson Papers; "Valley of Strontium 90," *Time*, 27 July 1959, p. 37; "Atomic Burying Grounds," *New Republic*, 10 Aug. 1959, pp. 5–6; *New York Times*, 16 July 1958, p. 8. See chap. 11 for additional discussion of the Animas River contamination.

33. CM 1528 (15 July 1959), Morse Salisbury to A. R. Luedecke, 24 July 1959, John A. McCone to the general manager, 30 Sept. 1959, Materials-12 (Waste Processing and Disposal), AEC/DOE.

34. Joseph A. Lieberman to Ernest B. Tremmel, 14 Mar. 1960, Box 2247, Floberg Office Files, AEC/DOE; Joseph A. Lieberman to David R. Toll, 18 May 1960, General Correspondence (Waste Disposal), JCAE Papers; AEC press release, 7 June 1960, AEC/NRC; *Annual Report to Congress of the Atomic Energy Commission for 1959* (Washington: Government Printing Office, 1960), p. 324; "Study Radioactive Wastes," *Science News Letter* 76 (25 July 1959), 51.

35. AEC-R 63 (10 Jan. 1961), AEC/NRC; Morse Salisbury to A. R. Luedecke, 18 Mar. 1960, File 2261, McCone Office Files, AEC/DOE; "The Huge and Ever-Increasing Problem of Radioactive Wastes," *Consumer Reports* 25 (Feb. 1960), 66–67; "The Deep Six," *Newsweek*, 15 Feb. 1960, pp. 92–95; "Hot Cargo," *Nation* 191 (3 Dec. 1960), 426–427; *New York Times*, 17 Jan. 1960, p. 26; *Wall Street Journal*, 18 Feb. 1960, p. 1; *Congressional Record*, 86th Cong., 2d sess., 1960, pp. A 3159–3160.

36. AEC-R 63, AEC-R 63/1 (24 Feb. 1961), AEC/NRC; "The Atomic Sewer," *Nation* 191 (6 Feb. 1960), 112.

37. H. C. Brown, memorandum for the files, 16 Mar. 1960, CM 1630 (20 June 1960), Materials-12 (Waste Processing and Disposal), AEC/DOE.

38. McCourt, "Test Case on Atomic Waste," p. 43.

39. AEC-R 42/23 (26 June 1960), AEC/NRC; E. B. White, "Letter from the East," *New Yorker*, 27 July 1957, p. 43; David F. Cavers, "Administrative Decisionmaking in Nuclear Facilities Licensing," *University of Pennsylvania Law Review* 110 (Jan. 1962), 340.

40. AEC 180/12 (3 Dec. 1959), AEC/NRC.

41. Ibid.

42. John A. McCone to the general manager, 17 Mar. 1960, CM 1573 (17 Dec. 1959), CM 1617 (6 May 1960), Materials-12 (Waste Processing and Disposal), A. R. Luedecke to the commissioners, 15 Apr. 1960, File 2261, McCone Office Files, AEC/DOE; AEC press release, 9 May 1960, AEC/NRC.

43. AEC 180/23 (10 May 1963), AEC press releases, 16 Nov. 1961, 1 May 1963,

AEC/NRC; CM 1630, Materials-12 (Waste Processing and Disposal), AEC/DOE; *New York Times*, 3 June 1961, p. 24; JCAE, *Hearings on Chemical Reprocessing Plant*, 88th Cong., 1st sess., 1963, pp. 47–50.

44. AEC 180/23, AEC/NRC; W. B. McCool to Ernest B. Tremmel, 17 May 1963, Dwight A. Ink to John O. Pastore, 23 May 1963, Materials-12 (Waste Processing and Disposal), AEC/DOE.

45. Richard G. Hewlett, "Federal Policy for the Disposal of Highly Radioactive Wastes from Commercial Power Plants: An Historical Analysis," unpublished paper, 1978, p. 24, Hanford Monthly Status and Progress Report to the Division of Production, October 1958, AEC/DOE; "Waste Management Operations, Hanford Reservation, Richland, Washington," Sept. 1974 (WASH-1538), draft, p. 11.1-C-134, AEC/NRC; *Annual Report to Congress of the Atomic Energy Commission*, 1960, pp. 301, 315; *Alternatives for Long-Term Management of Defense High-Level Radioactive Waste: Hanford Reservations* (ERDA 77-44) (Washington: Energy Research and Development Administration, 1977), pp. 2–7; Fred C. Shapiro, *Radwaste* (New York: Random House, 1981), pp. 48–50, 54–56; JCAE, *Hearings on Industrial Radioactive Waste Disposal*, pp. 165, 166, "202" Hearings, 88th Cong., 1st sess., 1963, p. 649.

46. AEC 180/13 (20 Sept. 1960), AEC/NRC; A. R. Luedecke to James T. Ramey, 15 June 1959, General Correspondence (Waste Disposal), R. L. Kirk to James T. Ramey, 21 Mar. 1961 (Committee Members—Holifield, Chet), JCAE Papers; Hewlett, "Federal Policy for the Disposal of Highly Radioactive Wastes," pp. 7–9; *Defense High-Level Radioactive Waste: Hanford Reservations*, pp. 2–7; JCAE, *"202" Hearings*, 88th Cong., 1st sess., 1963, p. 650; Shapiro, *Radwaste*, pp. 50–51, 60–61.

47. AEC 180/13, AEC/NRC.

48. Ibid.; A. R. Luedecke to H. H. Hess, 4 Jan. 1961, Materials-12 (Waste Processing and Disposal), AEC/DOE.

49. AEC 180/13, AEC/NRC.

XIII. IMPROVING THE REGULATORY PROCESS

1. U.S. Congress, Joint Committee on Atomic Energy, committee print, *A Study of AEC Procedures and Organization in the Licensing of Reactor Facilities*, 85th Cong., 1st sess., pp. 37–38, 108–109 (hereafter cited as JCAE print, *A Study of AEC Procedures*).

2. Appendix A to AEC 948 (17 Dec. 1956), AEC 948/1 (20 Dec. 1956), AEC/NRC; CM 1257 (20 Dec. 1956), CM 1258 (3 Jan. 1957), AEC/DOE.

3. AEC 948/3 (3 Apr. 1957), AEC 948/4 (1 May 1957), AEC/NRC; Lewis Strauss to Kenneth Fields, 6 May 1957 (Fields, Gen. Kenneth E. File), Lewis Strauss Papers, Herbert Hoover Library, West Branch, Iowa; CM 1282 (8 May 1957), AEC/DOE; JCAE print, *A Study of AEC Procedures*, pp. 45–46; Strauss to Carl T.

Durham, 13 June 1957, General Correspondence (Facility Licensing), Joint Committee on Atomic Energy (JCAE) Papers, Record Group 128 (Records of the Joint Committees of Congress), National Archives.

4. AEC 948/6 (15 Aug. 1957), AEC/NRC.

5. Ibid.

6. Ibid.

7. Ibid.; CM 1312 (30 Oct. 1957), AEC/DOE; AEC press release, 26 Dec. 1957, AEC/NRC.

8. "The Regulatory Program of the Atomic Energy Commission," Nov. 1960, printed in JCAE, committee print, *Improving The AEC Regulatory Process*, vols. 1 and 2, 87th Cong., 1st sess., 1961, 2:104, 130–135. For details on the state-agreements program and the creation of the Federal Radiation Council, see chaps. 9 and 10.

9. "The Regulatory Program of the Atomic Energy Commission," in JCAE print, *Improving the AEC Regulatory Process* 2:130–131, 146.

10. Ibid., pp. 120–122.

11. Ibid., pp. 104, 107–108; JCAE, *Hearings on Indemnity and Reactor Safety*, 86th Cong., 2d sess., 1960, p. 222.

12. AEC Manual, sec. 0103-12, "Functions and Delegations, Assistant General Manager for Regulation and Safety," sec. 0103-08, "Functions and Delegations, Division of Licensing and Regulation," 15 Feb. 1960, in JCAE print, *Improving the AEC Regulatory Process* 2:382–385. See also William H. Berman and Lee M. Hydeman, *The Atomic Energy Commission and Regulating Nuclear Facilities* (Ann Arbor: University of Michigan Law School, 1961), pp. 152–154.

13. JCAE, *Hearings on Indemnity and Reactor Safety*, 1960, pp. 222–223.

14. See above, chaps. 3 and 5. See also Berman and Hydeman, *Regulating Nuclear Facilities*, pp. 93–94.

15. "The Regulatory Program of the Atomic Energy Commission," in JCAE print, *Improving the AEC Regulatory Process* 2:151–153.

16. Ibid., pp. 112–119.

17. Ibid., pp. 151–153. See also Berman and Hydeman, *Regulating Nuclear Facilities*, pp. 105–107.

18. Examples of Safeguards Committee letter reports are: Rogers McCullough to Lewis L. Strauss, 5 Nov. 1957 (Report on National Advisory Committee for Aeronautics), McCullough to John A. McCone, 5 Aug. 1958 (Report on Rural Cooperative Power Association, Elk River, Minn.), McCullough to McCone, 15 Jan. 1959 (Report on Carolinas-Virginia Nuclear Powerplant), McCullough to Willard Libby, 12 July 1958 (Report on General Electric Test Reactor), ACRS File, AEC/NRC. See also reply from R. L. Doan, 5 Apr. 1961 in JCAE, committee print, *Views and Comments on Improving the AEC Regulatory Process*, 87th Cong., 1st sess., 1961, p. 35 (hereafter cited as JCAE print, *Views and Comments*).

19. For the hearing process before 1957, see chap. 3. Kenneth Culp Davis,

"Dueprocessitis in the Atomic Energy Commission," *American Bar Association Journal* 47 (Aug. 1961), 782–785.

20. JCAE print, *A Study of AEC Procedures*, pp. 23, 25, 206; JCAE, *Hearings on Government Indemnity and Reactor Safety*, 85th Cong., 1st sess., 1957, pp. 161, 263; S. 1648, 85th Cong., 1st sess., 1957; *Congressional Record*, 85th Cong., 1st sess., 1957, p. 3616; U.S. Congress, S. Rept. 296, 85th Cong., 1st sess., 1957, pp. 12–15, 24–25. See also JCAE print, *Improving the AEC Regulatory Process* 1:49.

21. "The Regulatory Program of the Atomic Energy Commission," in JCAE print, *Improving the AEC Regulatory Process* 2:141.

22. AEC 812/1 (23 June 1959), AEC/DOE; AEC-R 43/1 (28 Oct. 1959) CM-Reg. no. 55 (3 Nov. 1959), AEC/NRC. For a discussion of the historical development of the *ex parte* rule in AEC decision-making, see U.S. Nuclear Regulatory Commission, "A Study of the Separation of Functions and *Ex Parte* Rules in Nuclear Regulatory Commission Adjudications for Domestic Licensing" (NUREG-0670) (1980), pp. 15–29.

23. "The Regulatory Program of the Atomic Energy Commission," in JCAE print, *Improving the AEC Regulatory Process* 2:139; AEC press releases, 5 Aug. 1958, 7 July 1960, AEC/NRC.

24. See Berman and Hydeman, *Regulating Nuclear Facilities*, pp. 122–129, for an excellent discussion on the role of the examiner.

25. Hearing transcript, 8, 24 Oct. 1957, *Yankee Atomic Electric Co.*, AEC Docket no. 50-29, hearing transcript, 17 Jan. 1958, *General Electric Co.*, AEC Docket no. 50-70, hearing transcript, 16, 17 Jan., 21 Feb. 1958, *National Advisory Committee for Aeronautics*, AEC Docket no. 50-30, hearing transcript, 25 Mar., 11 June 1959, *Westinghouse Electric Co.*, AEC Docket no. 50-22, AEC/NRC; Berman and Hydeman, *Regulating Nuclear Facilities*, pp. 128–129; JCAE print, *Improving the AEC Regulatory Process* 1:21–22.

26. "Report on the Regulatory Program of the Atomic Energy Commission," in JCAE print, *Improving the AEC Regulatory Process* 2:411.

27. Hearing transcript, 26 May 1960, Second Intermediate Decision and Order for Limited Power Operations, 9 July 1960, *Yankee Atomic Electric Co.*, AEC Docket no. 50-29, AEC/NRC. At the operating-license stage of Commonwealth Edison's Dresden facility, Jensch devised a procedure whereby a hearing would be required at several different power-level steps before the reactor could go to full power. This procedural device, meant to keep AEC control over the final operating license while the burden of proof for safety continued to rest on the applicant, further formalized the licensing process and set a precedent for full-power operations of later reactors. Immediate Decision and Order for Limited Power Operations, 26 Sept. 1959, Motion for Reconsideration, 14 Oct. 1959, Supplemental Intermediate Decision, 12 Nov. 1959, *Commonwealth Edison Co.*, AEC Docket no. 50-10. See also memorandum of John S. Graham to commissioners, 20 Nov. 1959 in AEC-R 32/14 (1 Dec. 1959), AEC/NRC. Commonwealth

Edison was not happy with this procedure. See W. L. Oakley, memorandum for files, 20 Oct. 1959, in AEC-R 32/10 (12 Nov. 1959), AEC/NRC.

28. JCAE print, *Improving the AEC Regulatory Process* 1:vii, 31, 33–34, 48–52; James T. Ramey to Loren K. Olsen, 7 Nov. 1960, Olson to Ramey, 30 Nov. 1960, printed ibid. 2:575–587.

29. Amendment of Utilization Facility License (Amendment no. 14), 6 July 1960, Licensee's Petition for Reconsideration of Final Order, 1 Sept. 1960, *General Electric Co. (Vallecitos Boiling Water Reactor)*, AEC Docket no. 50-18, AEC/NRC.

30. W. B. McCool, memorandum to commissioners, 26 Oct. 1960, Commission Memorandum and Order, 2 Nov. 1960, AEC Docket no. 50-18, AEC/NRC.

31. 10 C.F.R. 50.59 (1963).

32. JCAE, *Hearings on Indemnity and Reactor Safety,* pp. 222–223.

33. The two parts of the AEC study were published in full in JCAE print, *Improving the AEC Regulatory Process* 2:87–422; CM 1685 (5 Jan. 1961), CM 1692 (31 Jan. 1961), AEC/DOE.

34. AEC press releases, 28 Feb. 1958, 16 May 1960, AEC/NRC; *New York Times,* 17 May 1960, p. 13; CM 1692 (31 Jan. 1961), AEC/DOE.

35. CM 1685, AEC/DOE; "Report on the Regulatory Program of the Atomic Energy Commission," in JCAE print, *Improving the AEC Regulatory Process* 2:399–402; *New York Times,* 22 Jan. 1961, p. 39.

36. CM 1685, AEC/DOE; *New York Times,* 5 Mar. 1961, p. 1.

37. CM 1692, AEC/DOE.

38. A. R. Luedecke to Commission, "Comments on the Regulatory Report," 26 Jan. 1961, Organization and Management (O&M)–7, CM 1692, CM 1693 (1 Feb. 1961), CM 1711 (10 Mar. 1961), AEC/DOE; AEC 132/35 (3 Mar. 1961), AEC press release, 16 Mar. 1961, AEC/NRC; Glenn Seaborg to John F. Kennedy, 16 Mar. 1961, President's Office Files (Atomic Energy Commission 1961), John F. Kennedy Papers, John F. Kennedy Library, Boston, Mass. For further agency implementation of the new regulatory organization, see AEC 132/37 (14 Apr. 1961), AEC/NRC; CM 1730 (25 Apr. 1961), AEC/DOE.

39. F. C. Schuldt to David Bell, 3 Feb. 1961, Harold Seidman to Elmer Staats, 15 Feb. 1961, File P7-1, Series 61.1a, David Bell to John F. Kennedy, 30 Mar. 1961, File F2-2, Record Group 51 (Records of the Bureau of the Budget), National Archives; Elmer Staats to Frederick G. Dutton, 16 Feb. 1961, Chet Holifield to John F. Kennedy, 21 Feb. 1961, William D. Carey to Dutton, 12 June 1961, White House Central Files (FG 202, Atomic Energy Commission), Kennedy Papers.

40. Schuldt to Bell, 3 Feb. 1961, File P7-1, Bell to Kennedy, 30 Mar. 1961, File F2-2, Series 61.1a, Bureau of Budget Records; Staats to Dutton, 16 Feb. 1961, White House Central Files (FG 202, Atomic Energy Commission), Kennedy Papers.

41. Clinton P. Anderson to John McCone, 30 Aug. 1960 in AEC 496/67 (2 Sept. 1960), James Ramey to W. B. McCool, 1 Sept. 1960, Legal-7-Reg. Proceedings, AEC/NRC; Ramey to Chet Holifield, 14 Feb. 1961, General Correspondence

(Facility Licensing), JCAE Papers; Ramey to Olson, 7 Nov. 1960, in JCAE print, *Improving the AEC Regulatory Process* 2:575–578. The AEC report was transmitted to the Joint Committee in February 1961; the Joint Committee study came out in March 1961.

42. "Report on the Regulatory Program of the Atomic Energy Commission," in JCAE print, *Improving the AEC Regulatory Process* 2:405–407, 410–411.

43. Ibid., pp. 413–420.

44. JCAE print, *Improving the AEC Regulatory Process* 1:3–5, 48–54, 62–64.

45. Ibid., pp. 64–68; Berman and Hydeman, *Regulating Nuclear Facilities* (the extracted parts are in JCAE print, *Improving the AEC Regulatory Process* 2:423–557; *New York Times*, 16 Mar. 1961, p. 20.

46. JCAE print, *A Study of AEC Procedures*, p. 46; JCAE print, *Improving the AEC Regulatory Process* 1:69–75.

47. JCAE print, *Improving the AEC Regulatory Process* 1:69.

48. Ibid., p. 70.

49. Ibid., p. 71.

50. Ibid., pp. 74–75.

51. JCAE print, *Views and Comments*, pp. v–viii.

52. Ibid., pp. 2, 9–10, 19–21, 33–34, 44, 49–50, 72, 81–84.

53. Draft hearing testimony, 9, 12, 14 June 1961, O&M-7, AEC/DOE; JCAE, *Improving the AEC Regulatory Process* 1:69; F. C. Schuldt to David Bell, 2, 9 June 1961, File P7-1, Series 61.1a, Bureau of Budget Records; William D. Carey to Frederick Dutton, 12 June 1961, White House Central Files (FG 202, Atomic Energy Commission), Kennedy Papers.

54. Carey to Dutton, 12 June 1961, Kennedy Papers.

55. JCAE, *Hearings on Radiation Safety and Regulation*, 87th Cong., 1st sess., 1961, pp. 269–286, 297–308.

56. Ibid., pp. 312–313.

57. Ibid., pp. 313–314.

58. Ibid., p. 314.

59. Ibid., pp. 372–389.

60. Glenn Seaborg to Chet Holifield, 24 July 1961, reproduced ibid., pp. 427–428; James Ramey to William Mitchell, 11 Aug. 1961, General Correspondence (Legislation: 87th S. 1947–88th S. 768), JCAE Papers; H.R. 8708 in *Congressional Record*, 87th Cong., 1st sess., 1961, p. 15879.

61. H.R. 8708; JCAE, *Hearings on Radiation Safety and Regulation*, pp. 427–428.

62. Seaborg to Holifield, 27 July 1961, Holifield to Seaborg, 7 Aug. 1961, reproduced in JCAE, *Hearings on Radiation Safety and Regulation*, pp. 428–430.

63. H.R. 8708; JCAE, *Hearings on Radiation Safety and Regulation*, pp. 313–314, 388–389.

64. H.R. 8708; JCAE, *Hearings on Radiation Safety and Regulation*, pp. 301, 429–430; CM-Reg. Information no. 16 (14 Aug. 1961), AEC/NRC.

65. H.R. 8708; S. 2419 in *Congressional Record*, 87th Cong., 1st sess., 1961,

p. 15882; Ramey to Mitchell, 11 Aug. 1961, Ramey to David Cavers, 11 Aug. 1961, 18 Aug. 1961, General Correspondence (Legislation: 87th S. 1947–88th S. 768), JCAE Papers; U.S. Congress, S. Rept. 1677, 87th Cong., 2d sess., 1962.

66. David Toll to James Ramey, 7 Mar. 1962, General Correspondence (Legislation: H.R. 8708–S. 2419), JCAE Papers; JCAE, *Hearing on AEC Regulatory Problems*, 87th Cong., 2d sess., 1962, pp. 27–28; H.R. 12336 in *Congressional Record*, 87th Cong., 2d sess., 1962, p. 11977; S. 3491 in *Congressional Record*, 87th Cong., 2d sess., 1962, p. 12235; S. Rept. 1677, *Congressional Record*, 87th Cong., 2d sess., 1962, pp. 15746, 16551.

67. White House press release, 19 Mar. 1962, David Bell to Kennedy, 3 May 1962, President's Office Files (Atomic Energy Commission 1962), Kennedy Papers; "Draft AEC Reorganization Plan," 1 Mar. 1962, Box 5, AEC Reorganization Problems–R. Jones File, Series 60.18, Bureau of Budget Records. For discussion of the report, see chap. 14.

68. Bell to Kennedy, 3 May 1961, Kennedy Papers. See also Ramey to Holifield, 14 Feb. 1961, General Correspondence (Facility Licensing), Melvin Price, speech to Atomic Industrial Forum, 6 Nov. 1961 (Speeches: Price, Melvin, vol. 3), Holifield to Kennedy, 13 Feb. 1962 (President), JCAE Papers.

69. Bell to Kennedy, 3 May 1962, Kennedy Papers; memorandum with draft letter, 4 May 1962, Commission to Bell, 16 May 1962 with Graham's 11 May 1962 enclosure, Office Files of Glenn T. Seaborg, AEC/DOE; Schuldt to Bell, 26 June 1962, Bell to Seaborg, 24 Aug. 1962, Box 5, AEC Reorganization Problems–R. Jones File, Series 60.18, Bureau of Budget Records.

70. Edward L. Clark to Steve McNichols, 22 Mar. 1961, File 29, U.S. Public Health Service Records, Division of Radiological Health, U.S. Public Health Service, Rockville, Maryland; Graham to Bell, 11 May 1962, AEC/DOE; Ralph Dungan to Kennedy, 3 May 1962, Bell to Kennedy, 3 May 1962, President's Office Files (Atomic Energy Commission 1962), Kennedy Papers.

71. Bell to Kennedy, 3 May 1962, President's Office Files (Atomic Energy Commission 1962), Kennedy Papers.

72. Dungan to Kennedy, 3 May 1962, President's Office Files (Atomic Energy Commission 1962), James T. Ramey to Ralph Dungan, 24 May 1962, White House Central Files (Atomic Energy 1961), Kennedy Papers; Schuldt to Roger Jones, 17 Jan. 1963, Box 5, AEC Reorganization Problems–R. Jones File, Series 60.18, Bureau of Budget Records; Harold P. Green, "Atomic Energy: Commission or Administrator?" *Bulletin of the Atomic Scientists* 18 (Dec. 1962), 33–37; Harold P. Green and Alan Rosenthal, *Government of the Atom* (New York: Atherton Press, 1963), pp. 76–78, 114; *New York Times*, 18 May 1962, p. 8; *Nucleonics Week*, 24 May 1962, p. 1.

73. Transcript of nomination of James Ramey to AEC, 8 Aug. 1962, General Correspondence (Hearings, Transcript), John Conway, memorandum to files, 23 Nov. 1962 (AEC—Reorganization and Personnel), JCAE Papers; Arthur Mur-

phy to George T. Mazuzan, 6 May 1982; *Nucleonics Week,* 22 Nov. 1962, p. 1. The consultants were New York lawyer Arthur Murphy, Columbia University political science professor Richard E. Neustadt, and Bell Telephone Laboratories president James B. Fisk.

74. Richard Neustadt to Elmer Staats, 20 Dec. 1962, Box 5, AEC Reorganization Problems–R. Jones File, Series 60.18, Bureau of Budget Records; *Nucleonics Week,* 31 Jan. 1963, p. 1; Harold Seidman, a senior staff member at the Budget Office, later confirmed the Joint Committee's view that abolition of the Commission was a direct threat to its powers: Seidman, *Policy, Position, and Power: The Dynamics of Federal Organization,* 2d ed. (New York: Oxford University Press, 1975), pp. 61–63.

75. Harold Price to Commission, 6 Sept. 1962, O&M-7 (Atomic Safety and Licensing Board), AEC/DOE; CM-Reg. no. 150 (9 Oct. 1962), AEC-R 4/16 (25 Oct. 1962), CM-Reg. Information no. 67 (29 Oct. 1962), CM-Reg. no. 154 (31 Oct. 1962), AEC-R 4/18 (27 Nov. 1962), CM-Reg. no. 158 (5 Dec. 1962), AEC press release, 6 Dec. 1962, AEC/NRC.

76. Summary notes of meeting with Atomic Safety Licensing panel members, 26 Nov. 1962, O&M-7 (Atomic Safety and Licensing Boards), AEC/DOE.

77. AEC press release, 17 May 1962, AEC/NRC.

78. JCAE print, *Improving the AEC Regulatory Process* 1:67, 74–75.

XIV. WATERSHED: THE 1962 REPORT TO THE PRESIDENT

1. Clinton P. Anderson to John F. Kennedy, 21 Nov. 1960, President's Office Files (Atomic Energy Commission 1961), Papers of John F. Kennedy, John F. Kennedy Library, Boston, Mass.

2. Ibid.

3. Chet Holifield to John F. Kennedy, 21 Feb. 1961, ibid.

4. Frederick G. Dutton to David Bell, Glenn Seaborg, and Jerome Wiesner, 21 Mar. 1961, Bell to John F. Kennedy, 22 Mar. 1961, File P7-2, F. C. Schuldt to Elmer B. Staats, 11 Oct. 1961, File P7-1, Series 61.1a, Bell to Kennedy, 17 Dec. 1961, Bureau of Budget budget review, n.d., Box 1, Series 61.1b, Record Group 51 (Records of the Bureau of the Budget), National Archives; *New York Times,* 4 Feb. 1962, p. 57; U.S. Congress, Joint Committee on Atomic Energy, *Hearings on Development, Growth, and State of the Atomic Energy Industry,* 87th Cong., 2d sess., 1962, pp. 6–21 (hereafter called JCAE, *"202" Hearings*). Administration reasons for the reductions included higher priority for defense expenditures, higher priority for nuclear-energy applications in space, the fact that the Pacific Gas and Electric Company had decided to build a 325-megawatt power reactor on the stated grounds of economic attractiveness, and that there was no reason to construct new reactors until more experience could be accumulated from reactors coming on line. F. C. Schuldt to David Bell, 6 Feb. 1962, Bell to Lee White, 13 Feb. 1962, File P7-2, Series 61.1a, Bureau of Budget Records; Howard

C. Brown, Jr., memorandum for file, 19 Feb. 1962, Proposed Presidential Statement Folder, Office Files of Glenn T. Seaborg, AEC/DOE.

5. Glenn Seaborg, speech to Joint Meeting of Atomic Industrial Forum–American Nuclear Society, Chicago, 8 Nov. 1961, AEC Commissioners' Speeches, AEC/NRC.

6. Ibid.

7. Howard C. Brown, Jr., "Note for the Chairman," with draft statement, 22 Dec. 1961, Brown to Robert E. Wilson, 11 Jan. 1962, with draft statement of 9 Jan. 1962, Brown to Seaborg, 16 Jan. 1962, with draft statement of 12 Jan. 1962, Proposed Presidential Statement Folder, Seaborg Office Files, AEC/DOE.

8. Draft statement, 23 Jan. 1962, Seaborg to David E. Bell, 26 Jan. 1962, with draft letter of transmittal, Seaborg to Kennedy, 26 Jan. 1962 and enclosed statement, Proposed Presidential Statement Folder, Seaborg Office Files, AEC/DOE.

9. Schuldt to Bell, 6 Feb. 1962, File P7-2, Series 61.1a, Bureau of Budget Records.

10. Holifield to Kennedy, 13 Feb. 1962, White House Central Files (FG 202, Atomic Energy Commission), Kennedy Papers.

11. Schuldt to Bell, 26 Feb., 16 Mar. 1962, File P7-2, Series 61.1a, Bureau of Budget Records, memorandum of telephone conversation between Fred Schuldt and Chris Henderson, 20 Feb. 1962, revised draft statements, 20, 28 Feb. 1962, Brown to Seaborg, 15 Mar. 1962, with draft letter, Kennedy to Seaborg, 15 Mar. 1962, memorandum of telephone conversation between Schuldt and Brown, 16 Mar. 1962, Proposed Presidential Statement Folder, Seaborg Office Files, AEC/DOE; Kennedy to Seaborg, 17 Mar. 1962, President's Office Files (Atomic Energy Commission 1962), Kennedy Papers.

12. JCAE, "202" Hearings, 1962, pp. 6–21. The Holifield letter is on pp. 6–8.

13. Holifield to Seaborg, 21 Mar. 1962, printed ibid., pp. 127–128; Craig Hosmer to John F. Kennedy, 8 Apr. 1962, Civilian Power Study File, Office Files of Robert Wilson, AEC/DOE; Schuldt to Bell, 28 Mar. 1962, Bell to Lee White, 23 May 1962, File P7-2, Series 61.1a, Bureau of Budget Records.

14. Seaborg to Holifield, 29 Mar. 1962, printed in JCAE, "202" Hearings, 1962, p. 128.

15. W. B. McCool, memorandum for file, 26 Mar. 1962, with attached memorandum for general manager from Seaborg, n.d., Research and Development–1 Policy, AEC/DOE.

16. Ibid.

17. W. C. Bartels, "Chronology of Meetings in Connection with Civilian Power Study," 13 Dec. 1962, Civilian Power Study and Report File, vol. 2, Office Files of Leland Haworth, Edward J. Bauser, memorandum for file, 26 July 1962, Ernest B. Tremmel, memorandum for file, 22 Aug. 1962, Research and Development–Civilian Nuclear Power, Seaborg Office Files, Holifield to Seaborg, 31 Aug. 1962, Haworth, memorandum for chairman, 24 Sept. 1962, Civilian Power Study,

Wilson Office Files, AEC/DOE; AEC press release, 4 May 1962, AEC/NRC; Appendix 7, "Information and Assistance from Organizations and Sources External to the Commission," Appendix 8, "Recommendations on Central Station Power Reactors by the General Advisory Committee," Appendix 1, "Fossil Fuel Resources of the United States," Appendix 3, "Overall Growth of Energy Requirements," in "Civilian Nuclear Power, Appendices to a Report to the President," printed in JCAE, committee print, *Nuclear Power Economics—1962 through 1967,* 90th Cong., 2d sess., 1968, pp. 244–246, 248–250, 171–199, 214–218.

18. Philippe G. Jacques to Pierre Salinger, 29 Aug. 1962, White House Central Files (Atomic Energy 1962), Kennedy Papers; Schuldt to Bell, 24 Sept. 1962, draft memorandum, Bell to Kennedy, 12 Nov. 1962, File P7-2, Series 61.1a, Bureau of Budget Records; "Civilian Nuclear Power—A Report to the President," 1962, in JCAE print, *Nuclear Power Economics—1962 through 1967,* pp. 99–167.

19. JCAE print, *Nuclear Power Economics,* pp. 116–121.

20. Ibid., pp. 124–126.

21. Ibid., pp. 122–123.

22. Ibid., pp. 134, 142–148.

23. Ibid., pp. 149–154.

24. Ibid., pp. 154–155.

25. Ibid., p. 160.

26. For press commentary on the report, see, for example, *New York Times,* 26 Nov. 1962, p. 28; *New York News,* 24 Nov. 1962, p. 15; *Washington Star,* 25 Nov. 1962, p. B4; *Science* 138 (14 Dec. 1962), 1231; *Nucleonics Week,* 26 Nov. 1962, p. 1; *Forum Memo,* Dec. 1962, p. 3.

27. Press briefing on civilian nuclear power, 21 Nov. 1962, note on press conference by J. Lyman, 28 Nov. 1962, Civilian Power Study and Report File, vol. 2, Haworth Office Files, AEC/DOE; *Nucleonics Week,* 28 Nov. 1962, p. 3.

28. Bell to Kennedy, 16 Nov. 1962, Bell to Ralph Dungan, 19 Nov. 1962, File P7-2, Series 61.1a, Bureau of Budget Records; McGeorge Bundy to Seaborg, 22 Nov. 1962, in JCAE, *"202" Hearings,* 88th Cong., 1st sess., 1963, p. 9; Kennedy to secretary of interior and others, 15 Feb. 1963 (AT 1963), Wiesner to Bundy, 3 May 1963 (AT 2—Industrial), White House Central Files, Kennedy Papers.

29. Philip Sporn to Robert Wilson, 22 Jan. 1963, Civilian Power Study File, Wilson Office Files, AEC/DOE.

30. David E. Lilienthal, "Whatever Happened to the Peaceful Atom?" 19 Feb. 1963, printed in JCAE, *"202" Hearings,* 1963, pp. 705–714.

31. Lewis L. Strauss, "My Faith in the Atomic Future," *Reader's Digest*, Aug. 1955, pp. 17–21.

32. JCAE print, *Improving the AEC Regulatory Process*, 87th Cong., 1st sess., 1961, 2:574.

33. Hazel Gaudet Erskine, "The Polls: Atomic Weapons and Nuclear Energy," *Public Opinion Quarterly* 27 (Summer 1963), 164.

34. JCAE, *"202" Hearings*, 1963, p. 714.

35. Ibid., pp. 714–742; David E. Lilienthal, *The Journals of David E. Lilienthal: The Harvest Years, 1959–1963* (New York: Harper and Row, 1971), p. 462.

SELECT BIBLIOGRAPHIC ESSAY

The following essay highlights the significant sources and is not meant as a recapitulation of the notes.

ATOMIC ENERGY COMMISSION RECORDS

The records of the Atomic Energy Commission provide a body of historical documentation that is rich in breadth and detail. Although many AEC documents still remain security classified, those dealing directly with the development of the licensing and regulatory system have been unclassified from the beginning of the private power program. The AEC sources cited in the notes all refer to unclassified material. In some files, however, classified and unclassified documents are mixed together and therefore are not readily accessible to private researchers. Most of those records have not been accessioned by the National Archives and remain under the control of the present agencies responsible for atomic-energy matters: the Department of Energy and the Nuclear Regulatory Commission. The Nuclear Regulatory Commission has placed copies of the records in its custody that are cited in the notes of this volume (as AEC/NRC), along with related materials, in its main Public Document Room, 1717 H Street Northwest, Washington, D.C. They are available there for public examination. The only exceptions are four Advisory Committee on Reactor Safeguards documents that could not be opened because they refer to personnel matters.

In 1974 the Energy Reorganization Act disbanded the Atomic Energy Commission and created in its place the Energy Research and Development Administration, now a part of the Department of Energy, and the Nuclear Regulatory Commission. As a result of this reorganization, the records of the AEC were split along functional lines: development records went to the Department of Energy in Germantown, Maryland, and regulatory records went to the Nuclear Regulatory Commission in Washington, D.C. The study of licensing and regulation, however, cannot be accomplished using only the regulatory records housed at the Nuclear Regulatory Commission. The very nature of the dual functions performed by the Atomic Energy Commission meant that many subjects did not neatly fall into one or the other functional type of records. To study licensing and regulation fully, the researcher must use the sources at both the Department of Energy and the Nuclear Regulatory Commission.

The most important series of records are the secretariat files. The secretariat received staff papers, memoranda, and correspondence for the Commission, scheduled Commission meetings, prepared minutes of meetings, and documented the action taken to fulfill Commission decisions. Each subject that came before the Commission was arranged with the pertinent documents in chronological order. These included internal memoranda, correspondence, staff papers, implementing papers, and summaries of actions taken. Often the subjects were cross-referenced to other subjects in the series, including staff working files. Using the secretariat files, a researcher can review at least the broad outlines of most policy development and in some instances acquire detailed knowledge about how the staff arrived at its positions.

Key documents in the secretariat subject series are the staff papers. Each one followed a specific format. It contained a statement of the issue, background data, alternatives to be considered, recommendations of the general manager, and appropriate appendixes. Since all staff recommendations went through the general manager (until 1961, when the director of regulation reported directly to the Commission on licensing and regulatory matters), it is sometimes difficult to determine the particular division of the staff where the paper originated. But even with this deficiency, the staff papers are invaluable documents.

The secretariat also prepared official minutes of Commission meetings, numbered in sequence from the first meeting in 1946. Regulatory matters were on the agenda at those meetings until September 1956, when the Commission started to hold separate meetings to handle the increasing regulatory business. The agendas of the regulatory meetings, however, covered only formal legal matters such as rule-making and licensing actions. The regular Commission meeting minutes continued to contain many subjects that related to regulatory issues.

At the beginning the Commission decided not to use verbatim transcripts of its formal meetings. Thus the minutes, compiled by the secretariat staff, must be relied on solely to review Commission discussions at the meetings. The minutes provide a summary of decisions and sometimes indicate positions taken by individual commissioners. For the period 1953–1957 the minutes are supplemented with verbatim transcripts of Commission meetings. Because of the increasing disagreement between Chairman Strauss and Commissioner Murray, the Commission decided to use both verbatim transcripts and minutes. Comparison of the minutes and the transcripts provides a good standard against which to judge the minutes for which there are no transcripts and indicates a high degree of accuracy for the minutes. After Murray's term expired in 1957, the Commission ceased making transcripts.

When the Advisory Committee on Reactor Safeguards became a statutory committee in 1957, it started making minutes of its meetings. In addition, several of the subcommittees of the main committee maintained minutes. Those records are essential in evaluating the important role the Safeguards Committee performed in the regulatory process. Safeguards Committee records are in the Nuclear Regulatory Commission.

Less formal and not as well organized are the office papers of individual commissioners. While the collections vary in usefulness and much of the material is often duplicated in the secretariat's subject files, there are occasional items that provide insights on some matters. The papers also reflect the interests of the individual commissioners.

Some records relating to individual licensed atomic-power facilities are available to researchers. Each facility has its own official documentation, maintained in a docket file at the Nuclear Regulatory Commission's Washington, D.C. headquarters. A duplicate docket is kept in the Commission's main public-document room. The files contain documents developed by the utility, vendor, and agency staff. They include items such as applications, safety reports, evaluations, and construction permits and operating licenses with amendments. Each docket is a documentary history in itself of a particular reactor facility and provides insight into the complicated task of licensing a plant.

OTHER GOVERNMENT RECORDS

Important documents on the regulatory aspects of atomic energy are contained in several other government collections. The organization that had the most pervasive influence on regulatory activities was the Joint Committee on Atomic Energy. Its extensive records are included in Record Group 128 (Records of the Joint Committees of Congress) at the National Archives in Washington, D.C. Although carefully screened by the committee staff before being deposited at the Archives, the Joint Committee papers yield many insights into regulatory matters by both individual members and the committee staff. The records are presently open through 1963, and some materials on later years can be examined with the assistance of the U.S. Senate Historical Office. Also at the National Archives are the records of the Bureau of the Budget (in Record Group 51). Particularly during the Kennedy administration, the Budget office was directly involved with legislative, organizational, and fiscal matters that influenced regulatory affairs. Detailed internal memoranda show the important link the Bureau provided between the Commission and the president's close advisers.

Some records at the Dwight D. Eisenhower Library in Abilene, Kansas and the John F. Kennedy Library in Boston are of importance. The White House Official File and the Ann Whitman File at the Eisenhower Library contain useful memoranda and correspondence on atomic energy and illuminate the close relationship between Lewis Strauss and the president. The White House Central Files and the President's Office Files at the Kennedy Library complement the records of the Bureau of the Budget and provide helpful documents on the often strained relations between the Joint Committee and the executive branch. Althouugh both libraries house valuable materials on military uses and promotion of peaceful applications of atomic energy, they have relatively little on regulatory issues.

A key collection of records on the subject of radiation protection and safety is maintained by the Division of Radiological Health of the United States Public Health Service in its library in Rockville, Maryland. The files are particularly rich in documenting the activities of the National Advisory Committee on Radiation and the Federal Radiation Council as well as the involvement of the Public Health Service in the fallout controversy and the efforts to protect uranium miners. The Service collected its materials in the preparation of a 1979 report, "Effects of Nuclear Weapons Testing on Health." They are available on microfilm for public examination.

PRIVATE PAPERS

A few key participants in the regulation of atomic energy have deposited personal collections at various libraries. By far the most useful are the papers of Lewis L. Strauss and Clinton P. Anderson. The Strauss papers are at the Herbert Hoover Library in West Branch, Iowa and are still in the process of being accessioned from the family. The papers are rich in correspondence with a variety of national figures and contain many memoranda for the files written by Strauss. The Anderson papers are at the Library of Congress, Washington, D.C. Although this collection includes many government reports and newspaper clippings, it also contains important correspondence and memoranda that are helpful on Anderson's role as a powerful member and sometimes chairman of the Joint Committee on Atomic Energy.

The Chet Holifield papers at the University of Southern California in Los Angeles, though less helpful than the Strauss and Anderson collections for the period covered in this volume, still contain some important material. They include information that supplements what is available on Joint Committee activities in the Committee's records at the National Archives and in the Anderson papers. The Holifield papers are much richer on regulatory issues in the late 1960s and early 1970s than on earlier years.

Two collections in the Bentley Library at the University of Michigan provide useful material on specific aspects of atomic regulation. The G. Mennen Williams papers document Michigan's participation in nuclear issues in the 1950s when Williams was governor. There is information on the participation by states in atomic regulation as well as on Michigan's role in the Power Reactor Development Company controversy of 1956. E. Blythe Stason, dean of the University of Michigan Law School, directed several studies on atomic regulation and sometimes served as an adviser to Williams and the Joint Committee on Atomic Energy. His papers not only trace his personal activities but also contain a wide assortment of materials on atomic development and regulation that he collected in the course of his work.

At Wayne State University's Walter P. Reuther Library, the Walter Reuther papers have valuable information on union perspectives on atomic-power development and regulation. They also document the union's decision to intervene in the PRDC case in 1956.

The Douglas Price papers at the Eisenhower Library have a few items on federal-state relations in atomic energy. Disappointing and not very useful are the papers of W. Sterling Cole at Cornell University and of Carl T. Durham at the University of North Carolina, both of whom were chairmen of the Joint Committee on Atomic Energy.

GOVERNMENT PUBLICATIONS

A valuable overview of the Commission's activities is provided in the Semiannual and Annual Reports to Congress that were required under the Atomic Energy Acts of 1946 and 1954. Indispensable reference sources are the legislative histories of the two basic atomic-energy laws: *Legislative History of the Atomic Energy Act of 1946, Public Law 585, 79th Congress,* compiled by James D. Nuse, 3 vols. (Washington: U.S. Atomic Energy Commission, 1965), and the *Legislative History of the Atomic Energy Act of 1954, Public Law 703, 83rd Congress,* compiled by Madeleine W. Losee, 3 vols. (Washington: U.S. Atomic Energy Commission, 1955).

The most important collection of published documents is the large volume of hearings and committee prints prepared by the Joint Committee on Atomic Energy. Beginning in 1956, the Joint Committee published annually an extremely useful handbook that included in its contents lists of all atomic-energy legislation to date, lists of current memberships for each Congress since 1946, and a cumulative list of its publications. The committee prints are the best guides to locate subjects that came before the Joint Committee.

Section 202 of the Atomic Energy Act required the Joint Committee to hold annual hearings on the "development, growth and state of the atomic energy industry." The "202" hearings, which usually lasted several days, included testimony not only from AEC officials but also from industry and labor leaders and other state and federal authorities. The published hearings contain not only testimony but also additional documentary materials supplied for the record. They provide a valuable overview of nuclear affairs.

Regulatory and licensing issues were the subject of several hearings throughout the years under study. Particularly noteworthy are the 1957 committee print, *A Study of AEC Procedures and Organization in the Licensing of Reactor Facilities,* which resulted from the PRDC controversy, and the subsequent *Hearings on Government Indemnity and Reactor Safety,* covering the hearings that culminated in the passage of the Price-Anderson Act. Again in 1961 the Joint Committee studied the licensing process and brought together an important group of documents in its two-volume print, *Improving the AEC Regulatory Process.* The result of this Joint Committee study and subsequent hearings was the creation of the Atomic Safety and Licensing Boards. The Joint Committee's hearings on radioactive fallout from weapons testing, particularly those held in 1957, provide an invaluable perspective on scientific views on and knowledge of the hazards of radiation in general and fallout in particular. They also trace growing doubts about the AEC's position on the dangers of exposure to radiation from bomb tests.

Committee prints and hearings delved into other atomic regulatory activities. Joint Committee publications on federal-state relations, employee radiation hazards, radiation-protection standards, problems of the uranium-mining and -milling industry, and waste disposal provide valuable information on regulatory issues.

The National Academy of Sciences published significant reports on controversial subjects relating to radiological safety. Its 1956 survey, *The Biological Effects of Atomic Radiation: A Report to the Public* is a milestone document and is particularly useful for understanding contemporary scientific assessments of radiation hazards. The 1960 updated version is also instructive. The National Academy also published two notable reports on radioactive waste, *Disposal of Radioactive Waste on Land* (1957) and *Radioactive Waste Disposal into Atlantic and Gulf Coastal Waters* (1959), the second of which aroused a public furor.

Essential for understanding the basis for radiation-protection standards are the handbooks prepared by the National Committee on Radiation Protection and published by the National Bureau of Standards, particularly *Maximum Permissible Amounts of Radioisotopes in the Human Body and Maximum Permissible Concentrations in Air and Water*, National Bureau of Standards, Handbook 52 (Washington, 1953), and *Permissible Dose from External Sources of Ionizing Radiation*, National Bureau of Standards, Handbook 59 (Washington, 1954). The background for those publications and other activities of the NCRP and ICRP can be studied in the correspondence, memoranda, summaries of meetings, and other primary material compiled in Lauriston S. Taylor, *Organization for Radiation Protection: The Operations of the ICRP and NCRP, 1928–1974* (Springfield, Va.: National Technical Information Service, 1979).

MEMOIRS

Very few of the personalities involved in the early history of nuclear regulation have published accounts of their experiences. Lewis L. Strauss's *Men and Decisions* (Garden City, N.Y.: Doubleday and Co., 1962) provides a sense of what motivated this controversial man. His bitterness toward

Senator Clinton P. Anderson is shown by Strauss's refusal to call his antagonist by name in the book; Anderson is always referred to as the "Junior Senator from New Mexico." Anderson's recollection, *Outsider in the Senate: Senator Clinton P. Anderson's Memoirs* (New York: World Publishing Co., 1970), is a chatty, informal memoir that is a useful supplement to his personal papers. Glenn T. Seaborg's *Kennedy, Khrushchev, and the Test Ban* (Berkeley, Los Angeles, London: University of California Press, 1981), is part memoir and part interpretative history. Though it focuses on the test-ban negotiations, it includes some valuable material on the fallout controversy. An excellent treatment of how early reactor-safety issues were handled is available in Edward Teller and Allen Brown, *The Legacy of Hiroshima* (Garden City, N.Y.: Doubleday and Co., 1962; reprint, Westport, Conn.: Greenwood Press, 1975). Teller has also contributed a helpful recollection in a published lecture, "The Reactor Safeguard Committee," in *Energy From Heaven and Earth* (San Francisco: W. H. Freeman and Co., 1979).

SECONDARY WORKS

The best history of the early Atomic Energy Commission has been written by the agency's historians. Richard G. Hewlett and Oscar E. Anderson, Jr., in *The New World, 1939–1946*, vol. 1 of *A History of the United States Atomic Energy Commission* (University Park: Pennsylvania State University Press, 1962), and Hewlett and Francis Duncan in *Atomic Shield, 1947–1952*, vol. 2 of *A History of the United States Atomic Energy Commission* (University Park: Pennsylvania State University Press, 1969), carry the story through 1952, quite properly emphasizing the military aspects of nuclear energy. In a later work, *Nuclear Navy, 1946–1962* (Chicago: University of Chicago Press, 1974), Hewlett and Duncan discuss the Shippingport power project. A manuscript, "Atoms for Peace and War," covering the Eisenhower years is presently in preparation by Department of Energy historians Hewlett (now retired) and Jack M. Holl. A much less thorough but very readable history of the agency is Corbin Allardice and Edward Trapnell, *The Atomic Energy Commission* (New York: Praeger Publishers, 1974). Also useful is Frank G. Dawson, *Nuclear Power, Development and Management of a Technology* (Seattle: University of Washington Press, 1976). Two Rand Corporation studies are helpful in understanding power-reactor development: Robert Perry et al., *Development and Commercialization of the Light Water Reactor, 1946–1976* (Santa Monica, Calif.: Rand Corporation, 1977) and Wendy Allen, *Nuclear Reactors for*

Generating Electricity: U.S. Development From 1946 to 1963 (Santa Monica, Calif.: Rand Corporation, 1977). Originally in the same series but later expanded and published separately is Elizabeth S. Rolph, *Nuclear Power and the Public Safety: A Study in Regulation* (Lexington, Mass.: D.C. Heath and Co., 1979). It is the best outline history of nuclear licensing and regulation published to date.

Specific subjects and institutions bearing on nuclear regulation and safety have been examined. A valuable study on the Joint Committee on Atomic Energy is Harold P. Green and Alan Rosenthal, *Government of the Atom* (New York: Atherton Press, 1963). Unfortunately it only covers Joint Committee activities to 1962. David Okrent, a longtime member of the Advisory Committee on Reactor Safeguards, focuses on the activities of the Safeguards Committee in *Nuclear Safety: The History of the Regulatory Process* (Madison: University of Wisconsin Press, 1981). This work includes many key documents on regulation and is useful both as a secondary overview from the position of the Safeguards Committee and as an account by a participant after 1964.

An excellent general introduction to radiation hazards can be found in Jack Schubert and Ralph E. Lapp, *Radiation: What It Is and How It Affects You* (New York: Viking Press, 1957). An able overview of the radiation-protection efforts of the National Committee on Radiation Protection and the International Commission on Radiological Protection is Lauriston S. Taylor, *Radiation Protection Standards* (Cleveland: CRC Press, 1971). More detailed accounts on early scientific efforts to understand radiation and provide protection against its hazards are Lawrence Badash, *Radioactivity in America: Growth and Decay of a Science* (Baltimore: Johns Hopkins University Press, 1979), a highly technical treatment of scientific inquiry in the first two decades of the twentieth century, and Daniel Paul Serwer, "The Rise of Radiation Protection: Science, Medicine, and Technology in Society, 1896–1935" (Ph.D. diss., Princeton University, 1977), a survey of initial attempts to limit exposure to radiation. Barton C. Hacker is preparing a study, "Elements of Controversy: A History of Radiation Safety in the Nuclear Weapons Testing Program," that promises to fill many gaps in the existing literature. Robert A. Divine's pioneering work, *Blowing on the Wind: The Nuclear Test Ban Debate, 1954–1960* (New York: Oxford University Press, 1978), focuses on Eisenhower's quest for arms control but is essential for understanding the broad international and domestic context in which radiation-protection standards evolved.

A broad discussion of radioactive-waste disposal is presented in an Atomic Energy Commission publication, Charles H. Fox, *Radioactive Wastes* (Washington: U.S. Atomic Energy Commission, 1965). A much more technical analysis can be found in C. B. Amphlett, *Treatment and Disposal of Radioactive Wastes* (New York: Pergamon Press, 1962). Sea disposal is well covered in Alton Frye, *The Hazards of Atomic Wastes: Perspectives and Proposals on Oceanic Disposal* (Washington: Public Affairs Press, 1962).

The Power Reactor Development Company reactor at Lagoona Beach, Michigan has been studied in two books. John G. Fuller, *We Almost Lost Detroit* (New York: Reader's Digest Press, 1975), is decidedly antinuclear in interpretation but presents much of the factual information on the early controversy. E. Pauline Alexanderson, the editor of *Fermi-1: New Age for Nuclear Power* (La Grange Park, Ill.: American Nuclear Society, 1979), has gathered essays on the company and the reactor that were written by participants in the venture. It is a good source for understanding the company's point of view.

Two books by William Berman and Lee Hydeman fall into the category of being both primary and secondary sources. *Federal and State Responsibilities for Radiation Protection: The Need for Federal Legislation* (Ann Arbor: University of Michigan Atomic Energy Research Project, 1959) and *The Atomic Energy Commission and Regulating Nuclear Facilities* (Ann Arbor: University of Michigan Law School, 1961) are excellent analyses. Both works were used as part of Joint Committee reviews that led to amendments to the Atomic Energy Act.

Works on nuclear technology and safety are plentiful. A handy reference is John F. Hogerton, *The Atomic Energy Deskbook* (New York: Reinhold Publishing Corp., 1963). Although twenty years old, it remains essential for understanding the state of the technology during that time. A more recent and equally valuable introduction to nuclear technology is Anthony V. Nero, Jr., *A Guidebook to Nuclear Reactors* (Berkeley, Los Angeles, London: University of California Press, 1979). Also useful for nuclear engineering is Henry C. Schwenk and Robert H. Shannon, *Nuclear Power Engineering* (New York: McGraw-Hill Book Co., 1957). Designed for use in basic engineering courses, the text is general in approach. Two highly technical volumes dealing specifically with reactor safety are T. J. Thompson and James G. Beckerley, eds., *The Technology of Nuclear Reactor Safety*, 2 vols. (Cambridge: MIT Press, 1964, 1973). The first covers reactor physics while the second delves into reactor materials and engineering. A less technical presentation is Charles G. Russell, *Reactor Safeguards* (New York: Pergamon Press, 1962).

Periodical literature provides much contemporary information. Especially useful are the *Bulletin of the Atomic Scientists* and *Nucleonics*. Many articles published in law journals are particularly rewarding for their analysis and perspective on the various issues of atomic licensing and regulation.

PERSONAL PARTICIPATION

Several willing participants have shared their views on different aspects of the atomic regulatory story, enabling us to develop a clearer perspective on many complex issues. We had the privilege of the guidance of Clifford Beck, Leo Goodman, Harold P. Green, Kenneth C. Hall, Chet Holifield, Lee Hydeman, Lyall Johnson, William Kennedy, Ralph E. Lapp, Robert Lowenstein, Arthur W. Murphy, William C. Parler, Eber Price, James T. Ramey, and Lauriston S. Taylor.

INDEX

ganization of, 4–9, 64–70, 193–196, 373–378; operating methods of, 6–8; field operations of, 10–11, 377; promotes atomic development, 13, 15–17, 18–19, 21, 59–60, 67, 69–70, 77–82, 418–422; assigned broad regulatory authority, 30; dual functions of, 31, 59, 60, 69–70, 90, 92, 93, 122, 159, 182, 194–196, 220, 251–253, 257, 290, 382, 391–393, 403–406, 418–424; relationship of with NCRP, 37–38, 56, 254; and 1953 sheep deaths, 41; Strontium 90 hazards assessed by, 42–43; issues 1955 report on fallout, 43, 50; risks of fallout, assurances on, 43, 44, 48, 51, 52–53, 58, 247, 254; on 1956 National Academy of Sciences report, 46; criticized for fallout statements, 50–51, 53, 247–250, 254; praised for research on fallout, 50, 51; conflicting responsibilities of, 51, 53; publishes fallout data, 52; revises radiation protection regulations, 56, 261, 333–335; public image of, 58, 257, 290, 301, 366, 373, 405, 423–424; establishes Safeguard Committee, 60–61; reactor hazards, early procedures of for assessing, 61–63; licensing procedures of, 63–67, 70–71, 76–77, 86–92, 122, 178–179, 191–193, 214–217, 378–379, 491 n. 27; creates regulatory staff, 64–70; prepares first regulations, 69–73; regulations of on production and utilization facilities, 73–76; requirements of for construction permit, 74–76; issues construction permits, 79–81; regulation of on special nuclear materials, 82–84; operators' licenses, regulations on, 84–85; research and development program of, 89–90, 126–128, 131–134, 145; and public participation in licensing, 91; authority of to insure private reactors, 94–95; investigates insurance question, 95; 1955 report of on insurance, 97–99; drafts insurance bill, 99; studies insurance question, 101; role of in re-

solving insurance question, 105; insurance proposals of, 108–112; favors unlimited indemnity, 112–116; estimates damage of accidents, 113–115; opposes Gore-Holifield, 119; reaction of to Safeguards Committee report on PRDC, 131–132; discusses request for Safeguards Committee report, 137–140; staff reviews PRDC application, 140–142; approves construction permit for PRDC, 142–143, 419–420; rules of for public participation in licensing, 150–151; holds separate regulatory meetings, 151–152; discusses intervention in PRDC case, 152–157; uses "separated staff" procedure, 154, 357, 381; refuses union access to restricted data, 158–159; declassifies documents in PRDC case, 159; signs contract with PRDC, 164–165; discusses union motion in PRDC case, 167–168; issues decision on PRDC, 168–172; Court of Appeals rules against, 173–175; appeals PRDC case to Supreme Court, 175–181; opposes release of Safeguards Committee documents, 184–190; opposes mandatory public hearings, 191–193; opposes separate agencies, 194–196, 391–393; reactor accidents, 1957 study of, 199–201, 203–208, 210–212, 421; supports indemnity legislation, 116–117, 201–203; opposes Anderson amendments to licensing, 210; supports amended Price-Anderson bill, 210–211; and establishing regulatory standards, 214–217, 245; approves plant sites, 220–221; drafts siting guidelines, 224–234; siting guidelines of criticized, 226; use of term "maximum credible accident" by, 229; publishes site criteria, 236; redrafts site criteria, 241; declassifies fallout information, 255, 470 n. 7; opposes use of FRC guides for fallout, 269, 273; internal controversy over Iodine-131, 271–272; denies exposure of children to excessive